THE GUINN
WHO'S WHO OF
SIXTIES
MUSIC

General Editor: Colin Larkin

GUINNESS PUBLISHING

Dedicated to Freddy Bienstock

First published in 1992 by
GUINNESS PUBLISHING LTD
33 London Road, Enfield, Middlesex EN2 6DJ, England

Reprinted 1994 (twice)

GUINNESS is a registered trademark of Guinness Publishing Ltd

British Library Cataloguing-in-Publication data
A catalogue record for this book is available from the British Library

ISBN 0-85112-578-6

Conceived, designed, edited and produced by
SQUARE ONE BOOKS LTD
Iron Bridge House, 3 Bridge Approach, Chalk Farm, London NW1 8BD
Editor and Designer: Colin Larkin
Picture Editor: Colin Larkin
Editorial and production assistants: Susan Pipe, John Eley, Aileen Tyler, Pat Perry,
Graham Lock, Jon Staines, Janice Newman, Johnny Rogan, Brian Hogg and Jane Ehrlich
Brian Hogg would like to thank Jacki Morton
Special thanks to Donald McFarlan and David Roberts of Guinness Publishing
and to Tony Gale of Pictorial Press
Logo concept: Darren Perry. Page make up: Tim Beard
This book has been produced on Apple Macintosh computers
using Quark Xpress and Microsoft Word
Image set by L & S Communications Ltd

Printed and bound in Great Britain by the Bath Press

EDITORS NOTE

The Guinness Who's Who Of Sixties Music forms a part of the multi-volume *Guinness Encyclopedia Of Popular Music*. A further 16 specialist single volumes are planned in the near future.
Also available:

The Guinness Who's Who Of Indie And New Wave Music
The Guinness Who's Who Of Heavy Metal
The Guinness Who's Who Of Jazz

In selecting entries for this work we have attempted to cover all artists who experienced major success in the 60s. Many artists only lasted a few years during that extraordinary decade and will forever be associated with the 60s; artists such as Sonny And Cher, Annette, Marianne Faithfull, Scott McKenzie and Buffalo Springfield. Dozens of others continued to be successful to a lesser degree throughout the 70s and 80s; for example the Kinks, the Hollies, the Searchers, the Troggs and Gene Pitney. They have still been included. The reader will note that jazz, blues, country and folk artists have been omitted from this decade. They will each have their own volume.
During the picture research I made an effort to avoid the obvious artists who have appeared in hundreds of publications over the years. We do not have photographs of the Beatles, Bob Dylan or the Rolling Stones, for example, but we have assembled with the help of Tony Gale of Pictorial Press, a broad and remarkable selection of 60s pop and rock artists. Tony was the location photographer present on dozens of the UK artist sessions, and many of these lesser known or long forgotten performers' pictures are being published for the first time. We have tried to convey the fashions and flavour of the 60s through the illustrations. All but 5 of the photographs are from Pictorial Press, the remaining items were supplied by Brian Hogg (another 60s luddite) with help from Jacki Morton.
In the preparation of this work contributions were received from, Peter Doggett, Brian Hogg, Jeff Tamarkin, Robert Pruter, Christopher Spencer, Dave Laing, Colin Larkin, Johnny Rogan, Dave McAleer, Steve Smith and Alan Clayson.
I would like to thank, in addition to the contributors; John Eley and Susan Pipe for an extraordinary effort in putting it all together at the end, and to Paola Simoneschi, Sallie Collins and Sarah Silvé for their production work. Donald McFarlan takes credit for finding Tim Beard who took a great deal of the strain away from us. Finally to Laura, Ben, Tom, Dan, Julian, Dick, Anne and George who were still my family at the very end.

Colin Larkin, August 1992

A

Allisons

Allisons

John Alford (b. 31 December 1939, London, England) and Bob Day (b. 2 February 1942, Trowbridge, Wiltshire, England). The pop duo played the rounds of coffee bars and youth clubs before being spotted by impresario Tito Burns, who became their manager. He saw their immediate potential as Everly Brothers lookalikes. Under the guise of brothers John and Bob Allison, they became overnight British sensations when their self-composed 'Are You Sure' became Britain's entry in the 1961 Eurovision Song Contest. They received a big wave of publicity when their song became runner-up in the competition. The record, produced by Jack Baverstock and arranged by Harry Robinson on Fontana, went to number 1 in Britain, sold over a million copies in Europe and narrowly missed the US chart. The duo, who were backed on stage by the Hunters, and who toured with Larry Parnes' stable of acts never returned to the Top 20. Their only other chart entries being their follow-up 'Words' and 'Lessons In Love' (a song from Cliff Richard's film

The Young Ones) in 1962. They have occasionally resurfaced over the years as writers, producers and artists but have had no further chart success.
Album: *Are You Sure* (1961).

Altamont Festival

6 December 1969, Altamont, California, USA. The free festival at the Altamont Raceway became the first major musical event since the peaceful 'happening' at Woodstock earlier that summer. Altamont tarnished the reputation of the new music revolution. Until then, all events had been violence-free and had allowed the older generation to reappraise their perception of pop music and its cultural trappings. The festival spirit died when Meredith Hunter, an 18-year-old black spectator, was horribly beaten and stabbed to death by a group of Hells Angels, while the Rolling Stones were onstage. Mick Jagger, only yards away, was oblivious to what was happening at his feet. When he finally called for help, it was too late. The Angels became involved after being recruited by the organizers to keep the peace as 'security' guards. Their fee was to be as much alcohol and drugs as they could consume. Consequently, it was later claimed that they were not in control of their horrific actions. Tempers had earlier become frayed when Santana's performance had been interrupted by a scuffle. The Jefferson Airplane, who followed, had their singer Marty Balin knocked unconscious by a blow from one of the Angels when he tried to stop another disturbance. Although the Angels were ultimately deemed responsible, they had themselves become victims of appalling organization. David Crosby defended their actions in a lengthy *Rolling Stone* interview. Mick Jagger has been the focus of a great deal of resentment from particular Hell's Angels groups who accuse the singer of shirking any responsibility for the incident and quickly shifting the blame. Consequently, Jagger has since received numerous death-threats and, supposedly, there is still a 'contract' out on his life. Other artists appearing in front of the unmanageable crowd of 300,000 included Crosby, Stills, Nash And Young and the Flying Burrito Brothers. Although the Grateful Dead were members of the organizing committee, they ended up not performing. The film of Altamont, *Gimme Shelter*, is an interesting, if gory piece of celluloid rock history.

Amboy Dukes

Originally from Detroit, Michigan, USA, the Amboy Dukes - John Drake (vocals), Ted Nugent (lead guitar), Steve Farmer (rhythm guitar), Rick Lober (keyboards), Bill White (bass) and Dave Palmer (drums) - achieved notoriety for their rendition of 'Baby Please Don't Go', which took Them's classic version as its inspiration, but added Ted Nugent's snarling guitar. A US Top 20 hit, its brashness set the tone for the group's subsequent albums on which Farmer's rather pretentious lyrics often undermined the music on offer. Frequent changes in personnel (Drake, Lorber and White were replaced, in turn, by Rusty Day, Andy Solomon and Greg Arama), made little difference to the Amboy Dukes' development as the group increasingly became an outlet for Nugent's pyrotechnics. He unveiled a new line-up in 1974 with *Call Of The Wild*, the first of two albums recorded for Frank Zappa's Discreet label. The guitarist then abandoned the band's name altogether and embarked on a solo career.

Albums: *The Amboy Dukes* (1968), *Journey To The Centre Of The Mind* (1968), *Migration* (1969), *Marriage On The Rocks* (1970), *Survival Of The Fittest* (c.70s), *Call Of The Wild* (1974), *Tooth, Fang And Claw* (1975).

Amen Corner

Hailing from Cardiff, Wales, this R&B-styled sextet comprised Andy Fairweather-Low (b. 1948; vocals), Blue Weaver (organ), Neil Jones (guitar), Clive Taylor (bass), Allen Jones (baritone saxophone), Mike Smith (tenor sax) and Dennis Bryn (drums). After hitting the charts with the bluesy 'Gin House' in 1967, Fairweather-Low became a pin-up and the group swiftly ploughed more commercial ground with a succession of hits including 'World Of Broken Hearts', 'Bend Me Shape Me' and 'High In The Sky'. What the pop press failed to reveal was the intense power-struggle surrounding the proprietorship of the group, and the menacingly defensive tactics of their manager Don Arden. After all the drama, the group moved from Decca to Andrew Oldham's Immediate label and enjoyed their only UK number 1 with 'Half As Nice' in 1969. After one final Top 10 hit, the energetic 'Hello Suzie', they split. Ironically, their pop star career ended on an anti-climactic note with the inappropriately-titled Beatles' cover 'Get Back'. Andy Fairweather-Low formed Fairweather and then went solo, while Blue Weaver found his way into the Strawbs. His keyboard work on their *Grave New World* was particularly noteworthy. The brass section became Judas Jump.

Albums: *Round Amen Corner* (1968), *National Welsh Coast Live Explosion Company* (1969), *Farewell To The Real Magnificent Seven* (1969).

Andrews, Chris

b. 1938, Romford, Essex, England. Originally lead singer in the early 60s outfit Chris Ravel And The Ravers, Andrews found greater success as a songwriter. Signed by manager Eve Taylor, he composed hits for her artists Adam Faith ('The First Time', 'We Are In Love', 'If He Tells Me', 'I Love Being In Love With You', 'Stop Feeling Sorry For Yourself', 'Someone's Taken Maria Away') and Sandie Shaw ('Girl Don't Come', 'Long Live Love' and 'Message Understood'). He scored chart success in his own right during 1965-66 with two catchy, upbeat numbers, 'Yesterday Man' and 'To Whom It Concerns'. Although he occasionally recorded additional solo singles, no further hits were forthcoming.

Albums: *Yesterday Man* (1965), *Who Is The Man* (1977).

Animals

Formed in Newcastle-upon-Tyne, England in 1963, when vocalist Eric Burdon (b. 4 May 1941, Walker, Newcastle, Tyne & Wear, England), joined local R&B band the Alan Price Combo. The Animals comprised Alan Price, (b. 19 April 1942, Fatfield, Co. Durham, England; piano), Hilton Valentine, (b. 22 May 1943, North Shields, Tyne & Wear, England; guitar), John Steel, (b. 4 February 1941, Gateshead, Co. Durham, England; drums) and Chas Chandler, (b. Bryan James Chandler, 18 December 1938, Heaton, Tyne & Wear, England; bass). Valentine had previously played with the Gamblers, while Burdon had played trombone together with Steel on trumpet, in college jazz bands. With their raucous and exciting stage act, they quickly attracted the attention of several music business entrepreneurs. R&B legend Graham Bond recommended them to his manager Ronan O'Rahilly. The group became stars at the legendary Club A-Go-Go in Newcastle. On one occasion they performed with Sonny Boy Williamson, (an album was released many years later of this explosive gig). By the end of 1963 they had moved to London to become an integral part of the fast-burgeoning club scene. After signing with producer Mickie Most they debuted with the energetic 'Baby Let Me Take You Home', (a version of Eric Von Schmidt's blues standard 'Baby Let Me Follow You Down'), which became a respectable hit. Their next release was to be both controversial and memorable. A pop song about a New Orleans brothel, lasting four-and-a-half minutes was at first resisted by their record company Columbia as being too long for radio play. Upon release, this record, Josh White's 'House Of The Rising Sun', leapt to the top of the charts all over the world, and ended up selling several million copies. The combination of Valentine's now legendary but simplistic guitar introduction and Price's shrill organ complemented Burdon's remarkably mature and blood curdling vocal. Over the next two years the Animals had seven further substantial hits on both sides of the Atlantic. Their memorable and dramatic version of a song Nina Simone popularized 'Don't Let Me Be Misunderstood' featured the autobiographical 'Club

A-Go-Go' on the b-side. Their choice of material was exemplary and many of their hits contained thought provoking lyrics, from the angst-ridden 'I'm Crying' to the frustration and urban despair of Cynthia Weill and Barry Mann's 'We Gotta Get Out Of This Place'. Their albums contained stirring renditions of classics by Chuck Berry, Sam Cooke, Jimmy Reed and Burdon's hero, Ray Charles. During this time Price departed (supposedly suffering from aerophobia), and was replaced by Dave Rowberry from the Mike Cotton Sound. Burdon still maintains that Price's departure was because he had taken ownership of the lucrative publishing rights to 'House Of The Rising Sun' and was therefore financially secure. Steel left in 1966, replaced by Nashville Teens drummer Barry Jenkins. The new band scored with the brilliant 'Its My Life' and the adventurous 'Inside Looking Out'. By 1967 Burdon and Valentine had become totally immersed in psychedelia, both musically and chemically. This alienated them from the rest of the group, (who preferred good old-fashioned alcohol), and led to its disintegration. Chandler went on to discover and manage the Jimi Hendrix Experience. Burdon, however, retained the name and immediately re-appeared as Eric Burdon And The New Animals. They found greater favour in the USA where the band was domiciled. The band courted the west coast sound and the school of bands from that period. 'San Franciscan Nights' perfectly echoed the moment with the lyrics: 'Strobe lights beam creates dreams, walls move, minds do too, on a warm San Franciscan night'. He further encapsulated his reverence in the song 'Monterey', cleverly eulogizing the epic Monterey Pop Festival of 1967. A number of interesting musicians passed through various line-ups of the New Animals, notably John Weider, Vic Briggs (formerly of Steampacket), Danny McCulloch, Zoot Money and Andy Summers. The tamed Burdon was now writing introspective and thought-provoking lyrics, although many of his previous fans could not take the former raver seriously. Long improvisational pieces began to appear in their live performances, with watered-down versions to be found on the albums *Winds Of Change, The Twain Shall Meet, Everyone Of Us* and *Love Is*. They disbanded at the end of 1968. Interestingly, the original line-up re-grouped twice, in 1977 and 1983. Both times new albums were released to an indifferent public. For the 1983 revival tour it was reported that Valentine had become so rusty on the guitar, that a lead guitarist was recruited. The Animals contribution to the 60s was considerable and at times their popularity threatened even the Beatles and Rolling Stones. 'The House Of The Rising Sun' gave them musical immortality, and will no doubt continue to be re-released at regular intervals.

Albums: *The Animals* (1964), *Animals On Tour* (1965), *Animal Tracks* (1965), *Most Of The Animals* (1966), *Animalization* (1966), *Animalisms* (1966), *Eric Is Here* (1967), *Winds Of Change* (1967), *The Twain Shall Meet* (1968), *Everyone Of Us* (1968), *Love Is* (1968), *In Concert From Newcastle* (1976), *Before We Were Rudely Interrupted* (1976), *The Ark* (1983), *Rip It To Shreds* (1984), *The Animals With Sonny Boy Williamson* (1988 - live recording from 1963). Selected compilations: *The EP Collection* (1989), *The Complete Animals* (1990), *Trackin' The Hits* (1990).

Further reading: *I Used To Be An Animal, But I'm All Right Now*, Eric Burdon, *Wild Animals*, Andy Blackford.

Annette

Annette

b. Annette Funicello, 22 October 1942, Utica, New York, USA. Initially billed as 'Annette', this singer/actress rose to fame under the aegis of the Walt Disney organization. A one-time Mousketeer, she enjoyed several hit singles between 1959 and 1961 which included two US Top 10 entries, 'Tall Paul' and 'O Dio Mio', as well as the enduring 'Pineapple Princess'. During the 60s Annette starred alongside Frankie Avalon in a series of 'quickie' beach films, including *Beach Party, Bikini Beach* (both 1964) and *How To Stuff A Wild Bikini* (1965), which combined slim plots, teenage themes and cameos from often-transitory pop stars. *The Monkey's Uncle*

(1964) drew its appeal from an appearance by the Beach Boys and musical contributions from their leader, Brian Wilson. The latter assisted songwriter/producer Gary Usher in creating material for *Muscle Beach Party*, Annette's strongest album, which featured back-up from girl-group, the Honeys. Funicello later appeared in the Monkees' cult film *Head* (1968), but was unable to sustain thespian and recording successes into the next decade.

Albums: *Annette Sings Anka* (1960), *Hawaiiannette* (1960), *Songs From Annette And Other Walt Disney Serials* (early 60s), *Tubby The Tuba And Other Songs About Music* (early 60s), *Annette, Italiannette* (early 60s), *Dance Annette* (early 60s), *The Story Of My Teens* (early 60s), *Teen Street* (early 60s), *Annette On Campus* (early 60s), *Annette At Bikini Beach* (early 60s), *Pajama Party* (early 60s), *Annette Sings Golden Surfin' Hits*, (early 60s) *Something Borrowed, Something Blue* (early 60s), *Annette Funicello* (early 60s), *Annette's Beach Party* (1963), *Muscle Beach Party* (1964).

Anthony, Richard

b. Richard Anthony Bush, 13 January 1938, Cairo, Egypt He forsook higher education in Paris to become a singer but was obliged to make ends meet with a variety of jobs and as a session saxophonist. He signed to Pathe-Marconi in 1958, but his debut single, 'La Rue Des Coeurs Perdus', fared poorly. However, he became popular with his native reproductions of US smashes such as Buddy Holly's 'Peggy Sue' and Lloyd Price's 'Personality'. He came into his own, however, with the twist craze with 'C'est Ma Fête' ('It's My Party') and an untranslated 'Let's Twist Again' established him as a rival to Johnny Halliday. After a million-selling French cover of Peter, Paul And Mary's '500 Miles Away From Home', he secured UK chart entries with 1963's 'Walking Alone' and reached the Top 20, with 'If I Loved You'. His revival of the Everly Brothers' 'Crying In The Rain' narrowly missed the charts. Concentration on this market adversely affected his domestic standing, until 1966's 'Fille Sauvage' (the Rolling Stones' 'Ruby Tuesday') brought him in from the cold. Both on tour and in the studio, he was backed for a long while by the Roulettes who impressed him with their playing on a French version of 'Concrete And Clay'. Anthony's career continued its ups and downs and his total record sales exceeded 12 million.

Selected album: *Disque D'Or* (70s).

Aphrodite's Child

Formed in Greece during the mid-60s, Aphrodite's Child consisted of Demis Roussos (b. 15 June 1947, Alexandria, Egypt; vocals), Vangelis Papathanassiou (b. Evangalos, Odyssey Papathanassiou, 29 March 1943, Valos, Greece; keyboards) and Lucas Sideras (b.

5 December 1944, Athens, Greece; drums). In 1968 the trio enjoyed a massive European hit with 'Rain And Tears', a haunting ballad memorable for Roussos' nasal, almost sobbing, falsetto. Although the single made little impression in Britain, the group did court a cult-like popularity, particularly in the wake of a second album, *It's Five O'Clock*. It was their 1972 release, *666*, that marked an artistic peak and this apocalyptical concept album, a double set, was applauded for its ambition and execution. Paradoxically, *666 - The Apocalypse Of St. John* was the trio's final recording. 'Break' from the album almost became a posthumous hit that year. Roussos subsequently found international fame as a purveyor of sweet, MOR material while Papathanassiou achieved notable solo success under the name of Vangelis. His instrumental and compositional dexterity reached its zenith with the soundtrack to the Oscar-winning British film *Chariots Of Fire*.

Albums: *Aphrodite's Child - Rain And Tears* (1968), *It's Five O'Clock* (1970), *666 - The Apocalypse Of St. John* (1972). Compilations: *The Best Of Aphrodite's Child* (1975), *Greatest Hits* (1981).

Applejacks

Applejacks

Formed in Solihull, West Midlands, this early 60s UK pop group comprised Martin Baggott (guitar), Philip Cash (guitar), Megan Davies (bass), Don Gould (organ), Al Jackson (vocals) and Gerry Freeman (drums). Signed by Decca A&R representative Mike Smith, they found Top 10 UK chart success in 1964 with the memorable 'Tell Me When'. The grand follow-up, 'Like Dreamers Do', was a song taken from the famous Lennon and McCartney Decca audition tape. It barely scraped the Top 20 in spite of its pedigree and the next single, 'Three Little Words' did no better. Always capable of finding a class demo the group turned to the Kinks' catalogue for Ray Davies's moody 'I Go To Sleep'. Its failure effectively signalled the Applejacks' doom and they duly returned to the northern club scene.

Album: *Tell Me When* (1964).

Archies

Created for mass consumption by bubblegum-pop genius Don Kirshner (the man who gave us the Monkees), the Archies were the ultimate manufactured pop group. They existed on television and on their record sleeves as pure animations, based on the comic book characters of the same name. The voices behind the singing cartoon characters were vocalists Ron Dante, Toni Wine and Andy Kim, who were later called upon for touring purposes. Kirshner was astute enough to employ solid commercial writers of some standing, including Jeff Barry and Ellie Greenwich. After several minor successes, the group released one of the biggest selling singles in the history of RCA Records. 'Sugar Sugar' became a transatlantic number 1, hogging the top spot in Britain for over two months. Back in the USA, where the television series was extremely popular, the group enjoyed another Top 10 hit with 'Jingle Jangle' before suffering the sharp plunge into obscurity common to animated creations.
Album: *Sugar Sugar* (1969).

P.P. Arnold and the Small Faces

Arnold, P.P

b. Patricia Arnold, 1946, Los Angeles, California, USA. This former church choir and talented session singer first came to the fore in 1966 as a member of Ike And Tina Turner's backing group, the Ikettes. Relocating to England, she was signed to Andrew Loog Oldham's Immediate label, and was backed on tour by the Nice. Her exceptional version of the Cat Stevens' ballad, 'The First Cut Is The Deepest', was a UK Top 20 hit in 1967 and she enjoyed a second major hit the following year with Chip Taylor's 'Angel Of The Morning', which was arranged by future Led Zeppelin bassist John Paul Jones. Highly regarded among her musical peers for the sheer power and clarity of voice, her first two albums were produced by Mick Jagger (the second in conjunction with Steve Marriott). Arnold repaid Marriott's production work by contributing some powerful vocals to the Small Faces' hit 'Tin Soldier'. Never

quite hitting the big time, Arnold concentrated increasingly on acting, appearing in such musicals as Jack Good's *Catch My Soul*, Tim Rice and Andrew Lloyd Webber's *Jesus Christ Superstar* and Lloyd Webber's *Starlight Express*. A session singer for many artists ranging from Dr John to Nils Lofgren and Freddie King, she returned to the UK charts in 1989 fronting the Beatmasters on 'Burn It Up'.
Albums: *First Lady Of Immediate* (1967), *Kafunta* (1968). Compilations: *Greatest Hits* (1978), *The P.P. Arnold Collection* (1988).

Artwoods

The collectability of the Artwoods' rare recorded works, has increased considerably over the past three decades. This competent UK-based R&B band had a brief moment of glory during the early 60s British beat group club scene. The band comprised Arthur 'Art' Wood (vocals), Keef Hartley (drums), Jon Lord (organ), Derek Griffiths (guitar) and Malcolm Pool (bass). Their only album contained workmanlike covers of regular R&B songs such as 'Can You Hear Me?' and 'If You've Got To Make A Fool Of Somebody', alongside bolder arrangements, including Jimmy Smith's, 'Walk On The Wild Side'. Lord demonstrated the seeds of what became a powerful organ style, with Deep Purple. Hartley, a technically brilliant drummer found limited success with John Mayall and his own unit, the Keef Hartley Band. Leader Wood disappeared from the music world, and is better known as the older brother of Ronnie Wood.
Album: *Art Gallery* (1965). Compilation: *The Artwoods* (1973).

Artwoods

Association

One of the most attractive pop/psychedelic harmony units of the mid-60s, the Association comprised Gary Alexander (lead vocals), Russ Giguere (vocals/guitar), Brian Cole (vocals/bass), Jim Yester (vocals/guitar), Ted Bluechel (drums) and Terry Kirkham (keyboards). After releasing two singles on small labels, 'Babe I'm Gonna Leave You' and a folk-rock version of Bob Dylan's 'One Two Many Mornings', they broke through with Tandyn Almer's evocative 'Along Comes Mary'. Its ascent to the US Top 10 coincided with allegations that it was a drug song. The Association's entire image was ambiguous; genuinely psychedelic in spirit, they also sang ballads and appeared in smart suits. With their strong line-up of singers/composers, they largely wrote their own material for albums. Terry Kirkham gave them their first number 1 single with 'Cherish' while their debut album *And Then ... Along Comes* (1967), produced by Curt Boettcher, displayed their harmonic talent to extraordinary effect. Considerable single success followed with another US chart-topper 'Windy' and a number 2 with 'Never My Love'. Their smooth balladeering was consistently balanced by odd psychedelic aberrations such as the genuinely weird 'Pandora's Golden Heebie Jeebies' on their second album *Renaissance*.

Never candidates for the hip elite, the group failed to attract a devoted following and by the late 70s their sales were dwindling. Garry Alexander left briefly for a trip to India and returned with a new name, 'Jules', while their long-standing producer Jerry Yester, brother of Jim, replaced Zal Yanovsky in the Lovin' Spoonful. Soldiering on, the Association continued to release quality singles such as 'Time For Living', but soon lost ground and major label status. A soundtrack for the movie *Goodbye Columbus* (1969) and a reasonable 'comeback' album, *Waterbeds In Trinidad* (1972) brought new hope but the death of founder member Brian Coles from drug abuse accelerated their eventual move on to the revivalist circuit.

Albums: *And Then ... Along Comes* (1966), *Renaissance* (1967), *Insight Out* (1967), *Birthday* (1968), *The Association* (1969), *Live* (1970), *Stop Your Motor* (1971), *Waterbeds In Trinidad* (1972). Compilations: *Greatest Hits* (1968), *Golden Heebie Jeebies* (1988).

Brian Auger And The Trinity

Auger, Brian
b. 18 July 1939, London, England. This respected jazz rock organist rose to prominence in 1962 leading the Brian Auger Trio. Rick Laird (bass) and Phil Kinorra (drums) completed an act which, within two years, had evolved into the Brian Auger Trinity with the addition on John McLaughlin (guitar) and Glen Hughes (saxophone). An unsettled period ensued, but by the end of 1964 the leader emerged fronting a new line-up completed by Vic Briggs (guitar), Rickie Brown (bass) and Mickey Waller (drums). The revamped Trinity completed several singles, notably 'Fool Killer' and 'Green Onions '65' before being absorbed into the revue-styled Steampacket. A third Trinity - Auger, Dave Ambrose (bass) and Clive Thacker (drums) - emerged in 1966 to pursue a successful career with vocalist Julie Driscoll which ran concurrent with the trio's own jazz-influenced desires. This direction was maintained with a 70s aggregation, Oblivion Express, which included guitarist Jim Mullen and drummer Robbie McIntosh, later of the Average White Band. Although UK success was not forthcoming, the unit was a popular attraction in the USA and Europe, but an unstable line-up hampered progress. Auger subsequently began a solo career but, despite embracing a dance-funk style on *Here And Now*, was unable to recapture the high profile he once enjoyed.

Albums: *Definitely What* (1968), *Befour* (1970), *Oblivion Express* (1971), *A Better Land* (1971), *Second Wind* (1972), *Closer To It* (1973), *Straight Ahead* (1974), *Live Oblivion Volume 1* (1974), *Live Oblivion Volume 2* (1974), *Reinforcements* (70s), *Happiness Heartaches* (1977), *Encore* (1978), *Here And Now* (1984). Compilations and archive sets: with Sonny Boy 'Rice Miller' Williamson and Jimmy Page *Don't Send Me No Flowers* (1968), *The Best Of Brian Auger And The Trinity* (1970), *Genesis* (1975), *Jam Session* (1975), *The Best Of Brian Auger* (70s), with Julie Driscoll *Open* (1967), *Streetnoise* (1968). Compilations: *Jools/Brian* (1968), *London 1964-1967* (1977), *The Road To Vauxhall 1967-1969* (1989).

Avalon, Frankie
b. Francis Avallone, 18 September 1939, Philadelphia, USA. The photogenic 50s teen idol started as a trumpet-playing child prodigy. His first recordings in 1954 were the instrumentals 'Trumpet Sorrento' and 'Trumpet Tarantella' on X-Vik Records (an RCA Records subsidiary). In the mid-50s, he appeared on many television and radio shows including those of Paul Whiteman, Jackie Gleason and Ray Anthony. He joined Rocco & The Saints and was seen singing with them in the 1957 film *Jamboree* (*Disc Jockey Jamboree* in the UK). Avalon signed to Chancellor Records and in 1958 his third single for them 'Dede Dinah' reached the US Top 10. It was the first of his 25 US chart entries, many of which were written by his hard-working manager,

Bob Marucci.

Despite the fact that he had a weak voice, he quickly became one of the top stars in the US and managed two chart toppers in 1959 'Venus' and 'Why', which were his only UK Top 20 entries. He had to wait until his 21st birthday in 1961 to receive the $100,000 he had earned to date and by that time he had passed his peak as a singer and turned his attention to acting. His acting career was also successful, with appearances in many films including a string of beach movies, alongside fellow 50s pop star Annette. He also appeared in the very successful 1978 film, **Grease**. He later recorded with little success on United Artists, Reprise, Metromedia, Regalia, Delite, Amos and Bobcat. Apart from his film and occasional television appearances, Avalon still performs on the supper-club circuit. Alongside his fellow Chancellor Records artist Fabian, he is often put down by rock critics, yet remains one of the American public's best loved 50s teen idols.

Selected albums: *Frankie Avalon* (1958), *The Young Frankie Avalon* (1959), *Swingin' On A Rainbow* (1959), *Young And In Love* (1960), *Summer Scene* (1960), *And Now About Mr. Avalon* (1961), *Italiano* (1962), *You Are Mine* (1962), *Frankie Avalon Christmas Album* (1962), *Muscle Beach Party* (1964 - film soundtrack), *I'll Take Sweden* (1965 - film soundtrack), *I Want You Near Me* (1970), *Bobby Sox To Stockings* (1984), *Frankie Avalon* (1987). Selected compilations: *A Whole Lotta Frankie* (1961), *15 Greatest Hits* (1964), *Best Of Frankie Avalon* (1984).

Bacharach, Burt

b. 12 May 1928, Kansas City, Missouri, USA. As a composer and arranger, Bacharach is rightly regarded as one of the most important figures in contemporary music. Although his father was a journalist, it was music rather than lyrics which were to prove Bacharach's forte. Bred in New York, Burt was a jazz aficionado and played in various ensembles during the 40s. He studied musical theory and composition at university and served in the US Army between 1950-52. Following his discharge, he worked as a pianist, arranger and conductor for a number of artists including Vic Damone, Steve Lawrence, Polly Bergen and the Ames Brothers. From 1956-58, Bacharach worked as musical director for Marlene Dietrich, a period in which he also registered his first

Burt Bacharach

hit as a composer. The song in question was the Five Blobs' 'The Blob', a tune written for a horror b-movie. Bacharach's co-composer on that hit was Mack David, but a more fruitful partnership followed when Burt was introduced to his collaborator's brother, Hal David. In 1958, Bacharach/David enjoyed their first hit with 'The Story Of My Life', a US Top 20 for Marty Robbins. In the UK, the song became an instant standard, courtesy of the chart-topping Michael Holliday and three other hit versions by Gary Miller, Alma Cogan and Dave King. Even greater success followed with Perry Como's reading of the engagingly melodic 'Magic Moments' which topped the UK charts for an astonishing eight weeks (number 4 in the US). Despite their chart-topping songwriting success, the Bacharach/David team did not work together exclusively until as late as 1962. In the meantime, Bacharach found a new songwriting partner, Bob Hilliard, with whom he composed several recordings for the Drifters. They also enjoyed minor success with Chuck Jackson's 'Any Day Now' (later recorded by Elvis Presley). It was during the early 60s that the Bacharach/David team recommenced their collaboration in earnest and many of their recordings brought success to both USA and UK artists. Frankie Vaughan's 'Tower Of Strength' gave them their third UK number 1, as well as another US Top 10 hit in a version by Gene

McDaniels. The highly talented Gene Pitney, himself a songwriter, achieved two of his early hits with the duo's 'The Man Who Shot Liberty Valence' and 'Twenty Four Hours From Tulsa'. Other well-known Bacharach/David standards from the early/mid-60s included 'Wives And Lovers' and 'What The World Needs Now Is Love' (successfully covered by Jack Jones and Jackie DeShannon, respectively).

From 1962 onwards the formidable Bacharach/David writing team steered the career of songstress Dionne Warwick with a breathtaking array of quality hit songs including 'Don't Make Me Over', 'Anyone Who Had A Heart', 'Walk On By', 'You'll Never Get To Heaven', 'Reach Out For Me', 'Are You There (With Another Girl)', 'Message To Michael', 'Trains And Boats And Planes', 'I Just Don't Know What To Do With Myself', Alfie', 'The Windows Of The World', 'I Say A Little Prayer', Valley Of The Dolls' and 'Do You Know The Way To San Jose?'. Interestingly, the songwriting duo maintained a quotient of number 1 singles in the UK, thanks to class covers by Cilla Black ('Anyone Who Had A Heart'), Sandie Shaw ('There's Always Something There To Remind Me'), the Walker Brothers ('Make It Easy On Yourself') and Herb Alpert ('This Guy's In Love With You'). Looking back at this remarkable series of hits, one notices the strength of Bacharach's melodies and the deftness of touch that so neatly complemented David's soul-tortured, romantic lyrics. Since writing the theme song to *The Man Who Shot Liberty Valence*, Bacharach/David were popular choices as composers of film scores. The comedy *What's New Pussycat?* brought them an Oscar nomination and another hit when the theme was recorded by Tom Jones. Dusty Springfield recorded numerous Bacharach songs on her albums throughout the 60s and together with Warwick, they were arguably the best interpreters of his material. Further hits and Academy Award nominations followed between 1967-68 with *Alfie* and *Casino Royale* (which featured 'The Look Of Love'). Finally, in 1969, a double Oscar celebration was achieved with the score from *Butch Cassidy And The Sundance Kid* and its award-winning standard 'Raindrops Keep Falling On My Head'.

Although there were opportunities to write further movie material during the late 60s, the duo were determined to complete their own musical, *Promises Promises*. The show proved enormously successful and enjoyed a lengthy Broadway run. Although Bacharach's reputation rests mainly on his songwriting, he has had a sporadic career as a recording artist. After a minor US hit with 'Saturday Sunshine'in 1963, he outmanoeuvred Billy J. Kramer And The Dakotas in the 1965 chart race involving 'Trains And Boats And Planes'. Personal appearances at such prestigious venues as the Greek Theatre in Los Angeles and the Riviera Hotel in Las Vegas have produced 'standing room only' notices, while television specials based on his songs proved very popular.

By 1970, Bacharach seemed blessed with the hit Midas touch and the Carpenters' beautiful reading of 'Close To You' suggested that a further wealth of standards would follow. Remarkably, however, this inveterate hitmaker would not enjoy another chart success for over 10 years. An acrimonious split with partner Hal David broke the classic songwriting spell. A barren period was possibly exacerbated by the concurrent break up of Burt's marriage to actress Angie Dickinson and the loss of his most consistent hitmaker Dionne Warwick. Bacharach's desultory decade was alleviated by a series of albums for A&M Records, which featured his own readings of his compositions. Although the late 60s recording *Make It Easy On Yourself* and the 1971 *Burt Bacharach* were chart successes, the curse of the 70s was once more evident when *Living Together* sold poorly. Worse followed when his musical *Lost Horizon* emerged as a commercial disaster. His succeeding albums *Futures* and *Woman* also fared badly and none of his new compositions proved chartworthy.

It was not until 1981 that Bacharach's dry run ended. At last he found a lyricist of genuine commercial fire in Carole Bayer Sager. Their Oscar-winning 'Arthur's Theme' (co-written with Peter Allen and singer Christopher Cross) returned Bacharach to the charts and in 1982 he married Sager. Together, they provided hits for Roberta Flack ('Making Love') and Neil Diamond ('Heartlight'). 1986 saw Bacharach re-enacting the success level so familiar during the late 60s, with two US number 1 hits 'That's What Friends Are For' (an AIDS charity record by Warwick and 'Friends' - Elton John, Gladys Knight and Stevie Wonder) and 'On My Own' (a duet between Patti Labelle and Michael McDonald).

Albums: *Hit Maker - Burt Bacharach* (1965), *Reach Out* (1967), *Make It Easy On Yourself* (1969), *Burt Bacharach* (1971), *Living Together* (1973), *Futures* (1977), *Woman* (1979). Compilations: *Portrait In Music* (1971), *Burt Bacharach's Greatest Hits* (1974).

Bachelors

Formed in Dublin, Eire in 1958, the group was originally known as the Harmony Chords and featured brothers Conleth Cluskey (b. 18 March 1941), Declan Cluskey (b. 12 December 1942) and John Stokes (b. Sean James Stokes, 13 August 1940). The Dublin-born trio initially worked as a mainstream folk act, all three playing harmonicas. In 1961, they were discovered in Scotland by entrepreneur Philip Solomon and his wife Dorothy. After a further period of struggle Solomon introduced them to Decca's A&R head Dick Rowe who recalls: 'They all played harmonicas and sang folk songs. They weren't an act you could sign to a pop record company. We went backstage afterwards and there were these three boys who looked at me as if I'd come from heaven and was going to open the door for them to walk in. I said, "God be with me at this moment", and I meant it'. After signing the trio, Rowe suggested a name change: 'I said, "What do girls like, Philip . . . Bachelors!".' With the assistance of producer Shel Talmy, the group scored a UK Top 10 hit with a revival of the Lew Pollack and Erno Rapee song 'Charmaine' in the summer of 1963. After three unsuccessful follow-ups ('Far Away', 'Whispering' and 'I'll See You') they struck again with a string of easy listening pop hits including several revivals suggested by Rowe: 'Diane', 'I Believe', 'Ramona', 'I Wouldn't Trade You For The World' and 'No Arms Can Ever Hold You'. In 1966, they revealed their former folk roots and surprisingly completely outmanoeuvred Simon And Garfunkel by taking 'The Sound Of Silence' to number 3 in the UK charts.

Working primarily with agent Dorothy Solomon, the Bachelors achieved great success on the cabaret circuit with a line-up that remained unchallenged for 25 years. However, in 1984, a dispute arose between the members and John Stokes was asked to leave. He duly took legal action against the brothers and the company Bachelors Ltd. During the hearing, Stokes' voice was likened to that of a 'drowning rat' but he received compensation and left with plans to form a duo. He was replaced by Peter Phipps who was inducted into the second generation New Bachelors. As Philip Solomon concluded: 'The Bachelors never missed a date in their lives. One of them even had an accident on their way to do a pantomime in Bristol and went on with his leg in plaster and 27 stitches in his head. That is professionalism'.

Albums: *The Bachelors (1963), The Bachelors Second Album* (1964), *Presenting: The Bachelors* (1964, US release), *The Bachelors And Sixteen Great Songs* (1964), *No Arms Can Ever Hold You* (1965, US release), *Marie* (1965, US release), *More Great Song Hits From The Bachelors* (1965), *Hits Of The Sixties* (1966), *Bachelors' Girls* (1966), *The Golden All Time Hits* (1967), *Live At Talk Of The Town* (1971), *Under And Over* (1971), with Patricia Cahill *Stage And Screen Spectacular* (1972). Compilations: *World Of The Bachelors* (1968), *World Of The Bachelors - Vol. Two* (1969), *World Of The Bachelors - Vol. Three* (1969), *World Of The Bachelors - Vol. Four* (1970), *World Of The Bachelors - Vol. Five* (1970), *The Very Best Of The Bachelors* (1974), *Focus On The Bachelors* (1979), *25 Golden Greats* (1979), *The Best Of The Bachelors* (1981), *The Bachelors Collection* (1985).

Joan Baez

Baez, Joan

b. 9 January 1941, Staten Island, New York, USA. The often used cliche'; the queen of folk to Bob Dylan's king, Joan's sweeping soprano is one of popular music's most distinctive voices. An impressive appearance at the 1959 Newport Folk Festival followed the singer's early performances throughout the Boston/New England club scene and established Baez as a vibrant interpreter of traditional material. Joan's first four albums featured ballads drawn from American and British sources, but as the civil rights campaign intensified, so the artist became increasingly identified with the protest movement. Her reading of 'We Shall Overcome', first released on *In Concert/Part 2*, achieved an anthem-like quality. This album also featured Dylan's, 'Don't Think Twice, It's All Right' and Baez then took the emergent singer on tour and their well-documented romance blossomed. Over the years she would interpret many of his songs, several of which, including 'Farewell Angelina' and 'Love Is Just A Four Letter Word', Dylan would not officially record. In the 60s she founded the Institute for the Study Of Nonviolence. Baez also featured early work by other contemporary writers, including Phil Ochs, brother-in-law Richard Farina, Tim Hardin and Donovan, and by the late 60s was composing her own material. The period was also marked by the singer's increasing commitment to non-violence and she was jailed on two occasions for participation in anti-war rallies. In 1968 Baez married David Harris, a peace activist who was later imprisoned for several years for draft resistance. The couple were divorced in 1972.

Although a version of the Band song, 'The Night They Drove Old Dixie Down', gave Joan a hit single in 1971, she found it hard to maintain a consistent commercial profile. Her devotion to politics continued as before and a 1973 release, *Where Are You Now My Son*, included recordings the singer made in North Vietnam. A 1975 collection, *Diamonds And Rust*, brought a measure of mainstream success. The title track remains her own strongest song. The story of her relationship with Dylan, it presaged their reunion, after ten years apart, in the legendary Rolling Thunder Revue. That in turn inspired her one entirely self-penned album, *Gulf Winds*, in which her songwriting continued to develop, often in new and unexpected directions. In 1989, she released an album celebrating 30 years of performing - *Speaking Of Dreams*, which found her duetting with her old friends Paul Simon and Jackson Browne and, surprisingly, with the Gypsy Kings in a rumba-flamenco cover of 'My Way'. However, Joan has preferred to concentrate her energies on humanitarian work rather than recording. In 1979 she founded Humanitas International, a rapid-response human rights group who first persuaded the US President Carter to send the Seventh Fleet to rescue Boat People. She has received numerous awards and honorary doctorates for her work. In the 80s and 90s Baez continued to divide her time between social activism and singing. She found a new audience among the young socially aware Europeans - 'The Children Of The Eighties', as she dubbed them in song. She retains a deserved respect for her early, highly influential releases.

Albums: *Joan Baez* (1960), *Joan Baez 2* (1961), *Joan Baez In Concert* (1962), *Joan Baez In Concert/Part 2* (1963), *Joan Baez 5* (1964), *Farewell Angelina* (1965), *Noel* (1966), *Joan* (1967), *Baptism* (1968), *Any Day Now* (1968), *David's Album* (1969), *Joan Baez In Italy* (1969), *24 July 1970 all Arena Civica di Milano* (1970), *One Day At A Time* (1970), *Blessed Are* (1971), *Carry It On* (1971), *Sacco And Vanzetti* (1971), *Come From The Shadows* (1972), *Where Are You Now My Son* (1973), *Gracias A La Vida (Here's To Life)* (1974), *Diamonds And Rust* (1975), *Live In Japan* (1975), *From Every Stage* (1976), *Gulf Winds* (1976), *Blowing Away* (1977), *Honest Lullaby* (1979), *European Tour* (1981), *Live Europe 83* (1983), *Very Early Joan* (1983), *Recently* (1988), *Diamonds And Rust In The Bullring* (1989), *Speaking Of Dreams* (1989). Compilations: *The First Ten Years* (1970), *The Ballad Book* (1972) *The Contemporary Ballad Book* (1974), *The Love Song* *Album* (1975), *The Best Of Joan Baez* (1977), *Spotlight On Joan Baez* (1980).

Further reading: *Daybreak - An Intimate Journal*, Joan Baez. *And A Voice To Sing With - A Memoir*, Joan Baez.

Baldry, Long John

b. 12 January 1941, London, England. Beginning his career playing folk and jazz in the late 50s, Baldry toured with Ramblin' Jack Elliott before moving into R&B. His strong, deep voice won him a place in the influential Blues Incorporated, following which he joined Cyril Davies's R&B All Stars. After Davies's death, Long John fronted the Hoochie Coochie Men which also included future superstar Rod Stewart, who went on to join Baldry in Steampacket (featuring Brian Auger and Julie Driscoll).

After a brief period with Bluesology (another promising outfit which boasted a young Elton John on keyboards), Baldry elected to go solo and record straightforward pop. Already well known on the music scene, he nevertheless cut an unusual pop star in 1967 with his sharp suits and imposing 6 foot 7 inch height. Composer/producer Tony Macaulay and his partner John McLeod presented the perfect song in 'Let The Heartaches Begin', a despairing ballad which Baldry belted out all the way to number 1 in the UK during late 1967. His chart career continued with the Olympic Games theme 'Mexico' the following year, which also made the Top 20. By the end of the 60s, however, the hits had ceased and another change of direction was ahead. Out went the suits and the neat, short haircut, replaced by furs and a beard as Long John belatedly attempted to establish himself with a new audience. With production assistance from former pals Rod Stewart and Elton John, he recorded a strong album, *It Ain't Easy*, but it failed to sell. After a troubled few years, he emigrated to Canada, where he performs on the club circuit.

Albums: *Long John's Blues* (1964), *Lookin' At Long John* (1966), *Let The Heartaches Begin* (1968), *Wait For Me* (1969), *It Ain't Easy* (1971), *Everything Stops For Tea* (1972), *Good To Be Alive* (1976), *Welcome To The Club* (1977), *Baldry's Out* (1979). Compilation: *Let The Heartaches Begin - The Best Of John Baldry* (1988).

Balls

Although this short-lived UK rock group barely managed a year of existence after being formed in February 1969, they are worthy of documentation as they were one of the first true 'supergroups', before that much-abused term was invented. The line-up of ex-Moody Blues, Denny Laine (vocals/guitar), ex-Move, Trevor Burton and Steve Gibbons (vocals) were augmented at various times by ex-Plastic Ono Band member Alan White (drums), Jackie Lomax, Richard Tandy (ELO), Mike Kelly (Spooky Tooth),

Keith Smart (drums) and Dave Morgan (bass). They released one single, in January 1971, financially backed by their creator/manager Tony Secunda. The energetic 'Fight For My Country' failed to sell, even though it was heavily plugged over the airwaves of the UK pirate radio station, Geronimo.

Band

When the Band emerged in 1968 with *Music From Big Pink*, they were already a seasoned and cohesive unit. Four of the group, Robbie Robertson (b. Jaime Robbie Robertson, 5 July 1943, Toronto, Ontario, Canada; guitar/vocals), Richard Manuel (b. 3 April 1943, Stratford, Canada, d. 7 March 1986; piano/drums/vocals), Garth Hudson (b. Eric Hudson, 2 August 1937, London, Ontario, Canada; organ) and Rick Danko (b. 9 December 1943, Simcoe, Canada; bass/vocals), had embraced rock 'n' roll during its first flush of success. One by one they joined the Hawks, a backing group fashioned by rockabilly singer Ronnie Hawkins, which included Levon Helm (b. Mark Levon Helm, 26 May 1942, Marvell, Arkansas, USA; drums/vocals). A minor figure in America, by the late 50s Hawkins had moved to Toronto where he pursued a career largely shaped around rabble-house cover versions. 'Bo Diddley' (1963) was a major hit in Canada, but the musicians flexed their independence during sessions for the subsequent *Mojo Man*, recording 'She's 19' and 'Farther Up The Road' with Helm taking the vocal. The quintet left Hawkins later that year and criss-crossed America's small town bars, performing for 'pimps, whores, rounders and flakeouts', as Hudson later recalled! Billed as the Canadian Squires or Levon And The Hawks, they developed a loud, brash repertoire, drawn from R&B, soul and gospel styles, while the rural life they encountered left a trail of impressions and images. The group completed a single, 'Leave Me Alone', under the former appellation, before settling in New York where 'Go Go Liza Jane' and 'The Stones I Throw' were recorded as Levon And The Hawks.

The quintet enjoyed the approbation of the city's famed Red Bird label. Robertson, Helm and Hudson supported blues singer John Hammond Jnr. on his debut single, 'I Wish You Would' (1964), while Levon's pacey composition, 'You Cheated, You Lied', was recorded by the Shangri-Las. The trio maintained their link with Hammond on the latter's fiery *So Many Roads* (1965), through which they were introduced to Bob Dylan. In August 1965 Robertson and Helm accompanied the singer for his Forest Hills concert and although the drummer reneged on further involvement, within months the remaining Hawks were at the fulcrum of Dylan's most impassioned music. They supported him on his 'electric' 1966 world tour and followed him to his Woodstock retreat where, reunited with Helm, they recorded the famous *Basement Tapes* whose lyrical, pastoral performances anticipated the style the quintet would soon adopt. *Music From Big Pink* restated traditional American music in an environment of acid-rock and psychedelia. Natural in the face of technocratic artifice, its woven, wailing harmonies suggested the fervour of sanctified soul, while the instrumental pulse drew inspiration from carnivals, country and R&B. The Band's deceptive simplicity was their very strength, binding lyrics of historical and biblical metaphor to sinuous, memorable melodies. The set included three Dylan songs, but is best recalled for 'The Weight' which, if lyrically obtuse, was the subject of several cover versions, notably from Jackie DeShannon and Spooky Tooth. *The Band* confirmed the quintet's unique qualities. Robertson had emerged as their principle songwriter, yet the panoramic view remained intact, and by invoking Americana past and present, the group reflected the pastoral desires of a restless generation. It contained several telling compositions - 'Across The Great Divide', 'The Unfaithful Servant' and 'The Night They Drove Old Dixie Down' - as well as 'Rag Mama Rag', an ebullient UK Top 20 hit. The Band then resumed touring, the perils of which were chronicled on *Stage Fright*. By openly embracing contemporary concerns, the quintet lacked their erstwhile perspective, but in 'The Rumour' they created one of the era's most telling portraits. Yet the group's once seamless sound had grown increasingly formal, a dilemma increased on *Cahoots*. Melodramatic rather than emotional, the set offered few highlights, although Van Morrison's cameo on '4% Pantomime' suggested a *bonhomie* distinctly absent elsewhere. It was followed by a warm in-concert set, *Rock Of Ages*, arranged by Allan Toussaint, and *Moondog Matinee*, a wonderful selection of favourite oldies. It served as a spotlight for Richard Manuel, whose emotional, haunting voice wrought new meaning from 'Share Your Love', 'The Great Pretender' and 'A Change Is Gonna Come'.

In 1974 the Band backed Bob Dylan on his acclaimed *Planet Waves* album and undertook the extensive tour documented on *Before The Flood*. The experience inspired a renewed creativity and *Northern Lights Southern Cross*, their strongest set since *The Band*, included 'Arcadian Driftwood', one of Robertson's most evocative compositions. However, the individual members had decided to dissolve the group and their partnership was sundered the following year with a gala performance at San Francisco's Winterland ballroom. The event, *The Last Waltz*, featured many guest contributions, including those by Dylan, Eric Clapton, Muddy Waters, Van Morrison, Neil Young, Joni Mitchell and Paul Butterfield, and was the subject of Martin Scorsese's film of the same name and a commemorative triple album. The Band also completed their contractual obligations with *Islands*, a somewhat tepid set notable only for 'Knockin' Lost John', which featured a rare lead vocal from Robertson. Levon Helm then pursued a dual career as a performer and actor, Rick Danko recorded an intermittently interesting solo album, while Hudson saved his talent for session appearances. Robbie Robertson scored soundtracks to several more Scorsese films, but kept a relatively low profile, refusing to join the ill-fated Band reunions of 1984 and 1985. A third tour ended in tragedy when, on 7 March 1986, Richard Manuel hanged himself in a motel room. His death inspired 'Fallen Angel' on Robertson's outstanding 'comeback' album, but despite the presence of Hudson and Danko elsewhere on the record, the guitarist refused to join his colleagues when they regrouped again in 1991.

Albums: *Music From Big Pink* (1968), *The Band* (1969), *Stage Fright* (1970), *Cahoots* (1971), *Rock Of Ages* (1972), *Moondog Matinee* (1973), *Northern Lights - Southern Cross* (1975), *Islands* (1977), with various artists *The Last Waltz* (1977). Compilations: *The Best Of The Band* (1976), *Anthology Volume 1* (1978), *Anthology Volume 2* (1980), *To Kingdom Come* (1989).

Bar-Kays

Jimmy King (b. 1949; guitar), Ronnie Caldwell (b. 1948; organ), Phalin Jones (b. 1949; saxophone), Ben Cauley (b. 1947; trumpet), James Alexander (bass) and Carl Cunningham (b. 1949; drums) were originally known as the River Arrows. Signed to Stax, the Bar-Kays were groomed as that label's second string houseband by Al Jackson, drummer in Booker T. And The MGs. The above sextet scored three R&B hits in 1967, spearheaded by the powerful, nagging instrumental 'Soul Finger' which deservedly crossed over into the US and UK pop charts. The Bar-Kays were employed as Otis Redding's backing group on tour, and the tragic plane crash in 1967, which took his life, also claimed King, Caldwell, Jones and Cunningham. Alexander, who fortuitously missed the flight, put a new line-up together with Ben Cauley, the sole survivor of the accident. The latter musician soon dropped out, leaving the bassist at the helm of a frequently changing line-up. Primarily a session group, the Bar-Kays provided the backing on many releases, including Isaac Hayes's *Shaft* and several of Albert King's 70s recordings. The group pursued a funk-based direction on their own releases with the addition of vocalist Larry Dodson, but while 'Son Of Shaft' reached the US R&B Top 10 in 1972, consistent success was only secured on their move to Mercury Records. Later singles, including 'Shake Your Rump To The Funk' (1976), 'Move Your Boogie Body' (1979) and 'Freakshow On The Dancefloor' (1984), were aimed squarely at the disco market. Since 1987 the group has featured Dodson, Harvey Henderson (tenor saxophone) and Winston Stewart (keyboards).

Albums: *Soul Finger* (1967), *Gotta Groove* (1969), *Black Rock* (1971), *Do You See What I See* (1972), *Cold Blooded* (1974), *Too Hot To Stop* (1976), *Flying High On Your Love* (1978), *Light Of Life* (1978), *Money Talks* (1978), *In Joy* (1979), *As One* (1980), *Night Cruisin'* (1981), *Propositions* (1982), *Dangerous* (1984), *Banging The Wall* (1985), *Contagious* (1987).

Barrett, Syd

b. Roger Keith Barrett, 6 January 1946, Cambridge, England. One of English pop's most enigmatic talents, Barrett embraced music in the early 60s as a member of Geoff Mutt And The Mottoes, a local group modelled on Cliff Richard And The Shadows. From there he joined an R&B act, the Hollering Blues, before moving to London to study at the Camberwell School of Art. In 1965, he joined three architectural students in a group he initially named the Pink Floyd Sound, but quickly dropped its superfluous suffix. He became the unit's undisputed leader, composing their early hit singles, 'Arnold Layne' and 'See Emily Play', as well as the bulk of *The Piper At The Gates Of Dawn*. An impulsive, impressionistic guitarist, his unconventional use of feedback, slide and echo did much to transfer the mystery and imagery of Pink Floyd's live sound into a studio equivalent. However, the strain of this position was too great for a psyche dogged by instability and an indulgence in hallucinogenic drugs. Barrett's behaviour grew increasingly erratic and in April 1968 he withdrew from the line-up. Tentative recording sessions were undertaken the following month, but it was another year before the artist seriously began work on a solo album. *The Madcap Laughs* was the product of two separate collaborations, firstly with producer Malcolm Jones, latterly with former colleagues Dave Gilmour and Roger Waters. The end result was an hypnotic, ethereal set on which Barrett's fragile performances were left basically unadorned or featured sympathetic support from the Soft Machine. By contrast *Barrett* was much more assertive wherein the singer's work was largely overdubbed by a band consisting of Gilmour, Rick Wright and Jerry Shirley. Although it lacked the poignancy of its predecessor, the album included the vitriolic 'Rats', one of Barrett's most chilling compositions.

The singer then returned to Cambridge where he remained in seclusion until 1972 and the formation of Stars, a short-lived unit which also featured Jack Monck (ex-Delivery) and Twink (ex-Tomorrow and Pretty Things). The trio made a disastrous debut supporting the MC5, and collapsed when Barrett failed to appear for a second gig. Rumours of new recordings have since proliferated at random, fuelled by his occasional appearance at the Abbey Road recording studios. He garnered a high profile in 1975 when Pink Floyd included a tribute - 'Shine On You Crazy Diamond' - on their best-selling *Wish You Were Here*, but Barrett's precarious mental state precludes any further active involvement in music. *Opel*, a 1988 release comprising of unissued masters and alternative takes, enhanced his reputation for startling, original work. Barrett was last rumoured to have returned to painting.

Albums: *The Madcap Laughs* (1969), *Barrett* (1970), *Opel* (1988).

Further reading: *Crazy Diamond: Syd Barrett And The Dawn Of Pink Floyd*, Mike Watkinson and Pete Anderson.

Barron Knights

Barron Knights

Formed in Leighton Buzzard, England, the Barron Knights rose from comparitive obscurity following their appearance on the bill of the Beatles' 1963 Christmas Show. Duke D'mond (b. Richard Palmer, 25 February 1945, Dunstable, Bedfordshire, England; vocals/rhythm guitar), Butch Baker (b. Leslie John Baker, 16 July 1941, Amersham, Buckinghamshire, England; guitar/banjo/vocals), 'P'nut' Langford (b. Peter Langford, 10 April 1943, Durham, Co Durham, England; guitar/vocals), Barron Antony (b. Antony Michael John Osmond, 15 June 1940, Abingdon, Berkshire, England; bass/vocals) and Dave Ballinger (b. 17 January 1941, Slough, Buckinghamshire, England; drums) scored a UK Top 3 hit the following year with 'Call Up The Groups', a parodic medley of contemporary releases by, among others, the Rolling Stones, the Searchers and the Dave Clark Five, based on the Four Preps US release, 'Big Draft'. Two similarly-styled singles, 'Pop! Go The Workers' and 'Merrie Gentle Pops', reached numbers 5 and 9 respectively in 1965, but the group failed to emulate this success with conventional

releases. The group were also the subject of one of the most bizarre high court actions in pop history when their original drummer, who had been hospitalized, sued the Barron Knights for engaging Ballinger. The Barron Knights pursued a lucrative career on the cabaret circuit throughout the late 60s and early 70s, before reviving the pastiche formula with two further Top 10 hits, 'Live In Trouble' (1977) and 'A Taste Of Aggro' (1978). A slick, show-business professionalism had now replaced the quintet's original perkiness, and they closed the decade one of Britain's most popular MOR attractions.

Albums: *Call Up The Groups* (1964), *The Barron Knights* (1966), *Scribed* (1967), *The Two Sides Of The Barron Knights* (1971), *Live In Trouble* (1977), *Knight Gallery* (1978), *Teach The World To Laugh* (1979), *Jesta Giggle* (1980), *Twisting The Knights Away* (1981), *Funny In The Head* (1984). Compilations: *Knights Of Laughter* (1979), *The Two Sides Of The Barron Knights* (1980), *Barron Knights* (1982), *The Best Of The Barron Knights* (1982).

Barry, Jeff

b. 3 April 1938, Brooklyn, New York, USA. Barry began his music career as a singer, completing several singles for RCA and Decca Records between 1959 and 1962. He also enjoyed concurrent success as a songwriter, most notably with 'Tell Laura I Love Her', a US Top 10 hit for Ray Peterson and a UK number 1 for Ricky Valance. In 1961 Barry was contracted to Trinity Music for whom he completed over 100 compositions and gained valuable experience in arranging, producing and recording demos. Although Jeff collaborated with several partners, his relationship with Ellie Greenwich would prove to be the most enduring. Together they wrote for Leslie Gore ('Maybe I Know'), the Four Pennies ('When The Boy's Happy') and the Exciters/Manfred Mann ('Do Wah Diddy') and, as the Raindrops, recorded a US Top 20 hit, 'The Kind Of Boy You Can't Forget'. However, the couple, who were now married, are best recalled for their classic work with Phil Spector which included the joyous 'Da Doo Ron Ron' and 'Then He Kissed Me' for the Crystals, 'Be My Baby' and 'Baby, I Love You' for the Ronettes and the monumenal 'River Deep Mountain High' for Ike And Tina Turner. Greenwich and Barry also wrote, and co-produced, releases on the Red Bird label for the Dixie Cups, Shangri-Las and Jelly Beans. It was also during this period that the duo 'discovered' Neil Diamond, whose early work they produced, but despite this professional commitment, their marriage ended in 1965. Barry then resumed his recording career with singles for United Artists and A&M, but achieved a greater degree of success in partnership with singer Andy Kim, writing, producing and performing for the Archies' cartoon series. The work with Greenwich has rightly stood the test of time having reached the pinnacle of stylish pop music diring the 60s.

Barry, John

b. Jonathan Barry Prendergast, 3 November 1933, York, Yorkshire, England. Renowned as one of the leading composers of film soundtrack music, Barry began his career leading the John Barry Seven. This rousing instrumental unit scored several notable UK hits between 1960-62, the best-known of which were 'Hit And Miss' and a version of the Ventures' Walk Don't Run' (both 1960). The former, which reached number 11 in the UK charts, was the theme to *Juke Box Jury*, BBC television's long-running record release show. Barry made regular appearances on several early pop programmes, including *Oh Boy* and *Drumbeat* and also enjoyed concurrent fame as a writer and arranger, scoring the distinctive pizzicato strings on numerous Adam Faith hits including the number 1 'What Do You Want' (1959). He also composed the soundtrack to *Beat Girl*, the singer's film debut, and later took up a senior A&R post with the independent Ember label. In 1962 Barry became musical director for *Dr. No*, the first of many James Bond films and although the bulk of this particular score was composed by Monty Norman, the highly evocative, and distinctive 'James Bond Theme' was Barry's own creation. He produced music for several subsequent Bond films, including *From Russia With Love*, *Goldfinger* and *You Only Live Twice*, the title songs from which provided hit singles for Matt Monro (1963), Shirley Bassey (1964) and Nancy Sinatra (1967). Such success led to a series of stylish soundtracks which encompassed contrasting moods and music, including *The Ipcress File*, *The Knack* (both 1965); *Born Free* (which won an Oscar in 1966); *Midnight Cowboy* (1969) and *Mary, Queen Of Scots* (1971). Although his theme songs have enjoyed a high commercial profile, it is Barry's imaginative incidental music which has assured his peerless reputation. By contrast he pursued another lucrative direction composing television commercials for disparate household items.

His consistency remained intact throughout the 70s and 80s, although several attendant films, including *King Kong* (1976) and *Howard The Duck* (1986), were highly criticized. 'Down Deep Inside', the theme from *The Deep* (1977), was a UK Top 5 hit for Donna Summer and this disco-influenced composition emphasized the writer's versatility. *Out Of Africa* (1985) and *The Living Daylights* (1987) demonstrated his accustomed flair while *Dances With Wolves* (1990) earned him an Oscar. His orchestrations combine elements of classical, jazz and popular themes and command the respect of enthusiastic aficionados.

Albums: as performer, composer, arranger or conductor *Six-Five Special* (1957), *Oh Boy* (1958), *Drumbeat* (1959), *Beat Girl* (1959), *Stringbeat* (1961), *Man In The Middle* (1962), *Dr. No* (1962), *It's All Happening* (1963), *Zulu* (1963), *Elizabeth Taylor In London* (1963), *From Russia With Love* (1963), *The Man In The Middle* (1964), *Goldfinger* (1964), *The Ipcress File* (1965), *Sophia Loren In Rome* (1965), *King Rat* (1965), *The Knack...& How To Get It* (1965), *Four In The Morning* (1965), *Thunderball* (1965), *Passion Flower Hotel* (1965), *The Wrong Box* (1966), *The Chase* (1966), *Born Free* (1966), *The Quiller Memorandum* (1966), *You Only Live Twice* (1967), *Dutchman* (1967), *The Whisperers* (1967), *Deadfall* (1968), *Petulia* (1968), *Boom* (1968), *The Lion In Winter* (1968), *On Her Majesty's Secret Service* (1969), *Midnight Cowboy* (1969), *The Last Valley* (1970), *Diamonds Are Forever* (1971), *Follow Me* (1971), *Lolita My Love* (1971), *The Persuaders* (1971), *Mary Queen Of Scots* (1971), *Alice's Adventures In Wonderland* (1972), *The John Barry Concert* (1972), *A Doll's House* (1973), *Billy* (1974), *The Dove* (1974), *The Man With The Golden Gun* (1974), *The Day Of The Locust* (1974), *Americans* (1975), *Robin And Marian* (1976), *King Kong* (1976), *The Deep* (1977), *The Game Of Death* (1978), *Starcrash* (1978), *The Black Hole* (1979), *Moonraker* (1979), *Inside Moves* (1980), *The Legend Of The Lone Ranger* (1981), *Frances* (1982), *High Road To China* (1983), *The Golden Seal* (1983), *Body Heat* (1983), *Until September* (1984), *Jagged Edge* (1985), *Out Of Africa* (1985), *A View To A Kill* (1985), *Peggy Sue Got Married* (1986), *Howard The Duck* (1986), *Golden Child* (1986), *Somewhere In Time* (1986), *Living Daylights* (1987), *Dances With Wolves* (1990). Compilations: *The Great Movie Sounds Of John Barry* (1966), *John Barry Conducts His Great Movie Hits* (1967), *Ready When You Are, John Barry* (1970), *John Barry Revisited* (1971), *Play It Again* (1974), *The Music Of John Barry* (1976), *The Very Best Of John Barry* (1977), *The John Barry Seven And Orchestra* (1979), *The Best Of John Barry* (1981), *The Big Screen Hits Of John Barry* (1981), *James Bond's Greatest Hits* (1982), *Music From The Big Screen* (1986), *Hit Or Miss* (1988), *The Film Music Of John Barry* (1989), *John Barry Themes* (1989).

Barry, Len

b. Leonard Borrisoff, 12 June 1942, Philadelphia, Pennsylvania, USA. Barry began his career as the anonymous vocalist on the Bosstones' 1958 single 'Mope-Itty Mope' before joining the Dovells between 1961-63. As a solo artist, his white soul vocals were best exemplified on the scintillating chart topper '1-2-3-' and the similarly paced 'Like A Baby'. With his sharp suits and clean-cut image, Barry seemed a Philadelphia teen idol chronologically cut adrift in 1965, and his contention that long-haired

groups were on the way out caused a few ripples in the pop press. Although he enjoyed another minor hit in the US with the **West Side Story** anthem 'Somewhere', the song had already charted in the UK courtesy of P.J. Proby. During the psychedelic boom in the late 60s, Barry went out of fashion and gradually toned down his lively stage act for cabaret purposes. By the end of the decade and through the 70s, he moved into production work.
Album: *1-2-3* (1965).

Lionel Bart and Shane Fenton

Bart, Lionel

b. Lionel Begleiter, 1 August 1930, East London, England. The comparative inactivity of Bart for many years has tended to cloud the fact that he is one of the major songwriters of 20th-century popular song. The former silk-screen printer was at the very hub of the rock 'n' roll and skiffle generation that came out of London's Soho in the mid-50s. As a member of the Cavemen with Tommy Steele he later became Steele's main source of non-American song material. In addition to writing the pioneering 'Rock With The Cavemen' he composed a series of glorious singalong numbers including 'A Handful Of Songs', 'Water Water' and the trite but delightfully innocent 'Little White Bull'. Much of Bart's work was steeped in the English music-hall tradition with a strong working class pride and it was no surprise that he soon graduated into writing songs for full-length stage shows. *Lock Up Your Daughters* and *Fings Ain't Wot They Used To Be* were two of his early successes, both appearing during 1959, the same year he wrote the classic 'Living Doll' for Cliff Richard. Bart was one of the first writers to introduce mild politics into his lyrics; beautifully transcribed with topical yet humorously ironic innocence, for example: 'They've changed our local Palais into a bowling alley and fings ain't wot they used to be.' As the 60s dawned Bart unconsciously embarked on a decade that saw him reach dizzy heights of success and made him one of the musical personalities of the decade. During the first quarter of the year he topped the charts with 'Do

You Mind' for Anthony Newley; a brilliantly simple and catchy song complete with Bart's own finger-snapped accompaniment. The best was yet to come when that year he launched *Oliver*, a musical based on Dickens's *Oliver Twist*. This became a phenomenal triumph, and remains one of the most successful musicals of all time. Bart's knack of simple melody combined with unforgettable lyrics produced a plethora of classics including the pleading 'Who Will Buy', the rousing 'Food Glorious Food' and the poignant 'As Long As He Needs Me' (also a major hit for Shirley Bassey, although she reputedly never liked the song). Bart was a pivotal figure throughout the swinging London scene of the 60s, although he maintains that the party actually started in the 50s. Lionel befriended Brian Epstein, the Beatles, the Rolling Stones, became an international star following *Oliver*'s success as a film (winning six Oscars) and was romantically linked with Judy Garland and Alma Cogan. Following continued, although lesser success, with *Blitz* and *Maggie May*, Lionel came down to reality when the London critics damned his 1965 musical *Twang*, based upon the life of Robin Hood. Bart's philanthropic nature made him a prime target for business sharks and he was wrested of much of his fortune by trusting too many people. By the end of the 60s the cracks were beginning to show; his dependence on drugs and alcohol increased and he watched many of his close friends die in tragic circumstances; Cogan with cancer, Garland through drink and drugs and Epstein's supposed suicide. In 1969, *La Strada* only had a short run in New York before Lionel retreated into himself, and for many years kept a relatively low profile, watching the 70s and 80s pass almost as a blur, only making contributions to *The Londoners* and *Costa Packet*. During this time the gutter press were eager for a kiss-and-tell story but Bart remained silent, a credible action considering the sums of money he was offered. During the late 80s Lionel finally beat his battle with booze and ended the decade a saner, wiser and healthier man. His renaissance started in 1989 when he was commissioned by a UK building society to write a television jingle. The composition became part of an award-winning advertisement, featuring a number of angelic children singing with Bart, filmed in pristine monochrome. The song 'Happy Endings' was a justifiable exhumation of a man who remains an immensely talented figure and whose work ranks with some of the greatest of the American 'musical comedy' songwriters.

Bass, Fontella

b. 3 July 1940, St. Louis, Missouri, USA. The daughter of gospel luminary Martha Bass, Fontella toured as keyboard player and singer with the Little Milton band during the early 60s. Simultaneously, she made several solo records, including one for Ike Turner's Prann label. When Milton's bandleader, Oliver Sain, left to form his own group, he took Fontella with him, and teamed her with another featured vocalist, Bobby McClure. The duo was subsequently signed to Checker, on which 'Don't Mess Up A Good Thing' and 'You'll Miss Me (When I'm Gone)' were hits in 1965. 'Rescue Me', a driving song, gave Fontella success in her own right that same year with an R&B number 1 and a UK/US Top 20 hit. Other solo hits, including 'Recovery', followed, but by the end of the decade she had moved to Paris with her husband, jazz trumpeter Lester Bowie. When they later returned to America, Fontella recorded a series of fine records for the Shreveport-based Ronn/Jewel/Paula complex. She has also worked with Bowie's *avant garde* group, the Art Ensemble Of Chicago. In 1985 she had resumed working for Oliver Sain in St. Louis.

Albums: *The New Look* (1966), *Les Stances A Sophie* (1970, film soundtrack), *Free* (1972).

Bassey, Shirley

b. 8 January 1937, Tiger Bay, Cardiff, Wales. Her early jobs included work in a factory's wrapping and packing department, while playing working men's clubs at weekends. After touring the UK in revues and Variety, Lancashire comedian Al Read included her in his 1955 Christmas Show at London's Adelphi Theatre, and his revue, *Such Is Life*, which ran for a year. Her first hit, in 1957, was the calypso-styled 'Banana Boat Song', followed by 'Kiss Me Honey Honey, Kiss Me' nearly two years later. With her powerful voice (she was sometimes called 'Bassey the Belter'), the unique Bassey style and phrasing started to emerge in 1959 with 'As I Love You' which topped the UK chart, and continued through to the mid-70s via such heart rending ballads as Lionel Bart's 'As Long As He Needs Me' (Nancy's big song from *Oliver*), 'You'll Never Know', 'I'll Get By', 'Reach For The Stars'/'Climb Every Mountain', 'What Now My Love', '(I) Who Have Nothing', George Harrison's, 'Something', 'For All We Know', and an Italian hit with a new lyric by Norman Newell, 'Never, Never, Never'. Her singles sales were such that, even into the 80s, her records had spent more weeks in the UK chart than those of any other female performer. Hit albums included *Shirley*, *Something*, *Something Else*, *Never Never Never*, *The Shirley Bassey Singles Album* and *25th Anniversay Album*. In 1962, she was accompanied on *Let's Face The Music* by top USA arranger/conductor Nelson Riddle. In live performances her rise to the top was swift and by the early 60s she was headlining in New York and Las Vegas. In 1964 Bassey had a big hit in the USA with 'Goldfinger', one of three songs she sang on the title sequences of James Bond movies. The others were

'Diamonds Are Forever' and 'Moonraker'. In 1969, she moved her base to Switzerland but continued to play major concert halls throughout the world. The American Guild Of Variety Artists voted her 'Best Female Entertainer' for 1976, and in the same year she celebrated 20 years as a recording artist with a 22-date British tour. In 1977, she received a Britannia Award for the 'Best Female Solo Singer In The Last 50 Years'.

In 1981, Bassey withdrew to her Swiss home and announced her semi-retirement, but continued to emerge occasionally throughout the 80s for television specials, concert tours, and a few albums including *Love Songs* and *I Am What I Am*. In one of pop's more unlikely collaborations, she was teamed wtih Yello in 1987 for the single, 'The Rhythm Divine'. In the 90s, with her provocative body language, ever more lavish gowns, and specialities such as 'Big Spender', 'Nobody Does It Like Me', 'Tonight' and 'What Kind Of Fool Am I', together with more contemporary material, the 'Tigress Of Tiger Bay' has shown herself to be a powerful and exciting performer.

Albums: *The Bewitching Miss Bassey* (1959), *Fabulous Shirley Bassey* (1960), *Shirley* (1961), *Shirley Bassey* (1962), *Let's Face The Music* (1962), *Shirley Bassey At The Pigalle* (1965), *Shirley Bassey Belts The Best!* (1965), *I've Got A Song For You* (1966), *Twelve Of Those Songs* (1968), *Live At The Talk Of The Town* (1970), *Something* (1970), *Something Else* (1971), *Big Spender* (1971), *It's Magic* (1971), *What Now My Love* (1971), *I Capricorn* (1972), *And I Love You So* (1972), *Never, Never, Never* (1973), *Live At Carnegie Hall* (1973), *Broadway, Bassey's Way* (1973), *Nobody Does It Like Me* (1974), *Good, Bad But Beautiful* (1975), *Love, Life And Feelings* (1976), *Thoughts Of Love* (1976), *You Take My Heart Away* (1977), *The Magic Is You* (1979), *As Long As He Needs Me* (1980), *As Time Goes By* (1980), *I'm In The Mood For Love* (1981), *Love Songs* (1982), *All By Myself* (1984), *I Am What I Am* (1984), *Playing Solitaire* (1985), *I've Got You Under My Skin* (1985), *Sings The Songs From The Shows* (1986), *Born To Sing The Blues* (1987), *Let Me Sing And I'm Happy* (1988), *Her Favourite Songs* (1988), *Keep The Music Playing* (1991). Compilations: *Golden Hits Of Shirley Bassey* (1968), *The Shirley Bassey Collection* (1972), *The Shirley Bassey Singles Album* (1975), *25th Anniversary Album* (1978), *21 Hit Singles* (1979), *Tonight* (1984), *Diamonds - The Best Of Shirley Bassey* (1988).

B. Bumble And The Stingers

This short-lived act was one of several US groups formed by pop svengali Kim Fowley as an outlet for his production/songwriting talents at Rendezvous Records. Their 1961 release, 'Bumble Boogie' (featuring Ernie Freeman at the piano), an adaptation of Nicolai Rimsky-Korsakov's 'Flight Of The Bumble Bee' reached number 21 in the US chart. It was, however, the following year's 'Nut Rocker' (with pianist Lincoln Mayorga), which brought them lasting fame. Although it only reached number 23 in the US, this propulsive instrumental, an irreverent boogie-woogie reading of Pyotr Ill'yich Tchaikovsky's *Nutcracker Suite*, fared much better in the UK where it soared to number 1 and, 10 years later, again reached the Top 20 on re-issue. The group - B. Bumble (who at this juncture was R.C. Gamble, b. 1940, Spiro, Oklahoma, USA), Terry Anderson (b. 1941, Harrison, Arkansas, USA; guitar), Jimmy King (b. 1938; rhythm guitar) and Don Orr (b. 1939; drums) - completed a British tour in 1962 that year.

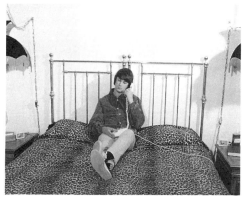

Beach Boys; Brian Wilson

Beach Boys

The seminal line-up comprised: Brian Wilson (b. 20 June 1942), Carl Wilson (b. 22 December 1946), Dennis Wilson (b. 4 December 1944, Hawthorne, California, USA), Al Jardine (b. 3 September 1942, Lima, Ohio, USA) and Mike Love (b. 15 March 1941, Baldwin Hills, California, USA). When the aforementioned, three brothers, one cousin and a schoolfriend, formed a casual singing group in 1961, they unconsciously created one of the longest running, compulsively fascinating and bitterly tragic sagas in popular music. As Carl And The Passions, the Pendletones and Kenny And The Cadets, they rehearsed and played highschool hops while the elder brother Brian began to demonstrate his songwriting ability. He was already obsessed with harmonics and melody, and would listen for hours to close harmony groups, especially the Four Freshmen and the Hi-Lo's. One of his earliest songs, 'Surfin'' (written at the suggestion of keen surfing brother Dennis), was released on a local label and the topical name, Beach Boys was innocently adopted. The domineering father of the brothers, Murray Wilson, immediately seized on their potential and appointed himself as manager, publicist and producer. After his own

abortive attempts at a career in music, he began to live his frustrated career dreams through his sons. 'Surfin'', with Murray's efforts, became a sizable local hit, and made the *Billboard* Hot 100. (number 75). His continuing efforts gained them a recording contract with Capitol Records during the summer of 1962. In addition to the developing group's conflicts, Nik Venet (the producer at Capitol) became embroiled immediately with Murray, and their ideas clashed. Over the next 18 months the Beach Boys had 10 US hits and released four albums of surfing and hot-rod songs, (each cover showed the photograph of neighbourhood friend, David Marks, who had temporarily replaced Al Jardine while he attended dentistry college). The Beach Boys' punishing work load began to affect the main songwriter Brian, who was additionally writing similar material for fellow surf/hot rodders Jan And Dean.

In 1963 the Beach Boys' phenomenon reached the UK in the shape of the single 'Surfin' USA', which mildly interrupted the Merseybeat domination. The predominantly working-class image of the British beat group scene was at odds with the clean and wholesome west coast perception blessed with permanent sunshine, fun and beautiful girls. During 1964 a further four albums were released, culminating in the *Christmas Album*. This represented a staggering eight albums in just over two years, six of which were arranged and produced by Brian, in addition to his having written 63 out of a total of 84 songs. In America, the Beatles had begun their unmatched domination of the charts, and in their wake came dozens of groups as the British invasion took place. The Beach Boys, more especially Brian, could only stand back in amazement. He felt so threatened that it drove him to compete against the Beatles. Eventually Brian gained some pyrrhic revenge, when in 1966 the Beach Boys were voted number 1 group in the world by the UK music press, pushing the Fab Four into second place.

Wilson's maturity as a composer was developing at a frightening pace with classic hits like 'I Get Around', 'California Girls' and 'God Only Knows'. The overall quality of albums such as *Summer Days And Summer Nights!!* and *Today* was extremely high. Many of Wilson's songs portrayed his own insecurity as an adolescent. Songs like, 'In My Room', 'Wouldn't It Be Nice' and 'Girl Don't Tell Me' found a receptive audience who could immediately relate to the lyrics. While their instrumental prowess was average, the immaculate combination of each member's voice, delivered a sound that was unmistakable. Both Carl and Brian had perfect pitch, even though Brian was deaf in one ear (reputedly caused through his father's beatings). In private the 'musical genius' was working on what was to be his self-intended masterpiece, *Pet*

Sounds. Released in August 1966, the high profile pre-publicity proved deserved and the reviews were outstanding. The music was also outstanding, but for some inexplicable reason, sales were not. It was later reported that Brian was devastated by the comparative commercial failure of *Pet Sounds* in his own country (US number 10), and mortified a year later when the Beatles' *Sgt Peppers Lonely Hearts Club Band* was released. It was not widely known that Brian had already experienced two nervous breakdowns, retired from performing with the group and had begun to depend on barbiturates. Even less public was the breakdown of his relationship with his father and the festering tension within the band. The brief recruitment of Glen Campbell, followed by Bruce Johnston, filled Brian's place in public. Through all this turmoil the Beach Boys rose to their peak at the end of 1966 with arguably their greatest achievement, 'Good Vibrations'. This glorious collage of musical pattern with its changes of tempo, unusual lyrics and incredible dynamics earned Brian and the band the respect of every musician. The group embarked on a major tour of Europe with a new single 'Heroes And Villains', another innovative excursion with more intriguing lyrics by Van Dyke Parks. Brian meanwhile attempted a counter attack on the Beatles, with a project to be known as 'Smile'. This became the band's albatross, although it was never officially released. The painstaking hours spent on this project is now one of pop's legendary tales. Parts of the material surfaced on their next three albums, and further tracks appeared on other collections up until 1971.

The conflict between Wilson and the band was surfacing more regularly. Mike Love in particular wanted the other Beach Boys to continue with their immaculate pop music, and argued that Brian was getting too 'far out'. Indeed Brian's reclusive nature, fast increasing weight and growing dependence on drugs added fuel to Love's argument. Observers felt that the band could not raise themselves to the musical level visualized in Brian's present state of mind. Many students of the Beach Boys saga feel, retrospectively, that at that point Brian should have completely broken away to concentrate on his symphonic ideas, and made his own records. The band meanwhile could have carried along the route that their fans loved. *Smiley Smile*, in 1967 and *Wild Honey* the following year were comparative failures in the charts by previous Beach Boys standards. Their music had lost its cohesiveness and their mentor and guiding light had by now retreated to his bed, where he stayed for many years. In Europe the group were still having hits, and even had a surprise UK chart topper in 1968 with 'Do It Again', with Mike Love's nasal vocals taking the lead on a song harping back to better times. Love had now become a devotee of the Maharishi Mahesh Yogi, while Dennis Wilson, who was emerging as a talented songwriter, became involved with Charles Manson; later to become notorious as a mass murderer. Dennis's naivety allowed him to be drained of money, parted from his home and ultimately threatened with his life. Manson and Wilson collaborated on a number of songs, notably 'Never Learn Not To Love' which, although a Beach Boys' b-side, had the ironic distinction of putting Charles Manson in the charts. To highlight their discontent, three of their next four singles were extraneous compositions, namely 'Bluebirds Over The Mountain', and a competent version of Huddie Ledbetters's 'Cottonfields'. The third non-original was the Phil Spector/Jeff Barry/Ellie Greenwich opus 'I Can Hear Music', featuring a passionate lead vocal from Carl, confirming his status as acting leader. He struggled to maintain this role for many years to come.

In April 1969 the Beach Boys left Capitol in a blaze of litigation. No new product would surface until August the following year and they had the ignominy of having an album rejected prior to that. *Sunflower* was an artistic triumph but a commercial disaster, on which Dennis contributed four songs including the sublime 'Forever'. Throughout the following 12 months they set about rebuilding their credibility in the USA, having lost much ground to the new wave bands from San Francisco. They started to tour constantly, even appearing with unlikely compatriots the Grateful Dead. Through determination and hard work they did the seemingly impossible and allied themselves with the hip *cognoscenti*.

The arrival of *Surf's Up* in July 1971 completed their remarkable renaissance. The title track, with surreal lyrics by Van Dyke Parks, was another masterpiece, while on the rest of the album it was Carl's turn to put in strong contributions with the beautiful 'Feel Flows' and 'Long Promised Road'. The record's strong ecological stance was years ahead of its time, and the critics were unanimous in favourably re-assessing them. As Dennis co-starred with James Taylor in the cult road movie *Two-Lane Blacktop* so Brian's life was deteriorating into mental instability. Miraculously the band were able to maintain their career which at times included only one Wilson, Carl, and no longer had the presence of the long-serving Bruce Johnston. The addition of Ricky Fataar, Blondie Chaplin and Daryl Dragon nevertheless gave the depleted band a fuller sound. One further album appeared before the outstanding *Holland* came in 1973. For this project the entire Beach Boys organization, including wives and children, moved to Holland for eight months of recording. Thankfully, even Brian was cajoled into going, because his composition 'Sail On Sailor' was a high point of the record. Murray Wilson died of a heart attack in June 1973, but Brian and Dennis declined to attend the funeral; they were greatly affected by his passing. At the same time the group's fortunes were once again in the descendent as a double live album was badly received. A year later an astonishing thing happened: a compilation, *Endless Summer* put together by Mike Love, unexpectedly rocketed to the top of the US charts. It spent 71 weeks on the lists, disappeared and returned again the following year to a high position staying for a further 78 weeks. This unparalleled success reinforced Love and Jardine's theory that all anybody wanted of the Beach Boys was surfing and car songs. With the addition of James William Guercio, formerly of Chicago and ex-producer of Blood, Sweat And Tears, the band enjoyed extraordinary concert tour success, and ended 1974 being voted Band of the Year by the influential magazine *Rolling Stone*. *Spirit Of America* (1975), another compilation of earlier tracks, enjoyed enormous success staying on the American charts over a year. Meanwhile Brian's condition had further deteriorated and he was now under the treatment of therapist Eugene Landy. The album *15 Big Ones* in July 1976 gave them a big hit with Chuck Berry's 'Rock And Roll Music'. The publicity centred on a tasteless 'Brian Is Back' campaign, the now obese Wilson being unwillingly pushed into the spotlight. It seemed obvious to all that Brian was not back; here was a sick, confused and nervous man being used as a financial tool. Subsequent albums; *The Beach Boys Love You* and *M.I.U. Album* attempted to maintain Brian's high profile as producer, but close observers were well aware that this was a total sham. The material was of average quality, although the former showed strong glimpses of Wilson's fascination for childlike innocence. In 1977 they signed a recording contract with CBS reputedly worth $8,000,000, on the terms that Brian Wilson contributed at least four new songs and a total of 70 per cent of all the material for each album. The first album under this contract was the patchy *LA (Light Album)*, with Bruce Johnston asked back, to bail them out on production duties. The album did manage to produce a sizeable hit with Al Jardine's 'Lady Lynda'. The most controversial track however was a re-make of 'Here Comes the Night', and this previously innocuous R&B song from *Wild Honey* was turned into an 11-minute extended disco extravaganza. This track alone cost $50,000 to produce. By now Dennis had a serious cocaine habit which hampered the recording of his own solo album *Pacific Ocean Blue*. It was released to excellent reviews, and was an album that Dennis put his heart into, using a host of musicians and singers, with the notable absence of the Beach Boys. Dennis now openly abused the other members of the band except for Brian, whom he defended resolutely. When Carl fell victim to cocaine and alcohol, the fragmentation of the group was at its height.

The next official work was *Keeping The Summer Alive*, a poor album, without the presence of Dennis who had left the group. He was now living with Christine McVie of Fleetwood Mac. During 1980 only Love and Jardine were present from the original group. Carl delivered his first solo album, a beautifully sung, well-produced record that flopped. One track, 'Heaven' later became a regular part of the Beach Boys' repertoire. In 1982, Brian Wilson was officially dismissed, and was admitted to hospital for detoxification, weighing a massive 320 pounds. In December 1983, Dennis Wilson tragically drowned while diving from his boat. Ironically, his death reportedly snapped Brian out of his stupor, and he gradually re-emerged to participate onstage. A clean and healthy looking band graced the back of the 1985 Steve Levine produced, *The Beach Boys*. Following this collection they found themselves without a recording contract, and decided to concentrate purely on being a major concert attraction, travelling the world. While no new albums appeared, they concentrated on singles, including an energetic, well-produced 'Rock And Roll To The Rescue', followed by their version of the Mamas And The Papas' classic 'California Dreaming', with Roger McGuinn featured on 12-string guitar. In 1987, they teamed up with rap act the Fat Boys for a remake of the Surfaris' 'Wipe Out'.

In 1988, a phoenix-like Brian Wilson returned with the solo album for which his fans had waited over 20 years. The much-publicized record showed a slim, healthy looking man. The critics and fans loved it, but the general public did not respond and the album sold only moderately well. At the same time the Beach Boys released 'Kokomo', which was included in the film *Cocktail*. They found themselves unexpectedly at the top of the US charts, for many weeks. In May 1990, the Beach Boys took Brian Wilson to court in an alleged attempt to wrest his $80 million fortune from him. They maintained that he was insane and unable to look after himself. His medical condition was confirmed (extreme introversion, pathological shyness and manic depression). Wilson defended the case but eventually reluctantly accepted a settlement by which he severed his links with the controversial Landy. The band's career has been rolling, like the tide their great songs evoked, constantly in and out, reaching incredible highs and extraordinary troughs. Through all the appalling experiences however they still reign supreme as the most successful American group in pop history.

Albums: *Surfin' Safari* (1962), *Surfin' USA* (1963), *Surfer Girl* (1963), *Little Deuce Coupe* (1963), *Shut Down Vol. 2* (1964), *All Summer Long* (1964), *Beach*

Boys Concert (1964), The Beach Boys' Christmas Album (1964), The Beach Boys Today! (1965), Summer Days (And Summer Nights!!) (1965), The Beach Boys' Party! (1965), Pet Sounds (1966), Smiley Smile (1967), Wild Honey (1967), Friends (1968), 20/20 (1969), Live In London (1970), Sunflower (1970), Surf's Up (1971), Carl And The Passions-So Tough (1972), Holland (1973), The Beach Boys In Concert (1973), 15 Big Ones (1976), The Beach Boys Love You (1977), M.I.U. Album (1978), LA (Light Album) (1979), Keepin' The Summer Alive (1980), Rarities (1983), The Beach Boys (1985), Still Cruisin' (1989). Compilations: Endless Summer (1974), Spirit Of America (1975), 20 Golden Greats (1976), The Very Best Of The Beach Boys (1983), Made In The USA (1986), Summer Dreams (1990).

Further reading: The Beach Boys And The California Myth, David Leaf. Heroes And Villains, The True Story Of The Beach Boys, Steven Gaines. The Beach Boys: Silver Anniversary, John Milward. The Beach Boys, John Tobler. Wouldn't It Be Nice, Brian Wilson.

Beatles

The origin of the phenomenon that became the Beatles can be traced back to 1957 when Paul McCartney (b. 18 June 1942) successfully auditioned at a church fete in Woolton, Liverpool for the guitarist's spot in the Quarrymen, a skiffle group featuring John Lennon (b. 9 October 1940). Within a year, two more recruits were added, a 15-year-old lead guitarist George Harrison (b. 25 February 1943) and an art school friend of Lennon's, Stuart Sutcliffe. After a brief spell as Johnny And the Moondogs, the inchoate ensemble rechristened themselves the Silver Beetles and, in April 1960, played before impresario Larry Parnes, winning the dubious distinction of a support slot on an arduous tour of Scotland with autumnal idol Johnny Gentle.

By the summer of 1960, the group had found a permanent name, the Beatles, a full-time drummer, Pete Best, and secured a residency at Bruno Koschminder's Indra Club in Hamburg. It was during this period that they honed their repertoire of R&B favourites and during exhausting six-hour-sets performed virtually every song they could remember. Already, the musical/lyrical partnership of Lennon/McCartney was bearing fruit, anticipating a body of work unparalleled in modern popular music. The image of the group was also subtly changing, most noticeably in their French-styled fringed haircuts or, as they were later known, the 'mop-tops', allegedly the creation of Sutcliffe's German fiancée Astrid Kirchherr. The first German sojourn ended when the under-age Harrison was deported in December 1960 and the others lost their work permits. During this turbulent period, they also parted company with quasi-manager Allan Williams, who had arranged many of their early gigs. Following a couple of months recuperation, the group reassembled for regular performances at the Cavern Club in Liverpool and briefly returned to Germany where they performed at the Top Ten club and backed Tony Sheridan on the single 'My Bonnie'. Meanwhile, Sutcliffe elected to leave the group and remain in Germany, surrendering his bass to the more accomplished McCartney.

During November 1961, local entrepreneur Brian Epstein saw the Beatles at the Cavern Club and soon after became their manager. Despite Epstein's enthusiasm, several major record companies passed on the Beatles, although the group were granted an audition with Decca on New Year's Day 1962. After some prevarication, the A&R department, headed by Dick Rowe, rejected the group in favour of Brian Poole And The Tremeloes. Other companies were even less enthusiastic than Decca which had at least taken the group seriously enough to finance a recording session. On 10 April, further bad news was forthcoming when the group heard that their erstwhile bassist Stuart Sutcliffe had died of a brain haemorrhage. The following day, the Beatles flew to Germany and opened a seven-week engagement at Hamburg's Star Club. By May, Epstein had at last found a Beatles convert in EMI producer George Martin, who signed the group to the Parlophone label. Three months later, drummer Pete Best was sacked amid considerable controversy and a public outcry from his vociferous local following. His replacement was Ringo Starr (b. Richard Starkey, 7 July 1940, Liverpool, England), the extrovert drummer from Rory Storm And The Hurricanes.

Towards the end of 1962, the Beatles broke through to the UK charts with their debut single, 'Love Me Do', and during the same month played the Star Club for the final time. Meanwhile, Epstein completed a deal with music publisher Dick James which led to the formation of the lucrative Northern Songs.

On 13 February 1963, the Beatles appeared on UK television's Thank Your Lucky Stars to promote their new single, 'Please Please Me', and were seen by six million viewers. It was a pivotal moment in their career at the start of a year in which they would spearhead a working-class assault on music, fashion and the peripheral arts. 'Please Please Me', with its distinctive harmonic blend and infectious group beat, soon topped the charts, signalling the imminent overthrow of the solo singer in favour of an irresistible wave of Mersey talent. From thereon, the Beatles would progress artistically and commercially with each successive record. After seven weeks at the top with 'From Me To You', they released the strident, wailing 'She Loves You', a rocker with a magical catchphrase ('Yeah, Yeah, Yeah') that was echoed in ever more frequent newspaper headlines.

'She Loves You' hit number 1, went down, then returned to the top seven weeks later as Beatlemania gripped the nation. The disc was finally despatched by 'I Want To Hold Your Hand', which boasted advance sales in excess of one million and entered the charts at number 1. Already, the Beatles were on their way to becoming the most consistent chart toppers of all time.

Until 1964 America had proven a barren ground for aspiring British pop artists with only fluke hits like the Tornados' 'Telstar'of any note. The Beatles changed that abruptly and decisively. 'I Want To Hold Your Hand' succeeded in America and backed by an airing on the top-rated *Ed Sullivan Show*, even eclipsed sales in the UK. Overnight, the group reached a level of popularity that even outshone their pre-eminence in Britain. By April, they held the first five places in the *Billboard* Hot 100, while in Canada they boasted nine records in the Top 10. Although the Beatles' chart statistics were fascinating in themselves, they barely articulated the group's importance. Single-handedly, they had established Liverpool as the music capital of the world and the beat boom soon traversed the UK and inexorably towards the USA. In common with Bob Dylan, the Beatles had taught the world that pop music could be intelligent and was worthy of serious consideration beyond the screaming hordes of teendom. With the onslaught of Beatles' merchandising, which spread to badges, dolls, chewing gum and even cans of Beatle breath, the group underlined the rich rewards that could be won and lost in the sale of ancillary goods. Perhaps most importantly of all, however, they broke the Tin Pan Alley monopoly of songwriting by steadfastly composing their own material. From the moment they overruled their producer and rejected Mitch Murray's 'How Do You Do It?' in favour of their own 'Please Please Me', Lennon/McCartney set in motion significant changes in the music publishing world which effectively revolutionized the industry. So prolific was their composing skill that they had sufficient surplus quality material to provide hits for fellow artists such as Billy J. Kramer, Cilla Black, the Fourmost and Peter And Gordon. As well as providing the Rolling Stones with one of their earliest hits, 'I Wanna Be Your Man', the Beatles encouraged their rivals to put pen to paper and win themselves some mechanical composers' royalties in the process.

By 1965, Lennon/McCarney's writing had matured to a startling degree and their albums were relying less on extraneous material. Previously, compositions by Chuck Berry, Buddy Holly, Carl Perkins, Bacharach And David, Leiber And Stoller and Goffin And King had nestled comfortably alongside instant Beatle standards, but with each successive release the group were leaving their earlier influences behind and moving towards uncharted pop territory. They carried their mass audience with them, and even while following traditional pop routes they always invested their work with originality. Their first two films, *A Hard Day's Night* and *Help!*, were not the usual pop celluloid cash-ins but were witty and inventive and achieved critical acclaim as well as box office success. The national affection bestowed upon the lovable mop tops was perhaps best exemplified by their 1965 appearance in the Queen's Honours List where they were each awarded MBEs for services to British industry. The year ended with the release of their first double-sided number 1, 'We Can Work It Out'/'Day Tripper', the coupling indicating how difficult it had now become to choose between a and b-sides.

What was most impressive about the Beatles was their symmetry, at once oppositional and complementary. On the ballad side there was McCartney, the composer of such sentimental standards as 'Yesterday' and 'I'll Follow The Sun', while Lennon displayed a more despairing personal angst on the bleak 'Baby's In Black' and the deceptively uptempo 'Help!', the first pop single to use the word 'insecure'. Both writers were massive influences on each other and showed themselves equally adept at crafting ballads and rockers, either alone or together. Even their handling of cover versions from Paul's wailing 'Kansas City' to John's screaming 'Twist And Shout' emphasized a dual talent at tackling diverse material.

Christmas 1965 saw the Beatles using the album format not as a collection of would-be hits or favourite covers, but as an artistic statement in itself. *Rubber Soul* was a startlingly diverse collection, ranging from the pointed satire of 'Nowhere Man' and the reflective 'In My Life' to the much covered 'Michelle', which provided the Overlanders with a UK number 1. As ever with the Beatles, there were some musical pointers to the future, not least Harrison's use of sitar on the punningly titled, quirky love song 'Norweigan Wood'. That same year, the Byrds, Yardbirds and Rolling Stones would incorporate Eastern-influenced sounds into their work and the music press would tentatively mention the decidedly unpoplike Ravi Shankar. Significantly, Shankar's champion George Harrison was allowed two writing credits on *Rubber Soul*, 'Think For Yourself' and 'If I Needed Someone' (also a hit for the Hollies).

During 1966, the Beatles continued performing their increasingly complex arrangements before scarcely controllable screaming fans, but the novelty of fandom was wearing frustratingly thin. In Tokyo, the group incurred the wrath of militant reactionary students who objected to their performance at Budokan. Several death threats were forthcoming and the quartet left Japan in poor spirits, unaware that worse was to follow. A visit to Manila ended in a near riot when the Beatles neglected to attend a palace party thrown by President Ferdinand Marcos, and before leaving the country they were set upon by angry patriots. Weeks later, they received further shock news indicating that Beatles records were being ceremoniously burned in the redneck southern states of America. The cause of the furore was Lennon's flippant observation on contemporary spiritual impoverishment: 'We are more popular than Jesus now'. Although his words passed unnoticed in Britain, their unfortunate reproduction in an American teenzine instigated assassination threats and a massed campaign by members of the Ku Klux Klan to stamp out the Beatle menace. By the summer of 1966, the group were exhausted and defeated and played their last official performance at Candlestick Park, San Francisco on 29 August.

The controversy surrounding their live performances did not detract from the quality of their recorded output. 'Paperback Writer' was another step forward with its gloriously elaborate harmonies and charmingly prosaic theme. It was soon followed by a double-sided chart topper, 'Yellow Submarine'/'Eleanor Rigby', the former a self-created nursery rhyme complete with mechanical sounds, and the latter a brilliantly orchestrated narrative of loneliness, untainted by mawkishness. The attendant album, *Revolver*, was equally varied with Harrison's caustic 'Taxman', McCartney's plaintive 'For No One' and 'Here, There And Everywhere' and Lennon's drug-influenced 'She Said She Said' and 'Tomorrow Never Knows', arguably the most effective evocation of an LSD experience ever captured on disc. After 1966, the Beatles retreated into the studio, no longer bound by the restriction of having to perform live. Their image as pin-up pop stars was also undergoing metamorphosis and when they next appeared in photographs, all four boasted moustaches, while Lennon unashamedly wore his notorious round glasses. A long hiatus was broken with their first recording in over six months, 'Penny Lane'/'Strawberry Fields Forever', arguably their finest single. Ironically, it broke their long run of consecutive UK number 1 hits, being held off the top by Engelbert Humperdinck's schmaltzy 'Release Me'. Nevertheless, the double-sided single was a landmark, brilliantly capturing the twin talents of Lennon and McCartney. Although their songwriting styles were increasingly contrasting, it was still the similarities that struck home most forcibly. Both songs were paeons to an old Liverpool, Paul recalling childhood memories of Penny Lane and John immortalising the orphanage Strawberry Fields. There were also absurdist elements in each song with 'Penny Lane' presenting a bustling landscape populated by various occupants including a fire

fighter wary of a shower of rain and a nurse selling poppies, who not only feels as though she is in a play, but actually is. 'Strawberry Fields Forever' was more philosophical with Lennon adopting an epiphenomenalist outlook ('Nothing is real') and dramatizing an inner dialogue characterized by stumbling qualifications ('That is, I think, I disagree'). Musically, the songs were similarly intriguing with 'Penny Lane' boasting the inclusion of a piccolo trumpet and shimmering percussive fade-out, while 'Strawberry Fields Forever' fused two radically different versions of the same song using reverse taped cellos to eerie effect.

It was intended that the Beatles' most innovative of singles would be the jewels in the crown of their next album, but by the summer of 1967 they had sufficient material to release 13 new tracks. *Sgt. Pepper's Lonely Hearts Club Band* turned out to be no mere pop album but a cultural icon embracing the constituent elements of 60s' youth culture: pop art, garish fashion, drugs, instant mysticism and freedom from parental control. The packaging of the album was a revelation in itself. Although the Beatles had previously experimented with collages on *Beatles For Sale* and *Revolver*, they took the idea to its logical extreme on *Sgt. Pepper* which included photos of every significant influence on their lives that they could remember. The album also offered a gatefold sleeve, cardboard cut-out figurines and, for the first time on a pop record, printed lyrics. The music itself was even more extraordinary and refreshing. Instead of the traditional breaks between each song, one track merged into the next, linked by studio talk, laughter, electronic noises and animal sounds - a continuous, chaotic activity of sound, ripped forth from the ingenuity of producer George Martin. The songs were essays in innovation and diversification, embracing the cartoon psychedelia of 'Lucy In The Sky With Diamonds', the music hall pastiche of 'When I'm 64', the circus atmosphere of 'Being For The Benefit Of Mr Kite', the eastern philosophical promise of 'Within You, Without You' and even a modern morality tale in 'She's Leaving Home'. Audio tricks and surprises abounded involving steam organs, orchestras, sitars and even farmyard animals and a pack of foxhounds in full cry at the end of 'Good Morning, Good Morning'. The album closed with the epic 'Day In The Life', the Beatles' most ambitious work to date, which used as its coda what Lennon described as 'a sound building up from nothing to the end of the world'. As a final gimmick, the orchestra was recorded beyond a 20,000 hertz frequency taking the final note beyond human ears to an audible level appreciated by canines. Even the phonogram was not allowed to interfere with the proceedings, for a record groove was cut back to repeat slices of backwards recorded tape which played on into infinity.

The summer of 1967 was astonishingly eventful, even by Beatles standards. While *Sgt Pepper's Lonely Hearts Club Band* topped the album charts, the group appeared on a live television broadcast playing their anthem of the period, 'All You Need Is Love'. The following week it entered the charts at number 1, echoing the old days of Beatlemania. There was sadness too that summer, for on 21 August, Brian Epstein was found dead, the victim of a cumulative overdose of the drug Carbitrol. With spiritual guidance from the Maharishi Mahesh Yogi, the Beatles took Epstein's death calmly and elected to look after their business affairs without a manager. The first fruits of their post-Epstein labour was the film *Magical Mystery Tour*, screened on Boxing Day 1967. While the phantasmogorical movie elicited mixed reviews, nobody could cavil about the music, initially released in the unique form of a double EP, featuring six well-crafted songs. The EPs effortlessly rose to number 2 in the UK, making chart history in the process. Ironically, the package was robbed of the top spot by the traditional Beatles' Christmas single, this time in the form of the catchy 'Hello Goodbye'.

1968 proved another notable year with the Beatles pursuing their latest project: Apple Corps. A mismanaged boutique came and went and on the record front they reverted to rock 'n' roll for their eleventh transatlantic number 1, 'Lady Madonna'. Later that year, the first Apple single emerged in the form of the rivetting 'Hey Jude', a moving ballad that evolved into a free-for-all singalong, clocking in at over seven minutes, with the distinction of being longest ever number 1 record at that time. There was also a third motion picture, *Yellow Submarine*, which took the form of a cartoon, the graphics being acclaimed as a milestone in animation technique. The soundtrack album contained a few desultory tracks issued the following year. With their prolific output, the group crammed the remainder of their most recent material on to a double album, *The Beatles*, released in a stark white cover. George Martin's perceptive overview of the work was that it would have made an excellent single album. It had some brilliant moments which displayed the broad sweep of Beatle talent from 'Back In The USSR', the affectionate tribute to Chuck Berry and the Beach Boys, to Lennon's tribute to his mother, 'Julia', and one of McCartney's finer moments as a tunesmith, 'Blackbird'. For once, Harrison vied with his partners for the best track nomination, courtesy of the shimmering 'While My Guitar Gently Weeps', which featured the additional guitar skills of Eric Clapton. Predictably, there was an ideal cover tune, 'Ob-La-Di, Ob-La-Da', which Marmalade gratefully took to number 1 in the UK, plus the breathless 'Helter Skelter', which took on symbolic force in the deranged mind of the psychotic Charles Manson. There were also a number of average songs which gave the impression that they required something more, plus some ill-advised doodlings such as the extraordinarily experimental 'Revolution No. 9' and the quirky 'Goodnight'. What *The Beatles* revealed was four musicians already working in an isolated neutrality.

The Beatles' profound fallibility as business executives was exemplified by the parlous state of their Apple empire which required the ruthlessness of Allen Klein to restore a semblance of order. The new realism that permeated the portals of Beatledom was even evident in their art. Like several contemporary artists, including Bob Dylan and the Byrds, they chose to end the 60s with a reversion to less complex musical forms. The return-to-roots minimalism was spearheaded by the appropriately titled, chart topping, 'Get Back', which included Billy Preston guesting on organ. During their next recording sessions, cameras were present and the Beatles ran through dozens of songs, many of which they had not played since the Hamburg days. When the sessions ended there were countless spools of tape which would not be reassembled until the following year. In the meantime, a select few witnessed the foursome's last 'public' performance on the rooftops of the Apple headquarters in Savile Row, London. Amid the uncertainty of 1969, the Beatles enjoyed their final UK number 1 with the wry 'Ballad Of John And Yoko', on which only Lennon and McCartney performed.

In a sustained attempt to cover the cracks that were becoming increasingly visible in their personal and musical relationships, the foursome reconvened for *Abbey Road*. The album was dominated by the song cycle on side 2 in which such fragmentary compositions as 'Mean Mr. Mustard', 'Polythene Pam', 'She Came In Through The Bathroom Window' and 'Golden Slumbers'/'Carry That Weight' gelled uneasily into a convincing whole. The concomitant hit single coupled Lennon's suggestive 'Come Together' with Harrison's McCartneyesque standard 'Something'. Significantly, the record only reached number 4 in the UK, the group's lowest chart-placing since 'Love Me Do' back in 1962. Such considerations were small compared to the fate of their other songs. The group could only watch helplessly as a wary Dick James surreptitiously sold Northern Songs to ATV. The priceless catalogue would continue to change hands over the years and not even the combined financial force of McCartney and Yoko Ono could finally wrest it from the outstretched hands of that millionaire superstar speculator Michael Jackson.

With various solo projects in the offing, the Beatles stumbled through 1970, their disunity betrayed to the world in the film *Let It Be*. The album, finally pieced together by producer Phil Spector, was a controversial and bitty affair, initially housed in a cardboard box containing a lavish book which increased the retail price to an alarmingly prohibitive level. Musically, the work revealed the Beatles looking back, poignantly and sadly, to better days. There was the sparse 'Two Of Us' and the primitive 'The One After 909', a song they used to play as the Quarrymen. There was an orchestrated 'Long And Winding Road' which provided a last US number 1 although McCartney pointedly preferred the non-orchestrated film version. And there was the aptly titled last official single, 'Let It Be', which entered the UK charts at number 2, only to drop to number 3 the following week. For many that was the final anti-climax before the inevitable yet still unexpected split. The acrimonious dissolution of the Beatles, like that of no other group before or since, symbolized the end of an era that they had dominated and helped create.

Albums: *Please Please Me* (1963), *With The Beatles* (1963), *A Hard Day's Night* (1964), *Beatles For Sale* (1964), *Help!* (1965), *Rubber Soul* (1965), *Revolver* (1966), *Sgt. Pepper's Lonely Hearts Club Band* (1967), *Magical Mystery Tour* (1968), *The Beatles* (1968), *Yellow Submarine* (1969), *Abbey Road* (1969), *Let It Be* (1970). Various compilations, retrospectives and archivist albums have also been issued.

Further selective reading: *The Beatles*, Hunter Davies. *Shout! The True Story Of The Beatles*, Philip Norman. *The Love You Make*, Peter Brown And Steven Gaines. *The Complete Beatles Recording Sessions*, Mark Lewisohn.

Beau Brummels

Formed in San Francisco in 1964, the Beau Brummels provided a vital impetus to the city's emergent rock circuit. Sal Valentino (b. Sal Spampinato, 8 August 1942, San Francisco, California, USA; vocals), Ron Elliott (b. 21 October 1943, Healdsburg, California, USA; guitar), Ron Meagher (b. 2 October 1941, Oakland, California, USA; bass) and John Petersen (b. 8 January 1942, Rudyard, Michigan, USA; drums) enjoyed a committed following within the city's Irish community prior to adding Declan Mulligan (b. County Tipperary, Eire; guitar) to the line-up. Local entrepreneurs, Tom Donahue and Bob Mitchell, saw their obvious topicality and signed the group to their fledgling Autumn label. 'Laugh Laugh', the Beau Brummel's debut single, broached the US Top 20, while its follow-up, 'Just A Little', reached number 8. Both songs bore an obvious debt to British Beat, but later, more adventurous compositions, including 'You Tell Me Why' and 'Don't Talk To Strangers', emphasized an American heritage. The group's early albums offered elements of folk, country and R&B. Producer Sylvester Stewart, later known as Sly Stone, sculpted a clear, resonant sound which outstripped that of many contemporaries. Elliott had also emerged as a distinctive songwriter, while Valentino's deep, tremulous delivery provided an unmistakable lead. Mulligan's premature departure did little to undermine this progress.

Autumn was wound-up in 1966 and the group's contract was sold to Warner Brothers. A new member, Don Irving, was featured on their next collection, *Beau Brummels 66*, but this sorry affair was a marked disappointment, consisting of throwaway readings of recent hits. Irving then left; and as the band now eschewed live appearances, Petersen opted for another local attraction, Harpers Bizzare. The remaining trio completed the exquisite *Triangle*, one of the era's most delicate and cultured albums, but the loss of Meagher reduced the group to that of Elliott and Valentino. Together they completed *Bradley's Barn*, an early excursion into country-rock, before embarking on separate careers. The original quintet regrouped in 1974, but once again Mulligan was an early casualty. He was replaced by Dan Levitt for the unit's reunion album, but the project was abandoned the following year. Since then the Beau Brummels have enjoyed several short-lived resurrections, but conflicting interests, coupled with Elliott's ill-health, have denied them a long-term future.

Albums: *Introducing The Beau Brummels* (1965), *Volume 2* (1965), *Beau Brummels 66* (1966), *Triangle* (1967), *Bradley's Barn* (1968), *The Beau Brummels* (1975). Compilations: *The Best Of The Beau Brummels* (1967), *The Best Of The Beau Brummels 1964-1968* (1981), *From The Vaults* (1982), *Autumn In San Francsico* (1985).

Beck, Jeff

b. 24 June 1944, Wallington, Surrey, England. As a former choir boy the young Beck was interested in music from an early age, becoming a competent pianist and guitarist by the age of 11. His first main band was the Tridents, who made a name for themselves locally. After leaving them Beck took on the seemingly awesome task of stepping into the shoes of Eric Clapton, who had recently departed from the 60s R&B pioneers, the Yardbirds. Clapton had a fiercely loyal following, but Beck soon had them gasping with his amazing guitar pyrotechnics, utilizing feedback and distortion. Beck stayed with the Yardbirds adding colour and excitement to all their hits until October 1966. The tension between Beck and the joint lead guitarist Jimmy Page was resolved during a US tour. Beck walked out and never returned. His solo career was launched in March 1967 with a different sounding Beck on a pop single 'Hi-Ho Silver Lining'. Jeff's unremarkable voice was heard on a sing-along number which was saved by his trademark guitar solo. The record was a sizeable hit and has subsequently demonstrated its perennial appeal to party-goers by re-entering the charts twice in 1972 and 1982. The follow-up, 'Tallyman' was also a minor hit, but by now Jeff's ambitions were in other directions. He retired from being a singing, guitar-playing, pop star and started a career that led him to become one of the world's leading rock guitarists. The Jeff Beck Group, formed in 1968, consisted of Beck, Rod Stewart (vocals), Ron Wood (bass), Nicky Hopkins (piano) and Mickey Waller (drums). This powerhouse quartet released *Truth*, which became a major success in the USA, resulting in the band undertaking a number of arduous tours. The second album *Cosa Nostra Beck-Ola* had similar success, although Stewart and Wood had now departed for the Faces. Beck also contributed some sparkling guitar and received equal billing with Donovan on the hit 'Goo Goo Barabajagal (Love Is Hot)'. In 1968 Jeff's serious accident with one of his hot-rod cars put him out of action for almost 18 months. A recovered Beck formed another group with Cozy Powell, Max Middleton and Bob Tench, and recorded two further albums, *Rough And Ready* and *Jeff Beck Group*. The latter became a sizeable hit. Beck was now fully accepted as a serious musician, and figured highly in various guitarist polls. In 1973 the erratic Beck musical style changed once again and he formed the trio Beck, Bogert And Appice with the two former members of Vanilla Fudge. Only one official album was released and Beck introduced yet another facet, this time forming an instrumental band. The result was the excellent *Blow By Blow*, thought by many to be his best work. His guitar work showed extraordinary technique combining rock, jazz and blues styles. *Blow By Blow* was a million seller and its follow-up, *Wired* had similar success. Having allied himself with some of the jazz/rock fraternity Beck teamed up with Jan Hammer for a frantic live album. Following its release Beck effectively retired for three years. He returned in 1980 with *There And Back*. His loyal fans had not deserted him, and, now rejuvinated, he found himself riding the album charts. During the 80s, Beck's appearances have been sporadic. He has appeared at charity functions and has spent much of his leisure time with automobiles. In one interview Beck stated that he could just as easily have been a car restorer. In the mid-80s he toured with Rod Stewart and was present on his version of 'People Get Ready'. The album *Flash* came in 1985, but proved his least successful to date. Jeff Beck has already ensured his place in the history book of guitarists and his no-nonsense approach to the music industry has earned him considerable respect. The release of a box-set in 1992, chronicling his career,

was a fitting tribute to this accomplished guitarist.
Albums: *Truth* (1968), *Cosa Nostra Beck-Ola* (1969), *Rough And Ready* (1971), *Jeff Beck Group* (1972), *Blow By Blow* (1975), *Wired* (1976), *Jeff Beck With The Jan Hammer Group Live* (1977), *There And Back* (1980), *Flash* (1985), with Terry Bozzio and Tony Hymas *Jeff Beck's Guitar Shop* (1989). Compilations: with Rod Stewart *The Late '60s* (1988), *Beckology* (1992).

Bee Gees

This hugely successful Anglo/Australian trio comprised of the twins Maurice and Robin Gibb (b. 22 December 1949, Isle Of Man, British Isles) and their elder brother Barry Gibb (b. 1 September 1946, Isle Of Man, British Isles). Hailing from a showbusiness family based in Manchester, England, they played as a child act in several of the city's cinemas. In 1958, the Gibb family emigrated to Australia and the boys performed regularly as a harmony trio in Brisbane, Queensland. Christened the Bee Gees, an abbreviation of Brothers Gibb, they signed to the Australian label Festival Records and released a series of singles written by the elder brother. While their single 'Spicks And Specks' was topping the Australian charts, the brothers were already on their way to London for a fateful audition before Robert Stigwood, a director of NEMS Enterprises, the company owned by Beatles svengali Brian Epstein. This, in turn, led to a record contract with Polydor and the swift release of 'New York Mining Disaster, 1941'. The quality of the single with its evocative, intriguing lyrics and striking harmony provoked premature comparison with the Beatles and gained the group a sizeable UK hit. During this period the trio were supplemented by Australian friends Colin Peterson (drums) and Vince Melouney (guitar). The second UK single, 'To Love Somebody', departed from the narrative power of their previous offering towards a more straightforward ballad style. Although the disc failed to reach the Top 40, the enduring quality of the song was evinced by a number of striking cover versions, most notably by Nina Simone, Eric Burdon And The Animals and Janis Joplin. The Beatlesque songs on their outstanding acclaimed UK debut, *The Bee Gees First* garnered further comparisons. Every track was a winner from the delightfully naive 'Cucumber Castle' to the sublime 'Please Read Me', while 'Holiday' had the beautiful stark quality of McCartney's 'Yesterday'. The 14 tracks, were all composed by the twins and Barry, still aged only 17 and 19 respectively. By October 1967, the group had registered their first UK number 1 with the moving 'Massachusetts', which showed off their ability as arrangers to particular effect. Aware of the changes occurring in the pop firmament, the group bravely experimented with different musical styles and briefly followed the

Beatles and the Rolling Stones along the psychedelic road. Their progressive forays confused their audience, however, and the double album *Odessa* failed to match the work of their major rivals. Their singles remained adventurous and strangely eclectic with the unusual tempo of 'World' followed by the neurotic romanticism of 'Words'. Both singles hit the Top 10 in the UK but signs of commercial fallibility followed with the relatively unsuccessful double a-side 'Jumbo'/'The Singer Not The Song'. Masters of the chart come-back, the group next turned to a heart-rending ballad about the final hour of a condemned prisoner. 'I've Gotta Get A Message To You' gave them their second UK number 1 and sixth consecutive US Top 20 hit. The stark but startling 'First Of May' followed, again revealing the Bee Gees willingness to tackle a mood piece in favour of an easily accessible melodic ballad. To complete their well-rounded image, the group showed their talent as composers, penning the Marbles' Top 10 UK hit 'Only One Woman'.

Without question, the Bee Gees were one of the most accomplished groups of the late 60s' but as the decade ended they fell victim to internal bickering and various pressures wrought by international stardom. Maurice Gibb married pop star Lulu and the group joined the celebrity showbusiness elite with all its attendant trappings of drink and drugs. Dissent among the brotherhood saw Robin Gibb embark on a solo career with brief success while the twins retained the group name. Remarkably, they ended the 60s with another change of style emerging with an authentic country standard in 'Don't Forget To Remember'. With Colin Peterson still in tow, Maurice and Barry worked on a much-publicized but ultimately insubstantial film, *Cucumber Castle*. This fractious period ended with a ludicrous series of law suits in which the drummer had the audacity to claim rights to the Bee Gees name. A year of chaos and missed opportunities ensued during which the group lost much of its impetus and following. Maurice and Barry both released one single each as soloists, but their efforts were virtually ignored. Their career in the UK was in tatters but after reuniting with Robin in late 1970 they went on to score two major US hits with 'Lonely Days' and the chart-topping 'How Can You Mend A Broken Heart'.

After a brief flurry of transatlantic hits in 1972 with 'My World' and 'Run To Me', the group's appeal diminished to an all-time low. Three hitless years saw them reduced to playing in cabaret at such inauspicious venues as the Batley Variety Club in Yorkshire. A switch from Polydor Records to Robert Stigwood's new label RSO encouraged the group to adopt a more American sound with the album *Life In A Tin Can*. Determined to explore a more distinctive style, the group were teamed with famed producer

Arif Mardin. *Mr. Natural*, recorded in London, indicated a noticeable R&B/soul influence which was extended on 1975's *Main Course*. Now ensconced in Miami, the group gathered together a formidable backing unit featuring Alan Kendall (guitar), Dennis Bryon (drums) and Blue Weaver (keyboards). 'Jive Talkin'', a pilot single from the album, zoomed to number 1 in the US and brought the trio back to the Top 10 in Britain. Meanwhile, fellow RSO artist Olivia Newton-John enjoyed a US hit with the group's country ballad 'Come On Over'. The Bee Gees were well and truly back.

The changes in their sound during the mid-70s was nothing short of remarkable. They had virtually reinvented themselves, with Mardin encouraging them to explore their R&B roots and experiment with falsetto vocals. The effect was particularly noticeable on their next US Top 10 hit 'Nights On Broadway' (later a hit for Candi Staton). The group were perfectly placed to promote and take advantage of the underground dance scene in the US, and their next album *Children Of The World* went platinum. The attendant single 'You Should Be Dancing' reached number 1 in the US, while the follow-up 'Love So Right' hit number 3. Not content to revitalize their own career the trio's soundtrack contributions also provided massive hits for Yvonne Elliman ('If I Can't Have You') and Tavares ('More Than A Woman'). The Bee Gees' reputation as the new gods of the discotheque was consummated on the soundtrack of the movie *Saturday Night Fever*, which sold in excess of 30 million copies. In their most successful phase to date, the group achieved a quite staggering run of six consecutive chart toppers: 'How Deep Is Your Love', 'Stayin' Alive', 'Night Fever', 'Too Much Heaven', 'Tragedy' and 'Love You Inside Out'. Their grand flurry continued with the movie *Grease*, for which they produced the chart-topping title track by Frankie Valli. Having already received Beatles comparisons during their early career, it was ill-advised of the group to take the starring role in the movie *Sgt. Pepper's Lonely Hearts Club Band*. The film proved an embarrassing detour for both the brothers and their co-star Peter Frampton.

As the 70s ended the Bee Gees increasingly switched their interests towards production. Although they released two further albums, *Spirits Having Flown* (1979) and *Living Eyes* (1981), far greater attention was being focused on their chart-topping younger brother Andy Gibb. A multi-million dollar dispute with their mentor Robert Stigwood was settled out of court following which the group contributed towards another movie soundtrack *Stayin' Alive*. With the group's activities put on hold, it was Barry who emerged as the most prolific producer and songwriter. He duetted with Barbra Streisand on the chart-topping 'Guilty' and composed and sang on 'Heartbreaker' with Dionne Warwick. The brothers, meanwhile, also wrote the Kenny Rogers and Dolly Parton US chart topper 'Islands In The Stream' and Diana Ross's excellent Motown pastiche 'Chain Reaction'. Seemingly content to stay in the background masterminding platinum discs for others, they eventually reunited in 1987 for the hugely successful *ESP*. The indisputable masters of melody, their 'come-back' single 'You Win Again' was warmly received by usually hostile critics who applauded its undoubted craftsmanship. The single gave the group their fifth UK number 1, a full eight years after their last chart topper, 'Tragedy'. Sadly, the death of younger brother Andy the following year added a tragic note to the proceedings. In deference to their brother's death they declined to attend an Ivor Novello Awards ceremony in which they were honoured for their Outstanding Contribution to British Music.

Looking back over the Bee Gees' career, one cannot fail to be impressed by the sheer diversification of their talents and their remarkable ability to continually reinvent themselves again and again. Like that other great family group the Beach Boys they have survived family feuds, dissension, tragic death, harsh criticism, changes in musical fashion and much else to become one of pop's ineffable institutions. Throughout all the musical changes they have undergone, the one constant has been their vocal dexterity, strength and an innate ability to arrange some wondrous pop melodies. The legacy of their performing, songwriting and production activities represents one of the richest tapestries in the entire history of modern popular music.

Albums: *Barry Gibb And The Bee Gees Sing And Play 14 Barry Gibb Songs* (1965), *Spicks And Specks* (1966), *The Bee Gees First* (1967), *Horizontal* (1968), *Idea* (1968), *Odessa* (1969), *Cucumber Castle* (1970), *Two Years On* (1970), *Trafalgar* (1971), *To Whom It May Concern* (1972), *Life In A Tin Can* (1973), *Mr Natural* (1974), *Main Course* (1975), *Children Of The World* (1976), *Here At Last . . . Bee Gees Live* (1977), *Saturday Night Fever* (1977), *Sgt. Pepper's Lonely Hearts Club Band* (1978), *Spirits Having Flown* (1979), *Living Eyes* (1981), *Stayin' Alive* (1983), *ESP* (1987), *High Civilisation* (1991). Compilations: *Rare Precious And Beautiful* (1968), *Rare Precious And Beautiful Vol. 2* (1968), *Rare Precious And Beautiful Vol. 3* (1969), *Best Of The Bee Gees* (1969), *Best Of The Bee Gees Vol. 2* (1973), *Bee Gees Gold Volume One* (1976), *Bee Gees Greatest* (1979), *The Early Days Vol. 1* (1979), *The Early Days Vol. 2* (1979), *The Early Days Vol. 3* (1979).

Bennett, Cliff

One of the most accomplished British R&B vocalists of his era, Cliff Bennett (b. 4 June 1940, Slough, England) formed the excellent Rebel Rousers in early 1961. Taking their name from a Duane Eddy hit of the period, the group comprised Mick King (lead guitar), Frank Allen (bass), Sid Phillips (piano/saxophone) and Ricky Winters (drums). With a repertoire of rock 'n' roll, blue-eyed soul and R&B, the group were briefly taken under the wing of madcap producer Joe Meek, with whom they recorded several unsuccessful singles. A succession of R&B covers brought no further success and, early in 1964, bassist Frank Allen departed to replace Tony Jackson in the Searchers. The Rebel Rousers continued their busy touring schedule at home and abroad and were finally rewarded with a Top 10 hit, 'One Way Love' in November 1964. This brassy, upbeat cover of the Drifters' original augured well for the future, but the follow up, 'I'll Take You Home', stalled at number 43. Abandoning the Drifters as source material, they covered other R&B artists, without noticeable success. A move to Brian Epstein's NEMs management secured them the invaluable patronage of the Beatles, and Paul McCartney stepped in to produce their sparkling reading of 'Got To Get You Into My Life' from the recently released *Revolver*. Peaking at number 6, the single was their second and last Top 10 hit. Thereafter, Bennett fell victim to changing musical fashions as beat groups were generally dismissed as anachronistic. The Rebel Rousers changed their name to the more prosaic Cliff Bennett and his Band and briefly sought success with contemporary writers such as Mark London and Roy Wood. By mid-1969, Bennett decided to dissolve his group and reinvent himself for the progressive market. The result was Toe Fat, a short-lived ensemble now best remembered for their tasteless album covers rather than their music. In 1972, Bennett tried again with Rebellion and, three years later, Shanghai, but commercial success proved elusive. Weary of traipsing around the country, Cliff eventually took up gainful employment in the advertising business, but still plays semi-professionally. Albums: *Cliff Bennett And The Rebel Rousers* (1965), *Drivin' You Wild* (1966), *Got To Get You Into Our Lives* (1967), *Cliff Bennett Branches Out* (1968).

Benton, Brook

b. Benjamin Franklin Peay, 19 September 1931, Camden, South Carolina, USA, d. 9 April 1988. A stylish, mellifluent singer, Benton's most ascendant period was the late 50s/early 60s. Although he began recording in 1953, Brook's first major hit came in 1959 on forging a songwriting partnership with Clyde Otis and Belford Hendricks. 'It's Just A Matter Of Time' reached the US Top 3 and introduced a remarkable string of success including 'So Many Ways' (1959), 'The Boll Weevil Song' (1961) and

'Hotel Happiness' (1962). Duets with Dinah Washington, 'Baby (You've Got What It Takes)', a million-seller, and 'A Rockin' Good Way (To Mess Around And Fall In Love)', topped the R&B listings in 1960. Benton's warm, resonant delivery continued to prove popular into the early 60s. A versatile vocalist, his releases encompassed standards, blues and spirituals, while his compositions were recorded by Nat 'King' Cole, Clyde McPhatter and Roy Hamilton. Brook remained signed to the Mercury label until 1964 before moving to RCA, then Reprise Records. Releases on these outlets failed to recapture the artist's previous success, but by the end of the decade Benton rose to the challenge of younger acts with a series of excellent recordings for Atlantic's Cotillion subsidiary. His languid, atmospheric version of 'Rainy Night In Georgia' (1970) was an international hit and the most memorable product of an artistically fruitful period. Benton continued to record for a myriad of outlets during the 70s, including Brut (owned by the perfume company), Stax and MGM. Although his later work was less incisive, the artist remained one of music's top live attractions. He died in April 1988, aged 56, succumbing to pneumonia while weakened by spinal meningitis.

Albums: *It's Just A Matter Of Time* (1959), *Brook Benton* (1959), *Endlessly* (1959), *So Many Ways* (1960), *Two Of Us - With Dinah Washington* (1960), *Songs I Love To Sing* (1960), *The Boll Weevil Song (& Eleven Other Great Hits)* (1961), *Sepia* (1961), *If You Believe* (1961), *Singing The Blues - Lie To Me* (1962), *There Goes That Song Again* (1962), *Born To Sing The Blues* (1964), *Laura (What's He Got That I Ain't Got)* (1967), *Do Your Own Thing* (1969), *Brook Benton Today* (1970), *Home Style* (1970), *The Gospel Truth* (1971), *Something For Everyone* (1973), *Sings A Love Story* (1975), *Mr. Bartender* (1976), *This Is Brook Benton* (1976), *Makin' Love Is Good For You* (1977), *Ebony* (1978), *Brook Benton Sings The Standards* (1984). Compilations: *Brook Benton's Golden Hits* (1961), *Golden Hits Volume Two* (1963), *Spotlight On Brook Benton* (1977), *The Incomparable Brook Benton* (1982), *Sixteen Golden Classics* (1986), *His Greatest Hits* (1987).

Berry, Chuck

b. Charles Edward Anderson Berry, 18 October 1926, St. Louis, Missouri, USA. A seminal figure in rock's evolution, Chuck Berry's influence as songwriter and guitarist is incalculable. His cogent songs captured adolescent life, yet the artist was 30-years-old when he commenced recording. Introduced to music as a child, Berry learned guitar while in his teens, but this period was blighted by a three-year spell in Algoa Reformatory following a conviction for armed robbery. On his release Berry undertook several blue-collar jobs while pursuing part-time spots in St. Louis bar bands. Inspired by Carl Hogan, guitarist in Louis Jordan's Timpani Five, and Charlie Christian, he continued to hone his craft and in 1951 purchased a tape recorder to capture ideas for compositions. The following year Berry joined Johnnie Johnson (piano) and Ebby Hardy (drums) in the houseband at the Cosmopolitan Club. Over the ensuing months the trio became a popular attraction, playing a mixture of R&B, country/hillbilly songs and standards, particularly those of Nat 'King' Cole, on whom Berry modelled his cool vocal style. The guitarist also fronted his own group, the Chuck Berryn Combo, at the rival Crank Club, altering his name to spare his father's embarassment at such worldly pursuits.

In 1955, during a chance visit to Chicago, Berry met bluesman Muddy Waters, who advised the young singer to approach the Chess label. Chuck's demo of an original song, 'Ida Mae', was sufficient to win a recording deal and the composition, retitled 'Maybellene', duly became his debut single. This ebullient performance was a runaway success, topping the R&B chart and reaching number 5 on the US pop listings. Its lustre was partially clouded by a conspiratorial publishing credit which required Berry to share the rights with Russ Fratto and disc jockey Alan Freed, in deference to his repeated airplay. This situation remained unresolved until 1986.

Berry enjoyed further hits with 'Thirty Days' and 'No Money Down', but it was his third recording session which proved highly productive, producing a stream of classics, 'Roll Over Beethoven', 'Too Much Monkey Business' and 'Brown-Eyed Handsome Man'. The artist's subsequent releases read like a lexicon of pop history - 'School Days' (a second R&B number 1), 'Reelin' And Rockin', 'Rock 'N' Roll Music' (all 1957), Sweet Little Sixteen', 'Johnny B. Goode' (1958), 'Back In The USA', 'Let It Rock' (1959), 'Bye Bye Johnny' (1960) are but a handful of the peerless songs written and recorded during this prolific period. In common with contemporary artists, Berry drew from both country and R&B music, but his sharp, often piquant lyrics, clarified by the singer's clear diction, introduced a new discipline to the genre. Such incomparable performances not only defined rock 'n' roll, they provided a crucial template for successive generations. Both the Beatles and Rolling Stones acknowledged their debt to Berry. The former recorded two of his compositions, taking one, 'Roll Over Beethoven', into the US charts, while the latter drew from his empirical catalogue on many occasions. This included 'Come On', their debut single, 'Little Queenie', 'You Can't Catch Me' and 'Around And Around', as well as non-Berry songs which nonetheless aped his approach. The Stones' readings of 'Route 66', 'Down

The Road Apiece' and 'Confessin' The Blues' were indebted to their mentor's versions while Keith Richards's rhythmic, propulsive guitar figures drew from Berry's style. Elsewhere, the Beach Boys re-wrote 'Sweet Little Sixteen' as 'Surfin' USA' to score their first million-seller while countless other groups scrambled to record his songs which somehow combined immediacy with longevity.

Between 1955-60, Berry seemed unassailable. He enjoyed a run of 17 R&B Top 20 entries, appeared in the films *Go Johnny Go, Rock, Rock, Rock* and *Jazz On A Summer's Day*, the last of which documented the artist's performance at the 1958 **Newport Jazz Festival**, where he demonstrated the famed 'duckwalk' to a bemused audience. However, personal impropriety undermined Berry's personal and professional life when, on 28 October 1961, he was convicted under the Mann Act of 'transporting an under-age girl across state lines for immoral purposes'. Berry served 20 months in prison, emerging in October 1963 just as 'Memphis Tennessee', recorded in 1958, was providing him with his first UK Top 10 hit. He wrote several stellar compositions during his incarceration, including 'Nadine', 'No Particular Place To Go', 'You Never Can Tell' and 'Promised Land', each of which reached the UK Top 30. Such chart success soon waned as the immediate R&B bubble burst and in 1966 Berry sought to regenerate his career by moving from Chess to Mercury. However, an ill-advised *Golden Hits* set merely featured re-recordings of old material, while attempts to secure a contemporary image on *Live At The Fillmore Auditorium* (recorded with the Steve Miller Band) and *Concerto In B. Goode* proved equally unsatisfactory. He returned to Chess in 1969 and immediately re-established his craft with the powerful 'Tulane'. *Back Home* and *San Francisco Dues* were cohesive selections and in-concert appearances showed a renewed purpose. Indeed, a UK performance at the 1972 Manchester Arts Festival not only provided half of Berry's *London Sessions* album, but also his biggest-ever hit. 'My Ding-A-Ling', a mildly ribald *double entendre* first recorded by Dave Bartholomew, topped both the US and UK charts, a paradox in the light of his own far superior compositions which achieved lesser commercial plaudits. It was his last major hit, and despite several new recordings, including *Rock It*, a much-touted release on Atco, Berry became increasingly confined to the revival circuit. He gained an uncomfortable reputation as a hard, shrewd businessman and disinterested performer, backed by pick-up bands with which he refused to rehearse. Tales abound within the rock fraternity of Berry's refusal to tell the band which song he was about to launch into. Pauses and changes would come about by the musicians watching Berry closely for an often disguised signal.

Berry has insisted for years upon pre-payment of his fee, usually in cash, and he will only perform an encore after a further negotiation for extra payment. Berry's continued legal entanglements resurfaced in 1979 when he was sentenced to a third term of imprisonment following a conviction for income tax evasion. Upon release he embarked on a punishing world tour, but the subsequent decade proved largely unproductive musically and no new recordings were undertaken. In 1986, the artist celebrated his 60th birthday with gala performances in St. Louis and New York. Keith Richard appeared at the former, although relations between the two men were strained, as evinced in the resultant documentary, *Hail! Hail! Rock 'N' Roll*, which provided an overview of Berry's entire career. Sadly, the 90s began with further controversy and allegations of indecent behaviour at the singer's Berry Park centre. Although these serve to undermine the individual, his stature as an essential figure in the evolution of popular music cannot be underestimated.

Albums: *After School Session* (1958), *One Dozen Berrys* (1958), *Chuck Berry Is On Top* (1959), *Rockin' At The Hops* (1960), *New Juke Box Hits* (1961), *Chuck Berry Twist* (1962), *More Chuck Berry* (1963), *Chuck Berry On Stage* (1963), *The Latest And Greatest* (1964), *St. Louis To Liverpool* (1964), with Bo Diddley *Two Great Guitars* (1964), *Chuck Berry In London* (1965), *Fresh Berrys* (1965), *Golden Hits* (1967, new recordings), *Chuck Berry In Memphis* (1967), *Live At The Fillmore Auditorium* (1967), *From St. Louis To Frisco* (1968), *Concerto In B. Goode* (1969), *Back Home* (1970), *San Francisco Dues* (1971), *The London Chuck Berry Sessions* (1972), *Bio* (1973), *Chuck Berry* (1975), *Live In Concert* (1978), *Rock It* (1979), *Rock! Rock! Rock 'N' Roll!* (1980), *Hail, Hail Rock 'N' Roll* (1988, film soundtrack). Compilations: *Chuck Berry's Greatest Hits* (1964), *Chuck Berry's Golden Decade* (1967), *Golden Decade, Volume 2* (1973), *Golden Decade, Volume 3* (1974), *Motorvatin'* (1977), *Spotlight On Chuck Berry* (1980), *Chess Masters* (1983), *Reelin' And Rockin' (Live)* (1984), *Rock 'N' Roll Rarities* (1986), *More Rock 'N' Roll Rarities* (1986), *Chicago Golden Years* (1988), *Decade '55 To '65* (1988), *The Great Twenty-Eight* (1990).

Further reading: *Chuck Berry - The Autobiography*, Chuck Berry.

Berry, Dave

b. David Holgate Grundy, 6 February 1941,Woodhouse, Sheffield, Yorkshire, England. With his long-serving backing group, the Cruisers, Berry was signed to Danny Betesh's Manchester-based Kennedy Street Enterprises and, after securing a deal with Decca Records, scored a hit with a version of Chuck Berry's 'Memphis Tennessee' in 1963. Covers of Arthur Crudup's 'My Baby Left Me' and

Burt Bacharach's 'Baby It's You' were also minor hits, but the big breakthrough came with Geoff Stevens's 'The Crying Game', which reached the UK Top 5 in August 1964. As well as Berry's wounded baritone, this record also highlighted Big Jim Sullivan's aptly tearful guitar legatos using a volume pedal-precursor of the wah-wah effect. Berry's stage act and image was strong for the period and featured the singer dressed in black, erotically contorting his body and playing with the microphone as though it were a writhing snake. Bobby Goldsboro's chirpy 'Little Things' and Ray Davies's 'This Strange Effect' - Holland's biggest-selling record ever - provided further chart success, which concluded with the much-covered B.J. Thomas opus, 'Mama', in 1966. In the late 70s, he was one of the few 60s stars held in any esteem in punk circles - epitomized by the Sex Pistols' revival of 'Don't Gimme No Lip Child', one of Berry's 1964 b-sides. The next decade saw a resumption of his recording career and he continues to tour abroad appearing frequently on the cabaret/revivalist circuit.

Albums: *Dave Berry* (1964), *The Special Sound Of Dave Berry* (1966), *One Dozen Berrys* (1966), *Dave Berry '68* (1968), *Hostage To The Beat* (1986). Compilation: *Berry's Best* (1988).

Berry, Mike

b. 1943, Hackney, London, England. Buddy Holly-influenced singer whose Joe Meek-produced recording debut was a Hollyesque cover of the Shirelles' 'Will You Still Love Me Tomorrow?' on Decca. He just missed the UK Top 20 in 1961 with his heartfelt 'Tribute To Buddy Holly' on HMV Records, a song supposedly given the seal of approval by Buddy at a seance! Berry was backed on this and other early recordings by the Outlaws, a noted group which included Ritchie Blackmore and Chas Hodges. Berry's biggest hit came in 1963 with the first of his two UK Top 10 hits, 'Don't You Think It's Time?', again written by spiritualist/songwriter Geoff Goddard and produced by Meek. Berry's records were picked up in the USA by Holly's old label Coral but did not reach the charts. In the 70s he became a well-known television actor, appearing regularly in television programmes such as the top children's show, *Worzel Gummidge*. In 1980, after a 17-year gap, he returned to the UK Top 10, this time on Polydor with a MOR revival of the standard 'The Sunshine Of Your Smile', produced by his old colleague Chas Hodges, now of Chas And Dave fame.

Albums: *Drifts Away* (1972), *Rocks In My Head* (1976), *I'm A Rocker* (1980), *Sunshine Of Your Smile* (1980), *Memories* (1982).

Bienstock, Freddy

b. 24 April 1928, Vienna, Austria. The music publishing branch of popular music is often criticised by the very artists the publishers represent. Not so for Freddy Bienstock, he has maintained respect and credibility for over five decades in waters infested with sharks. A young Ray Davies signed with Bienstock's Carlin Music at the age of 19, Davies stated 'I went to Carlin because I wanted to get paid for what I was doing, music publishers when I started were all Denmark Street'.

Bienstock started out as a lad working at the legendary Brill Building in the stockroom at Chappell Music in New York where his cousins Jean and Julian Aberbach were executives. They eventually left to form their own music company and Freddy joined them a few years later. His first manna from heaven came in 1955 when he was introduced to Colonel Tom Parker. Over the next few years Bienstock was instrumental in presenting new songs to Elvis Presley via the Hill and Range publishing company. This resulted in classics like 'Blue Suede Shoes' (Carl Perkins) and 'Jailhouse Rock' (Leiber And Stoller). Bienstock moved to London in 1957 to set up Belinda Music to handle the Aberbach's catalogue. Freddy eventually bought the list and founded Carlin Music in 1966. He originally wanted to name the company after his daughter Caroline but the Pirate Radio ship owner Ronan O'Rahilly had already registered the name. Freddy calmly removed the letters o and e to get round the Companies House legislation. One of his first signings was the Kinks, and it is to Bienstock's credit that he saw the future potential in the songwriting talent of Raymond Douglas Davies. Bienstock also acquired the Motown, Burt Bacharach, and Gamble And Huff catalogues in addition to many classic songs from the beat group era from Cliff Richard, the Shadows and the Animals. Great writers like Phil Spector, Ellie Greenwich, Jeff Barry, Doc Pomus and Mort Shuman also became part of the Carlin list. In 1980 he added over 100,000 American popular songs with the Redwood catalogue. This contained evergreens like 'As Time Goes By', 'Sweet Georgia Brown', 'Button Up Your Overcoat' and the Al Jolson perennial 'My Mammy'. Bienstock was able to purchase Chappells in 1984 provided that he agreed to suspend the Carlin operation. Outside purchasers were also taking an interest in Bienstock's Midas touch and in 1987 his board agreed to sell Chappells to Warner Brothers for many millions. Freddy now regrets the sale but wryly points out that the blow was softened by the huge profit they took.

Bienstock, however, shrewdly retained an outstanding collection with the Carlin catalogue and the company already had a firm foundation of classic rock 'n' roll, 60s pop, standards of American popular song and 70s progressive rock. Carlin's chief executive David Japp has consolidated this base by building on music from Europe, contemporary pop and film music. Bienstock is publisher to what is arguably the finest independent pop music catalogue in the world and he remains one of the peerless entrepreneurs in popular music history. Dave Davies stated in 1977: 'I dealt with a man called Freddy Bienstock. I think he's got a good ear, he's from Vienna'.

Big Brother And The Holding Company

Formed in September 1965, this pivotal San Franciscan rock group evolved out of 'jam' sessions held in the basement of a communal house. The original line-up featured Sam Andrew (b. 18 December 1941, Taft, California, USA; guitar/vocals), Peter Albin (b. 6 June 1944, San Francisco, California, USA; bass/vocals), Dave Eskerson (guitar) and Chuck Jones (drums), but within months the latter pair had been replaced, respectively, by James Gurley (b. c.1940, Detroit, Michigan, USA) and David Getz (b. 1938, Brooklyn, New York, USA). The restructured quartet initially eschewed formal compositions, preferring a free-form improvisation centred on Gurley's mesmeric finger-picking style, but a degree of discipline gradually evolved. The addition of Texas singer Janis Joplin in June 1966 emphasized this newfound direction and her powerful, blues-soaked delivery provided the perfect foil to the unit's intrumental power. Big Brother rapidly became one of the Bay Area's leading attractions, but naively struck an immoderate recording deal with the Chicago-based Mainstream label. Although marred by poor production, *Big Brother And The Holding Company* nonetheless contained several excellent performances, notably 'Bye Bye Baby' and 'Down On Me'. The quintet rose to national prominence in 1967 following a sensational appearance at the Monterey Pop Festival. Joplin's charismatic performance engendered a prestigious management deal with Albert Grossman who in turn secured their release from all contractual obligations. Big Brother then switched outlets to Columbia, for which they completed *Cheap Thrills* (1968). This exciting album topped the US charts, but despite the inclusion of in-concert favourites 'Piece Of My Heart' and 'Ball And Chain', the recording was fraught with difficulty. Joplin came under increased pressure to opt for a solo career as critics unfairly denegrated the musicians' abilities. The group broke up in November 1968 and while Sam Andrew joined the singer in her next venture, Albin and Getz joined Country Joe And The Fish. The following year the latter duo reclaimed the Big Brother name and with the collapse of an interim line-up, re-established the unit with ex-colleagues Andrew and Gurley. Several newcomers, including Nick Gravenites (vocals), Kathi McDonald (vocals), Dave Shallock (guitar) and Mike Finnegan (piano) augmented the quartet on an informal basis, but despite moments of inspiration, neither *Be A Brother* (1970) nor *How Hard It Is* (1971) recaptured former glories. The group was disbanded in 1972, but reconvened six years later at the one-off Tribal Stomp reunion. In 1987 singer Michelle Bastian joined Getz, Gurley, Andrew and Albin in a fully reconsituted Big Brother line-up still hoping to assert an independent identity.

Albums: *Big Brother And The Holding Company* (1967), *Cheap Thrills* (1968), *Be A Brother* (1970), *How Hard It Is* (1971). Compilations and archive collections: *Cheaper Thrills* (1984), *Joseph's Coat* (1986).

Big Three

Formed in Liverpool 1961 as an offshoot from Cass And The Cassanovas, the Big Three comprised Johnny Gustafson (vocals/bass), Johnny Hutchinson (vocals/drums) and Adrian Barber (guitar). During 1962, Barber relocated to Germany and was replaced by Brian Griffiths, who made his debut at the Star Club, Hamburg. A mini-legend in their native Liverpool, the Big Three were revered as one of the loudest, aggressive and visually appealing acts on the circuit. After signing with Beatles' manager Brian Epstein success seemed assured but their characteristic unruliness proved their undoing. They scored only two minor hits, a cover of Ritchie Barrett's R&B standard 'Some Other Guy' and professional hitmaker Mitch Murray's 'By The Way'. Although a live EP *At The Cavern* gave some indication of their power, their vinyl excursions failed to reveal their true potential. An acrimonious split with Epstein only months into their relatonship effectively put paid to their chances. By November 1963, Griffiths and Gustafson found alternative employment with the Seniors, leaving Hutchinson to recruit Paddy Chambers and Faron (of the Flamingos) as replacements. Less than a year later, the Big Three disbanded. The unlikely Gustafson later joined the Merseybeats, formed John And Johnny, then Quatermass and appeared again in the 70s as the bassist in Roxy Music.

Compilations: *Cavern Stomp* (1982), *I Feel Like Steppin' Out* (1986).

Bilk, Acker

b. Bernard Stanley Bilk, 28 January 1929, Pensford, Somerset, England. After playing as a semi-professional in Bristol, Bilk received his big break in the jazz world when he joined Ken Colyer as a clarinettist in 1954. Four years later, under the self-referential title 'Mr.' Acker Bilk, he enjoyed his first UK Top 10 hit with 'Summer Set'. Backed by the

Paramount Jazz Band, Bilk was at the forefront of the British trad jazz boom of the early 60s. With their distinctive uniform of bowler hats and striped waistcoats, Bilk and company enjoyed a number of UK hits including 'Buona Sera' and 'That's My Home'. It was with the Leon Young String Chorale, however, that Bilk achieved his most remarkable hit. 'Stranger On The Shore' was a US number 1 in May 1962 and peaking at number 2 in the UK it achieved an endurance record for its 55 weeks on the best-sellers list. Although the beat boom all but ended the careers of many trad jazzers, Bilk continued to enjoy a successful career in cabaret and even returned to the Top 10 as late as 1976 with 'Aria'. He continues to perform alongside contemporaries Kenny Ball and Chris Barber, recreating the UK number 1 album, *The Best Of Ball, Barber And Bilk* in 1962.

Albums: *Mr. Acker Requests* (1958), *Mr. Acker Marches On* (1958), *Mr. Acker Bilk Sings* (1959), *Mr. Acker Bilk Requests (Part One)* (1959), *Mr. Acker Bilk Requests (Part Two)* (1959), *The Noble Art Of Mr. Acker Bilk* (1959), *Seven Ages Of Acker* (1960), *Mr. Acker Bilk's Omnibus* (1960), *Acker* (1960), *A Golden Treasury Of Bilk* (1961), *Mr. Acker Bilk's Lansdowne Folio* (1961), *Stranger On The Shore* (1961), *Above The Stars And Other Romantic Fancies* (1962), *A Taste Of Honey* (1963), *Great Themes From Great European Movies* (1965), *Acker In Paris* (1966), *Blue Acker* (1968), *Some Of My Favourite Things* (1973), *That's My Desire* (1974), *Serenade* (1975), *The One For Me* (1976), *Invitation* (1977), *Meanwhile* (1977), *Sheer Magic* (1977), *Extremely Live In Studio 1* (1978), *Free* (1978), *When The Lights Are Low* (1978), with Max Bygraves *Twogether* (1980), *Unissued Acker* (1980), *Made In Hungary* (1980), *The Moment I'm With You* (1980), *Relaxin'* (1981), *Acker Bilk In Holland* (1985), *John, Paul And Acker* (1987), *On Stage* (1988), *That's My Home* (1988), with Chris Barber and Kenny Ball *The Ultimate!* (1991). Compilations: *The Best Of Ball, Barber And Bilk* (1962), *Golden Hour Of Acker Bilk* (1974) *Very Best Of Acker Bilk* (1978), *Evergreen* (1978), *Sheer Magic* (1979), *The Best Of Acker Bilk, Volume Two* (1979), *Mellow Music* (1980).

Birds

Formed in West Drayton, Middlesex, England in 1964. Ali McKenzie (vocals), Tony Munroe (guitar/vocals), Ron Wood (guitar/vocals), Kim Gardner (bass/vocals) and Pete McDaniels (drums) were originally known as the Thunderbirds, but truncated their name to avoid confusion with Chris Farlowe's backing group. One of the era's most powerful R&B groups, the Birds' legacy is confined to a mere four singles, but the excitement displayed on 'Leaving Here' and 'No Good Without You Baby' (both 1965), show their reputation is deserved. However, the group is better-known for a scurrilous publicity stunt wherein seven writs were served on the American Byrds, demanding they change their name and claiming loss of income. The US group naturally ignored the charges and the UK unit was latterly known as Bird's Birds. They broke up in October 1966 when Gardner joined Creation. Wood was also a member of this seminal pop-art unit in between his two spells with the Jeff Beck Group. Gardner achieved momentary fame in the 70s with Ashton, Gardner And Dyke and Badger, but it was Wood who enjoyed the greater profile, firstly with the Faces and latterly the Rolling Stones.
Album: *These Birds Are Dangerous* (1985).

Black, Bill

b. William Patton Black, 17 September 1926, Memphis, Tennessee, USA, d. 21 October 1965, Memphis, Tennessee, USA. Black was the bass-playing half of the Scotty And Bill team that backed Elvis Presley on his earliest live performances. After leaving Presley, Black launched a successful career of his own as leader of the Bill Black Combo. Initially playing an acoustic stand-up bass, Black was hired as a session musician by Sun Records, where he met Presley in 1954. He played on the earliest Sun tracks, including 'That's All Right'. Black toured with Presley alongside guitarist Scotty Moore; later drummer D.J. Fontana was added to the group. Black and Moore left Presley's employment in 1957 owing to what they felt was unfair payment. The Bill Black Combo was formed in 1959, with Black (electric bass guitar), Reggie Young (guitar), Martin Wills (saxophone), Carl McAvoy (piano) and Jerry Arnold (drums). Signed to Hi Records in Memphis, the group favoured an instrumental R&B-based sound tempered with jazz. Their first charting record was 'Smokie Part 2' in late 1959 but it was the follow-up, 'White Silver Sands' in the spring of 1960, that gave the group its biggest US hit, reaching number 9.
Black retired from touring in 1962 but the group kept performing under the same name without him, with Bob Tucker playing bass. The group also backed other artists, including Gene Simmons on the 1964 number 11 hit 'Haunted House'. Saxophonist Ace Cannon was a member of the combo for some time. The group continued playing even after Black died of a brain tumour in October 1965. The Bill Black Combo scored a total of 19 chart singles and was still working under the leadership of Tucker in the late 80s.
Selected albums: *Saxy Jazz* (1960), *Solid And Raunchy* (1962), *That Wonderful Thing* (1962), *Movin'* (1962), *Record Hop* (1962), *Let's Twist* (1962), *Untouchable Sound* (1963), *Plays The Blues* (1964), *Plays Chuck Berry* (1964), *Goes Big Band* (1964), *More Solid And Raunchy* (1965), *All Timers* (1966), *Black Lace* (1967), *King Of The Road* (1967), *The Beat Goes On* (1968),

Turn On Your Lovelight (1969), *Soulin' The Blues* (1969). Compilation: *Greatest Hits* (1963).

Cilla Black with Tom Jones and Harry H. Corbett

Black, Cilla

b. Priscilla White, 27 May 1943, Liverpool, England. While working as a part-time cloakroom attendant at Liverpool's Cavern club, in 1963, Priscilla appeared as guest singer with various groups, and was brought to the attention of Brian Epstein. The Beatles' manager changed her name and during the next few years ably exploited her girl-next-door appeal. Her first single, under the auspices of producer George Martin, was a brassy powerhouse reworking of the Beatles' unreleased 'Love Of The Loved', which hit the UK Top 30 in late 1963. A change of style with Burt Bacharach's 'Anyone Who Had A Heart' saw Cilla emerge as a ballad singer of immense power and distinction. 'You're My World', a translation of an Italian lyric, was another brilliantly orchestrated, impassioned ballad which, like its predecessor, dominated the UK number 1 position in 1964. In what was arguably the most competitive year in British pop history, Black was outselling all her Merseyside rivals, bar the Beatles. For her fourth single, Paul McCartney presented 'It's For You', a fascinating jazz waltz ballad which seemed a certain number 1, but stalled at number 8. By the end of 1964, Cilla was one of the most successful female singers of her era and continued to release superb quality covers, including a version of the Righteous Brothers' 'You've Lost That Lovin' Feelin'' and an excellent reading of Randy Newman's 'I've Been Wrong Before'. A consummate rocker and unchallenged mistress of the neurotic ballad genre, Black was unassailable at her pop peak, yet her chosen path was that of an 'all-round entertainer'. For most of 1965, she ceased recording and worked on her only film *Work Is A Four Letter Word*, but returned strongly the following year with 'Love's Just A Broken Heart' and 'Alfie'.

The death of Brian Epstein in 1967 and a relative lull in chart success might have blighted the prospects of a lesser performer, but Black was already moving into television work, aided by her manager/husband Bobby Willis. Her highly-rated television series was boosted by the hit title theme 'Step Inside Love', donated by Paul McCartney. Throughout the late 60s, she continued to register Top 10 hits, including the stoical 'Surround Yourself With Sorrow', the oddly-paced wish-fulfilling 'Conversations' and the upbeat 'Something Tells Me'. Like many of her former contemporaries, Cilla wound down her recording career in the 70s and concentrated on live work and television commitments. While old rivals such as Lulu, Sandie Shaw and Dusty Springfield were courted by the new rock elite, Black required no such patronage and entered the 90s as one of the highest paid family entertainers in the British music business with two major UK television shows, *Blind Date* and *Surprise Surprise*.

Albums: *Cilla* (1965), *Cilla Sings A Rainbow* (1966), *Sher-oo* (1968), *Surround Yourself With Cilla* (1969), *Sweet Inspiration* (1970), *Images* (1971), *Day By Day With Cilla* (1973), *In My Life* (1974), *It Makes Me Feel Good* (1976), *Modern Priscilla* (1978), *Surprisingly Cilla* (1985), *Love Songs* (1987). Compilation: *25th Anniversary Album* (1988).

Blackwell, Chris

b. 22 June 1937, London, England. Blackwell is the son of Middleton Joseph Blackwell, a distant relative of the power behind the Crosse & Blackwell food empire. Chris moved to Jamaica at the age of six months and his family lived in the affluent area of Terra Nova. Three years later, he returned to England to attend prep school and subsequently entered Harrow Public School. A mediocre scholar, he failed to get to university and spent the late 50s commuting between London and Kingston, uncertain of what to do with his life. During the summer of 1958 he was stranded on a coral reef near the Helshie Beaches. Dehydrated and sunburnt, he was rescued by members of a small Rastafarian community. He never forgot that formative incident and, in later life, displayed every willingness to deal directly with Rasta musicians and introduce their philosophy and culture to European and American audiences. Through his mother's friendship with writer Ian Fleming, Blackwell entered the film business during the early 60s, and worked with producer Harry Seltzman on the set of *Dr No*. Although he was offered the opportunity to work on further Bond films, Blackwell declined this invitation and instead turned to music.

In May 1962, he founded Island Records, borrowing the name from Alec Waugh's 50s novel *Island In The Sun*. After purchasing master recordings from Jamaican producers such as Leslie Kong, Coxsone Dodd and King Edwards, he issued them in the UK through Island. The company boasted a number of subsidiaries, including Jump Up, Black Swan and, most notably Sue, co-managed by producer Guy Stevens. Blackwell bought and promoted his own records, delivering them in his Mini Cooper. In Jamaica, his label achieved a number 1 hit with Laurel Aiken's 'Little Sheila'. Early signings included a host of Jamaican talent: Owen Gray, Jimmy Cliff, Derrick Morgan, Lord Creator and Bob Morley (aka Bob Marley). However, it was 14-year-old Millie Small, who provided Blackwell with his first UK breakthrough. The infectious 'My Boy Lollipop' sold six million copies, and precipitated Blackwell's move into the mainstream UK pop/R&B market. His first main band were the Spencer Davis Group, and he continued to manage Steve Winwood right through Traffic and into his highly successful solo career. Additionally Blackwell deserves major credit for his perseverance with many of his artists. Notably John Martyn, Robert Palmer, Nick Drake and Cat Stevens. He built up Island Records during the 70s simply by having a remarkably 'good ear'. Blackwell knew what he liked and he chose well with, Free, Mott The Hoople, Spooky Tooth and Fairport Convention. His contribution to exposing reggae and progressive rock to a wider market is inestimable.

Blodwyn Pig

Blodwyn Pig

During its short life, Blodwyn Pig made a valuable contribution to the British blues boom in the late 60s. The band was formed after guitarist Mick Abrahams (b. 7 April 1943, Luton, Bedfordshire, England), surprisingly departed the fast-rising Jethro Tull in 1969. His energetic and fluid playing blended well with the rest of the band; Jack Lancaster (saxophone), Andy Pyle (bass) and Ron Berg (drums). The fine debut *Ahead Rings Out* with its famous pig cover was a critical success, containing a healthy mixture of various styles of progressive blues. The Tull influenced 'Ain't Ya Comin Home' and the superb slide guitar of 'Dear Jill' were but two highlights. Lancaster's lengthy 'The Modern Alchemist'

showcased his jazz influence and saxophone skills. The band were a prolific live attraction, and Abrahams would delight the crowds with his exceptional showpiece, 'Cats Squirrel', probably the only time that a Cream number had been 'borrowed' and improved upon. Abrahams's solo was superior to Eric Clapton's, although this was a millstone he would constantly attempt to shed. The second album showed great moments, notably Abrahams's punchy 'See My Way'. Lancaster's advanced long pieces like 'San Francisco Sketches' ultimately gave the band a split direction. Abrahams departed and was replaced by Pete Banks formerly of Yes and Larry Wallis. Their direction was now led by Lancaster and they changed their name to Lancaster's Bomber, and finally, Lancaster, before they crash landed shortly afterwards. Four years later, Abrahams and Lancaster reformed Blodwyn Pig again, with Pyle and ex-Tull drummer Clive Bunker, but they had hardly got started when the signs that their day was long past became evident. While Lancaster eventually carved out a career as a producer, Abrahams set up his own financial consultancy business. However, Abrahams was not able to forsake the music business for too long and subsequently resurrected the group in the early 90s to play club dates, performing new material, utilizing the services of Dick Heckstall-Smith, plus former Piggies, Clive Bunker and Andy Pyle.
Albums: *Ahead Rings Out* (1969), *Getting To This* (1970).

Blood, Sweat And Tears

The jazz/rock excursions by one of the genre's leading pioneers came as a refreshing change to late 60s guitar dominated rock music. The many impressive line-ups of the band comprised (amongst others) David Clayton-Thomas (b. David Thomsett, 13 September 1941, Surrey, England; vocals), Al Kooper (b. 5 February 1944, New York, USA; keyboards/vocals), Steve Katz (b. 9 May 1945, New York, USA; guitar), Dick Halligan (b. 29 August 1943, New York, USA; trombone/flute/keyboards), Fred Lipsius (b. 19 November 1944, New York, USA; alto saxophone/piano), Bobby Colomby (b. 20 December 1944, New York, USA; drums), Jim Fielder (b. 4 October 1947, Denton, Texas, USA; bass), Lew Soloff (b. 20 February 1944, Brooklyn, New York, USA; trumpet), Chuck Winfield (b. 5 February 1943, Monessen, Pennsylvania, USA; trumpet), Jerry Hyman (b. 19 May 1947, Brooklyn, New York, USA; Trumpet) and Dave Bargeron (b. 6 September 1942, Athol, Massachusetts, USA; trumpet). The band was the idea of Al Kooper, who together with Katz, both from the Blues Project, created a monster that would soon outgrow them. Kooper departed soon after the debut *Child Is Father To The Man*, which contained two of his finest songs,

Blood Sweat And Tears

'I Can't Quit Her' and 'My Days Are Numbered'. The record was ultimately flawed by less than perfect vocals. *Blood Sweat And Tears* with Clayton-Thomas taking over the vocal chores was their finest work, which stands up today as a brilliantly scored and fresh-sounding record. Kooper, although working on the arrangements, missed out on the extraordinary success this record achieved. It topped the US album charts for many weeks during its two-year stay, sold millions of copies, won a Grammy award and spawned three major worldwide hits; 'You've Made Me So Very Happy', 'Spinning Wheel' and 'And When I Die'. The following two albums were both considerable successes, although basically more of the same, gutsy brass arrangements, occasional biting guitar solos and most of all Clayton-Thomas's growling effortless vocal delivery. Following *BS&T4*, Clayton-Thomas departed for a solo career, resulting in a succession of lead vocalists, including the former member of Edgar Winter's White Trash, Jerry LaCroix (b. 10 October 1943, Alexandria, Lousiana, USA). The fortunes of the band never returned to their former glory; even when Clayton-Thomas returned, their magic had gone. *New City* made a respectable showing in the album charts in the USA but the supper-club circuit ultimately beckoned. The band reformed briefly in 1988 to play a back catalogue; they deserve a place in rock history as both

innovators and brave exponents of jazz/rock.
Albums: *Child Is Father To The Man* (1968), *Blood, Sweat And Tears* (1969), *Blood, Sweat And Tears 3* (1970), *BS&T4* (1971), *New Blood* (1972), *No Sweat* (1973), *Mirror Image* (1974), *New City* (1975), *More Than Ever* (1976), *Brand New Day* (1977), *Nuclear Blues* (1980). Compilation: *Greatest Hits* (1972).

Bloomfield, Mike

b. 28 July 1944, Chicago, Illinois, USA d. 15 February 1981. For many, both critics and fans, Bloomfield was the finest white blues guitarist America has so far produced. Although signed to Columbia Records in 1964 as the Group (with Charlie Musslewhite and Nick Gravenites) it was his emergence in 1965 as the young, shy guitarist in the Paul Butterfield Blues Band that bought him to public attention. He astonished those viewers who had watched black blues guitarists spend a lifetime, and still not play with as much fluidity and feeling as Bloomfield. That same year he was an important part of musical history, when folk purists accused Bob Dylan of committing artistic suicide at the Newport Folk Festival. It was Bloomfield who was his electric lead guitarist, and it would be Bloomfield behind the electric guitar on Dylan's 60s masterpieces, *Highway 61 Revisited* and 'Like A Rolling Stone'. On leaving Butterfield in 1967 he immediately formed the seminal Electric Flag, although he had departed by the time the first album had begun to slide down the US charts. His 1968 album *Super Session* with Stephen Stills and Al Kooper became his biggest selling record. It led to a short but financially lucrative career with Kooper. The track 'Stop' on the album epitomized Bloomfield's style; clean, crisp, sparse and emotional. The long sustained notes were produced by bending the string with his fingers underneath the other strings so as not to affect the tuning. It was five years before his next satisfying work appeared, *Triumvirate,* with John Paul Hammond and Dr. John (Mac Rebennack). And so the pattern of Bloomfield's career began, no sooner had he become a star; than he became a recluse. Subsequent albums were distributed on small labels and did not gain national distribution. Plagued with a long-standing drug habit he occasionally supplemented his income by scoring music for pornographic movies. He also wrote three film music soundtracks, *The Trip* (1967), *Medium Cool* (1969) and *Steelyard Blues* (1973). Additionally he taught music at Stanford University in San Francisco, wrote advertising jingles and was an adviser to *Guitar Player* magazine. Bloomfield avoided the limelight, possibly because of his away-from-home insomnia, which hampered his touring, but mainly because of his intelligent perception of what he felt an audience wanted from him; 'Playing in front of strangers leads to idolatry, and idolatry is dangerous because the audience has a preconception of you, even though you cannot get a conception of them'. In 1975 he was cajoled into forming the 'supergroup' KGB with Rick Grech, Barry Goldberg and Carmine Appice. Predictably the whole affair was anathema to him and the album was an unmitigated disaster. Bloomfield then resorted to playing mostly acoustic music and had an extraordinarily prolific year when in 1977 he released five albums, the most notable being the critically acclaimed *If You Love These Blues, Play 'Em As You Please*, released through *Guitar Player* magazine. A second burst of activity occurred shortly before his tragic death when another three album's worth of material was recorded. Bloomfield was found dead in his car from a suspected accidental drug overdose, a sad end to a 'star' who had constantly avoided stardom in order to maintain his own integrity.

Albums: *Super Session* (1968), *The Live Adventures Of Mike Bloomfield And Al Kooper* (1969), *Fathers And Sons* (1969), with Barry Goldberg *Two Jews Blues* (1969), *It's Not Killing Me* (1969), with others *Live At Bill Graham's Fillmore West* (1969), *Triumvirate* (1973), *Try It Before You Buy It* (1975), *Bloomfield/Naftalin* (1976), *Mill Valley Session* (1976), *There's Always Another Record* (1976), *I'm Always With You* (1977), *If You Love These Blues, Play 'Em As You Please* (1977), *Analine* (1977), *Michael Bloomfield* (1977), *Count Talent And The Originals* (1977), *Mike Bloomfield And Woody Harris* (1979), *Between The Hard Place And The Ground* (1980), *Livin' In The Fast Lane* (1980), *Gosport Duets* (1981), *Red Hot And Blues* (1981), *Cruisin' For A Bruisin'* (1981), *Retrospective* (1984), *Junco Partners* (1984), as KGB *KGB* (1976).

Further reading: *The Rise And Fall Of An American Guitar Hero*, Ed Ward.

Blossom Toes

Brian Godding (guitar/vocals/keyboards), Jim Cregan (guitar/vocals), Brian Belshaw (bass/vocals) and Kevin Westlake (drums) were initially known as the Ingoes, but became Blossom Toes in 1967 on launching manager Giorgio Gomelsky's Marmalade label. *We Are Ever So Clean* was an enthralling selection, astutely combining English pop with a quirky sense of humour. The grasp of melody offered on 'Love Is' or 'What's It For' was akin to that of the Idle Race or Beatles, while the experimental flourish on 'What On Earth' or 'Look At Me I'm You' capture the prevailing flavour of 1967. *If Only For A Moment* marked the departure of Westlake, who was replaced, in turn, by John 'Poli' Palmer, then Barry Reeves. A noticeably heavier sound was shown to great effect on the revered 'Peace Lovin' Man', but the set was altogether less distinctive. The quartet was dissolved in 1970, but while Belshaw and Godding rejoined Westlake in B.B. Blunder, Cregan formed

Stud with Jim Wilson and Charlie McCracken, before joining Family. He later found fame with Cockney Rebel and Rod Stewart.

Albums: *We Are Ever So Clean* (1967), *If Only For A Moment* (1969). Compilation: *The Blossom Toes Collection* (1989).

Blue Cheer

Renowned as one of the world's loudest groups, Dickie Petersen (vocals/bass), Bruce Leigh Stephens (guitar) and Paul Whaley (drums) harboured dreams of a more conventional direction until seeing Jimi Hendrix perform at the celebrated Monterey Pop Festival. Taking their name from a potent brand of the hallucinogenic drug LSD, Blue Cheer made an immediate impact with their uncompromising debut album, which featured cacophonous interpretations of 'Summertime Blues' (US number 14) and 'Parchman Farm'. A second set, *Outsideinside*, was completed in the open air when the trio's high volume destroyed the studio monitors. Stephens left the group during the sessions for *New! Improved*, and his place was taken by former Other Half guitarist Randy Holden. *Blue Cheer* then unveiled a reconstituted line-up of Petersen, Burns Kellogg (keyboards), Bruce Stephens (bass) and Norman Mayall (drums/guitar). Stephens was then replaced by former Kak guitarist, Gary Yoder, for the quartet's fifth album, *The Original Human Being*. This impressive set featured the atmospheric, raga-influenced 'Babaji (Twilight Raga)', and is acclaimed as the group's most cohesive work. The band was dissolved during the early 70s, but reformed the following decade following an emotional reunion between Petersen and Whaley. Blue Cheer has continued to pursue the former's bombastic vision and a 1990 release, *Highlights And Lowlives*, united the group with Anthrax producer Jack Eudino.

Albums: *Vincebus Eruptum* (1968), *Outsideinside* (1968), *New! Improved! Blue Cheer* (1969), *Blue Cheer* (1970), *The Original Human Being* (1970), *Oh! Pleasant Hope* (1971), *Blitzkrieg Over Nuremburg* (1989), *Highlights And Lowlives* (1990). Compilations: *The Best Of Blue Cheer* (1982), *Louder Than God* (1987).

Blues Magoos

Formed in the Bronx, New York, USA in 1964 and initially known as the Bloos Magoos, the founding line-up consisted of Emil 'Peppy' Thielhelm (b. 16 June 1949; vocals/guitar), Dennis LaPore (lead guitar), Ralph Scala (b. 12 December 1947; organ/vocals), Ronnie Gilbert (b. 25 April 1946; bass) and John Finnegan (drums), but by the end of the year LaPore and Finnegan had been replaced by Mike Esposito (b. 1943, Delaware, USA) and Geoff Daking (b. 1947, Delaware, USA). The group quickly became an important part of the emergent

Greenwich Village rock scene and in 1966 secured a residency at the fabled Night Owl club. Having recorded singles for Ganim and Verve Forecast, the Magoos were signed to Mercury, where they became the subject of intense grooming. However, Vidal Sassoon-styled haircuts and costumes that lit-up onstage failed to quell an innate rebelliousness, though the group enjoyed one notable hit when '(We Ain't Got) Nothin' Yet' (1966) reached number 5 in the US chart. Its garage-band snarl set the tone for an attendant album, *Psychedelic Lollipop*, which contained several equally virulent selections. The Blues Magoos' dalliance with drugs was barely disguised and titles such as 'Love Seems Doomed' (LSD) and 'Albert Common Is Dead' (ACID) were created to expound their beliefs. By 1968 tensions arose within the group and they split up following the release of *Basic Blues Magoos*. The management team re-signed the name to ABC Records and, as Thielhelm had accumulated a backlog of material, suggested he front a revamped line-up. John Leillo (vibes/percussion), Eric Kaz (keyboards), Roger Eaton (bass) and Richie Dickon (percussion) completed *Never Goin' Back To Georgia*, while the same group, bar Eaton, was augmented by sundry session musicians for the disappointing *Gulf Coast Bound*. The Blues Magoos' name was discontinued when Peppy took a role in the musical *Hair*. As Peppy Castro he has since pursued a varied career as a member of Barnaby Bye, Wiggy Bits and Balance, while Cher and Kiss are among the artists who have recorded his songs.

Albums: *Psychedelic Lollipop* (1966), *Electric Comic Book* (1967), *Basic Blues Magoos* (1968), *Never Goin' Back To Georgia* (1969), *Gulf Coast Bound* (1970).

Blues Project

The Blues Project was formed in New York City in the mid-60s by guitarist Danny Kalb and took its name from a compendium of acoustic musicians on which he participated. Tommy Flanders (vocals), Steve Katz (guitar), Andy Kulberg (bass, flute), Roy Blumenfeld (drums), plus Kalb, were latterly joined by Al Kooper, fresh from adding the distinctive organ on Bob Dylan's 'Like A Rolling Stone'. The quintet was quickly established as the city's leading electric blues band, a prowess heard on their debut album *Live At the Cafe Au Go Go*. Flanders then left for a solo career and the resultant four-piece embarked on the definitive *Projections* album. Jazz, pop and soul styles were added to their basic grasp of R&B to create an absorbing, rewarding collection, but inner tensions undermined an obvious potential. By the time *Live At The Town Hall* was issued, Kooper had left the group to form Blood, Sweat And Tears, where he was subsequently joined by Katz. An unhappy Kalb also quit the group, but Kulberg and

Blumenfeld added Richard Greene (violin), John Gregory (guitar/vocals) and Don Kretmar (bass/saxophone) for a fourth collection, *Planned Obsolescence*. The line-up owed little to the old group, and in deference to this new direction, changed their name to Sea Train.

In 1971, Kalb reclaimed the erstwhile moniker and recorded two further albums with former members Flanders, Blumenfeld and Kretmar. This particular version was supplanted by a reunion of the *Projections* line-up for a show in Central Park, after which the Blues Project name was abandoned. Despite their fractured history, the group is recognized as one of the leading white R&B bands of the 60s.

Albums: *Live At The Cafe Au Go-Go* (1966), *Projections* (1967), *Live At The Town Hall* (1967), *Planned Obsolescence* (1968), *Lazarus* (1971), *Blues Project* (1972), *Reunion In Central Park* (1973).

Bob And Earl

Formed in Los Angeles in 1960 this duo comprised Bobby Day (b. Bobby Byrd, 1 July 1932, Fort Worth, Texas, USA) and Earl Lee Nelson. Day had previously formed the Hollywood Flames, a group best recalled for the rock 'n' roll hit 'Buzz-Buzz-Buzz' (1957) which featured Earl Nelson on lead vocal. Bobby then secured a solo hit with 'Rockin' Robin' before briefly joining Nelson in the original Bob And Earl. Bob Relf replaced Day when the latter resumed his own career. The Barry White produced 'Harlem Shuffle', the pairing's best-known song, was originally released in 1963. A minor hit in the US, the single proved more durable in Britain. Although it failed to chart when first released, a re-issue reached number 7 in 1969. Bob And Earl had meanwhile continued to record excellent singles, although the prophetically-titled 'Baby It's Over' (1966) was their only further hit. Nelson recorded under the name of Jay Dee for the Warner Brothers label in 1973, and also as Jackie Lee, charting in the US with 'The Duck' (1965), 'African Boo-Ga-Loo' (1968) and 'The Chicken' (1970). Relf wrote Love Unlimited's 1974 hit 'Walking In The Rain' and was latterly replaced by Bobby Garrett. The new duo continued to record together, and individually, during the 70s.

Album: *Harlem Shuffle* (1966).

Bob B. Soxx And The Blue Jeans

One of several groups created by famed producer Phil Spector, this short-lived trio consisted of two members of the Blossoms (Darlene Love and Fanita James), and soul singer Bobby Sheen. The Blue Jeans scored a US Top 10 hit in 1962 with a radical reading of 'Zip-A-Dee-Doo-Dah', wherein the euphoric original was slowed to a snail-like pace. Its success spawned an album which mixed restructured standards ('The White Cliffs Of Dover', 'This Land Is

Your Land') with original songs, of which 'Why Do Lovers Break Each Others Hearts' and 'Not Too Young To Get Married' were also issued as singles. The group made a contribution to Phil Spector's legendary *Christmas Album*.

Album: *Zip-A-Dee-Doo-Dah* (1963).

Bolan, Marc

b. Mark Feld, 30 July 1947, London, England, d. 16 September 1977. A former model in the halcyon 'Mod' era, Bolan began his singing career during the mid-60s folk boom. Initially dubbed 'Toby Tyler', he completed several unsuccessful demo discs before reportedly adopting his new surname from (Bo)b Dy(lan). The artist's debut single, 'The Wizard' (1965), revealed an early penchant for pop mysticism whereas its follow-up, 'The Third Degree', was indebted to R&B. Its b-side, 'San Francisco Poet', gave first airing to the distinctive, tremulous vocal warble for which Bolan became renowned and which flourished freely on his third single, 'Hippy Gumbo'. This slow, highly-stylized performance, produced by new manager Simon Napier-Bell, made no commercial impression, but was latterly picked up by the pirate station Radio London, whose disc jockey John Peel became a pivotal figure in Bolan's history. A series of demos was also undertaken at this point, several of which surfaced on *The Beginning Of Doves* (1974) and, with overdubs, on *You Scare Me To Death* (1981), but plans for a fourth single were postponed following the failure of its predecessor. Frustrated at his commercial impasse, the artist then opted to join Napier-Bell proteges John's Children in 1967. He composed their best-known single, 'Desdemona', but left the line-up after a matter of months to form Tyrannosaurus Rex. Here Bolan gave full rant to the 'underground' poetic folk-mysticism, redolent of author J.R.R. Tolkien, which 'Hippy Gumbo' had suggested. Such pretensions gave way to unabashed pop when the unit evolved into T. Rex three years later. Between 1970-73 this highly popular attraction enjoyed a run of 10 consecutive Top 5 singles, but Marc's refusal to alter the formula of his compositions resulted in an equally spectacular decline. Bolan was, nonetheless, one of the few established musicians to embrace punk and a contemporary television series, *Marc*, revived a flagging public profile. This ascendancy ended abruptly in September 1977 when the artist, as a passenger in a car driven by singer Gloria Jones, was killed when they crashed into a tree on Barnes Common, London.

Albums: *The Beginning Of Doves* (1974), *You Scare Me To Death* (1981), *Beyond The Rising Sun* (1984), *Love And Death* (1985), *The Marc Shows* (1989, television recordings). Compilation: *20th Century Boy* (1985 - provides an overview of the artist's entire career).

Graham Bond Organization

Bond, Graham

b. 28 October 1937, Romford, Essex, England, d. 8 May 1974, London, England. The young orphan was adopted from the Dr Barnardo's home and given musical tuition at school. The 'legendary' Graham Bond has latterly become recognized as one of the main instigators of British R&B along with Cyril Davies and Alexis Korner. His musical career began with Don Rendell's quintet in 1961 as a jazz saxophonist, followed by a stint with Korner's famous ensemble Blues Incorporated. By the time he formed his first band in 1963 he had made the Hammond organ his main instrument, although he showcased his talent at gigs by playing both alto saxophone and organ simultaneously. The seminal Graham Bond Organisation became one of the most respected units during 1964. The impressive line-up of Ginger Baker (drums), Jack Bruce (bass) and Dick Heckstall-Smith (saxophone - replacing John McLaughlin on guitar), played a hybrid of jazz, blues and rock that was musically and visually stunning. Bond was the first person in Britain to play a Hammond organ through a Leslie speaker cabinet and the first to use a Mellotron. The original Organisation made two superlative and formative albums *Sound Of '65* and *There's A Bond Between Us*. Both featured original songs mixed with standards. The band interpreted 'Walk On The Wild Side', 'Wade In The Water' and 'Got My Mojo Working'. Bond's own, 'Have You Ever Loved A Woman' and 'Walkin' In The Park' demonstrated his songwriting ability. Ironically such musicianship was unable to find a commercially acceptable niche. The jazz fraternity regarded Bond's band as too noisy and rock-based, while the pop audience found his music complicated and too jazzy. The small but loyal R&B club scene cognoscenti however, loved them. Ironically 30 years later the Tommy Chase Band are pursuing an uncannily similar road, now under the banner of jazz. As the British music scene changed, so the Organisation were penalized for staying close to their musical roots and refusing to adapt. Along the way, Bond had lost Baker and Bruce who had departed to form Cream, although the addition of Jon Hiseman on drums reinforced their musical pedigree. When Hiseman and Heckstall-Smith left to form Colosseum they showed their debt to Bond by featuring 'Walkin' In The Park' on their debut album. Disenchanted with the musical tide, Bond moved to the USA where he made two albums for the Pulsar label. Both records showed a veering away from jazz and R&B although the slightly more contemporary songs were an odd coupling with the Hammond organ. Neither album fared well and Graham returned to England in 1969. The music press welcomed his re-appearance, but a poorly attended Royal Albert Hall homecoming concert must have bitterly disheartened its subject. The new band; the Graham Bond Initiation, featured his wife Diane Stewart. The unlikely combination of astrological themes, R&B and public apathy doomed this promising unit. By now Graham had started on a slow decline into drugs, depression, mental disorder and dabblings with the occult. Following a reunion with Ginger Baker in his ill-fated Airforce project, and a brief spell with the Jack Bruce Band, Bond formed a musical partnership with Pete Brown; this resulted in one album and for a short time had a stabilizing effect on Bond's life. By 1974, following a nervous breakdown, drug addiction and two further unsuccessful conglomerations, Holy Magick and Magus, the cruellest of ironies happened on 8 May 1974; he was killed when he fell under the wheels of a London underground train at Finsbury Park station. Whether or not Graham Bond could ever have reached the musical heights of his 1964 band is open to endless debate. What has been acknowledged, is that he was an innovator, a catalyst and a major influence on British R&B.

Albums: *The Sound Of '65* (1965), *There's A Bond Between Us* (1966), *Mighty Grahame Bond* (1968), *Love Is The Law* (1968 - the latter two albums were re-packaged as *Bond In America* in 1971), *Solid Bond* (1970), *We Put The Majick On You* (1971), *Holy Magick* (1971), *Bond And Brown: Two Heads Are Better Than One* (1972), *This Is Graham Bond* (1978 - an edited version of *Bond In America*), *The Beginnings Of Jazz-Rock* (1977), *The Graham Bond Organisation* (1984), *Live At Klook's Kleek* (1988).

Further reading: *The Smallest Place In The World*, Dick Heckstall-Smith, *Graham Bond*; *The Mighty Shadow*, Harry Shapiro.

Bonds, Gary 'U.S.'

b. Gary Anderson, 6 June 1939, Jacksonville, Florida, USA. Having initially sung in various gospel groups, Bonds embraced secular music upon moving to Norfolk, Virginia. A successful spell in the region's R&B clubs resulted in a recording deal with local entrepreneur Frank Gauida, whose cavernous production technique gave Bonds's releases their distinctive sound. The ebullient 'New Orleans' set the pattern for the artist's subsequent recordings and its exciting, 'party' atmosphere reached an apogee on 'Quarter To Three', a US chart-topper and the singer's sole million-seller. Between 1961-62 Bonds scored further similar sounding hits with 'School Is Out', 'School Is In', 'Dear Lady Twist' and 'Twist Twist Senora', but his career then went into sharp decline. He remained a stalwart of the revival circuit until 1978 when long-time devotee Bruce Springsteen joined the singer onstage during a live engagement. Their friendship resulted in *Dedication*, produced by Springsteen's and E Street Band associate Miami Steve Van Zandt. The former contributed three original songs to the set, one of which, 'This Little Girl', reached the US Top 10 in 1981. Their collaboration was maintained with *On The Line*, which included Bonds'version of the Box Tops's 'Soul Deep', but he later asserted his independence with the self-produced *Standing In The Line Of Fire*.

Albums: *Dance Till Quarter To Three* (1961), *Twist Up Calypso* (1962), *Dedication* (1981), *On The Line* (1982), *Standing In The Line Of Fire* (1985). Compilations: *Greatest Hits Of Gary 'U.S.' Bonds* (1962), *Greatest Hits* (1981), *Gary 'U.S.' Bonds Meets Chubby Checker* (1981), *Certified Soul* (1982).

Bonzo Dog Doo-Dah Band

Although this eccentric ensemble was initially viewed as a 20s' revival act, they quickly developed into one of the era's most virulent satirists. Formed as the Bonzo Dog Dada Band in 1965 by art students Vivian Stanshall (b. 21 March 1943, Shillingford, Oxfordshire, England; vocals/trumpet/devices) and Rodney Slater (b. 8 November 1941, Crowland, Lincolnshire, England; saxophone), the group also included Neil Innes (b. 9 December 1944, Danbury, Essex, England; vocals/piano/guitar), Roger Ruskin Spear (b. 29 June 1943, Hammersmith, London, England; props/devices/saxophone) and 'Legs' Larry Smith (b. 18 January 1944, Oxford, England; drums). Various auxiliary members, including Sam Spoons (b. Martin Stafford Ash, 8 February 1942, Bridgewater, Somerset, England), Bob Kerr and Vernon Dudley Bohey-Nowell (b. 29 July 1932, Plymouth, Devon, England), augmented the line-up; the informality was such that no-one knew which members would turn up to perform on the group's early shows. In 1966, two early singles, 'My Brother Makes The Noises For Thè Talkies' and 'Alley Oop', reflected their transition from trad jazz to pop. *Gorilla*, the Bonzo's inventive debut album, still showed traces of their music-hall past, but the irreverent humour displayed on 'Jollity Farm' and the surrealistic 'The Intro And

The Outro', ('Hi there, happy you could stick around, like to introduce you to . . .') confirmed a lasting quality which outstripped that of contemporary 'rivals', the New Vaudeville Band, to whom Kerr, and others, had defected. A residency on the British television children's show, *Do Not Adjust Your Set*, secured the group's unconventional reputation and the songs they performed were later compiled on the *Tadpoles* album. The Bonzo Dog Band was also featured in the Beatles' film, *Magical Mystery Tour* performing the memorable 'Death Cab For Cutie' and in 1968 secured a UK Top 5 hit with 'I'm The Urban Spaceman', which was produced by Paul McCartney under the pseudonym Apollo C. Vermouth. Further albums, *The Doughnut In Granny's Greenhouse* and *Keynsham*, displayed an endearing eclecticism which derided the blues boom ('Can Blue Men Sing The Whites'), suburbia ('My Pink Half Of The Drainpipe') and many points in between, while displaying an increasingly rock-based bent. Newcomers Dennis Cowan (b. 6 May 1947, London, England), Dave Clague and Joel Druckman toughened the Bonzo's live sound, but the strain of compressing pre-war English middle class frivolousness (Stanshall), whimsical pop (Innes) and Ruskin Spear's madcap machinery into one unit ultimately proved too great. Although a re-convened line-up completed *Let's Make Up And Be Friendly* in 1972, this project was only undertaken to fulfil contractual obligations. The group had folded two years earlier when its members embarked on their inevitably divergent paths.

Albums: *Gorilla* (1967), *The Doughnut In Granny's Greenhouse* (1968), *Tadpoles* (1969), *Keynsham* (1969), *Let's Make Up And Be Friendly* (1972). Compilations: *The History Of The Bonzos* (1974), *The Bestiality Of The Bonzo Dog Band* (1989).

Booker T And The MGs

Formed in Memphis, Tennessee, USA in 1962 as a spin-off from the Mar-Keys, the group comprised Booker T. Jones (b. 11 December 1944, Memphis, Tennessee, USA; organ), Steve Cropper (b. 21 October 1941, Willow Spring, Missouri, USA; guitar), Lewis Steinberg (bass) and Al Jackson (b. 17 November 1945, Memphis, Tennessee, USA, d. 1 October 1975, Memphis, Tennessee, USA; drums). 'Green Onions', the MGs' renowned first hit, evolved out of a blues riff they had improvised while waiting to record a jingle. Its simple, smoky atmosphere, punctuated by Cropper's cutting guitar, provided the blueprint to a series of excellent records, including 'Jellybread', 'Chinese Checkers', 'Soul Dressing', Mo' Onions and 'Hip Hug-Her'. Pared to the bone, this sparseness accentuated the rhythm, particularly when Steinberg was replaced by Donald 'Duck' Dunn (b. 24 November 1941, Memphis,

Tennessee, USA). Their intuitive interplay became the bedrock of classic Stax, the foundation on which the label and studio sound was built. The quartet appeared on all of the company's notable releases, including 'In The Midnight Hour' (Wilson Pickett), 'Hold On I'm Comin'' (Sam And Dave) and 'Walkin' The Dog' (Rufus Thomas), on which Booker T. also played saxophone. Although Jones divided his time between recording and studying at Indiana University, he subsequently earned a BA in music; the MGs (Memphis Group) continued to chart consistently in their own right. 'Hang 'Em High' (1968) and 'Time Is Tight' (1969) were both US Top 10 singles, while as late as 1971 'Melting Pot' climbed into the same Top 50. The group split that year; Jones moved to California in semi-retirement, recording with his wife, Priscilla, while his three ex-colleagues remained in Memphis. In 1973 Jackson and Dunn put together a reconstituted group. Bobby Manuel and Carson Whitsett filled out the line-up, but the resultant album, *The MGs*, was a disappointment. Jackson meanwhile maintained his peerless reputation, particularly with work for Al Green and Syl Johnson, but tragically in 1975 he was shot dead in his Memphis home after disturbing intruders. Cropper, who had released a solo album, *With A Little Help From My Friends* in 1969, set up his TMI studio/label and temporarily seemed content with a low-key profile. He latterly rejoined Dunn, ex-Bar-Kay drummer Willie Hall and the returning Jones for *Universal Language*. Cropper and Dunn also played musicians roles in the film *The Blues Brothers* (1980). During the late 70s UK R&B revival, 'Green Onions' was re-issued and became a Top 10 hit in 1979. The 1981 MGs' album, *I Want You*, reached the R&B charts although each member still continued with his individual projects. The group did, however, complete some British concert dates in 1990. *Green Onions* and *Soul Dressing* show the group's definitive early style, *Soul Limbo* that of the later 60s. The *Best Of* collection crosses both eras.

Albums: *Green Onions* (1962), *Mo' Onions* (1963), *Soul Dressing* (1964), *My Sweet Potato* (1965), *And Now!* (1966), *In The Christmas Spirit* (1966), *Hip Hug Her* (1967), with the Mar-Keys *Back To Back* (1967), *Doing Our Thing* (1968), *Soul Limbo* (1968), *Uptight* (1968), *Booker T. Set* (1969), *McLemore Avenue* (1970), *Melting Pot* (1971), *The MGs* (1974), *Memphis Sound* (1975), *Union Extended* (1976), *Universal Language* (1977), *I Want You* (1981). Compilation: *The Best Of Booker T. And The MGs* (1984).

Box Tops

Formed in 1965, this Memphis-based quintet - Alex Chilton (b. 28 December 1950, Memphis, Tennessee, USA; guitar/harmonica/vocals), Gary Talley (b. 17 August 1949, Memphis, Tennessee,

USA; lead guitar), Billy Cunningham (b. 23 January 1950, Memphis, Tennessee, USA; rhythm guitar), John Evans (b. 1949; bass) and Danny Smythe (b. 1949; drums) - sprang to fame two years later when their debut single, 'The Letter', became an international hit. Although nominally a group, their appeal lay in Chilton's raspy delivery and Dan Penn's complementary production, a combination repeated on further successes, 'Neon Rainbow', 'Cry Like A Baby', 'Soul Deep' and the annoyingly infectious 'Choo-Choo Train'. Rick Allen (b. 28 January 1946, Little Rock, Arkansas, USA) replaced Evans in 1968, but the group's gifted singer remained its focal point. The Box Tops adeptly combined southern soul with pop, but any impetus faltered when their backroom mentors were drawn into other projects. The band broke up in 1969, but Chilton subsequently reappeared in the critically-acclaimed Big Star.

Albums: *The Letter/Neon Rainbow* (1967), *Cry Like A Baby* (1968), *Non Stop* (1968), *Dimensions* (1969). Compilations: *Super Hits* (1969), *Best Of The Box Tops* (1988), *Ultimate Box Tops* (1988).

Brel, Jacques

b. 8 April 1929, Brussels, Belgium, d. 10 October 1978. Brel remains both a figurehead and grey eminence of modern songwriting, despite a reluctance to either sing in English or, owing to his bitter opposition to the Vietnam war, perform in North America - or anywhere else after retiring from concert appearances in 1966. Although Flemish, he conversed in French. After studying commercial law, he married and spent several years in the family cardboard merchandising business until, nauseated by bourgeois convention, he made a new start in Paris as a singing composer. Buck-toothed and lanky, his deficit of obvious mass appeal was thrust aside by impressario Jacques Canetti who presented him regularly at Pigalle's Theatre Des Trois Baudets where he was accompanied by his own chord-slashing on guitar and a small backing combo. An instinctive sense of dramatic construction resulted in performances that, embracing fierce anger, open romanticism and world-weariness, captivated an audience that spread into a wider world after 'Quand On N'A Que L'Amour', his first record success. Other domestic hits such as 'Le Valse De Mille Temps', 'Les Bourgeois', 'Les Dames Patronesses' and 'Les Flamands' gave vent to social comment via a wryly watchful, literate lyricism. This remained intrinsically Gallic until US recording manager Nat Shapiro became evangelical about Brel to his CBS superiors, who authorized the issue of 1957's *American Debut* from which a substantial English-speaking following was to snowball. Brel was to leave his mark on the output of such diverse wordsmiths as Mort Shuman (an early and lifelong disciple), the Kinks'

Ray Davies, Leonard Cohen, David Bowie and - also the foremost interpreter of his work - Scott Walker. Brel was to reach a global market by proxy when his material was translated - and often emasculated as instanced by the Kingston Trio's 1964 rendition of 'Le Moribund' as 'Seasons In The Sun' (a UK number 1 for Terry Jacks a decade later), and the evolution of 'If You Go Away' into a cabaret 'standard'. He played two sell-out Carnegie Hall shows but was keener on extending himself through roles in movies like *Les Risques Du Metier* and *La Bande A Bonnet* (an account of a French anarchist movement at the turn of the century).

After he withdrew to the Polynesian Islands he would return fleetingly to Paris for one-take recording sessions but his work was kept before the public through a three-year Broadway run of the *Jacques Brel Is Alive And Well And Living In Paris* musical (that later became a film), and smaller tributes such as the Sensational Alex Harvey Band's use of 'Next' as title track of a 1975 album. In 1977, Brel was back in France for treatment for the cancer that would kill him the following year - a passing marked by a million-selling compilation album and a posthumous burgeoning of his popularity.

Compilations: *La Chanson Francais* (1979), *Music For The Millions* (1983), *Ses Plus Grandes Chansons* (1984), *Jacques Brel* (1986), *Le Plat Pays* (1988).

Brook Brothers

Geoffrey Brook (b. 12 April 1943) and Ricky Brook (b. 24 October 1940) were a pop duo from Winchester, Hampshire, England, who were often called the British Everly Brothers. The pair made their first appearance in a skiffle group in 1956 and started on the road to fame after winning a talent competition on Southern UK television's programme *Home Grown*. They first recorded in 1960 for Top Rank and their first single (which was an Italian hit for them) was a cover of the Brothers Four's US hit 'Greenfields'. They followed it with a double-sided cover 'Please Help Me I'm Falling'/'When Will I Be Loved'. They then moved to Pye with their producer Tony Hatch, and their second release on that label 'Warpaint' entered the UK Top 20, as did 'Ain't Gonna Wash For A Week' a few months later. Again, these were covers of US records with the originals coming from Barry Mann and Eddie Hodges respectively. The duo, backed by the Semi-Tones, toured with acts like Cliff Richard, Bobby Rydell and Jimmy Jones. They had three smaller UK hits in 1962-63, appeared in the film *It's Trad Dad* and recorded on Decca as the Brooks before fading from the scene. The crisp production of their canon of hits placed them above many of their contemporaries during their brief days of glory.

Arthur Brown

Brown, Arthur

b. 24 June 1942, Whitby, Yorkshire, England. A distinctive, uncompromising vocalist, Brown formed an R&B group - Blues And Brown - while studying philosophy at Reading University. He made his recording debut in 1965 with two contributions to a student 'Rag Week' flexi-disc, before moving to London where he fronted a succession of bands, known variously as the Southwest Five, the Arthur Brown Union and the Arthur Brown Set. In 1966 the singer moved to Paris where he began honing a theatrical and visual image. He was feted by the city's artisans and contributed two songs to *La Curee*, a Roger Vadim film which starred Jane Fonda.

Arthur returned to London in 1967 and formed the first Crazy World Of Arthur Brown with Vincent Crane (b. 21 May 1943, Reading, Berkshire, England, d. 14 February 1989; organ), Drachen Theaker (drums) and (later) Nick Greenwood (bass). They were quickly adopted by the 'underground' audience, where Brown's facial make-up, dervish dancing and fiery helmet garnered an immediate notoriety. Their popularity engendered a recording deal and the following year the group scored a surprise number 1 hit with the compulsive 'Fire'. The attendant album, *The Crazy World Of Arthur Brown*, contained many stage favourites, including 'Spontaneous Apple Creation' and 'Come And Buy',

but was marred by a poor production. Theaker and Crane then quit during a USA tour and although the latter would return to the fold, Carl Palmer, formerly of Chris Farlowe's Thunderbirds, joined as drummer. However, Brown's most successful group ended in 1969 when the newcomer and Crane formed Atomic Rooster.

The singer moved to Puddletown in Dorset, where a musically fertile commune had been established. Reunited with Theaker, Brown completed the experimental set latterly issued as *Strangelands*, before embarking on a new direction with Kingdom Come. This intermittently interesting group recorded three albums before breaking up. The singer resumed a solo career in 1974, but despite a memorable cameo as the Priest in Ken Russell's film, *Tommy*, subsequent recordings proved highly disappointing. His voice, which once stood comparison with those of Screaming Jay Hawkins, Little Richard and James Brown, was muted on the tired *Dance* album, and a reconciliation with Crane for *Chisholm In My Bosom* was little better. Arthur Brown then went into semi-retirement from the music business and settled in Austin, Texas where he pursues a career as a carpenter and decorator in partnership with former Mothers Of Invention drummer, Jimmy Carl Black.

Albums: *The Crazy World Of Arthur Brown* (1968), *Galactic Zoo Dossier* (1972), *The Journey* (1972), *Dance* (1974), *Chisholm In My Bosom* (1978), with Vincent Crane *Faster Than The Speed Of Light* (1980), *Requiem* (1982), *Strangelands* (1988). Compilation: *The Lost Ears* (1976, recordings from 1968-72).

Brown, James

b. 3 May 1928, Barnwell, South Carolina, USA. 'The Hardest Working Man In Show-Business', 'The Godfather Of Soul', 'The Minister Of The New New Super Heavy Funk' – such sobriquets only hint at the protracted James Brown legend. Convicted of theft at 16, he was imprisoned at the Alto Reform School, but secured an early release on the approbation of local singer, Bobby Byrd. Brown later joined his group, the Gospel Starlighters, who evolved into the Flames after embracing R&B. In 1955 they recorded a demo of 'Please Please Please' at WIBB, a Macon, Georgia, radio station. Local airplay was such that talent scout Ralph Bass signed the group to the King/Federal company. A recut version of the song was issued in March 1956. Credited to 'James Brown And The Famous Flames', it eventually climbed to number 5 in the USA R&B list. Releases which followed fared poorly until 1958 when 'Try Me' rose to number 1 in the same chart. Once again Brown found it hard to maintain this level of success, but 'I'll Go Crazy' and 'Think' (both 1960) put his progress on a surer footing. From thereon, until 1977, almost every 'official' single charted. However, it was an album, *Live At The Apollo* (1962) which assuredly established the singer. Raw, alive and uninhibited, this shattering collection confirmed Brown as the voice of black America. His singles continued to enthrall. Energetic songs like 'Night Train' and 'Shout And Shimmy', contrasted with such slower sermons as 'I Don't Mind' and 'Bewildered', but it was the orchestrated weepie, 'Prisoner Of Love' (1963), which gave James his first US Top 20 pop single. Such eminence allowed Brown a new manoeuvrability. Dissatisfied with his record label King, he ignored contractual niceties and signed with Smash. By the time his former outlet had secured an injunction, 'Out Of Sight' had become another national hit. More importantly, however, the single marked the beginning of a leaner, tighter sound which would ultimately discard accepted Western notions of harmony and structure. This innovative mid-60s' period is captured on film by his electrifying performance on the *TAMI Show*.

Throughout the 60s, James proclaimed an artistic freedom with increasingly unconventional songs including 'Papa's Got A Brand New Bag', 'I Got You (I Feel Good)', 'It's A Man's Man's Man's World' and 'Money Won't Change You'. In 1967 Alfred Ellis replaced Nat Jones as Brown's musical director and 'Cold Sweat' introduced further radical refinements to the group's presentation. With Clyde Stubblefield on drums, 'Say It Loud – I'm Black And I'm Proud' (1968), 'Mother Popcorn' (1969), and 'Get Up (I Feel Like Being A) Sex Machine' (1970) were each stripped down to a nagging, rhythmic riff, over which the singer soared; sometimes screaming, sometimes pleading, but always with an assertive urgency. In 1971 Brown moved to Polydor and unveiled a new backing band, the JBs. Led by Fred Wesley, it featured such seasoned players as Maceo Parker and St. Clair Pinckney, as well as a new generation of musicians. Elsewhere, former bassist William 'Bootsy' Collins defected with other ex-members to George Clinton's Funkadelic. Such changes, coupled with Sly Stone's challenge, simply reinforced Brown's determination. He continued to enjoy substantial hits; 1974 saw three successive number 1 R&B singles in 'The Payback', 'My Thang' and 'Papa Don't Take No Mess (Part 1)', and James also scored two film soundtracks, *Black Caesar* and *Slaughter's Big Rip Off*. However, as the decade progressed, his work became less compulsive, suffering a drop in popularity with the advent of disco. A cameo role in the movie *The **Blues Brothers*** marked time, and in 1980 Brown left the Polydor label.

Subsequent releases on such smaller labels as TK, Augusta Sound and Backstreet were only marginally successful. However, Brown returned with a vengeance in 1986 with 'Livin' In America', the theme song from the *Rocky IV* film soundtrack. An international hit single, it was followed by two R&B Top 10 entries, 'How Do You Stop' (1987) and 'I'm Real' (1988), the latter of which inspired a compulsive album of the same name. The Brown resurrection was abruptly curtailed that same year when the singer was arrested after a high-speed car chase. Charged with numerous offences, including illegal possession of drugs and firearms, aggravated assault and failure to stop for the police, he was sentenced to six-and-a-half years imprisonment at the State Park Correctional Centre. He was released in 1991, having reportedly written new material while incarcerated. James Brown's considerable influence has increased with the advent of hip-hop. New urban-based styles are indebted to the raw funk espoused by 'The Godfather of Soul', while Stubblefield's rhythmic patterns, particularly those on 1970's 'Funky Drummer', have been heavily sampled as have Brown's notorious whoops, screams, interjections and vocal improvisations. Artists as disparate as Public Enemy, George Michael, Sinead O'Connor and Candy Flip have featured beats pulled from Brown's impressive catalogue, one of the most enduring and exciting in the history of popular music.

Albums: *Please Please Please* (1959), *Try Me* (1959), *Think* (1960), *The Amazing James Brown* (1961), *James Brown Presents His Band/Night Train* (1961), *Shout And Shimmy* (1962), *James Brown And His Famous Flames Tour The USA* (1962), *Live At The Apollo* (1963), *Prisoner Of Love* (1963), *Pure Dynamite: Live At The Royal* (1964), *The Unbeatable James Brown* (1964), *Grits And Soul* (1964), *Out Of Sight* (1964), *Papa's Got A Brand New Bag* (1965), *I Got You (I Feel Good)* (1966), *James Brown Plays James Brown Today And Yesterday* (1966), *Mighty Instrumentals* (1966), *James Brown Plays New Breed (The Boo-Ga-Loo)* (1966), *Soul Brother No. 1: It's A Man's Man's Man's World* (1966), *James Brown Sings Christmas Songs* (1966), *The James Brown Show* (1967), *Raw Soul* (1967), *James Brown Plays The Real Thing* (1967), *Live At The Garden* (1967), *James Brown Presents His Show Of Tomorrow* (1968), *I Can't Stand Myself (When You Touch Me)* (1968), *Live At The Apollo, Volume 2* (1968), *James Brown Sings Out Of Sight* (1968), *Thinking About Little Willie John And A Few Nice Things* (1968), *A Soulful Christmas* (1968), *Say It Loud, I'm Black And I'm Proud* (1969), *Gettin' Down To It* (1969), *The Popcorn* (1969), *It's A Mother* (1969), *Ain't It Funky* (1970), *Soul On Top* (1970), *It's A New Day - Let A Man Come In* (1970), *Sex Machine* (1970), *Hey America* (1970), *Super Bad* (1971), *Sho' Is Funky Down Here* (1971), *Hot Pants* (1971), *Revolution Of The Mind/Live At The Apollo, Volume 3* (1971), *There It Is* (1972), *Get On The Good Foot* (1972), *Black Caesar* (1973), *Slaughter's Big Rip-Off* (1973), *The Payback* (1974), *Hell* (1974), *Reality* (1975), *Sex Machine Today*

(1975), *Everybody's Doin' The Hustle And Dead On The Double Bump* (1975), *Hot* (1976), *Get Up Offa That Thing* (1976), *Bodyheat* (1976), *Mutha's Nature* (1977), *Jam 1980's* (1978), *Take A Look At Those Cakes* (1979), *The Original Disco Man* (1979), *People* (1980), *Hot On The One* (1980), *Soul Syndrome* (1980), *Nonstop!* (1981), *Live In New York* (1981), *Bring It On* (1983), *Gravity* (1986), *James Brown And Friends* (1988), *I'm Real* (1988), *Love Over-Due* (1991). Compilations: *Soul Classics* (1972), *Soul Classics, Volume 2* (1973), *Solid Gold* (1977), *The Fabulous James Brown* (1978), *Can Your Heart Stand It?* (1981), *The Best Of James Brown* (1981), *The Federal Years, Part 1* (1984), *The Federal Years, Part 2* (1984), *Roots Of A Revolution* (1984), *Ain't That A Groove - The James Brown Story 1966-1969* (1984), *Doing It To Death - The James Brown Story 1970-1973* (1984), *Dead On The Heavy Funk 1974-1976* (1985), *The LP Of JB (Sex Machine And Other Soul Classics)* (1986), *In The Jungle Groove* (1986), *Motherlode* (1988), *Messin' With The Blues* (1991).
Further reading: *James Brown: The Godfather Of Soul*, James Brown with Bruce Tucker.

Brown, Joe

b. 13 May 1941, Swarby, Lincolnshire, England. Brown has sustained a career for over 30 years as a cheerful 'cockney' rock 'n' roll singer and guitarist. He was a popular live and television performer in the late 50s, a major UK recording star in the early 60s and is still a well-loved personality in the 90s. In 1956, this east London-based performer formed the Spacemen skiffle group, which became the backing outfit on Jack Good's top-rated television series *Boy Meets Girl* in 1959. At this point in his career, Brown was generally regarded as one of the finest guitarists in the UK and his services were frequently in demand. Re-christened Joe Brown And The Bruvvers, the group joined Larry Parnes's successful stable of artists (Parnes allegedly tried to rename him Elmer Twitch!) and signed to Decca Records. He first charted with a unique treatment of 'Darktown Strutters Ball' in 1960 and had a trio of UK Top 10 hits on the Pye Piccadilly label in 1962-63 with 'A Picture Of You', 'It Only Took A Minute' and 'That's What Love Will Do'. Being a happy and cheeky 'character' with a regional accent, it is likely that he could have had success in the USA in the way that Herman's Hermits did (Brown actually recorded 'I'm Henry The VIII, I Am' first). Brown's timing was just two years early, and before America was totally receptive to the 'British invasion'. As it was, his major hits were covered in the USA by acts like Paul Evans, the Kalin Twins and Bobby Goldsboro. He was voted 'Top UK Vocal Personality' in the *NME* poll in 1962 and 1963. He appeared in the film *What A Crazy World* and in the mid-60s starred in the hit musical *Charlie*

Girl. He has recorded sporadically since then on a variety of labels including MCA, Vertigo and Parlophone. During the early 70s Brown put together the country-rock band, Home Brew, which featured his wife Vicki, Ray Glynn (guitar), Pete Oakman (bass/violin), Jeff Peters (bass), Dave Hynes (drums) and Kirk Duncan (piano). Vikki was one of Britain's most successful and prolific backing session vocalists until her career was tragically curtailed by illness. She died from cancer in 1991. Brown has occasionally appeared on other artists' recordings; in 1982 he guested on George Harrison's *Gone Troppo*. His daughter Sam Brown has forged her own career as a notable rock singer.
Albums: *A Picture Of You* (1962), *Live* (1963), *Browns Home Brew* (1972), *Together* (1974), *Joe Brown Live* (1977). Compilations: *Joe Brown Collection* (1974), *Hits 'N' Pieces* (1988).

Brown, Pete

b. 25 December 1940, London, England. During the early 60s Brown was one of the leading 'beat poets'. His recitals at jazz fraternity gatherings and small clubs made him an important figure of the burgeoning 'underground' scene. His work came to national prominence as the lyricist of Jack Bruce's contributions to Cream. No one before or since has captured the essence of drug-induced lyrics in a better way. It was all the more remarkable as Brown had stopped all drug taking and drinking by the time he wrote this canon of songs. On *Disraeli Gears* Brown's outstanding nonsensical tales contributed to its prodigious success. Lines like, 'Its getting near dark, when light close their tired eyes' in 'Sunshine Of Your Love' and the powerful surrealism of 'SWLABR' (She Was Like A Bearded Rainbow), were but two examples of Brown's fertile hallucinogenic imagination. The superlative 'White Room' from *Wheels Of Fire* has stood the test of time and along with much of the Cream catalogue has enabled Brown to receive continuing financial reward for a series of classic rock songs. Some of his finest lyrics are to be found on Jack Bruce's solo debut *Songs For A Tailor* and *How's Tricks*, the former included the evocative 'Theme For An Imaginary Western' and the quirky 'Weird Of Hermiston'. During his most prolific time in the late 60s he also formed two bands which have now received belated critical acclaim. The Battered Ornaments featured the explorative guitar of Chris Spedding, while Piblokto! recorded two albums that are both valuable collector's items. Brown also worked with the pivotal R&B pioneer Graham Bond in a unit known as Bond And Brown. During the past years Brown has been involved with writing film scripts, but has recently returned to the music scene as well as continuing his long musical partnership with Jack Bruce. His contributions have lost none of their surreal sharpness as demonstrated on Bruce's *A Question Of Time* in 1989. Brown also continues to work with former Piblokto! colleague Phil Ryan, including musicals and film scores. He recently produced Dick Heckstall-Smith's *Where One Is*. Brown is a true original, retaining all the best qualities, humour and aspirations of the 60s underground scene with relevance three decades on.

Albums: *A Meal You Can Shake Hands With In The Dark* (1969), *Things May Come And Things May Go But The Art School Dance Goes On Forever* (1969), *Thousands On A Raft* (1970), *Two Heads Are Better Than One* (1972), *The 'Not Forgotten' Association* (1973), *Party In The Rain* (1983), *Ardours Of The Lost Rake* (1990). Compilation: *Before Singing Lessons 1969-1977* (1987).

Bruce, Tommy

b. 1939, London, England. This 60s' rock 'n' roll vocalist possessed an extraordinary voice which was described as a subtle blending of a corncrake, steam hammer and gravel polisher. Orphaned at the age of 10, he later worked for some years as a driver's mate in London's famous Covent Garden fruit market before his neighbour, the then actor and later successful songwriter Barry Mason, encouraged him to make the demo record that secured him a contract with Norrie Paramor at Columbia Records in 1960. His first release, the Fats Waller oldie 'Ain't Misbehavin'', was a UK number 2 hit and his follow-up, 'Broken Doll', also reached the UK Top 40, but was his last record to do so. The singer, who was either loved or hated, was often accused of emulating the Big Bopper. He hotly disputed this claim, saying he really did not know the late singer's work that well. Together with his group the Bruisers, he appeared on television programmes such as *Wham!!* and on many live shows, often under the auspices of impresario Larry Parnes. This unique cockney performer, who never claimed that he could actually sing, also recorded on Polydor in 1965, RCA in 1966 and CBS in 1969. Bruce is still to be found singing on rock 'n' roll revival and 60s' nostalgia shows.

Compilation: *Greatest Hits* (1985).

Buckinghams

Formed in Chicago, Illinois, USA in 1966, the Buckinghams originally consisted of Dennis Tufano (b. 11 September 1946, Chicago, Illinois, USA; vocals), Carl Giammarese (b. 21 August 1947, Chicago, Illinois, USA; lead guitar), Dennis Miccoli (organ), Nick Fortune (b. 1 May 1946, Chicago, Illinois, USA; bass) and Jon Jon Poulos (b. 31 March 1947, Chicago, Illinois, USA, d. 26 March 1980; drums). Although their first hit, 'Kind Of A Drag'

was their only gold disc, the group enjoyed a consistent run of US chart success throughout 1967, scoring two further Top 10 entries with 'Don't You Care' and 'Mercy Mercy Mercy'. Miccoli was latterly replaced by Marty Grebb (b. 2 September 1946, Chicago, Illinois, USA) before the Buckinghams' staid image was deemed passe by a more discerning audience. Yet despite those slick, commercial singles, their albums showed a desire to experiment. Produced and directed by Jim Guercio, such releases hinted at the brass arrangements this talented individual later brought to proteges Chicago. Unable to reconcile their image and ambitions, the quintet split up in 1970. Poulos later managed several local acts, but died of drug-related causes in 1980. Tufano and Giammarese continued working as a duo, while Grebb later worked with Chicago.

Albums: *Kind Of A Drag* (1967), *Time And Changes* (1967), *Portraits* (1968), *In One Ear And Gone Tomorrow* (1968), *Made In Chicago* (1969). Compilation: *The Buckingham's Greatest Hits* (1969).

Buckley, Tim

b. 14 February 1947, Washington, DC, USA, d. 29 June 1975. This effulgent talent began his solo career in the folk clubs of Los Angeles. He was discovered by manager Herb Cohen who secured the singer's recording deal with the prestigious Elektra label. *Tim Buckley* introduced the artist's skills, but his vision flourished more fully on a second selection, *Goodbye And Hello*. Although underscored by arrangements now deemed over-elaborate, the set features 'Morning Glory', one of Buckley's most evocative compositions, as well as the urgent 'I Never Asked To Be Your Mountain', a pulsating performance which indicated his future inclinations. With *Happy Sad* the singer abandoned the use of poetic metaphor, characteristic of its predecessor, to create a subtle, more intimate music. He forsook the services of long-time lyricist Larry Beckett, while Lee Underwood (guitar) and David Friedman (vibes) sculpted a sympathetic backdrop to Buckley's highly-personal, melancholic compositions. This expansive style was maintained on *Blue Afternoon* and *Lorca*, but while the former largely comprised of haunting, melodious folk-jazz performances, the latter offered a more radical, experimental direction. Its emphasis on improvisation inspired the free-from *Starsailor*, an uncompromising, almost atonal work, on which the singer's voice functioned as an extra instrument in a series of *avant garde* compositions. The set included the delicate 'Song To The Siren', which was successfully revived by This Mortal Coil in 1983. Buckley's work was now deemed uncommercial and, disillusioned, he sought alternative employment, including a spell as a chauffeur for Sly Stone. Paradoxically, the soul singer's brand of rhythmic funk proved significant, and when Buckley re-emerged with *Greetings From LA*, it marked a newfound fascination with contemporary black music. Sexually frank, this pulsating set was a commercial success, although its power was then diluted over two subsequent releases of only intermittent interest. Tim Buckley died in June 1975, having ingested a fatal heroin/morphine cocktail. His influence has increased with time and a recent archive selection, *Dream Letter*, culled from the singer's 1968 London performances, is a fitting testament to his impassioned creativity.

Albums: *Tim Buckley* (1966), *Goodbye And Hello* (1967), *Happy Sad* (1969), *Blue Afternoon* (1969), *Lorca* (1970), *Starsailor* (1970), *Greetings From LA* (1972), *Sefronia* (1973), *Look At The Fool* (1974), *Dream Letter-Live In London 1968* (1990). Compilation: *The Best Of Tim Buckley* (1983).

Buffalo Springfield

Buffalo Springfield

A seminal band in the development of American country/rock and folk/rock, though short-lived, the monumental influence of Buffalo Springfield rivals that of the Byrds. Although the line-up constantly changed, the main members throughout their three turbulent years comprised: Stephen Stills (b. 3 January 1945, Dallas, Texas, USA), Neil Young (b. 12 November 1945, Toronto, Canada), Richie Furay (b. 9 May 1944, Yellow Springs, Ohio, USA), Dewey Martin (b. 30 September 1942, Chesterville, Canada), Bruce Palmer (b. 1947, Liverpool, Canada) and Jim Messina (b. 5 December 1947, Maywood, California, USA). Furay and Stills worked together in the Au Go-Go Singers in the mid-60s, where they met Young, who at that time was a solo singer having previosly worked with Palmer in the Mynah Birds. They eventually congregated in Los Angeles in 1966 and following a series of gigs at the prestigious *Whiskey A Go-Go*, together with verbal endorsements from the Byrds' Chris Hillman and David Crosby the band were signed by Ahmet Ertegun to his Atco label. Any group containing three main songwriters

who could all play lead guitar was heading for trouble, and soon their egos clashed. Their problems were compounded by the continual immigration and drug problems of Palmer. At one point, their manager, Dick Davis masqueraded as bassist on the television. Eventually, Young's former associate Ken Koblin was recruited as a replacement. He, in turn, was replaced by Jim Fielder from the Mothers Of Invention. Their only major hit was in 1967; 'For What Its Worth (Hey Whats That Sound)' remains one of the finest 60s pop songs. This composition was an example of being the right song at the right time. Stills's plaintive yet wry and lethargic plea for tolerence was written after the police used heavy-handed methods to stop an anti-Vietnam student demonstration on Sunset Strip in 1966. The opening lyric 'There's something happening here, what it is ain't exactly clear, there's a man with a gun over there, telling me I've got to beware', innocently sets the scene. The chorus of 'Stop children, what's that sound everybody knows what's going down' became an anthem for west coast students who were unhappy with the Nixon government. Two albums were released although *Stampede* was recorded and only appeared in different form as a bootleg. *Last Time Around* was patched together by producer and latter day bassist Messina, after the band had broken up for the final time. *Buffalo Springfield Again* remains their finest work and is still highly favoured by the cogniscenti. The album demonstrated the developing talents of Stills and Young as major songwriters. Young, with his superb surreal mini-epics 'Expecting To Fly' and 'Broken Arrow' was equalled by Stills's immaculate 'Everdays' and the lengthy 'Bluebird' (Bluebird was Judy Collins). Furay also contributed, among others, the heavily countrified 'A Child's Claim To Fame'. Both the band and the album's essence however was encapsulated in one short track, 'Rock And Roll Woman' co-written by an uncredited David Crosby, who briefly appeared with the group as Young's substitute at the 1967 Monterey Pop Festival. The three lead guitars duelled together and the three lead vocals enmeshed brilliantly - all seemingly without ego, to produce for a brief moment what could have been America's greatest rival to the Beatles.

Albums; *Buffalo Springfield* (1967), *Buffalo Springfield Again* (1967), *Last Time Around* (1968). Compilation: *Retrospective* (1969).

Further reading: *Neil Young: Here We Are In The Years*, Johnny Rogan. *Crosby, Stills And Nash: The Authorized Biography*, Dave Zimmer.

Burke, Solomon

b. 1936, Philadelphia, Pennsylvania, USA. The former 'Wonder Boy Preacher', Burke's first recordings appeared on the New York-based Apollo

label. From 1955-59 he attempted various styles until a brisk rocker, 'Be Bop Grandma', attracted Atlantic Records. An eclectic performer, his reading of a sentimental country song, 'Just Out Of Reach' (1961), was a US Top 30 hit, but the following year the 'King of Soul' began asserting a defined soul direction with 'Cry To Me'. Burke's sonorous voice was then heard on a succession of inspired singles, including 'If You Need Me' (1963), 'Goodbye Baby (Baby Goodbye)' and the declamatory 'Everybody Needs Somebody To Love' (both 1964). This exceptional period culminated with 'The Price', an impassioned release which marked the end of Burke's relationship with producer Bert Berns. Although further strong records appeared, indeed 'Got To Get You Off My Mind' (1965) became his biggest hit, they lacked the drama of the earlier era. Still based in New York, Solomon was now overshadowed by Otis Redding, Sam And Dave and other acts who recorded at Stax and Fame. A belated Memphis session did provide a pop Top 50 entry in 'Take Me (Just As I Am)', but Burke left Atlantic for Bell in 1968. The ensuing album, *Proud Mary*, was a southern soul classic, while the title track, written by John Fogerty, charted as a single in the US. The 70s saw a switch to MGM, but his work there was marred by inconsistency. The same was true of his spells at Dunhill and Chess although his collaborations with Swamp Dogg on *From The Heart* brought his old power to mind. This rebirth continued on *Soul Alive*, where recorded in-concert, Solomon sounds inspired, infusing his 'greatest hits' with a newfound passion. A strong studio collection, *A Change Is Gonna Come*, followed 1987's European tour and displayed Burke's still-considerable talent. Two albums, *The Best Of Solomon Burke* (1966) and *Cry To Me* (1984), gather together his Atlantic singles, while *The Bishop Rides South* (1988) adds four extra tracks to the original *Proud Mary* album.
Albums: *Solomon Burke* (1962), *If You Need Me* (1963), *Rock 'N' Soul* (1964), *I Wish I Knew* (1968), *King Solomon* (1968), *Proud Mary* (1969), *Electronic Magnetism* (1972), *King Heavy* (1972), *We're Almost Home* (1972), *I Have A Dream* (1974), *Music To Make Love By* (1975), *Back To My Roots* (1975), *Soul Alive* (1985), *A Change Is Gonna Come* (1986), *Love Trap* (1987). Compilations: *Solomon Burke's Greatest Hits* (1962), *I Almost Lost My Mind* (1964), *The Best Of Solomon Burke* (1966), *King Of Rock 'N' Soul/From The Heart* (1981), *Cry To Me* (1984), *You Can Run But You Can't Hide* (1987), *The Bishop Rides South* (1988).
Further reading: *Sweet Soul Music*, Peter Guralnick.

Burton, James

b. 21 August 1939, Shreveport, Louisiana, USA. One of the most distinguished of rock and country-rock guitar players, Burton toured and recorded with Ricky Nelson, Elvis Presley and numerous other artists. His first recording was the highly influential 'Suzie Q' sung by Dale Hawkins in 1957. Burton also performed with country singer Bob Luman before moving to Los Angeles where he was hired to work with Nelson, then the latest teen sensation. For six years he toured and recorded with Nelson, perfecting a guitar sound known as 'chicken pickin''. This was achieved by dampening the strings for staccato sounding single-string riffs and solos. Among the best examples of this style are 'Hello Mary Lou', 'Never Be Anyone Else But You' and the more frantic, rockabilly-flavoured 'Believe What You Say'. During the late 60s and early 70s, Burton was much in demand as a session guitarist, working with Dale Hawkins on a comeback album as well as various artists including Buffalo Springfield, Judy Collins, John Phillips, Joni Mitchell, Michael Nesmith and Longbranch Pennywhistle, a group featuring future Eagles member Glenn Frey. Burton also played dobro on albums by P.F. Sloan and John Stewart. In addition, Burton's powerful rockabilly-influenced guitar work made a major contribution to the harsher country sound developed at this time by Merle Haggard. Burton made two albums of his own during these years, one in collaboration with steel guitarist Ralph Mooney.
During the 70s, Burton's work took him in contrasting directions. With pianist Glen D. Hardin (a former Crickets' member), he was a mainstay of Elvis Presley's touring and recording band from 1969-77, but he also played a leading role in the growing trend towards country/rock fusion. Burton's most significant performances in this vein came on the solo albums of ex-Byrds member Gram Parsons, *Grievous Angel* (1972) and *GP* (1973). After Parsons' death, Burton and Hardin toured with Emmylou Harris and backed her on several solo albums. As a session guitarist, Burton played on albums by Jesse Winchester, Ronnie Hawkins, Rodney Crowell, Phil from the Everly Brothers, J.J. Cale and Nicolette Larson.
Albums: *Corn Pickin' And Slick Slidin'* (1969), *The Guitar Sound Of James Burton* (1971).

Butler, Jerry

b. 8 December 1939, Sunflower, Mississippi, USA. Jerry, older brother of Billy Butler, moved to Chicago as a child and was later a part of the city's burgeoning gospel circuit. He subsequently joined several secular groups, including the Roosters, an aspiring trio of Sam Gooden and Richard and Arthur Brooks. Butler then suggested they add his friend, Curtis Mayfield, on guitar. Now called the Impressions, the quintet secured a Top 3 US R&B hit with the haunting 'For Your Precious Love'

(1958). However the label credit, 'Jerry Butler And The Impressions', caused friction within the group. A second single, 'Come Back My Love', was less successful and Butler left for a solo career. His early releases were minor hits until 'He Will Break Your Heart' reached number 1 in the US R&B and number 7 in the pop charts in 1960. The song was written by Mayfield who added guitar and sang backing vocals. Their differences clearly resolved, two subsequent hits, 'Find Another Girl' and 'I'm A Telling You' (both 1961), featured the same partnership. Mayfield's involvement lessened as the Impressions' own career developed, but Jerry's chart run continued. 'Make It Easy On Yourself' (1962) and 'I Stand Accused' (1964) were among his finest singles. Butler switched to Mercury in 1966 where he honed the style which won him his 'Ice Man' epithet. 'Hey Western Union Man' and 'Only The Strong Survive' topped the soul chart in 1968 and 1969, while duets with Gene Chandler and Brenda Lee Eager punctuated his early 70s' recordings. With his brother, Billy Butler, he formed the Butler Writers Workshop, which encouraged aspiring songwriters and musicians, amongst whom were, Martin Yancey and Chuck Jackson of the Independents and Natalie Cole. Jerry's releases on Motown preceded a more successful spell with Philadelphia International, while the 80s saw his work appear on Fountain and CTI. *Up On Love* (1980) mixes the best of Jerry's VeeJay singles with that first Impressions' hit. Butler is now an elected official in Chicago.

Albums: *Jerry Butler Esquire* (1959), *He Will Break Your Heart* (1960), *Love Me* (1961), *Aware Of Love* (1961), *Moon River* (1962), *Folk Songs* (1963), with Betty Everett *Delicious Together* (1964), *Soul Artistry* (1967), *Mr. Dream Merchant* (1967), *Jerry Butler's Golden Hits Live* (1968), *Just Beautiful* (1968), *The Soul Goes On* (1968), *The Ice Man Cometh* (1968), *Ice On Ice* (1970), *You & Me* (1970), *Special Memory* (1970), *Jerry Butler Sings Assorted Sounds By Assorted Friends And Relatives* (1971), with Gene Chandler *Gene & Jerry - One & One* (1971), *Melinda* (1972), *The Sagittarious Movement* (1971), *The Spice Of Life* (1972), with Brenda Lee Eagar *The Love We Have, The Love We Had* (1973), *The Power Of Love* (1973), *Sweet Sixteen* (1974), *Love's On The Menu* (1976), *Make It Easy On Yourself* (1976), *Suite For The Single Girl* (1977), *It All Comes Out In My Song* (1978), with Thelma Houston *Thelma And Jerry* (1977), with Houston *Two To One* (1978), *Nothing Says I Love You Like I Love You* (1978), *Best Love I Ever Had* (1981), *Ice 'N Hot* (1982). Compilations: *The Best Of Jerry Butler* (1962), *More Of The Best Of Jerry Butler* (1965), *Best Of Jerry Butler* (1970), *The Vintage Years* (1977, double album shared with the Impressions), *Up On Love* (1980), *Only The Strong Survive* (1985), *Whatever You Want* (1986), *Soul Workshop* (1986), *The Legendary*

Philadelphia Hits (1987).

Butterfield, Paul

b. 17 December 1942, Chicago, Illinois, USA, d. 3 May 1987. As a catalyst, Butterfield helped shape the development of blues music played by white musicians in the same way that John Mayall and Cyril Davis were doing in Britain. Butterfield had the advantage of standing in with Howlin' Wolf, Muddy Waters and his mentor Little Walter. Butterfield sang, composed and led a series of seminal bands throughout the 60s, but it was his earthy Chicago-style harmonica playing that gained him attention. He was arguably the first white man to play blues with the intensity and emotion of the great black blues harmonica players. Mike Bloomfield, Mark Naftalin, Elvin Bishop, David Sanborn and Nick Gravenites were some of the outstanding musicians that passed through his bands. His now infamous performance at the 1965 Newport Folk Festival gave him the distinction of being the man who supported Bob Dylan's musical heresy, by going electric. In 1973 his new venture *Better Days* went on the road to average response, and during subsequent years he struggled to find success. Ill health plagued him for some time, much of it caused by aggravating stomach hernias caused by his powerful harmonica playing. Butterfield's legacy stays, his influence untinged and much of his catalogue is still available. *East-West* remains his best-selling and most acclaimed work, although the rawness of the debut album also has many critical admirers.

Albums: *Paul Butterfield Blues Band* (1966), *East-West* (1966), *The Resurrection Of Pigboy Crabshaw* (1968), *In My Own Dream* (1968), *Keep On Movin'* (1969), *Live* (1971), *Sometimes I Just Feel Like Smilin'* (1971), *Offer You Can't Refuse* (1972), *Better Days* (1973), *It All Comes Back* (1973), *Better Days* (1973), *It All Comes Back* (1974), *Put It In Your Ear* (1976), *North South For Bearsville* (1981), *The Legendary Paul Butterfield Rides Again* (1986). Compilation: *Golden Butter - Best Of The Paul Butterfield Blues Band* (1972).

Byrds

Originally formed as a trio, the Jet Set, featured Jim (Roger) McGuinn (b. 13 July 1942, Chicago, Illinois, USA; vocals/lead guitar), Gene Clark (b. 17 November 1941, Tipton, Missouri, USA, d. 24 May 1991; vocals/tambourine/rhythm guitar) and David Crosby (b. 14 August 1941, Los Angeles, California, USA; vocals/rhythm guitar). Essentially ex-folkies caught up in the Beatle craze of 1964, they were signed to a one-off singles deal with Elektra Records which resulted in the commercially unsuccessful 'Please Let Me Love You', released under the pseudonym Beefeaters. By late 1964, the trio had expanded to include former bluegrass player turned bassist Chris Hillman (b. 4 December 1942, Los Angeles, California, USA) and drummer Michael Clarke (b. Michael Dick, 3 June 1944, Texas, USA). Under the supervision of manager/producer Jim Dickson, they recorded at Hollywood's World Pacific studios, slowly and painfully perfecting their unique brand of folk rock. In November 1964, they signed to CBS as the Byrds, and were placed in the hands of producer Terry Melcher. Their debut single, 'Mr Tambourine Man' was a glorious creation, fusing the lyrical genius of Bob Dylan with the harmonic and melodious ingenuity of the Beatles. McGuinn later described his vocal on the disc as a cross between that of John Lennon and Bob Dylan. By the summer of 1965, the single had topped both the US and UK charts and the Byrds found themselves feted as teen idols. They certainly looked the part with their immaculately groomed fringed haircuts and pop trappings which included Crosby's green, suede cape and McGuinn's rectangular granny glasses. To coincide with their British success a tour was hastily arranged on which the group were promoted as 'America's Answer To The Beatles'. This presumptuous and premature labelling backfired and during their exhausting visit they fell victim to over-expectant fans and tetchy critics. To make matters worse, their second single, 'All I Really Want To Do', suffered split sales due to an opportunistic cover from folk rock rival Cher. The group's management attempted to compensate for this setback by simultaneously promoting the b-side 'Feel A Whole Lot Better', a stunning slice of cynical romanticism which swiftly became a stage favourite. The Byrds' debut album *Mr Tambourine Man* was a surprisingly solid work which featured four Dylan covers, a striking re-arrangement of Pete Seeger's 'Bells Of Rhymney' and some exceptionally strong torch songs from Clark, including 'I Knew I'd Want You', 'Here Without You' and 'You Won't Have To Cry'. There was even a strange reworking of the wartime favourite 'We'll Meet Again', which ended the album on a bizarre yet amusing note.

After returning to the USA, the Byrds spent months in the studio before releasing their third single, the biblically-inspired 'Turn! Turn! Turn!', which gave them another US number 1. The album of the same name again showed the prolific Gene Clark in the ascendant with the charming 'The World Turns All Around Her' and the densely worded 'Set You Free This Time', their most sophisticated lyric to date and arguably their definitive self-penned folk rock statement. McGuinn's presence was also felt on the driving 'It Won't Be Wrong' and elegiac 'He Was A Friend Of Mine', with lyrics pertaining to the Kennedy assassination. An odd tribute to Stephen Foster closed the album in the form of a sarcastic 'Oh! Susanah'.

Byrds

By early 1966, the group had parted with producer Melcher and branched out from their stylized folk rock repertoire to embrace raga and jazz. The awesome 'Eight Miles High', with its John Coltrane-inspired lead break and enigmatic lyrics effectively elevated them to the artistic level of the Beatles and the Rolling Stones, but their chart rewards were severely qualified by a radio ban based on spurious allegations that their latest hit was a 'drug song'. In fact, the lyric had been written following their visit to England and the unusual imagery was based on their sense of culture shock. The b-side of the disc, 'Why', included some raga-like guitar work from McGuinn and during their press conference of the period the group were pictured studiously playing a sitar, although none of them had mastered the instrument. The setback over the banning of 'Eight Miles High' was worsened by the abrupt departure of leading songwriter Gene Clark, whose fear of flying and distaste for life on the road had proven intolerable burdens. Continuing as a quartet, the Byrds recorded *Fifth Dimension*, a clever amalgam of hard, psychedelic-tinged pop ('I See You' and 'What's Happening?!?!') and rich folk-rock orchestration ('Wild Mountain Thyme' and 'John Riley'). Their chart fortunes were already waning by this time and neither the quizzically philosophical '5-D (Fifth Dimension)' nor the catchy 'Mr Spaceman' made much impression on the charts. The Byrds, rather than promoting their latest album with endless tours, became more insular and suffered speculation that they were on the point of breaking up.

1967 proved the pivotal year in their career, commencing with the hit single, 'So You Want To Be A Rock 'N' Roll Star', an acerbic observation on the manufacturing of pop stars, complete with taped screams from their ill-fated UK tour and a guest appearance from Hugh Masekela on trumpet. Its b-side, 'Everybody's Been Burned', displayed Crosby's songwriting and vocal sensitivity with an exceptionally strong guitar solo from McGuinn and some stupendous jazz-inspired bass work from Hillman. Their fourth album, *Younger Than Yesterday*, proved their best yet, ably capturing the diverse songwriting skills of Crosby, McGuinn and Hillman and ranging in material from the raga-tinged 'Mind Gardens' to the country-influenced 'Time Between', the quirky space rock of 'CTA 102' and even an ironically retrospective Dylan cover, 'My Back Pages'. Their creative ascendancy coincided with intense inter-group rivalry, culminating in the dismissal of the ever controversial David Crosby, who would later re-emerge as part of the hugely successful Crosby, Stills And Nash. The Byrds, meanwhile, recruited former colleague Gene Clark, who lasted a mere three weeks before his aerophobia once more took its toll. Drummer Michael Clarke was dismissed from the group soon after, leaving McGuinn and Hillman to assemble the stupendous *The Notorious Byrd Brothers*, a classic example of artistic endeavour overcoming adversity. For this album, the Byrds used recording studio facilities to remarkable effect, employing phasing, close microphone technique and various sonic experiments to achieve the sound they desired. Producer Gary Usher who worked on this and their previous album contributed significantly towards their ascension as one of rock's most adventurous and innovative artists. Once again, however, it was the songs rather than the studio gimmickry that most impressed. Successful readings of Gerry Goffin and Carole King's 'Goin' Back' and 'Wasn't Born To Follow' were placed alongside Byrds' originals such as 'Change Is Now', 'Dolphin's Smile', 'Tribal Gathering' and 'Draft Morning'.

In early 1968, Hillman's cousin Kevin Kelley took over on drums and the talented Gram Parsons added musical weight as singer/composer/guitarist. Under Parsons' guidance, the group plunged headlong into country, recording the much-acclaimed *Sweetheart Of The Rodeo*. A perfectly timed reaction to the psychedelic excesses of 1967, the album predated Dylan's *Nashville Skyline* by a year and is generally accepted as the harbinger of country rock. Although Parsons directed the work and included one of his best compositions, 'Hickory Wind', his lead vocals on such country standards as 'You Don't Miss Your Water' and 'You're Still On My Mind' were replaced by those of McGuinn due to contractual complications. It was not until 1990 that the public heard the rough original vocals which were incorporated into a retrospective boxed-set package. McGuinn re-established the Bob Dylan links on *Sweetheart Of The Rodeo* by featuring two songs from the then unreleased *Basement Tapes*, 'You Ain't Going Nowhere' and 'Nothing Was Delivered'. The critical plaudits heaped upon the Byrds were not translated into sales, however, and further conflict ensued when Gram Parsons dramatically resigned on the eve of

their ill-advised tour of South Africa in the summer of 1968.

From 1965-68, the Byrds produced some of the greatest and most memorable work ever recorded in the history of popular music. Their remarkable ability to ride trends and incorporate stylistically diverse material ranging from folk and country to raga, jazz and space rock demonstrated a profound vision and wondrous spirit of adventure and innovation that few of their contemporaries could dream of, let alone match. Their work from this period still sounds fresh and contemporary which is a testament to their pioneering worth. Their achievement is all the more remarkable given the loss of several key personnel over the years. Rather than destroying the Byrds, their frequent and often inflammatory internal acrimony partly served as a creative catalyst, prompting a combative and proprietorial sense that resulted in some of the era's most spectacular recordings. Among their contemporaries only the Beatles could boast a body of work of such consistency, and the Byrds were probably unmatched in terms of musical diversity and eclecticism.

Late 1968 saw the group at their lowest ebb with Hillman quitting after a dispute with their new manager Larry Spector. The embittered bassist soon reunited with the errant Parsons in the Flying Burrito Brothers. McGuinn, meanwhile, assumed total control of the Byrds and assembled an entirely new line up featuring Clarence White (vocals/guitar), John York (vocals/bass) and Gene Parsons (vocals/drums). This new phase began promisingly enough with the single 'Bad Night At The Whiskey' backed by the McGuinn/Gram Parsons song 'Drug Store Truck Driving Man'. York lasted long enough to contribute to two albums, *Dr Byrds & Mr Hyde* and *Ballad Of Easy Rider*, before being replaced by journeyman Skip Battin. This stable line-up lasted from 1969-72 and re-established the Byrds' reputation with the hit single 'Chestnut Mare' and the best-selling album *(Untitled)*. Regular concert appearances brought the Byrds a strong groundswell support, but the quality of their early 70s output lacked consistency. After three successive albums with their first producer Melcher, they again severed their connections with him owing to his decision to include orchestration on *Byrdmaniax*. The Byrds hurriedly attempted to record a compensatory work *Farther Along* but it only served to emphasize their disunity. McGuinn eventually elected to dissolve the group after agreeing to participate in a recorded reunion of the original Byrds for Asylum Records. Released in 1973, *Byrds* received mixed reviews, prompting the group to revert to their various solo/offshoot ventures. That same year tragedy struck when ex-Byrd Clarence White was killed by a drunken driver. Less than three months later, Gram

Parsons died from a drug overdose.

The Byrds' legacy has continued in a host of new groups who either borrowed their Rickenbacker sound or traded off their folk/country roots. The individual members later featured in a host of offshoot groups such as Dillard And Clark, various permutations of the Flying Burrito Brothers, Manassas, Souther Hillman Furay and, of course, Crosby, Stills, Nash And Young. Ironically, the ex-Byrds (with the exception of Crosby) failed to exploit their superstar potential, even after reuniting again as McGuinn, Clark And Hillman. By the 80s, the individual members were either recording for small labels or touring without a record contract. Crosby, meanwhile, had plummeted into a narcotic netherworld of free-base cocaine addiction and after several seizures and arrests was confined to prison. He re-emerged reformed, corpulent and enthusiastic, and amid a flurry of activity set about resurrecting the Byrds monicker with McGuinn and Hillman. An acrimonious lawsuit with Michael Clarke ended with the drummer assuming the right to the group name. Although a proposed five-way reunion of the Byrds for a live album and world tour was mooted, the old conflicts frustrated its immediate fruition. However, McGuinn, Crosby and Hillman completed four songs in Nashville during August 1990 which were subsequently included on a boxed set featuring 90 songs. The nearest that the group reached to a full reunion was when they each turned up to be inducted at the rock 'n' roll Hall of Fame in January 1991.

Albums: *Mr Tambourine Man* (1965), *Turn! Turn! Turn!* (1965), *Fifth Dimension* (1966), *Younger Than Yesterday* (1967), *The Notorious Byrd Brothers* (1968), *Sweetheart Of The Rodeo* (1968), *Dr Byrds & Mr Hyde* (1969), *Ballad Of Easy Rider* (1969), *(Untitled)* (1970), *Byrdmaniax* (1971), *Farther Along* (1972). Three archive albums are also available: *Preflyte* (1969), *Never Before* (1989) and *In The Beginning* (1989). Compilations: *Greatest Hits* (1967), *Greatest Hits, Vol. II* (1971), *History Of The Byrds* (1973), *The Byrds Play Dylan* (1979), *The Original Singles* (1980), *The Original Singles, Vol. II* (1982), *The Byrds Collection* (1989), *The Byrds* (1990, four album box set).

Further reading: *Timeless Flight: The Definitive Biography Of The Byrds*, Johnny Rogan.

C

C., Roy

b. Roy Charles Hammond, 1943, New York City, New York, USA. A member of the Genies, with whom he recorded for several labels, Roy C's most enduring moment came with 'Shotgun Wedding' (1965). A US R&B Top 20 hit, it proved even more popular in the UK, reaching number 6 the following year making the Top 10 again in 1972. The singer later recorded, without luck, for Black Hawk and Shout, but 'Got To Get Enough (Of Your Sweet Love Stuff)' was a soul hit in 1971. Released on C's own Alaga label, he subsequently secured further success on Mercury Records. Roy also wrote 'Honey I Still Love You', a 1972 best-seller for the Mark IV.

Albums: *Sex And Soul* (1973), *More Sex And Soul* (1977).

Calvert, Reg

b. Yorkshire, England. Promoter Reg Calvert was one of the most eccentric, underrated and ultimately tragic figures of British 60s pop. He moved from Yorkshire to the south coast in the late 50s and signed up a series of young musicians. A specialist in 'xeroxed' pop acts, Calvert's artists were like travelling showbands, playing the hits of the day and imitating the style and looks of the élite stars on the television show *Oh Boy*. By the early 60s Calvert had bought a former stately home in the Midlands in which he housed a veritable battalion of teenage talent including, Danny Storm, Buddy Britten, Mike West, Carol Lane, Tanya Day, Gulliver's Travels, Robbie Hood And His Merrie Men and Mike West And The Silhouettes. After launching Screaming Lord Sutch as a political candidate, Calvert moved into pirate radio with Radio City and his increasing profile in the pop business enabled him to break in both the Fortunes and Pinkerton's Assorted Colours as hit acts. At one stage he launched a new version of Them before the ever vigilant Philip Solomon enforced his managerial right to the group name. At the peak of the British pirate radio boom Calvert seemed destined for great wealth and entrepreneurial fame but a dispute with a rival station headed by Major Oliver Smedley ended in tragedy. On 21 June 1967, Calvert visited Smedley's home and following a fracas was shot dead. Although Calvert never managed any great acts, his showmanship, sensationalism and invention were the match of any entrepreneur of the era.

Further reading: *Starmakers And Svengalis: The History*

Of British Pop Management, Johnny Rogan.

Canned Heat

This popular, but ill-fated blues/rock group was formed in 1965 by two Los Angeles-based blues aficionados: Alan Wilson (b. 4 July 1943, Boston, Massachusetts, USA; vocals/harmonica/guitar) and Bob 'The Bear' Hite (b. 26 February 1943, Torrance, California, USA; vocals). Wilson, nicknamed 'Blind Owl' in deference to his thick-lensed spectacles, was already renowned for his distinctive harmonica work and had accompanied Son House on the veteran bluesman's post 'rediscovery' album, *Father Of Folk Blues*. Wilson's obsession with the blues enabled him to have a massive archive blues collection by his early twenties. The duo was joined by Frank Cook (drums) and Henry Vestine (b. 25 December 1944, Washington, DC, USA; guitar), a former member of the Mothers Of Invention. They took the name Canned Heat from a 1928 recording by Tommy Johnson and employed several bassists prior to the arrival of Larry Taylor, an experienced session musician who had worked with Jerry Lee Lewis and the Monkees.

Canned Heat's debut album was promising rather than inspired, offering diligent readings of such 12-bar standards as 'Rollin' And Tumblin'', 'Dust My Broom' and 'Bullfrog Blues'. However, the arrival of new drummer Alfredo Fito (b. Adolfo De La Parra, 8 February 1946, Mexico City, Mexico) coincided with a newfound confidence displayed almost immediately on *Boogie With Canned Heat*. This impressive selection introduced the extended 'Fried Hookey Boogie', a piece destined to become an in-concert favourite, and the hypnotic remake of Jim Oden's 'On The Road Again', which gave the group a UK Top 10 and US Top 20 hit single in 1968. Wilson's distinctive frail high voice, sitar-like guitar introduction and accompanying harmonica has enabled this version to become a classic. A double set, *Livin' The Blues*, featured some of the group's finest moments, including an enthralling version of Charlie Patton's 'Pony Blues' and a 19-minute *tour de force* 'Parthenogenesis', which captured the quintet at their most experimental. However, it was Wilson's adaptation of a Henry Thomas song, 'Bulldoze Blues', which proved most popular. The singer retained the tune of the original, rewrote the lyric and emerged with 'Goin' Up The Country', whose simple message caught the prevalent back-to-nature attitude of the late 60s,. This evocative performance charted in the US and UK Top 20, and was one of the highlights of the successful Woodstock movie.

Between 1969-70 Canned Heat recorded four more albums, including a spirited collaboration with blues boogie mentor John Lee Hooker, and an enthralling documentary of their 1970 European tour. *Hallejujah*

boasted one of artist George Hunters's finest album covers. It also featured 'Get Off My Back', which in its day was used by hi-fi buffs to check their systems were in phase, as the cross-channel switching in the mix was outrageously overdone. *Future Blues* marked the arrival of guitarist Harvey Mandel, replacing Henry Vestine, who could no longer tolerate working with Larry Taylor. The reshaped band enjoyed two further UK hits with a cover of Wilbert Harrison's 'Let's Work Together', which reached number 2, and the cajun-inspired 'Sugar Bee', but were rocked by the suicide of Alan Wilson, whose body was found in Hite's backyard on 3 September 1970. His death sparked a major reconstruction within the group. Taylor and Mandel left to join John Mayall, the former's departure prompting Vestine's return, while Antonio De La Barreda became Canned Heat's new bassist. The new quartet completed *Historical Figures And Ancient Heads*, before Bob Hite's brother Richard replaced Barreda for the band's 1973 release, *The New Age*. The changes continued throughout the decade, undermining the band's strength of purpose. Bob Hite, the sole remaining original member, attempted to keep the group afloat, but was unable to secure a permanent recording deal. Spirits lifted with the release of *Human Condition*, but the years of struggle had taken their toll. On 5 April 1981, following a gig at the Palomino Club, the gargantuan vocalist collapsed and died of a heart attack. Despite the loss of many key members, the Canned Heat name has survived. Inheritors Larry Taylor and Fito De La Parra completed 1989's *Re-heated* album with two new guitarists, James Thornbury and Junior Watson. They now pursue the lucrative nostalgia circuit.

Albums: *Canned Heat* (1967), *Boogie With Canned Heat* (1968), *Livin' The Blues* (1968), *Hallelujah* (1969), *Vintage - Canned Heat* (1969, early recordings), *Future Blues* (1970), *Live At The Topanga Canyon* (1970), with John Lee Hooker *Hooker 'N' Heat* (1971), *Canned Heat Concert (Recorded Live In Europe)* (1971), *Memphis Heat* (1971), *Historical Figures And Ancient Heads* (1972), *The New Age* (1973), *Rollin' And Tumblin'* (1973), *One More River To Cross* (1974), *Human Condition* (1978), *Boogie Assault - Live In Australia* (1981), *Captured Live* (1981), with Hooker *Hooker 'N' Heat - Live* (1981), *Kings Of The Boogie* (1982), *Dog House Blues* (1983), *Re-Heated* (1989). Compilations: *Canned Heat Cook Book (The Best Of Canned Heat)* (1969), *The Very Best Of Canned Heat* (1973), *Greatest Hits* (1988), *The Best Of Hooker 'N' Heat* (1989), *Let's Work Together - The Best Of Canned Heat* (1989).

Cannon, Freddy

b. Freddy Picariello, 4 December 1940, Lynn, Massachusetts, USA. A frantic and enthusiastic vocalist, known as the 'last rock 'n' roll star' Cannon was the link between wild rock 'n' roll and the softer, Philadelphia-based sounds that succeeded it. The son of a dance-band leader, he fronted Freddy Karmon And The Hurricanes and played guitar on sessions for the G-Clefs. He was spotted by Boston disc jockey Jack McDermott who gave a song that Freddy and his mother had written, titled 'Rock 'N' Roll Baby', to top writing and production team Bob Crewe and Frank Slay, who improved it, retitled it 'Tallahassee Lassie', and renamed him Cannon. The record was released in 1959 on Swan, a label part owned by Dick Clark, who often featured Cannon on his US *Bandstand* television programme and road shows. The single was the first of 21 that 'Boom Boom' (as the ex truck driver was known) placed in the US charts over the next seven years. He had five US and four UK Top 20 singles, the biggest being his revival of 'Way Down Yonder In New Orleans' in 1959 and 'Palisades Park', written by television personality Chuck Barris, in 1962. His only hit album was the budget-priced *The Explosive! Freddy Cannon* in 1960 which has gone down in history as the first rock album to top the UK charts. Other labels he recorded on during his long career have been Warner Brothers, Buddah, Claridge (where he revived his two biggest hits), We Make Rock 'N' Roll Records, Royal American, MCA, Metromedia and Sire. He returned briefly to the charts in 1981 in the company of Dion's old group The Belmonts with a title that epitomized his work 'Let's Put The Fun Back Into Rock 'N' Roll'.

Albums: *The Explosive! Freddy Cannon* (1960), *Happy Shades Of Blue* (1960), *Freddy Cannon's Solid Gold Hits* (1961), *Freddy Cannon At Palisades Park* (1962), *Freddy Cannon Steps Out* (1963), *Freddy Cannon* (1964), *Action!* (1966). Compilation: *Freddy Cannon's Greatest Hits* (1966).

Captain Beefheart

b. Don Van Vliet, 15 January 1941, Glendale, California, USA. As a child he achieved some fame as a talented sculptor but for more than three decades the enigmatic and charismatic 'Captain', together with his various Magic Bands has been one of rock music's more interesting subjects. During his teens he met Frank Zappa, who shared the same interest in R&B, and while an attempt to form a band together fell through, Zappa (and members of the Mothers Of Invention, would crop up every now and again during Beefheart's career. The first Magic Band was formed in 1964, although it was not until 1966 that they secured a record contract. The unit comprised, in addition to Beefheart, Alex St. Clair Snouffer (guitar), Doug Moon (guitar), Paul Blakely (drums) and Jerry Handley (bass). The ensuing singles, including 'Diddy Wah Diddy', were a commercial

disaster and he was dropped by the record label A&M. Beefheart reappeared with the pioneering *Safe As Milk* in April 1967, and was immediately adopted by the underground scene as a mentor. The album was helped by Ry Cooder's unmistakable guitar and it was a critical success throughout the 'summer of love'. Beefheart found that Europe was more receptive to his wonderfully alliterated lyrics, full of nonsensical juxtaposition that defied the listener to decode. The follow-up, *Strictly Personal* has fallen from grace as a critics' favourite, but at the time it was one of the most advanced albums of the 60s. It is now regarded as more of a blues-based album, with a heavily phased recording that was at times hard to listen to. Titles such as 'Beatle Bones And Smokin' Stones' and 'Ah Feel Like Ahcid' were astonishing hallucinogenic voyages. It was with the remarkable *Trout Mask Replica* that Beefheart reached his peak. The double album, crudely recorded by Frank Zappa, contained a wealth of bizarre pieces, including 'Old Fart At Play', 'Veterans Day Poppy', 'Hair Pie Bake One' and 'Neon Meat Dream Of A Octofish'. Beefheart used his incredible octave range to great effect as he narrated and sang a wealth of lyrical 'malarkey'. The definitive Magic Band were present on this record, consisting of the Mascara Snake (unidentified, reputedly Beefheart's cousin), Antennae Jimmy Semens (Jeff Cotton), Drumbo (John French), Zoot Horn Rollo (Bill Harkelroad) and Rockette Morton (Mark Boston). It was reliably reported that the band recorded and played most of the tracks in one studio, while Beefheart added his lyrics in another (out of ear-shot). The structure and sound of many of the pieces was reminiscent of Ornette Coleman. At one stage on the record, Beefheart is heard laconically stating; 'Shit, how did the harmony get in there?' The listener required a high tolerance level, and while Beefheart and Zappa may have intended to inflict one of the greatest musical jokes of our time, the album is cherished as one of the classic albums from the psychedelic 60s.

A similar theme was adopted for *Lick My Decals Off, Baby* and *Spotlight Kid*, although the latter had a more structured musical format. This album contained the delightfully perceptive 'Blabber And Smoke', written by Jan Van Vliet commenting on her husband. Beefheart sings her lyrics, 'Why don't you stop acting like a silly dope, all you ever do is blabber and smoke'. Beefheart also received considerable attention by contributing the vocals to 'Willie The Pimp' on Zappa's *Hot Rats* in 1969. Following the release of the overtly commercial (by Beefheart standards) *Clear Spot* and a heavy touring schedule, the Magic Band split from Beefheart to form Mallard. The Captain signed to the UK Virgin Records label, releasing two albums, including the critically acclaimed *Unconditionally Guaranteed*. In 1975 Beefheart and

Frank Zappa released *Bongo Fury*, a superb live set recorded in Austin, Texas. However, the release of the album resulted in protracted litigation with Virgin Records, which won an injunction over Warner Brothers on the sale of the album in the UK. Beefheart began to spend more time with his other interest, painting. His colourful oils were in the style of Francis Bacon, and it eventually became his main interest. Beefheart has toured and recorded only occasionally and seemed destined to be an important cult figure until the release of *Ice Cream For Crow* in 1982. This excellent return to form saw him writing and performing with renewed fervour. The album glanced the UK charts but was ignored in his homeland. Since that time there have been no new recordings and Don Van Vliet, as he is now known, is a respected artist, exhibiting regularly. His paintings are now fetching considerable prices.
Albums: *Safe As Milk* (1967), *Strictly Personal* (1968), *Trout Mask Replica* (1969), *Lick My Decals Off, Baby* (1970), *The Spotlight Kid* (1972), *Clear Spot* (1972), *Mirror Man* (1973), *Unconditionally Guaranteed* (1974), *Bluejeans And Moonbeams* (1974), with Frank Zappa *Bongo Fury* (1975), *Shiny Beast (Bat Chain Puller)* (1978), *Doc At The Radar Station* (1980), *Ice Cream For Crow* (1982).
Further reading: *Captain Beefheart: The Man And His Music*, C.D. Webb.

Caravelles

Former office workers Lois Wilkinson (b. 3 April 1944, Sleaford, Lincolnshire, England) and Andrea Simpson (b. 1946) achieved international success with their distinctive version of 'You Don't Have To Be A Baby To Cry'. This light, breathy single reached the UK Top 10 in August 1963 where it formed an antidote to the more powerful, emergent British beat. Despite touring the USA, where the single was a number 3 hit, the duo was unable to maintain a consistent profile in spite of recording several excellent, if novelty-bound releases. Wilkinson began a solo career as Lois Lane, while Simpson maintained the Caravelles' name with a series of replacements and was actively performing throughout the 80s.
Album: *You Don't Have To Be A Baby To Cry* (1963).

Carlos, Wendy (Walter)

b. Walter Carlos, 1941. A former physicist, Carlos entered music by composing commercials and, having befriended electronics expert Dr. Robert A. Moog, later took up the latter's pivotal 60s' invention, the Moog synthesizer. He recorded *Switched On Bach* with the assistance of musicologist Benjamin Folkman and, despite the objection of purists, their unlikely transcription proved highly popular, topping the US classical chart for 94 weeks and remaining on its best-selling list throughout

1969-71. The blend of Bach's best-known fugues and movements to 20th-century technology sold in excess of 1 million copies and garnered three Grammy Awards for Best Classical Album, Best Engineered Recording and Best Performance by Instrumental Soloist. Similarly-styled follow-ups failed to match such success, and although Carlos was highly praised for *Sonic Seasonings*, a suite of four original, evocative compositions, her work is now confined to the experimental fringes. The artist's sex change incurred disproportionate publicity. On the 25th anniversary of Switched On Bach she recorded a second volume using today's state-of-the art technology.
Albums: *Switched On Bach* (1968), *The Well-Tempered Synthesizer* (1969), *A Clockwork Orange* (1972, film soundtrack), *Walter Carlos' Clockwork Orange* (1972), *Switched On Bach Volume 2* (1974), *Sonic Seasonings* (1972), *Brandenburg Concertos 3-5* (1976), *The Shining* (1980, film soundtrack), *Tron* (1982, film soundtrack), *Beauty And The Beast* (1986), *Switched On Bach II* (1992). Compilations: *Walter Carlos...By Request* (1977), *Best Of Carlos* (1983).

Carter And Lewis

John Carter (John Shakespeare) and Ken Lewis (Kenneth Hawker) were born in 1942 in Small Heath, Birmingham, England. They initially found fame leading Carter-Lewis And The Southerners, a group which briefly included guitarist Jimmy Page and recorded several singles including 'Sweet And Tender Romance' and 'Your Mama's Out Of Town' (both 1963). The duo's ability to create unabashed pop had been confirmed with 'Will I What?', a UK number 1 hit for Mike Sarne, and having disbanded their group, Carter/Lewis compositions were picked up by scores of acts, including the Marauders, Brenda Lee, P.J. Proby and the McKinleys, the last of whom they also produced. In 1964 the songwriters resurrected the idea of a group, forming the Ivy League with Perry Ford. This harmony trio enjoyed several hits, but lost momentum when first Carter, then Lewis, left the line-up in 1966. The pair resumed a back-room role with the Flowerpot Men, before scoring further success as composers and/or producers with, among others, White Plains and First Class. Carter and Lewis also became involved with commercials and jingles, either as a team, or as individuals.

Cascades

Formed in the late 50s in San Diego, California, USA. The Cascades were best known for their 1963 number 3 US hit 'Rhythm Of The Rain'. The group consisted of John Gummoe (vocals/guitar), Eddie Snyder (piano), Dave Stevens (bass), Dave Wilson (saxophone) and Dave Zabo (drums). They were discovered at a club called the Peppermint Stick in

1962 and signed to Valiant Records. Their first single, 'Second Chance', failed but 'Rhythm Of The Rain' did better, becoming a soft-rock classic that still receives radio airplay in the 90s. One other chart single for Valiant and one for RCA Records charted but the group was unable to repeat its main success. Two more albums recorded in the late 60s did not revive the group's fortunes. They disbanded in 1969, with only one original member remaining at the time.

Albums: *Rhythm Of The Rain* (1963), *What Goes On* (1968), *Maybe The Rain Will Fall* (1969).

Casinos

Formed in 1958 in Cincinnati, Ohio, USA. The Casinos originally consisted of Gene and Glen Hughes, Pete Bolton, Joe Patterson and Ray White. After gaining popularity locally, they signed with the small Terry Records and covered the Carla Thomas R&B ballad 'Gee Whiz', with no success. They then switched to the local Fraternity Records and recorded a series of singles which also failed commercially. The group, still sporting a clean-cut look and a 50s-orientated doo-wop sound, grew to nine members by the mid-60s, including Bob Armstrong, Tom Mathews, Bill Hawkins and Mickey Denton. Finally, in 1967, the group reached the US Top 10 with a cover of John D. Loudermilk's ballad, 'Then You Can Tell Me Goodbye'. The Casinos continued to record into the 70s and a version of the group was still performing in Cincinnati by the early 90s, but there have been no further hits.

Album: *Then You Can Tell Me Goodbye* (1967).

Castaways

Formed in Richfield, Minnesota, USA in 1962 with the express purpose of playing a fraternity party, the Castaways made one appearance on the US charts in 1965 with 'Liar, Liar', a 'garage-rock' gem marked by overbearing organ and heavily echoed vocals. Roy Hensley (guitar), Denny Craswell (drums) and Dick Roby (bass) originated the group, with Bob Folschow (guitar) and Jim Donna (keyboards) completing the line-up. Their only hit was also their first single, recorded for the local Soma label which was intended to gain the band a better footing from which to sell itself to local club owners. The group recorded several other singles but none charted. Denny Craswell left the band to join Crow in 1970, while the remaining four members still performed together in the late 80s and hope to eventually record an album. Meanwhile, 'Liar, Liar' remains popular, having received a boost in 1987 via placement in the film *Good Morning Vietnam*.

Casuals

Three times winners on *Opportunity Knocks*, British television's popular talent show of the late 60s, the Casuals subsequently left the UK for Italy, where they became a leading attraction. Alan Taylor (b. Halifax, Yorkshire, England; guitar/bass), Johnny Tebb (b. 1 October 1945, Lincoln, England; organ), Howard Newcombe (b. Lincoln, England; guitar/trumpet) and Robert O'Brien (b. Bridge Of Allan, Central Scotland; drums) were based in Milan for several years before returning to Britain in 1968, when their single, 'Jesamine', entered the charts. The song was originally recorded by the Bystanders, but the Casuals' inherently commercial reading coincided with a prevailing trend for emotional ballads. The single ultimately reached number 2 but later releases were less successful and 'Toy' (1968), which peaked at number 30; was their only other hit. The Casuals continued to record superior pop leader the Move leader Roy Wood wrote and produced the polished 'Caroline' (1969), but as the decade closed so their style of music grew increasingly anachronistic.

Album: *Hour World* (1969).

Chad And Jeremy

Chad Stewart (b. 10 December 1943, England; vocals/guitar/banjo/keyboards/sitar) and Jeremy Clyde (b. 22 March 1944, England; vocals/guitar) became acquainted as students at London's Central School of Speech and Drama. Inspired by a common interest in music, the pair began performing together with Stewart providing the musical accompaniment to Clyde's lyrics. Their early releases offered a brand of folk-influenced pop similar to that of Peter And Gordon, but the duo was unable to make commercial inroads in the UK. However, their quintessential English-ness inspired four US Top 30 hits, including 'Yesterday's Gone' and 'A Summer Song' the latter of which reached number 7. A concept album, *Of Cabbages And Kings*, produced by Gary Usher, signalled a switch to progressive styles, but this ambitious and sadly neglected work was not a commercial success and the pair broke up in 1969. Clyde, who made frequent appearances on the popular television show, *Rowan And Martin's Laugh-In*, later pursued an acting career, while Stewart began writing musicals.

Albums: *Yesterday's Gone* (1964), *Chad And Jeremy Sing For You* (1965), *Before And After* (1965), *I Don't Want To Lose You Baby* (1965), *More Chad And Jeremy* (1966), *Distant Shores* (1966), *Of Cabbages And Kings* (1967), *The Ark* (1968), *Three In An Attic* (1969, film soundtrack). Compilations: *The Best Of Chad And Jeremy* (1966), *5 Plus 10 Equals 15 Fabulous Hits* (1965), *Chad And Jeremy* (1968).

Chamberlain, Richard

b. George Richard Chamberlain, 31 March 1935, Los Angeles, California, USA. The well-known television

and film star had a brief spell as a successful recording artist in the early 60s. In 1960, after serving in Korea and attending the LA Conservatory of Music, he had his first television role in *Gunsmoke* and appeared in the film *The Secret Of The Purple Reef*. In 1961 he landed the lead role in the television series *Dr. Kildare*, which made the photogenic fresh-faced actor a top pin-up on both sides of the Atlantic. In 1962, his first single, a vocal version of the television series' theme song, 'Three Stars Will Shine Tonight' became the first of four UK and three US Top 40 singles for the pleasant-voiced MOR/pop singer. His debut album 'Richard Chamberlain Sings', on which he was accompanied by David Rose's 40-piece orchestra, also shot into the transatlantic Top 10s. Chamberlain, who at the height of his career as Dr. Kildare was reputedly receiving 2,500 letters a day, quickly faded from the pop scene but has gone on to star in many more television programmes and films.
Album: *Richard Chamberlain Sings* (1962).

Chambers Brothers

Born and raised in Lee County, Mississippi, USA, the four brothers, George (b. 26 September 1931; bass), Willie (b. 2 March 1938; guitar), Lester (b. 13 April 1940; harmonica) and Joe (b. 22 August 1942; guitar), moved to Los Angeles during the early 50s. The group's gospel-based origins were clearly heard in their first recordings, which included an unpolished reading of Curtis Mayfield's 'People Get Ready'. In 1965 they were joined by drummer Brian Keenan and an appearance at that year's Newport Folk Festival reinforced the group's 'R&B combo' approach, the basis for their later direction. The title track to a 1968 album, *Time Has Come Today*, with its exciting, extended instrumental break, introduced the Brothers to the white, counter-culture audience. They cultivated a hippie image and part of a subsequent album, *Love Peace And Happiness*, was recorded live at the Fillmore East, then one of rock's prestigious venues. The group continued to maintain their popularity into the 70s, but in embracing such a transient fashion they were unable to secure a committed following when tastes changed.
Albums: *People Get Ready* (1965), *Now* (1966), *Shout* (1968), *The Time Has Come* (1968), *A New Time - A New Day* (1963), with various artists *Love, Peace And Happiness* (1969), *Feeling The Blues* (1970), *New Generation* (1971), *Oh My God* (1972), *Unbounded* (1973), *Right Move* (1975). Compilation: *The Chamber Brothers Greatest Hits* (1971).

Chandler, Gene

b. Eugene Dixon, 6 July 1937, Chicago, Illinois, USA. Recalled for the gauche, but irresistible 1962 US number 1, 'Duke Of Earl', Chandler's million-selling single in fact featured the Dukays, a doo-wop

quintet he fronted (Eugene Dixon, Shirley Jones, James Lowe, Earl Edwards and Ben Broyles). His record company preferred to promote a solo artist and thus one of soul's most enduring careers was launched. Temporarily bedevilled by his 'dandy' image, the singer was rescued by a series of excellent Curtis Mayfield-penned songs. 'Rainbow' and 'Man's Temptation'. These were hits in 1963, but the relationship blossomed with 'Just Be True' (1964) and the sublime 'Nothing Can Stop Me' (1965), both US Top 20 singles. Chandler later recorded under the aegis of producer Carl Davis including '(The) Girl Don't Care', 'There Goes The Lover' and 'From The Teacher To The Preacher', a duet with Barbara Acklin. Switching to Mercury in 1970, 'Groovy Situation' became another major hit, while an inspired teaming with Jerry Butler was an artistic triumph. Chandler's career was revitalized during the disco boom when 'Get Down' was an international hit. Further releases, 'When You're Number 1' and 'Does She Have A Friend', consolidated such success, while recordings for Salsoul, with Jaime Lynn and Fastfire continued his career into the 80s.
Albums: *The Duke Of Earl* (1962), *Just Be True* (1964), *Live On Stage In '65* (1965, reissued as *Live At The Regal*), *The Girl Don't Care* (1967), *There Was A Time* (1968), *The Two Sides Of Gene Chandler* (1969), *The Gene Chandler Situation* (1970), with Jerry Butler *Gene And Jerry - One & One* (1971), *Get Down* (1978), *When You're Number One* (1979), *80* (1980), *Live At The Regal* (1986). Compilations: *Greatest Hits By Gene Chandler* (1964), *The Duke Of Soul* (1966), *Just Be True* (1980), *Stroll On With The Duke* (1984), *60s Soul Brother* (1986).

Channel, Bruce

b. 28 November 1940, Jacksonville, Texas, USA. Born into a musical family, Channel was actively performing while still in high school. He secured a six-month residency on the prestigious *Louisiana Hayride* show, which in turn resulted in a recording deal with Smash Records. In 1962 the singer scored a US chart-topper with the infectious 'Hey Baby' which also achieved gold record status on climbing to number 2 in the UK. Much of the song's appeal, however, was derived from its distinctive harmonica passage, which was played by Delbert McClinton. His plaintive style influenced that of several subsequent releases, including the Beatles' 'Love Me Do', although John Lennon later denied his influence. Channel's career floundered over the ensuing years and his releases were confined to low-key labels including Le Cam and Mel-O-Dy. He was signed to Mala in 1968, but although this made no difference to his fortune in America, the singer enjoyed another UK Top 10 hit with the exuberant 'Keep On'. Longtime fans were perplexed by a figure vowing to return with a blues group featuring McClinton and guitarist Bobby Turner, but Channel's newfound success proved short-lived, and the frantic 'Mr. Bus Driver' failed to chart. He has nonetheless continued to perform and in 1988 made a surprise guest appearance as a disc jockey on BBC Radio 2.

Albums: *Hey! Baby (And 11 Other Songs About Your Baby)* (1962), *Goin' Back To Louisiana* (1964), *Keep On* (1969).

Bruce Channel

Chantays

This US-based group was comprised of the Californian Santa Ana High School students Bob Spickard (lead guitar), Brian Carman (guitar/saxophone), Bob Marshall (piano), Warren Waters (bass) and Bob Welsh (drums). They formed the Chantays in 1962, and secured immortality with 'Pipeline' the following year. Initially released as the b-side to a vocal track, this atmospheric surfing instrumental brought a new level of sophistication to an often one-dimensional genre and deservedly became a hit in the USA and Britain. It was a standard the quintet were unable to repeat and although Steve Kahn replaced Welsh, the group broke up following a handful of unsuccessful releases. However a reformed line-up emerged during the 80s in the wake of a surfing resurgence.

Albums: *Pipeline* (1963), *Two Sides Of The Chantays* (1964). Compilation: *The Story Of Rock 'N' Roll* (1976).

Charlatans

The first of San Francisco's 'underground' groups, the Charlatans were formed in 1964 by George Hunter (autoharp/tambourine), Mike Wilhelm (guitar/vocals) and Richard Olsen (bass/clarinet/vocals). They were then augmented by pianist Michael Ferguson, whom Hunter had met in line at an unemployment office, and Sam Linde (drums). The incompatible Linde was replaced by Dan Hicks, by which time the group had adopted their striking visual image, reminiscent of turn-of-the-century western outlaws. Their waistcoats, stiff-necked collars, high boots and long hair so impressed the owner of the Red Dog Saloon, a bar in Virginia City, Nevada, that he booked them as his resident houseband. It was here that the group honed their melange of blues, folk, R&B and good-time music, while Ferguson's artwork for their debut performance is recognized as America's first psychedelic poster.

The Charlatans returned to San Francisco late in 1965 but their eminent position did not result in a coherent recording career. Demos for the local Autumn label were rejected, and although the quintet completed an album for Kama Sutra, the results were shelved. 'The Shadow Knows', a single issued against the group's preference, was the sole release by this pioneering line-up. Hicks, Ferguson and Hunter then left, disillusioned at this seeming impasse. Olsen and Wilhelm persevered and in 1969 completed the Charlatans' self-titled album with Darrell De Vore (piano) and Terry Wilson (drums). Although the group's erstwhile fire was muted, glimpses of their legacy appeared in 'Alabama Bound' and 'Fulsom Prison Blues'. The Charlatans then dissolved, but its individual members remained active. Hicks formed the impressive Dan Hicks And His Hot Licks, and while Wilhelm fronted Loose Gravel, Ferguson joined Lynne Hughes, barmaid at the Red Dog Saloon, in Tongue And Groove. Olsen became a producer at Pacific High Studios and Hunter, the group's visionary, founded the Globe Propaganda design company. Hunter's artwork graced numerous magnificent covers including *Happy Trails* (Quicksilver Messenger Service), *Hallelujah* (Canned Heat) and *Its A Beautiful Day*.(Its A Beautiful Day). Although the Charlatans were denied the plaudits garnered by those in their wake, the elan of San Francisco's renaissance is indebted to their influence.

Albums: *The Charlatans* (1969), *The Autumn Demos* (1982).

Charles, Ray

b. Ray Charles Robinson, 23 September 1930, Albany, Georgia, USA. Few epithets sit less comfortably than that of genius; Ray Charles has borne this title for over thirty years. As a singer, composer, arranger and pianist, his prolific work deserves no other praise. Born in extreme poverty, Ray was slowly blinded by glaucoma until, by the age of seven, he had lost his sight completely. He learned to read and write music in braille and was accomplished on several instruments by the time he left school. Orphaned at age 15, Charles drifted around the Florida circuit, picking up work where he could, before moving across the country to Seattle. Here he continued his itinerant career, playing piano at several nightclubs in a style reminiscent of Nat 'King' Cole.

Ray began recording in 1949 and this early, imitative approach was captured on several sessions. Three years later Atlantic Records acquired his contract, but initially the singer continued his 'cool' direction, baring only an occasional hint of the passions later unleashed. 'It Should've Been Me', 'Mess Around' and 'Losing Hand' best represent this early R&B era, but Ray's individual style emerged as a result of his work with Guitar Slim. This impassioned, almost crude blues performer sang with a gospel-based fervour that greatly influenced Charles' thinking. He arranged Slim's million-selling single, 'Things That I Used To Do', of which the riffing horns and unrestrained voice set the tone for Ray's own subsequent direction. This effect was fully realized in 'I Got A Woman' (1954), a song soaked in the fervour of the Baptist Church, but rendered salacious by the singer's abandoned, unrefined delivery. Its extraordinary success, commercially and artistically, inspired similarly compulsive recordings including 'This Little Girl Of Mine' (1955), 'Talkin' 'Bout You' (1957) and the lush and evocative 'Don't Let The Sun Catch You Crying' (1959), a style culminating in the thrilling call and response of 'What'd I Say' (1959). This acknowledged classic is one of the all-time great encore numbers to be found being performed by countless singers and bands in stadiums, clubs and bars all over the world. However, Charles was equally adept at slow ballads, as his heartbreaking intepretations of 'Drown In My Own Tears' and 'I Believe To My Soul' (both 1959) clearly show. Proficient in numerous styles, Ray's recordings embraced blues, jazz, standards and even country, as his muscular reading of 'I'm Movin' On' attested.

In November 1959, Charles left the Atlantic label for ABC Records, where he secured both musical and financial freedom. Commentators often note this as the point at which the singer lost his fire, but early releases for this new outlet simply continued his groundbreaking style. 'Georgia On My Mind' (1960) and 'Hit The Road Jack' (1961) were, respectively, poignant and ebullient, and established the artist as an international name. This stature was enhanced further in 1962 with the release of the massive selling album, *Modern Sounds In Country And Western*, a landmark collection which produced the million-selling single 'I Can't Stop Loving You'. Its success defined the pattern for Ray's later career; the edges were blunted, the vibrancy was stilled as Charles' repertoire grew increasingly inoffensive. There were still moments of inspiration, 'Let's Go Get Stoned' and 'I Don't Need No Doctor' brought a glimpse of a passion now too often muted, while *Crying Time*, Ray's first album since kicking his heroin habit, compared favourably with any Atlantic release. This respite was, however, temporary and as the 60s progressed so the singer's work became less compulsive and increasingly MOR. Like most artists, he attempted cover versions of Beatles' songs and had substantial hits with versions of 'Yesterday' and 'Eleanor Rigby'. Two 70s' releases, *A Message From The People* and *Renaissance*, did include contemporary material in Stevie Wonder's 'Living In The City' and Randy Newman's 'Sail Away', but subsequent releases reneged on this promise. Charles' 80s' work included more country-flavoured collections and a cameo appearance in the film *The Blues Brothers*, but the period is better marked by the singer's powerful appearance on the USA For Africa release, 'We Are The World' (1985). It brought to mind a talent too often dormant, a performer whose marriage of gospel and R&B prepared the basis for soul music. His influence is inestimable, his talent widely acknowledged and imitated by formidable white artists such as Steve Winwood, Joe Cocker, Van Morrison and Eric Burdon. Charles has been honoured with countless awards during his career including the Lifetime Achievement Award. He has performed rock, jazz, blues and country with spectacular ease but it is as 'father of soul music' that remains his greatest title.

Selected albums: *Hallelujah, I Love Her So* aka *Ray Charles* (1957), *The Great Ray Charles* (1957), with Milt Jackson *Soul Meeting* (1958), *Ray Charles At Newport* (1958), *Yes Indeed* (1958), *What'd I Say* (1959), *The Genius Of Ray Charles* (1959), *Ray Charles In Person* (1960), *Genius Hits The Road* (1960), *The Genius After Hours* (1961), *The Genius Sings The Blues* (1961), *Dedicated To You* (1961), *Genius + Soul = Jazz* (1961), with Betty Carter *Ray Charles And Betty Carter* (1961), *Modern Sounds In Country And Western Music* (1962), *Modern Sounds In Country And Western Music, Volume 2* (1962), *Ingredients In A Recipe For Soul* (1963), *Sweet And Sour Tears* (1964), *Have A Smile With Me* (1964), *Live In Concert* (1965), *Country And Western Meets Rhythm And Blues* aka *Together Again* (1965), *Crying Time* (1966), *Ray's Moods* (1966), *Ray Charles Invites You To Listen* (1967), *A Portrait Of Ray* (1968), *I'm All Yours, Baby!* (1969), *Doing His Thing* (1969), *My Kind Of Jazz* (1970), *Love Country Style* (1970), *Volcanic Action Of My Soul*

(1971), *A Message From The People* (1972), *Through The Eyes Of Love* (1972), *Come Live With me* (1974), *Renaissance* (1975), *Live In Japan* (1975), with Cleo Laine *Porgy And Bess* (1976), *True To Life* (1977), *Love And Peace* (1978), *Ain't It So* (1979), *Brother Ray Is At It Again* (1980), *Wish You Were Here Tonight* (1983), *Do I Ever Cross Your Mind* (1984), *Friendship* (1985), *Just Between Us* (1988). Compilations: *The Ray Charles Story* (1962), *A Man And His Soul* (1967), *25th Anniversary In Show Business Salute To Ray Charles* (1971), *The Right Time* (1987), *The Collection* (1990 - ABC recordings). In addition to these releases Charles' big band recorded the following: *My Kind Of Jazz* (1970), *Jazz Number II* (1973), *My Kind Of Jazz, Part 3* (1975).

Further reading: *Brother Ray*, Ray Charles and David Ritz.

Chubby Checker and Lulu

Checker, Chubby

b. Ernest Evans, 3 October 1941, Philadelphia, Pennsylvania, USA. Checker's musical career began in 1959 while working at a local chicken market. His employer introduced the teenager to songwriter Kal Mann, who penned the singer's debut single, 'The Class'. He was given his new name by the wife of disc jockey Dick Clark as a derivation of Fats Domino, Chubby Checker became one of several artists to enjoy the patronage of the influential *American Bandstand* show and the successful Cameo-

Parkway label. He achieved national fame in 1960 with 'The Twist', a compulsive dance-based performance which outgrew its novelty value to become an institution. The song, initially recorded in 1958 by Hank Ballard And The Midnighters, was stripped of its earthy, R&B connotation as Checker emphasized its carefree quality. 'The Twist' topped the US chart on two separate occasions (1960 and 1961), and twice entered the UK charts, securing its highest position, number 14, in 1962. 'Pony Time' (1961), a rewrite of Clarence 'Pine Top' Smith's 'Boogie Woogie', became Checker's second gold disc and second US number 1, before 'Let's Twist Again' established him as a truly international attraction. A Top 10 hit on both sides of the Atlantic, it became the benchmark of the twist craze, one of the memorable trends of the immediate pre-Beatles era. It inspired competitive releases by the Isley Brothers ('Twist And Shout'), Joey Dee ('Peppermint Twist') and Sam Cooke ('Twisting The Night Away') while Checker mined its appeal on a surprisingly soulful 'Slow Twistin'' (with Dee Dee Sharp) and 'Teach Me To Twist' (with Bobby Rydell). Eager for more dance-orientated success, he recorded a slew of optimistic singles including 'The Fly' (1961) and 'Limbo Rock' (1962), both of which sold in excess of one million copies. However, the bubble quickly burst, and records devoted to the Jet, the Swim and the Freddie were much less successful. Checker was latterly confined to the revival circuit, reappearing in 1975 when 'Let's Twist Again' re-entered the UK Top 5. The Fat Boys' single, 'The Twist (Yo Twist)', with Chubby guesting on vocals, climbed to number 2 in the UK in 1988.

Albums: *Chubby Checker* (1960), *Twist With Chubby Checker* (1960), *For Twisters Only* (1960), *It's Pony Time* (1961), *Let's Twist Again* (1961), *Bobby Rydell/Chubby Checker* (1961), *Twistin' Round The World* (1962), *For Teen Twisters Only* (1962), *Don't Knock The Twist* (1962, film soundtrack), *All The Hits (For Your Dancin' Party)* (1962), with Dee Dee Sharp *Down To Earth* (1962), *Limbo Party* (1962), *Let's Limbo Some More* (1963), *Beach Party* (1963), *Chubby Checker In Person* (1963), *Chubby's Folk Album* (1964), *Chubby Checker Discotheque* (1965), *The Other Side Of Chubby Checker* (1971), *The Change Has Come* (1982). Compilations: *Your Twist Party* (1961), *Chubby Checker's Biggest Hits* (1962), *Chubby Checker's Greatest Hits* (1972).

Chicken Shack

Chicken Shack was the product of eccentric guitarist Stan Webb, veteran of several R&B groups including the Blue 4, Sound Five and the Sounds Of Blue. The latter, active between 1964 and 1965, included Webb, Christine Perfect (b. 12 July 1943, Birmingham, England; piano/vocals) and Andy

Sylvester (bass), as well as future Traffic saxophonist Chris Wood. Webb and Sylvester then formed the core of the original Chicken Shack who enjoyed a long residency at Hamburg's famed Star Club before returning to England in 1967. Christine Perfect then rejoined the line-up which was augmented by several drummers until the arrival of Londoner, Dave Bidwell. Producer Mike Vernon then signed the quartet to his Blue Horizon label. *Forty Blue Fingers Freshly Packed And Ready To Serve* was finely balanced between original songs and material by John Lee Hooker and Freddie King, to whom Webb was stylistically indebted. *OK Ken?* emphasized the guitarist's own compositions, as well as his irreverence, as he introduces each track by impersonating well-known personalities, including John Peel, Harold Wilson and Kenneth Williams. The quartet also enjoyed two minor hit singles with 'I'd Rather Go Blind' and 'Tears In The Wind', the former of which featured a particularly moving vocal from Perfect, who then left for a solo career (later as Christine McVie). Her replacement was Paul Raymond from Plastic Penny. Ensuing releases, *100 Ton Chicken* and *Accept*, lacked the appeal of their predecessors and their heavier perspective caused a rift with Vernon, who dropped the band from his blues label. Friction within the line-up resulted in the departure of Raymond and Bidwell for Savoy Brown, a group Sylvester later joined.

Webb reassembled Chicken Shack with John Glassock (bass - ex-Jethro Tull) and Paul Hancox (drums) and embarked on a period of frenetic live work. They completed the disappointing *Imagination Lady* before Bob Daisley replaced Glassock, but the trio broke up, exhausted, in May 1973 having completed *Unlucky Boy*. The guitarist established a completely new unit for *Goodbye Chicken Shack*, before dissolving the band in order to join the ubiquitous Savoy Brown for a USA tour and the *Boogie Brothers* album. Webb then formed Broken Glass and the Stan Webb Band, but he has also resurrected Chicken Shack on several occasions, notably between 1977 and 1979 and 1980 and 1982, in order to take advantage of a continued popularity on the European continent which, if not translated into record sales, assures this instinctive virtuoso a lasting career. In the 90s, Stan 'The Man' Webb was once again delighting small club audiences with his latest version of Chicken Shack.
Albums: *Forty Blue Fingers Freshly Packed And Ready To Serve* (1968), *OK Ken?* (1969), *100 Ton Chicken* (1969), *Accept! Chicken Shack* (1970), *Imagination Lady* (1972), *Unlucky Boy* (1973), *Goodbye Chicken Shack* (1974), *The Creeper* (1978), *The Way We Are* (1979), *Chicken Shack* (1979), *Roadie's Concerto* (1981). Compilations: *Stan The Man* (1977), *The Golden Era Of Pop Music* (1977), *In The Can* (1980), *Collection:*
Chicken Shack (1988).

Chiffons

Formed in the Bronx, New York, USA, where all the members were born, erstwhile backing singers Judy Craig (b. 1946), Barbara Lee (b. 16 May 1947), Patricia Bennett (b. 7 April 1947) and Sylvia Peterson (b. 30 September 1946), are best recalled for 'He's So Fine', a superb girl-group release and an international hit in 1963. The song later acquired a dubious infamy when its melody appeared on George Harrison's million-selling single, 'My Sweet Lord'. Taken to court by the original publishers, the ex-Beatle was found guilty of plagiarism and obliged to pay substantial damages. This battle made little difference to the Chiffons, who despite enjoying hits with 'One Fine Day' (1963) and 'Sweet Talkin' Guy' (1966), were all too soon reduced to a world of cabaret and 'oldies' nights. They did, ironically, however, record their own version of 'My Sweet Lord'.
Albums: *He's So Fine* (1963), *One Fine Day* (1963), *Sweet Talkin' Guy* (1966). Compilations: *Everything You Ever Wanted To Hear...But Couldn't Get* (1984), *Doo-Lang Doo-Lang Doo-Lang* (1985), *Flips, Flops And Rarities* (1986), *Greatest Recordings* (1990).

Chipmunks

A fictional group, the Chipmunks were three cartoon characters, Alvin, Theodore and Simon, who were created by Ross Bagdasarian (b. 27 January 1919, Fresno, California, USA), a multi-faceted performer, who had earlier had an international hit as David Seville, with 'Witch Doctor', in early 1958. On that hit, Bagdasarian had manipulated a tape recorder so that normally sung vocals played back at a faster speed. Using the same technique, he experimented with the sound of three voices harmonizing at that faster speed and it reminded him of the chattering of chipmunks. Bagdasarian had recorded 'Witch Doctor' for Liberty Records (the three Chipmunks were named after Liberty executives) which released 'The Chipmunk Song' for the Christmas 1958 season. It reached number 1 in the US and was quickly followed by 'Alvin's Harmonica' which climbed to number 3. In all, the Chipmunks placed 15 songs on the US charts between 1958 and 1962, spawning a hit television programme. They continued well into the 60s, recording an album of Beatles songs. Bagdasarian died in January 1972 but the Chipmunks were revived in 1980 by his son, Ross Bagdasarian Jnr., and his partner Janice Karmen, this time recording albums of punk, country and current rock!
Albums: *Let's All Sing With The Chipmunks* (1959), *Sing Again With The Chipmunks* (1960), *Christmas With The Chipmunks* (1962), *Christmas With The Chipmunks - Volume Two* (1963), *The Chipmunks Sing The Beatles Hits* (1964), *The Chipmunks Sing With*

Children (1965), *Chipmunk Punk* (1980), *Urban Chipmunk* (1981), *A Chipmunk Christmas* (1981), *Chipmunk Rock* (1982), *Merry Christmas Fun With The Merry Chipmunks* (1984). Compilation: *Twenty All-Time Greatest Hits* (1982).

Chocolate Watch Band

The original line-up of this tempestuous pop group - Ned Torney (lead guitar/vocals), Mark Loomis (guitar/vocals), Jo Kemling (organ), Tom Antone (bass) and Gary Andrijasevich (drums) - was formed in San Jose, California, USA in 1964. The following year Antone, Torney and Kemling left to join another local outfit, the Other Side, while the latter group's guitarist, Dave 'Sean' Tolby, joined the Watch Band. Dave Aguliar (vocals) and Bill Flores (bass) completed its second incarnation. The reshaped quintet was then signed by producer Ed Cobb, already renowned for his work with the Standells. He matched the Watch Band's instinctive love of British R&B with a tough, almost metallic sound and the best of their work - 'Don't Need Your Lovin'', 'No Way Out' and 'Are You Gonna Be There (At The Love In)' - is among the finest to emerge from America's garage-band genre. The group's potential was undermined by personal and professional problems. Several Chocolate Watch Band masters featured studio musicians, while a substitute vocalist, Don Bennett, was also employed on certain sessions. The group did not achieve artistic control until the release of their third album, by which point Aguliar had been replaced by guitarist Danny Phay, another ex-member of the Other Side. However, *One Step Beyond* was a lacklustre effort and having survived a few further changes, the Chocolate Watch Band broke up in March 1970.

Albums: *No Way Out* (1967), *The Inner Mystique* (1968), *One Step Beyond* (1969). Compilations: *The Best Of The Chocolate Watch Band* (1983), *44* (1984).

Chocolate Watch Band

Christie, Lou

b. Lugee Alfredo Giovanni Sacco, 19 February 1943, Glen Willard, Pennsylvania, USA. A former student of classical music, Christie moved to New York in 1963 where he sang backing-vocals on a variety of sessions. Before beginning his string of hits, Christie recorded unsuccessfully with such groups as the Classics and Lugee and the Lions. Although his high falsetto was reminiscent of an earlier era, and similar to that used successfully by Frankie Valli and Del Shannon, 'The Gypsy Cried', the artist's debut solo single, achieved sales in excess of one million in 1963. The following year 'Two Faces Have I' proved equally successful but, unable to avoid the US military draft, Christie's career was interrupted. He achieved a third golden disc with 'Lightnin' Strikes' (1966), arguably his finest record, which pitted the singer's vocal histrionics against a solid, Tamla/Motown-styled backbeat. The single also charted in the UK, where its follow-up, 'Rhapsody In The Rain' (1966), was another Top 20 entry, despite a ban in deference to its 'suggestive lyric'. In 1969, this time signed to Buddah Records, Christie had his final Top 10 hit with 'I'm Gonna Make You Mine', his style virtually unchanged from the earlier hits. Numerous singles followed on small labels into the 80s, but Christie was unable to regain any commercial ground. A curious, almost anachronistic performer, Christie's best records exhibit more power when removed from their contemporary setting. He has spent most of the past two decades performing on the US rock 'n' roll revival circuit.

Albums: *Lou Christie* (1963), *Lightnin' Strikes* (1966), *Lou Christie Strikes Back* (1966), *Lou Christie Strikes Again* (1966), *Lou Christie Painter Of Hits* (1966), *I'm Gonna Make You Mine* (1969), *Paint America Love* (1971), *Lou Christie - Zip-A-Dee-Doo-Dah* (1974). Compilation: *This Is Lou Christie* (1969).

Clapton, Eric

b. Eric Patrick Clapp, 30 March 1945, Ripley, Surrey, England. The world's premier rock guitarist will be forever grateful to his grandparents, for it was they who bought him his first guitar. The young Eric was raised by his grandparents Rose and Jack Clapp after his natural mother could not face bringing up an illegitimate child at the age of 16. Eric received the £14 acoustic guitar for his 14th birthday, then proceeded to copy the great blues guitarists, note for note. His first band was the Roosters, a local R&B group whose members included Tom McGuinness, a future member of Manfred Mann, and latterly part of the Blues Band. Clapton stayed for eight months until he and McGuinness left to join Casey Jones And The Engineers. This brief sojourn ended in 1963 when Clapton was sought out by the Yardbirds, an aspiring R&B band, who needed a replacement for their guitarist Tony Topham. The reputation the Yardbirds then built was largely centred around Eric, who had already attained his nickname 'Slowhand' by the partisan crowd at Richmond's Crawdaddy club. Clapton stayed for 18 months until musical differences interfered. The Yardbirds were taking a more pop-orientated direction and Eric just wanted to play the blues. The perfect vehicle for his frustrations was John Mayall's Bluesbreakers, one of Britain's top blues bands. It was with Mayall that Clapton would earn a second nickname; 'God'! Rarely had there been such a meteoric rise to such an exalted position. Clapton only made one album with Mayall but the record is now a classic. *Bluesbreakers* shows Clapton on the now famous cover behind a copy of the *Beano* comic.

He was elevated to superstar status with the formation of Cream in 1966 and together with ex-Graham Bond Organisation members, Jack Bruce and Ginger Baker he created one of the most influential rock bands of our time. Additionally, as L'Angelo Mysterioso he played the beautiful lead solo on George Harrison's 'While My Guitar Gently Weeps' for the Beatles *The Beatles* ('The White Album'). Cream lasted just over two years, and shortly after their demise he was back again with Ginger Baker, this time as Blind Faith. The line-up was completed by Steve Winwood and Rick Grech. This 'supergroup' was unable to stay together for more than one self-titled album, although their financially lucrative American tour made the impending break-up easier to bear. During the tour Clapton befriended Delaney And Bonnie and decided he wanted to be their guitarist. He joined them before the sweat had dried, following his last Blind Faith gig in January 1970. He played on one album, *Delaney And Bonnie On Tour*, and three months later he had absconded with three of the former band to make the disappointing *Eric Clapton*, and then metamorphosed into Derek And The Dominos. This memorable unit, together with Duane Allman, recorded one of his most famous compositions: the perennial 'Layla'. This clandestine love song was directed at George Harrison's wife Pattie, with whom Clapton had become besotted. George, unaware of this, invited Eric to play at his historic Bangla Desh Concert in August 1971. Clapton then struggled to overcome a heroin habit that had grown out of control, since being introduced to the drug during the recording of *Layla And Other Assorted Love Songs*. During the worst moments of his addiction he began to pawn some of his precious guitars and spent up to £1,500 a week to feed his habit.

Pete Townshend of the Who was appalled to discover that Eric was selling his guitars and proceeded to try and rescue Clapton and his girl friend Alice Ormsby-Gore from certain death. Townshend organized the famous Eric Clapton At The Rainbow concert as part of his rehabilitation crusade, along with Steve Winwood, Rick Grech, Ron Wood and Jim Capaldi. His appearance broke two years of silence, and wearing the same suit he had worn at the Bangla Desh concert he played a majestic and emotional set. Although still addicted, this was to be the turning point in his life and following pleas from his girlfriend's father, Lord Harlech, he entered the famous Harley Street clinic home of Dr Meg Patterson for the initial treatment.

A rejuvenated Clapton began to record again and released the buoyant *461 Ocean Boulevard* in August 1974. The future pattern was set on this album; gone were the long guitar solos, instead they were replaced by relaxed vocals over shorter more compact songs. The record was an incredible success, a number 1 hit in the US and number 3 in the UK. The singles drawn from it were also hits, notably his number 1 US hit with Bob Marley's 'I Shot The Sheriff'. Also included was the autobiographical message to himself, 'Give Me Strength' and the beautifully mantric 'Let It Flow'. Clapton ended 1974 on a high note, not only had he returned from the grave, but he had finally succeeded in winning the heart of Pattie Harrison.

During 1975 he maintained his drug-free existence, although he became dependant on alcohol. That same year he had further hits with *There's One In Every Crowd* and the live *E.C. Was Here*. Both maintained his reputation. Since then Clapton has continued to grow in stature. During 1977 and 1978 he released two further big selling albums, *Slowhand* and *Backless*. Further single success's came with the gentle 'Lay Down Sally' and 'Promises', while other notable tracks were 'Wonderful Tonight', J.J. Cale's 'Cocaine', and John Martyn's 'May You Never'. Clapton had completely shrugged off his guitar hero persona and had now become an assured vocalist/songwriter, who, by chance, played guitar. A whole new audience, many of whom had never heard of the Yardbirds or Cream, saw Clapton as a clean healthy individual with no vices, and no cobwebs in his attic. Clapton found additional time to play at the Band's historic *Last Waltz* concert.

The 80s have been even kinder to Clapton with every album selling vast quantities and being critically well-received. *Another Ticket* and *Money And Cigarettes*, which featured Ry Cooder, were particularly successful during the beginning of the 80s. *Behind The Sun* benefited from the firm production hand of Clapton's close friend Phil Collins. Collins played drums on his next album, *August* which showed no sign of tiredness or lack of ideas. This particularly strong album contained the excellent hit 'Behind The Mask' and an exciting duet with Tina Turner on 'Tearing Us Apart', throughout the record Clapton's voice was in particularly fine form. *Journeyman* in 1989 went one better, not only were his voice and songs creditable but 'Slowhand' had discovered the guitar again. The album contains some of his finest playing. Not surprisingly it was a major success. Clapton has contributed to numerous artists albums over many years, including; John Martyn, Phil Collins, Duane Allman, Marc Benno, Gary Brooker, Joe Cocker, Roger Daltrey, Jesse Davis, Dr John (Mac Rebannack), Bob Dylan, Aretha Franklin, Rick Danko, Champion Jack Dupree, Howlin' Wolf, Sonny Boy Williamson, Freddie King, Alexis Korner, Ronnie Laine, Jackie Lomax, Christine McVie, the Mothers Of Invention, the Plastic Ono Band, Otis Spann, Vivian Stanshall, Stephen Stills, Ringo Starr, Leon Russell, Doris Troy, Roger Waters and many, many more. He also appeared as the Preacher in Ken Russell's film of Pete Townshend's rock-opera *Tommy*. Clapton has received a high-profile during the past few years with his touring, the Live Aid appearance, television documentaries, two biographies, and the now annual season of concerts at London's Royal Albert Hall. His 24 nights there in 1991 was a record. Such is his popularity that he could fill the Albert Hall every night for a year. As a final bonus to his many fans he plays three kinds of concerts, dividing the season with a series of blues nights, orchestral nights and regular nights. In the 90s Clapton's career went from strength to strength, although the tragic death of his son Conor in 1991 halted his career for some months. During December 1991 he toured Japan with George Harrison, giving Harrison the moral support that he had received more than a decade earlier. He has already earned the title of the greatest white blues guitarist of our time, but he is now on the way to becoming one of the greatest rock artists of our time. An encouraging thought for a man whose life had all but ended in 1973.

Albums: *What's Shakin'?* (1966, three tracks as the Powerhouse with Steve Winwood, Jack Bruce, Pete York and Paul Jones). *Eric Clapton* (1970), *Eric Clapton's Rainbow Concert* (1973), *461 Ocean Boulevard* (1974), *There's One In Every Crowd* (1975), *E.C. Was Here* (1975), *No Reason To Cry* (1976), *Slowhand* (1977), *Backless* (1978), *Just One Night* (1980), *Another Ticket* (1981), *Money And Cigarettes* (1983), *Backtrackin'* (1984), *Behind The Sun* (1985), *August* (1986), with Michael Kamen *Homeboy* (1989, television soundtrack), *Journeyman* (1989), *24 Nights* (1991), *Rush* (1992, film soundtrack). Compilations: *Time Pieces - The Best Of Eric Clapton* (1982), *History Of Eric Clapton* (1972), *Crossroads* (1988), *The Cream Of Eric Clapton* (1989).

Further reading: *Survivor*, Ray Coleman. *Eric Clapton: Lost In The Blues*, Harry Shapiro.

Clark, Dave, Five

One of the most popular British beat groups of the mid-60s, the Dave Clark Five's career stretched back

Dave Clark Five

as far as 1958. Originally a backing group for north London singer Stan Saxon, the Five comprised Dave Clark (b. 15 December 1942, London, England; drums/vocals), backed by various musicians, whose ranks included bassist Chris Wells and lead guitarist Mick Ryan. After splitting from Saxon, the Five established their own identity and nominated their date and place of formation as the South Grove Youth Club, Tottenham, London in January 1962. The evolving and finally settled line-up featured Mike Smith (b. 12 December 1943, London, England; organ/vocals), Rick Huxley (b. 5 August 1942, Dartford, Kent, England; bass guitar), Lenny Davidson (b. 30 May 1944, Enfield, Middlesex, England; lead guitar) and Denis Payton (b. 8 August 1943, London, England; saxophone). Smith's throaty vocals and Clark's incessant thumping beat were the group's most familiar trademarks. After losing out to Brian Poole And The Tremeloes with the much covered Contours' classic 'Do You Love Me', the group elected to record their own material. The Clark/Smith composition 'Glad All Over' proved one of the most distinctive and recognizable beat songs of its era and reached number 1 in the UK during January 1964. Its timing could not have been more opportune as the record fortuitously removed the Beatles' 'I Want To Hold Your Hand', after its six-week reign at the top. The national press, ever fixated with Beatles stories, pronounced in large headlines: 'Has The Five Jive Crushed The Beatles' Beat?'. The Five took advantage of the publicity by swiftly issuing the less memorable, but even more boot-thumping, 'Bits And Pieces', which climbed to number 2. Over the next couple of years, the group's chart career in the UK was erratic at best, though they enjoyed a sizeable Top 10 hit in 1965 with 'Catch Us If You Can' from the film of the same name in which they starred.

Even as their beat group charm in Britain faded, surprisingly new opportunities awaited them in the USA. A series of appearances on the *Ed Sullivan*

Show saw them at the forefront of the mid-60s beat invasion and they racked up a string of million sellers. A remarkable 17 **Billboard** Top 40 hits included 'Can't You See That She's Mine', 'Because', 'I Like It Like That' and their sole US number 1 'Over And Over'. Back in the UK, they enjoyed a belated and highly successful shift of style with the Barry Mason/Les Reed ballad, 'Everybody Knows'. Slipping into the rock 'n' roll revivalist trend of the early 70s, they charted with the medleys 'Good Old Rock 'N' Roll' and 'More Good Old Rock 'N' Roll', before bowing out in 1971.

The simultaneous strength and weakness of the group lay in their no-risk policy and refusal to surrender the hit-making formula for a more ambitious approach. Far from serious rivals to the Beatles, as their initial press implied, they were actually a limited but solid outfit who boasted an astute leader whose canny sense of the moment and business know-how enabled them to enjoy lucrative pickings in the US market long after their beat contemporaries had faded. Clark subsequently became a successful entrepreneur, both in the video market, where he purchased the rights to the pop show *Ready Steady Go!*, and onstage where his musical *Time* (starring Cliff Richard) enjoyed box office success.

Selected albums: *A Session With The Dave Clark Five* (1964), *Catch Us If You Can* (1965), *The Dave Clark Five's Greatest Hits* (1966), *Everybody Knows* (1968), *5x5 - Go!* (1969), *The Best Of The Dave Clark Five* (1970), *If Somebody Loves You* (1971), *25 Thumping Great Hits* (1977).

Clark, Petula

b. 15 November 1932, Epsom, Surrey, England. Her Welsh mother, a soprano, taught Petula to sing, which enabled her to commence a stage career at the age of seven and in broadcasting two years later. Her youthful image and crystal-clear enunciation were ideal for radio and by 1943, she had her own programme with the accent on wartime, morale-building songs. She made her first film, *Medal For The General*, in 1944 and then signed for the J. Arthur Rank Organization appearing in over 20 feature films, including the *Huggett* series, alongside other young hopefuls such as Anthony Newley and Alec Guinness. By 1949 she was recording, and throughout the 50s had several hits including 'The Little Shoemaker', 'Suddenly There's A Valley' 'With All My Heart' and 'Alone'. Around this period, Petula's success in France led to many concert appearances in Paris and recording, in French, for the Vogue label. Eventually, in 1959, at the age of 27 and unhappy with the British audiences' reluctance to see her as anything but a sweet adolescent, she moved to France, where she married Vogue's PR representative, Cluade Wolff. At the Olympia

Petula Clark

Theatre, Paris in 1960 she introduced her new sound, retaining the ultra-clear vocals, but adding to them electronic effects and a hefty beat. Almost immediately her career took off. She had a massive hit with 'Ya-Ya Twist', for which she received the Grand Prix du Disque, and by 1962 was France's favourite female vocalist, ahead even of the legendary Edith Piaf. Meanwhile, in Britain, Petula's versions of 'Romeo', 'My Friend The Sea' and 'Sailor', were chasing Elvis Presley up the charts. Her international breakthrough began in 1964 when songwriter/arranger Tony Hatch presented Petula with 'Downtown'. It became a big hit in western Europe, and a year later climbed to the top of the US charts, clinching her popularity in a country where she was previously unknown. The record sold over three million copies worldwide and gained a Grammy Award in the USA as the best rock 'n' roll single. Petula's subsequent recordings of other Hatch songs, written sometimes with his lyricist wife, Jackie Trent, such as 'Don't Sleep In The Subway', 'The Other Man's Grass', 'I Couldn't Live Without Your Love', 'My Love', and 'I Know A Place' all made the US Top 10. Her recording of 'This Is My Song', written by Charles Chaplin for the Marlon Brando/Sophia Loren epic, *A Countess From Hong Kong* (1967) reached number 1 in the UK charts. Tours of the USA and television guest shots followed. As well as hosting her own BBC television series, she was given her own US NBC television special *Petula*, in 1968. This was marred by the programme sponsor's request that a sequence in which she touched the arm of black guest Harry Belafonte, should be removed in deference to the southern States. The show was eventually transmitted complete. That same year Petula revived her film career when she appeared as Sharon, the 'Glocca Morra' girl in 'Yip' Harburg and Burton Lane's *Finian's Rainbow*, co-starring with Fred Astaire and Tommy Steele. While the film was generally regarded as too old fashioned for 60s audiences, Petula's performance, with just a touch of the blarney, was well received, as was her partnership with Peter O'Toole in MGM's 1969 re-make of *Goodbye, Mr. Chips*, marking her 30 years in show business. She was, by now, not only a major recording star, but an international personality, able to play all over the world, in cabaret and concerts. Between 1981 and 1982 she played the part of Maria in the London revival of Richard Rodgers/Oscar Hammerstein II's **The Sound Of Music**. It ran for 14 months, and was a great personal success. In 1989 PRT Records issued a 'radically remixed' version of her 60s hit, 'Downtown', with the original vocal accompanied by 'acid house' backing. It went to number 10 in the UK chart. To date she has sold over 30 million records worldwide and has been awarded more gold discs than any other British female singer. From early in her career she has written songs, sometimes under the pseudonym of Al Grant. So it was especially pleasing for Clark, in 1990, to write the music, and appear in the London West End musical, *Someone Like You*. The show opened in March to mixed reviews.

Albums: *Petula Clark Sings* (1956), *A Date With Pet* (1956), *You Are My Lucky Star* (1957), *Pet Clark* (1959), *Petula Clark In Hollywood* (1959), *In Other Words* (1962), *Petula* (1962), *Les James Dean* (1962), *Downtown* (1964), *I Know A Place* (1965), *The World's Greatest International Hits!* (1965), *The New Petula Clark Album* (1965), *Uptown With Petula Clark* (1965), *In Love* (1965), *Petula '65* (1965), *My Love* (1966), *Petula '66* (1966), *My Love* (1966), *Hello Paris, Vol. I* (1966), *Hello Paris, Vol. II* (1966), *Petula Clark Sings For Everybody* (1966), *I Couldn't Live Without Your Love* (1966), *Hit Parade* (1967), *Colour My World/Who Am I?* (1967), *These Are My Songs* (1967), *The Other Man's Grass Is Always Greener* (1968), *Petula* (1968), *Portrait Of Petula* (1969), *Just Pet* (1969), *Memphis* (1970), *The Song Of My Life* (1971), *Wonderland Of Sound* (1971), *Today* (1971), *Petula '71* (1971), *Warm And Tender* (1971), *Live At The Royal Albert Hall* (1972), *Now* (1972), *Live In London* (1974), *Come On Home* (1974), *C'est Le Befrain De Ma Vie* (1975), *La Chanson De Marie-Madeleine* (1975), *I'm The Woman You Need* (1975), *Just Petula* (1975), *Noel* (1975), *Beautiful Sounds* (1976), *Destiny* (1978), *An Hour In Concert With Petula Clark* (1983). Compilations: *Petula's Greatest Hits, Volume 1* (1968), *Petula Clark's 20 All Time Greatest* (1977), *Spotlight On Petula Clark* (1980), *100 Minutes Of Petula Clark* (1982), *Early Years* (1986), *The Hit Singles Collection* (1987), *My Greatest* (1989), *Downtown* (1989).

Classics IV

Formed in Jacksonville, Florida, USA, the Classics IV were 'discovered' by entrepreneur Bill Lowery upon their move to Atlanta in 1967. This strongly commercial quintet comprised: Dennis Yost (vocals), James Cobb (lead guitar), Wally Eaton (rhythm guitar), Joe Wilson (bass) and Kim Venable (drums). Seasoned session musicians, they had already worked on records by Lowrey proteges Tommy Roe, Billy Joe Royal and the Tams. Between 1968 and 1969, they enjoyed three soft-rock US hits with 'Spooky' (which sold in excess of one million copies), 'Stormy' and 'Traces', all extremely well arranged by producer Buddie Buie. For a time, lead singer Dennis Yost was billed independently of the group, as Gary Puckett and Diana Ross had been in the Union Gap and the Supremes during the same period. Despite expanding the line-up to that of an octet with Dean Daughtry, the eventual loss of major songwriter Cobb proved insurmountable. Yost failed to emerge as a star in spite of the new billing and, somewhat adrift in the early 70s, Classics IV enjoyed only one more minor hit, 'What Am I Crying For' (1972). James Cobb and Daughtry later formed the Atlanta Rhythm Section.
Albums: *Spooky* (1968), *Mamas And Papas/Soul Train* (1969), *Traces* (1969). Compilation: *Dennis Yost And The Classics IV/Golden Greats Volume 1* (1969).

Clay, Judy

b. Judy Guion, North Carolina, USA. Originally based in New York, Clay was part of the gospel group, the Drinkard Singers (featuring Dee Dee and Dionne Warwick, and Cissy Houston), prior to launching her solo career. She recorded several excellent 'uptown' soul singles, but her first success came in partnership with Billy Vera. Although a follow-up single, 'Country Girl - City Man', was actually a bigger pop hit, 'Storybook Children' (1967) remains their best-remembered release. On both of these singles the couple were backed by a vocal quartet, the Sweet Inspirations who featured former-Drinkard Cissy Houston, as well as Judy's sister Sylvia Shemwell. Clay was then teamed with William Bell in 1968 for the sublime 'Private Number'. This promising partnership was better received in the UK where the single reached the Top 10. Judy also recorded on her own and finally scored a minor solo hit in 1970 with 'Greatest Love'. She has since completely retired from music.

Album: with Billy Vera *Storybook Children* (1967).

Joe Cocker

Cocker, Joe

b. 20 May 1944, Sheffield, Yorkshire, England. The capricious but brilliant Cocker is felt by many to be the finest white soul singer Britain has yet produced. His roller coaster career started in 1961 with a little known local band the Cavaliers who changed their name to the clumsier, Vance Arnold And The Avengers and became known as a warm-up for big names such as the Hollies during the beat boom of 1963. Joe was spotted and offered a one single deal by Decca. This excellent record, a cover of the Beatles 'I'll Cry Instead' failed to sell and he was dropped. The sturdy Cocker refused to give in and formed the first Grease Band in 1966, comprising Vernon Nash (piano), Dave Memmott (drums), Frank Myles (guitar) and his future musical partner Chris Stainton (bass). After two years of solid club gigs building a reputation, they were rewarded with a recording session; however only Cocker and Stainton were needed and the rest of the band were told to stay at home. The single 'Marjorine' was a minor hit and Cocker and Stainton assembled a new Grease Band with Mickey Gee (guitar), Tommy Reilly (drums) and Tommy Eyre (keyboards). Once again a session was arranged; this time Gee and Reilly were banished. The resulting single took an age to record with session musicians including Jimmy Page and B.J.

Wilson. The single, John Lennon and Paul McCartney's 'With A Little Help From My Friends' went straight to the top of the UK charts in 1968. This *tour de force* features the finest blood-curdling scream on record, and 25 years on, is still a turntable hit.

The Grease Band had now enlisted the talented guitarist Henry McCullough (ex-Eire Apparent) who was able to copy Page's solo admirably. The band recorded their debut album with assistance from Steve Winwood and Jimmy Page and although it failed to chart in the UK it was a hit in the USA. Cocker and his band started touring America in 1969, they became huge stars through exposure on the **Ed Sullivan** *Show* and constant performing. The highlight of that year was Cocker's orgasmic performance at the Woodstock Festival. Few would deny that Cocker was one of the stars of the event; his astonishing delivery of 'With A Little Help From My Friends' is captured on the film of the festival. Joe stayed in the USA for many months. By the end of 1969 he had a further two hits with Dave Mason's 'Feelin' Alright' and Leon Russell's 'Delta Lady' together with another successful album *Joe Cocker*.

The 70s began with the famous Mad Dogs And Englishmen tour. Over 60 dates were played in as many days. A subsequent film and double album were released, although it was reported that Cocker was bankrupted by the whole charade. He then slid into a drink-and-drug stupor that lasted through most of the decade. Such was his stamina that he still regularly performed and continued to have hit records in America. In the UK he was largely forgotten apart form a loyal core of fans. He was deported from Australia during a 1972 tour, and was often so drunk onstage he was barely able to perform, even after throwing up in front of the audience. In the recording studio he was still able to find some magic and among the highlights of his catalogue of hits were Gregg Allman's 'Midnight Rider', 'You Are So Beautiful' and 'Put Out The Light'. His albums were patchy with only *I Can Stand A Little Rain* (1974) being totally satisfying. Amazingly, he survived the decade, and apart from a minor hit guesting with the Crusaders on 'I'm So Glad I'm Standing Here Today', little was heard from him until 1982. It was stated that it took two years for the alcohol to drain out of his body, but true or not, a thinner, older Cocker was seen promoting his best album for years, the critically well-received *Sheffield Steel*. Despite the plaudits, commercially, the album was a comparative failure. Cocker had little time to worry about its dismal showing for within weeks he was back at the top of the US charts duetting with Jennifer Warnes with the soundtrack to the film *An Officer And A Gentlemen*. The song 'Up Where We Belong' also restored him to the UK singles chart in 1983 after an absence of 13 years. He celebrated it with a belated return to his home town for a memorable concert. *Civilized Man* was another disappointment but while his albums are less successful his live performances are electrifying. His most satisfying recent album was *Unchain My Heart*, Cocker's interpretation of his mentor Ray Charles' classic was taken as a single but was only a moderate hit. *Night Calls* contained the Bryan Adam's song 'Feels Like Forever' and interesting Cocker-reworkings of the Beatles' 'You've Got To Hide Your Love Away' and Blind Faith's 'Can't Find My Way Home'. A wiser and sober Cocker continues into the 90s with his amazing voice intact and a constitution as strong as Sheffield steel.

Albums: *With A Little Help From My Friends* (1969), *Joe Cocker!* (1970), *Mad Dogs And Englishmen* (1970), *Cocker Happy* (1971), *Something To Say* (1973), *I Can Stand A Little Rain* (1974), *Jamaica Say You Will* (1975), *Stingray* (1976), *Live In LA* (1976), *Luxury You Can Afford* (1978), *Standing Tall* (1981), *Sheffield Steel* (1982), *Space Captain* (1982), *Countdown Joe Cocker* (1982), *An Officer And A Gentleman* (1983, film soundtrack), *Cocker* (1986), *Unchain My Heart* (1987), *Civilized Man* (1988), *One Night Of Sin* (1989), *Joe Cocker Live* (1990). Compilations: *Greatest Hits Volume 1* (1978), *Joe Cocker Platinum Collection* (1981), *The Very Best Of Joe Cocker* (1986), *Best Of Joe Cocker* (1988), *Joe Cocker Collection* (1986), *Connoisseur's Cocker* (1991).

Further reading: *Joe Cocker: With A Little Help From My Friends*, J.P. Bean.

Cogan, Alma

b. 19 May 1932, London, England, d. 26 October 1966. After appearing in the stage revues of *Sauce Tartare* and *High Button Shoes*, Cogan was spotted by A&R representative Wally Ridley and signed to HMV Records. Although she began her career as a balladeer, her breakthrough came with the novelty hit 'Bell Bottom Blues', which reached the Top 5 in the UK in 1954. A cover of Kitty Kallen's 'Little Things Mean A Lot' followed quickly and during that same year Cogan turned up with Frankie Vaughan on a couple of unsuccessful singles. Her lone UK number 1 occurred in the spring of 1955 with 'Dreamboat' and the following Christmas she was back with the novelty 'Never Do A Tango With An Eskimo'. A duet with Ronnie Hilton appeared on the b-side of his chart-topper 'No Other Love' and throughout this period Cogan earnestly covered a string of US hits including Jewel Akens' 'The Birds And The Bees' and Frankie Lymon And The Teenagers' 'Why Do Fools Fall In Love?'. By the end of the 50s, she had notched up 18 chart entries, more than any female singer of her era. Meanwhile, she was succeeding as a top variety star and enjoyed the

Alma Cogan

luxury of her own television programme. Another duet, this time with Ocher Nebbish, appeared on one of her b- sides. Nebbish was, in fact, famed composer Lionel Bart, who not only cast Alma in **Oliver!**, but planned to marry her, much to the astonishment of the showbiz community. The unlikely nuptials never occurred, and by the end of the 60s, Alma was no longer a chart regular. Always a candidate for the cover version game, she cut the bouncy 'Tell Him' but lost out to Billie Davis. Paul McCartney made a surprise appearance playing tambourine on the b-side of one of her singles and she repaid the compliment by cutting 'Eight Days A Week', a belated shot at chart fame that narrowly missed. In March 1966, doctors discovered that the singer had cancer. During a period of convalescence she wrote a number of songs under the pseudonym Al Western, including Ronnie Carroll's 'Wait For Me' and Joe Dolan's 'I Only Dream Of You'. At the peak of the *Man From UNCLE* television series, she cut the tribute disc to its star David McCallum. 'Love Ya Illya' by the pseudonymous Angela And The Fans received extensive airplay and barely missed the charts in 1966. That autumn, while working in Sweden, Alma collapsed and was sent home. On 26 October 1966, she lost her fight against cancer and died at London's Middlesex Hospital.

Albums: *I Love To Sing* (1958), *With You In Mind*

(1961), *Alma Sings With You In Mind* (1961), *How About Love* (1962). Compilations: *The Alma Cogan Collection* (1977), *The Second Collection* (1978), *The Very Best Of Alma Cogan* (1984), *Celebration* (1987). Further reading: *Alma Cogan* (a novel), Gordon Burn.

Cohen, Leonard

b. 1 September 1934, Montreal, Canada. A graduate in English Literature from McGill and Columbia Universities, Cohen first made an impression as a novelist. *The Favourite Game* (1963) and *Beautiful Losers* (1966) offered the mixture of sexual and spiritual longing, despair and black humour, prevalent in his lyrics. Two early songs, 'Suzanne' and 'Priests', were recorded by folksinger Judy Collins, and the former was also included on *The Songs Of Leonard Cohen*, the artist's impressive debut. The weary loneliness portrayed by his intonation was enhanced by the barest of accompaniment, while the literate, if bleak, subject matter endeared the artist to a generation of 'bedsit' singer/songwriter aficionados. The album also featured 'Sisters Of Mercy' and 'Hey, That's No Way To Say Goodbye', two haunting compositions destined to become classics of the genre. *Songs From A Room* maintained a similar pattern, but despite the inclusion of 'Story Of Isaac' and 'Bird On A Wire', lacked the commercial impact of its predecessor. The appeal of Cohen's lugubrious delivery had noticeably waned by the release of *Songs Of Love And Hate*, yet it contained two of his finest compositions in 'Joan Of Arc' and 'Famous Blue Raincoat'. The inclusion of 'Dress Rehearsal Rag', one of the artist's earliest songs, suggested an aridity and it was four years before Cohen completed another studio set. *New Skin For The Old Ceremony* showed his talent for wry, often chilling, observations undiminished and included the disconsolate 'Chelsea Hotel', an account of Cohen's sexual encounter with singer Janis Joplin. A second impasse in the artist's careed ended in 1977 with *Death Of A Ladies' Man*, an unlikely collaboration with producer Phil Spector. Although Cohen's songs retained their accustomed high standard, a grandiose backing proved ill-fitting and he later disowned the project. *Recent Songs* and *Various Positions* were excellent, if underrated collections, but the singer's career seemed confined to a small, committed audience until Jennifer Warnes, a former backing vocalist, released *Famous Blue Raincoat* in 1987. This commercially successful celebratory set comprised solely of Cohen's songs and served as a timely reminder of his gifts. His own next set, *I'm Your Man*, was thus afforded widespread attention and attendant live performances formed the core of a BBC television documentary. It revealed Cohen's artistry intact and suggested that his major compositions, far from becoming staid, have grown in stature with the passing of time.

Albums: *The Songs Of Leonard Cohen* (1968), *Songs From A Room* (1969), *Songs Of Love And Hate* (1971), *Live Songs* (1973), *New Skin For The Old Ceremony* (1974), *Death Of A Ladies' Man* (1977), *Recent Songs* (1979), *Various Positions* (1985), *I'm Your Man* (1988). Compilation: *Greatest Hits* (1975).
Further reading: *Leonard Cohen: Prophet Of The Heart*. L.S. Dorman and C.L. Rawlins.

Collectors

Formed in Vancouver, Canada in 1961 and originally known as the C-Fun Classics. The original line-up - Howie Vickers (vocals), Brian Russell (guitar), Claire Lawrence (saxophone), Glenn Miller (bass) and Gary Taylor (drums) - recorded locally with some success before unveiling a new name, the Collectors, with the single 'Looking At A Baby' in 1967. By this point Russell and Taylor had been replaced by Bill Henderson and Ross Turney. The Collectors were then drawn towards US west coast venues where they established a positive reputation for their complex arrangements, soaring harmonies and extended improvisations. Their debut album, *The Collectors* aka *New Vibrations From Canada* admirably displayed such diverse talents. The group's second album, *Grass And Wild Strawberries*, was a loosely framed concept album. Although their imaginative use of time signatures and woodwind garnered critical plaudits, this was not transferred into sales, and the Collectors' career trickled out with two non-album singles. The departure of Vickers prompted an internal rethink and the remaining quartet ditched the name and emerged as Chilliwack in 1971.
Albums: *The Collectors* aka *New Vibrations From Canada* (1968), *Grass And Wild Strawberries* (1969). Compilation: *Seventeenth Summer* (1986).

Collins, Judy

b. 1 May 1939, Seattle, Washington, USA. One of the leading female singers to emerge from America's folk revival in the early 60s, Judy Collins was originally trained as a classical pianist. Having discovered traditional music while a teenager, she began singing in the clubs of Central City and Denver, before embarking on a full-time career with engagements at Chicago's Gate Of Horn and New York's famed Gerde's. Signed to Elektra Records in 1961, Collins' early releases emphasized her traditional repertoire. However, by the release of *Judy Collins #3*, her clear, virginal soprano was tackling more contemporary material. This pivotal selection, which included Bob Dylan's 'Farewell', was arranged by future Byrds' guitarist Jim (Roger) McGuinn. *Judy Collins' Fifth Album* was the artist's last purely folk collection. Compositions by Dylan, Richard Farina, Eric Anderson and Gordon Lightfoot had gained the ascendancy, but Collins henceforth combined such talent with songs culled from theatre's bohemian fringes. *In My Life* embraced Jacques Brel, Bertolt Brecht, Kurt Weill and the then-unknown Leonard Cohen; on *Wildflower* she introduced Joni Mitchell and in the process enjoyed a popular hit with 'Both Sides Now'. These releases were also marked by Joshua Rifkin's studied string arrangements, which also became a feature of the singer's work. Collins' 1968 release, *Who Knows Where The Time Goes* is arguably her finest work. A peerless backing group, including Stephen Stills and Van Dyke Parks, added sympathetic support to her interpretations, while her relationship with the former resulted in his renowned composition, 'Suite: Judy Blue Eyes'. The singer's next release, *Whales And Nightingales*, was equally impressive, and included the million-selling single, 'Amazing Grace'. However, its sculpted arrangements were reminiscent of earlier work and although Collins' own compositions were meritorious, she was never a prolific writer. Her reliance on outside material grew increasingly problematic as the era of classic songwriters drew to a close and the artist looked to outside interests. She remained committed to the political causes born out of the 60s protest movement and fashioned a new career by co-producing *Antonia: Portrait Of A Woman*, a film documentary about her former teacher which was nominated for an Academy Award. Collins did secure another international hit in 1975 with a version of Stephen Sondheim's 'Send In The Clowns'. Although subsequent recordings lack her former perception, and indeed have grown increasingly infrequent, she remains a gifted interpreter.

Albums: *A Maid Of Constant Sorrow* (1961), *The Golden Apples Of The Sun* (1962), *Judy Collins #3* (1964), *The Judy Collins Concert* (1964), *Judy Collins' Fifth Album* (1965), *In My Life* (1966), *Wildflowers* (1967), *Who Knows Where The Time Goes* (1968), *Whales And Nightingales* (1970), *Living* (1971), *True Stories And Other Dreams* (1973), *Judith* (1975), *Bread And Roses* (1976), *Hard Times For Lovers* (1979), *Running For My Life* (1980), *Time Of Our Lives* (1982), *Home Again* (1984), *Trust Your Heart* (1987), *Fires Of Eden* (1990). Compilation: *Recollections* (1969), *Colours Of The Day: The Best Of Judy Collins* (1972), *So Early In The Spring, The First 15 Years* (1977), *Most Beautiful Songs Of Judy Collins* (1979), *Amazing Grace* (1985).

Further reading: *Trust Your Heart: An Autobiography*, Judy Collins.

Conley, Arthur

b. 1 April 1946, Atlanta, Georgia, USA. Recalled as something of a one-hit wonder, this Otis Redding protégé remains underrated. Initially signed to his mentor's Jotis label, further singles were leased to Volt and Stax before 'Sweet Soul Music' (1967) hit both the US R&B and pop charts. A thin reworking of Sam Cooke's 'Yeah Man', saw the song's original lyrics amended to pay homage to several contemporary soul singers. Although 'Funky Street' was a US Top 20 hit, Redding's tragic death forestalled Conley's progress. Minor successes followed throughout 1968 and 1969 before the singer switched to the Capricorn label in 1971. Conley's debut album, *Sweet Soul Music*, is a strong collection, highlighted by each of his first five singles and two Redding originals. Conley is still to be found on 60s package tour revivals

Albums: *Sweet Soul Music* (1967), *Shake, Rattle And Roll* (1967), *Soul Directions* (1968), *More Sweet Soul* (1968). Compilation: *Arthur Conley* (1988).

Further reading; *Sweet Soul Music*, Peter Guralnick.

Conniff, Ray

b. 6 November 1916, Attelboro, Massachusetts, USA. Taught to play the trombone by his father, Conniff studied arranging with the aid of a mail-order course while still at college. In 1934, after graduation, he worked with small bands in Boston before joining Bunny Berigan as trombonist/arranger in 1936. After a spell with Bob Crosby's Bobcats, Conniff spent four years with Artie Shaw and featured on several successful records including 'Concerto For Clarinet', 'Dancing In The Dark' and 'St James Infirmary'. During this period he was also studying at the New York Juilliard School of Music. After army service in World War II Conniff spent some time as an arranger with Harry James, then freelanced, while searching for a succcessful formula for making hit records. He joined Columbia Records in 1954, and worked with several of their artists including Johnny Ray, Rosemary Clooney, Guy Mitchell and Marty Robbins. In 1954 he provided the arrangement for Don Cherry's million-seller, 'Band Of Gold', and in 1956 was given the chance, by Columbia producer Mitch Miller, to make an album featuring his 'new sound'. The successful result, *'S Wonderful*, was a set of familiar songs with an orchestra, and a cleverly blended mixed chorus of wordless voices, sometimes used as extra instruments within the songs' arrangements. *'S Wonderful* was followed, naturally, by *'S Marvellous* and *'S Awful Nice*, all in the same vein. *It's The Talk Of The Town*, in 1960, featured a larger chorus, and for the first time they sang - words. From 1957-68 Conniff had 28 albums in the US Top 40, including, *Say It With Music (A Touch Of Latin)*, *Memories Are Made Of This*, and in 1966, the million-seller, *Somewhere My Love*. The album's title track, 'Lara's Theme' from the film *Doctor Zhivago* (1965), also made the US Top 10 singles chart. In 1969 he topped the UK album charts with *His Orchestra, His Chorus, His Singers, His Sound*, and in 1974 became the first American popular musician to record in

Russia, where he made *Ray Conniff In Moscow*, using a local chorus. More recent albums have included three Spanish sets, *Amor, Amor, Exclusivamente Latino* and *Fantastico*, and *The Nashville Collection* with country guest stars including Barbara Mandell, George Jones and Charly McClain who featured on songs as diverse as 'Oh, Lonesome Me' and 'Smoke Gets In Your Eyes'.

Albums: with Don Cherry *Swingin' For Two* (1956), *'S Wonderful!* (1957), *'S Marvelous* (1957), *'S Awful Nice* (1958), *Concert In Rhythm* (1958), *Broadway In Rhythm* (1959), *Hollywood In Rhythm* (1959), with Billy Butterfield *Conniff Meets Butterfield* (1959), *Christmas With Conniff* (1959), *It's The Talk Of The Town* (1960), *Concert In Rhythm - Volume II* (1960), *Young At Heart* (1960), *Hi-fi Companion Album* (1960), *Say It With Music (A Touch Of Latin)* (1960), *Memories Are Made Of This* (1961), *Somebody Loves Me* (1961), *So Much In Love* (1962), *'S Continental* (1962), *Rhapsody In Rhythm* (1962), *We Wish You A Merry Christmas* (1962), *The Happy Beat* (1963), with Butterfield *Just Kiddin' Around* (1963), *You Make Me Feel So Young* (1964), *Speak To Me About Love* (1964), *Invisible Tears* (1964), *Friendly Persuasion* (1965), *Music From Mary Poppins, The Sound Of Music, My Fair Lady & Other Great Movie Themes* (1965), *Love Affair* (1965), *Happiness Is* (1966), *Somewhere My Love* (1966), *Ray Conniff's World Of Hits* (1967), *En Espanol!* (1967), *This Is My Song* (1967), *Hawaiian Album* (1967), *It Must Be Him* (1968), *Honey* (1968), *Turn Around Look At Me* (1968), *I Love How You Love Me* (1969), *Jean* (1969), *Bridge Over Troubled Water* (1970), *Concert In Stereo/Live At The Sahara/Tahoe* (1970), *We've Only Just Begun* (1970), *Love Story* (1971), *Great Contemporary Instrumental Hits* (1971), *I'd Like To Teach The World To Sing* (1972), *Love Theme From The 'Godfather'* (1972), *Alone Again (Naturally)* (1972), *I Can See Clearly Now* (1973), *You Are The Sunshine Of My Life* (1973), *Harmony* (1973), *Evergreens* (1973), *Love Will Keep Us Together* (1975), *Plays The Carpenters* (1975), *Laughter In The Rain* (1975), *Send In The Clowns* (1976), *I Write The Songs* (1976), *Smoke Gets In Your Eyes* (1977), *If You Leave Me Now* (1977), *Sentimental Journey* (1978), *I Will Survive* (1979), *The Perfect Ten Classics* (1981), *The Nashville Connection* (1982), *Amor, Amor* (1984), *Exclusivamente Latino* (1984), *Fantastico* (1984), *Smoke Gets In Your Eyes* (1984), *Always In My Heart* (1988). Compilations: *'S Wonderful's 'S Marvellous* (1962), *Ray Conniff's Greatest Hits* (1969), *His Orchestra, His Chorus, His Singers, His Sound* (1969), *Happy Beat Of Ray Conniff* (1975), *The Ray Conniff Songbook* (1984).

Conrad, Jess

b. 1935, Brixton, London, England. Christened Jesse James, Conrad began his career as a repertory actor and film extra before being cast as a pop singer in a television play, *Rock-A-Bye Barney*. Initially, his singing voice was overdubbed by that of Gary Mills, but before long life imitated art and Conrad was transformed into a pop adonis. Championed by television producer Jack Good, he appeared in *Oh Boy!*, *Wham!* and *Boy Meets Girl*, which led to a recording contract with Decca Records and some minor early 60s hits with 'Cherry Pie', 'Mystery Girl' and 'Pretty Jenny'. When his recording career waned, he continued acting in low budget movies and pantomime, and in the 70's appeared in the musicals *Joseph And His Amazing Technicolour Dreamcoat* and *Godspell* as well as taking a cameo part in the Sex Pistols' celluloid excursion, *The Great Rock 'N' Roll Swindle*. One of Conrad's early singles, 'This Pullover' was belatedly named the worst single ever made in a novelty compilation of pop atrocities.

Album: *Jess For You* (1961).

Jess Conrad

Contours

The Contours formed as an R&B vocal group in Detroit in 1959, featuring lead vocalist Billy Gordon, Billy Hoggs, Joe Billingslea and Sylvester Potts. Hubert Johnson joined the line-up in 1960, and it was his cousin Jackie Wilson who secured the group an audition and then a contract with Motown Records in 1961. Initial singles proved unsuccessful, but in 1962 the dance-orientated number 'Do You Love Me' became one of the label's biggest hits to

Contours

date, topping the R&B charts and reaching number 3 in the US pop listing. The same frantic blend of R&B and the twist dance craze powered the follow-up, 'Shake Sherry', in 1963. Both songs heavily influenced the British beat group scene, with 'Do You Love Me' being covered by Brian Poole And The Tremeloes, Faron's Flamingos and the Dave Clark Five. Unfortunately the Contours were unable to capitalize on their early success, and their exciting, slightly chaotic sound lost favour at Motown, usurped by the choreographed routines and tight harmonies of acts like the Temptations and the Four Tops. As the Contours' line-up went through a rapid series of changes, they scored occasional R&B successes with 'Can You Jerk Like Me', Smokey Robinson's witty 'First I Look At The Purse', and the dance number 'Just A Little Misunderstanding'. Although 'It's So Hard Being A Loser' (1967) was the Contour's last official single, posthumous releases, particularly in Britain, kept their name alive. Former lead vocalist, Dennis Edwards, later enjoyed consistent success with the Temptations, and as a soloist. Versions of the Contours appeared on the revival circuit from 1972 onwards, and while Johnson committed suicide on 11 July 1981, a trio consisting of Billingslea, Potts and Jerry Green were still performing into the 80s. In 1988, 'Do You Love Me' returned to the US Top 20 on the strength of its inclusion in the film, *Dirty*

Dancing. The current line-up of Joe Billingslea, Sylvester Potts, Arthur Hinson, Charles Davis and Darrel Nunlee issued *Running In Circles* on Ian Levine's Motor City label in 1990. The former lead vocalist Joe Stubbs also recorded *Round And Round* for the same label.

Album: *Do You Love Me* (1962). Compilation: *Baby Hit And Run* (1974), *Running In Circles* (1990).

Cooke, Sam

b. Sam Cook, 22 January 1931, Clarksdale, Mississippi, USA, d. 11 December 1964, Los Angeles, California, USA. Cooke first performed publicly with his brother and two sisters in their Baptist quartet, the Soul Children. As a teenager he joined the Highway QCs, before replacing Robert 'R.H.' Harris in the Soul Stirrers. Between 1951-56 Cooke sang lead with this innovative gospel group. His distinctive florid vocal style was soon obvious on 'Touch The Hem Of His Garment' and 'Nearer To Thee'. The Soul Stirrers recorded for the Specialty label where the singer's popularity encouraged producer 'Bumps' Blackwell to provide Sam with pop material. 'Loveable'/'Forever' was issued as a single, disguised under the pseudonym 'Dale Cook' to avoid offending the gospel audience. Initially content, the label's owner, Art Rupe, then objected to the sweetening choir on a follow-up recording, 'You Send Me', and offered Cooke a release from his contract in return for outstanding royalites. The song was then passed to the Keen label, where it sold in excess of 2 million copies. Further hits, including 'Only Sixteen' and 'Wonderful World', followed. The latter was latter used extensively in a television jeans commercial and in 1986 the re-issue reached number 2 in the UK charts. Sam left the label for RCA where 'Chain Gang' (1960), 'Cupid' (1961) and 'Twistin' The Night Away' (1962), displayed a pop craft later offset by such grittier offerings as 'Bring It On Home To Me' and 'Little Red Rooster'. Cooke also founded the Sar and Derby labels on which the Simms Twins' 'Soothe Me' and the Valentinos' 'It's All Over Now' were issued. Cooke's own career remained in the acsendant with '(Ain't That) Good News' and 'Good Times' but the purity of such music made his tawdry fate all the more perplexing. On 11 December 1964, following an altercation with a girl he had picked up, the singer was fatally shot by the manageress of a Los Angeles motel. The ebullient 'Shake' became a posthumous hit, but its serene coupling, 'A Change Is Gonna Come', was a more melancholic epitaph. Arguably his finest composition, its title suggested a metaphor for the concurrent Civil Rights movement. Cooke's legacy continued through his various disciples - Johnnie Taylor, who had replaced Cooke in the Soul Stirrers, bore an obvious debt, as did Bobby Womack of the Valentinos. Sam's songs were interpreted by acts as diverse as Rod Stewart, the Animals and Cat Stevens, while the Rolling Stones' version of 'Little Red Rooster' echoed Cooke's reading rather than that of Howlin' Wolf. Otis Redding, Aretha Franklin, Smokey Robinson - the list of those acknowledging Cooke's skill is a testimony in itself. A seminal influence on soul music and R&B his effortless and smooth delivery has rarely been bettered. *Sam Cooke: A Man And His Music* provides an overview of the singer's whole career.

Albums: *Sam Cooke* (1958), *Sam Cooke Encore* (1959), *Tribute To The Lady* (1959), *Hit Kit* (1960), *I Thank God* (1960), *Wonderful World Of Sam Cooke* (1960), *Cooke's Tour* (1960), *Hits Of The 50s* (1960), *Swing Low* (1961), *My Kind Of Blues* (1961), *Twisting The Night Away* (1962), *Mr. Soul* (1963), *Night Beat* (1963), *Ain't That Good News* (1964), *Sam Cooke At The Copa* (1964), *Shake* (1965), *Try A Little Love* (1965), *Sam Cooke Sings Billie Holiday* (1976), *Live At Harlem Square Club* (1986). Compilations: *The Best Of Sam Cooke, Volume 1* (1962), *The Best Of Sam Cooke, Volume 2* (1965), *The Late And Great* (1969), *The Two Sides Of Sam Cooke* (1971), *This Is Sam Cooke* (1971), *The Golden Age Of Sam Cooke* (1976), *The Man And His Music* (1986).

Cortez, Dave 'Baby'

b. David Cortez Clowney, 13 August 1938, Detroit, Michigan, USA. Cortez played piano in church as a boy and progressed from there to Hammond organ, performing on the chittlin' circuit through the midwest and California in the late 50s. From 1955-57 he was with vocal group the Pearls and in 1956-57 also worked with the Valentines. In 1956 he made his first recording (under the name of Dave Clooney) for the Ember label. He recorded for RCA Victor in September 1959 and had a hit with Clock Records ('Happy Organ') in the same year. In 1962 he hit again with 'Rinky Dink', a crude 'Louie Louie'-type instrumental that sounds like a definition of 60s teen rock naïvety. He recorded an album for Chess Records in 1963 called, predictably, *Rinky Dink* and then signed with Roulette Records, who issued 'Shindig', 'Tweetie Pie' and 'In Orbit'. In February 1966 *The Fabulous Dave 'Baby' Cortez* appeared on Metro. In 1972 All Platinum released *Soul Vibration* with Frank Prescod (bass) and Bunky Smith (drums). Producer Joe Richardson gave the bass a funk depth comparable to reggae dub experiments. The hilarious dialogue of 'Tongue Kissing' plus liner notes by the organist's mum make the album a gem. Signed to the T-Neck label - a Buddha subsidiary - he worked with the Isley Brothers to produce *The Isley Brothers Go All The Way*. Since then, little has been heard of the man.

Albums: *Dave 'Baby' Cortez And His Happy Organ* (1959), *Dave 'Baby' Cortez* (1960), *Rinky Dink* (1962), *Organ Shindig* (1965), *Tweety Pie* (1966), *In Orbit With Dave 'Baby' Cortez* (1966), *The Fabulous Dave 'Baby' Cortez* (1966), *Soul Vibration* (1972).

Cougars

Formed in 1961 in Bristol, England, the Cougars consisted of Keith 'Rod' Owen (guitar/arranger), Dave Tanner (rhythm guitar), Adrian Morgan (bass) and Dave Hack (drums). An instrumental group in the mould of the Shadows, the quartet was signed to EMI by A&R manager Norrie Paramor following a talent contest. Their debut single, 'Saturday Night At The Duck Pond', a frenetic reworking of Tchaikovsky's 'Swan Lake', incurred a BBC ban on the grounds it 'defaced a classical melody', but nonetheless reached the number 33 spot in 1963. The same composer was the inspiration for several ensuing releases, including 'Red Square' and 'Caviare And Chips', but the group was unable to repeat its initial success.

Count Five

Formed in 1964 in San Jose, California, USA. The Count Five were a classic one-hit wonder whose Yardbirds-inspired psychedelic-punk hit 'Psychotic Reaction', reached the US Top 5 in 1966. The band's line-up consisted of Ken Ellner (b. 1948, Brooklyn, New York, USA; vocals/harmonica), Sean Byrne (b. 1947, Dublin, Eire; guitar/vocals), John Michalski (b. 1949, Cleveland, Ohio, USA; lead guitar), Roy Chaney (b. 1948, Indianapolis, Indiana, USA; bass) and Craig Atkinson (b. 1947, Springfield, Missouri, USA; drums). They first drew attention by wearing Dracula-style capes to their gigs. After recording one album, also titled *Psychotic Reaction*, they continued to release singles into 1968 before disbanding. Byrne returned to Eire and recorded on one album in 1973 as a member of Public Foot The Roman and in 1978 he turned up yet again for the group Legover on their album *Wait Till Nightime*.

Album: *Psychotic Reaction* (1966).

Country Joe And The Fish

Formed in Berkeley, California, USA in 1965, this imaginative quintet began life as the Instant Action Jug Band. Former folk singer Country Joe McDonald (b. 1 January 1942, El Monte, California, USA) established the group with guitarist Barry Melton (b. 1947, Brooklyn, New York, USA), the only musicians to remain in the line-up throughout its turbulent history. Part of a politically active family, McDonald immersed himself in the activism centred on Berkeley, and his group's earliest recording, 'I Feel Like I'm Fixin' To Die Rag' (1965), was a virulent attack on the Vietnam war. The following year an expanded line-up, McDonald, Melton, David Cohen (guitar/keyboards), Paul Armstrong (bass) and John

Country Joe And The Fish

Francis Gunning (drums) embraced electricity with a privately pressed EP. By 1967 Armstrong and Gunning had been replaced, respectively, by Bruce Barthol and Gary 'Chicken' Hirsh. This reshaped quintet was responsible for *Electric Music For The Mind And Body*, one of the 60s' 'west coast' era's most striking releases. Although politics were still prevailant on 'Superbird', this excellent collection also included shimmering instrumentals ('Section 43'), drug songs ('Bass Strings') and unflinching romanticism ('Porpoise Mouth'). It was followed by *I Feel Like I'm Fixin' To Die*, which not only featured a new version of that early composition, but also contained a poignant tribute to singer Janis Joplin. The controversial and outspoken McDonald instigated the famous 'fish cheer' which, more often than not, resulted in thousands of deliriously stoned fans spelling out not F.I.S.H but F.U.C.K with carefree abandon. Beset by internal problems, the group's disappointing third album, *Together*, marked the end of this innovative line-up. *Here We Are Again* was completed by various musicians, including Peter Albin and Dave Getz from Big Brother And The Holding Company, and although piecemeal, included the haunting country-tinged 'Here I Go Again' (later a hit for the 60s model, Twiggy). Mark Kapner (keyboards), Doug Metzner (bass) and Greg Dewey (drums - formerly of Mad River), joined McDonald and Melton in the summer of 1969. The new line-up was responsible for the group's final album, *C.J. Fish*, on which glimpses of the former fire were present. The 'classic' line-up, which appeared on the group's first three albums, was briefly reunited between 1976and 1977 but the resultant release, *Reunion*, was a disappointment. McDonald aside, Barry Melton has enjoyed the highest profile, recording several albums under his own name and performing with the San Francisco 'supergroup', the Dinosaurs.
Albums: *Electric Music For The Mind And Body* (1967), *I Feel Like I'm Fixin' To Die* (1967), *Together* (1968), *Here We Are Again* (1968), *C.J. Fish* (1969), *Reunion*

(1977). Compilations: *Greatest Hits* (1969), *The Life And Times Of Country Joe And The Fish From Haight-Ashbury To Woodstock* (1971), *Collectors' Items - The First Three EPs* (1980).

Countrymen

Formed in Hull, England in the early 60s, singing guitarists Alan Beach, David Kelsey and David Waite sported uniform waistcoats and embroidered shirts while performing commercial folk - 'I Know Where I'm Going', reached the lower reaches of the UK Top 50 in spring 1962. They were also noted as the first UK act to cover a Paul Simon opus when 'Carlos Dominguez' was issued in Britain a month prior to the version by the composer (as 'Jerry Landis') in May 1964. They were advantaged too by a virtual residency on UK television's *Five O'Clock Club* before being lost to the archives of oblivion when this ITV children's series ended.
Album: *The Countrymen* (1963).

Covay, Don

b. March 1938, Orangeburg, South Carolina, USA. Covay resettled in Washington during the early 50s and initially sang in the Cherry Keys, his family's gospel quartet. He crossed over to secular music with the Rainbows, a formative group which also included Marvin Gaye and Billy Stewart. Covay's solo career began in 1957 as part of the Little Richard revue. The most tangible result of this liaison was a single, 'Bip Bop Bip', on which Covay was billed as 'Pretty Boy'. Released on Atlantic, it was produced by Richard and featured the weight of his backing band, the Upsetters. Over the next few years Covay drifted from label to label. His original version of 'Pony Time', (credited to the Goodtimers), lost out to Chubby Checker's cover, but a further dance-oriented offering, 'Popeye Waddle', was a hit in 1962. Covay meanwhile honed his songwriting skill and formed partnerships with several associates including Horace Ott and Ronnie Miller. Such work provided Solomon Burke with 'I'm Hanging Up My Heart For You' while Gladys Knight And The Pips reached the US Top 20 with 'Letter Full Of Tears'. Covay's singing career continued to falter until 1964 when he signed with New York's Rosemart label. Still accompanied by the Goodtimers (Ace Hall, Harry Tiffen and George Clane), his debut single there, the vibrant 'Mercy Mercy', established his effortless, bluesy style. Atlantic subsequently bought his contract but while several R&B hits followed, it was a year before Covay returned to the pop chart. 'See-Saw', co-written with Steve Cropper and recorded at Stax, paved the way for other exceptional singles, including 'Sookie Sookie' and 'Iron Out The Rough Spots' (both 1966). Covay's late 60s' output proved less fertile, while the ill-founded Soul Clan, (with Solomon Burke, Wilson Pickett, Joe Tex and Ben E. King), ended after one single. Covay's songs still remained successful, Aretha Franklin won a Grammy for her performance of his composition, 'Chain Of Fools'. Covay switched to Janus in 1971; from there he moved to Mercury Records where he combined recording with A&R duties. *Superdude 1* (1973), a critics' favourite, reunited the singer with Horace Ott. Further releases appeared on the Philadelphia International (1976), U-Von (1977) and Newman (1980) labels, but while Randy Crawford and Bonnie Raitt resurrected his songs, Covay's own career continued to slide downhill.

Albums: *Mercy* (1964), *See Saw* (1966), with the Lemon Jefferson Blues Band *House Of Blue Lights* (1969), *Different Strokes* (1970), *Superdude 1* (1973), *Hot Blood* (1975), *Travellin' In Heavy Traffic* (1976). Compilations: *Sweet Thang* (1987), *Checkin' In With Don Covay* (1989).

Cowsills

Billed as 'America's First Family Of Music', the Cowsills were all born in Newport, Rhode Island, USA. The group featured Bill (b. 9 January 1948; guitar/vocals), Bob (b. 26 August 1949; guitar/vocals), Paul (b. 11 November 1952; keyboards/vocals), Barry (b. 14 September 1954; bass/vocals), John (b. 2 March 1956; drums) and Susan (b. 20 May 1960; vocals). Occasionally augmented by their mother Barbara (b. 1928; vocals), they came to the attention of writer/producer Artie Kornfeld who co-wrote and produced their debut single 'The Rain, The Park And Other Things' which reached number 2 in the US charts in December 1967. Featuring lyrics by Bill, their happy bouncy harmonies were evident on subsequent singles 'We Can Fly', 'In Need Of A Friend' and the 1968 Top 10 hit 'Indian Lake'. Their energetic interpretation of the title song from the rock musical *Hair* reached number 2 in May 1969 and proved to be their swansong. Shortly afterwards Bill left to pursue a career in composing. Before they split up in 1972, they became the inspiration for the NBC US television series *The Partridge Family* starrring David Cassidy, in 1970. In January 1985 Barbara died of emphysema, aged 56, in Tempe, Arizona, USA.

Albums: *The Cowsills* (1967), *We Can Fly* (1968), *Captain Sad And His Ship Of Fools* (1968), *The Cowsills In Concert* (1969), *On My Side* (1971). Compilation: *The Best Of The Cowsills* (1968).

Coxsone, Lloyd

An influential figure in the growth of the UK reggae scene, Coxsone ran the Sir Coxson sound system from 1962 and was one of Britain's pioneers of the 'talk-over' DJ style. During the 60s the sound system was resident at the Ram Jam club in Brixton where it helped to popularize the rock steady style in London. In the early 70s Coxsone's sound system had moved to the Roaring 20s club in Carnaby Street. Coxsone also recorded in his own right on tracks like 'Cruising' (Pyramid 1973). As a record producer he worked with such UK-based reggae singers as Louisa Mark and Fred Locks.

Floyd Cramer

Cramer, Floyd

b. 27 October 1933, Shreveport, Louisiana, USA. The style and sound of Cramer's piano playing is arguably one of the biggest influences on post 50s' country music. His delicate rock 'n' roll sound is achieved by accentuating the discord in rolling from the main note to a sharp or flat, known as 'slip note'. This is perfectly highlighted in his first major hit 'Last Date' in 1960. Cramer was already a vastly experienced Nashville session player, playing on countless records during the 50s. He can be heard on many Jim Reeves and Elvis Presley records, often with his long-time friend Chet Atkins. During the early 60s he regularly made the US charts. Two notable hits were the superb 'On The Rebound', which still sounds fresh and lively more than 30 years later, and his sombre reading of Bob Wills' 'San Antonio Rose'. After dozens of albums Cramer was still making commercially successful recordings into the 80s, having a further hit in 1980 with the theme from the television soap-opera *Dallas*. With Atkins,

Cramer remains Nashville's most prolific musician.

Albums: *Hello Blues* (1960), *Last Date* (1960), *On The Rebound* (1961), *America's Biggest Selling Pianist* (1961), *Floyd Cramer Get Organ-ized* (1962), *I Remember Hank Williams* (1962), *Swing Along With Floyd Cramer* (1963), *Comin' On* (1963), *Country Piano - City Strings* (1964), *Cramer At The Console* (1964), *Hits From The Country Hall Of Fame* (1965), *The Magic Touch Of Floyd Cramer* (1965), *Class Of '65* (1965), *The Distinctive Piano Style Of Floyd Cramer* (1966), *The Big Ones* (1966), *Class Of '66* (1966), *Here's What's Happening* (1967), *Floyd Cramer Plays The Monkees* (1967), *Class Of '67* (1967), *Floyd Cramer Plays Country Classics* (1968), *Class Of '68* (1968), *Floyd Cramer Plays MacArthur Park* (1968), *Class Of '69* (1969), *More Country Classics* (1969), *Floyd Cramer Country* (1976), *Looking For Mr. Goodbar* (1968), *The Big Ones - Volume 2* (1970), *Floyd Cramer With The Music City Pops* (1970), *Class Of '70* (1970), *Sounds Of Sunday* (1971), *Class Of '71* (1971), *Floyd Cramer Detours* (1972), *Class Of '72* (1972), *Super Country Hits Featuring Crystal Chandelier And Battle Of New Orleans* (1973), *Class Of '73* (1973), *The Young And The Restless* (1974), *In Concert* (1974), *Class Of '74 And '75* (1975), *Floyd Cramer And The Keyboard Kick Band* (1977), *Superhits* (1979), *Dallas* (1980), *Great Country Hits* (1981), *The Best Of The West* (1981). Compilations: *The Best Of Floyd Cramer* (1964), *The Best Of Floyd Cramer - Volume 2* (1968), *This Is Floyd Cramer* (1970), *The Big Hits* (1973), *Best Of The Class Of* (1973), *Spotlight On Floyd Cramer* (1974), *Piano Masterpieces 1900-1975* (1975), *All My Best* (1980), *Treasury Of Favourites* (1984), *Country Classics* (1984), *Our Class Reunion* (1987), *The Best Of Floyd Cramer* (1988), *Easy Listening Favorites* (1991).

Cream

Arguably the most famous trio in rock music, Cream comprised: Jack Bruce (b. John Symon Asher Bruce, 14 May 1943, Glasgow, Lanarkshire, Scotland; bass/vocals), Eric Clapton (b. Eric Patrick Clapp, 30 March 1945, Ripley, Surrey, England; guitar) and Ginger Baker (b. Peter Baker, 19 August 1940, Lewisham, London, England; drums). In their two-and-a-half years together, Cream made such an impression on fans, critics and musicians as to make them one of the most influential bands since the Beatles. They formed in the height of swinging London during the 60s and were soon thrust into a non-stop turbulent arena, hungry for new and interesting music after the Merseybeat boom had quelled. Cream were announced in the music press as a pop group, Clapton from John Mayall's Bluesbreakers, Bruce from Manfred Mann and Baker from the Graham Bond Organisation. Their debut single 'Wrapping Paper' was a comparatively weird pop song, and made the lower reaches of the charts

Cream

on the strength of its insistent appeal. Their follow-up single, 'I Feel Free' unleashed such energy that it could only be matched by Jimi Hendrix. The debut *Fresh Cream* confirmed the promise: this band are not what they seem. With a mixture of blues standards and exciting originals, the album became one of the records for any credible music fan to own. It reached number 6 in the UK charts. That same crucial year, *Disraeli Gears* with its distinctive day-glo cover went even higher, and firmly established Cream in the USA, where they would spend most of their touring life. This superb album showed a marked progression from their first, in particular the songwriting of Jack Bruce and his lyricist, former beat poet, Pete Brown. Landmark songs like 'Sunshine Of Your Love', 'Strange Brew' and 'SWLABR' (She Was Like A Bearded Rainbow), were performed with precision. Already rumours of a split prevailed as news filtered back from America of fights and arguments between Baker and Bruce. Meanwhile their live performances were nothing like they had thus far committed to vinyl. The long improvisational pieces, based around fairly simple blues structures were awesome. Each member had a least one party piece during concerts, Bruce with his frantic harmonica solo on 'Traintime', Baker with his trademark drum solo on 'Toad' and Clapton with his strident vocal and fantastic solo on 'Crossroads'. One disc of the superb two-record set *Wheels Of Fire* captured Cream live, at their inventive and exploratory best. Just a month after its release, while it sat on top of the US charts they announced they would disband at the end of the year following two final concerts. The famous Royal Albert Hall farewell concerts were fortunately captured on film, the posthumous *Goodbye* repeated the success of its predecessors, as did to a lesser degree the remaining live scrapings from the bottom of the churn. Cream came and went in one very long blink of an eye, leaving an indelible mark on rock music.

Albums: *Fresh Cream* (1966), *Disraeli Gears* (1967), *Wheels Of Fire* (1968), *Goodbye* (1969), *Live Cream*

(1970), *Live Cream, Volume 2* (1972). Compilations: *The Best Of Cream* (1969), *Heavy Cream* (1973), *Strange Brew - The Very Best Of Cream* (1986).

Creation

Revered as one of Britain's most inventive mod/pop-art acts, the Creation evolved out of Enfield, Middlesex, England beat group the Mark Four. Kenny Pickett (vocals), Eddie Phillips (lead guitar), Mick Thompson (rhythm guitar), John Dalton (bass) and Jack Jones (drums) completed four singles under this appellation before Dalton left to join the Kinks and Thompson abandoned music altogether. The remaining trio added Bob Garner, formerly of the Merseybeats, and Tony Sheridan and changed their name in 1966 upon securing a deal with producer Shel Talmy. The Creation's early singles, 'Making Time' and 'Painter Man', offered the same propulsive power as the Who, while Phillips' distinctive bowed guitar sound was later popularized by Jimmy Page. Although both releases were only minor hits in Britain, they proved highly successful on the Continent, but the group's undoubted promise was undermined by personality clashes between Pickett and Garner. The singer quit the group in June 1967 and although several strong records followed, they lacked the impact of earlier recordings. The group broke up in February 1968, but reformed the following month around Pickett, Jones, Kim Gardner (bass) and ex-Birds member, Ron Wood (guitar). This realignment, however, proved temporary and, impromptu reunions apart, the Creation broke up in June 1968.

Albums: *We Are Paintermen* (1967). Compilations: *The Best Of Creation* (1968), *66-67* (1973), *How Does It Feel To Feel* (1982), *Recreation* (1984).

Creedence Clearwater Revival

Although generally bracketed with the post-psychedelic wave of San Franciscan groups, Creedence Clearwater Revival boasted one of the region's longest pedigrees. John Fogerty (b. 28 May 1945, Berkeley, California, USA; lead guitar/vocals), Tom Fogerty (b. 9 November 1941, Berkeley, California, USA, d. 6 September 1990, Scottsdale, Arizona, USA; rhythm guitar/vocals), Stu Cook (b. 25 April 1945, Oakland, California, USA; bass) and Doug Clifford (b. 24 April 1945, Palo Alto, California, USA; drums) began performing together in 1959 while attending high-school. Initially known as the Blue Velvets, then Tommy Fogerty And The Blue Velvets, the quartet became a popular attraction in the Bay Area suburb of El Cerritto and as such completed a single, 'Bonita', for a local independent outlet. In 1964 they auditioned for the more prestigious Fantasy label, who signed them on the understanding they change their name to the more

topical Golliwogs to cash-in on the concurrent 'British Invasion'. Between 1965-67, the rechristened group recorded seven singles ranging from the Beatles-influenced 'Don't Tell Me No More Lies' to the compulsive 'Fight Fire' and 'Walk Upon The Water', two superb garage band classics. The quartet turned fully professional in December 1967 and in doing so became known as Creedence Clearwater Revival.

Their debut album reflected a musical crossroads. Revamped Golliwogs tracks and new John Fogerty originals slotted alongside several rock 'n' roll standards, including 'Suzie Q' and 'I Put A Spell On You', the former reaching number 11 in the US charts. *Bayou Country*, issued within a matter of months, was a more substantial affair, establishing Fogerty as a perceptive composer and CCR as America's consummate purveyors of late 60s pop. 'Proud Mary' reached the Top 10 in both the US and UK and in the process become the quartet's first gold disc. More importantly, it introduced the mixture of Southern creole styles, R&B and rockabilly through which the best of the group's work was filtered. *Green River* consolidated the group's new-found status and contained two highly successful singles, 'Green River' and 'Bad Moon Rising', the latter of which topped the UK charts. The set confirmed Fogerty's increasingly fertile lyricism which ranged from personal melancholia ('Lodi') to a plea for mutual understanding ('Wrote A Song For Everyone'). This social perspective flourished on the 'Fortunate Son', an acerbic attack on a privileged class sending others out to war, one of several highlights captured on *Willie And The Poor Boys*. By this point the group was indisputably America's leading attraction, marrying commercial success to critical approbation. 'Down On The Corner', a euphoric tribute to popular music, became their fifth US Top 10 single and confirmed a transformation from gutsy bar band to international luminaries.

CCR reached a peak with *Cosmo's Factory*. It included three gold singles, 'Travellin' Band', 'Up Around The Bend' and 'Looking Out My Back Door', as well as an elongated reading of the Tamla/Motown classic 'I Heard It Through The Grapevine'. The album defined the consummate Creedence sound: tight, economical and reliant on an implicit mutual understanding, and deservedly became 1970's best-selling set. However, relationships between the Fogerty brothers grew increasingly strained, reflected in the standard of the disappointing *Pendulum*. Although it featured their eighth gold single in 'Have You Ever Seen The Rain', the set lacked the overall intensity of its immediate predecessors, a sparkle only occasionally rekindled in 'Pagan Baby' and 'Molina'. Tom Fogerty left for a solo career in February 1971, but although those remaining continued to work as a trio, Creedence had lost much of its impetus. Major tours of the USA, Europe, Australia and Japan did ensue, but a seventh collection, *Mardi Gras*, revealed an artistic impasse. Cook and Clifford were granted democratic rights, but their uninspiring compositions only proved how much the group owed to John Fogerty's vision and Creedence Clearwater Revival was officially disbanded in July 1972. It was a dispiriting close to one of the era's most compulsive and successful groups, a combination rarely found. While the rhythm section followed low-key pursuits independently and together, their erstwhile leader began an erratic path, dogged by legal and contractual disputes, but which was marked by a deserved re-emergence in 1985.

Albums: *Creedence Clearwater Revival* (1968), *Bayou Country* (1969), *Green River* (1969), *Willie And The Poor Boys* (1969), *Cosmo's Factory* (1970), *Pendulum* (1970), *Mardi Gras* (1972), *Live In Europe* (1973), *Live At The Royal Albert Hall* aka *The Concert* (1980). Compilations: *Creedence Gold* (1972), *More Creedence Gold* (1973), *Chronicle* (1976), *Greatest Hits* (1979), *Creedence Country* (1981), *Creedence Clearwater Revival Hits Album* (1982), *The Creedence Collection* (1985), *Chronicle II* (1986). *The Golliwogs* (1975 - compiles the entire output of this early incarnation).

Further reading: *Inside Creedence*, John Hallowell.

Crickets

Despite being formed essentially to back Buddy Holly and to record his 'vocal group' songs, the Crickets have continued occasionally to record and tour as a unit ever since Holly's death in 1959. In addition to Holly, the original long-serving members were drummer Jerry Allison (b. 31 August 1939, Hillsboro, Texas, USA), bassist Joe B. Mauldin and guitarist Nicky Sullivan. When they were signed to Decca in 1957, it was decided that the tracks produced by Norman Petty should be released under two names, as Holly solo items (on Decca) and as the Crickets (on Coral). It was 'That'll Be The Day', credited to the Crickets which was the first number 1 hit. Other Crickets' successes with Holly on lead vocals included 'Oh Boy', 'Maybe Baby' and 'Think It Over'. However, by the end of 1958, Holly had moved to New York to concentrate on his solo career and the Crickets did not accompany him on his final tour. Petty and Jerry Allison had already begun recording independently of Holly, issuing 'Love's Made A Fool Of You' with Earl Sinks on lead vocals. On the later singles 'Peggy Sue Got Married' and 'More Than I Can Say' Sinks was replaced by Sonny Curtis (b. 9 May 1937, Meadow, Texas, USA; guitar/vocals who was an early Texas associate of Holly and Allison. Written by Curtis and Allison, 'More Than I Can Say' was a hit for Bobby Vee and in 1961 the

Crickets moved to Vee's label, Liberty and recorded an album of Holly numbers with the singer the following year. Glen D. Hardin (b. 18 April 1939, Wellington, Texas, USA; piano) joined at this point. The group also released a series of singles between 1962 and 1965. These made little impact in the USA but 'Please Don't Ever Change' (a Carole King/Gerry Goffin number) and 'My Little Girl' were Top 20 hits in Britain, where the group continued to tour.

There followed a five-year hiatus in the group's career as Curtis and Allison worked as songwriters and session musicians. They were persuaded to re-form the Crickets in 1970, to record a rock revival album for the Barnaby label. This led to a contract with Mercury and two albums containing mostly original country-rock style songs, such as Allison's powerfully nostalgic 'My Rockin' Days'. The producer was Bob Montgomery who had been Buddy Holly's earliest songwriting partner. The group now included singer/writer Steve Krikorian and two English musicians: guitarist Albert Lee and ex-Family and Blind Faith bassist Ric Grech.

The most recent phase of the Crickets' career was stimulated by the purchase from Paul McCartney's publishing company of Norman Petty's share of the Holly/Allison song catalogue. During the 80s, Allison led the band for revival tours and he returned to recording in 1987 with original bassist Mauldin and newcomer Gordon Payne on guitar and vocals. They released *Three-Piece* on Allison's own Rollercoaster label, which became *T-Shirt* on CBS with the addition of the title track, the winner of a UK songwriting competition organized by McCartney's company.

Selected albums: *In Style With The Crickets* (1961), *Bobby Vee Meets The Crickets* (1962), *Something Old, Something New, Something Borrowed, Something Else* (1963), *California Sun* (1964), *Rockin' 50s Rock 'N' Roll* (1970), *Bubblegum, Bop, Ballads And Boogies* (1973), *A Long Way From Lubbock* (1975), *Three-Piece* (1988), *T-Shirt* (1989).

Cropper, Steve

b. 21 October 1942, Willow Spring, Missouri, USA. This economical but effective guitarist was a founder member of the Mar-Keys, a high-school band whose instrumental single, 'Last Night', provided a cornerstone for the emerging Stax label in 1961. Cropper worked with several groups constructed around the company's house musicians, the most successful of which was Booker T. And The MGs. This latter unit not only scored several hits under its own identity, but over the next few years, was the muscle behind almost every performance released via the Stax studio. However, Cropper's prowess was not only confined to playing. His songwriting and

Steve Cropper

arranging skills were prevalent on many of these performances, including 'Knock On Wood' (Eddie Floyd), 'Sookie Sookie' (Don Covay), 'In The Midnight Hour' (Wilson Pickett) and 'Mr. Pitiful' and '(Sittin' On) The Dock Of The Bay' (Otis Redding). The MGs continued to record until the end of the decade, but they broke up when organist Booker T. Jones moved to California. Cropper preferred to maintain a low-key profile and although he recorded a pleasant solo album, *With A Little Help From My Friends*, he chose to concentrate on running his Memphis-based studio, TMI, rather than embrace the public acclaim he richly deserved. TMI subsequently folded and Cropper resettled in Los Angeles, returned to session work and production. He featured largely on the Rod Stewart's 1975 UK number 1, *Atlantic Crossing*. The surviving MGs were reunited following the death of drummer Al Jackson, and the group has since pursued this erratic existence. The guitarist was also a member of the Blues Brothers, a band formed by comedians John Belushi and Dan Ackroyd which led to the successful film of the same name. The group recorded three albums, following which Cropper released his second solo collection, *Playing My Thang*. Cropper has continued a low-key approach to his art during the 80s although he has made several live appearances in the UK in the early 90s, particularly in the wake of a revived interest

in the Blues Brothers. His distinctive sparse, clipped, high treble sound with his Fender Telecaster has been heard on literally hundreds of singles and albums. His reluctance to hog the limelight cannot disguise the fact that he is one of the major figures in soul music, remarkable in that he is an 'all-American white boy'.
Albums: with Albert King, 'Pops' Staples *Jammed Together* (1969), *With A Little Help From My Friends* (1971), *Playing My Thang* (1980).

Cryan' Shames

Two 60s' groups claimed the above name although a mis-spelling differentiated the British and American units. Formed in Chicago in 1965, the Cryan Shames - Tom 'Toad' Doody (b. 1945; vocals), Jim (Hook) Pilster (b. 1947; tambourine), Jim Fairs (b. 1948; lead guitar), Gerry Stone (b. 1945; rhythm guitar), Dave Purple (b. 1945; bass) and Dennis Conroy (b. 1948; drums) - made their debut with a version of 'Sugar And Spice', previously a hit for the Searchers. Although the single only rose to number 49 in the US charts, interest in the group proved sufficient to warrant an album. *Sugar And Spice* was a hurried affair, indebted to the Byrds and British beat, but the Cryan' Shames asserted a greater individuality on a second selection, *A Scratch In The Sky*. Here they showed an understanding of harmony pop akin to that of the Association, while the group's final album, *Synthesis*, blended such talent with some truly lavish instrumentation. The sextet was later hampered by personnel changes. Purple and Stone were replaced by Isaac Guillory (b. 27 February 1947, US Naval Base, Guantanamo Bay, Cuba) and Lenny Kerley, but such alterations had little effect on the group's ultimate progress. By 1970 they had split up; Guillory embarked on a solo career, Fairs began session work, Kerley and Conroy formed Possum River, and the brief career of the Cryan' Shames was ended.
Albums: *Sugar And Spice* (1966), *A Scratch In The Sky* (1967), *Synthesis* (1969). Compilation: *Sugar And Spice* (1988).

Crystals

This highly influential 60s US female vocal group were the product of Phil Spector, for his pioneering Philles record label. They along with the Ronettes were the definitive 'wall of sound' groups of the 60s. They came together after meeting in the legendary Brill Building where the group were preparing demos for the Aberbach's famous publishing company Hill and Range. The line-up comprised Dee Dee Kennibrew (b. Dolores Henry, 1945, Brooklyn, New York, USA), La La Brooks (b. 1946, Brooklyn, New York, USA), Pat Wright (b. 1945, Brooklyn, New York, USA), Mary Thomas (b.1946, Brooklyn, New York, USA) and Barbara Alston who was their manager's niece. Spector was impressed and produced the debut 'There's No Other (Like My Baby)' in 1961. At this time Spector was developing his unique sound by mixing numerous layers of vocals and instruments on to one mono track. The blurred result was demonstrated on 'Uptown' but it was taken to its glorious extreme on Gene Pitney's song 'He's A Rebel'. The latter featured the lead vocals of Darlene Wright (Love), and, as Spector owned the name, he could use who he wanted as the Crystals. It became a number 1 single in the USA (UK number 19). La la Brooks returned to the lead vocal on two further hits which have since become timeless classics, 'Da Doo Ron Ron (When He Walked Me Home)' and 'Then He Kissed Me', both major hits in 1963. The Beach Boys attempted a Spector-like production with their own version 'Then I Kissed Her', in 1967. The Crystals were soon overtaken when their mentor devoted more time to the Ronettes, and consequently their career faltered. New members passed through, including Frances Collins, and the band were prematurely banished to the nostalgia circuit.

Album: *He's A Rebel* (1963). Compilation: *Uptown* (1988)

Crystals

Cupid's Inspiration

Based in Stamford, Lincolnshire and initially known as the Ends, this pop attraction secured a recording deal with NEMS on the strength of vocalist T.

(Terry) Rice-Milton (b. 5 June 1946). The line-up was completed by Wyndham George (b. 20 February 1947; guitar), Laughton James (b. 21 December 1946; bass) and Roger Gray (b. 29 April 1949) and featured on 'Yesterday Has Gone' (1968), a song originally recorded by Little Anthony And The Imperials. Cupid's cover version rose to number 4 in the UK chart, during which time pianist Garfield Tonkin (b. 28 September 1946) was added to the group. However, despite enjoying a subsequent minor hit with 'My World', the quintet was unable to repeat the success of their powerful and catchy debut single. The line-up was disbanded at the end of the year, but within weeks Rice-Milton and Gray re-emerged alongside newcomers Bernie Lee (guitar) and Gordon Haskell (bass). A newfound, more 'progressive' style, failed to reverse declining fortunes and the unit disintegrated. Its vocalist began a short-lived solo career in 1970 with a revival of Cilla Black's 'You're My World', while Haskell, formerly of Fleur De Lys, later found fame with King Crimson.

Album: *Yesterday Has Gone* (1968).

Cymbal, Johnny

b. 3 February 1945, Ochiltree, Clyde, Scotland. Cymbal's family moved to Canada while he was a child. He became infatuated with music in his teens and in 1960 the singer, now living in Cleveland, Ohio, USA, secured a recording deal with MGM Records. His early releases included 'The Water Is Red', a macabre 'death disc' in which Cymbal's girlfriend was eaten by a shark. In 1963 the artist switched outlets to Kapp Records for whom he recorded 'Mr. Bass Man', a humorous paean to the vocalist carrying the bottom line in a harmony group, in this case one Ronnie Bright. The single, evocative of a passing singing style, reached number 16 in the US and number 24 in the UK, and has since become one of the most memorable novelty songs of the pre-Beatles era. However, despite a succession of subsequent releases, Cymbal was unable to secure another hit and instead forged a new career in songwriting. He penned 'Mary In The Morning', a US hit for Al Martino in 1967 and later produced several records for David Cassidy and Gene Pitney. Domiciled in Nashville since 1980, Cymbal now concentrates on country material.

Album: *Mr. Bass Man* (1963).

Cyrkle

Originally known as the Rondells, this accomplished harmony-pop group comprized of Lafayette College, Pennsylvania students Tom Dawes (b. 25 July 1944, Albany, New York, USA; vocals/guitar/banjo/sitar), Don Danneman (b. 9 May 1944, Brooklyn, New York, USA; piano/guitar) and Marty Fried (b. 1944 Wayside, New Jersey, USA; drums). Organist Earl

Pickens completed the line-up which took their Cyrkle name in 1966 upon striking a management deal with Brian Epstein, while John Lennon contributed its unique spelling. The quartet enjoyed a million-seller with the folk-rock styled 'Red Rubber Ball', composed by Paul Simon and Bruce Woodley of the Seekers, and although the Cyrkle scored further US chart success with 'Turn Down Day', their conservative appearance and approach was quickly overtaken by less conventional acts.

Albums: *Red Rubber Ball* (1966), *Neon* (1967).

D

Dana, Vic

b. 26 August 1942, Buffalo, New York, USA. As a young boy, Dana trained as a dancer, and at the age of 11 was spotted, performing in Buffalo, by Sammy Davis Jnr. Influenced by Davis, the Dana family moved to California, where young Dana worked on his dancing and also studied singing. In 1960, he toured as a solo act, appearing on the same bill as the Fleetwoods, and then signed for the same record company, Dolton. In the early 60s he had some success with 'Little Altar Boy', 'I Will' and 'More', before making the US Top 30 with 'Shangri-La' in 1964. The Top 10 hit 'Red Roses For A Blue Lady' followed in 1965, and 'I Love You Drops' in 1966. He also had a Top 20 album with *Red Roses For A Blue Lady*. In 1970 he switched to Liberty Records for 'If I Never Knew Your Name' and 'Red Red Wine'.

Albums: *More* (1963), *Shangri-La* (1964), *Red Roses For A Blue Lady* (1965).

Darin, Bobby

b. Walden Robert Cassotto, 14 May 1936, New York, USA, d. 20 December 1973. Darin's entry to the music business occurred during the mid-50s following a period playing in New York coffee houses. His friendship with co-writer/entrepreneur Don Kirshner resulted in his first single, 'My First Love'. A meeting with Connie Francis' manager George Scheck led to a prestigious television appearance on the Tommy Dorsey television show and a contract with Decca. An unsuccessful attempt to score a hit with a cover of Lonnie Donegan's 'Rock Island Line' was followed by a move towards pop novelty with 'Splish Splash'. Darin's quirky vocal ensured that his song was a worldwide hit, although

he was outsold in Britain by a rival version from comedian Charlie Drake. During this period, Darin also recorded in a group called the Ding Dongs, which prompted a dispute between Atco and Brunswick Records, culminating in the creation of a new group, the Rinky Dinks who were credited as the backing artists on his next single, 'Early In The Morning'. Neither that, nor its successor, 'Mighty Mighty', proved commercially viable, but the intervening Darin solo release, 'Queen Of The Hop', sold a million. The period charm of 'Plain Jane' presaged one of Darin's finest moments - the exceptional 'Dream Lover'. An enticing vocal performance allied to strong production took the song to number 1 in the UK and number 2 in the USA.

Already assured of considerable status as a pop artist, Darin dramatically changed direction with his next recording and emerged as a finger-clicking master of the supper club circuit. 'Mack The Knife', composed by Bertolt Brecht and Kurt Weill for the celebrated *Threepenny Opera*, proved a million seller and effectively raised Darin to new status as a 'serious singer' - he even compared himself favourably with Frank Sinatra, in what was a classic example of pop hubris. Darin's hit treatments of 'La Mer (Beyond The Sea)', 'Clementine', 'Won't You Come Home Bill Bailey?' and 'You Must Have Been A Beautiful Baby' revealed his ability to tackle variety material and transform it to his own ends.

In 1960, Darin adeptly moved into film and was highly praised for his roles in *Come September* (whose star Sandra Dee he later married), *State Fair, Too Late Blues, If A Man Answers, Pressure Point, Hell Is For Heroes* and *Captain Newman MD*. He returned to form as a pop performer with the lyrically witty 'Multiplication' and the equally clever 'Things'. In the meantime, he had recorded an album of Ray Charles' songs, including the standard 'What'd I Say'. During the beat boom era Darin briefly reverted to show tunes such as 'Baby Face' and 'Hello Dolly', but a further change of style beckoned with the folk-rock boom of 1965. Suddenly, Darin was a protest singer, summing up the woes of a generation with the surly 'We Didn't Ask To Be Brought Here'. Successful readings of Tim Hardin songs, including 'If I Were A Carpenter' and 'The Lady Came From Baltimore', and John Sebastian's 'Lovin' You' and 'Darling Be Home Soon' demonstrate his potential as a cover artist of seemingly limitless range. A more contemporary poet/political direction was evident on the album *Born Walden Robert Cassotto*, and its serious follow-up *Commitment*. As the 60s ended Darin was more actively involved in related business interests, although he still appeared regularly on television. One of the great vocal chameleons of pop music, Darin suffered from a weak heart and after several operations time finally caught up with the singer at Hollywood's Cedars of Lebanon Hospital in December 1973.

Albums: *Bobby Darin* (1959), *That's All* (1959), *This Is Darin* (1960), *Darin At The Copa* (1960), *For Teenagers Only* (1960), with Johnny Mercer *Two Of A Kind* (1961), *Love Swings* (1961), *Twist With Bobby Darin* (1962), *Darin Sings Ray Charles* (1962), *It's You Or No-One* (1962), *Oh Look At Me Now* (1962), *Earthy* (1962), *You're The Reason I'm Leaving* (1963), *Eighteen Yellow Roses* (1963), *From Hello Dolly To Goodbye Charlie* (1964), *Venice Blues* (1965), *In A Broadway Bag (Mame)* (1966), *If I Were A Carpenter* (1967), *Bobby Darin Something Special* (1967), *Born Walden Robert Cassotto* (1968), *Commitment* (1969). Compilations: *The Bobby Darin Story* (1961), *Things And Other Things* (1962), *Golden Folk Hits* (c.60s), *The Best Of Bobby Darin* (c.60s), *Greatest Moments* (1974), *The Versatile Bobby Darin* (1985), *The Legend Of Bobby Darin* (1985), *His Greatest Hits* (1985).

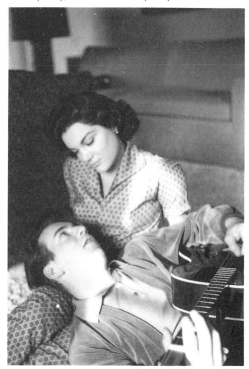

Bobby Darin and Connie Francis

Darren, James

b. James Ercolani, 3 October 1936, Philadelphia, Pennsylvania, USA. The photogenic actor/singer was signed to Columbia Pictures in the mid-50s, his first film being *Rumble On The Docks* in 1956. He first sang in the film *Gidget* in 1959 and the title song made the US chart. He starred in *Because They're Young* in 1960 and the epic *The Guns Of Navarone* in 1961. In 1962 he debuted in the US Top 20 with his lucky 13th single 'Goodbye Cruel World' and followed it with two more US Top 20 and UK Top 40 hits 'Her Royal Majesty', a Carole King song and 'Conscience', written by Barry Mann. Darren later recorded with little success on Warner Brothers in 1965, Kirshner in 1969, Buddah in 1970, MGM in 1973, Private Stock in 1975 (where he returned briefly to the US Top 100 in 1977) and RCA in 1978. This distinctively-voiced pop/MOR singer is perhaps now best remembered for playing the role of Tony Newman in the popular and often re-run 60s television series *The Time Tunnel*, although the memorable fairground atmosphere of 'Goodbye Cruel World' probably was his finest moment on record.

Albums: *Gidget Goes Hawaiian* (1961), *James Darren Vol 1* (c.60s), *Teenage Triangle* (1963), *Love Among the Young* (1962), *All* (1967).

Dave Dee, Dozy, Beaky, Mick And Tich

Formed in 1961 as Dave Dee And The Boston, this zany quintet found a settled hit line-up as: Dave Dee (b. David Harman, 17 December 1943, Salisbury, Wiltshire, England; vocals), Dozy (b. Trevor Davies, 27 November 1944, Enford, Wiltshire, England; bass), Beaky (b. John Dymond, 10 July 1944, Salisbury, Wiltshire, England; guitar), Mick (b. Michael Wilson, 4 March 1944, Amesbury, Wiltshire, England; lead guitar) and Tich (Ian Amey, 15 May 1944, Salisbury, Wiltshire, England). The group established their power as live performers during residencies at various Hamburg clubs in 1962. Their act featured rock 'n' roll spiced with comedy routines and an element of risque patter from their engaging frontman. While supporting the Honeycombs on a 1964 UK tour, they came to the attention of managers Howard & Blaikley (Ken Howard and Alan Blaikley) and were subsequently signed to Fontana Records by Jack Baverstock and assigned to producer Steve Rowland. After two unsuccessful singles, 'No Time' and 'All I Want', they hit the UK chart with the upbeat 'You Make It Move'. Thereafter, they had an incredible run of a dozen strong chart hits, all executed with a camp flair and costume-loving theatricalism that proved irresistible. With songs provided by Howard & Blaikley, they presented a veritable travelogue of pop, filled with melodramatic scenarios. 'Bend It' was their 'Greek' phase, and allowed Dave Dee to wiggle his little finger while uttering the curiously suggestive lyric; 'Zabadak' was an exotic arrangement sung in a unknown language; 'The Legend Of Xanadu' was a ripping yarn, which allowed Dee to brandish a bullwhip in live performance; 'Last Night In Soho' was a leather-boy motorbike saga portraying lost innocence in London's most notorious square mile.

The sheer diversity of the hits maintained the group's appeal but they lost ground at the end of the 60s and Dave Dee left for an unsuccessful solo career before venturing into A&R. The others continued as a quartet, but after one minor hit, 'Mr President', and an album, *Fresh Ear*, they broke up. A couple of brief nostalgic reunions later occurred, but not enough to encourage a serious re-launch.

Albums: *Dave Dee, Dozy, Beaky, Mick And Tich* (1966), *If Music Be The Food Of Love* (1967), *If No One Sang* (1968), *The Legend Of Dave Dee, Dozy, Beaky, Mick And Tich* (1969), *Together* (1969). Various hits compilations have been issued.

Dave Dee, Dozy, Beaky, Mick And Tich

David And Jonathan

Songwriting duo Roger Greenaway ('David') and Roger Cook ('Jonathan') began their partnership in 1965 after the demise of the former's beat group, the Kestrels, and enjoyed instant success when an early collaboration, 'You've Got Your Troubles', was a number 2 hit for the Fortunes. The pair began a performing/recording career at the end of the year, but paradoxically scored their first chart entry with a version of the Beatles''Michelle'. Although the Overlanders enjoyed a concurrent UK chart topper with the same song, David And Jonathan reached a respectable number 11, before securing a Top 10 slot with their self-penned follow-up, 'Lovers Of The World Unite'. Although the duo continued to record

under their adopted appellation, they found much greater commercial success with a series of crafted compositions including 'Gasoline Alley Bred' (the Hollies), 'Home Lovin' Man' (Andy Williams), 'I'd Like To Teach The World To Sing' (the New Seekers) and 'Something Tells Me (Somethin's Gonna Happen Tonight)' (Cilla Black). Such work was often undertaken with other songwriters, including Tony Macauley and Albert Hammond, but were copyrighted to the duo's Cookaway publishing company. Their commercial touch was maintained into the 70s with Blue Mink, a group comprising of session musicians fronted by Cook and Madeline Bell, and they remain one of the most efficacious pop songwriting teams the UK ever produced.

Albums: *David And Jonathan* (1966). Compilations: *Lovers Of The World Unite* aka *The Very Best Of David And Jonathan* (1984).

David And Jonathan

Davies, Cyril

b. 1932, Buckinghamshire, England, d. 7 January 1964. Along with Alexis Korner and Graham Bond, the uncompromising Davies was a seminal influence in the development of British R&B during the beat boom of the early 60s. His superb wailing and distorted harmonica shook the walls of many clubs up and down Britain. Initially he played with Alexis Korner's Blues Incorporated and then formed his own band, the All-Stars, featuring Long John Baldry, renowned session pianist Nicky Hopkins and drummer Mickey Waller. Their Chicago-based blues was raw, loud and exciting. Like Bond he died at a tragically young age, after losing his battle with leukaemia.

Album: *The Legendary Cyril Davies* (1970).

Davis, Billie

b. Carol Hedges, 1945, Woking, Surrey, England. Discovered by entrepreneur Robert Stigwood, this blue-eyed soul singer first came to chart prominence in 1962, duetting with Mike Sarne on the novelty hit, 'Will I What?'. The following year, she emerged in her own right with an upbeat rendition of the Exciters' 'Tell Him'. Although well poised to take advantage of the beat boom, Davis' strong voice proved insufficient to take the follow-up, 'He's The One' into the Top 30. Her romantic entanglement with former Shadows' guitarist Jet Harris gained considerable publicity, especially when both were involved in a car crash. With singles, however, further success proved elusive, although 'I Want You To Be My Baby' scraped into the lower chart regions in 1968. Thereafter, Davis concentrated strongly on the European market, particularly Spain, where she retained a healthy following.

Album: *Billie Davis* (1970).

Billie Davis

Davis, Sammy, Jnr.

b. 8 December 1925, Harlem, New York, USA, d. 16 May 1990, Los Angeles, California, USA. Davis Jnr. was a dynamic and versatile all-round entertainer and a trouper in the old-fashioned tradition. The only son of two dancers in a black vaudeville troupe, called Will Mastin's Holiday in Dixieland, Davis Jnr. made his professional debut with the group at the age of three, as 'Silent Sam, The Dancing Midget'. While still young he was coached by the legendary tap-dancer, Bill 'Bojangles' Robinson. Davis left the group in 1943 to serve in the US Army, where he encountered severe racial prejudice for the first, but not the last, time. After the war he rejoined his father

and adopted uncle in the Will Mastin Trio. By 1950 the Trio were headlining at venues such as the Capitol in New York and Ciro's in Hollywood with stars such as Jack Benny and Bob Hope, but it was Davis who was receiving the standing ovations for his singing, dancing, drumming, comedy and apparently inexhaustible energy. In 1954 he signed for Decca Records, and released two albums, *Starring Sammy Davis Jr*, (number 1 in the US chart), featuring his impressions of stars such as Dean Martin and Jerry Lewis, Johnnie Ray and Jimmy Durante; and *Just For Lovers*. He also made the US singles chart with 'Hey There', from *The Pajama Game* and in the same year he lost his left eye in a road accident. When he returned to performing in January 1955 wearing an eyepatch he was greeted even more enthusiastically than before. During that year he continued to reach the US Top 20 with 'Something's Gotta Give', 'Love Me Or Leave Me' and 'That Old Black Magic'. In 1956 he made his Broadway debut in the musical *Mr Wonderful*, music and lyrics by Jerry Bock, Larry Holofiener and George Weiss. Also in the show were the rest of the Will Mastin Trio, Sammy's uncle and Davis Snr. The show ran for nearly 400 performances and produced two hits, 'Too Close For Comfort', and the title song, which was very successful for Peggy Lee. Although generally regarded as the first popular American black performer to become acceptable to both black and white audiences, Davis attracted heavy criticism in 1956 over his conversion to Judaism, and later for his marriage to Swedish actress Mai Britt. He described himself as a 'one-eyed Jewish nigger'. Apart from a few brief appearances when he was very young, Davis started his film career in 1958 with *Anna Lucasta*, and was critically acclaimed in the following year for his performance as Sporting Life in *Porgy And Bess*. By this time Davis was a leading member of Frank Sinatra's 'inner circle', called variously, the 'Clan', or the 'Rat Pack'. He appeared with Sinatra in three movies, *Ocean's Eleven* (1960), *Sergeants 3* (1962), and *Robin And The Seven Hoods* (1964), but made, perhaps, a greater impact when he co-starred with another member of the 'Clan', Shirley MacLaine, in the Cy Coleman and Dorothy Fields' film musical, *Sweet Charity*. The 60s were good times for Davis, who was enormously popular on records and television, but especially 'live', at Las Vegas and in concert. In 1962 he made the US chart with the Anthony Newley/Leslie Bricusse number, 'What Kind Of Fool Am I?', and thereafter featured several of the their songs in his act. He sang Bricusse's nominated song, 'Talk To The Animals', at the 1967 Academy Awards ceremony, and collected the Oscar, on behalf of the songwriter, when it won. And in 1972, he had a million-selling hit record with the Newley/Bricusse song, 'The Candy Man', from the film, *Willy Wonka And The*

Chocolate Factory. He appeared again on Broadway in 1964 in *Golden Boy*, Charles Strouse and Lee Adams' musical adaptation of Clifford Odet's 1937 drama of a young man torn between the boxing ring and his violin. Also in the cast was Billy Daniels. The show ran for 569 performances in New York, and went to London in 1968. During the 70s he worked less, suffering, it is said, as a result of previous alcohol and drug abuse. He entertained US troops in the Lebanon in 1983, and five years later undertook an arduous comeback tour of the USA and Canada with Sinatra and Dean Martin. In 1989 he travelled further, touring Europe with the show, *The Ultimate Event*, along with Liza Minnelli and Sinatra. While he was giving everything to career favourites such as 'Birth Of The Blues', 'Mr Bojangles' and 'Old Black Magic' he was already ill, although he did not let it show. He died in May 1990.

Selected albums: *Starring Sammy Davis Jr* (1955), *Just For Lovers* (1955), *Mr. Wonderful* (1956, film soundtrack), *Here's Looking At You* (late 50s), with Carmen McRae *Boy Meets Girl* (late 50s), *It's All Over But The Swingin'* (late 50s), *Mood To Be Wooed* (late 50s), *All The Way And Then Some* (late 50s), *Sammy Davis Jr. At Town Hall* (1959), *Porgy And Bess* (1959), *Sammy Awards* (1960), *I Got A Right To Swing* (1960), *What Kind Of Fool Am I And Other Show-Stoppers* (1962), *Sammy Davis Jr. At The Cocoanut Grove* (1963), *As Long As She Needs Me* (1963), *Sammy Davis Jr. Salutes The Stars Of The London Palladium* (1964), *The Shelter Of Your Arms* (1964), with Count Basie *Our Shining Hour* (1965), *Sammy's Back On Broadway* (1965), *I've Gotta Be Me* (1969), *Sammy Davis Jr. Now* (1972), *Portrait Of Sammy Davis Jr.* (1972), *It's A Musical World* (1976), *The Song And Dance Man* (1977), *Sammy Davis Jr. In Person 1977* (1983), *Closest Of Friends* (1984). Compilations: *The Best Of Sammy Davis Jr.* (1982), *Collection* (1989), *The Great Sammy Davis Jr.* (1989).

Further reading: *Yes I Can*, Sammy Davis Jnr. *Why Me?*, Sammy Davis Jnr.

Davis, Spencer, Group

Formed in Birmingham in 1962 as the Rhythm And Blues Quartet the group featured Spencer Davis (b. 17 July 1942, Swansea, South Wales; guitar/vocals), Steve Winwood (b. 12 May 1948, Birmingham, England; guitar/organ/vocals), Muff Winwood (b. Mervyn Winwood, 15 June 1943, Birmingham, England; bass) and Pete York (b. 15 August 1942, Middlesbrough, Cleveland, England; drums). School teacher Davis, the elder Winwood brother and drummer York were already experienced performers with backgrounds in trad jazz, blues, modern jazz and skiffle. The group were gradually dwarfed by the younger Winwood's immense natural musical talent. While they were much in demand on the fast-

Spencer Davis Group

growing club scene as performers, their bluesy/pop records failed to sell, until they made a breakthrough in 1965 with 'Keep On Running', which reached number 1 in the UK. This was followed in quick succession by another chart-topper, 'Somebody Help Me', and three more notable hits 'When I Come Home', 'Gimme Some Lovin'', and 'I'm A Man'. In keeping with 60s pop tradition they also appeared in a low budget British film, *The Ghost Goes Gear*. Throughout their career they were managed by Chris Blackwell, founder of Island Records.

Amid press reports and months of speculation, Steve Winwood finally left to form Traffic in 1967. A soundtrack album *Here We Go Round The Mulberry Bush*, released that year, ironically had both Traffic and the Spencer Davis Group sharing the billing. Muff Winwood also left, joining Island as head of A&R. Spencer Davis soldiered on with the addition of Phil Sawyer, who was later replaced by Ray Fenwick from After Tea (guitar) and Eddie Hardin (keyboards). The latter had an uncannily similar voice to Steve Winwood. They were unable to maintain their previous success but had two further minor hits, 'Mr Second Class' and the richly psychedelia-phased 'Time Seller'. After a number of line-up changes including Dee Murray and Nigel Olsson, Hardin And York departed to form their own band, and enjoyed some success mainly on the continent during the progressive boom of 1969-70. Spencer Davis eventually went to live in America where he became involved in the business side, working in A&R for various major record companies. The Davis/York/Hardin/Fenwick team reformed briefly in 1973 with the addition of Charlie McCracken on bass, formerly with Taste, and made a further two albums. The infectious single 'Catch Me On The Rebop' almost become a belated hit. Today, York can still be found playing in various jazz style bands; his acknowledged talent as a drummer being regularly in demand. Spencer Davis is still making the occasional album from his base on the west coast of America. Muff Winwood is presently head of Artist Development at CBS Records and among his signings have been Shakin' Stevens, Bros, Paul Young and Terence Trent D'Arby. Steve Winwood after progressing through Blind Faith and Air Force is currently one of the most popular recording artists in the world.

Albums: *The First Album* (1965), *The Second Album* (1966), *Autumn '66* (1966), *Here We Go Round The Mulberry Bush* (1967), *With Their New Face On* (1967), *Gluggo* (1973), *Living In The Back Street* (1974). Compilation: *The Best Of The Spencer Davis Group* (1968).

Further reading: *Keep On Running: The Steve Winwood Story*, Chris Welch. *Back in The High Life: A Biography of Steve Winwood*, Alan Clayson.

Dee, Joey, And The Starliters

The US group that helped revitalize the Twist were Joey Dee (b. Joseph DiNicola, 11 June 1940, Passaic, New Jersey, USA; vocals), Carlton Latimer (keyboards), Willie Davis (drums), Larry Vernieri (backing vocals) and David Brigati (backing vocals). Formed in 1958, this lively and entertaining group took up residency at New York's famed Peppermint Lounge club in 1960, the year of their first recordings on Bonus and Scepter. In late 1961, a year after Chubby Checker's 'The Twist' topped the US chart, the wealthy socialites who frequented the club belatedly discovered the dance. Dee incorporated it into his act and even wrote a special club song 'Peppermint Twist'. The memorable, uplifting single shot to the top of the charts and *Doin' The Twist At The Peppermint Lounge* reached number 2. In 1962 the group, which now included a 10-piece dance team, starred in the low-budget films *Hey Let's Twist* and *Vive Le Twist* with the soundtrack album and title track of the former both hitting the US Top 20. They followed this with a breakneck version of the Isley Brothers' 'Shout', which reached number 6. Dee appeared in the film *Two Tickets To Paris* and his solo version of Johnny Nash's 'What Kind Of Love is This?', taken from it, became his fourth and final Top 20 entry in 1962. In all, this distinctive group, which never graced the UK Top 20, notched up nine US chart singles and three albums between 1961 and 1963. Dee opened his own club The Starliter in New York in 1964. That year he formed a new band which included Gene Cornish, Felix Cavaliere and Eddie Brigati, who became the very successful (Young) Rascals and a couple of years later he hired guitarist Jimi Hendrix for the group. Dee recorded on Jubilee in 1966 and Janus in 1973 and is now the spokesman of an association representing American 'oldies' acts.

Albums: *Doin' The Twist At The Peppermint Lounge* (1961), *Hey, Let's Twist* (1962), *Back At The Peppermint Lounge-Twistin* (1962), *All The World Is Twistin'* (1962), *Two Tickets To Paradise* (1962, film soundtrack), *Joey Dee* (1963), *Dance, Dance, Dance* (1963).

Deene, Carol

b. 1944, Thurnscoe, Yorkshire, England. The daughter of a singing miner. The clean-cut pop singer moved to London at the age of 16 and, after appearing on the Joan Regan television show in 1961, was snapped-up by HMV. Deene had four UK Top 50 entries in a 12-month period, all with cover versions, but none made the Top 20. The songs were 'Sad Movies' and 'Norman' (which were both John D. Loudermilk songs which had been US hits by Sue Thompson), 'Johnny Get Angry' (a US hit for Joanie Sommers) and 'Some People', which was originally performed by UK act Valerie Mountain & The Eagles in the film of the same name. In 1962 she had her own series as a disc jockey on Radio Luxembourg and was seen in the Acker Bilk film *Band Of Thieves*. She later had unsuccessful releases on Columbia in 1966, CBS in 1968, Conquest in 1969, Pye in 1970; and re-appeared in the late 70s on the Koala and Rim labels.

Deep Purple

Deep Purple

Deep Purple evolved in 1968 following sessions to form a group around former Searchers' drummer

Chris Curtis (b. 26 August 1942, Liverpool, England). Jon Lord (b. 9 June 1941, Leicester, England; keyboards) and Nick Simper (bass), veterans, respectively, of the Artwoods and Johnny Kidd And The Pirates, joined guitarist Ritchie Blackmore (b. 14 April 1945, Weston-super-Mare, England) in rehearsals for this new act, initially dubbed Roundabout. Curtis dropped out within days, and when Dave Curtis (bass) and Bobby Woodman (drums) also proved incompatible, two members of Maze, Rod Evans (vocals) and Ian Paice (drums), replaced them. Having adopted the Deep Purple name following a brief Scandinavian tour, the quintet began recording their debut album, which they patterned on USA group Vanilla Fudge. *Shades Of Deep Purple* thus included dramatic rearrangements of well-known songs, including 'Hey Joe' and 'Hush', the latter of which became a US Top 5 hit when issued as a single. Lengthy tours ensued as the group, all but ignored at home, steadfastly courted the burgeoning American concert circuit. *The Book Of Taliesyn* and *Deep Purple* also featured several excellent reworkings, notably of 'Kentucky Woman' (Neil Diamond) and 'River Deep Mountain High' (Ike And Tina Turner), but the unit also drew acclaim for its original material and the dramatic interplay between Lord and Blackmore. In July 1969 both Evans and Simper were axed from the line-up, which was then buoyed by the arrival of Ian Gillan (b. 19 August 1945, Hounslow, Middlesex, England; vocals) and Roger Glover (b. 30 November 1945, Brecon, Wales; bass) from the pop group Episode Six. Acknowledged by aficionados as the 'classic' Deep Purple line-up, the reshaped quintet made its album debut on the grandiose *Concerto For Group And Orchestra*, scored by Lord and recorded with the London Philharmonic Orchestra. Its orthodox successor, *Deep Purple In Rock*, established the group as a leading heavy-metal attraction and included such now-established favourites as 'Speed King' and 'Child In Time'. Gillan's powerful intonation brought a third dimension to their sound and this new-found popularity in the UK was enhanced when an attendant single, 'Black Night', reached number 2. 'Strange Kind Of Woman' followed it into the Top 10, while *Fireball* and *Machine Head* topped their respective chart. The latter included the riff-laden 'Smoke On The Water', now lauded as a seminal example of the hard rock oeuvre, and was the first release on the group's own Purple label. Although the platinum-selling *Made In Japan* captured their live prowess in full flight, relations within the band grew increasingly strained, and *Who Do We Think We Are?* marked the end of this highly-successful line-up. The departures of Gillan and Glover robbed Deep Purple of an expressive frontman and imaginative arranger, although Dave Coverdale (b. 22 September 1949,

Saltburn, Lancashire, England; vocals) and Glenn Hughes (late of Trapeze, bass) brought a new impetus to the act. *Burn* and *Stormbringer* both reached the Top 10, but Blackmore grew increasingly dissatisfied with the group's direction and in May 1975 left to form Rainbow. USA guitarist Tommy Bolin, formerly of the James Gang, joined Deep Purple for *Come Taste The Band*, but his jazz/soul style was incompatible with the group's heavy metal sound, and a now-tiring act folded in 1976 following a farewell UK tour. Coverdale then formed Whitesnake, Paice and Lord joined Tony Ashton in Paice Ashton And Lord, while Bolin tragically died of a heroin overdose within months of Purple's demise. Judicious archive and 'best of' releases kept the group in the public eye, as did the high profile enjoyed by its several ex-members. Pressure for a reunion bore fruit in 1984 when Gillan, Lord, Blackmore, Glover and Paice completed *Perfect Strangers*. A second set, *House Of Blue Lights*, ensued but recurring animosity between Gillan and Blackmore resulted in the singer's departure following the in-concert *Nobody's Perfect*. Former Rainbow vocalist, Joe Lynn Turner, was brought into the line-up for *Slaves And Masters* as Purple steadfastly maintained their revitalized career.

Albums: *Shades Of Deep Purple* (1968), *The Book Of Taliesyn* (1969), *Deep Purple* (1969), *Concerto For Group And Orchestra* (1970), *Deep Purple In Rock* (1970), *Fireball* (1971), *Machine Head* (1972), *Made In Japan* (1972), *Who Do We Think We Are?* (1973), *Burn* (1974), *Stormbringer* (1974), *Come Taste The Band* (1975), *Perfect Strangers* (1985), *House Of Blue Light* (1987), *Nobody's Perfect* (1988), *Slaves And Masters* (1990). Compilations: *Purple Passages* (1972), *24 Carat Purple* (1975), *Made In Europe* (1976), *Last Concert In Japan* (1977), *Powerhouse* (1978), *Singles: As & Bs* (1978), *When We Rock We Rock When We Roll We Roll* (1978), *Deepest Purple* (1980), *Live In London: Deep Purple* (1982), *Anthology: Deep Purple* (1985), *Scandinavian Nights* (1988), *Knebworth '85* (1991).

Dekker, Desmond

b. Desmond Dacris, 16 July 1942, Kingston, Jamaica. Dacris spent much of his orphaned childhood near Seaforth in St. Thomas before returning to Kingston, where he worked as a welder. His workmates encouraged him to seek a recording audition and after receiving rejections from leading producers Clement Dodd and Duke Reid, he found a mentor in the influential Leslie Kong. In 1963, the newly named Dekker released his first single 'Honour Your Father And Mother', which was also issued in the UK courtesy of Chris Blackwell's Island label. During the same period, Dekker teamed up with his backing group the Aces. Dekker enjoyed enormous success in Jamaica during the mid-late 60s with a formidable run of 20 number 1 hits to his credit.

Desmond Dekker

The emergence of rock steady in the latter half of 1966 propelled his James Bond inspired '007 (Shanty Town)' into the UK charts the following year. A catchy, rhythmically infectious articulation of the 'rude boy' street gang shenanigans, the single presaged Dekker's emergence as an internationally famous artist. In 1967, Dekker came second in the Jamaican Song Festival with 'Unity' and continued his chart-topping run in his home country with such titles as 'Hey Grandma', 'Music Like Dirt', 'Rudie Got Soul', 'Rude Boy Train' and 'Sabotage'.

1969 proved the year of Dekker's greatest international success. 'Get up in the morning, slaving for bread, sir, so that every mouth can be fed', was a patois-sung opening line which entranced and confused pop listeners on both sides of the Atlantic. The intriguing 'Israelites' was a club hit the previous year and by the spring of 1969 had become the first rock steady song to top the UK charts, a considerable achievement for the period. Even more astonishing was its Top 10 success in the USA, a country that had previously proved commercially out-of-bounds to Jamaican performers. Back in Britain, Dekker's follow up was the Top 10 hit 'It Mek'. Originally recorded the previous year under the title 'I It Mek', the track was remixed with additional brass and vocal dubs for UK chart consumption. Roughly translated as 'That's Why It Happened', 'It Mek' was inspired by

Desmond's sister Elaine, who fell off a wall at her home and cried 'like ice water'. Dekker enjoyed translating everyday observations in sharp, incisive lines. 'Israelites' similarly articulated the plight of the downtrodden working man, while 'Problems' was a rousing protest number with the refrain '*everyday* is problems'.

Dekker's success in the UK, buoyed by consistent touring, spearheaded the arrival of a number of Jamaican chart singles by such artists as the Harry J's All Stars, the Upsetters and the Pioneers. Until the arrival of Bob Marley, Dekker remained the most famous reggae artist on the international scene.

By 1969, Dekker had taken up residence in the UK where he was a regular club performer and continued to record his vocals over rhythm tracks recorded in Jamaica. A further minor success with 'Pickney Gal' was followed by a massive number 2 hit with the Jimmy Cliff composition 'You Can Get It If You Really Want', from the film *The Harder They Come*. When Dekker's long term manager/producer Kong died from heart failure in 1971, the artist joined the Cactus label. A reissue of 'Israelites' restored him to the UK Top 10 in 1975 and was followed by the pop/reggae 'Sing A Little Song', which reached number 16. During the 2-Tone phase in 1980, Dekker recorded *Black And Dekker* with Graham Parker's Rumour, but the experiment was not commercially successful. A follow-up, also on Stiff Records, *Compass Point*, was his last major attempt at chart action, though he remained a perennial performer of old hit material and has frequently been featured on compilation albums. In 1984, he was found bankrupt by a British court, and he publicly complained that he had failed to receive funds from his former manager. It was a sad moment for one of reggae's best-known personalities. His unmistakable falsetto vocal remains one of rock steady's most memorable, while his pioneering importance as the first major reggae artist to achieve international success deserves acknowledgement

Albums: *007 (Shanty Town)* (1967), *The Israelites* (1969), *This Is Desmond Dekker* (1969), *You Can Get It If You Really Want* (1970), *Black And Dekker* (1980), *Compass Point* (1981). Compilations: *Double Dekker* (1974), *Israelites* (1975), *Dekker's Sweet 16 Hits* (1978), *Original Reggae Hitsound* (1985), *Officially Live And Rare* (1987).

Denver, Karl

b. Angus McKenzie, 16 December 1934, Glasgow, Scotland. Denver, a former merchant seaman, was aged 23 before he began a career in show business. During his travels the singer accumulated a love of contrasting folk forms and his repertoire consisted of traditional material from the Middle East, Africa and China. Denver's flexible voice spanned several octaves and his unusual inflections brought much contemporary comment. The artist enjoyed four UK Top 10 hits during 1961/62, including 'Marcheta' and 'Wimoweh', the latter reaching number 4. Denver continued to enjoy minor chart success over the next two years, but he progressively turned to cabaret work. The singer has been based in Manchester for many years, which in part explains 'Lazyitis (One Armed Boxer)', his 1989 collaboration with the city's neo-psychedelic favourites, the Happy Mondays.

Albums: *Karl Denver* (1962), *Wimoweh* (early-60s), *Karl Denver At The Yew Tree* (early-60s), *With Love* (early-60s), *Karl Denver* (1970).

Karl Denver

DeShannon, Jackie

b. 21 August 1944, Hazel, Kentucky, USA. This highly talented singer and songwriter was introduced to gospel, country and blues styles while still a child. She was actively performing by the age of 15 and, having travelled to Los Angeles, commenced a recording career in 1960 with a series of releases on minor labels. Jackie's collaborations with Sharon Sheeley resulted in several superior pop songs including 'Dum Dum' and 'Heart In Hand' for Brenda Lee and 'Trouble' for the Kalin Twins. DeShannon then forged equally fruitful partnerships with Jack Nitzsche and Randy Newman, the former of which spawned 'When You Walk In The Room',

a 1964 smash for the Searchers. Resultant interest in the UK inspired several television appearances and DeShannon's London sojourn was also marked by several songwriting collaborations with Jimmy Page. Despite a succession of excellent singles, Jackie's own recording career failed to achieve similar heights, although her work continued to be covered by, Helen Shapiro, Marianne Faithfull, the Byrds and the Critters. DeShannon enjoyed a US Top 10 single with the Burt Bacharach/Hal David-penned 'What The World Needs Now Is Love' (1965), but her biggest hit came four years later when 'Put A Little Love In Your Heart' reached number 4 in the same chart. Although she continued to write and record superior pop, as evinced on *Jackie* and *Your Baby Is A Lady*, DeShannon was unable to sustain the same profile during the 70s and 80s. Her songs continued to provide hits for others, notably 'Bette Davis Eyes' (with Kim Carnes, 1981), 'Breakaway' (Tracey Ullman, 1983) and 'Put A Little Love In Your Heart' (Annie Lennox and Al Green, 1988). Jackie DeShannon's position as one of the 60s leading composers remains undiminished.

Albums: *Jackie DeShannon* (1963), *Breakin' It Up On The Beatles Tour* (1964), *Don't Turn Your Back On Me* (1964), *Surf Party* (1964, film soundtrack), *This Is Jackie DeShannon* (1965), *You Won't Forget Me* (1965), *In The Wind* (1965), *C'Mon Let's Live A Little* (1966, film soundtrack), *Are You Ready For This?* (1966), *New Image* (1967), *For You* (1967), *Me About You* (1968), *What The World Needs Now Is Love* (1968), *Laurel Canyon* (1969), *Put A Little Love In Your Heart* (1969), *To Be Free* (1969), *Songs* (1971), *Jackie* (1972), *Your Baby Is A Lady* (1974), *New Arrangement* (1975), *You're The Only Dancer* (1977), *Quick Touches* (1978). Compilations: *You Won't Forget Me* (1965), *Lonely Girl* (1970).

Deviants

Originally known as the Social Deviants, this pioneering British underground group merged R&B, pseudo-politics and an amateurism inspired by New York radicals, the Fugs. The 'Social' prefix was dropped in 1967 with the departure of Clive Muldoon and Pete Munroe, while the remaining core, Mick Farren (vocals), Sid Bishop (guitar), Cord Rees (bass) and Russell Hunter (drums) began work on the Deviants' debut album, *Ptooff*. This characteristically rabblehouse collection was initially issued on the group's own label and distributed through the network purveying the era's alternative publications, *International Times* and *Oz*. Rees was replaced by Duncan Sanderson for *Disposable*, memorable for Farren's call-to-arms composition, 'Let's Loot The Supermarket'. Canadian guitarist Paul Rudolph joined the group on Bishop's departure and the reconstituted quartet completed *Deviants* prior to embarking for America. Farren was fired during the tour and on their return his former colleagues dropped their erstwhile name and became the Pink Fairies upon the addition of former Pretty Things' drummer Twink. Farren, who pursued a multi-faceted career as a novelist, rock journalist and sometime musician, later re-established the Deviants' appellation for an EP, *Screwed Up* (1977) and an informal live performance captured on the *Human Garbage* album.

Albums: *Ptooff* (1967), *Disposable* (1968), *Deviants* (1969), *Human Garbage* (1984).

Diamond, Neil

b. 24 January 1941, Brooklyn, New York, USA. With a career as a hitmaker stretching across three decades, Diamond has veered between straightforward pop, a progressive singer-songwriter style and middle-of-the-road balladry. He attended the same high school as Neil Sedaka and Bobby Feldman of the Strangeloves and began songwriting as a young teenager. He made his first records in 1960 for local label Duel with Jack Packer as Neil And Jack. After college, Diamond became a full-time songwriter in 1962, recording unsuccessfully for CBS before 'Sunday And Me' produced by Leiber And Stoller for Jay And The Americans brought his first success as a composer in 1965. The following year, Diamond made a third attempt at a recording career, joining Bert Berns' Bang label. With Jeff Barry and Ellie Greenwich as producers, he released 'Solitary Man' before the catchy 'Cherry Cherry' entered the US Top 10. In 1967 the Monkees had multi million-sellers with Diamond's memorable 'I'm A Believer' and 'A Little Bit Me, A little Bit You'. Like his own 1967 hit, 'Thank The Lord For The Night', these songs combined a gospel feel with a memorable pop melody. In the same year, Diamond also showed his mastery of the country-tinged ballad with 'Kentucky Woman'.

After a legal dispute with Bang, Diamond signed to MCA Records' Uni label, moving from New York to Los Angeles. After a failed attempt at a progressive rock album (*Velvet Gloves And Spit*) he began to record in Memphis and came up with a series of catchy, and simple hits, including 'Sweet Caroline' (1969), 'Holly Holy' and two number 1s, 'Cracklin' Rosie' (1970) and 'Song Sung Blue' (1972). At the same time, Diamond was extending his range with the semi-concept album *Tap Root Manuscript* (on which Hollywood arranger Marty Paich orchestrated African themes) and the confessional ballad, 'I Am . . . I Said', a Top 10 single on both sides of the Atlantic. He was also much in demand for live shows and his dynamic act was captured on *Hot August Night*. Soon after its release, Diamond announced a temporary retirement from live appearances, and

spent the next three years concentrating on writing and recording. He moved into film work, winning a Grammy award for the soundtrack of *Jonathan Livingston Seagull* to which his long-time arranger Lee Holdridge also contributed. *Beautiful Noise* (on his new label, CBS) was a tribute to the Brill Building songwriting world of the 50s and 60s. It cost nearly half a million dollars to make and was produced by Robbie Robertson. Diamond also appeared in *The Last Waltz*, the star-studded tribute movie to the Band.

In 1978, he recorded his first duet since 1960 and his biggest hit single. The wistful 'You Don't Bring Me Flowers' had previously been recorded solo by both Diamond and Barbra Streisand but after a disc jockey had spliced the tracks together, producer Bob Gaudio brought the pair together for the definitive version which headed the US chart. Now at the peak of his success, Diamond accepted his first film acting role in a re-make of *The Jazz Singer*. The film was undistinguished although Diamond's performance was credible. The soundtrack album sold a million, in part because of 'America', a rousing, patriotic Diamond composition which he later performed at the Statue Of Liberty centenary celebrations. During the 80s, he increasingly co-wrote songs with Gilbert Becaud, David Foster and above all Carole Bayer Sager and Burt Bacharach. They collaborated on the ballad 'Heartlight' (1982), inspired by the film *E.T.* The next year, UB 40 revived one of his earliest songs 'Red Red Wine' and had a UK number 1. There were also disputes with CBS, which insisted on changes to two of Diamond's proposed albums, bringing in Maurice White to produce *Headed For The Future*. However, 'The Best Years Of Our Lives', written by Diamond alone, showed a return to the form of the 70s while he worked on his 1991 album with leading contemporary producers Don Was and Peter Asher. Diamond has neither courted nor has been fully accepted by the *cognoscenti*, his track record however speaks volumes; almost 60 hits in the USA, over 30 charting albums and is one of the Top 20 most successful artists ever in the USA. His success in the UK is comparable with 26 charting albums and a fiercely loyal fan base.

Albums: *The Feel Of Neil Diamond* (1966), *Just For You* (1967), *Velvet Gloves And Spit* (1968), *Brother Love's Travelling Salvation Show* (1969), *Touching You, Touching Me* (1969), *Gold* (1970), *Shilo* (1970), *Tap Root Manuscript* (1970), *Do It* (1971), *Stones* (1971), *Moods* (1972), *Hot August Night* (1972), *Double Gold* (1973), *Rainbow* (1973), *Jonathan Livingston Seagull* (1974), *Serenade* (1974), *Beautiful Noise* (1976), *And The Singer Sings His Song* (1976), *Love At The Greek* (1977), *I'm Glad You're Here With Me Tonight* (1977), *You Don't Bring Me Flowers* (1978), *September Morn* (1980), *The Jazz Singer* (1980), *On The Way To The*

Sky (1981), *Heartlight* (1982), *Primitive* (1984), *Headed For The Future* (1986), *Hot August II* (1987), *The Best Years Of Our Lives* (1989), *Lovescape* (1991). Selected compilations: *20 Golden Greats* (1978), *Diamonds* (1981), *Classics: The Early Years* (1983), *Red Red Wine* (1988), *Touching You Touching Me* (1988).

Dick And Dee Dee

This American boy/girl vocal duo was formed in 1961 by Dick St John Gostine (b. 1944, Santa Monica, California, USA) and Dee Dee Sperling (b. 1945, Santa Monica, California, USA) while they were at a local high school. The Gostine-written 'The Mountain's High' was originally released on the small local label Lama, but was picked up by Liberty and became a US hit. Gostine had already made some solo recordings for the label. The fact that they were still at college while this happened precluded touring, however. Visually, the duo dressed as high school kids for an end of term 'prom', and remained highly popular in the US for several years. They switched to Warner Brothers in 1962, and had several more hits before fading out of fashion in the mid-60s. Afterwards they retired from pop music.
Albums: *Songs We've Sung On Shindig* (c.60s), *Tell Me The Mountain's High* (c.60s), *Thou Shalt Not Steal* (c.60s), *Turn Around* (c.60s), *Young And In Love* (c.60s).

Diddley, Bo

b. Elias Bates (later known as Elias McDaniel), 30 December 1928, McComb, Mississippi, USA. After beginning his career as a boxer, where he received the soubriquet 'Bo Diddley', the singer worked the blues clubs of Chicago with a repertoire influenced by Louis Jordan, John Lee Hooker and Muddy Waters. In late 1954, he teamed up with Billy Boy Arnold and recorded demos of 'I'm A Man' and 'Bo Diddley'. Re-recorded at Chess Studios with a backing ensemble comprising Otis Spann (piano), Lester Davenport (harmonica), Frank Kirkland (drums) and Jerome Green (maraccas), the a-side 'Bo Diddley' became an R&B hit in 1955. Before long, Diddley's distorted, amplified, custom-made guitar, with its rectangular shape and pumping rhythm style became a familiar, much-imitated trademark, as did his self-referential songs with such titles as 'Bo Diddley's A Gunslinger', 'Diddley Daddy' and 'Bo's A Lumberjack'. His jive-talking routine with 'Say Man' (a US Top 20 hit in 1959) and 'Pretty Thing' and 'Hey Good Lookin'', which reached the lower regions of the UK charts in 1963. By then, Diddley was regarded as something of an R&B legend and found a new lease of life courtesy of the UK beat boom. The Pretty Things named themselves after one of his songs while his work was covered by such artists as the Rolling Stones, Animals, Manfred Mann,

Bo Diddley

Kinks, Yardbirds, Downliner's Sect and the Zephyrs. Diddley subsequently jammed on albums by Chuck Berry and Muddy Water,s and appeared infrequently at rock festivals. His classic version of 'Who Do You Love' became a staple cover for a new generation of USA acts ranging from Quicksilver Messenger Service to the Doors, Tom Rush and Bob Seger, while the UK's Juicy Lucy took the song into the UK Top 20.
Like many of his generation, Diddley attempted to update his image and in the mid-70s released *The Black Gladiator* in the uncomfortable guise of an ageing funkster. *Where It All Begins*, produced by Johnny Otis (whose hit 'Willie And The Hand Jive' owed much to Diddley's style), was probably the most interesting of his post 60s albums. In 1979, Diddley toured with the Clash and in 1984 took a cameo roll in the film *Trading Places*. A familiar face on the revival circuit, Diddley is rightly regarded as a seminal figure in the history of rock 'n' roll. His continued appeal to younger performers was emphasized by Craig McLachlan's hit recording of 'Mona' in 1990.
Albums: *Bo Diddley* (1962), *Go Bo Diddley* (1962), *Bo Diddley Is A Gunslinger* (1963), *Hey Bo Diddley* (1963), *Bo Diddley* (c.60s), *Bo Diddley Rides Again* (1963), *Bo Diddley's Beach Party* (1963), *Bo Diddley Goes Surfing* (1963), *Bo Diddley In The Spotlight*

(c.60s), *Hey Good Looking* (1964), *Let Me Pass* (1965), *The Originator* (c.60s), *Superblues* (c.60s), *The Super Super Blues Band* (1968), *Big Bad Bo* (1974), *Another Dimension* (1971), *The Bo Diddley London Sessions* (1973), *Two Guitar Greats* (1974), *The Black Gladiator* (1975), *Where It All Begins* (c.70s), *The 20th Anniversary Of Rock 'N' Roll* (1976), *Hey Bo Diddley* (1986). Various compilations have also been issued.

Dion

Dion And The Belmonts

b. Dion DiMucci, 18 July 1939, Bronx, New York, USA. During his peak, from 1958-63, Dion was the quintessential Italian-American New York City rocker and was, perhaps, the first major white rock singer who was not from a southern city. The career of one of America's legendary artists has spanned five decades, during which time he has made numerous musical style changes. Between 1958 and 1960 Dion And The Belmonts were one of the leading doo-wop groups. The Belmonts comprised Angelo D'Aleo (b. 3 February 1940, Bronx, New York, USA), Carlo Mastrangelo (b. 5 October 1938, Bronx, New York, USA), and Freddie Milano (b. 22 August 1939, Bronx, New York, USA). The slick besuited Italian look rivalled the black harmony groups that dominated the era. They had nine hits in two years, including two of the all-time great examples of white doo-wop, 'I Wonder Why' and 'No One Knows'. Their classic reading of the Doc Pomus and Mort

Shuman song 'Teenager in Love' with the memorable line of teenage despair; 'each night I ask, the stars up above, (bom, bom, bom, bom), why must I be a teenager in love?' It poignantly articulated growing pains in an era when conservative values were being challenged by a new moral climate.

In 1960 they attempted a version of 'When You Wish Upon A Star' from Walt Disney's *Pinocchio* and followed with a worthy cover of Cole Porter's 'In The Still Of The Night'. Dion left for a solo career in 1960 and immediately scored in the USA with 'Lonely Teenager'. The following year he had two consecutive hits that made him one of America's biggest artists. Both 'Runaround Sue' and 'The Wanderer' are rock classics; the former, warning everybody to keep away from Sue, while the latter warns Flo, Jane and Mary to steer clear of the wanderer. The similarity of the theme can be forgiven as they are both wonderfully uplifting songs, great dance records and two of the finest of the era. Dion sustained an incredible output of hits; in 1963 with seven major singles he was in the US charts for the entire year. In 1964 Dion disappeared from the scene to fight a serious addiction to heroin, a drug to which he had fallen victim in 1960. Although he and the Belmonts reunited briefly in 1967, little was heard of him until December 1968. He returned during a turbulent year in American history, the escalation of the Vietnam War had received strong opposition, particularly from the music world; and the assassination of Robert Kennedy was fresh in peoples' minds. The emotional Dick Holler song, 'Abraham, Martin And John' was a perfectly timed stroke of genius. This lilting folksy ballad barley left a dry eye as it climbed to number 4 in the US charts.

The following year a heroin-free Dion delighted festival and concert audiences with a striking solo act, accompanied on acoustic guitar. That same year the excellent *Dion* was released, including sensitive covers of songs by Bob Dylan, Joni Mitchell, Leonard Cohen, and a brave attempt at Jimi Hendrix's 'Purple Haze'. Dion's critical ranking was high but his commercial standing dwindled, and two acoustic-based albums were commercial disasters. Wily entrepreneurs encouraged another reunion with the Belmonts in 1973, and in 1975 Phil Spector produced 'Born To Be With You'. An album *Born To Be With You* (on Spector's own label), failed, and one underrated album, *The Return Of The Wanderer*, came in 1978 on Lifesong Records. For the next few years Dion became a devout, born-again, Christian and recorded sporadically, releasing Christian albums including *Inside Job* and *Kingdom Of The Street*. He returned to rock 'n' roll in 1988 playing with Bruce Springsteen and released the Dave Edmunds produced *To Frankie*; he toured the UK as recently as 1990. Dion is one of the few survivors from a school of American vocalists who had genuine talent, and should be forever applauded for a series of great uplifting songs that still sound remarkably fresh. He was elected to the Rock and Roll Hall of Fame in 1989.

Albums: Dion And The Belmonts: *Presenting Dion And The Belmonts* (1959), *Wish Upon A Star* (1960), *Together Again* (1967), *By Special Request* (1963), Compilation: *20 Golden Greats* (1980), *Reunion* (1973). Dion: *Alone With Dion* (1961), *Runaround Sue* (1961), *Lovers Who Wander* (1962), *Dion Sings His Greatest Hits* (1962), *Love Came To Me* (1963), *Ruby Baby* (1963), *Donna The Prima Donna* (1963), *Dion Sings To Sandy* (1963), *Dion* (1968), *Sit Down Old Friend* (1969), *Wonder Where I'm Bound* (1969), *You're Not Alone* (1971), *Sanctuary* (1971), *Suite For Late Summer* (1972), *Born To Be With You* (1975), *Sweetheart* (1976), *The Return Of The Wanderer* (1978), *Inside Job* (1980), *Kingdom Of The Street* (1985), *Velvet And Steel* (1986), *Yo Frankie!* (1989), *Bronx Blues: The Columbia Recordings (1962-1965)* (1991).

Further reading: *The Wanderer,* Dion DiMucci with Davin Seay.

Dixie Cups

Formed in New Orleans, Louisiana, USA in 1963, the Dixie Cups were a female trio best known for the original recording of the hit 'Chapel Of Love' in the early 60s. The group consisted of sisters Barbara Ann Hawkins (b. 23 October 1943) and Rosa Lee Hawkins (b. 24 September 1944) and their cousin Joan Marie Johnson (b. January 1945, New Orleans, Louisiana, USA). Having sung together in church and at school, the girls formed a group called the Meltones for a high school talent contest in 1963. There they were discovered by Joe Jones, a New Orleans singer who had secured a hit himself with 'You Talk Too Much' in 1960. He became their manager and signed the trio with producers/songwriters Jerry Leiber and Mike Stoller, who were then starting their own record label, Red Bird, with industry veteran George Goldner.

The Dixie Cups recorded Jeff Barry and Ellie Greenwich's 'Chapel Of Love' despite the fact that both the Ronettes and the Crystals had failed to have hits with the song and was described by co-producer Mike Leiber as 'a record I hated with a passion'. Released as the debut Red Bird single, the trio's first single reached number 1 in the USA during the summer of 1964. (The trio later claimed that they received only a few hundred dollars for their part in the recording.) Following that hit, the Dixie Cups toured the USA and released a number of follow-up singles for Red Bird, four of which charted. 'People Say', the second one, made number 12 and the last 'Iko Iko', a traditional New Orleans chant, reached number 20. The song was subsequently used in soundtracks for a number of films, in common with 'Chapel Of Love'.

After Red Bird closed down in 1966, the Dixie Cups signed with ABC-Paramount Records. No hits came of the association, and the trio have not recorded since, although they continue to perform (the two sisters are the only originals still in the act).

Albums: *Chapel Of Love* (1964), *Iko Iko* (reissue of first album) (1965), *Ridin' High* (1966).

Dodd, Ken

b. 8 November 1927, Liverpool, England. Primarily a stand-up comedian, Dodd also had a successful recording career singing romantic ballads in a warm mezzo-tenor voice. His only comedy record - as the Diddy Men in 1965 - was a flop. He grew up in Liverpool and sang in a church choir before developing a comedy act as Professor Yaffle Chuckabutty, Operatic Tenor and Sausage Knotter, in which he sang comic versions of well-known songs. Dodd worked in sales before becoming a professional comic in 1954, playing theatres and summer shows at Blackpool's Central Pier, where he topped the bill in 1958. This led to appearances at the London Palladium and a television series in the 60s. Like other comedians of his generation, Dodd was a competent singer and frequently closed his shows with a romantic ballad.

In 1960 he signed to Decca and recorded 'Love Is Like A Violin', a 20s ballad which became a Top 10 hit. This was followed by 'Once In Every Lifetime' (1961) and 'Pianissimo' (1962). He next switched to EMI's Columbia label, where Geoff Love was the musical director for the minor hits 'Still' (1963) and the calypso-flavoured 'Happiness' (1964). But the biggest hit of his career was the contrasting 'Tears', a weepie of a ballad produced by Norman Newell. After five weeks at number 1 in the UK, it was displaced by the Rolling Stones' 'Get Off Of My Cloud'. In one of pop's most innovative eras, 'Tears' was the biggest selling single in the UK that year. First recorded in 1929 by Rudy Vallée, 'Tears' sold nearly two million copies for Dodd and led to six more Top 20 singles in the next few years. Among these were translations of three Italian Ken Dodd hits ('The River', 'Broken Hearted' and 'When Love Comes Round Again') and 'Promises', based on Beethoven's *Pathetique Sonata*. During the 80s, Dodd had one minor hit with 'Hold My Hand' (1981). In 1990, he hit the headlines following a controversial High Court action brought by the Inland Revenue, which he won.

Selected albums: *Tears Of Happiness* (1965), *Hits For Now And Always* (1966), *For Someone Special* (1967), *Now And Forever* (1983).

Donahue, Tom

b. 21 May 1928, South Bend, Indiana, USA, d. 28 April 1975. Affectionately known as 'Big Daddy' in deference to his massive girth, Donahue played a pivotal role in the evolution of San Franciscan music. He arrived in the city in 1961, having already established himself as a leading disc jockey with Philadelphia's top station WBIG. At KYA he befriended colleague Bob Mitchell, and together they began promoting concerts at the Cow Palace auditorium. The Beatles and the Rolling Stones were two of the acts presented there. Donahue and Mitchell founded Autumn Records in 1964. They scored a national hit with Bobby Freeman's 'C'mon And Swim', before embracing nascent American rock with the Beau Brummels. Fellow disc jockey Sylvester Stewart, aka Sly Stone, produced many of the label's acts. The entrepreneurs also established a North Beach club, Mothers, which showcased some of the early acts synonymous with the San Franciscan sound, including the Great Society. However, they singularly failed to sign other important acts, including the Charlatans, the Grateful Dead and Dino Valenti, despite recording demos with them. This hesitancy was one of the factors contributing to Autumn's demise. Mitchell died in 1966, but Donahue retained his influential position. He managed several artists, including Ron Nagle, Sal Valentino and the aforementioned Valenti, and revolutionized radio at station KSAN-FM by adopting a bold 'album' format. He masterminded an ambitious touring revue, the *Medicine Ball Caravan*, which later spawned a film, and Donahue remained a fixture within the city until his premature death from a heart attack, in 1975.

Donovan

Donovan

b. Donovan Leitch, 10 May 1946, Glasgow, Scotland. Uncomfortably labelled 'Britain's answer to Bob Dylan' the young troubadour did not fit in well with the folk establishment. Instead, it was the pioneering UK television show *Ready Steady Go* that adopted Donovan, and from then on success was assured. His first single 'Catch The Wind' launched a career that lasted through the 60s with numerous hits, developing as fashions changed. The expressive 'Colours' and 'Turquoise' continued his hit folk image, although hints of other influences began to creep into his music. Donovan's finest work, however, was as ambassador of 'flower power' with memorable singles like 'Sunshine Superman' and 'Mellow Yellow'. His subtle drug references endeared him to the hippie movement, although some critics felt his stance was just a bit fey and insipid. He enjoyed several hits with light material such as the calypso influenced 'There Is A Mountain' and 'Jennifer Juniper' (written for Jenny Boyd during a much publicized sojourn with the guru, Maharishi Mahesh Yogi). Donovan's drug/fairy tale imagery reached its apotheosis on the Lewis Carroll influenced 'Hurdy Gurdy Man'. As the 60s closed, however, he fell from commercial grace. Undeterred, Donovan found greater success in the USA; indeed, many of his later records were first issued in America and some gained no UK release. His collaboration with Jeff Beck on 'Goo Goo Barabajagal (Love Is Hot)' showed a more gutsy approach, while a number of the tracks on the boxed set *A Gift From A Flower To A Garden* displayed a jazzier feel. He had previously flirted with jazz on his b-sides, notably the excellent 'Sunny Goodge Street' and 'Preachin' Love'. *Cosmic Wheels* in 1973 was an artistic success; it sold well and contained his witty 'Intergalactic Laxative'. In anticipation of continued success, *Essence To Essence* was a bitter disappointment, and thereafter Donovan ceased to be a major concert attraction.

In 1990 after many inactive years the Happy Mondays bought him back into favour by praising his work and invited him to tour with them in 1991. Their irreverent tribute 'Donovan' underlined this new-found favouritism. Shortly before this, he was back on television as part of a humorous remake of 'Jennifer Juniper' with UK comedians Trevor and Simon. A new album was released and a flood of reissues arrived; for the moment at least the cognoscenti decreed that Donovan was 'okay' again. He undertook a major UK tour in 1992.

Albums: *What's Bin Did And What's Bin Hid* (1965), *Catch The Wind* (1965), *Fairytale* (1965), *Sunshine Superman* (1966), *Mellow Yellow* (1967), *Wear Your Love Like Heaven* (1967), *For Little Ones* (1967), *A Gift From A Flower To A Garden* (1967), *Donovan In Concert* (1968), *Hurdy Gurdy Man* (1968), *Barabajagal* (1969), *Open Road* (1970), *HMS Donovan* (1971), *Brother Sun, Sister Moon* (1972 film soundtrack), *Colours* (1972), *The Pied Piper* (1973 film soundtrack), *Cosmic Wheels* (1973), *Essence To Essence* (1973), *7-Tease* (1974), *Slow Down World* (1976), *Donovan* (1977), *Neutronica* (1981), *Love Is The Only Feeling*

(1981), *Lady Of The Stars* (1984). Selected compilations: *Universal Soldier* (1967), *The Golden Hour Of Donovan* (1971), *The Donovan File* (1977), *Spotlight On Donovan* (1981), *Greatest Hits And More* (1989), *The EP Collection* (1990), *Donovan Rising* (1990), *25 Years In Concert* (1991).

Doonican, Val

b. Michael Valentine Doonican, 3 February 1928, Waterford, Eire. Doonican learned to play the mandolin and guitar as a boy, and later toured northern and southern Ireland in various bands before travelling to England in 1951 to join an Irish vocal quartet, the Four Ramblers. He wrote the group's vocal arrangements as well as singing and playing guitar in their BBC radio series *Riders Of The Range*. In the late 50s, on the advice of Anthony Newley, he went solo, and appeared on television in *Beauty Box*, and on radio in *Dreamy Afternoon*; later re-titled, *A Date With Val*. In 1963 he was recommended to impresario Val Parnell, by comedian Dickie Henderson, and gained a spot on ITV's top-rated television show *Sunday Night At The London Palladium*. He made an immediate impact with his friendly, easy-going style and in 1964 commenced an annual series for BBC television, which ran until the 80s. He soon became one of the most popular entertainers in the UK, and was voted Television Personality Of The Year three times. The closing sequence of his TV show, in which he sang a song while seated in a rocking chair, was especially effective. The idea was later used as a self-depreciating album title: *Val Doonican Rocks, But Gently*. Later, in the age of video tape, he still preferred his shows to be transmitted 'live'. His first record hit, 'Walk Tall', in 1964, was followed by a string of chart entries through to the early 70s, including 'The Special Years', 'Elusive Butterfly', 'What Would I Be', 'Memories Are Made Of This', 'If The Whole World Stopped Loving', 'If I Knew Then What I Know Now' and 'Morning'. Equally popular, but not chart entries, were a number of novelty songs such as 'O'Rafferty's Motor Car', 'Delaney's Donkey' and 'Paddy McGinty's Goat', written by the prolific English team of Bob Weston & Bert Lee.

Selected albums: *Lucky 13 Shades Of Val Doonican* (1964), *Gentle Shades Of Val Doonican* (1966), *Val Doonican Rocks, But Gently* (1967), *Val* (1968), *Sounds Gentle* (1969), *The Magic Of Val Doonican* (1970), *This Is Val Doonican* (1971), *Morning Has Broken* (1973), *Song Sung Blue* (1974), *I Love Country Music* (1975), *Life Can Be Beautiful* (1976), *Some Of My Best Friends Are Songs* (1977), *Quiet Moments* (1981), *Val Sings Bing* (1982), *The Val Doonican Music Show* (1984), *By Request* (1987). Compilations: *The World Of Val Doonican* (1969), *The World Of Val Doonican, Volume Two* (1969), *The World Of Val Doonican, Volume Three* (1970), *The World Of Val Doonican, Volume Four* (1971), *The World Of Val Doonican, Volume Five* (1972), *Rocking Chair Favourites* (1973), *Spotlight On Val Doonican* (1974), *Focus On Val Doonican* (1976), *Memories Are Made Of This* (1981), *Forty Shades Of Green* (1983), *The Very Best Of Val Doonican* (1984), *Twenty Personal Favourites For You* (1986), *It's Good To See You* (1988).

Further reading: *The Special Years*, Val Doonican.

Doors

'When the doors of perception are cleansed, man will see things as they truly are, infinite.' This quote from poet William Blake was an inspiration to Jim Morrison (b. James Douglas Morrison, 8 December 1943, Melbourne, Florida, USA, d. 3 July 1971, Paris, France), a student of theatre arts at the University of California and an aspiring musician. His dream of a rock band entitled 'the Doors' was fulfilled in 1965, when he sang a rudimentary composition, 'Moonlight Drive', to fellow scholar Ray Manzarek (b. 12 February 1935, Chicago, Illinois, USA; keyboards). Impressed, he invited Morrison to join his campus R&B band, Rick And The Ravens, which also included the organist's two brothers. Ray then recruited drummer John Densmore (b. 1 December 1945, Los Angeles, California, USA), and the reshaped unit recorded six Morrison songs at the famed World Pacific studios. The session featured several compositions which the group subsequently re-recorded, including 'Summer's Almost Gone' and 'End Of The Night'. Manzarek's brothers disliked the new material and later dropped out of the group. They were replaced by Robbie Krieger (b. 8 January 1946, Los Angeles, California, USA), an inventive guitarist, who Densmore met at a meditation centre. Morrison was now established as the vocalist and the quartet began rehearsing in earnest.

The Doors' first residency was at the London Fog on Sunset Strip, but they later found favour at the prestigious Whisky-A-Go-Go. They were, however, fired from the latter establishment, following a performance of 'The End', Morrison's chilling, oedipal composition. Improvised and partly spoken over a raga/rock framework, it proved too controversial for timid club owners, but the group's standing within the music fraternity grew. Local rivals Love, already signed to Elektra Records, recommended the Doors to the label's managing director, Jac Holtzman who, despite initial caution, signed the group in 1966.

The Doors, released the following year, unveiled a group of many contrasting influences. Manzarek's thin sounding organ (he also performed the part of bassist with the aid of a separate bass keyboard) recalled the garage-band style omnipresent several months earlier, but Krieger's liquid guitar playing and Densmore's imaginative drumming were already clearly evident. Morrison's striking, dramatic voice added power to the exceptional compositions, which included the pulsating 'Break On Through' and an 11-minute version of 'The End'. Cover versions of material, including Willie Dixon's 'Back Door Man' and Bertolt Brecht/Kurt Weill's 'Alabama Song (Whisky Bar)', exemplified the group's disparate influences.

The best-known track, however, was 'Light My Fire', which, when trimmed down from its original seven minutes, became a number 1 single in the USA. Its fiery imagery combined eroticism with death, and the song has since become a standard. Its success created new problems and the Doors, perceived by some as underground heroes, were tarred as teenybop fodder by others. This dichotomy weighed heavily on Morrison who wished to be accepted as a serious artist. A second album, *Strange Days*, showcased 'When The Music's Over', another extended piece destined to become a *tour de force* within the group's canon. The quartet enjoyed further chart success when 'People Are Strange' broached the US Top 20, but it was 1968 before they secured another number 1 single with the infectious 'Hello I Love You'. The song was also the group's first major UK hit, although some of this lustre was lost following legal action by Ray Davies of the Kinks, who claimed infringement of his own composition, 'All Day And All Of The Night'.

The action coincided with the Doors' first European tour. A major television documentary, *The Doors Are Open*, was devoted to the visit and centred on their powerful performance at London's Chalk Farm Roundhouse. The group showcased several tracks from their third collection, *Waiting For The Sun*, including the declamatory 'Five To One', and a fierce protest song, 'The Unknown Soldier', for which they also completed an uncompromising promotional film. However, the follow-up album, *The Soft Parade*, on which a horn section masked several unremarkable songs, was a major disappointment, although the tongue-in-cheek 'Touch Me' became another US Top 3 single and 'Wishful Sinful' was a Top 50 hit.

Continued commercial success exacted further pressure on Morrison, whose frustration with his role as a pop idol grew more pronounced. His anti-authoritarian persona combined with a brazen sexuality and notorious alcohol and narcotics consumption to create a character bedevilled by doubt and cynicism. His confrontations with middle America reached an apogee in July 1969 when, following a concert at Miami's Dinner Key auditorium, the singer was indicted for indecent exposure, public intoxication and profane, lewd and lascivious conduct. Although Morrison was later acquitted of all but the minor charges, the incident clouded the group's career when live dates for the next few months were cancelled.

Paradoxically, this furore re-awoke the Doors' creativity. *Morrison Hotel*, a tough R&B-based collection, matched the best of their early releases and featured seminal performances in 'Roadhouse Blues' and 'You Make Me Real'. *Absolutely Live*, an in-concert set edited from a variety of sources, gave the impression of a single performance and exhibited the group's power and authority. However Morrison, whose poetry had been published in two volumes, *The Lords* and *The New Creatures*, now drew greater pleasure from this more personal artform. Having completed sessions for a new album, the last owed to Elektra, the singer escaped to Paris where he hoped to follow a literary career and abandon music altogether. Tragically, years of hedonistic excess had taken its toll and on 3 July 1971, Jim Morrison was found dead in his bathtub, his passing recorded officially as a heart attack.

LA Woman, his final recording with the Doors, is one of their finest achievements. Recorded in the group's workshop, its simple intimacy resulted in some superb performances, including 'Riders On The Storm', whose haunting imagery and stealthy accompaniment created a timeless classic. The survivors continued to work as the Doors, but while *Other Voices* showed some promise, *Full Circle* was severely flawed and the group soon dissolved. Densmore and Krieger formed the Butts Band, with whom they recorded two albums before splitting to pursue different paths. Manzarek undertook several projects as either artist, producer or manager, but the spectre of the Doors refused to die. Interest in the group flourished throughout the decade and in 1978 the remaining trio supplied newly recorded music to a series of poetry recitations, which Morrison had taped during the *LA Woman* sessions. The resultant album, *An American Prayer*, was a major success and prompted further such archive excursions as *Alive She Cried*, a compendium of several concert performances and *The Doors Live At Hollywood Bowl*. The evocative use of 'The End' in Francis Ford Coppola's Vietnam war film, *Apocalypse Now* (1979), also generated renewed interest in the group's legacy; and indeed it is on those first recordings that the Doors' considerable reputation, and influence, rest. Since then the Doors' catalogue has never been out of print, and future generations of rock fans will almost certainly use them as a major role model. In 1991, director Oliver Stone's film biography *The Doors*, starring Val Kilmer confirmed Morrison as one of the 60s' great cultural icons.

Albums: *The Doors* (1967), *Strange Days* (1967), *Waiting For The Sun* (1968), *The Soft Parade* (1969), *Morrison Hotel* (1970), *Absolutely Live* (1970), *LA*

Woman (1971), *Other Voices* (1971), *Full Circle* (1972), *An American Prayer* (1978), *Alive She Cried* (1983), *The Doors Live At The Hollywood Bowl* (1987). Compilations: *13* (1971), *Weird Scenes Inside The Goldmine* (1972), *The Best Of The Doors* (1974), *Greatest Hits* (1980), *The Doors* (1991 - original soundtrack).

Further reading: *No-One Here Gets Out Alive*, Danny Sugerman and Jerry Hopkins. *The Doors - The Illustrated History*, Danny Sugerman.

Dorsey, Lee

b. Irving Lee Dorsey, 24 December 1926, New Orleans, Louisiana, USA, d. 1 December 1986. An ex-boxer (nicknamed 'Kid Chocolate'), turned singer, Dorsey first recorded for Joe Banashak's Instant label. One song, 'Lottie Mo', became a regional hit and led to a contract with Fury. The infectious 'Ya Ya' (1961) was a number 1 US R&B and pop Top 10 single. A year later a version by Petula Clark, retitled 'Ya Ya Twist' reached the UK Top 20. Dorsey's next release 'Do-Re-Mi' (regularly performed by Georgie Fame and Dusty Springfield) was also a hit, although this time reaching no higher than 27 in the *Billboard* pop chart, and subsequent releases on Fury Records were less successful. His career stalled temporarily when Fury collapsed but Lee re-emerged in 1965 with the classic 'Ride Your Pony' on the Amy label. Written by Allen Toussaint and produced by Marshall Sehorn, this combination created a series of impeccable singles, which blended crisp arrangements with the singer's easy delivery. In 1966 he reached the peak of his success in the UK by scoring four Top 40 hits, including two Top 10 singles with 'Working In The Coalmine' and 'Holy Cow', both of which reached the US R&B and pop charts. 'Everything I Do Gohn Be Funky (From Now On)' became Dorsey's last substantial hit in 1969, although the title track to his excellent 'concept' album, 'Yes We Can', did reach the R&B Top 50. Lee continued to record for Polydor and ABC and remained a popular figure, so much so that he guested on the 1976 debut album by Southside Johnny And The Asbury Dukes and supported the Clash on their 1980 tour of north America. Sadly, he died of emphysema in December 1986.

Albums: *Ya Ya* (1962), *Ride Your Pony/Get Out My Life Woman* (1966), *Working In The Coalmine/Holy Cow* (1966), *The New Lee Dorsey* (1966), *Yes We Can* (1970), *Night People* (1978). Compilations: *The Best Of Lee Dorsey* (1966), *Gohn Be Funky* (1985), *All Ways Funky* (1982), *Holy Cow! The Best Of Lee Dorsey* (1985), *Am I That Easy To Forget?* (1987), *Can You Hear Me* (1987).

Douglas, Craig

b. Terence Perkins, 12 August 1941, Newport, Isle Of Wight, England. After moving to London in the mid-50s, Douglas came under the wing of agent Bunny Lewis, appeared on the television show *6.5 Special*, and won a record contract with Decca before moving to Dick Rowe's label, Top Rank. Covering American hits was the classic route to chart success, and in 1959 Douglas scored with Dion's 'A Teenager In Love' and reached number 1 with Sam Cooke's 'Only Sixteen'. He co-starred with Helen Shapiro in the film *It's Trad Dad* (1961). Several more hits followed but after four consecutive number 9s with 'A Hundred Pounds Of Clay', 'Time', 'When My Little Girl Is Smiling' and 'Our Favourite Melodies', Craig felt the sting of the approaching beat boom. He then travelled the world, returning for a career in cabaret in the UK, where he still resides.

Albums: *Craig Douglas* (1960), *Bandwagon Ball* (1961), *Our Favourite Melodies* (1962).

Downliners Sect

Formed in 1962, this enduring UK act was initially known as the Downliners, but the original line-up fell apart following a brief tour of US air bases. Founder members Don Craine (vocals, rhythm guitar) and Johnny Sutton (drums) then reshaped the group around Keith Grant (bass) and Terry Gibson (lead guitar) and, having added the 'Sect' suffix, the quartet secured a residency at London's Studio 51 club. A privately pressed EP, *A Nite In Great Newport Street*, captured their brash interpolation of Chicago R&B, and was a contributory factor to a subsequent recording deal with EMI. A version of Jimmy Reed's 'Baby What's Wrong' became the unit's first single in June 1964, by which time Ray Sone (harmonica) had been added to the line-up. The Sect's brazen musical approach, redolent of the contemporaneous Pretty Things, was showcased on their debut album, but not only did its irreverance anger purists, Craine's everpresent deerstalker hat and autoharp also did little to attract a younger, more fashion-conscious audience. The group, however, seemed unmoved by such considerations and in 1965 further confused any prospective audience with *The Country Sect*, an album of folk and country material, and *The Sect Sing Sick Songs* EP, which included the ghoulish 'I Want My Baby Back', and 'Leader Of The Sect', a riposte to the Shangri-Las' death-disc, 'Leader Of The Pack'. Ray Sone left the group prior to recording *The Rock Sect's In* which neatly combined almost all of the unit's diverse styles. It is now notable for the inclusion of 'Why Don't You Smile Now', which was part-composed by Lou Reed and John Cale prior to their founding the Velvet Underground. The Sect, however, were still struggling to find commercial success and the line-up disintegrated when two pop-oriented singles, 'Glendora' and the Graham Gouldman-penned 'Cost Of Living', failed to chart.

Gibson and Sutton were replaced, respectively, by Bob Taylor and Kevin Flanagan, while pianist Matthew Fisher, later of Procol Harum, was also briefly a member. Craine abandoned his creation following the release of 'I Can't Get Away From You', after which Grant and the prodigal Sutton took the group to Sweden, where they recorded a handful of tracks before disbanding altogether. Craine and Grant revived Sect in 1976 in the wake of the pub rock/R&B phenomenon, and the resultant *Showbiz* invoked the gutsy styles of Dr. Feelgood or Count Bishops. The duo continued to lead the group throughout the 80s, and they are also an integral part of the British Invasion All-Stars with former members of the Yardbirds, Creation and Nashville Teens. However, it is their 60s recordings which afford the Sect their cult-based appeal.

Albums: *The Sect* (1964), *The Country Sect* (1965), *The Rock Sect's In* (1966), *Showbiz* (1979). Compilation: *Be A Sect Maniac* (c.80s), *Savage Return* (1991).

Drifters

Formed in 1953 in New York, USA, at the behest of Atlantic Records, this influential R&B vocal group was initially envisaged as a vehicle for ex-Dominoes' singer, Clyde McPhatter. Gerhart Thrasher, Andrew Thrasher and Bill Pinkney completed the new quartet which, as Clyde McPhatter and the Drifters, scored a number 1 R&B hit with their debut single, 'Money Honey'. Follow-up releases, including 'Such A Night', 'Lucille' and 'Honey Love' (a second chart-topper), also proved highly successful, while the juxtaposition of McPhatter's soaring tenor against the frenzied support of the other members provided a link between gospel and rock 'n' roll styles. The leader's interplay with bassist Pinkey breathed new life into 'White Christmas', the group's sixth R&B hit, but McPhatter's induction into the armed forces in 1954 was a blow the Drifters struggled to withstand. The vocalist opted for a solo career upon leaving the services, and although his former group did enjoy success with 'Adorable' (number 1 R&B 1955), 'Steamboat' (1955), 'Ruby Baby' (1956) and 'Fools Fall In Love' (1957), such recordings featured a variety of lead singers, including David Baughn and Johnny Moore. A greater emphasis on pop material ensued, but tension between the group and manager, George Treadwell, resulted in an irrevocable split. Having fired the extant line-up in 1958, Treadwell, who owned the copyright to the Drifters' name, invited another act, the Five Crowns, to adopt the appellation. Ben E. King (tenor), Charlie Thomas (tenor), Doc Green Jnr. (baritone) and Elsbury Hobbs (bass), plus guitarist Reggie Kimber, duly became 'the Drifters', and declared their newfound role with 'There Goes My Baby'. Written and produced by Leiber And Stoller, this pioneering release contained a Latin rhythm and string section, the first time such embellishments had appeared on an R&B recording. The single not only topped the R&B chart, it also reached number 2 on the US pop listings, and anticipated the 'symphonic' style later developed by Phil Spector.

Further excellent releases followed, notably 'Dance With Me' (1959), 'This Magic Moment' (1960) and 'Save The Last Dance For Me', the last-named of which topped the US pop chart and reached number 2 in the UK. However, King left for a solo career following 'I Count The Tears' (1960), and was replaced by Rudy Lewis, who fronted the group until his premature death in 1964. The Drifters continued to enjoy hits during this period and songs such as 'Sweets For My Sweet', 'When My Little Girl Is Smiling', 'Up On The Roof' and 'On Broadway' were not only entertaining in their own right, but also provided inspiration, and material, for many emergent British acts, notably the Searchers, who took the first-named song to the top of the UK chart. Johnny Moore, who had returned to the line-up in 1963, took over the lead vocal slot from Lewis. 'Under The Boardwalk', recorded the day after the latter's passing, was the Drifters' last US Top 10 pop hit, although the group remained a popular attraction. Bert Berns had taken over production from Leiber and Stoller, and in doing so brought a soul-based urgency to their work, as evinced by 'One Way Love' and 'Saturday Night At The Movies' (1964). When he left Atlantic to found the Bang label, the Drifters found themselves increasingly overshadowed by newer, more contemporary artists and, bedevilled by lesser material and frequent changes in personnel, the group began to slip from prominence. However their career was revitalized in 1972 when two re-released singles, 'At The Club' and 'Come On Over To My Place', reached the UK Top 10. A new recording deal with Bell was then secured and British songwriters/producers Tony Macauley, Roger Cook and Roger Greenaway fashioned a series of singles redolent of the Drifters' 'classic' era. Purists poured scorn on their efforts, but, between 1973 and 1975, the group, still led by Moore, enjoyed six UK Top 10 hits, including 'Come On Over To My Place', 'Kissin' In The Back Row Of The Movies', 'Down On The Beach Tonight' and 'There Goes My First Love'. This success ultimately waned as the decade progressed, and in 1982 Moore left the line-up. He was replaced, paradoxically, by Ben E. King who in turn brought the Drifters back to Atlantic. However, despite completing some new recordings, the group found it impossible to escape its heritage, as evinced by the numerous 'hits' repackages and corresponding live appearances on the cabaret and nostalgia circuits.

Selected albums: *Save The Last Dance For Me* (1961), *The Good Life With The Drifters* (1964), *I'll Take You*

Where The Music's Playing (1965), *Souvenirs, Love Games* (1975), *There Goes My First Love* (1975), *Every Night's A Saturday Night* (1976), *Greatest Hits Live* (1984). There have been numerous compilations, including - *The Drifters Greatest Hits, Our Biggest Hits* (1964), *The Drifters' Golden Hits, Rockin' And Driftin', Good Gravy* (1964), *The Drifters' Story, 24 Original Hits, Diamond Series: The Drifters* (1988).

Driscoll, Julie

b. 8 June 1947, London, England. Driscoll was employed by producer/manager Giorgio Gomelsky as administrator of the Yardbirds' fan club when the former suggested a singing career. Her singles included a version of the Lovin' Spoonful's 'Didn't Want To Have To Do It' (1965) and an early Randy Newman composition 'If You Should Ever Leave Me' (1967), but this period is better recalled for Julie's membership of Steam Packet, an R&B-styled revue which also featured Long John Baldry, Rod Stewart and the Brian Auger Trinity. Driscoll remained with the last-named act when the larger unit folded, and in 1968 scored a number 5 hit with Bob Dylan's 'This Wheel's On Fire'. Her striking appearance engendered much publicity, but a cool, almost disinterested vocal style formed the ideal counterpoint to Auger's jazz-based ambitions. 'Jools' left the group following the release of *Streetnoise* in order to pursue a more radical direction. She contributed to B B Blunder's *Workers Playtime*, and released the excellent *Julie Driscoll*, which featured support from members of the Soft Machine, Nucleus and Blossom Toes as well as pianist Keith Tippett, whom the singer later married. She has since appeared on many of her husband's *avant garde* jazz creations, notably Centipede's *Septober Energy* (1971) and the expansive *Frames* (1978) as well appearing and recording with Brian Eley and the experimental vocal quartet, Voice.
Albums: with Brian Auger *Open* (1967), with Auger *Streetnoise* (1968). Solo *Julie Driscoll* (1971). Compilations: *Jools/Brian* (1968), both shared with Brian Auger *London 1964-1967* (1977), *The Best Of Julie Driscoll* (1982), both with the Brian Auger Trinity *The Road To Vauxhall 1967-1969* (1989).

Dubliners

This Dublin, Eire band featured Barry MacKenna (b. 16 December 1939), Luke Kelly (b. 16 November 1939), ex-draughtsman John Sheahan (b. 19 May 1939), Ciaran Bourke and former teacher Ronnie Drew. They formed in 1962, in the back of O'Donoghues' bar in Merron Row, Dublin and were originally named the Ronnie Drew Group. The members were known faces in the city's post-skiffle folk haunts before pooling their assorted singing and fretboard skills in 1962. They played various theatre bars, made several albums for Transatlantic and gained a strong following on the Irish folk circuit. After an introduction by Dominic Behan, they were signed by manager Phil Solomon and placed on his label, Major Minor. Throughout their collective career, each member pursued outside projects - among them Kelly's stints as an actor and MacKenna's 'The Great Comic Genius', a solo single issued after the Irishmen transferred from Transatlantic to the Major Minor label in 1966. During this time they received incessant plugging on the pirate Radio Caroline. Bigoted folk purists were unable to regard them with the same respect as the similarly motivated Clancy Brothers And Tommy Makem after the Dubliners were seen on *Top Of The Pops* promoting 1967's censored 'Seven Drunken Nights' and, next, 'Black Velvet Band'. 'Never Wed An Old Man' was only a minor hit but high placings for *A Drop Of The Hard Stuff* and three of its successors in the album list were a firm foundation for the outfit's present standing as a thoroughly diverting international concert attraction. A brain haemorrhage forced Bourke's retirement in 1974, and Drew's return to the ranks (after a brief replacement by Jim McCann) was delayed by injuries sustained in a road accident. Nevertheless, Drew's trademark vocal - 'like coke being crushed under a door' - was heard on the group's 25th anniversary single, 'The Irish Rover', a merger with the Pogues that signalled another sojourn in the Top 10.
Selected albums: *A Drop Of The Hard Stuff* (1967), *Best Of The Dubliners* (1967), *More Of The Hard Stuff* (1967), *Drinkin' And Courtin'* (1968), *Very Best Of The Dubliners* (1975), *Dubliners In Concert* (1982), *The Dubliners 25 Years Celebration* (1987), *20 Greatest Hits: Dubliners* (1989), *20 Original Greatest Hits* (1988), *20 Original Greatest Hits Vol. 2* (1989).

Dupree, Simon, And The Big Sound

Formed in Portsmouth, England by the Shulman brothers, Derek (b. 11 February 1947, Glasgow, Scotland; lead vocals), Ray (b. 3 December 1949, Portsmouth, Hampshire, England; lead guitar) and Phil (b. 27 August 1937, Glasgow, Scotland; saxophone/trumpet). The siblings had led several local groups, including the Howlin' Wolves and Roadrunners, before a newly acquired manager suggested the above appellation in 1966. Eric Hine (keyboards), Pete O'Flaherty (bass) and Tony Ransley (drums) completed the line-up which then became a regular attraction in London's soul and R&B clubs. 'I See The Light', 'Reservations' and 'Daytime Nightime' (penned by Manfred Mann drummer Mike Hugg) were all radio hits and a *de rigueur* compendium of dance-floor favourites *Without Reservations*, preceded the sextet's switch to flower-power with 'Kites'. The group disliked the song's overt trappings - gongs, finger cymbals and Jackie

Chan's Chinese narration - but it became their biggest hit, rising to number 9 in 1967. Subsequent singles failed to emulate this success, but the band achieved a measure of notoriety the following year when their psychoactive single, 'We Are The Moles', credited pseudonymously to the Moles, was assumed to be the Beatles in disguise. The unit was disbanded in 1969 when Derek Shulman, tired of being 'Simon Dupree', suffered a nervous breakdown. Upon recovery he joined his brothers in Gentle Giant.
Album: *Without Reservations* (1967). Compilations: *Amen* (1982), *Kites* (1987).

Dylan, Bob

b. Robert Allen Zimmerman, 24 May 1941, Duluth, Minnesota, USA. Unquestionably one of the most influential figures in the history of popular music, Dylan effectively began his musical career after dropping out of the University of Minnesota in 1960. He soon assimilated a mass of musical and literary influences, ranging from the rock 'n' roll of Little Richard and Elvis Presley to the talking blues of Woody Guthrie, the melancholy lyricism of Hank Williams, the irreverential howling of the beat poets and the startling imagery of the French symbolists. Adopting the persona of the folk troubadour, he moved from Minneapolis to New York in January 1961 and appeared at various coffee houses in Greenwich Village. After playing harmonica on albums by Harry Belafonte and Carolyn Hester, he was auditioned by producer John Hammond and signed to Columbia Records.
In March 1962, *Bob Dylan* was released. A stunning debut, it neatly encapsulated his recent influences, with songs inspired or borrowed from Village folkies Ric Von Schmidt and Dave Van Ronk, plus the poignant blues of Blind Lemon Jefferson and, significantly, two Dylan compositions: the delightfully satiric 'Talkin' New York Blues' and the reverential tribute 'Song To Woody'.
By the end of the year Dylan recorded his debut single 'Mixed Up Confusion', an electric rocker which was rapidly withdrawn for fear of conflicting with his image as the young messiah of folk. Meanwhile, Dylan was hailed by his contemporaries as a civil rights activist and began penning songs such as 'Blowin' In The Wind', later an international hit for Peter, Paul And Mary. The trio were managed by Dylan's great mentor, Albert Grossman, whose forceful entrepreneurial proprietorship protected the performer from unwanted business or personal influences.
The Freewheelin' Bob Dylan, marked the emergence of Dylan the poet in such songs as the apocalyptic 'A Hard Rain's A-Gonna Fall' and the bitter finger-pointing 'Masters Of War'. The cover of the album portrayed the singer arm-in-arm with lover Suze

Rotolo, who would soon be replaced in the performer's affections by Joan Baez. The Queen of Folk avidly promoted Dylan, whose prolific output continued with *The Times They Are A-Changin'*. A notably mature work, the album displayed many facets of Dylan's writing talent, not least his ability to transform downtrodden figures like Hattie Carroll or Hollis Brown into universal symbols of tragic injustice. While the title track and 'When The Ship Comes In' ushered in a new mood of optimism, it was not insignificant that the 'rapidly fading' old order was swept aside in similes and images taken from the Old Testament. Nor were the closing lines of the final track 'Restless Farewell' to be ignored: 'I'll bid farewell and not give a damn'.
Dylan's farewell to the agitprop of the Greenwich Village folk movement was voiced most forcibly on 'My Back Pages' from his 1964 album, *Another Side Of Bob Dylan*. The chorus, 'I was so much older then, I'm younger than that now', suggested that the black and white certainties previously espoused by the singer on such songs as 'Masters Of War' required more delicate shading. 'Chimes Of Freedom', despite its title, was no mere rallying cry, but a song steeped in dense imagery that signalled a new direction. Other tracks such as 'All I Really Want To Do' and 'Motorpsycho Nightmare' stressed Dylan's humour and wordplay, while the closing tracks, 'I Don't Believe You', 'Ballad In Plain D' and 'It Ain't Me Babe', were powerful outpourings of disillusionment and insouciant vindictiveness in the wake of a broken relationship.
The change in Dylan's attitude and art were mirrored by the mini-revolution taking place on the popular music front. On a visit to Britain in 1964, Dylan first fully appreciated the originality of the Beatles, and responded to the irresistible rise of the new beat groups. In July 1964, the Animals topped the UK charts with an electric version of 'House Of The Rising Sun', a track which they had learned from Dylan's own reading of the song, included on his first album. During that same period the fledgling Byrds were rehearsing at World Pacific Studios under the auspices of producer Jim Dickson, who was encouraging them to electrify an as yet unreleased Dylan tune, 'Mr Tambourine Man'. These folk rock experiments had a profound effect on the composer who, during the next three years, would produce a trilogy of albums, whose marriage of lyrical sophistication and musical punch represents the finest sustained body of work in rock music history.
Bringing It All Back Home (1965) coincided with the rise of Dylan to the status of a popular culture hero. The first side of the album contained some of his most impressive early rock workouts with 'Subterranean Homesick Blues' and 'Maggie's Farm', while the primarily acoustic side two featured four of

his greatest songs: 'Mr Tambourine Man', 'Gates Of Eden', 'It's Alright Ma (I'm Only Bleeding)' and 'It's All Over Now, Baby Blue'. He was now not only an albums artist, but also a frequent visitor to the pop charts with four Top 20 hits in 1965 alone, including the six minute 'Like A Rolling Stone', a track often cited as the best single ever made. Dylan even looked the consummate rock star with his dark glasses, sharply mod-ish clothes, enigmatic persona and brooding arrogance. The film of his 1965 UK tour, *Don't Look Back*, captured the essence of Dylan's charismatic charm, while disguising none of his petulance or impatience. For the next 12 months he needed all his egotistical strength to survive the brickbats of the more regressive elements of his old audience, who responded to his electric music with ill-disguised contempt. After a stormy reception at the 1965 Newport Folk Festival, Dylan set off on a world tour backed by the Band (then known as the Hawks). This virtually unknown Canadian outfit proved the perfect complement for Dylan's rock experimentation. His stage performances were immensely powerful and daringly uncompromising, often taking the form of a war of attrition between the performer and his audience. The celebrated 1966 UK tour, which saw a disgruntled spectator scream 'Judas!' from the rear of the auditorium while hecklers catcalled in conflicting celebration, epitomized the folk-rock schism.

Dylan's reply to his critics was in the quality of his recorded output. *Highway 61 Revisited* fused the cut and thrust R&B of 'From A Buick 6' and 'Tombstone Blues' with the satiric bite of 'Ballad Of A Thin Man' and the surreal imagery of 'Desolation Row'. Less than one year later, the double album *Blonde On Blonde* completed this remarkable phase in Dylan's career with a flourishing assortment of songs ranging from intense speculations on personal relationships ('Just Like A Woman', 'One Of Us Must Know'), to the hip wordplay of 'Stuck Inside Of Mobile With The Memphis Blues Again', the dry wit of 'Rainy Day Women Nos. 12 & 35' and 'Leopard Skin Pillbox Hat', and the philosophical speculations of 'Visions Of Johanna'. Uniquely for a pop LP of its period, the album included an entire side devoted to one song, the epic 'Sad Eyed Lady Of The Lowlands', inspired by Dylan's wife Sara Lowndes, whom he had married only months before.

The punishing schedule that Dylan had undertaken during 1966 was abruptly curtailed on 29 July following a motorcycle accident near his home in Woodstock. For the next two years he disappeared from the public eye amid exaggerated rumours that he was disfigured, brain damaged or perhaps dead. In fact, Dylan was far from creatively inactive during this long hiatus, but spent much time recording privately at his home with members of the Band. Freed from the pressure of live commitments and recording schedules, Dylan explored an impressive array of different musical styles from country and blues to cajun and folk. The tone and theme of the material was equally diverse, embracing on the one hand surreal comedy ('Please Mrs Henry', 'Open The Door Homer', 'Quinn The Eskimo' and 'Million Dollar Bash'), yet also displaying soul-searchingly introspective musings on guilt and redemption ('Tears Of Rage', 'I Shall Be Released' and 'Too Much Of Nothing'). It remains uncertain how many songs were completed during this period, although hours of tapes were recorded in the basement of Big Pink, a house in West Saugerties rented by the Band. A double album selection of this material was belatedly released in 1975 as *The Basement Tapes*.

The death of Woody Guthrie in late 1967 brought Dylan out of his self-imposed retreat to appear in a tribute concert early the following year. His re-emergence coincided with the firing of his long term manager Albert Grossman and the release of *John Wesley Harding*, a stark but brilliant work, which challenged and effectively reversed the pseudo-poeticism and psychedelic excesses prevalent in rock during the previous year. Moving away from the convoluted imagery that had characterized his previous work, Dylan chose sharp aphorisms and used quasi-allegorical figures such as John Wesley Hardin, St. Augustine and Tom Paine to express his search for fulfilment. Biblical phraseology dominated the album, most notably in the richly symbolic 'All Along The Watchtower' and 'Ballad Of Frankie Lee And Judas Priest'. Not for the first time, Dylan ended the album with a hint of his future direction in 'I'll Be Your Baby Tonight'. A seemingly unambiguous love song, it suggested a new Dylan, content, demon free and uncharacteristically mellow.

The transition was completed on *Nashville Skyline*, released in April 1969. This unlikely excursion into country music, complete with a Johnny Cash duet on a surprisingly effective reworking of 'Girl From The North Country', revealed the full extent of Dylan's diversity. For those who had previously complained about his unorthodox vocal style or lack of melodic content, there was some serious revision underway. Remarkably, the singer's voice had deepened, almost beyond recognition, and his crooning sounded assured and attractive. More importantly, on songs such as 'Lay Lady Lay' and 'I Threw It All Away' he showed a melodic skill, previously suspected but never fully revealed in such an accessible form. The ultimate achievement of *Nashville Skyline*, however, was its capacity to bring both Dylan's canon and the burgeoning country rock scene, to a wider audience. While the cream of the 60s counter culture assembled near Dylan's home for the Woodstock festival, the singer, in common with the Beatles and the Rolling

Stones, declined to appear. Instead, he chose another festival in the unlikely setting of the Isle Of Wight, England. With close-cropped hair, a beard and wearing a baggy white suit, the singer played a short set in a relaxed manner. The concert anticipated Dylan's next move, arguably his most bizarre yet.

Self Portrait may have been a double set but it hardly compared with *Blonde On Blonde*. The album consisted of a hotch potch of old songs like 'She Belongs To Me' and 'Like A Rolling Stone' played live in desultory fashion, some curious covers of Richard Rodgers and Lorenz Hart's 'Blue Moon' and Simon And Garfunkel's 'The Boxer', and even a couple of instrumentals. Within such an uninspiring context, the compensatory charm of 'Copper Kettle' and 'Days Of 49' seemed almost negligible. As a deliberate attempt at demystifying his guru status the album could be seen as a perverse success for it garnered a wealth of critical abuse. Greil Marcus began his review in **Rolling Stone** with: 'What is this shit?' On another level *Self Portrait* resembled nothing less than an official bootleg and may well have reflected Dylan's periodic antipathy towards the public dissemination of his privately recorded moments which had begun with the release a few months earlier of the first bootleg record, Great White Wonder.

The uneven and uncomplicated *New Morning*, released in October 1970, was of sufficient quality to prompt cries of celebration from some reviewers, including Ralph J. Gleason who stated in *Rolling Stone*: 'We've got Dylan back again'. Others perceived the work as a retreat into the cosiness of family life or a further rejection of his former status. The belated appearance of his novel *Tarantula* in 1971 served as a reminder of the verbal dexterity of his mid-60s work and fulfilled an almost nostalgic function. For a time, Dylan himself seemed to conjure the ghosts of his past, re-entering the political arena with the anthemic protest 'George Jackson', and appearing at George Harrison's benefit concert for the starving in Bangladesh. In contrast to his recent work he sang stirring versions of 'Mr Tambourine Man', 'Blowin' In The Wind' and 'A Hard Rain's A-Gonna Fall'. Thereafter, however, he maintained a peculiarly low profile while critics dissected his past work and pondered on the passing of a musical legend. Dylan, meanwhile, was working with director Sam Peckinpah on the film *Pat Garrett And Billy The Kid*, in which he played Billy's sidekick, Alias. The soundtrack album contained an evocative hit single 'Knockin' On Heaven's Door', the singer's first chart entry in almost two years.

With the termination of his CBS contract imminent, Dylan surprised many industry observers by signing an albums deal with David Geffen's label Asylum. Columbia responded with petulant indignation by releasing *Dylan*, a compilation containing several lamentable 1970 outtakes including the maestro's amusing version of Elvis Presley's 'A Fool Such As I' and Joni Mitchell's 'Big Yellow Taxi'. At a time when Dylan's critical reputation needed a boost, it was a sad nadir. However, 1974 saw Dylan return to the centre stage with a blistering series of concerts across America which attracted his best coverage in years. A studio album, *Planet Waves*, re-established his standing, primarily thanks to two versions of the classic 'Forever Young', plus 'Dirge' and 'Wedding Song', two of his most passionately intense outpourings. The live double, *Before The Flood*, released five months later, was almost equally well received and by the autumn CBS had re-signed the artist. Dylan immediately began work on *Blood On The Tracks*, his most sustained album since the mid-60s. It contained some scorching narratives ('Tangled Up In Blue', 'Lily, Rosemary And The Jack Of Hearts'), fascinatingly ambiguous love songs ('If You See Her Say Hello', 'Shelter From The Storm') and a seething epic 'Idiot Wind', whose savage imagery and accusingly triumphant tone recalled the genius of 'Like A Rolling Stone'.

By the winter of 1975, Dylan was back on the road playing small clubs with the Rolling Thunder Revue, an eclectic ensemble, which included along its spiralling route Roger McGuinn, Arlo Guthrie, Joan Baez, Mick Ronson, Ronee Blakley, Joni Mitchell and Allen Ginsberg. In January 1976, the new album *Desire* opened with 'Hurricane', a punchy paean to the imprisoned boxer Ruben Carter, and ended with 'Sara', an urgent plea to a wife who would shortly commence divorce proceedings. With the assistance of co-writer Jacques Levy, Dylan penned an evocative travelogue of drama from the streets of Brooklyn to the pyramids of Egypt, taking in Mozambique, Durango and Black Diamond Bay along the way. The music was equally colourful thanks to the hauntingly expressive violin work of Scarlet Rivera and the wailing background vocals of Emmylou Harris and Ronee Blakley.

A second tour with Rolling Thunder commenced in April 1976, but the recorded results, *Hard Rain*, failed to capture the eccentric charm of the revue. Dylan's next project, the four hour movie *Renaldo And Clara*, seemed baffling, uncoordinated and indulgent, to some, though others hailed it as a work of sprawling genius. Dylan also appeared on film in Martin Scorsese's celebrated documentary of the Band's musical farewell, *The Last Waltz*. 1978 saw Dylan undertaking an extensive world tour, which coincided with *Street-Legal*, an interesting set ranging in mood from the brooding 'Senor (Tales Of Yankee Power)' to the plaintive pleading of 'Baby Stop Crying' and the curiously celebratory 'Changing Of The Guard'.

Dylan ended the decade on a dramatic note by converting to Christianity. Entering the studio in May 1979, he worked with producer Jerry Wexler and Dire Straits' Mark Knopfler on his 'born again' album *Slow Train Coming*. A subsequent concert tour was notable for Dylan's staunch refusal to play his old songs. Some of the old radicals in his audience voiced the same cries of disillusioned bewilderment or outrage that the Greenwich Village folkies had uttered when Dylan went electric in 1965, but, once again, the quality of the material was undeniable. 'Precious Angel' was a stirring statement of faith and, in common with the other songs in his repertoire, eschewed bland, beatific platitudes in favour of challenging comments on man's shortcomings. 'Gotta Serve Somebody' and 'When You Gonna Wake up' were brilliantly rhetorical putdowns, which showed Dylan taking on the non-believers with the same voice in which he had castigated the subjects of 'Positively 4th Street' and 'Like A Rolling Stone'. This was Dylan at his acerbic best.

The sharpness of Dylan's tongue was less evident on *Saved* (1980), which was the closest he ever reached to recording a pure gospel album. The underrated *Shot Of Love* (1981) had a delightfully refreshing 'back-to-basics' production and the minimalist feel suited Dylan's new material. Among the tracks was an elegiac tribute to the controversial comedian Lenny Bruce, a seemingly inappropriate secular subject, whose presence clearly indicated that Dylan's fundamentalism was far less pronounced than the majority of his followers assumed. His impatience with atheistic intolerance was still effectively voiced in the sarcastic 'Property Of Jesus', but by the time of the next release of the next album, *Infidels*, political concerns seemed uppermost in the artist's mind. A slicker production, the album saw Dylan tackling the state of trade unions and American nationalism rather than concerning himself with spiritual redemption.

Although no longer billed as the spokesperson of his generation, Dylan's contribution to popular music was emphasized in the five album retrospective *Biograph*, released in 1985. That same year the anticlimactic *Empire Burlesque* appeared, much of its contents wrapped in predictably arranged backing vocals, which gave a bland uniformity to much of the material. The capacity of Dylan to confound his audience with periodic disappointment had been evident since *Self Portrait* and even earlier in certain faltering live performances, but such fallibility had never been seen on such a global scale as the closing of Live Aid concert in July 1985. Backed by a ragged Ron Wood and Keith Richard's, Dylan stumbled through a short acoustic set which was almost inexplicably lacklustre. His reputation was further dented by a critically panned movie, *Hearts Of Fire*, and a poorly received album, *Knocked Out Loaded*.

Despite a collaboration with songwriter Carol Bayer Sager and a welcome return to the narrative form, courtesy of the 11-minute 'Brownsville Girl', co-written with the playwright Sam Shepard, the album found few champions. Dylan nevertheless continued to tour, appearing at benefits for Farm Aid and Sun City and even turning up at a poetry festival in Moscow. While critics bemoaned the recent quality of his studio output, Dylanologists pointed to a wealth of material languishing in the vaults which testified to his continued greatness.

Down In The Groove (1988) settled none of the arguments, being mainly composed of old blues songs and personal favourites. Its spontaneity was appealing, its timing perhaps unfortunate. Further evidence of Dylan's love of improvisation was heard on *The Traveling Wilburys- Volume One,* on which he collaborated with Jeff Lynne, Tom Petty, George Harrison and Roy Orbison.

Throughout the late 80s, Dylan continued to tour, appearing with both Tom Petty And The Heartbreakers and the Grateful Dead. Some concerts were deemed inspired, others mediocre. Yet, there was no doubting the importance of Dylan's live work in the context of his art. More than any other performer he had used the stage as a means of redefining his work and was now well known for twisting his lyrics into new unfamiliar metres, or changing the meaning of lines or entire songs through stress or intonation. Songs such as 'It Ain't Me Babe' or 'It's All Over Now, Baby Blue' could thus be presented as testaments of celebration, apathy, disillusionment or plain disgust, depending upon Dylan's unpredictable and often eccentric inflexions. The inherent ambiguity in his best material was brilliantly evinced via live performances and added a new dimension to his work.

It was not until the end of the decade that the experiments and aberration of recent years crystallized into a universally accepted work of excellence. *Oh Mercy* (1989) brought back the musical and lyrical 'mystery' to Dylan's work that always separated him from his lesser songwriting contemporaries. The production by Daniel Lanois brought a shadowy resonance to the proceedings which perfectly complemented the air of sinister inevitability that permeated 'Man In A Long Black Coat'. The Old Testament imagery could again be found on 'Ring Them Bells' and 'Shooting Star', but Dylan was no longer dealing in cast iron certainties. 'What Was It You Wanted' seemed strangely quizzical, while the beautiful 'Most Of The Time' presented a series of positive statements undermined by the qualifications implicit in its title ('I can survive and I can endure and I don't even think about her . . . most of the time').

If *Oh Mercy* showed an underlying quest motif, then

this was even more evident in his live performances, particularly the amusingly nicknamed 'Never Ending Tour' on which Dylan embarked in 1988 with a back-to-basics three-piece band, initially inspired by guitarist G.E. Smith. *Under The Red Sky* found few friendly critics when released, although time has healed what could have merely been anger at him not delivering another *Oh Mercy*, and the album is now seen as good, if not great. Dylan's punishingly exhaustive, almost obsessional touring schedule, compounded by radical alterations in his set on a nightly basis has resulted in live work of magnificent stature as well as prompting unanswerable questions about his motivations which in themselves enhance the mystique that he has sustained over 30 years as a performing artist. In addition to the glut of books published to celebrate Dylan's 50th birthday, CBS/Legacy released *The Bootleg Series, Vols 1-3, Rare And Unreleased 1961-1991* - an outstanding boxed set of his entire career composed entirely of previously unreleased tracks and alternate versions. If there ever had been any serious doubters about Dylan's achievements, this collection made amends in spectacular fashion.

Albums: *Bob Dylan* (1962), *The Freewheelin' Bob Dylan* (1963), *The Times They Are A-Changin'* (1964), *Another Side Of Bob Dylan* (1964), *Bringing It All Back Home* (1965), *Highway 61 Revisited* (1965), *Blonde On Blonde* (1966), *John Wesley Harding* (1968), *Nashville Skyline* (1969), *Self Portrait* (1970), *New Morning* (1970), *Dylan* (1973), *Planet Waves* (1974), *Before The Flood* (1974), *Blood On The Tracks* (1975), *The Basement Tapes* (1975), *Desire* (1976), *Hard Rain* (1976), *Street-Legal* (1978), *Slow Train Coming* (1979), *At Budokan* (1979), *Saved* (1980), *Shot Of Love* (1981), *Infidels* (1983), *Real Live* (1984), *Empire Burlesque* (1985), *Knocked Out Loaded* (1986), *Down In The Groove* (1988), *Dylan And The Dead* (1989), *Oh Mercy* (1989), *Under The Red Sky* (1990). Various compilations have also been issued, *More Bob Dylan Greatest Hits* (1972) and *Biograph* (1985) contained some new material, while *The Bootleg Series, Vols 1-3, Rare And Unreleased 1961-1991* (1991) consisted entirely of unreleased performances.

Selected further reading: *Tarantula*, Bob Dylan. *Writings And Drawings*, Bob Dylan. *Bob Dylan*, Anthony Scaduto. *Song And Dance Man*, Michael Gray. *A Retrospective*, Craig McGregor. *On The Road With Bob Dylan*, Larry Sloman. *No Direction Home*, Robert Shelton. *Complete Lyrics*, Bob Dylan. *All Across The Telegraph - A Bob Dylan Handbook*, ed. Michael Gray and John Bauldie. *Wanted Man - In Search Of Bob Dylan*, ed. John Bauldie. *Performing Artist*, Paul Williams. *A Dylan Companion*, ed. Liz Thomson. *Oh No! Not Another Bob Dylan Book*, Patrick Humphries and John Bauldie.

E

Earls

Although 'Remember Then' was their only hit, the Earls were one of the most accomplished white doo-wop groups of the early 60s. The lead singer Larry Chance (b. Larry Figueiredo, 19 October 1940, Philadelphia, Pennyslvania, USA) formed the group in New York's Bronx area in the late 50s. The other members were first tenor Robert Del Din (b. 1942), second tenor Eddie Harder (b. 1942), baritone Larry Palumbo (b. 1941) and bass John Wray (b. 1939). For their first single, the group revived the Harptones' 1954 R&B hit 'Life Is But A Dream'. This was released by the local Rome label in 1961. The following year, the group moved to another New York label, Old Town, and made 'Remember Then' which reached the Top 30. The Earls continued to release singles on Old Town until 1965, but the only record to make an impact was a maudlin version of 'I Believe', dedicated to Palumbo, who had died in a parachute accident. With various personnel changes, including the addition of Hank DiScuillo on guitar, Larry Chance continued to lead the group on occasional records for Mr G and ABC. With their big hit on numerous oldies compilations during the 70s, the Earls appeared on rock revival shows. 'Remember Then' was a UK Top 20 hit in 1979 for revivalist band Showaddywaddy.

Album: *Remember Me Then* (1962).

Earth Opera

Formed in Boston, New England, USA in 1967, Earth Opera revolved around Peter Rowan (vocals/guitar) and David Grisman (b. 1945, Hackensack, New Jersey, USA; mandocello/mandolin). Both were veterans of the bluegrass and old-time circuit; Rowan with Bill Monroe And The Bluegrass Boys and the Mother State Bay Entertainers, and Grisman as leader of the New York Ramblers and member of the Even Dozen Jug Band. The two musicians worked as a duo, performing Rowan's original songs, before adding John Nagy (bass) and Bill Stevenson (keyboards/vibes). *Earth Opera* was produced by fellow folk music associate Peter Siegel, who shared an unerring empathy with the material. Rowan's lyrical, highly visual compositions were enhanced by his unusual, expressive tenor, particularly on the graphic 'Death By Fire' and 'The Child Bride'. Elsewhere the material reflected the questioning rootlessness prevalent in the immediate post-1967 era.

Drummer Paul Dillon was then added to the line-up, but Bill Stevenson left the group prior to recording a second album. Although worthy, *The Great American Eagle Tragedy* featured a roughshod horn section which altered the tone of several songs, with only one track, 'Mad Lydia's Waltz', retaining the delicacy of the previous set. The collection was marked by its uncompromising title track, a lengthy impassioned attack on the Vietnam War. A compulsive example of the genre, replete with images of terror and madness, this accomplished piece overshadowed much of the remaining content, although Rowan's talent was equally obvious on 'Home To You' and 'Sanctuary From The Law'. The former contained the memorably quirky lyric, 'It's tired and I'm getting late'. Earth Opera broke up soon after the set was issued. Rowan later joined Sea Train, before enjoying a successful solo career, while Grisman became a leading figure in traditional music circles.
Albums: *Earth Opera* (1968), *The Great American Eagle Tragedy* (1969).

Easybeats

Formed in Sydney, Australia in 1964, this beat group comprised Harry Vanda (b. Harold Wandon, 22 March 1947, The Hague, Holland; guitar), Dick Diamonde (b. 28 December 1947, Hilversum, Holland; bass), Steve Wright (b. 20 December 1948, Leeds, Yorkshire, England; vocals), George Young (b. 6 November 1947, Glasgow, Scotland; guitar) and Gordon 'Snowy' Fleet (b. 16 August 1946, Bootle, Lancashire, England; drums). Originally known as the Starfighters, they changed their name after the arrival of Fleet, who modelled their new style on that of the Liverpool beat groups of the period. After a series of hits in their homeland, including six number 1 singles, the group relocated to England in the summer of 1966 and were offered the opportunity to work with top pop producer Shel Talmy. The combination resulted in one of the all-time great beat group singles of the '60s: 'Friday On My Mind'. Strident guitars, clever counter harmonies and a super-strong beat were the ingredients that provided the disc with its power. Following a solid push on pirate radio, it peaked at number 6 in the UK. Unfortunately, the group found it difficult to follow up their hit and their prospects were not helped after splitting with Talmy during the recording of their first UK-released album. When they finally returned to the UK charts in 1968, it was with the ballad 'Hello How Are You', the mood of which contrasted sharply with that of their first hit. Lack of morale and gradual line-up changes subtly transformed the group into a vehicle for key members Vanda and Young, who were already writing material for other artists. In 1969, after an Australian tour, the Easybeats split up. Ironically, they enjoyed a US hit some months later

with 'St Louis'. In the wake of their demise, Vanda/Young went into production, released records under a variety of pseudonyms and were largely responsible for the Australian success of such artists as John Paul Jones and William Shakespeare. George Young and his two brothers, Angus and Malcolm, were part of the original line-up of AC/DC, while Vanda/Young found success in their own right during the early 80s as Flash In The Pan.
Selected albums: *Easy* (1965), *It's 2 Easy* (1966), *Volume 3* (1966), *The Best Of The Easybeats, Plus Pretty Girl* (1967), *Friday On My Mind* (1967), *Vigil* (1968), *Friends* (1969), *The Shame Just Drained* (1977), *Absolute Anthology* (1980), Compilations: *Rock Legend* (1980), *Best Of The Easybeats* (1986).

Eclection

Eclection

Formed in London in 1967, Eclection took their name from the contrasting backgrounds of its original line-up. Although Mike Rosen (guitar), Kerilee Male (vocals), Georg Hultgren (bass) and Gerry Conway (drums) were not well-known figures, guitarist Trevor Lucas had established himself on the folk circuit following his arrival from Australia. The quintet used his undoubted talent to forge an imaginative folk/rock style which showed influences from both British and American sources. Kerilee Male left the group in October 1968, following the release of Eclection's debut album. Her replacement was Dorris Henderson, a black American singer who had previously recorded two folk-influenced collections with guitarist John Renbourn. A further change occurred when John 'Poli' Palmer succeeded Mike Rosen, but the group was sadly unable to fulfill its obvious potential. In October 1969 Palmer left to join Family, and Eclection simply folded. Lucas and Conway soon resurfaced in Fotheringay, while Hultgren later changed his surname to Kajanus and found fame with the pop group Sailor. In the 70s Henderson attempted to revive Eclection with different musicians, but she was largely unsuccessful.
Album: *Eclection* (1968).

Duane Eddy

Eddy, Duane

b. 26 April 1938, Corning, New York, USA. The legendary simple 'twangy' guitar sound of Duane Eddy has made him one of rock 'n' roll's most famous instrumental artists. The sound was created after hearing Bill Justis's famous 'Raunchy' (the song that George Harrison first learned to play). Together with producer Lee Hazelwood, Eddy co-wrote a deluge of hits mixed with versions of standards, using the bass strings of his Grestch guitar recorded through an echo chamber. The debut 'Movin' 'N' Groovin'' made the lower end of the US chart, and for the next six years Eddy repeated this formula with greater success. His backing group, the Rebel Rousers was a tight, experienced unit with a prominent saxophone sound played by Jim Horn and Steve Douglas, completed by pianist Larry Knechtel. Among their greatest hits were 'Rebel-Rouser', 'Shazam', 'Peter Gunn', 'Ballad Of Paladin' and 'Theme From Dixie'. The latter was a variation on the Civil War standard written in 1860. One of Eddy's most memorable hits was the superlative theme music for the film *Because They're Young*, brilliantly combining his bass notes with evocative strings. The song has been used by UK disc jockey Johnny Walker as his theme music for over 25 years and this classic still sounds fresh. Eddy's '(Dance With The) Guitar Man' was another major hit, which was unusual for the fact that the song had lyrics, sung by a female group. Eddy's albums played heavily on the use of 'twang' in the title, but that was exactly what the fans wanted.

The hits dried up in 1964 at the dawn of the Beatles' invasion, and for many years his sound was out of fashion. An attempt in the contemporary market was lambasted with *Duane Goes Dylan*. Apart from producing Phil Everly's excellent *Star Spangled Springer* in 1973, Eddy travelled the revival circuit, always finding a small but loyal audience in the UK. Tony Macauley wrote 'Play Me Like You Play Your Guitar' for him in 1975, and after more than a decade he was back in the UK Top 10. He slipped back into relative obscurity but returned to the charts in 1986 when he was flattered to be asked to play with the electro-synthesizer unit Art Of Noise, all the more complimentary was that it was his song, 'Peter Gunn'. The following year Jeff Lynne produced his first album for many years, being joined by Paul McCartney, George Harrison and Ry Cooder, all paying tribute to the man who should have legal copyright on the word 'twang'.

Selected albums: *Have Twangy Guitar Will Travel* (1958), *Especially For You* (1958), *The 'Twang's The 'Thang'* (1959), *Songs Of Our Heritage* (1960), *$1,000,000 Worth Of Twang* (1960), *Girls! Girls! Girls!* (1961), *$1,000,000 Worth Of Twang Volume 2* (1962), *Twistin' And Twangin'* (1962), *Twisting With Duane Eddy* (1962), *Twangy Guitar-Silky Strings* (1962), *Dance With The Guitar Man* (1963), *In Person* (1963), *Surfin' With Duane Eddy* (1963), *Twang A Country Song* (1963), *Twanging Up A Storm!* (1963), *Lonely Guitar* (1964), *Water Skiing* (1964), *Best Of* (1965), *Twangsville* (1965), *Duane Goes Bob Dylan* (1965), *Duane A Go Go* (1965), *Biggest Twang Of Them All* (1966), *Roaring Twangies* (1967), *Twangy Guitar* (1970), *Legends Of Rock* (1975), *Twenty Terrific Twangies* (1981), *Duane Eddy* (1987), *Greatest Hits* (1991).

Electric Flag

The brief career of the much vaunted Electric Flag was begun in 1967 by the late Mike Bloomfield, following his departure from the influential Paul Butterfield Blues Band. The original group comprised of Bloomfield (b. 28 July 1944, Chicago, Illinois, USA, d. 15 February 1981; guitar), Buddy Miles (drums/vocals), Nick Gravenites (b. Chicago, Illinois, USA; vocals), Barry Goldberg (keyboards), Harvey Brooks (bass), Peter Strazza (tenor saxophone), Marcus Doubleday (trumpet) and Herbie Rich (baritone saxophone). All members were well-seasoned professionals coming from a variety of musical backgrounds. Their debut at the 1967 Monterey Pop Festival was a noble start. Their excellent *A Long Time Comin'* was released in 1968 with additional members Stemziel (Stemsy) Hunter and Mike Fonfara and was a significant hit in the USA. The tight brassy-tinged blues numbers were laced with Bloomfield's sparse but bitingly crisp Fender Stratocaster guitar. Tracks such as 'Killing Floor' were perfect examples of vintage Flag. The band was unable to follow this release, and immediately began to fall apart, with founder Bloomfield being the first to go. Buddy Miles attempted to hold the band together but the second album was a pale shadow of their debut, with only 'See To Your Neighbour' showing signs of a unified performance. Miles then left to form the Buddy Miles Express, while Gravenites became a songwriting legend in San Francisco. Harvey Brooks, following years of session work, including the Bloomfield/Kooper/Stills *Super Session*, turned up as a member of Sky. An abortive Flag reunion produced the lacklustre and inappropriately titled *The Band Kept Playing*.

Albums: *The Trip* (1967, film soundtrack), *A Long Time Comin'* (1968), *The Electric Flag* (1969), *The Band Kept Playing* (1974).

Electric Prunes

Formed in Los Angeles in 1965, the Electric Prunes originally consisted of Jim Lowe (b. San Luis Obispo, California, USA; vocals/guitar/autoharp), Ken Williams (b. Long Beach, California, USA; lead guitar), James 'Weasel' Spagnola (b. Cleveland, Ohio, USA; guitar), Mark Tulin (b. Philadelphia, Pennsylvania, USA; bass) and Michael Weakley aka Quint (drums), although the latter was quickly replaced by Preston Ritter (b. Stockton, California, USA). The quintet made its debut with the low-key 'Ain't It Hard', before scoring two US Top 20 hits with 'I Had Too Much To Dream (Last Night)' and 'Get Me To The World On Time'. These exciting singles blended the drive of garage/punk rock, the rhythmic pulse of the Rolling Stones and the experimentalism of the emerging psychedelic movement. Such performances were enhanced by Dave Hassinger's accomplished production. The Prunes debut album was hampered by indifferent material, but the excellent follow-up, *Underground*, featured three of the group's finest achievements, 'Hideaway', 'The Great Banana Hoax' and 'Long Day's Flight'. However the Prunes were sadly unable to sustain their hit profile and grew increasingly unhappy with the artistic restrictions placed on them by management and producer. Ritter was replaced by the prodigal Quint before the remaining original members dropped out during sessions for *Mass In F Minor*. This acclaimed combination of Gregorian styles and acid rock was composed and arranged by David Axelrod, who fulfilled the same role on a follow-up set, *Release Of An Oath*. An entirely new line-up - Ron Morgan (guitar), Mark Kincaid (b.

Topeka, Kansas, USA; guitar), Brett Wade (b. Vancouver, British Columbia, Canada; bass) and Richard Whetstone (b. Hutchinson, Kansas, USA; drums) - completed the lacklustre *Just Good Old Rock 'N' Roll*, which bore no trace of the founding line-up's sense of adventure. The Electric Prunes' name was then abandoned.

Albums: *The Electric Prunes (I Had Too Much To Dream Last Night)* (1967), *Underground* (1967), *Mass In F Minor* (1967), *Release Of An Oath* (1968), *Just Good Old Rock 'N' Roll* (1969). Compilation: *Long Day's Flight* (1986).

Elektra Records

Founded in New York, USA in 1950 by student and traditional music enthusiast Jac Holtzman, this much respected label initially showcased recordings drawn from America's rich heritage. Early releases included Jean Ritchie's *Songs Of Her Kentucky Mountain Family* and Ed McCurdy's *Songs Of The Old West*, but the catalogue also boasted collections encompassing material from international sources. Elektra also made several notable jazz and blues recordings but, as the 50s progressed, became renowned for its interest in contemporary folk. It thus attracted many of the performers from the Greenwich Village and New England enclaves, notably Judy Collins, Tom Paxton, Koerner, Ray And Glover, Fred Neil and Phil Ochs, before embracing electric styles in 1966 with the Paul Butterfield Blues Band and Love. Elektra then became established on America's west coast and its transformation from folk to rock was confirmed the following year with the Doors. Subsequent signings included the MC5, Rhinoceros, the Stooges and Earth Opera, while the label achieved concurrent commercial success with Bread. Elektra also became an important outlet for many singer-songwriter's, and its catalogue included superior releases by David Ackles, Tom Rush, Tim Buckley, Harry Chapin Incredible String Band and Carly Simon. In 1971 Elektra was absorbed into the WEA conglomerate and incongruous releases by the New Seekers and Queen robbed the company of its individuality. Two years later, and with the departure of Holtzman, the label was amalgamated with Asylum and for much of the decade remained the junior partner. Television's *Marquee Moon* rekindled memories of the outlet's classic era, while during the 80s Elektra was responsible for releases by 10000 Maniacs, the Screaming Blue Messiahs and the Pixies (US only). The label was unwilling, or unable, to shake off its early heritage which was commemorated in a series of boxed sets under the umbrella title *The Jac Holtzman Years*. Elektra's 40th anniversary was celebrated with *Rubiayat*, in which representatives from the current roster performed songs drawn from the 'classic' era.

Recommended listening: *What's Shakin'* (1966), *Select Elektra* (1967), *Begin Here* (1969), *O Love Is Teasing: Anglo-American Mountain Balladry* (1983), *Bleecker & MacDougal: The Folk Scene Of The 60s* (1983), *Crossroads: White Blues In The 60s* (1985), *Elektrock: The Sixties* (c.1985).

Elgins

US-born Johnny Dawson, Cleo Miller and Robert Fleming, later replaced by Norbert McClean, sang together in three Detroit vocal groups in the late 50s, the Sensations, the Five Emeralds and the Downbeats. Under the last of these names, they recorded two singles for Motown in 1959 and 1962. Also in 1962, Saundra Mallett (later Saundra Mallett Edwards) issued 'Camel Walk' for Tamla, backed by the Vandellas. Motown suggested that she join forces with the Downbeats, and the new group was named the Elgins - after the title originally used by the Temptations when they first joined Motown.

In the fiercely competitive climate of Motown Records in the mid-60s, the Elgins were forced to wait three years before they could issue a single, but 'Darling Baby' - written and produced by Holland/Dozier/Holland - reached the R&B Top 10 early in 1966. 'Heaven Must Have Sent You', which also exhibited the traditional Motown sound of the period, matched that success, but after one further hit in 1967, the group split up. In 1971, the group enjoyed two surprise UK Top 20 hits when Motown reissued 'Heaven Must Have Sent You' and the former b-side 'Put Yourself In My Place'. The Elgins reformed to tour Britain, with Yvonne Allen (a former session vocalist) taking the place of Saundra Mallett; but plans for the revitalized group to renew their recording career foundered. In 1989 Yvonne Allen, Johnny Dawson, Norman Mclean and Jimmy Charles recorded a new arrangement of 'Heaven Must Have Sent You' for producer Ian Levine. They continued working for his Motor City label in the 90s, releasing *Take The Train* and *Sensational*. The original lead vocalist on all their Motown material, Saundra Edwards, was also recording for the same label.
Album: *Darling Baby* (1966), *Take The Train* (1990), *Sensational* (1991).

Elliott, Bern, And The Fenmen

Formed in Erith, Kent, England in 1961, Bern Elliott And The Fenmen spent much of their early years playing in German clubs. Signed to Decca in 1963, they scored a UK Top 20 hit with their debut single, 'Money', arguably the finest cover version of this recurrent beat group favourite. A rendition of 'New Orleans' provided another chart entry, but the singer and backing group broke up following the release of 'Good Times'. While the Fenmen: Alan Judge (guitar), Wally Allen (guitar), Eric Willmer (bass) and Jon Povey (drums) - continued to record in an engaging, close-harmony style, Elliott formed a new group, the Klan, around Dave Cameron (organ), Tim Hamilton (guitar), John Silby-Pearce (bass) and Pete Adams (drums). Despite several excellent singles, including 'Voodoo Woman' (1965), the vocalist was unable to regain initial success. Former colleagues Allen and Povey later found fame in the Pretty Things.
Album: *The Beat Years* (1988).

Ellis, Shirley

b. 1941, Bronx, New York, USA. Before striking out on a solo career in 1963, Ellis served an apprenticeship singing with an unsuccessful vocal group, the Metronones. Her strong voice was used for good effect on dance-floor ravers 'The Nitty Gritty' (number 4 R&B and number 8 pop in 1963) and '(That's) What The Nitty Gritty Is' (number 14 R&B 1964), and her future looked bright. Ellis, however, soon found herself in novelty song territory with catchy ditties written by her husband/manager Lincoln Chase, namely 'The Name Game' (number 4 R&B and number 3 pop in 1965) and 'The Clapping Song (Clap Pat Clap Slap)' (number 16 R&B and number 8 pop in 1965). The latter was the only UK success for Ellis, amazingly hitting twice, in 1965, when it reached number 6, and on an EP in 1978. The Belle Stars, a female group, successfully revived 'The Clapping Song' in 1982.
Albums: *In Action* (1964), *The Name Game* (1965), *Sugar, Let's Shing A Ling* (1967).

Ellison, Lorraine

b. 1943, Philadelphia, Pennsylvania, USA. Lorraine recorded with two gospel groups, the Ellison Singers and the Golden Chords, but left the latter in 1964 to pursue a solo career. 'I Dig You Baby' (1965) was a minor hit, but it was the powerful 'Stay With Me' (1966) that established her reputation. Written and produced by Jerry Ragavoy, this intense, dramatic ballad defined deep soul. Ellison's awe-inspiring vocal plea was a spectacular one-off performance. Nothing in her subsequent recordings emulated its naked emotion and even the excellent 'Heart Be Still' (1967) was an anti-climax. Afterwards, Ellison never charted again, not even with the original version of 'Try Just A Little Bit Harder' (1968), which rock singer Janis Joplin later re-made with great success. Ellison's compositions on which she often collaborated with Sam Bell from the Enchanters, were recorded by Howard Tate and Garnet Mimms.
Albums: *Heart And Soul* (1966), *Stay With Me* (1969), *Lorraine Ellison* (1974). Compilation: *The Best Of Philadelphia's Queen* (1976).

Epstein, Brian

b. Brian Samuel Epstein, 1934, Liverpool England, d. 27 August 1967. One of the most famous pop managers in music business history, Epstein began his working life as a provincial shopkeeper, overseeing the North End Road Music Stores (NEMS) in central Liverpool. His life took a new direction on Saturday 28 October 1961 when a customer requested a record entitled 'My Bonnie' by a group called the Beatles. When Brian subsequently attended one of their gigs at the Cavern club in Matthew Street he was drawn into the alien netherworld of leather-clad beat groups and, against the advice of his friends, became a pop manager. His early efforts at promoting the Beatles proved haphazard, but using his influence with record companies he secured a number of interviews with important A&R representatives. A slew of rejections followed, but Decca Records at least offered the Beatles an audition before finally turning them down. Epstein took his revenge by crediting the unfortunate Dick Rowe with the immortal words: 'Groups of guitarists are on the way out'.

Epstein's tardiness in securing a record deal did not diminish his abilities in other areas. He transformed the Beatles into a more professional outfit, banned them from swearing or eating on stage and even encouraged the establishment of a rehearsed repertoire. Perhaps his most lasting contribution at this point was persuading them to replace their menacing, black leather garb with smart, grey lounge suits, with eye-catching matching collars. By the spring of 1962, Epstein at last won a record deal thanks to the intuitive intervention of producer George Martin. A near crisis followed shortly afterwards when Epstein had to oversee the dismissal of drummer Pete Best, who was replaced by Ringo Starr. During October 1962, a management contract was belatedly finalized with the Beatles by which Epstein received 25 per cent of their earnings, a figure he maintained for all future signings. Weeks later, he struck a deal with music publisher Dick James which culminated in the formation of Northern Songs, a company dealing exclusively with compositions by John Lennon and Paul McCartney. In an extremely clever and unusual deal for the period, the powers agreed on a 50/50 split: half to Dick James and his partner Charles Emmanuel Silver; 20 per cent each to Lennon and McCartney, and 10 per cent to Epstein.

Long before the Beatles became the most successful entertainers in British music history, Epstein had signed his second group Gerry And The Pacemakers. Scouring the Cavern for further talent he soon added Tommy Quickly, the Fourmost, Billy J. Kramer And The Dakotas, the Big Three and Cilla Black. The spree of NEMS signings during 1963 was the most spectacular managerial coup since Larry Parnes' celebrated discoveries during the late 50s. More importantly, the artists dominated the UK charts throughout the year, logging an incredible nine number 1 hits spanning 32 weeks at the top. By early 1964, Beatlemania had crossed from Britain to America and NEMS had transformed from a small family business into a multi-million pound organization. The strength of the company ensured that the Beatles had few administrative problems during the Epstein era. Scrupulously fair, he even allowed his charges a 10 per cent interest in NEMS. One area where Epstein was deemed fallible was in the merchandising agreements that he concluded on behalf of the Beatles. Ironically, it was due to delegating the matter to the inexperienced solicitor David Jacobs that the group found themselves receiving a mere 10 per cent of the sums received by the company set up to merchandise goods in their name. By the mid-60s, licences had been granted for every product that the American merchandising mentality could conceive. This meant not only badges, dolls and toys, but even cans of Beatle breath. The lost revenue that Brian had allowed to slip through his fingers was gruesomely revealed in the pages of the *Wall Street Journal*. According to their figures, Americans spent approximately $50 million on Beatles goods up until the end of 1964, while the world market was estimated at roughly £40 million. Although Epstein attempted to rectify the poor merchandising deal through litigation and even contributed massive legal expenses from his own pocket, the stigma of the unfortunate deal remained. Few pointed out that it was less Epstein's error than that of the inexperienced Jacobs, who had agreed to the arrangement without consulting his client.

The merchandising dispute has all too often eclipsed Epstein's achievements in other areas. It deserves to be remembered that he effectively ushered in the era of stadium rock with the Beatles' Hollywood Bowl concert, an event which changed rock economics for ever. Even while the Beatles were conquering the New World, Epstein was expanding his empire. Although he signed a couple of unsuccessful artists, most of the NEMS stable enjoyed tremendous success. The career of Cilla Black was a tribute to Epstein's creative management. He helped her adapt to the rigours of showbusiness success with a feminine solicitude typical of a would-be dress designer. More importantly, however, he immediately recognized her lasting charm as the unpretentious, girl-next-door, an image that another manager might have suppressed. Epstein's expert exploitation of her appeal paved the way for her eventual acceptance and success as a television host.

When the Beatles ceased touring after the summer of 1966, Epstein's role in their day-to-day lives was minimal. For a time, he attempted to find satisfaction in other areas, purchasing the Savile Theatre in London's Shaftesbury Avenue and alternating serious drama with Sunday pop shows. Ever puzzling, Epstein even sponsored an Anglo-Spanish bullfighter named Henry Higgins and astonished his colleagues by attempting to persuade the perpetually nervous Billy J. Kramer to pursue an acting career. NEMS, meanwhile, ceased to inspire the entrepreneur and he inexplicably offered a 51 per cent controlling interest to the Australian adventurer Robert Stigwood. By 1967, Epstein was losing control. Drug dependence and homosexual guilt brought him to the verge of a nervous breakdown and attempted suicide. He even suffered at the hands of the press for advocating the use of the drug LSD. On August Bank Holiday 1967 the Beatles were in north Wales attending a course in transcendental meditation with their new mentor the Maharishi Mahesh Yogi. Brian, meanwhile, was lying dead at his London home. The inquest subsequently found that he had died from a cumulative overdose of the sleep-inducing drug Carbitrol. Although suicide was suspected and some fanciful conspiracy theories have suggested the remote possibility of foul play, the coroner concluded with a prosaic verdict of accidental death from 'incautious self-overdoses'.

In spite of his foibles, Epstein is rightly regarded as a great manager, possibly the greatest in British pop history. Judged in the context of his era, his achievements were remarkable. Although it is often claimed that he did not exploit the Beatles' earning power to its maximum degree, he most certainly valued their reputation above all else. During his tenure as manager, he insulated them from corporate avarice and negotiated contracts that prevented EMI from marketing cheap reissues or unauthorized compilations. In this sense, he was the complete antithesis of Elvis Presley's manager, Colonel Tom Parker, who allowed his artist to atrophy through a decade of bad movies. As the custodian of the Beatles' international reputation, Epstein's handling of their career was exemplary. For Epstein, honour meant more than profit and he brought an integrity to pop management that few of his successors have matched. Further reading: *Starmakers & Svengalis: The History Of British Pop Management*, Johnny Rogan. *Brian Epstein*, Ray Coleman.

Equals

Twins Derv and Lincoln Gordon (b. 29 June 1948, Jamaica; vocals and rhythm guitar respectively), Eddie Grant (b. 5 March 1948, Guyana; lead guitar), Patrick Lloyd (b. 17 March 1948, Holloway, London, England; rhythm guitar) and John Hall (b. 25 October 1947, Holloway, London, England; drums) began playing together in 1965 on a council estate in Hornsey Rise, north London. Their best-remembered single, 'Baby Come Back', was recorded the following year as a b-side, but the quintet's early releases made little impression. Over the ensuing months the group became highly regarded on the Continent, where they toured extensively. 'Baby Come Back' became a major hit in Germany during 1967 and later topped the charts in Holland and Belgium. This propulsive, infectious song was then reissued in Britain where it eventually rose to number 1. Although the Equals enjoyed other hits, only 'Viva Bobby Joe' (1969) and 'Black Skinned Blue-Eyed Boys' (1970) reached the Top 10 as their reliance on a tested formula wore thin. Chief songwriter Grant left for a solo career in 1971, after which the group underwent several changes in personnel before finding security on the cabaret circuit. However, their career was resurrected in 1978 when Grant, by then a self-sufficient artist and entrepreneur, signed them to his Ice label for *Mystic Synster*.

Albums: *Unequalled Equals* (1967), *Equals Explosion* aka *Equal Sensation/Sensational Equals* (1968), *Equals Supreme* (1968), *Baby Come Back* (1968), *Equals Strike Back* (1969), *Equals At The Top* (1970, *Equals Rock Around The Clock* (1974), *Doin' The 45s* (1975), *Born Ya* (1976), *Mystic Synster* (1978). Compilations: *The Best Of The Equals* (1969), *Greatest Hits* (1974).

Equals

Escorts

Terry Sylvester (vocals/guitar), John Kinrade (lead guitar) and Mike Gregory (b. 1947; vocals/bass) formed the Escorts at Liverpool's Rose Lane school in 1962. They were originally augmented by drummer John Foster, aka Johnny Sticks, a cousin of Ringo Starr, replaced by Pete Clark (b. 1947) in 1963. The quartet made their debut in April 1964 with a powerful intepretation of 'Dizzie Miss Lizzie', before scoring a minor hit two months later with 'The One To Cry'. Their next release, 'I Don't Want To Go On Without You', was also recorded by the Moody Blues, who secured the chart entry. This undermined the Escorts' confidence, and subsequent releases, although carefully crafted, proved unsuccessful. The group's line-up was also unstable. Terry Sylvester left for the Swinging Blue Jeans, from where he later replaced Graham Nash in the Hollies and by mid-1966, John Kinrade and Mike Gregory were the sole original members. Paddy Chambers (guitar, ex-Big Three, Paddy, Klaus And Gibson) and Paul Comerford (drums, ex-Cryin' Shames) completed the group featured on 'From Head To Toe', the Escorts' final single. This accomplished performance featured Paul McCartney on tambourine, but the quartet split up within weeks of its release.

Album: *3 Down 4 To Go* (1973). Compilation: *From The Blue Angel* (1982).

Evans, Maureen

b. 1940, Cardiff, Wales. Evans began her singing career on the Embassy label, which made budget-priced recordings of contemporary hits for the UK Woolworths' chain-store. She later enjoyed chart success in her own right, beginning in 1960 with 'The Big Hurt', and peaking two years later with 'Like I Do'. This perky offering, more teen-oriented than Evans's normal fare, reached the UK Top 3, but later releases failed to emulate its success. Her rather dated style was quickly surpassed by younger-minded artists, although 'Never Let Him Go', one of the singer's final releases, was an excellent interpretation of a David Gates' song.

Album: *Like I Do* (1963).

Everett, Betty

b. 23 November 1939, Greenwood, Mississippi, USA. Having moved to Chicago in the late 50s, Everett recorded unsuccessfully for several local labels, including Cobra and One-derful. Her hits came on signing to VeeJay Records where 'You're No Good' (1963) and 'The Shoop Shoop Song (It's In His Kiss)' (1964) established her pop/soul style. A duet with Jerry Butler, 'Let It Be Me' (1964), consolidated this position, but her finest moment came with 'Getting Mighty Crowded', a punchy Van McCoy song. Her career faltered on VeeJay's collapse, and an ensuing interlude at ABC Records was unproductive. However in 1969, 'There'll Come A Time' reached number 2 in the R&B charts, a momentum which continued into the early 70s with further releases on UNI and Fantasy Records. Betty's last chart entry was in 1978 with 'True Love (You Took My Heart)'. Cher took her version of 'The Shoop Shoop Song' to the top of the charts in 1991.

Albums: *It's In His Kiss* (1964), with Jerry Butler *Delicious Together* (1964), *There'll Come A Time* (1969), *Love Rhymes* (1974), *Black Girl* (1974), *Happy Endings* (1975). Compilations: *The Very Best Of Betty Everett* (1965), *Betty Everett* (1974 - VeeJay

recordings), *Hot To Handle* (1982), with Lillian Offitt *1957-1961* (1986).

Everly Brothers

Everly Brothers

Don (b. 1 February 1937, Brownie, Kentucky, USA) and Phil (b. 19 January 1939, Chicago, Illinois, USA), the world's most famous rock 'n' roll duo had already experienced a full career before their first record 'Bye Bye Love' was released. As sons of popular country artists Ike and Margaret, they were pushed into the limelight from an early age. They would regularly appear on their parents' radio shows throughout the 40s and accompanied them on many tours. In the mid-50s as rockabilly was evolving into rock 'n' roll the boys moved to Nashville, the mecca for such music. Don had a minor hit when Kitty Wells recorded his composition 'Thou Shalt Not Steal' in 1954.

In 1957 they were given a Felice and Boudleaux Bryant song that was finding difficulty in being placed. They took 'Bye Bye Love' and made it their own; it narrowly missed the US number 1 position and scored in the UK at number 6. The brothers then embarked on a career that made them second only to Elvis Presley in the rock 'n' roll popularity stakes. Their blend of country and folk did much to sanitize and make respectable a phenomenon to which many parents showed hostility. America, then still a racially segregated country, was not ready for its white teenagers to listen to black-based rock music. The brothers' clean looks and even cleaner harmonies did much to change people's attitudes. They quickly followed this initial success with more irresistible Bryant songs, 'Wake Up Little Susie', 'All I Have To Do Is Dream', 'Bird Dog', 'Problems', 'So Sad' and the beautiful 'Devoted To You'. The brothers were supremely confident live performers both with their trademark Gibson Dove and later black J50 guitars. By the end of the 50s they were the world's number 1 vocal group.

Amazingly, their career gained further momentum when, after signing with the newly-formed Warner Brothers Records for $1 million, they delivered a song that was catalogued WB1. This historical debut was the superlative 'Cathy's Clown', written by Don. No Everly record had sounded like this before; the echo-laden production and the treble-loaded harmonies stayed at number 1 in the US for 5 weeks. In the UK it stayed on top for over two months, selling several million and making it one of the most successful records of all time. The brothers continued to release immaculate records, many of them reached the US Top 10, although in England their success was even greater, with two further number 1's during 1961. Again the echo and treble dominated in two more classics, 'Walk Right Back' and a fast-paced reworking of the former Bing Crosby hit 'Temptation'. At the end of 1961 they were drafted into the US Marines, albeit for only six months, and resumed by making a European tour. Don became dependent on drugs, the pressures from constant touring and recording began to show; during one historic night at London's East Ham Granada, in England, a nervous Phil performed solo. The standard 'food poisoning/exhaustion' excuse was used. What was not known by the doting fans, was that Don had attempted a suicidal drug overdose twice in 48 hours. Phil completed the tour solo. Don's addiction continued for another three years, although they were able to work during part of this time.

The advent of the beat boom pushed the brothers out of the spotlight and while they continued to make hit records, none came near their previous achievements. The decline was briefly halted in 1965 with two excellent major UK hits, 'The Price Of Love' and 'Love Is Strange'. The former, a striking chart topper, sounded like their early Warner sound, while the latter harked back even earlier, with a naive but infectious call and answer, talking segment. In 1966 they released Two Yanks In England, a superb album which contained eight songs by Nash/Clarke/Hicks of the Hollies; surprisingly the album failed to chart. The duo were recognized only for their superb singles, and many of their albums were less well-received. The stunning Stories We Could Tell, with an array of guest players, threatened to extend their

market into the rock mainstream, but it was not to be. After a few years of declining fortunes and arrival at the supper-club circuit, the brothers acrimoniously parted. Following a show at Knotts Berry Farm, California in 1973 during which a drunken Don had insulted Phil, the latter walked off, smashed one of his beloved Gibsons and vowed, 'I will never get on a stage with that man again'. The only time they met over the next 10 years was at their father's funeral. Both embarked on solo careers with varying degrees of accomplishment. Their country-flavoured albums found more favour with the Nashville audience of their roots. Don and his band, the Dead Cowboys, regularly played in Nashville, while Phil released the critically acclaimed Star Spangled Springer. Inexplicably the album was a relatively poor seller, as was his follow-up Mystic Line. Phil made a cameo appearance in the film Every Which Way But Loose, performing with actress Sondra Locke. While Don maintained a steady career, playing with ex-Heads, Hands And Feet maestro Albert Lee, Phil concentrated on writing songs. 'She Means Nothing To Me' was a striking duet with Cliff Richard which put the Everly name back in the UK Top 10. Rumours began to circulate of a reunion, which was further fueled by a UK television advertisement for an Everlys' compilation. In June 1983 they hugged and made up and their emotional reunion was made to an ecstatic wet-eyed audience at London's Royal Albert Hall. The following year EB84 was released and gave them another major hit with Paul McCartney's 'Wings Of A Nightingale'. In 1986 they were inducted into the Rock 'n' Roll Hall Of Fame and the following year Phil gave Don a pound of gold and a handmade guitar for his 50th birthday. The Everly Brothers' influence over a generation of pop and rock artists is inestimable; they set the standard for close harmony singing which has rarely been bettered. They now perform regularly together, and to date the ceasefire has held.

Albums: *The Everly Brothers* (1958), *Songs Our Daddy Taught Us* (1958), *It's Everly Time* (1960), *The Fabulous Style Of The Everly Brothers* (1960), *A Date With The Everly Brothers* (1961), *Both Sides Of An Evening* (1961), *Instant Party* (1962), *Christmas With The Everly Brothers And The Boys Town Choir* (1962), *The Everly Brothers Sing Great Country Hits* (1963), *Gone Gone Gone* (1965), *Rock 'N' Soul* (1965), *Beat 'N' Soul* (1965), *In Our Image* (1966), *Two Yanks In England* (1966), *The Hit Sound Of The Everly Brothers* (1967), *The Everly Brothers Sing* (1967), *Roots* (1969), *The Everly Brothers Show* (1970), *End Of An Era* (1971), *Stories We Could Tell* (1972), *Pass The Chicken And Listen* (1973), *The Most Beautiful Songs Of The Everly Brothers* (1973), *Don's And Phil's Fabulous Fifties Treasury* (1974), *The Exciting Everly Brothers* (1975), *Living Legends* (1977), *The New Album* (1977), *The*

Sensational Everly Brothers (1979), The Everly Brothers Reunion Concert (1984), Nice Guys (1984), EB84 (1984), Born Yesterday (1986), Some Hearts (1989). Selected compilations: The Very Best Of The Everly Brothers (1965), The Golden Hits Of The Everly Brothers (1962), The Everly Brothers Original Greatest Hits (1970), The Very Best Of The Everly Brothers (1964), Walk Right Back With The Everlys (1976), Hidden Gems (1990), Perfect Harmony (1990). Solo albums: Don Everly Don Everly (1970), Sunset Towers (1974), Brother Juke Box (1977). Phil Everly Star Spangled Springer (1973), Phil's Diner (There's Nothing Too Good For My Baby) (1974), Mystic Line (1975), Living Alone (1979), Phil Everly (1983).
Further reading; Walk Right Back, Roger White.

Exciters

Exciters

Formed in the Jamaica district of Queens, New York City. This aptly-named group which included Herb Rooney (b. 1941, New York City, New York, USA), Brenda Reid (b. 1945), Carol Johnson (b. 1945) and Lillian Walker (b. 1945) first came to prominence with the vibrant 'Tell Him', a US Top 5 hit in 1962 (also a hit in the UK for Billie Davis in 1963). Produced by Leiber And Stoller and written by Bert Berns (under his pseudonym Bert Russell), the single's energy established the pattern for subsequent releases. 'Do Wah Diddy' (later a hit by Manfred Mann) and 'He's Got The Power' took elements from both uptown soul and the girl-group genre, but later singles failed to fully exploit this powerful combination. The group had lesser hits with 'I Want You To Be My Boy' (1965), a revival of 'A Little Bit Of Soap' (1966) and 'You Don't Know What You're Missing (Till It's Gone)' (1969), but failed to recapture the verve of those first releases. The group re-entered the UK charts in 1975 with 'Reaching For The Best'. Ronnie Pace and Skip McPhee later replaced Johnson and Walker, while Rooney and Reid (his wife) had a minor 1978 hit as Brenda And Herb, releasing one album in 1979, In Heat Again.

Albums: Tell Him (1963), The Exciters (1965), Caviar And Chitlins (1969), Black Beauty (1971), Heaven Is Where You Are (1976), The Exciters (1977). Compilations: The Hit Power Of The Exciters (1986), Tell Him (1991).

F

Fabares, Shelley

b. Michelle Fabares, 19 January 1944, Santa Monica, California, USA. Fabares, whose music career was highlighted by the 1962 number 1 song 'Johnny Angel', was the niece of actress Nanette Fabray. Turning to acting herself, Fabares landed roles in such 50s' films as Never Say Goodbye, Rock, Pretty Baby and Summer Love before being offered the part of Mary Stone in the US television situation comedy The Donna Reed Show in 1958. As the show's popularity rose, both she and series co-star Paul Petersen signed recording contracts with Colpix Records. Fabares was given the ballad 'Johnny Angel', written by Lee Pockriss and Lyn Duddy, and after its debut on the television show, the single quickly rose to number 1. Three follow-up singles did not fare nearly as well, nor did the two albums she recorded for Colpix. In 1964 Fabares married record producer Lou Adler, who arranged a record deal for Fabares with VeeJay Records. There were no hits and Fabares then became the first artist signed to his new Dunhill Records label. Again there were no hits and Fabares returned to acting, working with Herman's Hermits in their film Hold On and with Elvis Presley in Girl Happy, Spinout and Clambake. She divorced Adler in the late 60s and continued to work in film and television. In the late 80s and early 90s she was a member of the cast of Coach, a popular television situation comedy.
Albums: Shelley! (1962), The Things We Did Last Summer (1962).

Fabian

b. 6 February 1943, Philadelphia, USA. Fabiano Forte Bonaparte, almost despite himself, was among the more endurable products of the late 50s when the North American charts were infested with a turnover of vapid boys-next-door - all hair spray, doe eyes and coy half-smiles - groomed for fleeting stardom. Fabian was 'discovered' by two local talent scouts, Peter De Angelis and Bob Marucci, in Frankie Avalon's Teen And Twenty youth club in 1957.

Enthralled by the youth's good looks, the pair shortened his name and contracted him to their Chancellor Records where a huge budget was allocated to project him as a tamed Elvis Presley. Accompanied by the Four Dates, Fabian's first two singles - 'I'm In love' and 'Lilly Lou' - were only regional hits but a string of television performances on Dick Clark's nationally-broadcast *American Bandstand* plus a coast-to-coast tour had the desired effect on female teenagers, and Fabian found himself suddenly in **Billboard**'s Top 40 with 'I'm A Man,' composed by the top New York songwriting team, Doc Pomus/Mort Shuman who also delivered more lucrative hits in 'Turn Me Loose' and 'Hound Dog Man', the main theme from Fabian's silver screen debut of the same name.

More substantial movie roles came Fabian's way after his recording career peaked with 1959's million-selling 'Tiger' and *Hold That Tiger*. As well as the predictable teenpics with their vacuous story-lines and mimed musical sequences, he coped surprisingly well as John Wayne's sidekick in 1960's *North To Alaska* and with Bing Crosby and Tuesday Weld in *High Time*. Fabian's decline was as rapid as his launch after Congress pinpointed him as an instance of one of the exploited puppets in the payola scandal. Questioned at the time, Fabian made matters worse by outlining the considerable electronic doctoring necessary to improve his voice on record. 1960 brought his first serious miss in 'About This Thing Called Love' and an iredeemable downward spiral mitigated by 1962's 'Kissin' And Twistin'' and other small hits. Nevertheless, he could be spotted in in films like the 1962 war epic *The Longest Day* but more commensurate with his talent were such as *Fireball 500* (a 1966 hot-rod epic with his old friend Frankie Avalon) and 1965's *Ride The Wild Surf*.
Album: *Hold That Tiger* (1959).

Fairport Convention

The unchallenged inventors of British folk-rock have struggled through tragedy and changes, retaining the name that now represents not so much who is in the band, but what it stands for. The original group of 1967 comprised Iain Matthews (b. Ian Matthews MacDonald, 16 June 1946, Scunthorpe, Lincolnshire, England; vocals), Judy Dyble (b. 13 February 1949, London, England; vocals), Ashley 'Tyger' Hutchings (b. 26 January 1945, Muswell Hill, London, England; bass), Richard Thompson (b. 3 April 1949, London, England; guitar/vocals), Simon Nicol (b. 13 October 1950, Muswell Hill, London, England; guitar/vocals) and Martin Lamble (b. 28 August 1949, St. Johns Wood, London, England, d. 12 May 1969; drums). The band originally came to the attention of the London 'underground' club scene by sounding like a cross between the Jefferson Airplane and the Byrds.

Fairport Convention

As an accessible alternative they immediately took to people's hearts. American producer Joe Boyd signed them and they released the charming 'If I Had A Ribbon Bow'. On their self-titled debut they introduced the then little-known Canadian songwriter Joni Mitchell to a wider audience. The album was a cult favourite, but like the single, it sold poorly. Judy Dyble departed and was replaced by former Strawbs vocalist, Sandy Denny (b. Alexandra Denny, 6 January 1948, Wimbledon, London, England, d. 21 April 1978). Denny brought a traditional folk-feel to their work which began to appear on the superlative *What We Did On Our Holidays*. This varied collection contained some of their finest songs: Denny's version of 'She Moved Through The Fair', her own 'Fotheringay', Matthews' lilting 'Book Song', the superb 'I'll Keep It With Mine' and Thompson's masterpiece 'Meet On The Ledge'. This joyous album was bound together by exemplary musicianship, of particular note was the guitar of the shy and wiry Thompson. Matthews left soon after its release, unhappy with the traditional direction the band were pursuing. Following the album's critical acclaim and a modest showing in the charts, they experienced tragedy a few months later when their Transit van crashed, killing Martin Lamble and their friend and noted dressmaker Jeannie Franklyn. *Unhalfbricking* was released and, although not as strong as the former, it contained two excellent readings of Bob Dylan songs, 'Percy's Song' and 'Si Tu Dois Partir' (If You Gotta Go, Go Now). Sandy contributed two songs, 'Autopsy' and the definitive, and beautiful, 'Who Knows Where The Time Goes'. More significantly, *Unhalfbricking* featured guest musician, Dave Swarbrick, on fiddle and mandolin. The album charted, as did the second Dylan number; by now the band had opened the door for future bands like Steeleye Span, by creating a climate that allowed traditional music to be played in a rock context. The songs that went on their next album were premièred on John Peel's BBC radio show *Top Gear*. An excited Peel stated that their performance would 'sail them into uncharted waters'; his judgement proved correct. The live-set was astonishing - they played jigs and reels, and completed all 27 verses of the traditional 'Tam Lin', featuring Swarbrick, now a full-time member, plus the debut of new drummer, Dave Mattacks (b. March 1948, Edgeware, Middlesex, England). The subsequent album *Liege And Lief* was a milestone; they had created British folk-rock in spectacular style. This, however, created problems within the band and Hutchings left to form Steeleye Span and Sandy departed to form Fotheringay with ex-Eclection and future husband Trevor Lucas. Undeterred, the band recruited Dave Pegg on bass and Swarbrick became more prominent both as lead vocalist and as an outstanding fiddle player. From their communal home in Hertfordshire they wrote much of the next two album's material although Thompson left before the release of *Angel Delight*. They made the *Guinness Book Of Records* in 1970 with the longest-ever title 'Sir B. McKenzies's Daughter's Lament For The 77th Mounted Lancer's Retreat From The Straits Of Loch Knombe, In The Year Of Our Lord 1727, On The Occasion Of The Announcement Of Her Marriage To The Laird Of Kinleakie'. *Full House* was the first all-male Fairport album and was instrumentally strong with extended tracks like 'Sloth' becoming standards. The concept album *Babbacombe Lee,* although critically welcomed, failed to sell and Simon Nicol left to form the Albion Band with Ashley Hutchings. Swarbrick struggled on, battling against hearing problems. With such comings and goings of personnel it was difficult to document the exact changes. The lack of any animosity from ex-members contributed to the family atmosphere, although by this time record sales were dwindling. Sandy Denny rejoined, as did Dave Mattacks (twice), but by the end of the 70s the name was put to rest. The family tree specialist Pete Frame has documented their incredible array of line-ups. Their swan-song was at Cropredy in Oxfordshire in 1979. Since then an annual reunion has taken place and is now a major event on the folk calendar. The band have no idea which ex-members will turn up! They have continued to release albums, making the swan-song a sham. With Swarbrick's departure, his position was taken by Ric Sanders in 1985 who rapidly quietened his dissenters by stamping his own personality on the fiddler's role. Some of the recent collections have been quite superb, including *Gladys Leap*, with Simon Nicol back on lead vocals, and the instrumental *Expletive Delighted*. With the release in 1990 of *The Five Seasons*, the group had established the longest lasting line-up in their history. The Fairports are now as much a part of the folk music tradition as the music itself.

Albums: *Fairport Convention* (1968), *What We Did On Our Holidays* (1969), *Unhalfbricking* (1969), *Liege And Lief* (1969), *Full House* (1970), *Angel Delight* (1971), *Babbacombe Lee* (1971), *Rosie* (1973), *Nine* (1973), *Live Convention (A Moveable Feast)* (1974), *Rising For The Moon* (1975), *Gottle O'Geer* (1976), *Live At The LA Troubadour* (1977), *A Bonny Bunch Of Roses* (1977), *Tipplers Tales* (1978), *Farewell, Farewell* (1979), *Moat On The Ledge* (1981), *Gladys Leap* (1985), *Expletive Delighted* (1986), *House Full* (1986), *Heyday: The BBC Radio Sessions 1968-9* (1987), *'In Real Time' - Live '87* (1988), *Red And Gold* (1988), *Five Seasons* (1990). Compilations: *History Of Fairport Convention* (1972), *The Best Of Fairport Convention* (1988).

Further reading: *Meet On The Ledge*, Patrick Humphries.

Adam Faith and Connie Francis

Faith, Adam

b. Terence Nelhams, 23 June 1940, Acton, London, England. During the British 'coffee bar' pop music phenomenon of the late 50s two artists reigned supreme; Cliff Richard and Adam Faith. While the former has shown astonishing staying power the young Faith had a remarkable run of hit records during the comparatively short time before he retired from singing. In seven years he made the UK chart 24 times, opening his career with two chart toppers. Both, 'What Do You Want' and 'Poor Me' lasted only two minutes; both featured the infectious

pizzicato strings of John Barry's orchestra, both were written by Les Vandyke (alias Johnny Worth) and both featured the hiccuping delivery with the word, 'baby' pronounced 'bybeee'. This became Adam's early 'gimmick'. Faith's continued success rivalled that of Cliff's, when in a short period of time he appeared in three films *Beat Girl*, *Never Let Go* and *What A Whopper*, and made a surprisingly confident appearance, being interviewed by John Freeman in a serious BBC television programme, *Face To Face*. Adults were shocked to find that during this conversation, this lucid teenager admitted to pre-marital sex and owned up to listening to Sibelius. The following year, still enjoying chart hits, he appeared in the film *Mix Me A Person*. His career continued until the dawn of the Beatles, then Faith was assigned the Roulettes (featuring a young Russ Ballard). Songwriter Chris Andrews proceeded to feed Adam with a brief second wave of infectious beat-group hits most notably 'The First Time'. In the mid-60s he gave up singing and went into repertory theatre and in 1971 became an acting star in the UK television series *Budgie*. Additionally Faith has produced records for Roger Daltrey and Lonnie Donegan and managed Leo Sayer. His two supporting actor roles in *Stardust* and *McVicar* bought him critical success in addition to appearing in *Yesterday's Hero*. For a number of years he has been a wealthy financial consultant, although in the 90s he returned to the stage with *Budgie* and to television, as lead actor in *Love Hurts*. Faith still works on the perimeter of the musical world. While he will readily admit that his vocal range was limited, his contribution to popular music was significant insofar that he was the first British teenager to confront a hostile world of respectable parents and adults and demonstrate that pop singers were not all mindless layabouts and boneheads.
Selected albums: *Adam* (1960), *Beat Girl* (1961, film soundtrack), *Adam Faith* (1962), *Faith Alive* (1965), *I Survive* (1974). Compilations: *20 Golden Greats* (1981), *Not Just A Memory* (1983), *The Adam Faith Singles Collection: His Greatest Hits* (1990).
Further reading: *Poor Me*, Adam Faith.

Faithfull, Marianne

b. 29 December 1946, Hampstead, London, England. Ex-convent schoolgirl Faithfull began her singing career upon meeting producer Andrew Loog Oldham at a London party. She was thus introduced into the Rolling Stones' circle and a plaintive Jagger/Richard song, 'As Tears Go By', became her debut single in 1964. This folksy offering reached number 9, the first of four UK Top 10 hits which also included 'Come And Stay With Me' (penned by Jackie DeShannon) and the pounding 'Summer Nights'. Her albums reflected an impressive balance between folk and rock, featuring material by Donovan, Bert Jansch and

Marianne Faithfull

Tim Hardin, but her doomed relationship with Mick Jagger undermined ambitions as a performer. Marianne also pursed thespian aspirations appearing on stage in Chekhov's *Three Sisters* and on celluloid in the title role of *Girl On A Motorcycle*, but withdrew from the public eye following a failed suicide attempt upon her break with Jagger. Drug problems bedeviled her recovery, but Marianne re-emerged in 1976 with *Dreamin' My Dreams*, a mild country set on which she was backed by the Grease Band. A further period of seclusion followed but the singer rekindled her career three years later with the impressive *Broken English*. The once-virginal voice was now replaced by a husky drawl, particularly effective on the atmospheric title track and her version of Shel Silverstein's 'The Ballad Of Lucy Jordan', a minor UK hit. Faithfull's later releases followed a similar pattern, but nowhere was the trauma of her personal life more evident than on *Blazing Away*, a live album on which the singer reclaimed songs from her past. Recorded live in Brooklyn's St. Ann's Cathedral, her weary intonation, although artistically effective, contravened the optimism of those early recordings.
Albums: *Come My Way* (1965), *Marianne Faithfull* (1965), *Go Away From My World* (1965), *Faithfull Forever* (1966), *North Country Maid* (1966), *Loveinamist* (1967), *Dreamin' My Dreams* (1976), *Faithless* (1977), *Broken English* (1979), *Dangerous Acquaintances* (1981), *A Child's Adventure* (1983), *Strange Weather* (1987), *Blazing Away* (1990). Compilations: *The World Of Marianne Faithfull* (1969), *Marianne Faithfull's Greatest Hits* (1969, US release), *As Tears Go By* (1981), *Summer Nights* (1984), *The Very Best Of Marianne Faithfull* (1987), *Rick Kid's Blues* (1988).
Further reading: *As Tears Go By*, Mark Hodkinson.

Fame, Georgie

b. Clive Powell, 26 June 1943, Leigh, Lancashire, England. Entrepreneur Larry Parnes, gave the name to this talented organist during the early 60s following a recommendation from songwriter Lionel Bart.

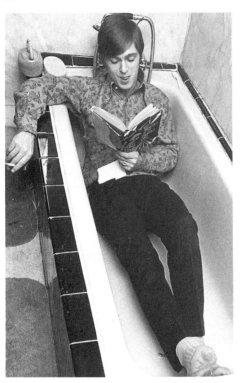

Georgie Fame

Parnes already had a Power, a Wilde, an Eager and a Fury. All he now needed was Fame. It took a number of years before Georgie and his band the Blue Flames had commercial success, although he was a major force in the popularizing of early R&B, bluebeat and ska at London's famous Flamingo club. The seminal *Rhythm And Blues At The Flamingo* was released in 1964. Chart success came later that year with a UK number 1, 'Yeh Yeh'. Fame's jazzy nasal delivery, reminiscent of Mose Alison, made this record one of the decade's classic songs. He continued with another eleven hits, including two further UK chart toppers, 'Get Away' and 'The Ballad Of Bonnie And Clyde', the latter of which was his only US Top 10 single in 1968. The former maintained his jazz feel, which continued on such striking mood pieces as 'Sunny' and 'Sitting In The Park'. Thereafter, he veered towards straight pop. His recent change of record labels had attempted to re-market him and at one stage teamed him with the Harry South Big Band. While his albums showed a more progressive style his singles became lightweight, the nadir being when he teamed up with Alan Price to produce some catchy pop songs. Fame has also played straight jazz at Ronnie Scott's club, performed a tribute to Hoagy Carmichael with singer Annie Ross, and has sung over Esso advertisements. It was four years before a new album appeared. In recent times Georgie has been content touring with Van Morrison as keyboard player, given a brief cameo to perform the occasional hit. During the renaissance of the Hammond B3 organ (an instrument that Fame had originally pioneered in the London clubs) during the jazz boom of the early 90s it was announced that Georgie had recorded a new album, its subsequent release to favourable reviews and regular concert appearances indicates a new phase. The album was recorded to the highest standards and featured smooth contributions from Steve Gadd, Robben Ford, Richard Tee, Jon Hendricks and Boz Scaggs. A reggae reworking of 'Yeh Yeh' and a graceful version of Carmichael's 'Georgia' are but two outstanding tracks. Van Morrison duets with Fame on the former's classic, 'Moondance'.

Albums: *Rhythm And Blues At The Flamingo* (1963), *Fame At Last* (1964), *Yeh Yeh* (1965), *Sweet Things* (1966), *Sound Venture* (1966), *Get Away* (1966), *Hall Of Fame* (1967), *Two Faces Of Fame* (1967), *The Ballad Of Bonnie And Clyde* (1968), *The Third Face Of Fame* (1968), *Seventh Son* (1969), *Georgie Does His Things With Strings* (1970), *Going Home* (1971), *Fame And Price, Price And Fame Together* (1971), *All Me Own Work* (1972), *Georgie Fame* (1974), *That's What Friends Are For* (1979), *Georgie Fame Right Now* (1979), *Closing The Gap* (1980), with Annie Ross *Hoagland* (1981), *In Goodman's Land* (1983), *Rhythm And Blues At The Flamingo* (1984), *My Favourite Songs* (1984), *No Worries* (1988), *Cool Cat Blues* (1991). Compilations: *20 Beat Classics* (1982), *The First Thirty Years* (1990).

Family

Highly respected and nostalgically revered, Family were one of Britain's leading progressive rock bands of the late 60s and early 70s. They were led by the wiry yet vocally demonic Roger Chapman (b. 8 April 1942, Leicester, England), a man whose stage presence could both transfix and terrify his audience, who would duck from the countless supply of tambourines he would destroy and hurl into the crowd. Chapman was ably supported by Rick Grech (b. 1 November 1946, Bordeaux, France, d. 17 March 1990; violin/bass), Charlie Whitney (b. 24 June 1944, Leicester, England; guitar), Rob Townsend (b. July 7 1947, Leicester, England; drums) and Jim King (b. Kettering, Northamptonshire, England; flute/saxophone). The band was formed in 1962 and known variously as the Roaring Sixties and the Farinas, finally coming together as Family in 1967 with the arrival of Chapman and Townsend. Their first album released in 1968 was given extensive exposure on John Peel's influential BBC radio programme, resulting in this Dave Mason-produced collection becoming a major cult record. Chapman's remarkable strangulated vibrato caused heads to turn. Following the release of their most successful album *Family Entertainment* they experienced an ever changing personnel of high pedigree musicians when Rick Grech departed to join Blind Faith in 1969, being replaced by John Weider, who in turn was supplanted by John Wetton in 1971, then Jim Cregan in 1972. Poli Palmer superseded Jim King in 1969 who was ultimately replaced by Tony Ashton in 1972. Throughout this turmoil they maintained a high standard of recorded work and had singles success with 'No Mules Fool', 'Strange Band', 'In My Own Time' and the infectious 'Burlesque'. Family disintegrated after their disappointing swan-song *Its Only A Movie*, Chapman and Whitney departing to form Streetwalkers. While their stage performances were erratic and unpredictable, the sight of Roger Chapman performing their anthem 'The Weaver's Answer' on a good night was unforgettable and one that rock fans who saw them will cherish.

Albums: *Music In A Doll's House* (1968), *Family Entertainment* (1969), *A Song For Me* (1970), *Anyway* (1970), *Fearless* (1971), *Bandstand* (1972), *It's Only A Movie* (1973). Compilation: *Best Of Family* (1974).

Family Tree

Bob Segarini (guitar/vocals), Mike Olsen (keyboards), Bill Whittington (bass) and Newman Davis (drums) formed Family Tree in 1965. This San Franciscan rock group was bedevilled by internal unrest, and by the time their debut album was released, Segarini was the only remaining original member. *Miss Butters* unveiled the anglophile persuasion which marked his subsequent music, but was deemed out of step with the prevailing musical trend. Mike Dure (guitar), Jim De Cocq (keyboards), Bill 'Kootch' Troachim (bass) and Vann Slatter (drums) completed the band's final line-up, which broke apart in 1970. Segarini and De Cocq formed Roxy, while founder member Olsen found fame as virtuoso Lee Michaels.

Album: *Miss Butters* (1968).

Fantastic Baggys

The Fantastic Baggys was a recording outlet for songwriting team P.F. Sloan (herein known as 'Flip') and Steve Barri. The duo supplied surfing act Jan And Dean with several compositions, notably 'Summer Means Fun' and 'From All Over The World', and added backing harmonies on several sessions, factors which in turn inspired this concurrent career. Bob Myman (drums) and Jerry Cargman completed the nominal Baggys' line-up, but the venture was, in essence, studio-based. The Sloan/Barri team wrote arranged and produced every track on *Tell 'Em I'm Surfin'*, but the duo quickly tired of their creation and ceased using the name following the release of the Gary Paxton-penned 'It Was I' (1965). However, the Fantastic Baggys had proved highly popular in South Africa and a second album, *Ride The Wild Surf*, was compiled the following year. Although five tracks, drawn from singles and out-takes, did feature Sloan and Barri, more than half the set featured anonymous musicians aping the original group. By the release of *Surfer's Paradise*, the ruse had run its course. Here any connection was even more tenuous and the sole Sloan/Barri performance, 'Only When Your Lonely', was mistakenly drawn from another studio project, the Grass Roots. When the album proved commercially moribund, the Baggy's appellation was mercifully abandoned.

Albums: *Tell 'Em I'm Surfin'* (1964), *Ride The Wild Surf* (1964, film soundtrack), *Surfer's Paradise* (1967). Compilation: *Surfin' Craze* (1983).

Fardon, Don

b. Don Maughn c.1943, Coventry, West Midlands, England. As the vocalist with the Sorrows, Maughn was featured on this cult group's most durable release, the pulsating 'Take A Heart'. A number 21 hit in September 1965, its hypnotic, throbbing beat was maintained on subsequent releases, several of which the singer co-composed. Here, however, he preferred to use an alternative surname, Fardon, which was then retained for the artist's solo career. His version of John D. Loudermilk's '(The Lament Of The Cherokee) Indian Reservation', gave him his first and only US hit single in 1968, reaching the Top 20. He broke into the UK charts in 1970 with 'Belfast Boy', a homage to the talented, but troubled footballer, George Best. This success paved the way for the re-issue of 'Indian Reservation' which when resurrected, climbed to a respectable number 3 and became one of that year's most distinctive chart entries. Yet despite several further releases, some of which were remakes of former Sorrows' material, Fardon was unable to secure consistent success.

Albums: *Lament Of The Cherokee* (1968, reissued in 1988 as *Indian Reservation*), *I've Paid My Dues* (1970), *Released* (1970).

Farlowe, Chris

b. John Henry Deighton, 13 October 1940, London, England. Farlowe's long career began during the 50s skiffle boom when the John Henry Skiffle Group won the all-England championship. He then formed the original Thunderbirds, which remained semi-professional until 1962 when they embarked on a month's engagement in Frankfurt, Germany. Farlowe then met Rik Gunnell, owner of London's Ram Jam and Flamingo clubs, and the singer quickly became a stalwart of the city's R&B circuit. He made his recording debut that year with the pop-oriented 'Air Travel', but failed to secure commercial success until 1966 when his version of the Rolling Stones' song,

'Out Of Time', produced by Mick Jagger, soared to the top of the UK charts. Several minor hits, including 'Ride On Baby' (1966) and 'Handbags And Gladrags' (1967), followed, as well as a brace of pop/soul albums, but Farlowe's intonation proved too craggy for popular consumption. He and the Thunderbirds - which between 1964 and 1967 featured Albert Lee (guitar), Dave Greenslade (organ), Bugs Waddell (bass), Ian Hague (drums) and Jerry Temple (congas) - remained one of the country's most impressive R&B acts, although session musicians were increasingly employed for recording purposes. By 1968 the unit had been reduced to that of Farlowe, Lee, Pete Solley (keyboards) and Carl Palmer (drums), but two years later the singer founded an all-new group, the Hill. The venture's sole album, *From Here To Mama Rosa*, was not a commercial success and Chris then joined ex-colleague Greenslade in Colosseum. This jazz-rock group disbanded in 1971, and having briefly switched allegiances to Atomic Rooster, Farlowe retired from rock to pursue an interest in military and Nazi memorabilia. He re-emerged in 1975 with *The Chris Farlowe Band, Live*, but has conspicuously failed to find a satisfactory niche for his powerful, gritty voice. Cameo appearances during the 80s on sessions for Jimmy Page engendered the widely acclaimed *Out Of The Blue* and *Born Again* which together served notice that the singer's talent remained intact.
Albums: *Chris Farlowe And The Thunderbirds* aka *Stormy Monday* (1966), *Fourteen Things To Think About* (1966), *The Art Of Chris Farlowe* (1966), *The Fabulous Chris Farlowe* (1967), *Paint It Farlowe* (1968), *From Here To Mama Rosa* (1970), *The Chris Farlowe Band, Live* (1976), *Out Of The Blue* (1985), *Born Again* (1988), *Waiting In The Wings* (1992). Compilations: *The Best Of Chris Farlowe* (1968), *Out Of Time* (1975), *Out Of Time-Paint It Black* (1977), *Hot Property (The Rare Tracks)* (1983), *Mr. Soulful* (1986), *Buzz With The Fuzz* (1987).

Feliciano, José

b. 10 September 1945, Lares, Puerto Rico. After early fame as a flamenco-style interpreter of pop and rock material, Feliciano turned more to mainstream Latin music, becoming one of the most popular artists in the Spanish-speaking world. He was born blind and as a child moved to New York's Spanish Harlem. He learned guitar and accordion and from 1962 performed a mixture of Spanish and American material in the folk clubs and coffeehouses of Greenwich Village. Signed to RCA, he released a gimmicky single 'Everybody Do The Click' before recording an impressive debut album in 1964. Its impassioned arrangements of recent hits were continued on *Feliciano!* With jazz bassist Ray Brown among the backing musicians, Feliciano's Latin treatment of the Doors' 'Light My Fire' became his first hit. It was followed by a version of Tommy Tucker's R&B standard 'Hi Heel Sneakers' and such was Feliciano's popularity that he was chosen to sing 'The Star-Spangled Banner' at the 1968 baseball World Series. However, the application of his characteristic Latin-jazz styling to the US national anthem caused controversy among traditionalists.
In the UK, where he recorded a 1969 live album, Feliciano's version of the Bee Gees' 'The Sun Will Shine' was a minor hit, but the 70s saw RCA promoting Feliciano's Spanish-language material throughout Latin America. He recorded albums in Argentina, Mexico and Venezuela and had a television show syndicated throughout the continent. He also sang the theme music to the television series *Chico And The Man*. In parallel with the Latin albums, Feliciano continued to record English-language songs, notably on *Compartments*, produced by Steve Cropper. In 1976, Feliciano switched labels to Private Stock where producer Jerry Wexler was brought in to re-create the feeling of José's early work on Sweet Soul Music. When Motown set up its own Latin music label in 1981 Feliciano headed the roster, recording the Rick Jarrard-produced *Romance In The Night* as well as Grammy-winning Latin albums. In 1987 he signed a three-pronged deal with EMI to record classical guitar music and English pop (*I'm Never Gonna Change*) as well as further Spanish-language recordings (*Tu Immenso Amor*). He also pursued his jazz interests, recording *Steppin' Out* for Optimism.
Albums: *The Voice And Guitar Of José Feliciano* (1964), *A Bag Full Of Soul* (1965), *Feliciano!* (1967), *Feliciano 10 To 23* (1969), *Alive Alive-O* (1969), *Souled* (1969), *Fireworks* (1970), *That The Spirit Needs* (1971), *José Feliciano Sings* (1972), *Compartments* (1973), *And The Feeling's Good* (1974), *Just Wanna Rock 'N' Roll* (1974), *Sweet Soul Music* (1976), *Jose Feliciano* (1980), *Escenas De Amor* (1982), *Romance In The Night* (1983), *Los Exitos De José Feliciano* (1984), *Tu Immenso Amor* (1987), *I'm Never Gonna Change* (1989), *Steppin' Out* (1990). Compilations: *The Best Of José Feliciano* (1985), *Portrait* (1985).

Felix, Julie

b. 14 June 1938, Santa Barbara, California, USA. Felix arrived in the UK during the early 60s at a time when several US folksingers, including Paul Simon and Jackson C. Frank, had also relocated to London. Her early recordings revealed a commercial, rather than innovative talent, a fact emphasized by weekly appearances on television's *The Frost Report* (1967/68). She followed the liberal tradition of Tom Paxton or Pete Seeger, rather than that of the radical left, although was an early champion of the folk-styled singer/songwriter movement, notably Leonard

Cohen and was proclaimed as 'Britain's Leading Lady of Folk'. Her humanitarian beliefs had however been put to practical use by the singer's tour of the African states of Kenya and Uganda, working for the Christian Aid and Freedom From Hunger charities. Felix enjoyed two successful British television series in her own right, *Once More With Felix* (1969/70) and *The Julie Felix Show* (1971), and scored a UK Top 20 hit in 1970 with a version of 'El Condor Pasa', produced by pop svengali Mickie Most. The singer's 'wholesome' image was tarred by a conviction for possession of marijuana, but she continued a prolific recording career, albeit to less publicity, into the 80s, as well as performing for Women's Rights, Green and environmental benefits, and founding Britain's first 'New Age Folk Club'.

Albums: *Julie Felix* (1964), *2nd Album* (1965), *3rd Album* (1966), *Julie Felix Sings Dylan And Guthrie* (1966), *Changes* (1966), *Julie Felix In Concert* (1967), *Flowers* (1968), *This World Goes Round And Round* (1969), *Going To The Zoo* (1970), *Clotho's Web* (1971), *Lightning* (1974), *London Palladium* (1974), *Hota Chocolata* (1977), *Blowing In The Wind* (1982), *Bright Shadows* (1989). Compilations: *The World Of Julie Felix* (1969), *The World Of Julie Felix Volume 2* (1970), *The Most Collection* (1972), *This Is Julie Felix* (1970), *This Is Julie Felix Volume 2* (1974), *Amazing Grace* (1987).

Fenton, Shane

b. Bernard Jewry, 1942, London, England. Fenton achieved his first notable success after securing a spot on *Saturday Club*, BBC radio's influential show. Backed by the Fentones and sporting a distinctive silver lamé suit, the singer quickly became a part of Britain's pre-beat enclave beside other home-grown talent including Cliff Richard, Marty Wilde, Duffy Power and Billy Fury. Fenton scored a UK Top 30 hit in 1961 with the mythologizing 'I'm A Moody Guy', but despite several similarly-structured releases, only 'Cindy's Birthday' (1962) broached the UK Top 20. Deemed passé on the rise of the Beatles, Fenton eked out a living from the rock 'n' roll/cabaret circuit until revitalizing his career in the 70s under a new guise, Alvin Stardust.

Fever Tree

Although a Texas group, Fever Tree made its mark with a tribute to the Summer of Love's host city with their 1968 anthem 'San Francisco Girls (Return Of The Native)'. Comprised of Rob Landes (keyboards), Dennis Keller (vocals), E.E. Wolfe (bass), John Tuttle (drums) and Michael Knust (guitar), the psychedelic group formed in Houston, Texas, in the mid-60s as Bostwick Vine. The name change came in 1967 and the group subsequently signed with Chicago-based Mainstream Records. Two unsuccessful singles were recorded, and the group then signed to Uni Records, and recorded their self-titled debut album in 1968. 'San Francisco Girls (Return Of The Native)' was penned by Vivian Holtzman, one of the group's producers. Although only a minor chart hit, it received much airplay on the new FM rock stations and on John Peel's *Top Gear* radio programme in the UK. The group recorded four albums, three of which charted in the USA, before splitting up in 1970. Interest in the group was renewed in the mid-80s psychedelic revival, and compilation albums were issued in both the USA and UK.

Albums: *Fever Tree* (1968), *Another Time, Another Place* (1968), *Creation* (1969), *For Sale* (1970). Compilations: *Best Of Fever Tree* (1985), *San Francisco Girls* (1986).

Fifth Dimension

Originally known as the Versatiles and later as the Vocals, Marilyn McCoo (b. 30 September 1944, Jersey City, New Jersey, USA), Florence LaRue (b. 4 February 1944, Philadelphia, Pennsylvania, USA), Billy Davis Jnr. (b. 26 June 1940, St. Louis, Missouri, USA), Lamont McLemore (b. 17 September 1940, St. Louis, Missouri, USA) and Ron Townsend (b. 29 January 1941, St. Louis, Missouri, USA), were a soul-influenced harmony group, based in Los Angeles. They sprang to fame in 1967 as an outlet for the then unknown talents of songwriter Jimmy Webb. Ebullient singles on the pop charts including; 'Go Where You Wanna', 'Up Up And Away' and 'Carpet Man', established their fresh voices which wrapped themselves around producer Bones Howe's dizzy arrangements. Having completed two albums of Webb originals, the group then took to another composer, Laura Nyro, whose soul-styled songs, 'Stoned Soul Picnic', 'Sweet Blindness' (both 1968), 'Wedding Bell Blues' (1969) and 'Save The Country' (1970) continued the Fifth Dimension's success and introduced the group to the R&B charts. These popular recordings were punctuated by 'Aquarius/Let The Sunshine In', a medley of songs from the rock musical **Hair** which topped the US chart in 1969 and reached number 11 in Britain that same year. In 1971 the group reached number 2 in the US with the haunting 'One Less Bell To Answer'. From then on, however, the MOR elements within their style began to take precedence and the quintet's releases grew increasingly bland. In 1976 Marilyn McCoo and Billy Davis Jnr. (who were now married) left for a successful career both as a duo and as solo artists. They had a US number 1 hit together in 1976 with 'You Don't Have To Be A Star' which was followed up in 1977 by their last Top 20 hit, 'Your Love'. Marilyn went on to host the US television show *Solid Gold* for much of the early 80s.

Albums: *Up Up And Away* (1967), *Magic Garden*

(1967), *Stoned Soul Picnic* (1968), *Age Of Aquarius* (1969), *Fantastic* (1970), *Portrait* (1970), *Love's Lines, Angles And Rhymes* (1971), *Live!* (1971), *Individually And Collectively* (1972), *Living Together, Growing Together* (1973), *Earthbound* (1975). Compilations: *The July 5th Album* (1970), *Reflections* (1971), *Greatest Hits On Earth* (1972, combines Soul City and Bell label tracks), *Greatest Hits* (1988).

Fischer, Larry 'Wild Man'

b. 1945. Fischer was a prominent fixture on Los Angeles' Sunset Strip during the late 60s. This imposing figure, part-eccentric, part-LSD casualty, was renowned for composing songs to order in return for small change. He became associated with Frank Zappa who produced Larry's uncompromising debut, *An Evening With Wild Man Fischer*. Contemporary opinion was divided on its merits. Some critics deemed it voyeuristic, while others proclaimed it a work of art and a valid documentary. Caught in the middle was an ecstatic performer, elated that his 50s-style compositions were finally recorded. Fischer made several live appearances with Zappa's group, the Mothers Of Invention, but it was seven years before he recorded again. Having completed a single, advertising the Rhino Records store, he was signed to their fledgling label. Three further albums continued the disquieting atmosphere of that first release.

Albums: *An Evening With Wild Man Fischer* (1968), *Wild Mania* (1978), *Pronounced Normal* (1981), *Nothing Crazy* (1984).

Flamin' Groovies

This unflinchingly self-assured act evolved from an aspiring San Francisco-based garage band, the Chosen Few. Roy Loney (b. 13 April 1946, San Francisco, California, USA; vocals), Tim Lynch (b. 18 July 1946, San Francisco, California, USA; guitar), Cyril Jordan (b. 1948, San Francisco, California, USA; guitar), George Alexander (b. 18 May 1946, San Mateo, California, USA; bass) and Ron Greco (drums) subsequently flirted with a new appellation, Lost And Found, before breaking up in the summer of 1966. All of the group, bar Greco, reassembled several months later as the Flamin' Groovies. New drummer Danny Mihm (b. San Francisco, Califonia, USA) joined from another local act, Group 'B', and the new line-up embarked on a direction markedly different from the city's prevalent love of extended improvisation. The Groovies remained rooted in America's immediate beat aftermath and bore traces of the Lovin' Spoonful and the Charlatans. Having completed a promising private pressing, the group recorded their official debut, *Supersnazz*, which also revealed a strong debt to traditional rock 'n' roll. The group's subsequent albums, *Flamingo* and *Teenage Head*, were influenced by Detroit's MC5 and offered a more contemporary perspective. The latter set drew complementary reviews and was compared favourably with the Rolling Stones' *Sticky Fingers*, but it marked the end of the original line-up. Loney and Lynch were replaced, respectively, by Chris Wilson and James Farrell. Denigrated at home, the Groovies enjoyed a cult popularity in Europe and a series of superb recordings, including the seminal anti-drug song, 'Slow Death', were recorded during a brief spell in Britain. Several of these performances formed the basis of *Shake Some Action*, the Groovies' majestic homage to 60s' pop, which remains their finest and most accomplished work. New drummer David Wright had replaced a disaffected Mihm, while the group's harmonies and reverberating instrumental work added an infectious sparkle. The group then adopted former Charlatan Mike Wilhelm in place of Farrell. However subsequent releases relied on a tried formula where a plethora of cover versions disguised a lack of original songs. The Groovies were then perceived as a mere revival band and the resultant frustration led to the departure of Wilson, Wilhelm and Wright. Jordan and Alexander continued relatively undeterred, adding Jack Johnson (guitar) and Paul Zahl (drums) from Roky Erickson's backing band. The reconstituted Groovies toured Europe, Australia and New Zealand and completed a handful of new recordings, including *One Night Stand*. However, despite promises of a greater prolificacy, the group has been unable to secure a permanent recording deal. Paradoxically, Roy Loney has enjoyed a flourishing performing career, honing a style not dissimilar to that of *Supersnazz* and *Flamingo*.

Albums: *Sneakers* (1968), *Supersnazz* (1969), *Flamingo* (1970), *Teenage Head* (1971), *Shake Some Action* (1976), *Flamin' Groovies Now* (1978), *Jumpin' In The Night* (1979), *One Night Stand* (1986). Compilations: *Still Shakin'* (1976), *Slow Death - Live* aka *Bucketful Of Brains* (1983), *Studio '68* (1984), *Studio '70* (1984), *Roadhouse* (1986), *The Rockfield Sessions* (1989).

Flaming Youth

This short-lived UK act comprised of Gordon Smith (guitar), Brian Chatton (keyboards), Ronnie Caryl (bass) and Phil Collins (drums). Their sole recording, *Ark 2*, was an ambitiously packaged concept album, written and arranged by Ken Howard/Alan Blakley, a team better known for creating the unashamed pop of the Herd and Dave Dee, Dozy, Beaky, Mick And Tich. The project was the subject of considerable hype, but its new musical departure proved unconvincing and prematurely doomed Flaming Youth's career. The group was effectively disbanded when Collins successfully auditioned for Genesis in 1970.

Album: *Ark 2* (1969).

Flee-Rekkers

Originally known as the Ramblers, then Statesiders, this primarily instrumental unit based in the UK was led by Peter Fleerackers, a Dutch-born tenor saxophonist. Elmy Durrant (tenor saxophone), Dave 'Tex' Cameron (lead guitar), Ronald Marion (rhythm guitar), Derek Skinner (bass) and Phil Curtis (drums) completed the line-up signed by producer Joe Meek in 1960. 'Green Jeans', a raucous version of the traditional 'Greensleeves', reached number 23 that year, but despite a series of competent singles reminiscent of Johnny And The Hurricanes, this was the group's only chart entry. 'Fireball', arranged by Tony Hatch, became the unit's final release in 1963, by which time Alan Monger and Mickey Waller had replaced Marion and Curtis. Cameron, Durrant and Monger later enjoyed success in Germany with the Giants, but Fleerackers failed to pursue a high profile career in music. Although Skinner joined the popular Spotniks, it was left to newcomer Waller to achieve greater fame with Jeff Beck and Rod Stewart.
Album: *Joe Meek's Fabulous Flee-Rekkers* (1991).

Fleetwood Mac

The original Fleetwood Mac was formed in July 1967 by Peter Green (b. Peter Greenbaum, 29 October 1946, Bethnel Green, London, England; guitar) and Mick Fleetwood (b. 24 June 1947, London, England; drums), both of whom had recently left John Mayall's Bluesbreakers. They secured a recording deal with Blue Horizon Records on the strength of Green's reputation as a blues guitarist before the label's overtures uncovered a second guitarist, Jeremy Spencer (b. 4 July 1948, Hartlepool, Cleveland, England), in a semi-professional group, the Levi Set. A temporary bassist, Bob Brunning, was recruited into the line-up, until a further Mayall acolyte, John McVie (b. 26 November 1945, London, England), was finally persuaded to join the new unit. Peter Green's Fleetwood Mac, as the group was initially billed, made its debut on August 12, 1967 at Windsor's National Jazz And Blues Festival. Their first album, *Fleetwood Mac*, released on Blue Horizon in February the following year, reached the UK Top 5 and established a distinctive balance between Green's introspective compositions and Spencer's debt to Elmore James. A handful of excellent cover versions completed an album that was seminal in the development of the British blues boom of the late 60s.

The group also enjoyed two minor hit singles with 'Black Magic Woman', a hypnotic Green composition later popularized by Santana, and a delicate reading of 'Need Your Love So Bad', first recorded by Little Willie John. Fleetwood Mac's second album, *Mr. Wonderful*, was another triumph, but while Spencer was content to repeat his established style, Green, the group's leader, extended his compositional boundaries with several haunting contributions, including the heartfelt 'Love That Burns'. His guitar playing, clean and sparse but always telling, was rarely better, while McVie and Fleetwood were already an instinctive rhythm section. *Mr. Wonderful* also featured contributions from Christine Perfect (b. 12 July 1943, Birmingham, England), pianist from Chicken Shack, and a four-piece horn section, as the group began to leave traditional blues behind. A third guitarist, Danny Kirwan, (b. 13 May 1950, London, England), was added to the line-up in September 1968. The quintet scored an immediate hit when 'Albatross', a moody instrumental reminiscent of 'Sleep Walk' by Santo And Johnny, topped the UK charts. The single, which reached number 2 when it was reissued in 1973, was the group's first million seller.

Fleetwood Mac then left Blue Horizon, although the company subsequently issued *Blues Jam At Chess*, on which the band jammed with several mentors, including Buddy Guy, Otis Spann and Shakey Horton. Following a brief interlude on Immediate Records, which furnished the hypnotic 'Man Of The World', the quintet made their debut on Reprise with 'Oh Well', their most ambitious single to date, and the superb *Then Play On*. This crafted album unveiled Kirwan's songwriting talents and his romantic leanings offset the more worldly Green. Although pictured, Jeremy Spencer was notably absent from most of the sessions, although his eccentric vision was showcased on a self-titled solo album.

Fleetwood Mac now enjoyed an international reputation, but it was a mantle too great for its leader to bear. Peter Green left the band in May 1970 as his parting single, the awesome 'The Green Manalishi', became another Top 10 hit. He was replaced by Christine Perfect, now married to John McVie, and while his loss was an obvious blow, Kirwan's songwriting talent and Spencer's sheer exuberance maintained a measure of continuity on a fourth album, *Kiln House*. However in 1971 the group was rocked for a second time when Spencer disappeared mid-way through an American tour. It transpired he had joined a religious sect, the Children Of God and while Green deputized for the remainder of the tour, a permanent replacement was found in a Californian musician, Bob Welch (b. 31 July 1946, California, USA).

The new line-up was consolidated on two melodic albums, *Future Games* and *Bare Trees*. Neither release made much impression with UK audiences who continued to mourn the passing of the Green-led era, but in America the group began to assemble a strong following for their new-found transatlantic sound. However, further changes occurred when Kirwan's chronic stage-fright led to his dismissal. Bob Weston, a guitarist from Long John Baldry's backing band, was his immediate replacement, while the line-up was also bolstered by former Savoy Brown vocalist, Dave Walker. The group, however, was unhappy with a defined frontman and the singer left after only eight months, having barely completed work on their *Penguin* album. Although not one of the band's strongest collections, it does contain an excellent Welch composition, 'Night Watch'.

The remaining quintet completed another album, *Mystery To Me*, which was released at the time of a personal nadir within the group. Weston, who had been having an affair with Fleetwood's wife, was fired midway through a prolonged US tour and the remaining dates were cancelled. Their manager, Clifford Davis, assembled a bogus Mac to fulfil contractual obligations, thus denying the 'real' group work during the inevitable lawsuits. Yet despite the inordinate pressure, Perfect, Welch, McVie and Fleetwood returned with *Heroes Are Hard To Find*, a positive release which belied the wrangles surrounding its appearance. Nonetheless the controversy proved too strong for Welch, who left the group in December 1974. His departure robbed Fleetwood Mac of an inventive songwriter whose American perspective helped redefine the group's approach.

It was while seeking prospective recording studios that Fleetwood was introduced to Stevie Nicks and Lindsey Buckingham via the duo's self-named album. Now bereft of a guitarist, he recalled Buckingham's expertise and invited him to replace Welch. Lindsey accepted on condition that Nicks also join, thus cementing Fleetwood Mac's most successful line-up. *Fleetwood Mac*, released in 1975, was a promise fulfilled. The newcomers provided easy, yet memorable compositions with smooth harmonies while the British contingent gave the group its edge and power. A succession of stellar compositions, including 'Over My Head', 'Say You Love Me' and the dramatic 'Rhiannon', confirmed a perfect balance had been struck giving the group their first in a long line of US Top 20 singles. The quintet's next release, *Rumours*, proved more remarkable still. Despite the collapse of two relationships - the McVies were divorced, Buckingham and Nicks split up - the group completed a remarkable collection which laid bare the traumas within, but in a manner neither maudlin nor pitiful. Instead the ongoing drama was charted by several exquisite songs; 'Go Your Own Way', 'Don't Stop', 'Second Hand News' and 'Dreams', which re.ained both melody and purpose. An enduring release, *Rumours* has sold upwards of 25 million copies and is second to Michael Jackson's *Thriller* as the best-selling album of all time.

Having survived their emotional anguish, Fleetwood Mac was faced with the problem of following-up a phenomenon. Their response was *Tusk*, an ambitious double-set which showed a group unafraid to experiment, although many critics damned the collection as self-indulgent. The title track, a fascinating instrumental, was an international hit, although its follow-up, 'Sara', a composition recalling the style of *Rumours*, was better received in the USA than the UK. An in-concert selection, *Fleetwood Mac: Live*, was released as a stop-gap in 1980 as rumours of a complete break-up flourished. It was a further two years before a new collection, *Mirage*, appeared by which point several members were pursuing independent ventures. Buckingham and Nicks, in particular, viewed their own careers with equal importance and *Mirage*, a somewhat self-conscious attempt at creating another *Rumours*, lacked the sparkle of its illustrious predecessor. It nonetheless yielded three successful singles in 'Hold Me', 'Gypsy' and Buckingham's irrepressible 'Oh Diane'.

Five years then passed before a new Fleetwood Mac album was issued. *Tango In The Night* was a dramatic return to form, recapturing all the group's flair and invention with a succession of heartwarming performances in 'Little Lies', 'Family Man' and 'You And I (Part 2)'. Christine McVie contributed a further high-point with the rhythmic sing-a-long 'Anyway'. The collection was, however, Lindsey Buckingham's swan-song, although his departure from the band was not officially confirmed until June 1988. By that point two replacement singer/guitarists, ex-Thunderbyrd Rick Vito (b. 1950) and Billy Burnette (b. 7 May 1953), had joined the remaining quartet. The new line-up's debut, *Behind The Mask*, ushered in a new decade and era for this tempestuous group, that gained strength from adversity and simply refused to die. Its success confirmed their status as one of the major groups in the history of popular music.

Albums: *Fleetwood Mac* (1968), *Mr. Wonderful* (1968), *English Rose* (1969), *Then Play On* (1969), *Blues Jam At Chess* aka *Fleetwood Mac In Chicago* (1969), *Kiln House* (1970), *Future Games* (1971), *Bare Trees* (1972), *Penguin* (1973), *Mystery To Me* (1973), *Heroes Are Hard To Find* (1974), *Fleetwood Mac* (1975), *Rumours* (1977), *Tusk* (1979), *Fleetwood Mac Live* (1980), *Mirage* (1982), *Live In Boston* (1985), *London Live '68* (1986), *Tango In The Night* (1988), *Behind The Mask* (1989). Compilations: *The Pious Bird Of Good Omen* (1969), *The Original Fleetwood Mac* (1971), *Fleetwood Mac's Greatest Hits* (1971), *The Vintage Years* (1975), *Albatross* (1977), *Man Of The World* (1978), *Best Of* (1978), *Cerurlean* (1985), *Greatest Hits: Fleetwood Mac* (1988).

Further reading: *Fleetwood: My Life And Adventures With Fleetwood Mac*, Mick Fleetwood with Stephen Davis.

Flower Pot Men

Flowerpot Men

This UK group was formed in 1967 by the Carter And Lewis songwriting team to exploit the concurrent flower-power boom. The ensuing single, 'Let's Go To San Francisco', became a Top 5 hit and a quartet of session vocalists - Tony Burrows, Robin Shaw, Pete Nelson and Neil Landon - then assumed the name. Despite this undoubtedly mercenary instigation, the group completed several well-sculpted releases, notably 'A Walk In The Sky'. An instrumental section, comprising of Ged Peck (guitar), Jon Lord (organ), Nick Simper (bass) and Carlo Little (drums), accompanied the singers on tour, but this line-up was dissolved when Lord and Simper founded Deep Purple. Burrows later reverted to session work, and while Landon resurfaced in Fat Mattress, Shaw and Nelson retained their relationship with Carter And Lewis in White Plains.
Album: *Let's Go To San Francisco* (1988).

Floyd, Eddie

b. 25 June 1935, Montgomery, Alabama, USA. A founder member of the Detroit-based Falcons, Floyd was present on both their major hits, 'You're So Fine' (1959) and 'I Found A Love' (1962). Eddie then recorded solo for Lupine in Detroit and Safice in Washington DC, before moving to Memphis in 1965 to join the Stax organization. He first made his mark there as a composer, penning Wilson Pickett's '634-5789' among others. During Floyd's recording tenure at Stax, he enjoyed the use of the session bands Booker T. And The MGs and the Mar-Keys. He opened his account with 'Things Get Better' (1965), followed by the anthem-like 'Knock On Wood' (1966), one of soul's enduring moments. Probably the only time lightning and frightning can be coupled without sounding trite; 'just like thunder and lightning, the way you love me is frightning think I'd better knock on wood'. Although subsequent releases failed to match its success, a series of powerful singles, including 'Love Is A Doggone Good Thing' (1967)

and 'Big Bird' (1968), confirmed his stature both as performer and songwriter. Although Floyd's compositions were recorded by several acts, his next US Top 20 pop hit came with Sam Cooke's 'Bring It On Home To Me' in 1968. Eddie stayed with Stax until its bankruptcy in 1975, whereupon he moved to Malaco. His spell there was thwarted by commercial indifference and he left the label for Mercury in 1977, but met with no better results. Briefly relocated to London, he recorded under the aegis of Mod resurrectionists Secret Affair, before surfacing in New York with the album *Try Me* (1985). In 1990 Floyd appeared live with a reformed Booker T. And The MGs.
Albums: *Knock On Wood* (1967), *I've Never Found A Girl* (1968), *You've Got To Have Eddie* (1969), *California Girl* (1970), *Down To Earth* (1971), *Baby Lay Your Head Down* (1973), *Soul Street* (1974), *Experience* (1977), *Chronicle* (1979), *Try Me* (1985), *Flashback* (1988). Compilations: *Rare Stamps* (1968), *The Best Of Eddie Floyd* (1988).

Folks Brothers

To be labelled a one-hit wonder is something of an insult, but to be a one-record wonder is an accolade. The Jamaican artists who have made one perfect recording and then vanished, leaving a reputation forever untarnished by later lapses, could be counted on the fingers of one hand. The Folks Brothers are among that number: in 1961 or early 1962 they recorded 'Oh Carolina', a unique and perfect single, and never appeared again. The record has Count Ossie's Rastafarian drummers thundering out complex African cross-rhythms, Owen Gray contrastingly American-styled on piano, and the Brothers, a soulful lead singer and two lighter-voiced male accompanists, delivering the song. The b-side, though credited to the Brothers, is a routine early ska instrumental and Ruddy & Sketto's 'Chubby', which sounds as if it was recorded at the same session, has a quite different vocal sound. Prince Buster, who produced the session, doubtless knows the answer to the mystery but, until he can be induced to tell all, 'Oh Carolina' will remain a magnificent mystery.

Fontana, Wayne

b. Glyn Ellis, 28 October 1945, Manchester, England. After changing his name in honour of Elvis Presley's drummer D.J. Fontana, Wayne was signed to the appropriately named Fontana Records by A&R head Jack Baverstock. Wayne's backing group, the Mindbenders from the horror film of the same name, were as accomplished as their leader and provided a gritty accompaniment. Specializing in R&B covers, the group finally broke through with their fifth release, the Major Lance cover 'Um, Um, Um, Um, Um', which reached number 5 in the UK. The 1965 follow-up, 'The Game Of Love', hit number 2 and spearheaded a Kennedy Street Enterprises Manchester invasion of the US which lifted the group to number 1. Thereafter, the group struggled, with 'Just A Little Bit Better' being their only hit. In October 1965, Wayne decided to pursue a solo career, first recording the Bert Berns/Jerry Ragavoy ballad 'It Was Easier To Hurt Her' before finding hit success with Jackie Edwards' catchy 'Come On Home'. Erratic progress followed, with only the Graham Gouldman composition 'Pamela Pamela' breaking a run of misses. After giving up music during the early 70s, Fontana joined the revivalist circuit, though his progress was frequently dogged by personal problems. Albums: *Wayne Fontana And The Mindbenders* (1965),*The Game Of Love* (1965 - US release), *Eric, Rick Wayne And Bob* (1966), *Wayne One* (1966), *Wayne Fontana* (1967).

Fortunes

Originally formed in March 1963 as a trio, this UK beat group comprised; Glen Dale (b. 24 April 1943, Deal, Kent, England; guitar); Rod Allen (b. Rodney Bainbridge, 31 March 1944, Leicester, England; bass) and Barry Pritchard (b. 3 April 1944, Birmingham, England; guitar). The group had come together at Clifton Hall, the pop academy in the Midlands masterminded by their manager Reg Calvert. After perfecting their harmonic blend, the group recruited David Carr (b. 4 August 1943, Leyton, Essex, England; keyboards) and Andy Brown (b. 7 July 1946, Birmingham, England; drums) and toured consistently in the Midlands. Their debut single, 'Summertime Summertime' passed without notice, but the follow-up 'Caroline' was taken up as the theme song for the pirate radio station of the same name. By 1965 the group had broken into the UK and US Top 10 with 'You've Got Your Troubles' and modestly stated their ambition of recording pop ballads and harmonious standards. 'Here It Comes Again' and 'This Golden Ring' displayed their easy listening appeal and suggested the possibility of a long-term showbusiness career. Unfortunately, the group was hampered by the departure of vocalist Glen Dale who went on to pursue an unsuccessful solo career. To make matters worse, their manager was shot dead in a dispute over the ownership of the UK pirate station Radio City. The group continued and after switching record labels scored an unexpectedly belated USA hit with 'Here Comes That Rainy Day Feeling Again' in 1971. Back in the UK, they also enjoyed their first hits in over five years with 'Freedom Come Freedom Go' and 'Storm In A Teacup' and have since sustained their career, albeit with changing personnel, on the cabaret circuit. Compilations: *Remembering* (1976), *Best Of The Fortunes* (1983), *Music For The Millions* (1984), *Greatest Hits* (1985).

Foundations

Foundations

Formed in January 1967, the Foundations were discovered by London record dealer Barry Class as they rehearsed in the Butterfly, a club sited in a basement below his office. He introduced the group to songwriters Tony Macauley and John MacLeod whose composition, 'Baby, Now That I've Found You', became the unit's debut release. An engaging slice of commercial pop/soul, the single soared to the top of the UK charts and by February 1968 had reached number 9 in the USA, with global sales eventually passing three million.

The group's multi-racial line-up included Clem Curtis (b. 28 November 1940, Trinidad, West Indies; vocals), Alan Warner (b. 21 April 1947, London, England; guitar), Tony Gomez (b. 13 December 1948, Colombo, Sri Lanka; organ), Pat Burke (b. 9 October 1937, Jamaica, West Indies; tenor saxophone/flute), Mike Elliot (b. 6 August 1929, Jamaica, West Indies; tenor saxophone), Eric Allan Dale (b. 4 March 1936, Dominica, West Indies; trombone), Peter Macbeth (b. 2 February 1943, London, England; bass) and Tim Harris (b. 14 January 1948, London, England; drums). Dale was a former member of the Terry Lightfoot and Alex Welsh jazz bands while Elliot had backed Colin Hicks, brother of British rock 'n' roll singer Tommy

Steele. This mixture of youth and experience drew much contemporary comment. The Foundations scored a second multi-million seller in 1968 with 'Build Me Up, Buttercup'. Written by Macauley in partnership with Manfred Mann's Michael D'Abo, this compulsive song reached number 2 in Britain before topping the US chart for two weeks. The unit enjoyed further success with several similarly-styled releases including 'Back On My Feet Again' and 'Any Old Time' (both 1968), but their momentum faltered when Curtis embarked on an ill-starred solo career. He was replaced by Colin Young (b. 12 September 1944, Barbados, West Indies), but the departure of Elliot signalled an internal dissatisfaction. 'In The Bad Bad Old Days' (1969) returned the group to the UK Top 10, but that year's minor hit, 'Born To Live And Born To Die', was their last chart entry. The septet split up in 1970 when the rhythm section broke away to form the progressive group Pluto. A completely new line-up later resurrected the Foundations' name with little success.

Albums: *From The Foundations* (1967), *Digging The Foundations* (1969). Compilations: *The Foundations* (1968), *The Golden Hour Of The Foundations* (1973), *Back To The Beat* (1983), *The Best Of The Foundations* (1987).

Fourmost

Originally known as the Blue Jays, then the Four Jays, then the Four Mosts; Brian O'Hara (b. 12 March 1942, Liverpool, England; lead guitar/vocals), Mike Millward (b. 9 May 1942, Bromborough, Cheshire, England, d.1966; rhythm guitar/vocals), Billy Hatton (b. 9 June 1941, Liverpool, England; bass) and Dave Lovelady (b. 16 October 1942, Liverpool, England; drums) achieved momentary fame under the management wing of Brian Epstein. Two commercial John Lennon/Paul McCartney songs, 'Hello Little Girl' and 'I'm In Love', served as their initial a-sides, but the unflinchingly chirpy 'A Little Lovin'' became the quartet's biggest hit on reaching number 6 in April 1964. An archetypal merseybeat group, the Fourmost's later releases veered from Tamla/Motown ('Baby I Need Your Lovin'') to George Formby ('Aunt Maggie's Remedy') and their unswerving 'show business' professionalism was deemed anachronistic in the wake of the R&B boom. The death in 1966 of leukæmia victim Millward undermined the unit's confidence and despite McCartney's continued patronage - he produced their 1969 rendition of 'Rosetta' - the Fourmost were later consigned to cabaret and variety engagements.

Album: *First And Fourmost* (1965). Compilation: *The Most Of The Fourmost* (1982).

Four Pennies

This Lancastrian born Blackburn beat group, the Four Pennies, comprised of Lionel Morton (14 August 1942, Blackburn, Lancashire, England; vocals/rhythm guitar), Fritz Fryer (b. David Roderick Carnie Fryer, 6 December 1944, Oldham, England; lead guitar), Mike Wilsh (b. 21 July 1945, Stoke-on-Trent, England; bass) and Alan Buck (b. 7 April 1943, Brierfield, Lancashire, England; drums). They scored a notable UK number 1 hit in 1964 with 'Juliet' - a Morton-penned ballad which was originally the b-side of the less-immediate 'Tell Me Girl' that had a stark simplicity which enhanced its plaintive qualities. The quartet enjoyed three further Top 20 entries with 'I Found Out The Hard Way', 'Black Girl' (both 1964) and 'Until It's Time For You To Go' (1965), but were unable to sustain a long career. Fryer, having briefly fronted a new act, Fritz, Mike and Mo, later became a successful record producer, while Morton made frequent appearances in children's television programmes.

Albums: *Two Sides Of The Four Pennies* (1964), *Mixed Bag* (1966).

Four Seasons

Four Seasons

This highly-acclaimed USA vocal group first came together in 1956 with a line-up comprising vocalists Frankie Valli (b. Francis Castelluccio, 3 May 1937, Newark, New Jersey, USA), brothers Nick and

Tommy DeVito (b. 19 June 1936, Bellville, New Jersey, USA) and Hank Majewski. Initially known as the Variatones, then the Four Lovers, they enjoyed a minor USA hit with 'You're The Apple Of My Eye', composed by Otis Blackwell. After being dropped by RCA Records, they recorded a single for Epic, following which Valli departed in 1958. As a soloist he released 'I Go Ape', composed by singer Bob Crewe. Meanwhile, the Four Lovers released several records under pseudonymous names during which Nick DeVito and Majewski departed to be replaced by Nick Massi (b. 19 September 1935, Newark, New Jersey, USA) and Bob Gaudio (b. 17 December 1942, Bronx, New York, USA), a former member of the Royal Teens. After combining with Crewe and Gaudio, the group evolved into the Four Seasons, recording the single 'Spanish Lace' for the End label, before signing with VeeJay. There, they released 'Sherry', which reached number 1 in the USA in September 1962. A brilliant, example of falsetto, harmony pop, the track established the group as one of America's most popular. Two months later, they were back at the top with the powerful 'Big Girls Don't Cry' and achieved the same feat the following March with 'Walk Like A Man'. All these hits were underpinned by lustrous, soaring harmonies and thick up-front production, which gave the Seasons a sound unique in pop. Their international fame continued throughout 1964 when they met fierce competition from the Beatles. A sign of their standing was evinced by VeeJay's release of a battle of the bands album featuring the Seasons and the Beatles. Significantly, when the Fab Four held four of the Top 5 positions in the **Billboard** chart during early 1964, the Four Seasons represented the solitary competition with 'Dawn (Go Away)' at number 3. The sublime 'Rag Doll' brought them back to the top in the summer of 1964.

In 1965, Nick Massi left the group and was replaced by Joe Long. It was during this period that they playfully released a version of Bob Dylan's 'Don't Think Twice It's All Right' under the pseudonym Wonder Who. Valli, meanwhile, was continuing to enjoy solo hits. By the end of the 60s, the group reflected the changing times by attempting to establish themselves as a more serious act with *Genuine Imitation Life Gazette*. The album was poorly received, however, and following its release Gaudio replaced Crewe as producer. When Tommy DeVito left in 1970, the lucrative Four Seasons back catalogue and rights to the group name rested with Valli and Gaudio. A brief tie-up with Berry Gordy's Motown label saw the release of *Chameleon*, which despite favourable reviews sold poorly. Meanwhile, Valli was receiving unexpected success in the UK thanks to a Northern Soul dancefloor revival of 'You're Ready Now', which reached number 11 in

1971. Throughout the early 70s, membership of the Four Seasons was erratic, and Gaudio retired from performing in 1974 to concentrate on producing. Despite impending deafness, Valli was back at number 1 in 1975 with 'My Eyes Adored You'. With an old track from *Chameleon*, 'The Night', adding to the glory and the latest group line-up charting with 'Who Loves You', it was evident that the Four Seasons were as popular as ever. Immense success followed as the group became part of the disco boom sweeping America. The nostalgic 'December 1963 (Oh What A Night)' was a formidable transatlantic number 1 in 1976, but the following year, Valli left the group to concentrate on his solo career. While he again hit number 1 in the USA with the Barry Gibb film theme, *Grease*, the Four Seasons continued with drummer Gerry Polci taking on lead vocals. Valli returned to the group for a double album recorded live at Madison Square Garden. A team-up with the Beach Boys on the single 'East Meets West' in 1984 was followed by a studio album, *Streetfighter*, which featured Valli. Still going strong, the Four Seasons have become an institution whose illustrious history spans several musical eras from the barber shop harmonies of the 50s to the disco beat of the 70s and beyond.

Selected albums: *Sherry And 11 Others* (1962), *Ain't That A Shame And 11 Others* (1963), *The 4 Seasons Greetings* (1963), *Born To Wander* (1964), *Dawn And 11 Other Great Songs* (1964), *Rag Doll* (1964), *Entertain You* (1965), *The Four Seasons Sing Big Hits By Bacharach, David And Dylan* (1966), *Working My Way Back To You* (1966), *Lookin' Back* (1967), *Chrismas Album* (1967), *Genuine Imitation Life Gazette* (1969), *Edizione D'Oro* (1969), *Chameleon* (1972), *Inside You* (1976), *Who Loves You* (1976), *Helicon* (1977), *Reunited Live* (1981), *Streetfighter* (1975). Numerous compilations have also been issued.

Four Tops and Brian Epstein

Four Tops

Levi Stubbs (b. c.1938, Detroit, Michigan, USA), Renaldo 'Obie' Benson (b. 1947, Detroit, Michigan,

USA), Lawrence Peyton (b. c.1938, Detroit, Michigan, USA) and Abdul 'Duke' Fakir (b. c.1938, Detroit, Michigan, USA), first sang together at a party in Detroit in 1954. Calling themselves the Four Aims, they began performing at supper clubs in the city, with a repertoire of jazz songs and standards. In 1956, they changed their name to the Four Tops to avoid confusion with the popular singing group the Ames Brothers, and recorded a one-off single for the R&B label Chess. Further unsuccessful recordings appeared on Red Top, Columbia and Riverside between 1958-62, before the Four Tops were signed to the Motown jazz subsidiary, Workshop, in 1963. Motown boss Berry Gordy elected not to release their initial album, *Breaking Through*, in 1964, and suggested that they record with the label's Holland/Dozier/Holland writing and production team. The initial release from this liaison was 'Baby I Need Your Loving', which showcased the group's strong harmonies and the gruff, soulful lead vocals of Levi Stubbs, it reached the US Top 20. The following year, another Holland/Dozier/Holland song, 'I Can't Help Myself', topped the charts, and established the Four Tops as one of Motown's most successful groups.

Holland/Dozier/Holland continued to write and produce for the Four Tops until 1967. The pinnacle of this collaboration was 'Reach Out I'll Be There', a transatlantic hit in 1966. This represented the peak of the traditional Motown style, bringing an almost symphonic arrangement to an R&B love song; producer Phil Spector described the record as black (Bob) Dylan. Other major hits like 'It's The Same Old Song' and 'Bernadette' were not as ambitious, although they are still regarded as Motown classics today. In 1967, the Four Tops began to widen their appeal with soul-tinged versions of pop hits, such as the Left Banke's 'Walk Away Renee' and Tim Hardin's 'If I Were A Carpenter'. The departure of Holland/Dozier/Holland from Motown later that year brought a temporary halt to the group's progress, and it was only in 1970, under the aegis of producer/writers like Frank Wilson and Smokey Robinson, that the Four Tops regained their hit status with a revival of the Tommy Edwards' hit, 'It's All In The Game', and the socially aware ballad, 'Still Waters'. That same year, they teamed up with the Supremes for the first of three albums of collaborations.

Another revival, Richard Harris's hit 'MacArthur Park', brought them success in 1971, while Renaldo Benson also co-wrote Marvin Gaye's hit single 'What's Going On'. But after working with the Moody Blues on 'A Simple Game', in 1972, the Four Tops elected to leave Motown when the corporation relocated its head office from Detroit to California. They signed a deal with Dunhill, and immediately

restored their chart success with records that marked a return to their mid-60s style, notably the theme song to the 'blaxploitation' movie *Shaft In Africa*, 'Are You Man Enough'. Subsequent releases were less dynamic, and for the remainder of the 70s the Four Tops enjoyed only sporadic chart success, though they continued touring and performing their Motown hits. After two years of inactivity at the end of the decade, they joined Casablanca Records, and immediately secured a number 1 soul hit with 'When She Was My Girl', which revived their familiar style. Subsequent releases in a similar vein also charted in Britain and America.

In 1983, the group performed a storming medley 'duel' of their 60s hits with the Temptations during the Motown 25th Anniversary television special. They re-signed to the label for the aptly titled *Back Where I Belong*, one side of which was produced by Holland/Dozier/Holland. But disappointing sales and disputes about the group's musical direction led them to leave Motown once again for Arista, where they found immediate success in 1988 with the singles 'Indestructible' and 'Loco In Acapulco', the latter taken from the soundtrack to the film *Buster*. The Four Tops have retained a constant line-up since their inception, and the group's immaculate choreography and harmonies have ensured them ongoing success as a live act from the mid-60s to the present day - notably in Britain and Europe, where they have always been held in higher regard than in their homeland.

Albums: *Four Tops* (1965), *Second Album* (1965), *On Top* (1966), *Live!* (1966), *On Broadway* (1967), *Reach Out* (1967), *Yesterday's Dreams* (1968), *Now* (1969), *Soul Spin* (1969), *Still Waters Run Deep* (1970), *Changing Times* (1970), with the Supremes *The Magnificent Seven* (1970), with the Supremes *The Return Of The Magnificent Seven* (1971), with the Supremes *Dynamite* (1971), *Nature Planned It* (1972), *Keeper Of The Castle* (1972), *Main Street People* (1973), *Meeting Of The Minds* (1974), *Live And In Concert* (1974), *Night Lights Harmony* (1975), *Catfish* (1976), *The Show Must Go On* (1977), *At The Top* (1978), *Tonight* (1981), *One More Mountain* (1982), *Back Where I Belong* (1983), *Magic* (1985), *Hot Nights* (1986), *Indestructible* (1988). Numerous compilations are available.

Foxx, Inez And Charlie

Inez Foxx (b. 9 September 1942, Greensboro, North Carolina, USA) and Charlie Foxx (b. 23 October 1939, Greensboro, North Carolina, USA). A brother and sister duo, Inez was a former member of the Gospel Tide Chorus. Her first solo single, 'A Feeling', was issued on Brunswick Records, credited to 'Inez Johnston'. Charlie was meanwhile a budding songwriter and his reworking of a nursery rhyme,

'Mockingbird', became their first single together. Released on the Sue label subsidiary Symbol, it was a US Top 10 hit in 1963, although it was not until 1969 that the song charted in the UK Top 40. Their immediate releases followed the same contrived pattern but later recordings for Musicor/Dynamo, in particular 'I Stand Accused', were more adventurous. However, their final hit together, '(1-2-3-4-5-6-7) Count The Days' (1967), was modelled closely on that early style. Solo again, Inez continued to record for Dynamo before signing with Stax/Volt in 1972. Although apparently uncomfortable with their recording methods, the results, including the *Inez Foxx In Memphis* album, were excellent.

Albums: *Mockingbird* (1963), *Inez And Charlie Foxx* (1965), *Come By Here* (1965). Compilation: *The Best Of Charlie And Inez Foxx* (1986). Solo album: Inez Foxx *In Memphis* (1972).

Charlie And Inez Foxx

Francis, Connie

b. Concetta Rosa Maria Franconero, 12 December 1938, Newark, New Jersey, USA. A popular singer of tearful ballads and jaunty up-tempo numbers, Francis was one of the most successful female artists of the 50s and 60s. She began playing the accordion at the age of four, and was singing and playing professionally when she was 11. After winning an *Arthur Godfrey Talent Show*, she changed her name, at Godfrey's suggestion. Signed for MGM Records in 1955, her first record was a German import, 'Freddy', which was also recorded by Eartha Kitt and Stan Kenton. 'Majesty Of Love', her 10th release, a duet with Marvin Rainwater, was her first US chart entry. In 1957 she was persuaded by her father, against her will, to record one of his favourites, the 1923 song 'Who's Sorry Now', by Harry Ruby, Bert Kalmar and Ted Snyder. It went to number 4 in the US charts and number 1 in the UK, and was the first of a string of hits through to 1962. These included re-workings of more oldies, such as 'My Happiness', 'Among My Souvenirs' and 'Together'. Among her more jaunty, upbeat songs were 'Stupid Cupid' (another UK number 1 coupled with 'Carolina Moon') and 'Where The Boys Are' by the new songwriting team of Neil Sedaka and Howard Greenfield. Her other US Top 10 entries included 'Lipstick On Your Collar', 'Frankie', 'Mama', 'Everybody's Somebody's Fool' (her first US number 1), 'My Mind Has A Heart Of Its Own' (another US number 1), 'Many Tears Ago', 'Breakin' In A Brand New Broken Heart', 'When The Boy In Your Arms (Is The Boy In Your Heart)', 'Don't Break The Heart That Loves You' (US number 1), 'Second Hand Love' and 'Vacation'. Francis made her film debut in 1960 with *Where The Boys Are*, and followed it with similar 'frothy' comedy musicals such as *Follow The Boys* (1963), *Looking For Love* (1964) and *When The Boys Meet The Girls* (1965). Outdated by the 60s beat boom, she worked in nightclubs in the late 60s, and did much charity work for UNICEF and similar organizations, besides entertaining US troops in Vietnam. She also extended her repertoire, and kept her options open, by recording albums in several languages, including French, Spanish and Japanese, and one entitled, *Connie Francis Sings Great Jewish Favorites*. Late 70s issues included more country music selections, including *Great Country Hits* with Hank Williams Jnr.

In 1974 she was the victim of a rape in her motel room after performing at the Westbury Theatre, outside New York. She later sued the motel for negligence, and was reputedly awarded damages of over three million dollars. For several years afterwards she did not perform in public, and underwent psychiatric treatment for long periods. She returned to the Westbury in 1981, to an enthusiastic reception, and resumed performing in the USA and abroad, including appearances at the London Palladium in 1989; and in Las Vegas in the same year, where she received a standing ovation after a mature performance ranging from her opening number, 'Let Me Try Again', to the climactic, 'If I Never Sing Another Song'. In 1991 she was featured in a full-page advertisement in the trade magazine *Variety*, confirming that she was still working.

Albums: *Who's Sorry Now?* (1958), *The Exciting*

Connie Francis (1959), *My Thanks To You* (1959), *Christmas In My Heart* (1959), *Italian Favorites* (1960), *More Italian Favorites* (1960), *Rock 'N' Roll Million Sellers* (1960), *Country And Western Golden Hits* (1960), *Spanish And Latin American Favorites* (1960), *Connie Francis At The Copa* (1961), *Connie Francis Sings Great Jewish Favorites* (1961), *Songs To A Swingin' Band* (1961), *Never On Sunday And Other Title Songs From Motion Pictures* (1961), *Folk Song Favorites* (1961), *Do The Twist* (1962), *Second Hand Love And Other Hits* (1962), *Country Music Connie Style* (1962), *Modern Italian Hits* (1963), *Follow The Boys* (1963, film soundtrack), *German Favorites* (1963), *Award Winning Motion Picture Hits* (1963), *Great American Waltzes* (1963), *In The Summer Of His Years* (1964), *Looking For Love* (1964, film soundtrack), with Hank Williams Jnr. *Great Country Favorites* (1964), *A New Kind Of Connie* (1964), *Connie Francis Sings For Mama* (1965), *When The Boys Meet The Girls* (1965, film soundtrack), *Movie Greats Of The Sixties* (1966), *Live At The Sahara In Las Vegas* (1966), *Love Italian Style* (1967), *Happiness* (1967), *My Heart Cries For You* (1967), *Hawaii Connie* (1968), *Connie And Clyde* (1968), *Connie Sings Bacharach And David* (1968), *The Wedding Cake* (1969), *Connie Francis Sings Great Country Hits, Volume Two* (1973), *Sings The Big Band Hits* (1977), *I'm Me Again - Silver Anniversary Album* (1981), *Connie Franicis And Peter Kraus, Volumes 1 & 2* (1984), *Country Store* (1988). Compilations: *Connie's Greatest Hits* (1960), *More Greatest Hits* (1961), *Connie Francis Sings* (1962), *Mala Femmena And Connie's Big Hits From Italy* (1963), *The Very Best Of Connie Francis* (1963), *The All Time International Hits* (1965), *20 All Time Greats* (1977), *Connie Francis In Deutschland* (1988, eight-album box set), *The Very Best Of Connie Francis, Volume Two* (1988).
Further reading: *Who's Sorry Now?*, Connie Francis.

Frank, Jackson C.

b. 1943, Buffalo, New York, USA. Frank was one of several American folk performers, including Shawn Phillips and Paul Simon, who temporarily lived in Britain during the mid-60s. Indeed, Simon produced *Jackson C. Frank*, the artist's lone album, which showcased his gift for melody and a lyrical perception. Released in 1965, several of its songs, including 'Blues Run The Game' and 'You Never Wanted Me', have since been recognized as standards. Folksinger Sandy Denny befriended Frank and regularly performed his compositions both as a solo act and on joining Fairport Convention. Jackson's final British appearance of note came in September 1968 at the Royal Festival Hall. Billed as 'An Evening Of Contemporary Song', he shared the stage with Joni Mitchell, Al Stewart and the Fairports, but returned to the United States without consolidating his undoubted early promise.

Album: *Jackson C. Frank* (1965 - re-issued in 1978 as *Jackson Frank Again*). Compilation: *Blues Run The Game* (1987).

Aretha Franklin

Franklin, Aretha

b. 25 March 1942, Memphis, Tennessee, USA. Aretha's music is steeped in the traditions of the church. Her father, Cecil L. Franklin was a Baptist preacher, famed throughout black America for his fiery sermons and magnetic public appearances. He knew the major gospel stars, Mahalia Jackson and Clara Ward, who in turn gave his daughter valuable tutelage. At 12, Aretha was promoted from the choir to become a featured soloist. Two years later she began recording for JVB and Checker. Between 1956-60, her output consisted solely of devotional material but the secular success of Sam Cooke encouraged a change of emphasis. Franklin auditioned for John Hammond, who signed her to Columbia. Sadly, the company was indecisive on how best to showcase her remarkable talent. They tried blues, cocktail jazz, standards, pop songs and contemporary soul hits, each of which wasted the singer's natural improvisational instincts. There were some occasional bright spots; 'Running Out Of Fools' (1964) or 'Cry Like A Baby' (1966), but in both cases content succeeded over style. A disillusioned Franklin joined Atlantic in 1966 where the magnificent 'I Never Loved A Man (The Way I

Loved You)' declared her liberation. All these songs were recorded at Muscle Shoals and the houseband's contribution was suitably sparse while Aretha simply wailed ecstatically. The single soared into the US Top 10 and, coupled with the expressive 'Do Right Woman – Do Right Man', it announced the arrival of a major artist. The releases which followed – 'Respect', 'Baby I Love You', '(You Make Me Feel Like) A Natural Woman', 'Chain Of Fools' and '(Sweet Sweet Baby) Since You've Been Gone' – confirmed her authority and claim to being the 'Queen Of Soul'

Despite Franklin's professional success, her personal life grew confused. Her relationship with husband and manager Ted White disintegrated and while excellent singles like 'Think' still appeared, others betrayed a discernible lethargy. She followed 'Think' with the sublime 'I Say A Little Prayer' giving power and authority to simple yet delightful lyrics; 'the moment I wake up, as I put on my make-up, I say a little prayer for you'. By 1970, however, she had regained her powers as 'Call Me', 'Spirit In The Dark' and 'Don't Play That Song' ably testified. An album, *Aretha Alive At The Fillmore West* (1971), meanwhile restated her in-concert power. The following year another live appearance resulted in *Amazing Grace*, a double gospel set recorded with James Cleveland and the Southern California Community Choir. Its passion encapsulated her career to date. Franklin continued to record strong material throughout the early 70s and enjoyed three R&B chart-toppers, 'Angel', 'Until You Come Back To Me (That's What I'm Gonna Do)' and 'I'm In Love'. Sadly, the rest of the decade was marred by recordings which were at best predictable, at worst dull. Her cameo role in the film *The **Blues Brothers***, however, rekindled her flagging career. Aretha moved to Arista in 1980 and immediately regained a commercial momentum with 'United Together' and two confident albums, *Aretha* and *Love All The Hurt Away*. 'Jump To It', 'Get It Right', 'Freeway Of Love' and 'Who's Zooming Who' continued her rejuvenation, while duets with the Eurythmics and George Michael kept her in the pop charts in the mid-80s. Aretha Franklin may now lack the instinct of her classic Atlantic recordings, but as *One Lord One Faith One Baptism* (1987) proved, she is still a commanding singer. Franklin possesses an astonishing voice that has often been wasted on poor choice of material.

Albums: *Aretha* (1961), *Electrifying* (1962), *The Tender, Moving And Swinging Aretha Franklin* (1962), *Laughing On The Outside* (1963), *Unforgettable* (1964), *Songs Of Faith* (1964), *Running Out Of Fools* (1964), *Yeah!!!* (1965), *Queen Of Soul* (1965), *Once In A Lifetime* (1965), *Soul Sister* (1966), *Take It Like You Give It* (1967), *Take A Look* (1967), *I Never Loved A Man The Way That I Love You* (1967), *Aretha Arrives* (1967), *Aretha: Lady Soul* (1968), *Aretha Now* (1968), *Aretha In Paris* (1968), *Soul '69* (1969), *Today I Sing The Blues* (1969), *Soft And Beautiful* (1969), *I Say A Little Prayer* (1969), *Aretha Franklin Live* (1969), *This Girl's In Love With You* (1970), *Spirit In The Dark* (1970), *Two Sides Of Love* (1970), *Aretha Live At The Fillmore West* (1971), *Young, Gifted And Black* (1971), *Amazing Grace* (1972), *Hey Now Hey (The Other Side Of The Sky)* (1973), *Let Me Into Your Life* (1974), *With Everything I Feel In Me* (1974), *You* (1975), *Sparkle* (1976), *Sweet Passion* (1977), *Satisfaction* (1977), *Almighty Fire* (1978), *La Diva* (1979) *Aretha* (1980), *Love All The Hurt Away* (1981), *Jump To It* (1982), *Get It Right* (1983), *Who's Zoomin' Who?* (1985), *Aretha Franklin* (1986), *One Lord, One Faith, One Baptism* (1987), *Through The Storm* (1989). Compilations: *Aretha's Gold* (1969), *Aretha's Greatest Hits* (1971), *The First 12 Sides* (1973), *Ten Years Of Gold* (1976), *Legendary Queen Of Soul* (1983), *The Collection* (1986), *Never Grow Old* (1987), *20 Greatest Hits* (1987), *Aretha Franklin's Greatest Hits 1960-1965* (1987).

Fred, John, And His Playboy Band

b. 8 May 1941, Baton Rouge, Louisiana, USA. John Fred was a 6 foot 5 inch, blue-eyed soul singer who originally worked with Fats Domino's backing group in the late 50's. During the early 60's various versions of the Playboy Band recorded for small independent record labels but it was not until the end of 1967 that success finally came with the international hit, 'Judy In Disguise'. An amusing satire on the Beatles' 'Lucy In The Sky With Diamonds', the single beat off a rival version by Amboy Dukes. Although the Playboy Band were generally perceived as a novelty group, they were tight and well organized and Fred's blue-eyed soul vocals were evident on their album *Agnes English,* which included a rasping version of 'She Shot A Hole In My Soul'. By the end of the 60s the group split and Fred went on to become a producer.
Album: *Agnes English* (1968).

Freddie And The Dreamers

This Lancastrian, Manchester born and raised group, comprising of Freddie Garrity (b. 14 November 1940; vocals), Roy Crewsdon (b. 29 May 1941; guitar), Derek Quinn (b. 24 May 1942; guitar), Pete Birrell (b. 9 May 1941; bass) and Bernie Dwyer (b. 11 September 1940; drums), was briefly renowned for its mixture of beat music and comedy. Garrity formed the group in 1959 and it remained semi-professional until passing a BBC audition in 1963. Although their debut, 'If You Gotta Make A Fool Of Somebody', was an R&B favourite (James Ray and Maxine Brown), subsequent releases were tailored to the quintet's effervescent insouciant image. 'I'm Telling

You Now' and 'You Were Made For Me' also reached the UK Top 3, establishing the group at the height of the beat boom. Although Garrity displayed his songwriting skill with such strong ballads as 'Send A Letter To Me', his work was not used for a-side recordings. Further hits followed in 1964 with 'Over You', 'I Love You Baby', 'Just For You', and the Christmas season favourite 'I Understand'. The group's appeal declined in the UK but early in 1965, they made a startling breakthrough in America where 'I'm Telling You Now' topped the charts. American audiences were entranced by Garrity's zany stage antics (which resulted in frequent twisted ankles) and eagerly demanded the name of his unusual dance routine. "It's called the Freddie", he innocently replied. A US Top 20 hit rapidly followed with 'Do The Freddie'. Although the group appeared in a couple of films, *Just For You* And *Cuckoo Patrol*, their main audience was in pantomime and cabaret. They broke up at the end of the decade, but Garrity and Birtles remained together in the children's show *Little Big Time*. During the mid-70s the group was revived by Freddie Garrity, with new personnel, for revival concerts at home and abroad. In 1988, Garrity began a parallel career of performing in cabaret and an acting career.
Albums: *Freddie And The Dreamers* (1963), *You Were Made For Me* (1964), *Freddie And The Dreamers* (1965, US release), *Sing-Along Party* (1965), *Do The Freddie* (1965), *Seaside Swingers* aka *Everyday's A Holiday* (1965, film soundtrack), *Frantic Freddie* (1965), *Freddie And The Dreamers In Disneyland* (1966), *Fun Lovin' Freddie* (1966), *King Freddie And His Dreaming Knights* (1967), *Oliver In The Underworld* (1970). Compilations: *The Best Of Freddie And The Dreamers* (1982), *The Hits Of Freddie And The Dreamers* (1988).

Free

Formed in the midst of 1968's British blues boom, Free originally included Paul Rodgers (b. 12 December 1949, Middlesbrough, Cleveland, England; vocals), Paul Kossoff (b. 14 September 1950, London, England, d. 19 March 1976; guitar), Andy Fraser (b. 7 August 1952, London, England; bass) and Simon Kirke (b. 28 July 1949, Shrewsbury, Shropshire, England; drums). Despite their comparative youth, the individual musicians were seasoned performers, particularly Fraser, a former member of John Mayall's Bluesbreakers. Free gained early encouragement from Alexis Korner, but having completed an earthy debut album, *Tons Of Sobs*, the group began honing a more individual style with their second set. The injection of powerful original songs, including 'I'll Be Creeping', showed a maturing talent, while Rodgers' expressive voice and Kossoff's stinging guitar enhanced a growing reputation.

The quartet's stylish blues/rock reached its peak on *Fire And Water*. This confident collection featured moving ballads; 'Heavy Load', 'Oh I Wept' and compulsive, uptempo material, the best-known of which is 'All Right Now'. An edited version of this soulful composition reached number 2 in the UK and number 4 in the US in 1970, since when the song has become one of pop's most enduring performances making periodic appearances in the singles chart. A fourth set, *Highway*, revealed a mellower perspective enhanced by an increased use of piano at the expense of Kossoff's guitar. This was due, in part, to friction within the group, a factor exacerbated when the attendant single, 'The Stealer', failed to emulate its predecessor. Free split up in May 1971, paradoxically in the wake of another successful single, 'My Brother Jake', but regrouped in January the following year when spin-off projects faltered, although Kossoff and Kirke's amalgamation (Kossoff, Kirke, Tetsu And Rabbit) proved fruitful.
A sixth album, *Free At Last*, offered some of the unit's erstwhile fire and included another UK Top 20 entrant, 'Little Bit Of Love'. However Kossoff's increasing ill-health and Fraser's departure for the Sharks undermined any newfound confidence. A hastily convened line-up consisting of Rodgers, Kirke, John 'Rabbit' Bundrick (keyboards) and Tetsu Yamauchi (b. 1946, Fukuoka, Japan; bass) undertook a Japanese tour, but although the guitarist rejoined the quartet for several British dates, his contribution to Free's final album, *Heartbreaker*, was muted. Kossoff embarked on a solo career in October 1972; Wendel Richardson from Osibisa replaced him on a temporary basis, but by July the following year Free had ceased to function. Rodgers and Kirke subsequently formed Bad Company.
Albums: *Tons Of Sobs* (1968), *Free* (1969), *Fire And Water* (1970), *Highway* (1971), *Free Live* (1971), *Free At Last* (1972), *Heartbreaker* (1973). Compilations: *The Free Story* (1974), *Completely Free* (1982), *All Right Now* (1991).

Friends Of Distinction

Formed in 1968 by Floyd Butler (b. 5 June 1941, San Diego, California, USA), Harry Elston (b. 4 November 1938, Dallas, Texas, USA), Jessica Cleaves (b. 10 December 1948, Los Angeles, California, USA) and Barbara Jean Love (b. 24 July 1941, Los Angeles, California, USA). This smooth vocal quartet began working together in the Ray Charles' revue. Stylistically similar to the Fifth Dimension, the Friends scored a million-selling hit with a vocal version of Hugh Masekela's 'Grazing In The Grass' (1969). Two further releases, 'Going In Circles' and 'Love Or Let Me Be Lonely', were also substantial hits, before their sweet-harmony, MOR soul established them as a cabaret attraction.

Albums: *Grazin'* (1969), *Highly Distinct* (1969), *Real Friends* (1970), *Whatever* (1970), *Friends And People* (1971).

Fuller, Bobby

b. 22 October 1943, Baytown, Texas, USA. An inventive and compulsive musician, Bobby Fuller made his recording debut in 1961. 'You're In Love' was the first of several outings for local independent labels, but the artist's development was more apparent on the many demos completed in his home-based studio. Fuller later moved to Los Angeles where his group, the Bobby Fuller Four - Randy Fuller (bass), Jim Reese (rhythm guitar) and DeWayne Quirico (drums) - became a leading attraction, infusing Buddy Holly-styled rockabilly with the emergent British beat. Their early releases were regional hits, nevertheless in January 1966 the unit reached the US Top 10 with an ebullient reading of the Crickets' 'I Fought The Law'. This pop classic, later covered by the Clash, was followed up by a Top 30 hit, 'Love's Made A Fool Of You'. The singer's stature now seemed assured, but on 18 July that same year any hope for a bright future was cut short when Fuller's badly beaten body was discovered in a parked car in Los Angeles. His death was attributed to asphyxia through the forced inhalation of gasoline, but further investigations as to the perpetrators of this deed remain unresolved.

Albums: *KRLA King Of The Wheels* (1965), *I Fought The Law* aka *Memorial Album* (1966), *Live Again* (1984). Compilations: *The Best Of The Bobby Fuller Four* (1981), *The Bobby Fuller Tapes, Volume 1* (1983), *Memories Of Buddy Holly* (1984), *The Bobby Fuller Instrumental Album* (1985).

Fury, Billy

b. Ronald Wycherley, 17 April 1940, Dingle, Liverpool, England, d. 28 January 1983. An impromptu audition in a Birkenhead dressing room resulted in Wycherley joining Larry Parnes' management stable. The entrepreneur provided the suitably enigmatic stage name, and added the aspirant to the bill of a current package tour. Fury enjoyed a UK Top 20 hit with his debut single, 'Maybe Tomorrow', in 1959 and the following year completed *The Sound Of Fury*, which consisted entirely of the artist's own songs. Arguably Britain's finest example of the rockabilly genre, it owed much of its authenticity to sterling support from guitarist Joe Brown, while the Four Jays provided backing vocals. However Fury found his greatest success with a series of dramatic ballads which, in suggesting a vulnerability, enhanced the singer's undoubted sex appeal. His stylish good looks complimented a vocal prowess blossoming in 1961 with a cover version of Tony Orlando's 'Halfway To Paradise'. This superior

Billy Fury

single, arranged and scored by Ivor Raymonde, established a pattern which would provide Fury with 16 further UK Top 30 hits, including 'Jealousy' (1961), 'Last Night Was Made For Love' (1962), 'Like I've Never Been Gone' (1963), 'It's Only Make Believe' (1964) and 'In Thoughts Of You' (1965). Billy also completed two exploitative pop movies, *Play It Cool* (1962) and *I've Gotta Horse* (1964) and remained one of Britain's leading in-concert attractions throughout the early-60s. Supported initially by the Tornados, then the Gamblers, the singer showed a wider repertoire live than his label would allow on record. Bedevilled by ill-health and overtaken by changing musical fashions, Fury's final Top 30 hit came in 1966 with 'Give Me Your Word'. The following year he left Decca for Parlophone, debuting with a Peter And Gordon song, 'Hurtin' Is Lovin''. Subsequent recordings included David Bowie's 'Silly Boy Blue', the Bee Gees' 'One Minute Woman' (both 1968) and Carole King's 'Why Are You Leaving' (1970), but the singer was unable to regain his erstwhile success. In 1971 he underwent open-heart surgery, but recovered to record 'Will The Real Man Stand Up' on his own Fury label and played the part of Stormy Tempest in the film *That'll Be The Day* (1973). A second major operation in 1976 forced Billy to retire again, but he re-emerged at the end of the decade with *Memories*, new recordings of his best-known songs, and several live and television appearances. In 1981 Fury struck a new deal with Polydor, but his health was rapidly deteriorating and on 28 January 1983 he succumbed to a fatal heart attack. Unlike many of his pre-Beatles contemporaries, the artist's reputation has grown over the years, and Billy Fury is now rightly regarded as one of the finest rock 'n' roll singers Britain ever produced.

Albums: *Sound Of Fury* (1960), *Billy Fury* (1960), *Halfway To Paradise* (1961), *Billy* (1963), *We Want Billy* (1963), *I've Got A Horse* (1965), *The One And Only* (1983). Compilations: *The Best Of Billy Fury* (1967), *The World Of Billy Fury* (1972), *The Billy Fury Story* (1977), *Billy Fury - The Golden Years* aka *Memories* (1979), *The World Of Billy Fury Volume 2* (1980), *Hit Parade* (1982), *The Missing Years 1967-1980* (1983), *The Billy Fury Hit Parade* (1983), *Loving You* (1984), *The Other Side Of Billy Fury* (1984), *Stick 'N' Stones* (1985), *The EP Collection* (1985), *Jealousy* (1986), *The Collection* (1987), *The Best Of Billy Fury* (1988), *The Sound Of Fury + 10* (1988).

G

Gainsbourg, Serge

b. 2 April 1928, Paris, France, d. 2 March 1991. Gainsbourg was a frustrated painter who eked a living as a bar pianist before joining the band hired for the musical *Milord L'Arsoille* starring Michele Arnaud. Eventually given a reluctant singing role, his stage-fright was interpreted by the audience as part of the act. His subsequent self-penned hit parade successes included 'Poinconneur Des Lilacs', 'La Chanson De Prevert' (a homage to the renowned French poet) and 'La Javanaise' but, an unlikely looking pop star with his heavy-lidded homeliness, he preferred to compose for others. More prestigious than songs for Regine, Valerie Lagrange and Dominique Walter were those commissioned by such as Juliette Greco, Sacha Distel, Johnny Halliday, Claude Francois and also English language vocalists, Petula Clark and Dionne Warwick. 'Je T'Aime . . . Moi Non Plus' was intended for Brigitte Bardot but she was unwilling to simulate the sounds of sexual congress that it required. Instead, Gainsbourg recorded it himself as an album track with film actress Jane Birkin, the 'constant companion' he had met on the set of 1967's *Slogan*. Issued as a single in 1969, publicity earned via a BBC ban caused its abrupt

deletion by Fontana but, unworried by moral opprobrium, other labels seized the opportunity to take up the slack as it swept to number 1 all over Europe and hovered around the middle of the US Hot 100. It would enjoy a further few weeks in the UK Top 40 when reissued in 1974. Other Gainsbourg records were confined to home charts - though the artist's occasional outrages on Gallic chat-shows were thought newsworthy in those areas that remembered his erotic duet.

David Garrick

Garrick, David

b. 1946, Liverpool, England. Opera-trained Garrick began his career at the famed Cavern club, where he performed as a member of the Dions, before moving to London on securing a deal with the Piccadilly label as a solo artist. Two unsuccessful singles were released before the singer scored a UK Top 30 hit with 'Lady Jane', originally recorded by the Rolling Stones, in June 1966. Garrick enjoyed a second chart entry with 'Dear Mrs. Applebee', a boyish performance redolent of Herman's Hermits, which sold a million copies in Germany. Despite sharing management with the Kinks and enjoying a front page advertisement for 'I Found A Love', further chart success proved elusive. Album: *A Boy Called David* (1966).

Gaye, Marvin

b. Marvin Pentz Gay Jnr., 2 April 1939, Washington

DC, USA, d. 1 April 1984. Gaye was named after his father, a minister in the Apostolic Church. The spiritual influence of his early years played a formative role in his musical career, particularly from the 70s onwards, when his songwriting shifted back and forth between secular and religious topics. He abandoned a place in his father's church choir to team up with Don Covay and Billy Stewart in the R&B vocal group the Rainbows. In 1957, he joined the Marquees, who recorded for Chess under the guidance of Bo Diddley. The following year the group were taken under the wing of producer and singer Harvey Fuqua, who used them to re-form his doo-wop outfit, the Moonglows. When Fuqua moved to Detroit in 1960, Gay went with him: Fuqua soon joined forces with Berry Gordy at Motown, and Marvin became a session drummer and vocalist for the label.

In 1961, he married Gordy's sister, Anna, and was offered a solo recording contract. Renamed Marvin Gaye, he began his career as a jazz balladeer, but in 1962 he was persuaded to record R&B, and notched up his first hit single with the confident 'Stubborn Kind Of Fellow', a Top 10 R&B hit. This record set the style for the next three years, as Gaye enjoyed hits with a series of joyous, dance-flavoured songs which cast him as a smooth, macho Don Juan figure. He also continued to work behind the scenes at Motown, co-writing Martha And The Vandellas' hit 'Dancing In The Street', and playing drums on several early recordings by Little Stevie Wonder. In 1965, Gaye dropped the call-and-response vocal arrangements of his earlier hits and began to record in a more sophisticated style. 'How Sweet It Is (To Be Loved By You)' epitomized his new direction, and it was followed by two successive R&B number 1 hits, 'I'll Be Doggone' and 'Ain't That Peculiar'. His status as Motown's best-selling male vocalist left him free to pursue more esoteric avenues on his albums, which in 1965 included a tribute to the late Nat 'King' Cole and a collection of Broadway standards.

To capitalize on his image as a ladies' man, Motown teamed Gaye with their leading female vocalist, Mary Wells, for some romantic duets. When Wells left Motown in 1964, Gaye recorded with Kim Weston until 1967, when she was succeeded by Tammi Terrell. The Gaye/Terrell partnership represented the apogee of the soul duet, as their voices blended sensuously on a string of hits written specifically for the duo by Nikolas Ashford and Valerie Simpson. Terrell developed a brain tumour in 1968, and collapsed onstage in Gaye's arms. Records continued to be issued under the duo's name, although Simpson allegedly took Terrell's place on some recordings. Through the mid-60s, Gaye allowed his duet recordings to take precedence over his solo work, but in 1968 he issued the epochal 'I Heard It Through

The Grapevine', a song originally released on Motown by Gladys Knight And The Pips, though Gaye's version had actually been recorded first. With its tense, ominous rhythm arrangement, and Gaye's typically fluent and emotional vocal, the record represented a landmark in Motown's history - not least because it became the label's biggest-selling record to date. Gaye followed up with another number 1 R&B hit, 'Too Busy Thinking 'Bout My Baby', but his career was derailed by the insidious illness and eventual death of Tammi Terrell in March 1970. Devastated by the loss of his close friend and partner, Gaye spent most of 1970 in seclusion. The following year, he emerged with a set of recordings which Motown at first refused to release, but which eventually became his most successful solo album.

On 'What's Going On', a number 1 hit in 1971, and its two chart-topping follow-ups, 'Mercy Mercy Me (The Ecology)' and 'Inner City Blues', Gaye combined his spiritual beliefs with his increasing concern about poverty, discrimination and political corruption in American society. To match his shift in subject matter, Gaye evolved a new musical style, which influenced a generation of black performers. Built on a heavily percussive base, Gaye's arrangements mingled jazz and classical influences into his soul roots, creating a fluid instrumental backdrop for his sensual, almost despairing vocals. The three singles were all contained on *What's Going On*, a conceptual masterpiece on which every track contributed to the spiritual yearning suggested by its title. After making a sly comment on the 1972 USA Presidential election campaign with the single 'You're The Man', Gaye composed the soundtrack to the 'blaxploitation' thriller, *Trouble Man*. His primarily instrumental score highlighted his interest in jazz, while the title song provided him with another hit single.

Gaye's next project saw him shifting his attention from the spiritual to the sexual with *Let's Get It On*, which included a quote from T.S. Eliot on the sleeve and devoted itself to the art of talking a woman into bed. Its explicit sexuality marked a sea-change in Gaye's career; as he began to use cocaine more and more regularly, he became obsessed with his personal life, and rarely let the outside world figure in his work. Paradoxically, he continued to let Motown market him in a traditional fashion by agreeing to collaborate with Diana Ross on a sensuous album of duets in 1973 - though the two singers allegedly did not actually meet during the recording of the project. The break-up of his marriage to Anna Gordy in 1975 delayed work on his next album. *I Want You* was merely a pleasant reworking of the *Let's Get It On* set, albeit cast in slightly more contemporary mode. The title track was another number 1 hit on the soul charts, however, as was his 1977 disco extravaganza,

Marvin Gaye

'Got To Give It Up'. Drug problems and tax demands interrupted his career, and in 1978 he fled the USA mainland to Hawaii in a vain attempt to salvage his second marriage. Marvin devoted the next year to the *Here My Dear* double album, a bitter commentary on his relationship with his first wife. Its title was ironic: he had been ordered to give all royalties from the project to Anna as part of their divorce settlement.

With this catharsis behind him, Gaye began work on an album to be called *Lover Man*; but he cancelled its release after the lukewarm sales of its initial single, the sharply self-mocking 'Ego Tripping Out', which he had presented as a duet between the warring sides of his nature. In 1980 under increasing pressure from the Internal Revenue Service, Gaye moved to Europe where he began work on an ambitious concept album, *In My Lifetime*. When it emerged in 1981, Gaye accused Motown of remixing and editing the album without his consent, of removing a vital question-mark from the title, and of parodying his original cover artwork. The relationship between artist and record company had been shattered, and Gaye left Motown for Columbia in 1982. Persistent reports of his erratic personal conduct and reliance on cocaine fuelled pessimism about his future career, but instead he re-emerged in 1982 with a startling single, 'Sexual Healing', which combined his passionate soul

vocals with a contemporary electro-disco backing. The subsequent album, *Midnight Love*, offered no equal surprises, but the success of the single seemed to herald a new era in Gaye's music. He returned to the USA, where he took up residence at his parents' home. The intensity of his cocaine addiction made it impossible for him to work on another album, and he fell into a prolonged bout of depression. He repeatedly announced his wish to commit suicide in the early weeks of 1984, and his abrupt shifts of mood brought him into heated conflict with his father, rekindling animosity that had festered since Gaye's adolescence. On 1 April 1984, another violent disagreement provoked Marvin Gay Snr. to shoot his son dead, a tawdry end to the life of one of soul music's premier performers.

Motown and Columbia collaborated to produce two albums based on Marvin's unfinished recordings. *Dream Of A Lifetime* mixed spiritual ballads from the early 70s with sexually explicit funk songs from a decade later; while *Romantically Yours* offered a travesty of Gaye's original intentions in 1979 to record an album of big band ballads. Though Gaye's weighty canon is often reduced to a quartet of 'I Heard It Through The Grapevine', 'Sexual Healing', *What's Going On* and *Let's Get It On*, his entire recorded output signifies the development of black music from raw rhythm and blues, through sophisticated soul to the political awareness of the early 70s, and the increased concentration on personal and sexual politics thereafter. Gaye's remarkable vocal range and fluency remains a touchstone for all subsequent soul vocalists, and his 'lover man' stance has been frequently copied and parodied.

Albums: *The Soulful Moods Of Marvin Gaye* (1961), *That Stubborn Kinda Fellow* (1963), *Recorded Live: On Stage* (1964), *When I'm Alone I Cry* (1964), with Mary Wells *Together* (1964), *Hello Broadway* (1965), *How Sweet It Is To Be Loved By You* (1965), *A Tribute To The Great Nat King Cole* (1965), *Moods Of Marvin Gaye* (1966), with Kim Weston *Take Two* (1966), with Tammi Terrell *United* (1967), *In The Groove* (1968), with Terrell *You're All I Need* (1968), *MPG* (1969), *That's The Way Love Is* (1970), *What's Going On* (1971), *Trouble Man* (1972), *Let's Get It On* (1973), with Diana Ross *Diana And Marvin* (1973), *Live* (1974), *I Want You* (1976), *Live At The London Palladium* (1977), *Here My Dear* (1978), *In Our Lifetime* (1981), *Midnight Love* (1982), *Dreams Of A Lifetime* (1985), *Romantically Yours* (1985). Numerous compilations have also been issued.

George, Barbara

b. 16 August 1942, New Orleans, Louisiana, USA. Barbara George is best remembered for her 1961 R&B number 1 hit, 'I Know', released on the small AFO (All For One) label. George was discovered by

Jessie Hill, another New Orleans R&B artist, himself known for the hit 'Ooh Poo Pah Doo'. Hill brought George to AFO, where label head Harold Battiste at first did not see much potential in the girl. They recorded 'I Know' in spite of this and it was heard by Sue Records owner Juggy Murray, who agreed to distribute the record. 'I Know' not only reached the top of the R&B chart but was an enormous success in the US pop charts. George was unable to follow her hit with any other significant records, however, and by the end of the 60s she had retired from music, save for a brief return in the early 80s.

Album: *I Know You Don't Love Me Anymore* (1962).

Gerry Marsden

Gerry And The Pacemakers

Liverpudlians Gerry Marsden (b. Gerard Marsden, 24 September 1942; guitar/vocals), Freddie Marsden (b. 23 October 1940; drums) and John 'Les' Chadwick (b. 11 May 1943; bass) formed the original Pacemakers in 1959. Two years later they were joined by Les Maguire (b. 27 December 1941, Wallasey, Cheshire; piano) and having completed highly successful spells in German beat clubs, became the second group signed to Brian Epstein's management stable. The effervescent 'How Do You Do It', rejected as unsuitable by the Beatles, gave the more pliant Pacemakers a number 1 hit. Further chart-toppers 'I Like It' and 'You'll Never Walk Alone' (both 1963) followed in quick succession

earning the group the distinction of becoming the first act to have their first three releases reach number 1. The latter song, taken from the musical *Carousel*, was later adopted as the anthem of Liverpool Football Club. Although the group's lone album revealed a penchant for R&B, their singles often emphasized Gerry Marsden's cheeky persona. The exceptions included two excellent in-house compositions 'Don't Let The Sun Catch You Crying' (1964) and 'Ferry Cross The Mersey' (1965), the theme song to the Pacemakers' starring film. A follow-up release, 'I'll Be There', was the quartet's final Top 20 entry and in 1967 Gerry embarked on a solo career. He remained a popular figure in television and on the cabaret circuit, but regained the national spotlight in 1985 following the Bradford City Football Club fire tragedy, when a charity recording, credited to the Crowd and featuring an all-star cast, took a new version of 'You'll Never Walk Alone' to the top of the UK chart for the second time. Another re-recording of an earlier hit for charity, 'Ferry Cross The Mersey', this time for the victims of the Hillsborough crowd disaster, involving supporters of Liverpool FC in 1989, reached number 1.

Albums: *How Do You Like It* (1963), *Second Album* (1964), *I'll Be There!* (1965), *Ferry Cross The Mersey* (1965, film soundtrack), *Girl On A Swing* (1965), *20 Year Anniversary Album* (1983). Compilations: *Don't Let The Sun Catch You Crying* (1964, US release), *Gerry And The Pacemakers' Greatest Hits* (1965), *The Best Of Gerry And The Pacemakers* (1977), *The Very Best Of Gerry And The Pacemakers* (1984), *Hit Singles Album* (1986), *The EP Collection* (1987), *The Singles Plus* (1987).

Gilberto, Astrud

b. 1940, Bahia, Brazil. Gilberto's career began by accident in March 1963 during a recording session featuring her husband, guitarist Joao Gilberto, and saxophonist Stan Getz. A projected track, 'The Girl From Ipanema', required a singer conversant with English and although strictly a non-professional, Astrud was coaxed into performing the soft, *sang-froid* vocal. Her contribution was considered relatively unimportant - early pressings of the resultant *Stan Getz/Joao Gilberto* did not credit the singer - even when the track was issued as a single the following year. 'The Girl From Ipanema' eventually reached the US Top 5 and UK Top 20, garnering sales in excess of one million and forever binding the artist to the subject of the song. Astrud later toured with Getz; their collaboration was chronicled on *Getz A-Go-Go*, but she later pursued an independent career, bringing her distinctive, if limited, style to a variety of material, including standards, Brazilian samba/bossa nova and contemporary songs from Tim Hardin, Jimmy Webb and the Doors. Gilberto was the subject of renewed attention when 'Ipanema' re-entered the UK charts in 1984 as a result of the UK bossa nova/jazz revival perpetrated by artists such as Everything But The Girl, the Style Council, Weekend and Sade.

Albums: *The Astrud Gilberto Album* (1965), *The Shadow Of Your Smile* (1965), *I Haven't Got Anything Better To Do* (1968), *Look To The Rainbow* (1986), with James Last *Plus* (1986), *So & So* (1988). Compilations: *Once Upon A Summertime* (1971), *That Girl From Ipanema* (1977), *The Best Of Astrud Gilberto* (1982), *The Essential Astrud Gilberto* (1984), *Compact Jazz* (1987).

Astrud Gilberto

Gilmer, Jimmy, And The Fireballs

Best known for the US number 1 hit 'Sugar Shack', with the group the Fireballs in 1963, Jimmy Gilmer (b. 1940, LaGrange, Illinois, USA; piano/vocals) began singing as a child after his family moved south to Amarillo, Texas. He studied music at the Musical Arts Conservatory and in 1957 formed his own band while attending Amarillo College, where he studied engineering. While at Norman Petty's recording studios in Clovis, New Mexico, in 1960, Gilmer was introduced to the Fireballs George Tomsco, Stan Lark and Doug Roberts and soon replaced departing vocalist Chuck Tharp. Signed to Dot Records, and now billed as Jimmy Gilmer And The Fireballs, they recorded 'Sugar Shack' in 1963, which hit number 1

for five weeks, becoming the year's most successful single. After a couple of follow-up singles, including the Top 20 'Daisy Petal Pickin'', and six albums, the group reverted to the name Fireballs. Without Gilmer, they had another Top 10 single, 'Bottle Of Wine', in 1967 but by the end of the 60s they had disbanded.

Albums: *Sugar Shack* (1963), *The Sugar Shackers* (1963), *Sensational* (1963), *Buddy's Buddy* (1964), *Lucky 'leven* (1965), *Folk Beat* (1965), *Campusology* (1966).

Golden Earring

Formed in The Hague, Netherlands in 1961 by George Kooymans (b. 11 March 1948, The Hague, Netherlands; guitar/vocals) and Rinus Gerritsen (b. 9 August 1946, The Hague, Netherlands; bass/vocals) along with Hans Van Herwerden (guitar) and Fred Van Der Hilst (drums). The group, initially known as the Golden Earrings, subsequently underwent several changes before they secured a Dutch Top 10 hit with their debut release, 'Please Go' (1965). By this point Kooymans and Gerritsen had been joined by Frans Krassenburg (vocals), Peter De Ronde (guitar) and Jaap Eggermont (drums) and the revitalized line-up became one of the most popular 'nederbeat' attractions. Barry Hay (b. 16 August 1948, Fyzabad, India; lead vocals, flute, saxophone, guitar) replaced Krassenburg in 1966, while De Ronde also left the group as they embraced a more radical direction. The group's first Dutch number 1 hit, 'Dong-Dong-Di-Ki-Di-Gi-Dong' came in 1968 and saw them branching out from their homeland to other European countries as well as a successful tour of the USA. Eggermont left the group to become a producer and was eventually supplanted by Cesar Zuiderwijk (b. 18 July 1948, The Hague, Netherlands) in 1969 as Golden Earring began courting an international audience with their compulsive *Eight Miles High*, which featured an extended version of the famous Byrds' song.

After years of experimenting with various music styles, they settled for a straight, hard rock sound and in 1972 Golden Earring were invited to support the Who on a European tour. They were subsequently signed to Track Records and the following year scored a Dutch number 1/UK Top 10 hit with 'Radar Love' which subsequently found its way into the US Top 20 in 1974. Despite this, they were curiously unable to secure overseas success, which was not helped by a consistently unstable line-up. Robert Jan Stips augmented the quartet between 1974 and 1976 and on his departure Eelco Gelling joined as supplementary guitarist. By the end of the decade, however, the group had reverted to its basic line-up of Kooymans, Gerritsen, Hay and Zuiderwijk which continued to forge an imaginative brand of rock and their reputation as a top European live act was reinforced by *Second Live*. With the release of *Cut* in 1982, Golden Earring earned themselves a US Top 10 hit with 'Twilight Zone'. This was followed by a triumphant tour of the United States and Canada, where further chart success was secured with 'Lady Smiles'. With various members able to indulge themselves in solo projects, Golden Earring have deservedly earned themselves respect throughout Europe and America as the Netherland's longest surviving and successful rock group.

Albums: *Just Earrings* (1965), *Winter Harvest* (1967), *Miracle Mirror* (1968), *On The Double* (1969), *Eight Miles High* (1970), *Golden Earring* (1971), *Seven Tears* (1971), *Together* (1972), *Moontan* (1973), *Switch* (1975), *To The Hilt* (1975), *Rock Of The Century* (1976), *Contraband* (1976), *Mad Love* (1977), *Live* (1977), *Grab It For A Second* (1978), *No Promises . . . No Debts* (1979), *Prisoner Of The Night* (1980), *Second Live* (1981), *Cut* (1982), *N.E.W.S. (North East West South)* (1984), *Something Heavy Going Down - Live From The Twilight Zone* (1984), *The Hole* (1986). Compilations: *Greatest Hits* (1968), *Best Of Golden Earring* (1970), *Greatest Hits Volume 2* (1971), *Hearring Earring* (1973), *The Best Ten Years: Twenty Hits* (1975), *The Golden Earring Story* (1978), *Greatest Hits Volume 3* (1981). Solo albums: George Kooymans *Jojo* (1971), *Solo* (1987). Barry Hay *Only Parrots, Frogs And Angels* (1972). Rinus Gerritsen and Michel Van Dijk *De G.V.D. Band* (1979), *Labyrinth* (1985).

Goldie And The Gingerbreads

Formed in Brooklyn, New York, USA in 1963, Goldie And The Gingerbreads made their debut at the city's famed Peppermint Lounge. They were discovered by British group the Animals who, impressed by the quartet's musical abilities, suggested they move to the UK. Goldie Zelkowitz (b. 1943, Brooklyn, New York, USA; vocals), Carol McDonald (b. 1944, Wilmington, Delaware, USA; guitar), Margo Crocitto (b. 1943, Brooklyn, New York, USA; organ) and Ginger Panebianco (b. 1945, Long Island, New York, USA; drums) arrived in London in November 1964 and their debut single was issued the following year in the wake of successful appearances at the Crazy Elephant and Flamingo clubs. Animals' keyboard player Alan Price produced the excellent 'Can't You Hear My Heart Beat?', a UK Top 30 entry, but two further singles failed to gain the same success. The group toured with the Rolling Stones and Kinks, but despite their undoubted dexterity - Crocitto made several session appearances - they were unfairly perceived as a novelty. The quartet split up in October 1965 when Goldie embarked on a solo career, but the remaining trio maintained contact and the group continued to record upon returning to New York, releasing 'Song To The Moon'/'Walking In Different Circles' in 1967. They later re-emerged during the 70s as part of Isis, an all-woman group.

Good, Jack

b. 1931, London, England, This founder of British pop television was president of Oxford University Drama Society and then a stand-up comic before enrolling on a BBC training course. His final test film was centred on Freddie Mills. The late boxer was also an interlocutor on 1957's *6.5 Special*, a magazine series for 'teenagers produced by Good and Josephine Douglas. While he became evangelical about rock 'n' roll, Good's staid superiors obliged him to balance the pop with comedy sketches, string quartets and features on sport and hobbies. He was fired for flaunting Corporation dictates by presenting a stage version of the show. Snapped up by ITV, he broke ground with *Oh Boy!* which introduced Cliff Richard, Marty Wilde and other homegrown rockers to the nation. So swiftly did its atmospheric parade of idols - mostly male - pass before the cameras that the screaming studio audience, urged on by Good, scarcely had pause to draw breath. While overseeing the less exciting *Boy Meets Girls* and *Wham!*, Good branched out into publishing - and record production of such as Billy Fury's *Sound Of Fury*.

1962 found Good in North America where he worked intermittently as an actor - notably on Broadway in C.P. Snow's *The Affair* and, in 1967, as a hotelier in *Clambake*, an Elvis Presley vehicle. His self-financed pilot programme, *Young America Swings The World*, fell on stony ground but, after Brian Epstein commissioned him for *Around The Beatles*, he superintended the nationally-broadcast pop showcase *Shindig* which, as well as 'discoveries' like the Righteous Brothers and Sonny And Cher, represented a media breakthrough for diverse black artists from Howlin' Wolf to the Chambers Brothers - and held its own in a ratings war against *The Beverley Hillbillies* on a main rival channel. Leaving *Shindig* to fend for itself, his most interesting career tangent of the later 60s was *Catch My Soul*, 1968's rock adaptation in a Los Angeles theatre of Shakespeare's *Othello* with Jerry Lee Lewis as Iago. For a season in London, P.J. Proby assumed the Lewis role with Good himself as the Moor. Back in the USA, he ticked over with one-shot television specials concerning, among others, Andy Williams, the Monkees and 1970's Emmy award-winning classical/pop hybrid of Ray Charles, Jethro Tull, the Nice and the LA Philharmonic. On an extended visit to England from his Santa Fe home, Good put on *Elvis*, a biographical musical starring, initially, Proby and Shakin' Stevens before daring an updated reconstruction of *Oh Boy!* (later transferred to television) at the same London West End theatre. By the 80s, income from the inspired Good's less frequent television and stage ventures underwrote another vocational episode - as a painter. In the early 90s it was reported that Good was taking up the priesthood to become a monk.

Good Rats

This US group was formed while the members were at college in 1964 by Peppi and Mickey Marchello both from Long Island, New York, USA. Their debut was a mixture of rock 'n' roll and progressive rock. A succession of poor selling albums coupled with regular changes of record labels hampered their commercial prospects. They broke up for three years during 1969-72. By the time of their fourth and best album - *From Rats To Riches* - (which was later issued on Radar in the UK), the line-up was the gruff-voiced Peppi, Mickey (guitar), John 'the Cat' Gatto (guitar), Lenny Kotke (bass) and Joe Franco (drums). This album was recorded on Long Island in late 1977 with Flo And Eddie (Mark Volman and Howard Kaylan) producing. Although their place in the market was never clear they were essentially a good old-fashioned, basic US rock 'n' roll band.
Albums: *The Good Rats* (1968), *Tasty* (1974), *Ratcity In Blue* (1976), *From Rats To Riches* (1978), *Birth Comes To Us All* (1978), *Live At Last* (1980), *Great American Music* (1981).

Gore, Lesley

b. 2 May 1946, New York City, USA and raised in Tenafly, New Jersey. Having secured a recording contract with Mercury on the basis of a privately financed demonstration disc, Gore enjoyed a sensational debut when 'It's My Party' topped the US chart, reached number 9 in the UK in 1963 and grossed sales in excess of one million. This tale of adolescent trauma has retained its timeless appeal - the singer's birthday celebrations are irrevocably marred on losing boyfriend Johnny to Judy - and it remains one of the era's most memorable releases. The vengeful follow-up, 'Judy's Turn To Cry', earned another gold disc, but successive releases, including 'You Don't Own Me', a powerful call for independence, and 'Maybe I Know', confirmed that the singer was not simply a novelty act. Gore made several appearances in teen-oriented films and television shows, including *Batman*, but her career was marred by periods of inactivity. She re-emerged in 1972 with *Something Else Now*, released on Motown's Mowest subsidiary and three years later was briefly re-united with producer/songwriter Quincy Jones, who had produced her early Mercury recordings, which resulted in the exceptional 'Immortality'. Despite the frailty exhibited on her debut single, Lesley Gore's is now viewed by commentators as an early champion of women's rights.
Albums: *I'll Cry If I Want To* (1963), *Lesley Gore Sings Of Mixed-Up Hearts* (1963), *Boys, Boys, Boys* (1964), *Girl Talk* (1964), *My Town, My Guy And Me* (1965), *Lesley Gore Sings All About Love* (1966), *California Nights* (1967), *Someplace Else Now* (1972). Compilations: *The Golden Hits Of Lesley Gore* (1965), *The Golden Hits Of Lesley Gore, Volume 2* (1968).

Bill Graham

Graham, Bill

b. Wolfgang Wolodia Grajonca, 8 January 1931, Berlin, Germany, d. 25 October 1991. Born into a Russian-Jewish family, Graham arrived in New York during 1941, a refugee from Nazi persecution. After earning a degree in business administration, he moved to the west coast. By 1965 he was managing the San Francisco Mime Troupe, organizing the requisite benefit gigs to keep the revue afloat. Such work brought him into contact with the nascent rock fraternity and Graham began promoting concerts at the city's Fillmore Auditorium. The venue became the leading showcase for the 'San Francisco Sound', exemplified by Jefferson Airplane, Quicksilver Messenger Service, the Grateful Dead and Big Brother And The Holding Company. Graham, in turn, became a leading impresario, and by 1968 had bought the larger Carousel Ballroom, renaming it the Fillmore West. Within weeks he had opened a corresponding Fillmore East in a vacant cinema on New York's Second Avenue.
As a hard-headed entrepreneur, he often came into conflict with the free-loading hippie idealism inherent in running a music venue. Yet Graham often confounded his critics by contributing to local help organizations in the form of benefits. In addition, the presentation of concerts at his venues paved the way for future promoters by way of introducing light shows, showing films between acts, free apples and taking a personal interest in the musicians giving a professional performance. He was also instrumental in efforts to integrate black artists on billings, so introducing many musicians to a

predominantly white audience. These artists included B.B. King, Leon Thomas, Raahsan Roland Kirk, Miles Davis, Muddy Waters and Ravi Shanker.

By the end of 1971, Graham had closed down both halls and determined to retire from a business for which he was losing respect. The final performances at the Fillmore West were captured on the film and accompanying album box-set, *Fillmore - The Last Days* (1972). The sabbatical was brief and during the next decade he was involved in national tours by Bob Dylan and Crosby, Stills, Nash And Young, as well as major one-off events. Such work culminated on 13 July, 1985 when Graham organized the American segment of the Live Aid concert for famine relief. A controversial and outspoken character, he also pursued a successful career in management, guiding, at different times, the paths of the Jefferson Airplane, Santana, Van Morrison and Dylan.

Graham's tragic death in a helicopter crash occurred while returning from a Huey Lewis And the News concert he had promoted, in South County, California. It robbed the rock music business of one its most legendary characters and greatest promoters. His funeral service was attended by members of the Grateful Dead, Santana and Quicksilver Messenger Service who offered musical tributes.

Grant, Julie

Out of the early 60s vintage UK pop vocalists came Patsy Ann Noble, Tanya Day and Julie Grant. The latter found some success with a string of singles for Pye Records. Her half-beehive hairstyle and angular eye make-up was seen regularly on package tours and UK television. Her manager was Eric Easton, who briefly managed the Rolling Stones, with whom she shared the bill on their first major package tour. Her 1962 cover of the Drifters' 'Up On The Roof' made the UK hit parade but was overtaken by Kenny Lynch's version. Nevertheless, she bounced back with 'Count On Me' reaching number 24 - her highest (and penultimate) chart placing. However, after 1964's 'Come To Me', a tempestuous ballad, was heard often on the BBC Light Programme as it wended its way to the edge of the Top 30, Grant's fortunes on record declined irrecoverably.

Grapefruit

Formed in Britain during 1967, Grapefruit originally comprised of three former members of harmony group Tony Rivers And The Castaways - John Perry (b. 16 July 1949, London, England; lead guitar/vocals), Pete Sweetenham (b. 24 April 1949, London, England; rhythm guitar/vocals) and Geoff Sweetenham (b. 8 March 1948, London, England; drums) - and songwriter George Alexander (b. 28 December 1946; Glasgow, Scotland; bass/vocals). The quartet, named by John Lennon, was the first act

signed to the Beatles' Apple publishing company whose faith was confirmed when Grapefruit's debut single, 'Dear Delilah', became a UK Top 30 hit. Alexander's penchant for high-quality British pop was matched by Terry Melcher's sympathetic production, but despite several equally excellent follow-up releases, the group's only other chart entry was 'C'mon Marianne', originally recorded by the Four Seasons. By 1969 Mick Fowler (keyboards) had been added to the unit while Geoff Sweetenham was later replaced by Bobby Ware. *Deep Water* revealed an unsatisfactory soul/rock perspective and Alexander subsequently disbanded the line-up. He joined former Easybeats' members George Young and Harry Vanda (Young and Alexander were brothers) for a variety of projects issued under different names. The Grapefruit appellation was briefly revived in 1971 for 'Universal Party', a melodic pop song redolent of the act's initial releases although it failed to make a similar impact on the singles chart.

Albums: *Around Grapefruit* (1968), *Deep Water* (1969).

Grass Roots

Although several Californian groups claimed this sobriquet, including the embryonic Love, it was appropriated by songwriters P.F. Sloan and Steve Barri, who employed the name pseudonymously on several folk-rock performances. When 'Where Were You When I Needed You?' reached the US Top 30 in 1966, the need for a permanent line-up arose and the duo enticed Warren Entner (b. 7 July 1944, Boston, Massachusetts, USA; vocals/guitar), Creed Bratton (b. 8 February 1943, Sacramento, California, USA; guitar), Rob Grill (b. 30 November 1944, Los Angeles, California, USA; vocals/bass) and Rick Coonce (b. Erik Michael Coonce, 1 August 1947, Los Angeles, California, USA; drums) to adopt the Grass Roots' name. The new unit enjoyed immediate success with 'Let's Live For Today', a remake of an Italian hit. This distanced the quartet from their mentors, but although Sloan's input lessened dramatically, Barri retained his role as producer. The Grass Roots then became one of America's leading commercial attractions with a series of confident, if undemanding, performances, including 'Midnight Confessions' (1968), 'Bella Linda' (1968), 'I'd Wait A Million Years' (1969) and 'Sooner Or Later' (1971). The group remained a popular attraction into the 80s, although the verve of their early work had, by then, evaporated.

Albums: *Where Were You When I Needed You?* (1966), *Let's Live For Today* (1967), *Feelings* (1968), *Lovin' Things* (1969), *Leaving It All Behind* (1969), *Move Along* (1972), *A Lotta' Mileage* (1973). Compilations: *Golden Grass (Their Greatest Hits)* (1968), *More Golden Grass* (1970), *Their Sixteen Greatest Hits* (1974).

Grateful Dead

The enigmatic and mercurial Grateful Dead evolved from Mother McCree's Uptown Jug Champions to become the Warlocks in 1965. The legendary name was chosen from a randomly opened copy of the *Oxford English Dictionary*, the juxtaposition of words evidently appealed to members of the band. The original line-up comprised: Jerry Garcia (b. Jerome John Garcia, 1 August 1942, San Francisco, California, USA; lead guitar), Bob Weir (b. Robert Hall, 16 October 1947, San Francisco, California, USA; rhythm guitar), Phil Lesh (b. Philip Chapman, 15 March 1940, Berkeley, California, USA; bass), Ron 'Pigpen' McKernan (b. 8 September 1945, San Bruno, California, USA. d. 8 March 1973; keyboards) and Bill Kreutzmann (b. 7 April 1946, Palo Alto, California, USA; drums). The Grateful Dead have been synonymous with the San Francisco/Acid Rock scene since its inception in 1965 when they took part in Ken Kesey's Acid Tests. Stanley Owsley manufactured the then legal LSD and plied the band with copious amounts. This hallucinogenic opus was duly recorded onto tape over a six-month period, and documented in Tom Wolfe's book *The Electric Kool-Aid Acid Test*. Wolfe stated that 'They were not to be psychedelic dabblers, painting pretty pictures, but true explorers'.

Their music, which started out as straightforward rock and R&B, germinated into a hybrid of styles, but has the distinction of being long, wandering and improvisational. By the time their first album was released in 1967 they were already a huge cult band. *Grateful Dead* sounds raw in the light of 90s record production, but it was a brave, early attempt to capture a live concert sound on a studio album. The follow-up *Anthem Of The Sun* was much more satisfying. On this 'live' record, 17 different concerts and four different live studios were used. The non-stop suite of ambitious segments with tantalizing titles such as 'The Faster We Go The Rounder We Get' and 'Quadlibet For Tenderfeet' was an artistic success. Their innovative and colourful album covers were amongst the finest examples of San Franciscan art, utilizing the talents of Kelley Mouse Studios (Alton Kelley and Stanley Mouse). The third album contained structured songs and was not as inaccessible as the palindrome title *Aoxomoxoa* suggested. Hints of a mellowing Grateful Dead surfaced on 'China Cat Sunflower' and the sublime 'Mountains Of The Moon', complete with medieval-sounding harpsichord. In concert, the band were playing longer and longer sets, sometimes lasting six hours with only as many songs.

Their legion of fans, now known as 'Deadheads' relished the possibility of a marathon concert. It was never ascertained who imbibed more psychedelic chemicals, the audience or the band. Nevertheless the sounds produced sometimes took them to breathtaking heights of musical achievement. The interplay between Garcia's shrill, flowing solos and Lesh's meandering bass lines complemented the adventurous chords of Weir's rhythm guitar. The band had now added a second drummer, Micky Hart and a second keyboard player Tom Constanten to accompany the unstable McKernan. It was this line-up that produced the seminal *Live Dead* in 1970. Their peak of improvisation is best demonstrated on the track 'Dark Star'. During its 23 minutes of recorded life, the music simmers, builds and explodes four times, each with a crescendo of superb playing from Garcia and his colleagues. On the two following records *Workingman's Dead* and *American Beauty*, a strong Crosby, Stills And Nash harmony influence prevailed. The short, country-feel songs brought Garcia's pedal steel guitar to the fore (he had recently guested on Crosby, Stills, Nash And Young's *Déjà Vu*). Paradoxically the 'Dead' reverted to releasing live sets by issuing a second double album closely followed by the triple, *Europe '72*. After years of ill-health through alcohol abuse, McKernan died in 1973. He was replaced by Keith Godcheaux from Dave Mason's band, who together with his wife Donna on vocals compensated for the tragic loss. *Wake Of The Flood* in 1973 showed a jazz influence and proved to be their most commercially successful album to date. With this and subsequent studio albums the band produced a mellower sound. It was not until *Terrapin Station* in 1977 that their gradual move towards lethargy was averted. Producer Keith Olsen expertly introduced a fuller, more orchestrated sound.

As a touring band the Grateful Dead continued to prosper, but their studio albums began to lose direction. For their funky *Shakedown Street* they enlisted Lowell George. Although the band had been with the band for some years, Keith and Donna Godcheaux had never truly fitted in. Donna had trouble with her vocal pitch, resulting in some excruciating performances, while Keith began to use hard drugs. They were asked to leave at the end of 1979 and on 21 July 1980, Keith was killed in a car crash. *Go To Heaven* (1980) with new keyboard player Brent Mydland betrayed a hint of disco-pop. The album sleeve showed the band posing in white suits which prompted 'Deadheads' to demand: 'Have they gone soft?' Ironically, it was this disappointing record that spawned their first, albeit minor, success in the US singles chart with 'Alabama Getaway'. All of the band had experimented with drugs for many years and, unlike many of their contemporaries, had survived. Garcia, however, succumbed to heroin addiction in 1982. This retrospectively explained his somnolent playing and gradual decline as a guitarist, together with his often weak and shaky vocals. By the mid-80s, the band had become amorphous but still commanded a massive following. Garcia eventually collapsed and came close to death when he went into a diabetic coma in 1986.

The joy and relief of his survival showed in their first studio album in seven years, *In The Dark*. It was a stunning return to form, resulting in a worldwide hit single 'Touch Of Grey', with Garcia singing his long time co-songwriter Robert Hunter's simplistic yet honest lyric: 'Oh well a touch of grey, kinda suits you anyway, that's all I've got to say, it's alright'. The band joined in for a joyous repeated chorus of 'I will survive' followed by 'We will survive'. They were even persuaded to make a video and the resulting exposure on MTV introduced them to a whole new generation of fans. The laconic Garcia humorously stated that he was 'appalled' to find they had a smash hit on their hands. While *Built To Last* (1989) was a dull affair, they continued to play to vast audiences. They have since received acclaim as the largest grossing band in musical history. In August 1990 Mydland died from a lethal combination of cocaine and morphine. Remarkably this was the third keyboard player to die in the band. Mydland's temporary replacement was Bruce Hornsby until Vince Welnick was recruited full-time. In 1990, the band's live album catalogue was increased with the release of the erratic *Without A Net*. The transcendental Grateful Dead have lasted, throughout the many difficult stages in their long career and, health permitting, their future is assured.

Albums: The *Grateful Dead* (1967), *Anthem Of The Sun* (1968), *Aoxomoxoa* (1969), *Live/Dead* (1970), *Workingman's Dead* (1970), *Vintage Dead* (1970, early live recordings), *American Beauty* (1970), *Historic Dead* (1971, early live recordings), *Grateful Dead* (1971), *Europe '72* (1972), *History Of The Grateful Dead, Volume 1 - (Bear's Choice)* (1973), *Wake Of The Flood* (1973), *From The Mars Hotel* (1974), *Blues For Allah* (1975), *Steal Your Face* (1976), *Terrapin Station* (1977), *Shakedown Street* (1978), *Go To Heaven* (1980), *Reckoning* (1981), *Dead Set* (1981), *In The Dark* (1987), *Built To Last* (1989), with Bob Dylan *Dylan And The Dead* (1990), *Without A Net* (1990). Compilations: *Skeletons From The Closet* (1974), *What A Long Strange Trip It's Been: The Best Of The Grateful Dead* (1977),
Further reading: *Grateful Dead - The Music Never Stopped*, Blair Jackson.

Grease Band

The Grease Band was formed in 1966 to back singer Joe Cocker but the original line-up - Frank Myles (guitar), Vernon Nash (piano), Chris Stainton (bass) and Dave Demmott (drums) - underwent several changes over the ensuing years. Henry McCullough (guitar), Alan Spenner (bass) and Bruce Rowlands (bass) joined Stainton in the group's best-known incarnation, but this unit split from Cocker in 1970 at the end of an arduous American tour. Spenner, Rowlands and McCullough were then joined by guitarist Neil Hubbard as the Grease Band embarked on an independent career. The group's brand of blues-rock was perfectly captured on their debut album and they enjoyed a reputation as an exciting live attraction. Stainton remained an associate member, although Mick Weaver, aka Wynder K. Frog, subsequently augmented the line-up. John 'Pugwash' Weathers came in for the defecting Rowlands, but the band broke up in December 1971 when McCullough joined Wings.

Albums: *The Grease Band* (1971), *Amazing Grease* (1975, previously unissued recordings).

Great Society

The Great Society was formed in August 1965 by Grace Slick (b. Grace Wing, 30 October 1939, Evanston, Illinois, USA; vocals/piano/recorder/guitar), her husband Jerry (drums) and his brother Darby Slick (lead guitar). David Minor (rhythm guitar) and Bard DuPont (bass) completed the original line-up, although the latter was replaced by Peter Vandergelder, who also doubled on saxophone. One of the first San Franciscan rock groups, the quintet was active for 13 months during which they issued a solitary single, 'Someone To Love' (later known as 'Somebody To Love') on Tom Donahue's Autumn Records/Northbeach label. This intriguing Darby Slick composition achieved fame when it was adopted by Jefferson Airplane, the group Grace joined in October 1966. The Great Society split up on her departure, but two live collections, released solely in the wake of the singer's subsequent fame, show a group of rare imagination. The first album features 'White Rabbit', another composition Grace introduced to her new-found companions, which is preceded by a lengthy instrumental passage performed in an eastern, raga style that typified the Great Society's approach to many of their songs. Indeed, on the break-up of the group Darby Slick, Vandergelder and Minor went to study music in India, while Jerry was briefly a member of Final Solution before returning to film work.

Albums: *Conspicuous Only In Its Absence* (1968), *How It Was* (1968). Compilation: *Live At The Matrix* (1989).
Further reading: *The Jefferson Airplane And The San Francisco Sound*, Ralph J. Gleeson. *Grace Slick - The Biography*, Barbara Rowe.

Groundhogs

The original Groundhogs emerged in 1963 when struggling UK beat group the Dollarbills opted for a more stylish name; Tony 'T.S.' McPhee (b. 22 March

1944, Humberstone, Lincolnshire, England; guitar), John Cruickshank (vocals/harp), Bob Hall (piano), Pete Cruickshank (b. 2 July 1945, Calcutta, India; bass) and Dave Boorman (drums) also adopted a 'John Lee' prefix in honour of mentor John Lee Hooker, whom the quintet subsequently backed in concert and on record. John Lee's Groundhogs recorded two singles before breaking up in 1966. McPhee completed several solo tracks with producer Mike Vernon before rejoining Pete Cruickshank in Herbal Mixture, a short-lived, pseudo-psychedelic group. In 1968 the two musicians formed the core of a reformed Groundhogs alongside Steve Rye (vocals/harmonica) and Ken Pustelnik (drums). The new unit made its debut with the rudimentary *Scratching The Surface*, but were then cut to a trio by Rye's departure. A second set, *Blues Obituary*, contained two tracks, 'Mistreated' and 'Express Man', which became in-concert favourites as the group embarked on a more progressive direction. This was confirmed with *Thank Christ For The Bomb*, the Groundhogs' powerful 1970 release which cemented a growing popularity. McPhee composed the entire set and his enthusiasm for concept albums was maintained with its successor, *Split*, which examined schizophrenia. Arguably the group's definitive work, this uncompromising selection included the classic 'Cherry Red'. Pustelnik left the group following the release of *Who Will Save The World?* in 1972. Former Egg drummer Clive Brooks (b. 28 December 1949, London, England) was an able replacement, but although the Groundhogs continued to enjoy a fervent popularity, their subsequent recordings lacked the fire of those early releases. The trio was also beset by managerial problems and broke up in 1975, although McPhee maintained the name for two disappointing releases, *Crosscut Saw* and *Black Diamond*.

The guitarist resurrected the Groundhogs' sobriquet in 1984 in the wake of interest in an archive release, *Hoggin' The Stage*. Although Pustelnik was one of several musicians McPhee used for touring purposes, the most effective line-up was completed by Dave Anderson (bass), formerly of Hawkwind, and drummer Mike Jones. McPhee has in recent years appeared as a solo performer as part of a 70s nostalgia tour.

Albums: *Scratching The Surface* (1968), *Blues Obituary* (1969), *Thank Christ For The Bomb* (1970), *Split* (1971), *Who Will Save The World?* (1972), *Hogwash* (1972), *Solid* (1974), *Crosscut Saw* (1976), *Black Diamond* (1976), *Razor's Edge* (1985), *Back Against The Wall* (1987), *Hogs On The Road* (1988). Compilations: *Groundhogs Best 1969-1972* (1974), *Hoggin' The Stage* (1984).

GTOs

An acronym for Girls Together Outrageously, this all-female US septet were lauded in 1967 as part of Frank Zappa's Bizarre roster. After meeting the overtly polite Tiny Tim, they immediately abandoned their surnames and became Miss Pamela, Miss Christine, Miss Sparks, Miss Mercy, Miss Cynderella, Miss Lucy and Miss Linda. Their novelty value clearly appealed to Zappa, who produced their sole album *Permanent Damage* in 1969. By the end of those sessions they had broken up, but their flirtations with the rock elite continued. Miss Christine was pictured on the inside sleeve of Todd Rundgren's *Runt,* appeared crawling from a tomb on the cover of Zappa's *Hot Rats* and was sniped at in the Flying Burrito Brothers' 'Christine's Tune' (later retitled 'Devil In Disguise' in deference to her death from a drug overdose). Miss Cynderella was briefly married to John Cale, Miss Mercy and Miss Pamela joined the Hot Burrito Chorus on 'Hippie Boy', as well as appearing on the sleeve of *The Gilded Palace Of Sin*. Pamela then sang on tour with the Pink Fairies, married singer Michael De Barras of Silverhead and in 1989 penned a dubious groupie kiss-and-tell, *I'm With The Band*.

Album: *Permanent Damage* (1969).

Guess Who

Guess Who

The Guess Who was Canada's most popular rock band of the 60s and early 70s. The group had its roots in a band called Chad Allan And The Reflections, formed in Winnipeg, Canada in 1962. That group itself came out of two others, Allan And The Silvertones and the Velvetones. The original line-up of Chad Allan And The Reflections consisted of Allan (b. Allan Kobel; guitar/vocals), Jim Kale (bass), Randy Bachman (guitar), Bob Ashley (piano) and Garry Peterson (drums). Their first single, 'Tribute To Buddy Holly', was released on the Canadian American label in Canada in 1962. Singles for the Quality and Reo labels followed. By 1965 the group had changed its name to Chad Allan and the

Expressions and recorded a cover of Johnny Kidd And The Pirates' 'Shakin' All Over', released on Quality Records in Canada and picked up by Scepter Records in the USA. It became a number 1 single in Canada and number 22 in the USA. Ashley left the group and was replaced by Burton Cummings, formerly of the Canadian group the Deverons, who shared lead vocal duties with Allan for a year. In 1966 the group released its first album, *Shakin' All Over*. In order to give the impression to potential buyers that the group was English, Quality printed 'Guess Who?' on the cover, prompting the group to take those words as its new name. In 1966 Allan departed the group. He was briefly replaced by Bruce Decker, another ex-Deveron, who quickly left, leaving the group as a quartet with Cummings as chief vocalist.

Although they faded from the US charts for three years, the Guess Who remained popular in Canada. In 1967 they scored their first UK chart single, with 'His Girl', on the King label. A brief, disorganized UK tour left the group in debt, and it returned to Canada, recording Coca-Cola commercials and appearing on the television programme *Let's Go*, which boosted their Canadian popularity even further. They continued to release singles in Canada on Quality, and on Amy and Fontana Records in the US. In 1968, with financial backing from producer Jack Richardson, the Guess Who recorded *Wheatfield Soul* in New York, released in Canada on Richardson's own Nimbus 9 label. The third single from the album, 'These Eyes', written by Cummings and Bachman, reached number 1 in Canada and earned the group a US contract with RCA Records. The single reached number 6 in the US in spring of 1969. That year, the group's second album, *Canned Wheat Packed By The Guess Who*, also charted, as did 'Laughing', the b-side of 'These Eyes', itself a Top 10 hit, and 'Undun', which reached number 22 in the US. The group's busy year was wrapped up with a number 5 single, 'No Time'.

In March 1970, the hard-rocking 'American Woman' became the Guess Who's only US number 1 The b-side 'No Sugar Tonight' also received considerable radio airplay. *American Woman* became the group's only Top 10 album in the US during this time. In July 1970 Bachman left the group, finding the group's rock lifestyle incompatible with his Mormon religion. He resurfaced first with Chad Allan in a new group called Brave Belt and finally with Bachman Turner Overdrive (minus Allan), which itself - ironically - became a popular hard rock group in the 70s. A Guess Who album recorded while Bachman was still in the group was cancelled. Bachman was replaced in the Guess Who by guitarists Kurt Winter and Greg Leskiw. Another US Top 10 single, 'Share The Land', finished up 1970 for the group. They continued to release charting singles and albums in

the early 70s, including 'Albert Flasher' and 'Rain Dance' in 1971, and their *Greatest Hits* reached number 12. In 1972 Leskiw and Kale left the group, replaced by Don McDougall and Bill Wallace, respectively. In 1974 Winter and McDougall left, replaced by Domenic Troiano, former guitarist of the James Gang. That year, the single 'Clap For The Wolfman', written for US disc jockey Wolfman Jack, reached number 6 in the USA. It was to prove the group's final hit. In 1975 Cummings disbanded the Guess Who and began a solo career.

In 1979 a new Guess Who group, featuring Allan, Kale, McDougall and three new members, recorded and toured but were not successful. Similar regroupings (minus Cummings) also failed. A 1983 Guess Who reunion aroused some interest and resulted in an album and concert video, and Bachman and Cummings toured together in 1987, failing to win large audiences.

Albums: *Shakin' All Over* (1965), *It's Time* (1966), *A Wild Pair* (1967), *Wheatfield Soul* (1968), *Canned Wheat Packed By The Guess Who* (1969), *American Woman* (1970), *Share The Land* (1970), *So Long, Bannatyne* (1971), *Rockin'* (1972), *Live At The Paramount (Seattle)* (1972), *Artificial Paradise* (1973), *#10* (1973), *Road Food* (1974), *Flavours* (1975), *Power In The Music* (1975), *Together Again* (1974). Compilations: *The Best Of The Guess Who* (1971), *The Best of The Guess Who, Volume II* (1974), *The Greatest Of The Guess Who* (1977), *The Guess Who Collection* (1988).

Gun

This late 60s high-powered UK trio had an interesting ancestry for two of their number were the offspring of the Kinks' irreverent and exuberant road manager Sam Curtis. Paul Curtis (b. Paul Gurvitz, 6 July 1947) and Adrian Curtis (b. Adrian Gurvitz, 26 June 1949) joined drummer Louie Farrell (b. Brian Farrell, 12 December 1947) at a time when the boundaries between pop and progressive music were still a matter of hot debate. Gun were featured on John Peel's influential BBC radio show, *Top Gear*, and enjoyed a strong chart hit with the driving, riff-laden 'Race With The Devil' in 1968, which was uncannily similar to Moby Grape's 'Can't Be So Bad'. Uncertain of their appeal in the pop market, they came unstuck with their follow-up, the frantic 'Drives You Mad', and when 'Hobo' also flopped, it was clear that their chart days were over. Their record label attempted to market them as counter culture heroes with advertisements proclaiming 'the revolutionaries are on CBS', but the group failed to establish themselves as albums artists. After dissolving the group in the early 70s, Adrian Gurvitz teamed up with Ginger Baker to form the Baker Gurvitz Army, and later achieved a hit single, 'Classic', as a soloist in

1982.
Album: *Gunsight* (1969).

Guthrie, Arlo

b. 10 July 1947, Coney Island, New York, USA. The eldest son of folksinger Woody Guthrie, Arlo was raised in the genre's thriving environment. His lengthy ballad, 'Alice's Restaurant Massacre', part humorous song, part narrative, achieved popularity following the artist's appearance at the 1967 Newport Folk Festival. The composition became the cornerstone of Arlo's debut album, and inspired a feature film, but the attendant publicity obscured the performer's gifts for melody. An early song, 'Highway In The Wind', was successfully covered by Hearts And Flowers as Arlo emerged from under the shadow of his father. *Running Down The Road*, produced by Van Dyke Parks, indicated a newfound maturity, but his talent truly flourished on a series of excellent 70s recordings, notably *Hobo's Lullaby*, *Last Of The Brooklyn Cowboys*, and *Amigo*. Although offering a distillation of traditional music - wedding folk and country to ragtime, blues and Latin - such recordings nonetheless addressed contemporary concerns. 'Presidential Rag' was a vitriolic commentary on Watergate and 'Children Of Abraham' addressed the Arab/Israeli conflict. The singer enjoyed a US Top 20 hit with a reading of Steve Goodman's 'City Of New Orleans' (1972) and, if now less prolific, Arlo Guthrie remains a popular figure on the folk circuit.

Albums: *Alice's Restaurant* (1967), *Arlo* (1968), *Running Down The Road* (1969), *Alice's Restaurant* (1969, film soundtrack), *Washington County* (1970), *Hobo's Lullaby* (1972), *Last Of The Brooklyn Cowboys* (1973), *Arlo Guthrie* (1974), with Pete Seeger *Together In Concert* (1975), *Amigo* (1976), *Outlasting The Blues* (1979), *Power Of Love* (1981). Compilations: *Arlo Guthrie* (1972), *The Best Of Arlo Guthrie* (1977).

H

Hardin, Tim

b. 23 December 1941, Eugene, Oregon, USA, d. 29 December 1980. Hardin arrived in New York following a tour of duty with the US Marines. He initially studied acting, but dropped out of classes to develop his singing and songwriting talent. By 1964 he was appearing regularly in New York's Greenwich Village cafés, where he forged a unique blend of

Tim Hardin

poetic folk/blues. Hardin's first recordings were made in 1964 although the results of this traditional-based session were shelved for several years and were only issued, as *This Is Tim Hardin*, in the wake of the singer's commercial success. His debut album, *Tim Hardin 1*, was a deeply poignant affair, wherein Tim's frail, weary intonation added intrigue to several magnificent compositions, including 'Don't Make Promises', 'Misty Roses' (sensitively covered by Colin Blunstone) and 'Hang On To A Dream' (which became a regular part of the Nice's live performances) as well as the much-covered 'Reason To Believe'. *Tim Hardin 2*, featured his original version of 'If I Were A Carpenter', an international hit in the hands of Bobby Darin and the Four Tops, which confirmed Hardin's position as a writer of note. However the artist was deeply disappointed with these releases and reportedly broke down upon hearing the finished master to his first selection. Tim's career then faltered on private and professional difficulties. As early as 1970 Hardin had alcohol and drug problems. A live album, *Tim Hardin 3*, was followed by a fourth set featuring lesser material recorded at the same performance. A conceptual work, *Suite For Susan Moore And Damion* reclaimed something of his former fire but his gifts seemed to desert him following its release. Hardin's high standing as a songwriter has resulted in his work being interpreted by a plethora of artists over the past four decades, including Wilson Phillips and Rod Stewart ('Reason to Believe') and Scott Walker ('Lady Came From Baltimore'). As Hardin's own songs grew less incisive, he began interpreting the work of other songwriters, including Leonard Cohen, but his resigned delivery, once so alluring, now seemed maudlin. Beset by heroin addiction, his remaining work is a ghost of that early excellence. Tim Hardin died, almost forgotten and totally underrated, in December 1980 of a heroin overdose.

Albums: *Tim Hardin 1* (1966), *Tim Hardin 2* (1967), *Tim Hardin 3 Live In Concert* (1968), *Tim Hardin 4* (1969), *Suite For Susan Moore And Damion/We Are - One, One, All In One* (1969), *Bird On A Wire* (1971), *Painted Head* (1973), *Nine* (1974), *The Shock Of Grace* (1981), *The Homecoming Concert* (1982). Compilations: *Best Of Tim Hardin* (1969), *Memorial Album* (1982).

Francoise Hardy

Hardy, Françoise

b. 17 January 1944, Paris, France. After graduating from the Le Bruyère College, Hardy pursued a musical career as a singer-songwriter. Signed to the prestigious French record label Vogue, she scored an international million-selling hit in 1962 with the self-composed 'Tous Les Garçons Et Les Filles'. Three years later, she enjoyed her only major UK hit with the softly-sung 'All Over The World'. A major star in her home country, she extended her appeal thanks to

various modelling assignments and appearances in several films by Roger Vadim. Her international recording career gradually declined towards the end of the 60s due to stage fright.

Selected albums: *Golden Hour Presents The Best Of Françoise Hardy* (1974), *Greatest Hits* (1984), *The Françoise Hardy Hit Parade* (1984), *In Vogue* (1988), *All Over the World* (1989).

Harmony Grass

Formed in Essex, England during 1968, this close harmony pop group developed from Tony Rivers And The Castaways, a superior beat attraction heavily influenced by the Beach Boys. Longtime associate Ray Brown (bass) joined Rivers (lead vocals) in a venture completed by third former Castaway, Kenny Rowe (second bass), and newcomers Tony Ferguson (lead guitar), Tom Marshall (rhythm guitar/piano) and Bill Castle (drums). Signed to RCA, the sextet enjoyed a UK Top 30 hit in 1969 with their debut single, 'Move In A Little Closer', which was produced by Chris Andrews, previously successful with Sandie Shaw and Adam Faith. However, despite recording several equally high-class singles, including a cover version of Paul Simon's 'Cecilia', Harmony Grass was unable to consolidate this early commercial promise. Rivers later pursued a career as a successful session singer, while the rump of his erstwhile group evolved into Capability Brown and J.J. Foote.

Album: *This Is Us* (1969).

Harper, Roy

b. 12 June 1941, Manchester, England. Although introduced to music through his brother's skiffle group, Harper's adolescence was marked by a harrowing spell in the Royal Air Force. Having secured a discharge by feigning insanity, he drifted between mental institutions and jail, experiences which left an indelible mark on later compositions. Harper later began busking around Europe, and secured a residency at London's famed Les Cousins club on returning to Britain. His debut album, *The Sophisticated Beggar* (1966), was recorded in primitive conditions, but contained the rudiments of the artist's later, highly personal, style. *Come Out Fighting Genghis Smith* was released as the singer began attracting the emergent underground audience, but he was unhappy with producer Shel Talmy's rather fey arrangements. *Folkjokeopus* contained the first of Harper's extended compositions, 'McGoohan's Blues', but the set as a whole was considered patchy. *Flat, Baroque And Berserk* (1970) introduced the singer's long association with the Harvest label. Although he would later castigate the outlet, they allowed him considerable artistic licence and this excellent album, considered by Harper as his first 'real work', offered contrasting material, including the uncompromising 'I Hate The White Man' and 'Tom Tiddler's Ground', as well as the jocular 'Hell's Angels', which featured support from the Nice. *Stormcock*, arguably the performer's finest work, consists of four lengthy, memorable songs which feature sterling contributions from arranger David Bedford and guitarist Jimmy Page. The latter remained a close associate, acknowledged on 'Hats Off To Harper' from *Led Zeppelin III*, and he appeared on several succeeding releases, including *Lifemask* and *Valentine*. Although marred by self-indulgence, the former was another remarkable set, while the latter reaffirmed Harper's talent with shorter compositions. An in-concert album, *Flashes From The Archives Of Oblivion* completed what was arguably the artist's most rewarding period. *HQ* (1975) introduced Trigger, Harper's short-lived backing group consisting of Chris Spedding (guitar), Dave Cochran (bass) and Bill Bruford (drums). The album included 'When An Old Cricketer Leaves The Crease',in which a colliery brass band emphasized the melancholia apparent in the song's cricketing metaphor. A second set, *Commercial Break*, was left unreleased on the group's demise. The singer's next release, *Bullinamingvase*, centred on the ambitious 'One Of Those Days In England', but it is also recalled for the controversy surrounding the flippant 'Watford Gap' and its less-than-complimentary remarks about food offered at the subject's local service station. The song was later removed. It was also during this period that Harper made a memorable cameo appearance on Pink Floyd's *Wish You Were Here*, taking lead vocals on 'Have A Cigar'. Harper's subsequent work, while notable, has lacked the passion of this period and *The Unknown Soldier*, a bleak and rather depressing set, was the prelude to a series of less compulsive recordings, although his 1990 album, *Once*, was critically acclaimed as a return to form. Roy Harper remains a wayward, eccentric talent who has steadfastly refused to compromise his art. Commercial success has thus eluded him, but he retains the respect of many peers and a committed following.

Albums: *The Sophisticated Beggar* (1966), *Come Out Fighting Genghis Smith* (1967), *Folkjokeopus* (1969), *Flat, Baroque And Berserk* (1970), *Stormcock* (1971), *Lifemask* (1973), *Valentine* (1974), *Flashes From The Archives Of Oblivion* (1974), *HQ* (1975 - retitled *When An Old Cricketer Leaves The Crease*), *Bullinamingvase* (1977), *The Unknown Soldier* (1980), *Work Of Heart* (1981), with Jimmy Page *Whatever Happened To Jugula* (1985), *Born In Captivity* (1985), *Descendants Of Smith* (1988), *Loony On The Bus* (1988), *Once* (1990). Compilations: *Harper 1970-1975* (1978), *In Between Every Line* (1986).

Harpers Bizarre

Evolving from Santa Cruz band the Tikis, the original Harpers Bizarre emerged in late 1966 with a line-up comprising lead vocalist/guitarist Ted Templeman (b. Theodore Templeman, 24 October 1944), vocalist/guitarist Dick Scoppettone (b. 5 July 1945), vocalist/bassist Dick Young (9 January 1945), vocalist/guitarist Eddie James and former Beau Brummels' drummer/vocalist John Peterson. A sprightly cover of Simon And Garfunkel's '59th Street Bridge Song (Feelin' Groovy)' brought them a US Top 20 hit and became a perennial radio favourite. Their first album, boasting the arranging skills of Leon Russell and the composing talents of Randy Newman, backed by Harpers' exceptional vocal talent, proved an enticing debut. After covering Van Dyke Parks' 'Come To The Sunshine', they worked with the man himself on the hit follow-up, a revival of Cole Porter's 'Anything Goes'. An album of the same name combined similar standards with material by Parks and Newman. After two more albums, the group split in 1969 with Templeman becoming a name staff producer for Warner Brothers Records. Three members of the original line-up reunited briefly six years later for the album *As Time Goes By*.

Albums: *Feelin' Groovy* (1967), *Anything Goes* (1967), *The Secret Life Of Harpers Bizarre* (1968), *Harpers Bizarre 4* (1969), *As Time Goes By* (1976).

Harris, Anita

b. 3 June 1942, Midsomer Norton, Somerset/Avon, England. After attending Hampshire School of Drama, and training as a dancer for two years, Harris travelled to the USA at the age of 16 and danced in the chorus at the El Rancho in Las Vegas. On her return to England she joined the Cliff Adams Singers in the late 50s, at about the time they were starting their long-running series on BBC Radio. After singing with the Granadiers, along with Gerry Dorsey before his metamorphosis into Engelbert Humperdinck, she went solo, working the UK club and theatre circuit. Shortly after winning the Gold Medal for Britain at the San Remo Song Festival, she had a UK Top 10 hit in 1967 with Tom Springfield's 'Just Loving You'. This was also the title of her 1968 Top 30 album which, when re-released in 1976, sold over a million copies. Other minor 60s singles hits included 'Playground', 'Anniversary Waltz' and 'Dream A Little Dream Of Me'. Popular on television, she starred in several series, including *The Saturday Crowd*, with Leslie Crowther; *Magic Box*, with David Nixon; and an innovative children's programme, *Jumbleland*, devised by her writer-director husband, Mike Margolis. Harris also appeared as Nurse Clarke in the 1968 film comedy, *Carry On Doctor*. In the early 70s she twice played

Peter Pan in National Theatre Productions, and established herself as one of the leading 'principal boys' in traditional Christmas pantomimes. In the early 80s she garnered excellent reviews for her cabaret act, particularly for several appearances at London's Talk Of The Town venue, and the Savoy Hotel. In 1982 she was named Performer Of The Year, by the Variety Club Of Great Britain, and in 1984 headlined in the Club's Ball Of The Year. In 1990, she starred in a touring version of *Nightingale*, a musical based on the life of Florence Nightingale.

Album: *Just Loving You* (1967), *Anita Is Peter* (1975). Compilation: *I Love To Sing* (1976), *The Best Of Anita Harris* (1977).

Jet Harris

Harris, Jet, And Tony Meehan

Terence 'Jet' Harris (b. 6 July 1939, Kingsbury, Middlesex, England; guitar) and Daniel Joseph Anthony Meehan (b. 22 March 1943, Hampstead, London, England; drums) began their partnership in 1959 as members of the Shadows. Meehan left the group in October 1961 to take up an A&R position at Decca, and the following year Harris began a solo career with 'Besame Mucho'. 'The Man With The Golden Arm' gave the guitarist a UK Top 20 hit prior to reuniting with Meehan in 1963. The duo's debut single, 'Diamonds' was a startling instrumental composition which topped the UK charts, while two ensuing releases, 'Scarlett O'Hara' and 'Applejack',

also reached the Top 5. Each performance matched Harris' low-tuned Fender Jaguar guitar with Meehan's punchy drum interjections, and although a bright future was predicted, a serious car crash undermined Harris' confidence and the pair split up. Existing contracts were fulfilled by the Tony Meehan Combo, although Harris did resume recording with 'Big Bad Bass'. His subsequent career was blighted by personal and professional problems and successive attempts at rekindling former glories fell flat. Meehan, meanwhile, enjoyed an increasingly backroom role as a producer and arranger.

Compilations: *Remembering: Jet Harris And Tony Meehan* (1976), *The Jet Harris And Tony Meehan Story Volumes 1 & 2* (1976), *Diamonds* (1983).

Harris, Richard

b. 1 October 1932, Limerick, Eire. Although better-known as an actor, Harris nonetheless drew praise for his starring role in the musical *Camelot* (1967). The following year he began a recording career upon meeting US songwriter Jimmy Webb, the first fruit of which was 'MacArthur Park'. This lengthy, melodramatic composition reached the US and UK Top 5 with sales in excess of 1 million and drew its appeal from a contrast between the singer's cracked vocal and a sweeping, sumptuous backing. The Harris/Webb partnership was maintained on *A Tramp Shining*, and *The Yard Went On Forever*, but subsequent singles, including the haunting 'Didn't We', failed to match the success of the first release. The singer scored a US Top 50 entry with 'My Boy' in 1970, and appeared in the stage production of *Tommy*.Now having concentrated solely on thespian pursuits (and being a reformed alcoholic) he remains a brilliant racontour.

Albums: *A Tramp Shining* (1968), *The Yard Went On Forever* (1969), *Love Album*, (1970), *My Boy* (1971), *Slides, I, In The Membership Of My Days* (c.70s), *Jonathan Livingston Seagull* (c.70s), *The Prophet* (1974). Compilation: *Richard Harris - His Greatest Performances* (1979).

Harris, Rolf

b. 30 March 1930, Perth, Australia. A talented cartoonist and artist, Harris moved to London in the late 50s to pursue a showbusiness career. A regular on children's television, he was instantly recognizable with his horn-rimmed spectacles, goatee, fast-talking manner and lightning sketching abilities. In 1960, his novelty recording 'Tie Me Kangeroo Down, Sport', complete with exaggerated Australian accent, was a worldwide Top 10 hit and million seller. Two years later, Harris struck again with the atmospheric 'Sun Arise', based on an aboriginal chant. Awarded the MBE and later the OBE, Harris was a distinguished representative of British Variety but seemed an unlikely figure for further 60s chart success. Amazingly, however, he brought the decade to an end with the best-selling UK single of 1969: 'Two Little Boys'. Written as early as 1903 by USA songwriters, Edward Madden and Theodore Morse, the song topped the UK charts for a sterling six weeks. Harris failed to discover a suitable hit follow-up but returned to the UK number 1 spot in 1985 as a member of the Crowd, whose charity recording of 'You'll Never Walk Alone' topped the charts in its first week of release.

Albums: *Sun Arise* (1963), *All Together Now* (1965), *The Man With The Microphone* (1966), *The Rolf Harris Show* (1968).

Alex Harvey And The Soul Band

Harvey, Alex

b. 5 February 1935, Gorbals, Glasgow, Scotland, d. 4 February 1982. Having left school at the age of 15, Harvey undertook a multitude of occupations until opting for music. Inspired by Jimmie Rodgers, Woody Guthrie and Cisco Houston, he became acquainted with several musicians who rehearsed regularly at the city's Bill Patterson Studios. In 1955 Harvey joined saxophonist Bill Patrick in a group that combined rock 'n' roll and trad jazz. Known jointly as the Clyde River Jazz Band or the Kansas City Skiffle Band, depending on the booking, the unit later evolved into the Kansas City Counts, and joined the Ricky Barnes All-Stars as pioneers of the Scottish

rock 'n' roll circuit. By the end of the decade, and with their singer the obvious focal point, the group had became known as Alex Harvey's (Big) Soul Band, the appellation derived from a new form of small combo jazz championed by Horace Silver. The band's repertoire consisted of Ray Charles, the Isley Brothers and urban R&B while their innovative use of conga drums and other percussive instruments emphasized the swinging nature of their sound. Having become popular in Scotland and the north of England, Harvey then moved to Hamburg where he recorded *Alex Harvey And His Soul Band* in October 1963. Curiously this excellent set did not feature the singer's regular group, but musicians drawn from Kingsize Taylor And The Dominoes. The following year Alex returned to the UK. His group made its London debut on 6 February 1964 and for several months remained a highly popular attraction in the capital. However another opportunity to capture them on record was lost when *The Blues* consisted of largely solo material with support derived solely from Harvey's younger brother, Leslie. This disparate set included suitably idiosyncratic readings of 'Danger Zone', 'Waltzing Matilda' and 'The Big Rock Candy Mountain'. Despite initial intentions to the contrary, Harvey dissolved the Soul Band in 1965 with a view to pursuing a folk-based direction. However subsequent releases, including 'Agent 00 Soul' and 'Work Song', continued the artist's love of R&B. Having briefly fronted the houseband at Glasgow's Dennistoun Palais, Alex returned to London in 1967 to form the psychedelic Giant Moth. The remnants of this short-lived combo - Mox (flute), Jim Condron (guitar/bass) and George Butler (drums) - supported the singer on two invigorating singles, 'Someday Song' and 'Maybe Someday'. Stung by their commercial failure, Harvey took a job in the pit band for the musical ***Hair*** which in turn inspired *Hair Rave Up Live From The Shaftesbury Theatre*. The singer re-established his own career in 1969 with the uncompromising *Roman Wall Blues*. This powerful set included the original version of 'Midnight Moses', a composition which the singer brought to his next substantial group, the Sensational Alex Harvey Band. Galvanized by the tragic death of his brother Leslie while on stage with Stone The Crows, Harvey formed SAHB with Tear Gas, a struggling Glasgow hard rock band. Together they became one of the most popular live attractions of the early 70s until ill-health took its toll of their irrepressible leader. He abandoned the group in October 1977 to resume a less frenetic solo career, but *The Mafia Stole My Guitar* failed to recapture former glories. Harvey succumbed to a fatal heart attack on 4 February 1982 in Belgium at the end of a four-week tour of Europe. His death robbed rock of one of its most enigmatic and endearing characters.

Albums: *Alex Harvey And His Soul Band* (1964), *The Blues* (1964), *Hair Rave Up Live From The Shaftesbury Theatre* (1969), *Roman Wall Blues* (1969), *The Mafia Stole My Guitar* (1979) Compilation: *The Alex Harvey Collection* (1986),

Hatch, Tony

b. 1939, Pinner, England. Hatch earned one lowly British Top 50 entry under his own name (with 1962's 'Out Of This World', a light orchestral outing) before emerging as a respected songwriter, arranger and producer. While on National Service, he had been permitted to leave his London barracks most afternoons to continue as a freelance musical director with Top Rank and then Pye - for which he had supervised two domestic smashes in 1961 for the Brook Brothers, while gaining lesser accolades with the Kestrels. In 1963, he joined those digging pop gold around Merseyside. An ill-judged choice of recorded repertoire for the Undertakers was mitigated by a novel arrangement of 'I Could Write A Book' (from *Pal Joey*) for the Chants and much more so by his propagation of the Searchers' international hit parade run - which included his composition 'Sugar And Spice' (under the pseudonym 'Fred Nightingale') as their stabilizing second single. He was, however, more at home with the middle-of-the-road sophistications of Petula Clark's 'Downtown' smash of 1964. He continued writing memorable hit songs for her for many years. Professional and personal joys merged the following year through the chart-topping 'Where Are You Now (My Love)' which he co-wrote with Jackie Trent, its singer and his future spouse. Buoyed by two lesser UK hits for, the Hatches had fun as a husband-and-wife recording team - notably with 1967's 'Long Is The Lonely Night' and their theme song 'The Two Of Us' - plus cabaret turn's until the 70s when Tony was contracted by ITV to pass acerbic but well-qualified comment on acts arrayed in *New Faces*, a long-running Saturday evening talent show. In 1974 he wrote and produced the number 1 hit for Sweet Sensation 'Sad Sweet Dreamer'. His longest running success has been with television theme songs: three notable songs set to give him pop immortality are *Mr And Mrs*, *Crossroads* and *Neighbours*.

Havens, Richie

b. Richard Pierce Havens, 21 January 1941, Bedford-Stuyvesant, Brooklyn, New York, USA. Havens' professional singing career began at the age of 14 as a member of the McCrea Gospel Singers. By 1962 he was a popular figure on the Greenwich Village folk circuit with regular appearances at the Cafe Wha?, Gerdes, and The Fat Black Pussycat. Havens quickly developed a distinctive playing style, tuning his guitar to the open E chord which in turn inspired an insistent percussive technique and a stunningly deft right hand technique. A black singer in a predominantly white idiom, Havens' early work combined folk material with New York-pop inspired compositions. His soft, yet gritty, voice adapted well to seemingly contrary material and two early releases, *Mixed Bag* and *Something Else Again*, revealed a blossoming talent. However, the artist established his reputation interpreting songs by other acts, including the Beatles and Bob Dylan, which he personalized through his individual technique. Havens opened the celebrated Woodstock Festival and his memorable appearance was a highlight of the film. A contemporaneous release, *Richard P. Havens 1983*, was arguably his artistic apogee, offering several empathic cover versions and some of the singer's finest compositions. He later established an independent label, Stormy Forest, and enjoyed a US Top 20 hit with 'Here Comes The Sun'. A respected painter, writer and sculptor, Havens currently pursues a lucrative career doing voice-overs for US television advertisements.

Albums: *Richie Havens Record* (1965), *Electric Havens* (1966), *Mixed Bag* (1967), *Something Else Again* (1968), *Richard P. Havens 1983* (1969), *Stonehenge* (1970), *Alarm Clock* (1971), *The Great Blind Degree* (1971), *Richie Havens On Stage* (1972), *Portfolio* (1973), *Mixed Bag II* (1974), *The End Of The Beginning* (1976), *Mirage* (1977), *Connections* (1980), *Common Ground* (1984), *Simple Things* (1987). Compilations: *A State Of Mind* (1971), *Richie Havens Sings The Beatles And Dylan* (1990).

Hawkins, Edwin, Singers

As directors of music at their Berkeley church, the Ephresian Church of God in Christ, Edwin Hawkins (b. August 1943, Oakland, California, USA) and Betty Watson, began in 1967 to absorb the leading soloists from other San Francisco-based choirs to inaugurate the North California State Youth Choir. In 1969, the 50 strong ensemble recorded an album to boost their funds, and when San Francisco DJ Tom Donahue began playing one of its tracks, 'Oh Happy Day', the assemblage found itself with both a record contract with the Buddah label and a surprise international hit. Although renamed the Edwin Hawkins Singers, the featured voice belonged to Dorothy Combs Morrison (b. 1945, Longview, Texas) and much of the single's attraction comes from her powerful delivery. The singer subsequently embarked on a solo career which failed to maintain its initial promise while Hawkins, deprived of such an important member, struggled in the wake of this 'novelty' hit, although they enjoyed a period of great demand for session singing. One such session put them back into the US charts in 1970 whilst guesting on Melanie's Top 10 hit 'Lay Down (Candle In The

Wind)'. It was to be their last chart appearance to date and eventually to group's fortunes faded. The Singers, now somewhat reduced, continue to tour and occasionally record.

Albums: *Oh Happy Day* (1969), *Lets Us Go Into The House Of The Lord* (1969), *Peace Is Blowing In The Wind* (1969), *Live At The Yankee Stadium* (1969, one side of double album), *I'd Like To Teach The World To Sing* (1972), *New World* (1973), *Live - Amsterdam* (1974), *Live At The Bitter End, N.Y.* (1974), *Wonderful* (1977), *Love Alive II* (1979), *Imagine Heaven* (1982), *Live With The Oakland Symphony Orchestra* (1982), *Give Us Peace* (1982). Edwin Hawkins solo: *Children (Get Together)* (1971), *Love Alive* (1977). Compilation: *The Best Of The Edwin Hawkins Singers* (1985).

Hazlewood, Lee

b. Barton Lee Hazlewood, 9 July 1929, Mannford, Oklahoma, USA. Hazlewood, the son of an oil worker, served in Korea and, on his return, became a DJ in Phoenix. He set himself up as an independent record producer and wrote 'The Fool', 'Run Boy Run' and 'Son Of A Gun' for Sanford Clark. On Clark's recordings, Hazlewood was experimenting with ways of recording Al Casey's guitar, often using echo. In 1957, after 'The Fool' had become a US pop hit for the Dot label, Hazlewood formed his own Jamie label, with publisher Lester Sill and television host Dick Clark. Hazlewood created the 'twangy guitar' by slowing down Duane Eddy's notes and deepening his sound. Hazlewood and Eddy co-wrote many instrumental hits including 'Rebel Rouser', 'Cannon Ball', 'Shazam!' and, with a minimal lyric, 'Dance With The Guitar Man'. Eddy was the first major performer to include musicians' names on album sleeves and, similarly, Hazlewood was acknowledged as the producer. Eddy also backed Hazlewood on a single, 'The Girl On Death Row'/'Words Mean Nothing'. Much of Eddy's success stemmed from his regular appearances on Dick Clark's *American Bandstand*, and Clark's payola allegations harmed Eddy's career. Hazlewood formed his LHI label and he produced the *Safe At Home* album by the International Submarine Band (including Gram Parsons). At Reprise in 1965, he wrote and produced US hits by Dean Martin ('Houston') and Dino, Desi And Billy, which included Martin's son ('I'm A Fool'). When Hazlewood was assigned to Nancy Sinatra, the daughter of the label's owner, who had made several unsuccessful singles, he promised to get her hits. Nicknaming her 'Nasty Jones', he gave her 'These Boots Are Made For Walkin'', which had been written for a man, and said, 'You gotta get a new sound and get rid of this babyness. You're not a virgin anymore so let's do one for the truck drivers. Bite the words'. Sinatra's boots stomped over the

international charts, and she followed it with other Hazlewood songs including 'How Does That Grab You, Darlin'', 'Sugartown' and 'Lightning's Girl'. Their duets include the playful 'Jackson' and the mysterious 'Some Velvet Morning' and 'Lady Bird'. The partnership folded because Sinatra tired of singing Hazlewood's songs, although she has made few records since. Hazlewood, whose singing voice is as deep as Eddy's guitar, tried for the US country charts with a cover of 'Ode To Billie Joe', and he also produced Waylon Jennings' *Singer Of Sad Songs*. His own albums include *Trouble Is A Lonesome Town*, a sombre collection about the characters in a western town, and *Requiem For An Almost Lady*, a sincere tribute to a girlfriend who had died. His *Poet, Fool Or Bum* album was dismissed in one word by the *New Musical Express* - 'Bum'. One track, 'The Performer', emphasized his disillusionment and he moved to Sweden, making records for that market.

Albums: *Trouble Is A Lonesome Town* (1963), *The N.S.V.I.P.'s* (1965, soundtrack), *Lee Hazlewood Sings Friday's Child* (1966), *The Very Special World Of Lee Hazlewood* (1966), *Hazlewoodism - Its Cause And Cure* (1966), *Love And Other Crimes* (1968), with Nancy Sinatra *Nancy And Lee* (1968), *Cowboy In Sweden* (1970), with Ann-Margret *The Cowboy And The Lady* (1971), *Forty* (1971), *Requiem For An Almost Lady* (1971), with Nancy Sinatra *Did You Ever?* (1971), *13* (1972), *I'll Be Your Baby Tonight* (1973), *Poet, Fool Or Bum* (1973), *The Stockholm Kid* (1974), *A House Safe For Tigers* (1975, soundtrack), *20th Century Lee* (1976), *Movin' On* (1977), *Back On The Street Again* (1977).

Head, Roy

b. 1 September 1941, Three Rivers, Texas, USA. This respected performer first formed his group, the Traits, in 1958, after moving to San Marcos. The line-up included Jerry Gibson (drums) who later played with Sly And The Family Stone. Head recorded for several local labels, often under the supervision of famed Texas producer Huey P. Meaux, but it was not until 1965 that Head scored a national hit when 'Treat Her Right' reached number 2 on both US pop and R&B charts. This irresistible song, with its pumping horns and punchy rhythm, established the singer alongside the Righteous Brothers as that year's prime blue-eyed soul exponent. Head's later releases appeared on a variety of outlets, including Dunhill and Elektra, and embraced traces of rockabilly ('Apple Of My Eye') and psychedelia ('You're (Almost) Tuff'). However, by the 70s he had honed his style and was working as a country singer and in 1975 he earned a notable US C&W Top 20 hit with 'The Most Wanted Woman In Town'.

Albums: *Roy Head And The Traits* (1965), *Treat Me*

Right (1965), *A Head Of His Time* (1968), *Same People* (1970), *Dismal Prisoner* (1972), *Head First* (1976), *Tonight's The Night* (1977), *Boogie Down* (1977), *Rock 'N' Roll My Soul* (1977), *In Our Room* (1979), *The Many Sides Of Roy Head* (1980). Compilations: *His All-Time Favourites* (1974), *Treat Her Right* (1988).

Bobby Hebb

Hebb, Bobby

b. 26 July 1941, Nashville, Tennessee, USA. An accomplished musician and songwriter, Hebb appeared on the *Grand Ole Opry* at 12 and studied guitar with Chet Atkins. He later moved to New York, ostensibly to play with Mickey And Sylvia. When that duo split, a new combination emerged: Bobby And Sylvia. This short-lived unit was followed by several solo Hebb releases which culminated in 'Sunny' (1966). Written in memory of his brother Hal, who died the day after the assassination of John F. Kennedy, this simple, melancholic song reached number 2 in the US and number 12 in the UK. It was recorded by many artists, including Cher and Georgie Fame, whose version reached number 13 in the UK in 1966. Despite his tag as 'the song a day man', Bobby chose the country standard, 'A Satisfied Mind', as the follow-up. It fared less well commercially, although the singer later secured a reputation in UK northern soul circles with 'Love Me' and 'Love Love Love', which reached the Top 40 in the UK in 1972. Hebb returned to the fringes

of the soul chart with 'Sunny 76', a reworking of his best-known moment.
Album: *Sunny* (1966).

Hedgehoppers Anonymous

Formed in November 1963 and originally known as the Trendsetters, this short-lived quintet consisted of ex-members of the Royal Air Force. Mick Tinsley (b. 16 December 1940), Ray Honeyball (b. 6 June 1941), Leslie Dash (b. 3 April 1943), Alan Laud (b. 13 March 1946) and John Stewart (b. 18 March 1941) were managed by Jonathan King, who wrote and produced their UK Top 5 hit 'It's Good News Week' in 1965. A somewhat contrived cash-in on the then-current 'protest' trend, the single was undeniably catchy, but the group was unable to repeat its success. Although a follow-up, 'Don't Push Me', was given considerable airplay, it failed to chart and the quintet disbanded soon afterwards.

Heinz

b. Heinz Burt, 24 July 1942, Germany. Bassist Heinz was a founder member of the Tornados, a studio group assembled by UK producer Joe Meek. The quintet enjoyed international fame with 'Telstar', but the photogenic dyed-blond Heinz was then groomed for a solo career. Although his debut disc, 'Dreams Do Come True', failed to chart despite magnanimous publicity, the singer later enjoyed a UK Top 5 hit with the 'tribute' to the late Eddie Cochran, 'Just Like Eddie' (1963). An immoderate vocalist, Heinz was bolstered by a crack studio group, the Outlaws, and was accompanied live by the Wild Boys, which included guitarist Ritchie Blackmore. However further minor hits, 'Country Boy' (1963), 'You Were There' (1964) and 'Diggin' My Potatoes' (1965), revealed his limitations and an acrimonious split with Meek ended his chart career. Burt has nonetheless remained popular through rock 'n' roll revival shows and cabaret.
Album: *Tribute To Eddie* (1964).
Compilation: *Remembering...Heinz* (1977).

Hendrix, Jimi

b. Johnny Allen Hendrix, 27 November 1942, Seattle, Washington, USA, d. 18 September, 1970. His father subsequently changed his son's name to James Marshall Hendrix. More superlatives have been bestowed upon Hendrix than almost any other rock star. Unquestionably one of music's most influential figures, Jimi Hendrix brought an unparalleled vision to the art of playing electric guitar. Self-taught and with the burden of being left-handed with a right-handed guitar he spent hours absorbing the recorded legacy of southern-blues practitioners, from Robert Johnson to Muddy Waters, Howlin' Wolf to B.B. King. The aspiring musician joined several local R&B

Jimi Hendrix Experience

bands while still at school, before enlisting as a paratrooper in the 101st Airborne Division. It was during this period that Hendrix met Billy Cox, a bass player upon whom he would call at several stages in his career. Together they formed the King Kasuals, an in-service attraction later resurrected when both men returned to civilian life. Hendrix was discharged in July 1962 after breaking his right ankle. He began working with various touring revues backing, among others, the Impressions, Sam Cooke and the Valentinos. He enjoyed lengthier spells with the Isley Brothers, Little Richard and King Curtis, recording with each of these acts, but was unable to adapt to the discipline their performances required. Despite such individuality, the experience and stagecraft gained during this formative period proved essential to the artist's subsequent development.

By 1965, Jimi was living in New York. In October he joined struggling soul singer Curtis Knight, signing a punitive contract with the latter's manager, Ed Chaplin. This ill-advised decision would return to haunt the guitarist. In June the following year Hendrix, now calling himself Jimmy James, formed a group initially dubbed the Rainflowers, then Jimmy James And The Blue Flames. The quartet, which also featured future Spirit member Randy California, was appearing at the Cafe Wha? in Greenwich Village when Chas Chandler was advised to see them. The Animals' bassist immediately recognized the guitarist's extraordinary talent and persuaded him to come to London in search of a more receptive audience. Hendrix arrived in England in September 1966. Chandler became his co-manager, in partnership with Mike Jeffries (aka Jeffreys), and immediately began auditions for a suitable backing group. Noel Redding (b. 25 December 1945, Folkstone, Kent, England) was selected on bass, having recently failed to join the New Animals, while John 'Mitch' Mitchell (b. 9 July 1947, Ealing, Middlesex, England), a veteran of the Riot Squad and Georgie Fame's Blue Flames, became the trio's drummer.

The new group, dubbed the Jimi Hendrix Experience, made its debut the following month at Evereux in France. On returning to England they began a string of club engagements which attracted pop's aristocracy, including Pete Townshend and Eric Clapton. In December the trio released its first single, the brilliantly understated 'Hey Joe', but its UK Top 10 placing encouraged a truly dynamic follow-up in 'Purple Haze'. The latter was memorable for its pyrotechic guitar work and psychedelic-influenced lyrics, such as the famous line: ''Scuse me while I kiss the sky'.

His trademark Fender Stratocaster and Marshall Amplifier were punished night after night. Having fulfilled pop's requirements, the group enhanced its reputation with exceptional live appearances. Here Hendrix drew on black music's cultural heritage to produce a startling visual and audio bombardment. Framed by a halo of long, wiry hair, his slight figure was clad in colourful, de rigueur psychedelic garb, and although never a demonstrative vocalist, his delivery was curiously effective. Hendrix's playing technique drew its roots from the blues artists, but it encompassed an emotional palette far greater than any contemporary guitarist. Eric Clapton, Jeff Beck and Pete Townshend all tried: but Hendrix *did it*, while they stood aghast. Rapier-like runs vied with measured solos, matching energy with ingenuity, while a plethora of technical possibilities - distortion, feedback and even sheer volume - brought texture to his overall approach. His technique was so impressive it was irrational. This assault was enhanced by a flamboyant stage persona in which Hendrix used the guitar as a physical appendage. He played his instrument behind his back, between his legs or, in simulated sexual ecstasy, on the floor. Such practices brought criticism from radical quarters, who claimed the artist had become an 'Uncle Tom', employing tricks to carry favour with a white audience. These accusations had denied a similar showmanship from generations of black performers, from Charley Patton to T-Bone Walker, but Hendrix prevailed and in doing so created a climate to allow future stars such as Michael Jackson and Prince to express themselves fully.

Redding's clean, uncluttered bass lines provided the backbone to Hendrix's improvisations, while Mitchell's anarchic drumming, as unfettered as his leader's guitar work, was an innovatory foil. Their concessions to the pop world now receding, the Experience completed an astonishing debut album which ranged from the apocalyptical vision of 'I Don't Live Today', the blues of 'Red House' to the funk of 'Fire' and 'Foxy Lady'. Jimi Hendrix returned to America in June 1967 to appear, sensationally, at the Monterey Pop Festival. During one number (Dylan's 'Like A Rolling Stone') he paused and informed the crowd that he was re-tuning his guitar, later in the same song he admits forgetting the words. Such cheek, humour and unparalleled confidence endeared him to the crowd. His performance was a sensation, best remembered for his largesse in picking the guitar with his teeth and then burning it with lighter fuel.

He was now fêted in his homeland, and following an ill-advised tour supporting the Monkees, the Experience enjoyed reverential audiences in the country's nascent concert circuit. *Axis: Bold As Love*, revealed a lyrical capability, notably the title track, the jazz-influenced 'Up From The Skies', and 'Little Wing', a delicate love song bathed in emotion through the delicate tones of his guitar, which offered a gentle perspective closer to that of the artist's shy, offstage demeanour. Released in December 1967, the collection completed a triumphant year, artistically and commercially, but within months the fragile peace began to fragment. In January 1968, the Experience embarked on a gruelling American tour encompassing 54 concerts in 47 days. Hendrix was now tiring of the wild man image which had brought initial attention, but his desire for a more eloquent art was perceived as diffident by spectators anticipating gimmickry. An impulsive artist, he was unable to disguise below-par performances, while his relationship with Redding grew increasingly fraught as the bassist rebelled against the set patterns he was expected to play.

Electric Ladyland, the last official Experience album, was released in October. This extravagant double set was initially deemed 'self-indulgent', but is now recognized as a major work. It revealed the guitarist's desire to expand the increasingly limiting trio format, and contributions from members of Traffic (Chris Wood and Steve Winwood) and Jefferson Airplane (Jack Casady) embellished several selections. The collection featured a succession of classic-styled performances - 'Gypsy Eyes', 'Crosstown Traffic' - while the astonishing 'Voodoo Chile (Slight Return)', a posthumous number 1 single, showed how Hendrix had brought rhythm, purpose and mastery to the recently invented wah-wah pedal. *Electric Ladyland* included two UK hits, 'The Burning Of The Midnight Lamp' and 'All Along The Watchtower'. The former dared to tell us in the plausible lyric that 'traffic lights turn blue' before the listener realises. The latter, an urgent restatement of a Bob Dylan song, was particularly impressive, and received the ultimate accolade when the composer adopted Hendrix's interpretation when performing it live on his 1974 tour.

Despite such creativity, the guitarist's private and professional life was becoming problematic. He was arrested in Toronto for possessing heroin, but although the charges were later dismissed, the proceedings clouded much of 1969. Chas Chandler had meanwhile withdrawn from the managerial partnership and although Redding sought solace with a concurrent group, Fat Mattress, his differences with Hendrix were now irreconcilable. The Experience played its final concert on June 29 1969; Jimi subsequently formed the Gypsies Sons And Rainbows with Mitchell, Billy Cox (bass), Larry Lee (rhythm guitar), Juma Sultan and Jerry Velez (both percussion). This short-lived unit closed the Woodstock Festival, during which Hendrix performed his famed rendition of the 'Star Spangled Banner'. Perceived by some critics as a political statement, it came as the guitarist was increasingly subjected to pressures from different radical quarters. In October he formed an all-black group, Band Of Gypsies, with Cox and drummer Buddy Miles, intending to accentuate the African-American dimension in his music. The trio made its debut on 31 December 1969, but its potential was marred by Miles' comparatively flat, pedestrian drumming and unimaginative compositions. Part of the set was issued as *Band Of Gypsies*, but despite the inclusion of the exceptional 'Machine Gun', this inconsistent album was only released to appease former manager Chaplin, who acquired the rights in part-settlement of a miserly early contract.

The Band Of Gypsies broke up after a mere three concerts and initially Hendrix confined his efforts to completing his Electric Ladyland recording studio. He then started work on another double set, the unreleased *First Rays Of The New Rising Sun*, and later resumed performing with Cox and Mitchell. His final concerts were largely frustrating, as the aims of the artist and the expectations of his audience grew increasingly divergent. His final UK appearance, at the Isle Of Wight festival, encapsulated this dilemma, yet at times the music produced at this concert was truly mesmerizing.

The guitarist returned to London following a short European tour. On 18 September 1970, his girlfriend, Monika Danneman, became alarmed when she was unable to rouse him from sleep. An ambulance was called, but Hendrix was pronounced dead on arrival at a nearby hospital. The inquest recorded an open verdict, death caused by suffocation due to inhalation of vomit. Eric Burdon claimed at the time to possess a suicide note but this has never been confirmed.

Two posthumous releases, *Cry Of Love* and *Rainbow Bridge*, mixed portions of the artist's final recordings with masters from earlier sources. These were fitting tributes, but many others were tawdry cash-ins, recorded in dubious circumstances, mispackaged, mistitled and serving only to dilute his outstanding career. This imbalance has been redressed of late with the release of fitting archive recordings, but the Hendrix legacy also rests in his prevailing influence on fellow musicians. Many, notably white, guitarists, have adopted superficially his trademarks, but Jimi's influence on black performers, from Miles Davis to George Clinton and Prince, has in turn inspired new and compulsive music. Hendrix has influenced and appears likely to influence rock music more than any other individual, and remains a colossal legend.

Albums: *Are You Experienced?* (1967), *Axis: Bold As Love* (1967), *Electric Ladyland* (1968), *Band Of Gypsies* (1970). The rest of the extensive Hendrix catalogue was compiled after his death. *Cry Of Love* (1971), *Experience* (1971), *Isle Of Wight* (1971), *Rainbow Bridge* (1971), *Hendrix In The West* (1971), *More Experience* (1972), *War Heroes* (1972), *Soundtrack Recordings From The Film Jimi Hendrix* (1973), *Loose Ends* (1974), *Crash Landing* (1975), *Midnight Lightnin'* (1975), *Nine To The Universe* (1980), *The Jimi Hendrix Concerts* (1982), *Jimi Plays Monterey* (1986), *Band Of Gypsies 2* (1986), *Live At Winterland* (1987), *Radio One* (1988), *Live And Unreleased* (1989). Compilations: *Smash Hits* (1968), *The Essential Jimi Hendrix* (1978), *The Essential Jimi Hendrix Volume Two* (1979), *The Singles Album* (1983), *Kiss The Sky* (1984), *Cornerstones* (1990).

Further reading: *Hendrix - A Biography*, Chris Welch. *Jimi - An Intimate Biography Of Jimi Hendrix*, Curtis Knight. *Jimi Hendrix - Voodoo Child Of The Aquarian Age*, David Henderson. *Crosstown Traffic/Jimi Hendrix And Post-War Pop*, Charles Shaar Murray. *Jimi Hendrix - Electric Gypsy*, Harry Shapiro and Caesar Glebbeek. *The Hendrix Experience*, Mitch Mitchell and John Platt. *Are You Experienced*, Noel Redding and Carol Appleby.

Herd

This UK group originally formed in 1965 as a quintet featuring Terry Clark (vocals), Andy Bown (bass), Gary Taylor (guitar) and Tony Chapman (drums). After several line-up shuffles, Bown took over on lead vocals and organ, occasionally relieved by the new guitarist Peter Frampton. In 1967, however, songwriting managers Ken Howard and Alan Blaikley, were taken on in place of Billy Gaff and immediately promoted the reluctant Frampton to centre stage. A near miss with the psychedelic 'I Can Fly' was followed by a portentous adaptation of *Orpheus In The Underworld* (retitled 'From The Underworld'), which became a UK Top 10 hit. Having translated Virgil into pop, Howard And Blaikley next took on Milton for 'Paradise Lost'. Despite their strange mix of literate pop and jazz rhythms, the Herd were marketed for teenzine consumption and Frampton was voted the 'Face of '68' by *Rave* magazine. Not surprisingly, a more straightforward hit followed with 'I Don't Want Our Loving To Die'. Ambivalent feelings about their pop star status convinced them to dump Howard and Blaikley in favour of the mercurial Andrew Oldham,

but their next single, the Frampton-composed 'Sunshine Cottage', missed by a mile. A brief tie-up with yet another manager, Harvey Lisberg, came to nothing and by this time Frampton had left to form Humble Pie. For a brief period, the remaining members struggled on, but to no avail. Bown later teamed up with Andy Fairweather-Low and appeared on the road with Status Quo, while Taylor and Steele guested on various sessions.

Album: *Paradise Lost* (1968).

Herman's Hermits, Dusty Springfield, Dave Berry and Brian Poole

Herman's Hermits

Originally known as the Heartbeats, they were discovered in 1963 by manager Harvey Lisberg and his partner Charlie Silverman. After restructuring the group, Herman's Hermits emerged as Peter Noone (b. 5 November 1947, Manchester, England; vocals), Karl Green (b. 31 July 1947, Salford, Manchester, England; bass), Keith Hopwood (b. 26 October 1946, Manchester, England; rhythm guitar), Lek Leckenby (b. 14 May 1946, Leeds, England; lead guitar) and Barry Whitwam (b. 21 July 1946, Manchester, England; drums). A link with producer Mickie Most and an infectious cover of Earl Jean's US hit, 'I'm Into Something Good' gave the quintet a UK number 1 in 1964. By early 1965, the group had settled into covering 50s high-school songs such as the Rays' 'Silhouettes' and Sam Cooke's 'Wonderful World', when an extraordinary invasion of America saw them challenge the Beatles as a chart act with over 10 million record sales in under 12 months. A plethora of non-stop hits over the next two years, including the vaudevillian 'Mrs Brown You've Got A Lovely Daughter' and 'I'm Henry VIII, I Am', effectively transformed them into teen idols. Director Sam Katzman even cast them in a couple of movies, *When The Boys Meet The Girls* (co-starring Connie Francis) and *Hold On!* Although their music-hall inspired US chart-toppers were not issued as singles in the UK, they enjoyed a run of hits penned by the leading commercial songwriters of the day. 'A Must

To Avoid' and 'No Milk Today' were inventive as well as catchy, though by 1968-69 their repertoire had become more formulaic. The hits continued till as late as 1970 when Peter Noone finally decided to pursue a solo career. Thereafter, Herman's Hermits drifted into cabaret, where they can still be found in 1990.
Albums: *Herman's Hermits* (1965), *Both Sides Of Herman's Hermits* (1966), *There's A Kind Of Hush* (1967), *Mrs Brown You've Got A Lovely Daughter* (1968). Additional US albums: *Introducing Herman's Hermits* (1965), *Herman's Hermits On Tour* (1965), *Hold On!* (1966), *Blaze* (1967).

High Tide

Formed in 1969 this UK group comprised: Tony Hill (guitar), Simon House (violin), Peter Pavli (bass) and Roger Hadden (drums). Signed as part of Liberty Records' attempt to climb on the progressive bandwagon, *High Tide* was more than a credible debut, complete with Mervyn Peake-styled sleeve illustrations. The unique blending of guitar and violin was for many an unaccustomed taste. However, the dramatic and powerful songs laced with Hill's Jim Morrison-like vocals appealed to the UK progressive market. By the time of the second album though, the formula had worn thin and the band broke up, with House eventually joining Hawkwind.
Albums: *Sea Shanties* (1969), *High Tide* (1970), *Interesting Times* (1986), *The Flood* (c.80s), *Ancient Gates* (c.80s), *A Fierce Native* (1990). Tony Hill solo, *Playing For Time* (1991).

Highwaymen

This self-contained folk quintet comprised Dave Fisher (b. 1940, New Haven, Connecticut, USA); Steve Butts (b. 1940, New York, New York, USA); Chan Daniels (b. 1940, Buenos Aires, Brazil d. 2 August 1975); Bobby Burnett (b. 1940, Mystic, Connecticut, USA) and Steve Trott (b. 1940, Mexico City, Mexico). The group recorded their self-titled album for United Artists in 1961 whilst still students at the Wesleyan University in Middletown, Connecticut, where they had first met. Their haunting version of an old slave song 'Michael', arranged by Fisher, took them to the top on both sides of the Atlantic in 1961, despite a UK cover version by Lonnie Donegan. They followed their gold record with another 19th-century folk song 'Cotton Fields'. It too made the US Top 20 but it was to be their last major success. The group, whose repertoire included folk songs from around the world, sang in English, French, Spanish and Hebrew. For them, music was never much more than a hobby and they continued their studies rather than pursuing full-time musical careers. They unsuccessfully re-recorded 'Michael' in 1965 before recording for a brief time on

ABC.
Albums: *The Highwaymen* (1961), *Standing Room Only!* (1962), *Hootenanny With The Highwaymen* (1963).

Hill, Vince

b. 16 April 1939, Coventry, England. Hill's various jobs included pastry cook, wheelwright and coalminer. He did his National Service in the Royal Signals and sang with the regimental band in Europe and the Far East. After demobilization he toured in Leslie Stuart's 19th-century musical comedy *Floradora*, later joining trumpeter Teddy Foster's band as vocalist. In 1958 Hill joined another two boys and a girl to form the Raindrops vocal group, and appeared regularly on BBC Radio's *Parade Of The Pops* for two years. He received his big chance on the television show *Stars And Garters*, eventually turning solo in 1962, scoring a minor hit single that year with 'The River's Run Dry'. He later signed for Columbia and had success with 'Take Me To Your Heart Again', 'Heartaches' and 'Merci Cheri' in 1966, followed by the major number 2 hit, 'Edelweiss' plus 'Roses Of Picardy' and 'Love Letters In The Sand', in 1967. In 1970 Hill gained the Most Popular Singer Award while representing Britain at the Rio Song Festival, and in 1971 had more chart success with 'Look Around' from the movie *Love Story*. In 1973 he had his own television series for the first time, entitled *They Sold A Million* which ran for 15 weeks. He has a highly-rated cabaret act and in 1984 entertained on the QE2's world cruise.
Albums: *Heartaches* (1966), *Edelweiss* (1967), *You Forgot To Remember* (1969), *Look Around And You'll Find Me There* (1971), *In My Thoughts Of You* (1972), *Mandy* (1975), *Wish You Were Here* (1975), *Midnight Blue* (1976), *This Is My Lovely Day* (1978), *While The Feeling's Good* (1980), *I'm The Singer* (1985), *I Will Always Love You* (1987). Compilations: *The Vince Hill Collection* (1976), *That Loving Feeling* (1978), *The Very Best Of Vince Hill* (1979), *20 Golden Favourites* (1980), *Greatest Hits: Vince Hill, An Hour Of Hits* (1986).

Hollies

Formed in Manchester in 1962 by childhood friends Allan Clarke (b. 15 April 1942, Salford, Lancashire, England; vocals), and Graham Nash (b. 2 February 1942, Blackpool, Lancashire, England; vocals/guitar). They had already been singing together locally for a number of years as a semi-professional duo under a number of names such as the Guytones, the Two Teens and Ricky And Dane. They enlarged their unit by adding Eric Haydock (b. 16 September 1944, Burnley, Lancashire, England; bass) and Don Rathbone (drums), to became the Fourtones and then the Deltas. Following the recruitment of local guitar hero Tony Hicks from the Dolphins (b. 16

December 1943, Nelson, Lancashire, England) they became the Hollies. Almost immediately they were signed to the same label as the Beatles, the prestigious Parlophone. Their first two singles were covers of the Coasters '(Ain't That) Just Like Me' and 'Searchin''. Both made the UK charts and the group set about recording their first album. At the same time Rathbone left to become their road manager and was replaced by Bobby Elliott (b. 8 December 1942) from Shane Fenton (Alvin Stardust) And The Fentones. The group's excellent live performances throughout Britain had already seasoned them for what was to become one of the longest beat group success stories in popular music. Their first two albums contained the bulk of their live act and both albums became long-time residents in the UK charts. Meanwhile the band was scoring a train of singles hits that would continue between 1963 and 1974, and their popularity almost rivalled that of the Beatles and Rolling Stones. Infectious, well produced hits such as Doris Troy's 'Just One Look', 'Here I Go Again' and the sublime 'Yes I Will' all contained their trademark, soaring harmonies. The voices of Clarke, Hicks and Nash combined to make one of the most distinctive sounds to be heard in popular music.

As their career progressed the aforementioned developed into a strong songwriting team, and wrote most of their own b-sides (under the pseudonym, L. Ransford). On their superb third collection, *Hollies* in 1965 their talents blossomed with 'Too Many People' an early song about over-population. Their first UK number 1 came in 1965 with 'I'm Alive' and was followed within weeks by Graham Gouldman's uplifting yet simple take 'Look Through Any Window'. By Christmas 1965 the group experienced their first lapse when their recording of George Harrison's 'If I Needed Someone' just scraped the UK Top 20 and brought with it some bad press. Both the Hollies and John Lennon took swipes at each other, venting frustration at the comparative failure of a Beatles song. Early in 1966, the group enjoyed their second number 1, 'I Can't Let Go' which topped the **New Musical Express** chart jointly with the Walker Brothers' 'The Sun Ain't Gonna Shine Anymore'. 'I Can't Let Go', co-written by Chip Taylor, had already appeared on the previous year's *Hollies* and was one of their finest recordings, combining soaring harmonies with some exceptionally strong, driving guitar work.

The enigmatic and troublesome Eric Haydock was sacked in April 1966 and was replaced by Hicks' former colleague in the Dolphins, Bernie Calvert. The Hollies, success continued unabated with Graham Gouldman's 'Bus Stop', the exotic 'Stop! Stop! Stop!' and the poppier 'On A Carousel', all UK Top 5 hits, and (at last) became major hits in the US charts. The Hollies were quick to join the 'flower

Hollies; Graham Nash

power' bandwagon, as a more progressive feel had already pervaded their recent album, *For Certain Because*, but with *Evolution* their beads and kaftans were everywhere. That same year (1967) the release of the excellent *Butterfly* showed signs of discontent. Inexplicably the album failed to make the charts in either the UK or the US. It marked two distinct types of songs from the previously united team of Nash/Clarke/Hicks. On one hand there was a Clarke influenced song 'Charley And Fred' and on the other an obvious Nash composition like 'Butterfly'. Nash took a more ambitious route. His style was perfectly highlighted with the exemplary 'King Midas In Reverse' an imaginative song complete with brass and strings. It was, by Hollies standards, a surprising failure (UK number 18). The following year during the proposals to make *Hollies Sing Dylan*, Nash announced his departure for Crosby, Stills And Nash. His replacement was Terry Sylvester of the Escorts. Allan Clarke was devastated by the departure of his friend of more than 20 years and after seven further hits, including 'He Ain't Heavy He's My Brother', Clarke decided to leave for a solo career. The band soldiered on with the strange induction of Mickael Rickfors from Sweden. In the USA the million selling 'Long Cool Woman (In A Black Dress)' narrowly missed the top spot, ironic also because Allan Clarke was the vocalist on this older number taken from the successful album *Distant Light*.

Clarke returned after an abortive solo career which included two average albums, *My Real Name Is 'Arold* and *Headroom*. The return was celebrated with the worldwide hit, 'The Air That I Breathe', composed by Albert Hammond. Over the next five years the Hollies pursued the supper club and cabaret circuit as their chart appearances began to dwindle. Although their albums were well produced they were largely unexciting and sold poorly. In 1981 Sylvester and Calvert left the group. Sensing major problems ahead, EMI suggested they put together a Stars On 45-type segued single. The ensuing 'Holliedaze' was a hit, and Graham Nash was flown over for the television promotion. This reunion prompted the album *What Goes Around*, which included a minor hit with the Supremes' 'Stop In The Name Of Love'. The album was justifiably slammed by the critics, and only made the US charts because of Nash's name.

Following this, the Hollies went back to the oldies path, until in 1988 a television beer commercial used 'He Ain't Heavy', and once again they were at the top of the charts for the first time in over a dozen years. The Hollies' catalogue of hits, like those of the Beach Boys, Beatles and Kinks will continue to be re-issued for future generations. Their longevity is assured for their expertly crafted, harmonic songs represent some of the greatest music in mid-60s pop.

Albums: *Stay With The Hollies* (1964), *In The Hollies' Style* (1964), *The Hollies* (1965), *Would You Believe* (1966), *For Certain Because* (1966), *Evolution* (1967), *Butterfly* (1967), *The Hollies Sing Dylan* (1969), *Hollies Sing Hollies* (1969), *Reflection* (1969), *Confessions Of The Mind* (1970), *Distant Light* (1971), *The Hollies* (1972), *Romany* (1972), *The Hollies* (1974), *Another Night* (1975), *Write On* (1976), *Russian Roulette* (1976), *Hollies Live Hits* (1977), *A Crazy Steal* (1978), *Evolution* (1978), *The Other Side Of The Hollies* (1978), *Confessions Of The Mind* (1978), *Five Three One-Double Seven O Four* (1979), *Long Cool Woman In A Black Dress* (1979), *Buddy Holly* (1980), *What Goes Around* (1983). Selected compilations: *The Hollies' Greatest* (1968), *The Hollies Greatest Hits Vol.2* (1972), *The History Of The Hollies* (1975), *The Best Of The Hollies EPs* (1978), *20 Golden Greats* (1978), *The EP Collection* (1987).

Holloway, Brenda

b. 21 June 1946, Atascadero, California, USA. Brenda Holloway began her recording career with three small Los Angeles labels, Donna, Catch and Minasa, in the early 60s, recording under the aegis of producer Hal Davis. In 1964, Holloway made an uninvited performance at a disc jockeys' convention in California, where she was spotted by a Motown talent scout. She signed to the label later that year, becoming its first west coast artist. Her initial Tamla single, 'Every Little Bit Hurts', established her bluesy soul style, and was quickly covered by the Spencer Davis Group in Britain. She enjoyed further success in 1964 with 'I'll Always Love You', and the following year with 'When I'm Gone' and 'Operator'. Her consistent record sales led to her winning a place on the Beatles' 1965 USA tour, but subsequent Tamla singles proved less successful.

Holloway began to devote increasing time to her songwriting, forming a regular writing partnership with her sister Patrice, and Motown staff producer Frank Wilson. This combination produced her 1968 single 'You've Made Me So Very Happy', a song which proved more successful via the million-selling cover version by the white jazz-rock group, Blood, Sweat And Tears. In 1968, Holloway's contract with Motown was terminated. The label issued a press release stating that the singer wished to sing for God, though Holloway blamed business differences for the split. She released a gospel album in 1983 and worked with Ian Levine from 1987. She teamed with Jimmy Ruffin in 1989 for a duet 'On The Rebound'.

Albums: *Every Little Bit Hurts* (1964), *The Artistry Of Brenda Holloway* (1968), *All It Takes* (1991).

Hondells

The Hondells were a non-existent group when they released their Top 10 single 'Little Honda' in 1964. The mastermind behind the record was producer Gary Usher, a friend and songwriting partner of Beach Boys leader Brian Wilson. Usher had created a series of surf music records using a revolving team of musicians and singers and assigning different group names to the finished products. The Hondells were one such creation. Usher and his hired hands for the day recorded a version of the Brian Wilson song extolling the virtues of Honda motorcycles, which was released on Mercury Records and reached number 9 in the US. With the record a success, the company asked Usher to assemble a touring group of Hondells. He hired Ritchie Burns, one of the background singers on the record, to lead the group. Burns still had not quit his job at a bank when the album cover photos were taken, and he had friends of his (who were not involved with the record) to pose for its cover. The Hondells continued to make records, and appeared on popular television programmes and in a number of 'beach party' films, including *Beach Blanket Bingo*. Only two further singles charted, 'My Buddy Seat' in 1964-65, and a cover of the Lovin' Spoonful's 'Younger Girl' in 1966. Following this release the group assembled to masquerade as the Hondells began to sing and play on the records, recording a version of Bob Lind's 'Cheryl's Going Home'. Subsequent singles on Columbia Records and Amos did not chart and only the first of the Hondells' albums made the charts. The

group and the name Hondells were retired in 1970.
Albums: *Go Little Honda* (1964), *The Hondells* (1965).

Honeybus

Honeybus

Originally managed by one-time Them drummer Terry Noon, Honeybus was a vehicle for minor hit songwriters Pete Dello and Ray Cane. Following the recruitment of Colin Hare (vocals/guitar) and Peter Kircher (drums), the group was signed to the hip Decca subsidiary Deram Records. Their second single, 'Do I Still Figure In Your Life', with its plaintive lyric and striking string arrangement, received extensive airplay but narrowly failed to reach the Top 50. The similarly-paced 'I Can't Let Maggie Go' fared better, entering the charts in March 1968 and peaking at number 8. Rather than exploiting the group's hit success, however, Pete Dello dramatically left Honeybus only months later. Deprived of their main songwriter and gifted arranger, the group failed to escape the one-hit-wonder trap, but almost broke through with 'Girl Of Independent Means'. After advice from their management they folded in 1969. The post-demise release, *Story* (1970), testifies to their fledgling talent. Their single moment of chart glory was later resurrected as the long-running theme for a UK television bread commercial.
Album: *Story* (1970).

Honeycombs

Formed in north London in November 1963, the group was originally known as the Sherabons and comprised: Denis D'ell (b. Denis Dalziel, 10 October 1943, London, England; vocals), Anne 'Honey' Lantree (b. 28 August 1943, Hayes, Middlesex, England; drums), John Lantree (b. 20 August 1940, Newbury, Berkshire, England; bass), Alan Ward (b. 12 December 1945, Nottingham, England; lead guitar) and Martin Murray (rhythm guitar), later replaced by Peter Pye (b. 12 July 1946, London, England). Producer Joe Meek had selected one of their songs as a possible single and the group's chances were enhanced following a management agreement with Ken Howard and Alan Blaikley. Although several record companies passed on the quintet's debut, 'Have I The Right', Pye Records' managing director Louis Benjamin agreed to release the disc. First, though, there was the obligatory name change, with Benjamin selecting Honeycombs after a track by Jimmie Rodgers. The fact that the focus of attention in the group was the red-haired drummer 'Honey' made the re-christening even more appropriate. When 'Have I The Right' hit number 1 in the UK in the summer of 1964, the group's pop star future seemed assured. However, a dramatic flop with the follow-up 'Is It Because' caused concern and although Howard and Blaikley came to the rescue with 'That's The Way', the group faltered amid line-up changes and poor morale, before moving inexorably towards cabaret and the revivalist circuit.
Album: *All Systems Go* (UK) *Here Are The Honeycombs* (USA) (1965). Compilation: *Meek And Honey* (1983).

Honeys

Arguably the definitive female surf group, the Honeys were formed in California, USA as the Rovell Sisters in 1961. Marilyn, Diane and Barbara Rovell initially appeared at amateur talent shows, but embarked on a more substantial career when a cousin, Sandra Glantz aka Ginger Blake, replaced Barbara. The newcomer, a budding songwriter, brought the trio to producer Gary Usher, who in turn introduced the group to Beach Boys svengali, Brian Wilson. Now dubbed the Honeys, a term for 'female surfer', the trio embarked on a series of exemplary singles, each of which featured Wilson as either producer, arranger or composer. They included a reworking of a Stephen Foster standard, retitled 'Surfin' Down The Swanee River' (a number 1 in Denmark), 'Pray For Surf' and 'The One You Can't Have', a superb attempt at emulating the Phil Spector 'wall-of-sound'. Such releases were commercially unsuccessful but the Honeys remained in demand as backing vocalists for the Beach Boys, Jan And Dean and Bruce Johnston. Their ties within this close-knit circle were enhanced in December 1964 when Brian Wilson and Marilyn

Rovell were married. A 1969 single, 'Goodnight My Love', anticipated the style the Rovells then followed as (American) Spring. Ginger Blake, meanwhile, pursued a parallel career, singing back-up with several live acts before establishing her own song publishing company. The trio was reunited during the early 80s for *Ecstasy*, but this disappointing album owed more to brash rock than earlier achievements.
Album: *Ecstasy* (1983).

Hopkin, Mary

b. May 3 1950, Pontardawe, Glamorgan, Wales. Hopkin's career began while still a schoolgirl. Briefly a member of a local folk/rock band, she completed several Welsh-language releases before securing a slot on the televised talent show, 'Opportunity Knocks'. Model Twiggy was impressed by Hopkin's performance and recommended the singer to Paul McCartney as a prospective signing for the newly-formed Apple label. 'Those Were The Days', a traditional song popularised by Gene Raskin of The Limelighters, was selected as the artist's national debut and this haunting, melancholic performance, deftly produced by McCartney, duly topped both the UK and US charts in 1968. Her follow up single, 'Goodbye', reached number 2 the following year, but despite its excellent versions of Donavan's 'Happiness Runs' and 'Lord Of The Reedy River', the concurrent *Post Card* showed a singer constrained by often inappropriate material. Nevertheless, the Mickie Most produced 'Temma Harbour' was another Top 10 hit, while 'Knock, Knock, Who's There?' Britain's entry to the 1970 Eurovision Song Contest, peaked at number 2. 'Think About Your Children' penned by Most's protégés Hot Chocolate, was Hopkin's last Top 20 entry as the singer became increasingly unhappy over the style of her releases. However, a second album *Earth Song/Ocean Song*, was more representative of Hopkin's talent and sympathetic contributions from Ralph McTell and Danny Thompson enhanced its enchanting atmosphere. Paradoxically, the set was issued as her contract with Apple expired and having married producer Tony Visconti, Mary retired temporarily from recording. She resumed her career in 1972 with 'Mary Had A Baby' and enjoyed a minor hit four years later with 'If You Love Me'. The singer also added backing vocals on several sessions, notably David Bowie's 'Sound And Vision', before joining Mike Hurst (ex-Springfields) and Mike D'Albuquerque (ex-ELO) in Sundance. Having left this short-lived aggregation, Hopkin resurfaced in 1983 as a member of Oasis. Peter Skellern and Julian LLoyd Webber were also members of this act which enjoyed a Top 30 album, but was brought to a premature end when Hopkin was struck by illness. Mary's subsequent work includes an appearance on George Martin's production of *Under Milk Wood*, but she remains indelibly linked to her million-selling debut hit.

Albums: *Post Card* (1969), *Earth Song/Ocean Song* (1971). Compilations: *Those Were The Days* (1972) *The Welsh World Of Mary Hopkin* (1979)

H.P. Lovecraft

This imaginative group formed in Chicago, Illinois, USA by George Edwards (guitar/vocals) and David Michaels (keyboards/woodwind/vocals). They made their debut in 1967 with a folk-rock reading of 'Anyway That You Want Me', a Chip Taylor composition successfully revived by the Troggs. The duo was initially backed by a local outfit, the Rovin' Kind, until Tony Cavallari (lead guitar), Jerry McGeorge (bass, ex-Shadows Of Knight) and Michael Tegza (drums) completed the new venture's line-up. Their debut album, *H.P. Lovecraft*, fused haunting, folk-based material to graphic, contemporary compositions. It featured stirring renditions of 'Wayfaring Stranger' and 'Let's Get Together', but the highlight was 'The White Ship', a mesmerizing adaptation of a short story penned by the author from whom the quintet took its name. McGeorge was replaced by Jeffrey Boylan for *H.P. Lovecraft II*. This enthralling set included 'At The Mountains Of Madness', in which the group's distinctive harmonies cultivated an eerie, chilling atmosphere. Commercial indifference sadly doomed their progress and the quintet disintegrated, although Tezga re-emerged in 1971 with three new musicians, Jim Dolinger (guitar), Michael Been (bass) and Marty Grebb (keyboards). Now dubbed simply Lovecraft, the unit completed *Valley Of The Moon*, a set that bore little relation to those of its pioneering predecessor In 1975 the drummer employed a completely new line-up for *We Love You Whoever You Are*, before finally laying the name to rest.
Albums: *H.P. Lovecraft* (1967), *H.P. Lovecraft II* (1968), as Lovecraft *Valley Of The Moon* (1971), as Lovecraft *We Love You Whoever You Are* (1975), as H.P. Lovecraft *Live - May 11, 1968* (1992).

Humperdinck, Engelbert

b. Arnold George Dorsey, 2 May 1936, Madras, India. Originally known as Gerry Dorsey, this singer had attempted to achieve mainstream success in the UK during the 50s. He was a featured artist on the television series *Oh Boy*, toured with Marty Wilde and recorded a failed single, 'I'll Never Fall In Love Again'. It was during this period that he first met Gordon Mills, a singer in the Viscounts who later moved into songwriting and management. By 1963, Dorsey's career had hit rock bottom. The beat boom hampered his singing career and to make matters worse he fell seriously ill with tuberculosis. Mills, meanwhile, was beginning to win international success for Tom Jones and in 1967 decided to help his old friend Gerry Dorsey. Soon after, the singer was rechristened Engelbert Humperdinck, a name featured a duet with Gloria Gaynor.

Selected albums: *Release Me* (1967), *The Last Waltz* (1967), *A Man Without Love* (1968), *Engelbert* (1969), *Engelbert Humperdinck* (1969), *We Made It Happen* (1970), *Another TIme, Another Place* (1971), *Live At The Riviera* (1972), *Engelbert Humperdinck - His Greatest Hits* (1974), *Getting Sentimental* (1975), *Remember I Love You* (1987), *The Engelbert Humperdinck Collection* (1987).

Englebert Humperdinck

inspired by the composer of Hansel And Gretel, and relaunched as a balladeer. His first single for Decca 'Dommage Dommage' failed to chart, but received considerable airplay. There was no mistake with the follow-up, 'Release Me', which sold a million copies in the UK alone, dominated the number 1 spot for five weeks and, most remarkably, prevented the Beatles from reaching the top with the magnificent 'Penny Lane'/'Strawberry Fields Forever'. Humperdinck's follow-up 'There Goes My Everything' climbed to number 2 in the UK and by the end of the summer he was back at the top for a further five weeks with 'The Last Waltz'. The latter once again sold in excess of a million copies in the UK alone. In a year dominated by psychedelia and experimentation in rock, Humperdinck was the biggest selling artist in England. His strong vocal and romantic image ensured regular bookings and brought a further series of UK Top 10 hits including 'Am I That Easy To Forget', 'A Man Without Love', 'Les Bicyclettes De Belsize', 'The Way It Used To Be' and 'Winter World Of Love'. Although he faded as a hit-making artist after the early 70s, his career blossomed in America where he was a regular on the lucrative Las Vegas circuit. Like his stablemate Tom Jones he went through a long period without recording, which ended in 1987 with the release of a comeback album, *Remember I Love You*, which

Brian Hyland

Hyland, Brian

b. 12 November 1943, Woodhaven, Queens, New York, USA. A demonstration disc, recorded with the artist's high-school group the Delphis, alerted Kapp Records to Hyland's vocal talent. In 1960 he enjoyed a US chart topper with 'Itsy Bitsy Teenie Weenie Yellow Polkadot Bikini', one of the era's best-known 'novelty' recordings which subsequently sold over one million copies. Having switched outlets to the larger ABC Paramount, the singer enjoyed further success with 'Let Me Belong To You (1961 - a US Top 20 hit) 'Ginny Come Lately' (1962 - a UK Top 10 hit), before securing a second gold award for 'Sealed With a Kiss'. Its theme of temporary parting was empathetic to the plight of many lovestruck teenagers and the song returned to the UK Top 10 in 1975 before being revived in 1990 by Jason Donovan. Hyland continued to enjoy US chart entries, notably with 'The Joker Went Wild' and

'Run, Run, Look And See' (both 1966), but reasserted his career in 1970 with a sympathetic version of the Impressions' 'Gypsy Woman'. This third million-seller was produced by long-time friend Del Shannon, who co-wrote several tracks on the attendant album, but this rekindled success proved shortlived and the artist later ceased recording.

Albums: *The Bashful Blonde* (1960), *Let Me Belong To You* (1961), *Sealed With A Kiss* (1962), *Country Meets Folk* (1964), *Here's To Our Love* (1964), *Rockin' Folk* (1965), *The Joker Went Wild* (1966), *Tragedy* (1969), *Stay And Love Me All Summer* (1969), *Brian Hyland* (1970). Compilations: *Golden Decade 1960-1970* (1988), *Ginny O Ginny* (1988).

I

Idle Race

Dave Pritchard (guitar), Greg Masters (bass) and Roger Spencer (drums) spent several years in the Nightriders, backing Birmingham singer Mike Sheridan. Their frontman left for a solo career in 1966, but with the addition of guitarist/composer Jeff Lynne (b. 30 December 1947, Birmingham, West Midlands, England), the restructured group embarked on an enthralling, independent direction. The quartet took the name the Idle Race in the wake of an unsuccessful debut single released under their former appellation. By 1967 Lynne had become the unit's focal point, contributing the bulk of their original material and shaping its sound and direction. *The Birthday Party* showcased his gift for melody and quirky sense of humour, facets prevalent in two of its undoubted highlights, 'Follow Me Follow' and 'The Skeleton And The Roundabout'. The guitarist's grasp on the group was strengthened with their second album, *Idle Race*, which he produced. This evocative selection featured some of Lynne's finest compositions, many of which bore a debt to the Beatles, but without seeming plagiaristic. Any potential, however, was bedevilled by public indifference. Repeated overtures to join the Move ultimately proved too strong for Lynne to ignore. Highly commercial pop songs like 'Come With Me' and 'At The End Of The Road' surprisingly failed to become hits.

Lynne's departure in January 1970 to form the Electric Light Orchestra precipitated several changes. Pritchard, Masters and Spencer drafted Mike Hopkins and Roy Collum into the line-up, the latter of whom

was then replaced by Dave Walker. This reshaped quintet was responsible for *Time Is*, a progressive rock collection at odds with the erstwhile unit's simple pop. Walker then left for Savoy Brown and his place was taken by Birmingham veteran Steve Gibbons. Founder members Pritchard and Spencer abandoned their creation, Bob Lamb and Bob Wilson from Tea And Symphony joined, before a third member of that august ensemble, Dave Carroll, replaced Mike Hopkins. When Greg Masters quit the Idle Race in 1971, their link with the past was finally severed and the group became known as the Steve Gibbons Band.

Albums: *The Birthday Party* (1968), *Idle Race* (1969), *Time Is* (1971). Compilations: *Imposters Of Life's Magazine* (1976), *Light At The End Of The Road* (1985).

Frank Ifield

Ifield, Frank

b. 30 November 1936, Coventry, Warwickshire, England. The most successful recording artist in the UK during the early 60s, Ifield is now also one of the most underrated. At the age of nine, his family emigrated to Australia, and Ifield entered show business during his teens. He first came to prominence in Australia during 1957 with 'Whiplash', a song about the 1851 Australian goldrush which was later used as the theme for a long-running television series. After returning to England in the late 50s, Ifield was signed to the EMI subsidiary Columbia Records and soon found success working with producer Norrie Paramor. After scoring minor hits with 'Lucky Devil' and 'Gotta Get A Date', he broke through spectacularly with the chart-topping 'I Remember You'. The song had a wonderfully elegiac feel, complemented by Ifield's relaxed vocal and a pleasing harmonica break. The track dominated the UK chart listings staying at number 1 for a staggering seven weeks and was the first record ever to sell a million copies in England alone. The song also charted in America, a rare feat for a British-based singer in the early 60s. Late in 1962, Ifield was back at the top of the UK charts for a further five weeks with 'Lovesick Blues', which betrayed his love of C&W and emphasized his extraordinary ability as a yodeller. His engaging falsetto became something of a trademark, which differentiated him from other UK vocalists of the period. A revival of Gogi Grant's 'The Wayward Wind' put Ifield into the record books. No artist in British pop history had ever logged three consecutive number 1 records before, but during February 1963 Ifield achieved that honour. Ironically, he shared the number 1 spot jointly with the Beatles' 'Please Please Me', and it was their abrupt rise that year which tolled the death knell for Ifield as a regular chart contender. He secured a fourth UK number 1 with the breezy 'Confessin''. Thereafter, the material chosen for him seemed weaker and his chart career atrophied. He became the most celebrated victim of the beat boom that was sweeping the UK and never regained the seemingly unassailable position that he enjoyed in the early 60s. He continued his career, playing regularly in pantomime and in stage productions like *Up Jumped A Swagman*, before reverting to cabaret work. In the 90s following lengthy bouts of ill health, Ifield was residing in Cornwall and performing only occasionally.

Selected albums: *I'll Remember You* (1963), *Born Free* (1963), *Blue Skies* (1964), *Greatest Hits* (1964).

Impressions

Formed in Chicago in 1957 and originally known as the Roosters, this group comprised Jerry Butler (b. 8 December 1939, Sunflower, Mississippi, USA), Curtis Mayfield (b. 3 June 1942, Chicago, Illinois, USA), Sam Gooden (b. 2 September 1939, Chattanooga, Tennessee, USA), and brothers Richard Brooks and Arthur Brooks (both born Chattanooga, Tennessee, USA). Curtis Mayfield and Jerry Butler first met in the choir of the Travelling Soul Spiritualists Church, from where they formed the Modern Jubilaires and Northern Jubilee Singers. The two teenagers then drifted apart, and while Curtis was involved in another group, the Alphatones, Butler joined Gooden and the Brooks brothers in the Roosters. Mayfield was subsequently

installed as their guitarist. Dubbed the Impressions by their manager, the group's first single for Abner/Falcon, 'For Your Precious Love', was a gorgeous ballad and substantial hit, reaching number 11 in the US pop chart in 1958. The label credit, which read 'Jerry Butler And The Impressions', caused internal friction and the two sides split after one more release. While Butler's solo career gradually prospered, that of his erstwhile colleagues floundered. He and Mayfield were later reconciled on Jerry's 1960 single, 'He Will Break Your Heart', the success of which, and other Curtis-penned songs, rekindled the Impressions' career. Signed to ABC-Paramount in 1961, they scored a hit with the haunting 'Gypsy Woman'. Subsequent releases were less well received until 'It's All Right' (1963) soared to number 1 in the R&B chart and to number 4 in pop chart. The group was now a trio of Mayfield, Gooden and Fred Cash, and their rhythmic harmonies were set against Johnny Pate's stylish arrangements. Magnificent records – including 'I'm So Proud', 'Keep On Pushing', 'You Must Believe Me' (all 1964) and 'People Get Ready' (1965) – showed how Mayfield was growing as an incisive composer, creating lyrical songs which were alternately poignant and dynamic. During this period the Impressions scored what was to be their last US pop Top 10 hit, 'Amen', which was featured in the film *Lilies Of The Field*. Mayfield then set up two short-lived record companies, Windy C, in 1966 and Mayfield, in 1967. However, it was the singer's third venture, Curtom, which proved most durable. In the meantime, the Impressions had emerged from a period when Motown had provided their prime influence. 'You Been Cheatin'' (1965) and 'You Always Hurt Me' (1967), however good in themselves, lacked the subtlety of their predecessors, but were part of a transition in Mayfield's musical perceptions. Statements, previously implicit, would be granted a much more open forum. 'This Is My Country' (1968), 'Mighty Mighty Spade And Whitey' (1969) and 'Check Out Your Mind' (1970) were tougher, politically-based performances, while his final album with the group, the quintessential *Young Mod's Forgotten Story*, set the framework for his solo work. Mayfield's replacement, Leroy Hutson, left in 1973. Reggie Torian and Ralph Johnson were subsequently added, and the new line-up topped the R&B chart in 1974 with 'Finally Got Myself Together (I'm A Changed Man)'. 'First Impressions' (1975) became their only British hit, but the following year Johnson left. Although Mayfield, Butler, Cash and Gooden have, on occasions, reformed, the latter pair have also kept their version of the Impressions active.

Albums: *The Impressions* (1963), *The Never Ending Impressions* (1964), *Keep On Pushing* (1964), *People Get Ready* (1965), *One By One* (1965), *Riding High*

(1966), *The Fabulous Impressions* (1967), *We're A Winner* (1968), *This Is My Country* (1968), *The Versatile Impressions* (1969), *The Young Mod's Forgotten Story* (1969), *Check Out Your Mind* (1970), *Times Have Changed* (1972), *Preacher Man* (1973), *Finally Got Myself Together* (1974), *Three The Hard Way* (1974), *First Impressions* (1975), *It's About Time* (1976), *Loving Power* (1976), *Come To My Party* (1979), *Fan The Fire* (1981). Compilations: *The Impressions Greatest Hits* (1965), *The Best Of The Impressions* (1968), *Your Precious Love* (1981).

Incredible String Band

This UK folk group was formed in 1965 in Glasgow, Scotland, at 'Clive's Incredible Folk Club' by Mike Heron (b. 12 December 1942, Glasgow, Scotland), Robin Williamson (b. 24 November 1943, Edinburgh, Scotland) and Clive Palmer (b. Glasgow, Scotland). In 1966 the trio completed *The Incredible String Band*, a collection marked by an exceptional blend of traditional and original material, but they split up upon its completion. Heron and Williamson regrouped the following year to record the exceptional *5000 Spirits Or The Layers Of The Onion*. On this the duo emerged as a unique and versatile talent, employing a variety of exotic instruments to enhance their global folk palate. Its several highlights included Mike's 'Painting Box' and two of Robin's most evocative compositions, 'Way Back In The 1960s' and 'First Girl I Loved'. The latter was later recorded by Judy Collins. A *de rigueur* psychedelic cover encapsulated the era and the pair were adopted by the emergent underground. Two further releases, *The Hangman's Beautiful Daughter* and *Wee Tam And The Big Huge*, consolidated their position and saw Williamson, in particular, contribute several lengthy, memorable compositions. *Changing Horses*, as its title implies, reflected a growing restlessness with the acoustic format and the promotion of two previously auxiliary members, Licorice McKechnie (harp/violin/percussion) and Rose Simpson (bass/violin/percussion), indicated a move to a much fuller sound. The album polarized aficionados with many lamenting the loss of an erstwhile charm and idealism. *I Looked Up* continued the transformation to a rock-based perspective although *U*, the soundtrack to an ambitious ballet-cum-pantomime, reflected something of their earlier charm. 1971's *Liquid Acrobat As Regards The Air* was stylistically diverse and elegiac in tone. Dancer-turned-musician Malcolm Le Maistre was introduced to the group's circle and, with the departure of both Rose and Licorice, a keyboard player, Gerald Dott, joined the String Band for *Earthspan*. By this point the group owed little to the style of the previous decade although Williamson's solo, *Myrrh*, invoked the atmosphere of *Wee Tam* rather than the apologetic rock of *No Ruinous Feud*. The two founding members were becoming estranged both musically and socially and in 1974 they announced the formal end of their partnership.

Albums: *The Incredible String Band* (1966), *5000 Spirits Or The Layers Of The Onion* (1967), *The Hangman's Beautiful Daughter* (1968), *Wee Tam And The Big Huge* (1968), *Changing Horses* (1969), *I Looked Up* (1970), *U* (1970), *Be Glad For The Song Has No Ending* (1970), *Liquid Acrobat As Regards The Air* (1971), *Earthspan* (1972), *No Ruinous Feud* (1973), *Hard Rope And Silken Twine* (1974), *On Air* (1991 - rare BBC recordings). Compilations: *Relics Of The Incredible String Band* (1970), *Seasons They Change* (1976).

Iron Butterfly

During the progressive music revolution in the late 60s one of the most surprising successes was that of Iron Butterfly. They arguably invented the term 'heavy' music following the release of their debut in 1968. The band was formed by Doug Ingle (b. 9 September 1947, Omaha, Nebraska, USA; organ/vocals) who added Ron Bushy (b. 23 September 1941, Washington DC, USA; drums), Eric Brann (b. 10 August 1950, Boston, Massachusetts, USA; guitar), Lee Dorman (b. 19 September 1945, St. Louis, Missouri, USA; bass/vocals) and briefly Danny Weiss. Their second release *In-A-Gadda-Da-Vida* (In The Garden Of Eden) became a multi-million seller and was for a number of years the biggest selling record in Atlantic Records' catalogue. This 17-minute title number contained every ingredient that any late-progressive rock fan could want - it was manna from heaven: classical influenced organ with Indian undertones, solid beat, screeching guitar part, barbed-wire feedback and an overlong drum solo. It was magnificent then, but 20 years some critics might argue that it has not stood up well. The follow-up *Ball* was a similar though lesser success. This album contained a better collection of songs, notably, the invigorating 'It Must Be Love' and the subtle 'Soul Experience'. Brann departed after a poor live album and was replaced by two guitarists: Larry 'Rhino' Reinhardt (b. 7 July 1948, Florida, USA) and Mike Pinera (b. 29 September 1948, Florida, USA). No further success ensued. *Metamorphosis* was a confused collection recorded when the band was disintegrating. The band reformed in the mid-70s with two disappointing albums but Iron Butterfly ultimately suffered from an identity crisis.

Albums: *Heavy* (1968), *In-A-Gadda-da-Vida* (1968), *Ball* (1969), *Iron Butterfly Live* (1970), *Metamorphosis* (1970), *Scorching Beauty* (1975), *Sun And Steel* (1976). Compilations: *Evolution* (1971), *Star Collection* (1973).

Irwin, Big Dee

b. Defosca Erwin, 4 August 1939, New York City, New York, USA. The corpulent R&B singer first made his mark as lead for the doo-wop group, the Pastels, who hit with two sumptuous ballads, 'Been So Long' (1957) and 'So Far Away' (1958). As a solo artist, he is recalled for a series of tongue-in-cheek singles, the most successful of which was a version of the Bing Crosby hit 'Swingin' On A Star' in 1963, an irreverent performance on which he was joined by a perky, Little Eva. Irwin's other releases included 'Everybody's Got A Dance But Me', on which he begrudged the dance-based releases of other artists, and 'Happy Being Fat', where Eva, once again, provided the spiky interjections. Irwin later enjoyed intermittent success as a songwriter, including 'What Kind Of Boy', recorded on the Hollies' debut album.

Isley Brothers

Isley Brothers

Three brothers, O'Kelly (b. 25 December 1937, d. 31 March 1986), Rudolph (b. 1 April 1939) and Ronald Isley (b. 21 May 1941) began singing gospel in their hometown of Cincinnati, USA, in the early 50s, accompanied by their brother Vernon, who died in a car crash around 1957. Moving to New York the following year, the trio issued one-shot singles before being signed by the RCA Records production team, Hugo And Luigi. The Isleys had already developed a tight vocal unit, with Rudolph and O'Kelly supporting Ronald's strident tenor leads in a call-and-response style taken directly from the church. The self-composed 'Shout' - with a chorus based on an ad-libbed refrain which had won an enthusiastic response in concert - epitomised this approach, building to a frantic crescendo as the brothers screamed out to each other across the simple chord changes. 'Shout' sold heavily in the black market, and has since become an R&B standard, but RCA's attempts to concoct a suitable follow-up were unsuccessful. The group switched labels to Wand in 1962, where they scored a major hit with an equally dynamic cover of the Top Notes' 'Twist And Shout',

an arrangement that was subsequently copied by the Beatles. In the fashion of the times, the Isleys were forced to spend the next two years recording increasingly contrived rewrites of this hit, both on Wand and at United Artists. A brief spell with Atlantic in 1964 produced a classic R&B record, 'Who's That Lady?', but with little success. Tired of the lack of control over their recordings, the Isleys formed their own company, T-Neck Records, in 1964 - an unprecedented step for black performers. The first release on the label, 'Testify', showcased their young lead guitarist, Jimi Hendrix, and allowed him free rein to display his virtuosity and range of sonic effects. But the record's experimental sound went unnoticed at the time, and the Isleys were forced to abandon both T-Neck and Hendrix, and sign a deal with Motown. They were allowed little involvement in the production of their records and the group were teamed with the Holland/Dozier/Holland partnership, who effectively treated them as an extension of the Four Tops, and fashioned songs for them accordingly. This combination reached its zenith with 'This Old Heart Of Mine' in 1966, a major hit in the USA, and a belated chart success in Britain in 1968. UK listeners also reacted favourably to 'Behind A Painted Smile' and 'I Guess I'll Always Love You' when they were reissued at the end of the 60s. Such singles were definitive Motown; a driving beat, an immaculate houseband and several impassioned voices. But although the Isleys' records always boasted a tougher edge than those by their stablemates, little of their work for Motown exploited their gospel and R&B heritage to the full.

Tired of the formula and company power games, the Isley's reactivated T-Neck in 1969 along with a change of image from the regulation mohair suits to a freer, funkier 'west coast' image, reflected in their choice of repertoire. At this point too, they became a sextet, adding two younger brothers, Ernie (b. 7 March 1952; guitar) and Marvin (bass) as well as a cousin, Chris Jasper (keyboards). While their mid-60s recordings were enjoying overdue success in Britain, the Isleys were scoring enormous US hits with their new releases, notably 'It's Your Thing' and 'I Turned You On'. These records sported a stripped-down funk sound, inspired by James Brown And The JBs, and topped with the brothers' soaring vocal harmonies. They issued a succession of ambitious albums in this vein between 1969 and 1972, among them a live double set which featured extended versions of their recent hits, and *In The Beginning*, a collection of their 1964 recordings with Jimi Hendrix.

In the early 70s, the Isleys incorporated a variety of rock material by composers like Bob Dylan, Stephen Stills and Carole King into their repertoire. Their dual role as composers and interpreters reached a peak in 1973 on *3+3*, the first album issued via a distribution deal with CBS Records. The record's title reflected the current make-up of the group, with the three original vocalists supported by a new generation of the family, Ernie (guitar/drums), Marvin and Chris Jasper. Ernie Isley's powerful, sustained guitarwork, strongly influenced by Jimi Hendrix, became a vital ingredient in the Isleys' sound, and was featured heavily on the album's lead single, 'That Lady', a revamped version of their unheralded 1964 single on Atlantic. *3+3* also contained soft soul interpretations of material by Seals And Croft, James Taylor and the Doobie Brothers. An important key track was the Isleys' own 'Highway Of My Life', which demonstrated Ronald's increasing mastery of the romantic ballad form.

Having established a winning formula, the Isleys retained it through the rest of the 70s, issuing a succession of slick, impressive soul albums which were divided between startlingly tough funk numbers and subdued Ronald Isley ballads. *The Heat Is On* in 1975 represented the pinnacle of both genres: the angry lyrics of 'Fight The Power', a US Top 10 single, contrasted sharply with the suite of love songs on the album's second side, aptly summarised by the title of one of the tracks, 'Sensuality'. 'Harvest For The World' (1976) proved to be one of the Isleys' most popular recordings in Britain, with its stunning blend of dance rhythm, melody and social awareness. This song hit the charts in 1988 with the Christians. In the late 70s, the increasing polarization of the rock and disco markets ensured that while the Isleys continued to impress black record buyers, their work went largely unheard in the white mainstream. 'The Pride', 'Take Me To The Next Phase', 'I Wanna Be With You' and 'Don't Say Goodnight' all topped the specialist black music charts without registering in the US Top 30, and the group responded in kind, concentrating on dance-flavoured material to the exclusion of their ballads. 'It's A Disco Night', a UK hit in 1980, demonstrated their command of the idiom, but a growing sense of self-parody infected the Isleys' music in the early 80s. Conscious of this decline, Ernie and Marvin Isley and Chris Jasper left the group in 1984 to form the successful Isley/Jasper/Isley combination. The original trio soldiered on, but the sudden death of O'Kelly Isley from a heart attack on 31 March 1986 brought their 30-year partnership to an end. Ronald and Rudolph dedicated their next release, *Smooth Sailin'*, to him, and the album produced another black hit in Angela Wimbush's ballad, 'Smooth Sailin' Tonight'. Wimbush now assumed virtual artistic control over the group, and she wrote and produced their 1989 release *Spend The Night,* which was effectively a Ronald Isley solo album. In 1986 the Housemartins

had a UK number 1 hit with 'Caravan Of Love'. The artistic innovations of the Isley Brothers, continued by the second generation of the family in Isley/Jasper/Isley, belie the conservatism of their releases since the late 70s. The group represented the apogee of gospel-inspired soul on their early hits; pioneered the ownership of record labels by black artists; and invented a new funk genre with their blend of dance rhythms and rock instrumentation in the early 70s. Their series of US hits from the 50s to the 90s is one of the major legacies of black American music.

Albums: *Shout* (1959), *Twist And Shout* (1962), *The Fabulous Isley Brothers - Twisting And Shouting* (1964), *Take Some Time Out - The Famous Isley Brothers* (1964), *This Old Heart Of Mine* (1966), *Soul On The Rocks* (1967), *It's Our Thing* (1969), *Doin' Their Thing* (1969), *The Brothers Isley* (1969), *Live At Yankee Stadium* (1969), *Get Into Something* (1970), *In The Beginning* (1970), *Givin' It Back* (1971), *Brother Brother Brother* (1972), *Live* (1972), *3+3* (1973), *Live It Up* (1974), *The Heat Is On* (1975), *Harvest For The World* (1976), *Go For Your Guns* (1977), *Showdown* (1978), *Winner Takes All* (1979), *Go All The Way* (1980), *Grand Slam* (1981), *Inside You* (1981), *The Real Deal* (1982), *Between The Sheets* (1983), *Masterpiece* (1985), *Smooth Sailin'* (1987), *Spend The Night* (1989). Selected compilations: credited to the Isley Brothers And Jimi Hendrix *In The Beginning* (1970), *Rock Around The Clock* (1975), *Super Hits* (1976), *Forever Gold* (1977), *The Best Of The Isley Brothers* (1978), *Timeless* (1979), *Let's Go* (1986), *Greatest Motown Hits* (1987).

It's A Beautiful Day

This San Francisco-based unit centred on the virtuoso skills of violinist David LaFlamme, formerly of Dan Hicks And His Hot Licks. Patti Santos (vocals), Hal Wagenet (guitar), Linda LaFlamme (keyboards), Mitchell Holman (bass) and Val Fluentes (drums) completed the line-up which won a major recording deal in the wake of its appearance on Cream's farewell concert bill. *It's A Beautiful Day* was marked by the inclusion of 'White Bird', the haunting opening track with which the act is inexorably linked. The instrumental 'Bombay Calling' and 'Wasted Union Blues' were other stand-out tracks. Elsewhere, a pot-pourri of musical styles revealed their undoubted versatility, a facet continued on *Marrying Maiden*. However, the appeal of the leader's extravagant soloing quickly paled as numerous departures undermined an early sense of purpose, rendering later releases, *Choice Quality Stuff* and *Live At Carnegie Hall* superfluous. LaFlamme later abandoned his creation as a protracted lawsuit with former manager Matthew Katz destroyed any lingering enthusiasm. Late period members Bud

Cockrell (bass) and David Jenkins (guitar) resurfaced in Pablo Cruise, while both LaFlamme and Santos enjoyed low-key solo careers. The violinist briefly resuscitated the band in 1978 under the sarcastic title It Was A Beautiful Day.

Albums: *It's A Beautiful Day* (1969, reissued as *1001 Nights* in 1974), *Marrying Maiden* (1970), *Choice Quality Stuff/Anytime* (1971), *It's A Beautiful Day At Carnegie Hall* (1972), *It's A Beautiful Day...Today* (1973). Compilations: *It's A Beautiful Day* (1979).

Ivy League

Formed in 1964, the Ivy League was an outlet for songwriters John Carter (b. John Shakespeare, 20 October 1942, Birmingham, England) and Ken Lewis (b. James Hawker, 3 December 1942, Birmingham, England). The duo's talent had been established through compositions for several acts, including Mike Sarne's UK novelty hit, 'Will I What', and their own beat group, Carter-Lewis And The Southerners, which featured guitarist Jimmy Page. Perry Ford (b. Bryan Pugh, 1940, Lincoln, England), a former member of Bert Weedon's backing band, completed the Ivy League line-up which scored three UK hits in 1965 with 'Funny How Love Can Be' (number 8), 'That's Why I'm Crying' (number 22) and 'Tossing And Turning' (number 3). Their close harmony, falsetto style was modelled on that of the Four Freshmen and Four Seasons and while obviously competent, grew increasingly out-of-step as contemporary pop progressed. The trio reached a creative peak with the atmospheric 'My World Fell Down', but John Carter was now tiring of his creation. Tony Burrows replaced him in 1966 and although Ken Lewis left the group several months later, Perry Ford remained at its helm until the end of the decade, fronting an ever changing line-up. By then, however, the Ivy League had been surpassed by newer Carter/Lewis projects including the Flowerpot Men and White Plains.

Albums: *This Is The Ivy League* (1965). Compilation: *The Best Of The Ivy League* (1988).

J

Jackson, Chuck

b. 22 July 1937, Latta, South Carolina, USA. Jackson travelled the traditional 50s route into soul music, via a spell in the gospel group, the Raspberry Singers. In 1957, he joined the hit doo-wop combo, the Dell-

Chuck Jackson

Vikings, taking a prominent role on their USA Top 10 success 'Whispering Bells'. His strong baritone vocals enabled him to launch a solo career with Beltone Records in 1960, before signing to the more prestigious Wand label the following year. Jackson's early 60s singles for Wand epitomized the New York uptown soul style, with sophisticated arrangements - often crafted by Burt Bacharach - supporting his sturdy vocals with female vocalists and orchestras. He enjoyed enormous success in the R&B market for several years with a run of hits which have become soul classics, like 'I Don't Want To Cry', 'I Wake Up Crying', 'Any Day Now' and 'Tell Him I'm Not Home', though only the majestic 'Any Day Now', co-written by Bacharach, crossed into the USA Top 30. In 1965 he was teamed with Maxine Brown on a revival of Chris Kenner's R&B favourite, 'Something You Got', the first of three hit duets over the next two years. Their partnership was severed in 1967 when Jackson joined Motown, a decision he later described as 'one of the worst mistakes I ever made in my life'. Although he notched up a minor hit with Freddie Scott's 'Are You Lonely For Me Baby?' in 1969, the majority of his Motown recordings found him pitched against unsympathetic backdrops in a vain attempt to force him into the label's formula. Jackson left Motown in 1971 for ABC, where again he could muster just one small hit, 'I Only Get This

Feeling' in 1973. Another switch of labels, to All-Platinum in 1975, produced the chart entry 'I'm Wanting You, I'm Needing You' in his traditional style. In 1980, he joined EMI America, where his most prominent role was as guest vocalist on two hit albums by Gary 'U.S.' Bonds. In the late 80s Jackson was one of many ex-Motown artists signed to Ian Levine's Motor City label, with whom he released two singles.

Albums: I Don't Want To Cry (1961), Any Day Now (1962), Encore (1963), Chuck Jackson On Tour (1964), Mr Everything (1965), with Maxine Brown Saying Something (1965), A Tribute To Rhythm And Blues (1966), A Tribute To Rhythm And Blues Vol. 2 (1966), with Maxine Brown Hold On We're Coming (1966), Dedicated To The King (1966), album split with Tammi Terrell The Early Show (1967), Chuck Jackson Arrives (1968), Goin' Back To Chuck Jackson (1969), Teardrops Keep Falling On My Heart (1970), Through All Times (1974), Needing You, Wanting You (1975), The Great Chuck Jackson (1977), I Wanna Give You Some Love (1980). Compilations: Mr. Emotion (1985), A Powerful Soul (1987).

Jackson, Deon

b. 26 January 1946, Ann Arbor, Michigan, USA. This versatile performer was discovered by producer Ollie McLaughlin, who also guided the careers of Del Shannon and Barbara Lewis. An accomplished drummer and clarinettist, Jackson established himself as a singer and composer with 'Love Makes The World Go Round', a smooth, melodic mid-tempo single which reached the US R&B Top 3 and peaked at number 11 in the US pop chart in 1966. Despite undoubted promise, Jackson was only able to secure two further chart entries when 'Love Takes A Long Time Growing' (1966) and 'Ooh Baby' (1967) only managed to scrape in at the lower regions of the charts. From there this talented musician's career faded and Jackson now makes a living playing cocktail lounge and nightclub piano spots.

Album: Love Makes The World Go Round (1966). Compilation: His Greatest Recordings (1984).

Jackson, Wanda

b. Wanda Jean Jackson, 20 October 1937, Maud, Oklahoma, USA. Jackson started her career as one of the rawest of female rockabilly singers before going on to successful work in both country and gospel music. Her family moved to California when she was four, settling in the city of Bakersfield, but moved back to Oklahoma when she was 12. There Jackson won a talent contest which led to her own radio programme. Country singer Hank Thompson liked her style and hired her to tour with his band. In 1954 Jackson signed to Decca Records, recording 15 country tracks; one of which, 'You Can't Have My

Love', a duet with Billy Gray, made the country Top 10. The following year Jackson joined Red Foley's touring company and met Elvis Presley. He advised her to change her style to the new rock 'n' roll. When she signed with Capitol Records in 1956, she recorded a number of singles, one side of each a rocker, the other a honky-tonk country number. Only one of these rockabilly records, 'I Gotta Know', made the country charts, but her other recordings for Capitol, such as 'Honey Bop', 'Fujiyama Mama' and 'Hot Dog That Made Him Mad', are prized by collectors decades later. Only one, 'Let's Have A Party', earlier recorded by Elvis, made the US pop charts when Capitol belatedly released it in 1960. Backed by the Blue Caps, this song is delivered in raucus style and it remains an extraordinary vocal delivery. That same year Jackson chose to stay with country and recorded her own composition, 'Right Or Wrong', which has since become a hit for both Ronnie Dove and George Strait. 'Right Or Wrong' and 'In The Middle Of a Heartache' became the last of Jackson's Top 10 country songs in 1961-62, although she placed 30 singles in that chart in total. She recorded nearly two dozen albums for Capitol in the 60s. By the early 70s Jackson began recording Christian music for Capitol and later the Word and Myrrh labels, returning to rock 'n' roll for one album, Rock 'N' Roll Away Your Blues, in 1984.

Selected albums: Wanda Jackson (1958), Rockin' With Wanda (1960), There's A Party Goin' On (1961), Right Or Wrong (1961), Lovin' Country Style (1962), Wonderful Wanda (1962), Love Me Forever (1963), Two Sides Of Wanda Jackson (1964), Blues In My Heart (1964), Wanda Jackson Sings Country Songs (1966), Salutes The Country Music Hall Of Fame (1966), Reckless Love Affair (1967), You'll Always Have My Love (1967), The Best Of Wanda Jackson (1967), Cream Of The Crop (1968), The Happy Side Of... (1969), Closer To Jesus (1967), In Person At Mr. Lucky's In Phoenix, Arizona (1969), Many Moods Of... (1969), Country! (1970), Woman Lives For Love (1970), I've Gotta Sing (1971), I Wouldn't Want You Any Other Way (1972), Praise The Lord (1972), When It's Time To Fall In Love Again (1973), Country Keepsakes (1973), Now I Have Everything (1974), Rock 'N' Roll Away Your Blues (1984), Her Greatest Country Hits (1985), Early Wanda Jackson (1986), Rockin' In The Country: The Best Of... (1990).

Jackson Five

The Jackson Five comprised of five brothers, Jackie (b. Sigmund Esco Jackson, 4 May 1951), Tito (b. Toriano Adaryll Jackson, 15 October 1953), Jermaine (b. 11 December 1954), Marlon (b. 12 March 1957) and Michael Jackson (b. 29 August 1958). Raised in Gary, Indiana, USA, by their father Joe, a blues guitarist, they began playing local clubs in 1962, with youthful prodigy Michael as lead vocalist. Combining dance routines influenced by the Temptations with music inspired by James Brown, they first recorded for the Indiana-based Steeltown label before auditioning for Motown Records in 1968. Bobby Taylor recommended the group to Motown, although the company gave Diana Ross public credit for their discovery. A team of Motown writers known as the Corporation composed a series of songs for the group's early releases, all accentuating their youthful enthusiasm and vocal interplay. Their debut single for Motown, 'I Want You Back', became the fastest-selling record in the company's history in 1969, and three of their next five singles also topped the American chart. Michael Jackson was groomed for a simultaneous solo recording career, which began in 1971, followed by similar excursions for Jermaine and elder brother Jackie. As the group's appeal broadened, they became the subjects of a cartoon series on American television, *The Jackson 5*, and hosted a television special, *Goin' Back To Indiana*.

After the dissolution of the Corporation in 1971, the group recorded revivals of pop and R&B hits from the 50s, and cover versions of other Motown standards, before being allowed to branch out into more diverse material, such as Jackson Browne's 'Doctor My Eyes'. They also began to record their own compositions in the early 70s, a trend which continued until 1975, by which time they were writing and producing most of the songs on their albums.

The Jackson Five reached the peak of their popularity in Britain when they toured there in 1972, but after returning to America they suffered decreasing record sales as their music grew more sophisticated. By 1973, they had dropped the teenage stylings of their early hits, concentrating on a cabaret approach to their live performances while on record they perfected a harder brand of funk. The group's recording contract with Motown expired in 1975. Feeling that the label had not been promoting their recent records, they signed to Epic Records. Jermaine Jackson, however, who was married to the daughter of Motown boss Berry Gordy, chose to leave the group and remain with the company as a solo artist. Gordy sued the Jackson Five for alleged breach of contract in 1976, and the group were forced to change their name to the Jacksons. The case was settled in 1980, with the brothers paying Gordy $600,000, and allowing Motown all rights to the 'Jackson Five' name.

Albums: *Diana Ross Presents The Jackson 5* (1969), *ABC* (1970), *Third Album* (1970), *Christmas Album* (1970), *Maybe Tomorrow* (1971), *Goin' Back To Indiana* (1971), *Lookin' Through The Windows* (1972), *Skywriter* (1973), *Get It Together* (1973), *Dancing Machine* (1974), *Moving Vibrations* (1975), *Anthology* (1976), *Joyful Jukebox Music* (1976). Compilation: *Greatest Hits* (1971).

James, Etta

b. Jamesetta Hawkins, 25 January 1938, Los Angeles, California, USA. James's introduction to performing followed an impromptu audition for Johnny Otis, backstage at San Francisco's Fillmore Auditorium. 'Roll With Me Henry', her 'answer' to the Hank Ballard hit, 'Work With Me Annie', was re-titled 'The Wallflower' in an effort to disguise its risqué lyric and became an R&B number 1. 'Good Rockin' Daddy' provided another hit, but the singer's later releases failed to chart. Having secured a deal with the Chess group of labels, James unleashed a series of powerful songs including 'All I Could Do Was Cry' (1960), 'Stop The Wedding' (1962) and 'Pushover' (1963). She also recorded several duets with Harvey Fuqua. Heroin addiction sadly blighted both her personal and professional life, but in 1968 Chess took her to the Fame studios. The resultant *Tell Mama*, was a triumph, and pitted James's abrasive voice with the exemplary Muscle Shoals houseband. Its highlights included the proclamatory title track, a pounding version of Otis Redding's 'Security' (both of which reached the R&B Top 20) and the despairing 'I'd Rather Go Blind', which was later a Top 20 UK hit for Chicken Shack. The 1973 album *Etta James* earned her a US Grammy nomination, despite her continued drug problems, something she would not overcome until the mid-80s. A 1977 album, *Etta Is Betta Than Evah*, completed her Chess contract, and she moved to Warner Brothers. *Deep In The Night*, was a critics' favourite. A live album, *Late Show*, released in 1986, featured Shuggie Otis and Eddie 'Cleanhead' Vinson. A renewed public profile followed her appearance at the opening ceremony of the Los Angeles Olympics in 1988 and was followed by *Seven Year Itch*, her first album for Island Records in 1989. This, and the subsequent release, *Stickin' To My Guns*, found her back on form, aided and abetted once more by the Muscle Shoals team.

Albums: *At Last!* (1961), *Second Time Around* (1961), *Etta James* (1962), *Etta James Sings For Lovers* (1962), *Etta James Rocks The House* (1964), *Queen Of Soul* (1965), *Tell Mama* (1968), *Etta James Sings Funk* (1970), *Losers Weepers* (1971), *Etta James* (1973), *Come A Little Closer* (1974), *Etta Is Betta Than Evah!* (1978), *Deep In The Night* (1978), *Changes* (1980), *Good Rockin' Mama* (1981), *Tuff Lover* (1983), *Blues In The Night* (1986), *Late Show* (1986), *Seven Year Itch* (1989), *Stickin' To My Guns* (1990). Compilations: *Etta James Top Ten* (1963), *Peaches* (1973), *Good Rockin' Mama* (1981), *Chess Masters* (1981), *Tuff Lover* (1983), *R&B Queen* (1986), *Her Greatest Sides, Volume One* (1987), *R&B Dynamite* (1987), *Chicago Golden Years* (1988), *On Chess* (1988).

James, Jimmy, And The Vagabonds

Jimmy James (b. September 1940, Jamaica), enjoyed local success with two self-composed singles, 'Bewildered And Blue' and 'Come Softly To Me', before arriving in England in 1964. He joined the multi-racial Vagabonds - Wallace Wilson (lead guitar), Carl Noel (organ), Matt Fredericks (tenor saxophone), Milton James (baritone saxophone), Phillip Chen (bass), Rupert Balgobin (drums) and Count Prince Miller (vocals/MC) - and the new unit became a leading attraction at UK soul venues during the 60s. The group was managed and produced by the early Who mentor, Peter Meaden. Although they failed to secure a substantial chart hit, the Vagabonds' early albums were impressive, infectious re-interpretations of contemporary releases, featuring material by the Impressions, the Miracles and Bobby Bland. Such a function, however enthusiastic, lost its impetus when the original artists gained popular acclaim. 'Red Red Wine' gave the group a belated, if minor, success in 1968, but the unit was latterly dubbed *passé*. Chen later enjoyed a fruitful association with Rod Stewart, while James scored two hits in 1976 alongside another set of Vagabonds with 'I'll Go Where The Music Takes Me' and 'Now Is The Time', the latter of which reached the UK Top 5. The singer has since pursued a career as a cabaret attraction.

Albums: *The New Religion* (1966), *Open Up Your Soul* (1968), *London Swings* (1968, one side only), *You Don't Stand A Chance* (1975), *Now* (1976), *Life* (1977), *Dancin' Till Dawn* (1979). Compilations: *This Is Jimmy James* (1968), *Golden Hour Of Jimmy James* (1979).

James, Tommy, And The Shondells

Tommy James formed his first group Tommy And The Tornadoes at the age of 13, by which time he had already recorded his debut single, 'Long Pony Tale'. The Shondells comprised of James, Larry Coverdale (guitar), Craig Villeneuve (keyboards), Larry Wright (bass) and Jim Payne (drums) and were assembled to fulfil weekend engagements, but they secured a deal with the local Snap label in 1962. Their first release, 'Hanky Panky', was a regional success, but a chance discovery four years later by Pittsburg disc jockey Bob Mack led to its becoming a national smash, selling in excess of 1 million copies. Now signed to the Roulette label, James assembled a new Shondells which, following defections, settled around a nucleus of Eddie Gray (guitar), Ronnie Rossman (keyboards), Mike Vale (bass) and Pete Lucia (drums). The addition of producer/songwriting team Ritchie Cordell and Bo Gentry resulted in a string of classic, neo-bubblegum hits, including 'I Think We're Alone Now', 'Mirage' (both gold discs from 1967) and 'Out Of The Blue' (1968). The

Tommy James And The Shondells

group's effortless grasp of hooklines and melody culminated with the pulsating 'Mony Mony' (1968), a UK number 1 which invoked the style of the classic garage-band era. James then assumed complete artistic control of his work, writing, arranging and producing the psychedelic-influenced 'Crimson And Clover'. This haunting, atmospheric piece, described by the singer as 'our second renaissance', topped the US chart and garnered sales of over five million copies. This desire to experiment continued with two further gold-selling singles, 'Sweet Cherry Wine', 'Crystal Blue Persuasion' (both 1969) and the album *Cellophane Symphony*. In 1970 the group and singer parted on amicable terms. The latter continued under the name Hog Heaven, while an exhausted James retired to a farm before launching a solo career. 'Draggin' The Line' (1971) provided a US Top 5 hit although subsequent releases from the early 70s failed to broach the Top 30. In 1980 the singer scored another million-seller with 'Three Times In Love', since when he has continued to record, albeit with less success. Tommy James And The Shondells' power was encapsulated in their danceability and bracing fusion of soulful voices, garage group riffs, effervescent pop and occasional bubblegum appeal. This pop pourri legacy was picked up by younger artists over a decade on when Joan Jett charted with 'Crimson And Clover' and both Billy Joel and

Tiffany took Shondells' covers back to number 1 in the US charts.

Albums: *Hanky Panky* (1966), *It's Only Love* (1967), *I Think We're Alone Now* (1967), *Gettin' Together* (1968), *Mony Mony* (1968), *Crimson & Clover* (1968), *Cellophane Symphony* (1969), *Travelin'* (1970). The Shondells solo: *Hog Heaven* (1971). Compilations: *Something Special! The Best Of Tommy James And The Shondells* (1968), *The Best Of Tommy James And The Shondells* (1969), *Anthology* (1990), *Tommy James: The Solo Recordings 1970-1981* (1991).

James Gang

Formed in 1967 in Cleveland, Ohio, USA, the embryonic James Gang comprised of Glenn Schwartz (guitar/vocals), Tom Kriss (bass/vocals) and Jim Fox (drums/vocals). Schwartz left in April 1969 to join Pacific Gas And Electric, but Joe Walsh proved a more than competent replacement. *Yer Album* blended group originals with excellent interpretations of material drawn from Buffalo Springfield ('Bluebird') and the Yardbirds ('Lost Women'). The group enjoyed the approbation of Pete Townshend, who admired their mature cross-section of British and 'west coast' rock. Kriss was replaced by Dale Peters for *The James Gang Rides Again*, an excellent, imaginative amalgamation of rock, melody and instrumental dexterity. Here Walsh emerged as the group's director, particularly on the second side which also marked his maturation as a songwriter. Keyboards were added to create a dense, yet more fluid sound as the group embraced themes drawn from country and classical music. *Thirds* was another highlight, including the excellent 'Walk Away', but when a retreat to hard rock proved unconvincing, Walsh quit to pursue solo ambitions. He later found fame as a member of the Eagles. Two Canadians - Roy Kenner (vocals) and Dom Troiano (guitar) - joined Fox and Peters for *Straight Shooter* and *Passin' Thru*, but both sets were viewed as disappointing. Troiano was then replaced by Tommy Bolin, formerly of Zephyr, whose exemplary technique provided new bite and purpose. *Bang*, which featured eight of the newcomer's songs, was a marked improvement, but still lacked the verve and conviction of the Walsh era. *Miami*, released in July 1974, coincided with Bolin's departure to Deep Purple, following which the James Gang was dissolved. The ever optimistic Fox and Peters resurrected the name the following year, adding Bubba Keith (vocals) and Richard Shack (guitar), but finally dropped the name following the undistinguished *Jesse Come Home*.

Albums: *Yer Album* (1969), *The James Gang Rides Again* (1970), *Thirds* (1971), *James Gang Live In Concert* (1971), *Straight Shooter* (1972), *Passin' Thru'* (1972), *Bang* (1973), *Miami* (1974), *Newborn* (1975),

Jesse Come Home (1976). Compilations: *The Best Of The James Gang Featuring Joe Walsh* (1973), *16 Greatest Hits* (1973), *The True Story Of The James Gang* (1987).

Jan And Dean

Jan And Dean

Jan Berry (b. 3 April 1941, Los Angeles, California, USA) and Dean Torrence (b. 10 March 1940, Los Angeles, California, USA). Students at Emerson Junior High School, Berry and Torrence began singing together on an informal basis. They formed an embryonic group, the Barons, with Bruce Johnston and Sandy Nelson, but its members gradually drifted away, leaving Jan, Dean and singer Arnie Ginsburg to plot a different course. The trio recorded 'Jennie Lee' in 1958. A homage to the subject of Ginsburg's affections, a local striptease artist, the single became a surprise hit, reaching number 8 in the US chart. Although featured on the song, Torrance was drafted prior to its success, and the pressing was credited to Jan And Arnie. Subsequent releases failed to achieve success and the pair split up. Berry and Torrance were reunited the following year. They completed several demos in Berry's makeshift studio and, having secured the production and management services of local entrepreneur Lou Adler, the reshaped duo enjoyed a Top 10 entry with 'Baby Talk'. Jan And Dean scored several minor hits over the ensuing four years until a 1963 release, 'Linda', heralded a departure in their style. Here the duo completed all the backing voices, while the lead was sung in falsetto. The sound was redolent of the Beach Boys and the two acts' immediate future became entwined.

Brian Wilson co-wrote 'Surf City', Jan And Dean's first number 1 hit. This glorious summer hit evokes fun, sunshine and 'two girls for every boy'.The Beach Boys' leader also made telling contributions to several other notable classics, including 'Drag City', 'Dead Man's Curve' and 'Ride The Wild Surf', although Berry's contribution as writer, and later producer, should not be underestimated. However, despite the promise of a television series, and a role in the film *Easy Come - Easy Go*, relations between he and Torrance became increasingly strained. Dean added fuel to the fire by singing lead on 'Barbara Ann', an international hit pulled from the informal *Beach Boys Party*. The exploitative 'Batman' single, released in January 1966, was the last session the pair recorded together. Within weeks Jan Berry had crashed his sports car receiving appalling injuries. He incurred severe brain damage, but although recovery was painfully slow, the singer did complete a handful of singles during the early 70s. Torrance, meanwhile, kept the Jan And Dean name alive with several new recordings, but failed to recapture the duo's erstwhile success and subsequently found his true vocation with his highly respected design company, Kittyhawk Graphics. However, the pair were reunited in 1978 when they undertook the support slot for that year's Beach Boys' tour.

Selected albums: *Jan And Dean* (1960), *Jan And Dean's Golden Hits* (1962), *Jan And Dean Take Linda Surfin'* (1963), *Surf City (And Other Swinging Cities)* (1963), *Drag City* (1964), *Dead Man's Curve/New Girl In School* (1964), *Ride The Wild Surf* (1964), *The Little Old Lady From Pasadena* (1964), *Golden Hits Volume 2* (1965), *Command Performance - Live In Person* (1965), *Folk 'N' Roll* (1966), *Filet Of Soul - A 'Live' One* (1966), *Jan And Dean Meet Batman* (1966), *Popsicle* (1966), *Save For A Rainy Day* (1967), *The Jan And Dean Anthology Album* (1971), *Gotta Take That One Last Ride* (1973), *Ride The Wild Surf (Hits From Surf City, USA)* (1976).

Jay, Peter, And The Jaywalkers

Originally based in East Anglia, England, the Jaywalkers - Peter Miller (lead guitar), Tony Webster (rhythm guitar), Mac McIntyre (tenor saxophone/flute), Lloyd Baker (piano/baritone saxophone), Geoff Moss (acoustic bass), Johnny Larke (electric bass), and Peter Jay (drums), pre-dated the British beat boom. They scored a minor hit in 1962 with 'Can Can 62', but despite an unquestioned competence, their rather stilted act became increasingly anachronistic. The group attempted a more contemporary image with several R&B-based releases, and in 1966 a restructured line-up emerged under the name Peter Jay And The New Jaywalkers. Now reduced to a quintet, the unit featured vocalist Terry Reid, but despite an impressive appearance on the Rolling Stones' UK tour, they disbanded by the end of that year.

Jay And The Americans

This New York-based act was formed in 1961 when former Mystics' vocalist John 'Jay' Traynor joined ex-Harbor Lites duo Kenny Rosenberg, aka Kenny Vance, and Sandy Yaguda, aka Sandy Deane. Howie Kane (b. Howard Kerschenbaum) completed the line-up which in turn secured a recording deal through the aegis of the songwriting and production team, Leiber And Stoller. Jay And The Americans scored a US Top 5 hit with their second single, the dramatic 'She Cried', but a series of misses exacerbated tension within the group and in 1962 Traynor left for a low-key solo career. Bereft of a lead vocalist, the remaining trio recruited David Black from the Empires. Dubbed 'Jay' to infer continuity, Black introduced fifth member Marty Saunders (guitar) to the line-up, and the following year established his new role with the powerful 'Only In America'. Initially intended for the Drifters, the song's optimism was thought hypocritical for a black act and the Americans' vocal was superimposed over the original backing track. In 1964 Artie Ripp assumed the production reins for the quintet's 'Come A Little Bit Closer', a US Top 3 entry. The following year the group was assigned to Gerry Granahan who in turn secured a greater degree of consistancy. 'Cara Mia', 'Some Enchanted Evening' and 'Sunday And Me', (the last named penned by Neil Diamond) all reached the US Top 20, and although 'Livin' Above Your Head' was less successful, this enthralling performance is now recognized as one of the unit's finest recordings. The quintet's brand of professional pop proved less popular as the 60s progressed although revivals of 'This Magic Moment' (1968) and 'Walkin' In The Rain' (1969) were US Top 20 hits. The latter featured the musical talents of Donald Fagen and Walter Becker, later of Steely Dan, but at that point members of the Americans' studio band. By the turn of the decade the unit's impetus was waning and with Vance embarking on solo recordings, Sanders writing and Deane producing, Jay Black was granted the rights to the group's name. Further recordings did ensue, but although chart entries have long since ended, he continues to perform on the nostalgia circuit.

Albums: *She Cried* (1962), *Jay And The Americans At The Cafe Wha?* (1963), *Come A Little Bit Closer* (1964), *Blockbusters* (1965), *Sunday And Me* (1966), *Livin' Above Your Head* (1966), *Wild, Wild Winter* (1966, film soundtrack), *Try Some Of This* (1967),

Sands Of Time (1969), *Wax Museum* (1970). Compilations: *Jay And The Americans' Greatest Hits* (1965), *Very Best Of* (1979), *Jay And The Americans' Greatest Hits Volume Two* (1966), *Come A Little Bit Closer* (1990).

Jay And The Techniques

Formed in Allentown, Pennsylvania, USA in the mid-60s, Jay And The Techniques were an inter-racial pop group best known for the Top 10 debut single 'Apples, Peaches, Pumpkin Pie' in 1967. The group consisted of vocalist Jay Proctor and six other members: Karl Landis, Ronald Goosly, John Walsh, George Lloyd, Charles Crowl and Dante Dancho. The group built a following in the northeast and was discovered by producer Jerry Ross, who arranged to have them signed to Smash Records, a subsidiary of Mercury Records. 'Apples, Peaches, Pumpkin Pie', was their biggest hit, reaching number 6 in the US in 1967. 'Keep The Ball Rolling' was, like the first, based on a children's game, and it climbed to number 14. The formula held up for one further game-orientated single, 'Strawberry Shortcake', which scraped into the Top 40 in 1968. A final chart success, 'Baby Make Your Own Sweet Music', ended their run on the pop charts in 1968, but a revived Jay And The Techniques placed, 'Number Onederful', on the R&B charts in 1976, on Event Records. That was the group's swan song.
Albums: *Apples, Peaches, Pumpkin Pie* (1967), *Love, Lost & Found* (1968).

Jefferson Airplane

Along with the Grateful Dead, the Airplane are regarded as the most successful San Francisco band of the late 60s. The group were formed in 1965 by Marty Balin (b. Martyn Jerel Buchwald, 30 January 1942, Cincinnati, Ohio, USA; vocals/guitar). The other members in the original line-up were Paul Kantner (b. 17 March 1941, San Francisco, California, USA; guitar/vocals) and Jorma Kaukonen (b. 23 December 1940, Washington DC, USA; guitar/vocals). Bob Harvey and Jerry Peloquin gave way to Alexander 'Skip' Spence and Signe Anderson (b. Signe Toly Anderson, 15 September 1941 Seattle, Washington, USA). Their replacements; Spencer Dryden (b. 7 April 1938, New York, USA; drums) and Jack Casady (b. 13 April 1944, Washington DC, USA), made up a seminal band that blended folk and rock into what became known as west-coast rock. Kantner, already a familiar face on the local folk circuit and Balin formerly of the Town Criers and co-owner of the Matrix club, soon became highly popular locally, playing gigs and benefits organised by promoter Bill Graham. Eventually they became regulars at the Fillmore Auditorium and the Carousel Ballroom both a short distance from their communal home in the Haight Ashbury district. Anderson departed shortly after the release of their moderately successful debut *Takes Off* and was replaced by Grace Slick (b. Grace Barnett Wing, 30 October 1939, Chicago, Illinois, USA; vocals). Slick was already well known with her former band, the Great Society and donated two of their songs, 'White Rabbit' and 'Somebody To Love' to the Airplane. Both titles were on their second influential collection *Surrealistic Pillow*, and both became US Top 10 hits. They have now achieved classic status as definitive songs from that era. 'White Rabbit's' lyrics combined the harmless tale of *Alice In Wonderland* with an LSD trip. Their reputation was enhanced by a strong performance at the legendary Monterey Pop Festival in 1967. This national success continued with the erratic *After Bathing At Baxters* and the brilliant *Crown Of Creation*. The latter showed the various writers in the band maturing and developing their own styles. Balin's 'If You Feel', Kaukonen's 'Ice Cream Phoenix' and Slick's tragi-comic 'Lather' gave the record great variety. This album also contained 'Triad' a song their friend David Crosby had been unable to get on a Byrds album. They maintained a busy schedule and released a well-recorded live album *Bless Its Pointed Little Head* in 1969. The same year they appeared at another milestone in musical history; the Woodstock Festival. Later that year they were present at the infamous Altamont Festival, where a group of Hells Angels killed a young spectator and attacked Balin.

Slick and Kantner had now become lovers and their hippie ideals and political views were a major part of *Volunteers*. While it was an excellent album it marked the decline of Balin's presence in the band. Additionally, Dryden departed and the offshoot Hot Tuna began to take up more of Casady and Kaukonen's time. Kantner released a concept album *Blows Against The Empire*, bearing the name, Paul Kantner And The Jefferson Starship. The 'Starship' consisted of various Airplane members, plus Jerry Garcia, David Crosby, Graham Nash, *et al*. This majestic album was nominated for the science fiction Hugo Award. Slick meanwhile gave birth to a daughter, China, who later in the year graced the cover of Slick And Kantner's *Sunfighter*.

Following a greatest hits selection, *Worst Of* and the departure of Balin, the band released the cleverly packaged *Bark*. Complete with brown paper bag, the album offered some odd moments, notably Slick's 'Never Argue With A German', sung in spoof German and Covington's 50s sounding acappella, 'Thunk'. It also marked the first release on their own Grunt label. The disappointing *Long John Silver* was followed by a gutsy live outing, *30 Seconds Over Winterland*. This was the last album to bear their name, although an interesting compilation consisting of single releases and studio out-takes later appeared as *Early Flight*. Hot Tuna became Jack and Jorma's main interest and Grace and Paul released further 'solo' albums. The name change evolved without any fuss and one of the most inventive bands in history prepared for a second take-off as the Jefferson Starship. The Airplane title was resurrected in 1989 when Slick, Kaukonen, Casady, Balin and Kantner reformed and released *Jefferson Airplane* to an indifferent audience. By the early 90s Hot Tuna had reformed, Kantner was rebuilding his Jefferson Starship and Grace had apparently retired from the music business.

Albums: *Jefferson Airplane Takes Off* (1966), *Surrealistic Pillow* (1967), *After Bathing At Baxter's* (1967), *Crown Of Creation* (1968), *Bless Its Pointed Little Head* (1969), *Volunteers* (1969), *Bark* (1971), *Long John Silver* (1972), *30 Seconds Over Winterland* (1973), *Early Flight* (1974), *Jefferson Airplane* (1989). Compilations: *Worst Of Jefferson Airplane* (1970), featuring Jefferson Airplane and Starship *Flight Log (1966-1976)* (1977), *2400 Fulton Street* (1987).

Further reading: *The Jefferson Airplane And The San Francisco Sound*, Ralph J. Gleason. *Grace Slick - The Biography*, Barbara Rowes.

Jethro Tull

Jethro Tull was formed in Luton, England in 1967 when Ian Anderson (b. 10 August 1947, Edinburgh, Scotland; vocals/flute) and Glenn Cornick (b. 24 April 1947, Barrow-in-Furness, Cumbria, England; bass), members of a visiting Blackpool blues group, John Evan's Smash, became acquainted with Mick Abrahams (b. 7 April 1973, Luton, Bedfordshire, England; guitar/vocals) and Clive Bunker (b. 12 December 1946, Blackpool, Lancashire, England; drums), Abrahams' colleague in local attraction, McGregor's Engine, completed the original line-up which made its debut in March the following year with 'Sunshine Day'. This commerically-minded single, erroneously credited to Jethro Toe, merely hinted at developments about to unfold. A residency at London's famed Marquee club and a sensational appearance at that summer's Sunbury Blues Festival confirmed a growing reputation, while 'Song For Jeffrey', the quartet's first release for the Island label, introduced a more representative sound. Abrahams' rolling blues licks and Anderson's distinctive, stylized voice combined expertly on *This Was* - for many Tull's finest collection. Although the material itself was derivative, the group's approach was highly exciting, with Anderson's propulsive flute playing, modelled on jazzman Raahsan Roland Kirk, particularly effective. The album reached the UK Top 10, largely on the strength of Tull's live reputation in which the singer played an ever-increasing role. His exaggerated gestures, long, wiry

hair, ragged coat and distinctive, one-legged stance cultivated a compulsive stage personality to the extent that, for many spectators, Jethro Tull was the name of this extrovert frontman and the other musicians merely his underlings. This impression gained credence through the group's internal ructions. Mick Abrahams left in November 1968 and formed Blodwyn Pig. When future Black Sabbath guitarist Tony Iommi proved incompatible, Martin Barre (b. 17 November 1946) joined Tull for *Stand Up*, their excellent, chart-topping, second album. The group was then augmented by John Evan (b. 28 March 1948; keyboards), the first of Anderson's Blackpool associates to be invited into the line-up. *Benefit*, the last outwardly blues-based album, duly followed and this period was also marked by the group's three UK Top 10 singles, 'Living In The Past', 'Sweet Dream' (both 1969) and 'The Witch's Promise' (1970). Cornick then quit to form Wild Turkey and Jeffrey Hammond-Hammond (b. 30 July 1946), already a legend in Tull's lexicon through their debut single, 'Jeffrey Goes To Leicester Square' and 'For Michael Collins, Jeffrey And Me', was brought in for *Aqualung*. Possibly the group's best-known work, this ambitious concept album featured Anderson's musings on organized religion and contained several tracks which remained long-standing favourites, including 'My God' and 'Locomotive Breath'.

Clive Bunker, the last original member, bar Anderson, left in May 1971. A further John Evan-era acolyte, Barriemore Barlow (b. 10 September 1949), replaced him as Jethro Tull entered its most controversial period. Although *Thick As A Brick* topped the US chart and reached number 5 in the UK, critics began questioning Anderson's reliance on obtuse concepts. However, if muted for this release, the press reviled *A Passion Play*, damning it as pretentious, impenetrable and the product of an egotist and his neophytes. Such rancour obviously hurt. Anderson retorted by announcing an indefinite retirement, but continued success in America, where the album became Tull's second chart-topper, doubtlessly appeased his anger. *War Child*, a US number 2, failed to chart in the UK, although *Minstrel In The Gallery* proved more popular. *Too Old To Rock 'N' Roll, Too Young To Die* marked the departure of Hammond-Hammond in favour of John Glascock (b. 1953, London, England, d. 17 November 1979), formerly of the Gods, Toe Fat and Chicken Shack. Subsequent releases, *Songs From The Wood* and *Heavy Horses*, reflected a more pastoral sound as Anderson abandoned the gauche approach marking many of their predecessors. David Palmer, who orchestrated each Tull album, bar their debut, was added as a second keyboards player as the group embarked on another highly-successful phase culminating in November 1978 when a concert at

New York's Madison Square Garden was simultaneously broadcast around the world by satellite. However, Glascock's premature death in 1979 during heart surgery ushered in a period of uncertainty, culminating in an internal re-alignment. In 1980 Anderson began a projected solo album, retaining Barre and new bassist Dave Pegg (ex-Fairport Convention), but adding Eddie Jobson (ex-Curved Air and Roxy Music; keyboards) and Marc Craney (drums). Longtime cohorts Barlow, Evan and Palmer were left to pursue their individual paths. The finished product, *A*, was ultimately issued under the Jethro Tull banner and introduced a productive period which saw two more group selections, plus Anderson's solo effort, *Walk Into Light*, issued within a two-year period. Since then Jethro Tull has continued to record and perform live, albeit on a lesser scale, using a nucleus of Anderson, Barre and Pegg. *Catfish Rising* in 1991, although a disappointing album was a return to their blues roots. The singer has also become a renowned entrepreneur, owning tracts of land on the west coast of Scotland and the highly-successful Strathaird Salmon processing plant.
Albums: *This Was* (1968), *Stand Up* (1969), *Benefit* (1970), *Aqualung* (1971), *Thick As A Brick* (1972), *A Passion Play* (1973), *War Child* (1974), *Minstrel In The Gallery* (1975), *Too Old To Rock 'N' Roll Too Young To Die* (1976), *Songs From The Wood* (1977), *Heavy Horses* (1978), *Live - Bursting Out* (1978), *Storm Watch* (1979), *A* (1980), *The Broadsword And The Beast* (1982), *Under Wraps* (1984), *Crest Of A Knave* (1987), *Rock Island* (1989), *Live At Hammersmith* (1991), *Catfish Rising* (1991). Compilations: *Living In The Past* (1972), *M.U.: Best Of Jethro Tull* (1976), *Repeat, The Best Of Jethro Tull - Volume II* (1977), *Original Masters* (1985), *20 Years Of Jethro Tull* (1988, box set). Ian Anderson solo: *Walk Into The Light* (1983).

Johnny And The Hurricanes

Formed by tenor saxophonist Johnny Paris (b. 1940, Walbridge, Ohio, USA), this instrumental group went through a series of line-up changes from 1957-63. With bassist Lionel 'Butch' Mattice and drummer Tony Kaye, the group recorded the single 'Crossfire' under the name the Orbits in 1959. Under their new name, Johnny And The Hurricanes, they followed-up with the rivetting 'Red River Rock', which featured the trademark sound of rasping saxophone, combined with the swirling organ of Paul Tesluk. After enlisting new drummers Don Staczek and Little Bo Savitch along the way, the group continued the hit run in the USA and UK with such instrumentals as 'Reveille Rock', 'Beatnik Fly', 'Down Yonder', 'Rocking Goose' and 'Ja-Da'. In 1963, an entirely new group of Johnny Paris-led Hurricanes toured the UK comprising Eddie Wagenfeald (organ), Billy Marsh (guitar), Bobby Cantrall (bass) and Jay Drake (drums).

By this time, however, their instrumental sound was becoming anachronistic and they were soon consumed by the beat boom, which swept the UK/USA. Various line-ups of Hurricanes continued for live performances and cabaret.
Album: *Stormsville* (1960).

John's Children

Formed in Leatherhead, Surrey, England in 1964, John's Children's earliest antecedent was known as the Clockwork Onions. Louie Grooner (vocals), Andy Ellison (harmonica), Geoff McClelland (guitar), Chris Dawsett (bass) and Chris Townson (drums) made up this short-lived ensemble. The following year they emerged under a new name, the Silence, wherein Ellison (now vocalist), McClelland and Townson were joined by bassist John Hewlett. The group became John's Children in 1966 after meeting manager/producer Simon Napier-Bell. They made their debut in October with 'The Love I Though I'd Found', an experimental composition made memorable by a start-stop, staccato tempo. This unusual release was known by its original title, 'Smashed Blocked', in American and Europe. A debut album, entitled *Orgasm*, was then readied for release. The set consisted of rudimentary material overdubbed by fake applause, but was withheld until 1970 in deference to its questionable quality and then-controversial title. The group's second single, 'Just What You Want, Just What You Get', was a minor UK hit, but marked the departure of McClelland. His replacement was Napier-Bell protege and budding singer-songwriter, Marc Bolan, whose spell in John's Children, although brief, proved contentious. His first offering, 'Desdemona' incurred a BBC ban over the line 'lift up your skirt and fly', and when a second composition, 'A Midsummer Night's Scene', had been recorded unsatisfactorily, Bolan left to form Tyrannosaurus Rex. His former colleages then released the felicitous flower-power anthem, 'Come And Play With Me In The Garden', before exhuming another Bolan song, 'Go Go Girl', from an earlier session. A final John's Children line-up - Ellison, Hewlett, Townson (now guitar) and Chris Colville (drums) completed several outstanding engagements before breaking up. Ellison embarked on a brief solo career, later re-emerging with Townson in 1974 as Jet and from there on to Radio Stars. John Hewlett became a successful manager with Sparks, while also handling Jook, a less celebrated ensemble which also featured Chris Townson.
Album: *Orgasm* (1971). Compilation: *A Midsummer Night's Scene* (1987, contains all of the group's singles).

Johnson, Marv

b. Marvin Earl Johnson, 15 October 1938, Detroit, Michigan, USA. The gospel training which Johnson received as a teenager in the Junior Serenaders was a major influence on his early R&B releases. In 1958, he formed a partnership with the young Berry Gordy, who was then working as a songwriter and producer for Jackie Wilson. Gordy produced Johnson's earliest releases on Kudo, and launched his Tamla label with Marv's single 'Come To Me', which became a hit when it was licensed to United Artists. Johnson remained with the label until 1965, scoring a run of chart entries in early 60s with 'You Got What It Takes', 'I Love The Way You Move', and 'Move Two Mountains' - all produced by Gordy.

Johnson's tracks showcased his delicate tenor vocals against a female gospel chorus, and he maintained this style when he signed to Gordy's Motown stable in 1965. His initial release on the Gordy Records label, the soul favourite 'I Miss You Baby', was a US hit, though it proved to be a false dawn. His subsequent USA releases failed, and Johnson eventually abandoned his recording career in 1968. Ironically, the UK Tamla-Motown label chose this moment to revive Johnson's 1966 recording, 'I'll Pick A Rose For My Rose', which became an unexpected Top 20 hit amidst a dramatic revival in the label's popularity in Britain. Johnson quickly travelled to the UK to capitalize on this success, before retiring to become a sales executive at Motown. After almost two decades working behind the scenes in the music business, he returned to performing in 1987, touring with the 'Sounds Of Motown' package and re-recording his old hits for the Nightmare label. He was teamed with Carolyn Gill (of the Velvelettes) by record producer Ian Levine to release 'Ain't Nothing Like The Real Thing' in 1987. He released *Come To Me* on Levine's Motor City label.

Albums: *Marvellous Marv Johnson* (1960), *More Marv Johnson* (1961), *I Believe* (1966), *I'll Pick A Rose For My Rose* (1969), *Come To Me* (1990).

Jones, Jack

b. John Allen Jones, 14 January 1938, Los Angeles, California, USA. A popular singer from the early 60s, Jones has one of the finest, and most versatile, light baritone voices in popular music. The son of actress Irene Hervey and actor/vocalist Allan Jones, Jack studied singing while still at high school. After graduation in 1957, he joined his father's act, making his first appearance at the Thunderbird Hotel, Las Vegas. He left after eight months, and worked in small clubs and lounges, even bowling alleys, and also appeared in the minor musical film, *Juke Box Rhythm*. Jones was spotted, third on the bill, in a San Francisco club, by arranger-conductor Pete King, who recommended him to Kapp Records. Shortly afterwards, Jones started a six-month stint in the US Air Force, and, during that time, recorded 'Lollipops And Roses', which won him a Grammy in 1962 for Best Performance By A Male Singer. *Cash Box* magazine voted him Most Promising Vocalist in 1962 and 1963; he had a minor hit with 'Call Me Irresponsible', and won another Grammy, for 'Wives And Lovers' (1964), which was also the title of a best-selling album, along with 'Dear Heart', 'The Impossible Dream' and 'Lady'. Other 60s chart successes, through until 1967, included 'The Race Is On' and *My Kind Of Town*. Jones also sang the title songs for the movies *Where Love Has Gone* and *Love With A Proper Stranger* and the winning entry of the Golden Globe Awards, 'Life Is What You Make It', from the film, *Kotch*. In 1967, he switched from Kapp to RCA, and continued to make highly regarded albums, including *Without Her*, the first for his new label. He also appeared frequently on television with artists such as Jerry Lewis and Bob Hope, and was a part of Hope's troupe which entertained the US Forces in Vietnam in December 1965. In concert, Jones was an accomplished performer, skilfully mixing old standards, 'My Romance' and 'People Will Say We're In Love', with more up-to-date songs 'Light My Fire', 'I Think It's Gonna Rain Today', 'What Are You Doing The Rest Of Your Life' and 'What I Did for Love'. He also had a slick line in patter; for instance, when rejecting the inevitable request for 'The Donkey Serenade': 'We don't have that one, but I'll sing you another song that has a lot of the same notes in it!'. In fact, he would sing it, but at a much greater pace than his father ever did, occasionally prefacing the song with lines like: 'I don't know if you know this, but my father recorded 'The Donkey Serenade' on the night that I was born. It's true - he was on a very tight schedule!' Jones was extremmely popular in the UK, and toured regularly from 1973. Although he never had a Top 75 single there, he made the charts, during the 70s, with *A Song For You*, *Breadwinners*, *Together*, *Harbour*, *The Full Life* and *All To Yourself*. *Breadwinners*, with songs by David Gates, was typical of the way that Jones selected material from the best writers of the 60s and 70s, including Michel Legrand, Alan And Marilyn Bergman, John Lennon and Paul McCartney, Nilsson, Leonard Cohen, Burt Bacharach and Hal David, Randy Newman, Jimmy Webb, Paul Williams, Tony Hatch and Jackie Trent. Later releases included *Deja Vu*, *The Full Life*, *Fire and Rain*, *Magic Moments*, *Nobody Does It Better*, *Songs Of Love* and *In Person At The Sands Las Vegas*. In the 80s and early 90s, he continued to thrive in Las Vegas, at venues such as the Golden Nugget and the Desert Inn. During such performances he added contemporary numbers including 'Wind Beneath My Wings' and Andrew Lloyd Webber's 'Music Of The

Night' to hoary old favourites such as the *Love Boat* theme. Early in 1991, he played Sky Masterson in a west coast production of **Guys And Dolls**, and, later in the year, appeared at several UK theatres, including the London Palladium.

Albums: *Call Me Irresponsible* (1963), *Wives And Lovers* (1963), *Bewitched* (1964), *Where Love Has Gone* (1964), *Dear Heart* (1965), *My Kind Of Town* (1965), *There's Love & There's Love & There's Love* (1965), *For The 'In' Crowd* (1966), *The Impossible Dream* (1966), *Jack Jones Sings* (1966), *Lady* (1967), *Our Song* (1967), *Without Her* (1967), *If You Ever Leave Me* (1968), *Where Is Love?* (1968), *A Time For Us* (1969), *A Song For You* (1972), *Breadwinners* (1972), *Together* (1973), *Write Me A Love Song Charlie* (1974), *In Person, Sands, Las Vegas* (1974), *Harbour* (1974), *The Full Life* (1977), *All To Yourself* (1977), *Christmas Album* (1978), *I've Been Here All The Time* (1980), *Deja Vu* (1982), *Fire And Rain* (1985). Compilations: *What The World Needs Now Is Love!* (1968), *Best Of Jack Jones* (1978), *The Jack Jones Special Collection* (1980), *The Very Best Of Jack Jones* (1981), *Magic Moments* (1984), *Love Songs* (1985), *Golden Classics* (1986).

Jones, Jimmy

b. 2 June 1937, Birmingham, Alabama, USA. Jones, who had spent a long apprenticeship singing in the R&B doo-wop groups, became a rock 'n' roll star in the early 60s singing 'Handy Man' and other hits with a dramatic and piercingly high falsetto. He began his career as a tap dancer, and in 1955 joined a vocal group, the Sparks Of Rhythm. In 1956 Jones formed his own group, the Savoys, which were renamed the Pretenders in 1956. With all these groups, tracks were recorded in the prevailing doo-wop manner but with no discernable success beyond a few local radio plays in the New York/New Jersey area. Success finally came when Jones began a solo career, signing with MGM's Cub subsidiary in 1959 and hitting with his debut, 'Handy Man' (number 3 R&B/number 2 pop in 1960). Retaining the same falsetto style, he followed-up with 'Good Timin'' (number 8 R&B/number 3 pop in 1960), but the fall off in sales was considerable for his two other US chart entries, 'That's When I Cried' (number 83 pop 1960) and 'I Told You So' (number 85 pop 1961). In the UK, Jones's chart success was exceptional compared to most of his US contemporareies. In 1960 'Handy Man' reached number 3, 'Good Timin'' number 1, 'I Just Go For You' number 35, 'Ready For Love' number 46 and 'I Told You So' number 33. 'Handy Man' was revived on the charts twice, by Del Shannon in 1964 and by James Taylor in 1977.
Album: *Good Timin'* (1960).

Jones, Tom

b. Thomas Jones Woodward, 7 June 1940,

Tom Jones and Mama Cass

Pontypridd, Mid-Glamorgan, Wales. One of the most famous pop singers of the past three decades, Jones began his musical career in 1963 as vocalist in the group Tommy Scott And The Senators. The following year, he recorded some tracks for Joe Meek, which were initially rejected by record companies. He was then discovered by Decca A&R producer/scout Peter Sullivan and, following the recommendation of Dick Rowe, was placed in the hands of the imperious entrepreneur Phil Solomon. That relationship ended sourly, after which Scott returned to Wales. One evening, at the Top Hat Club in Merthyr Tydfil, former Viscounts vocalist Gordon Mills saw Scott's performance and was impressed. He soon signed the artist and changed his name to Tom Jones. His first single, 'Chills And Fever' failed to chart but, early in 1965, Jones's second release 'It's Not Unusual', composed by Mills and Les Reed, reached number 1 in the UK. The exuberant arrangement, reinforced by Jones's gutsy vocal and a sexy image, complete with hair ribbon, brought him instant media attention. Jones enjoyed lesser hits that year, with ballads 'Once Upon A Time' and 'With These Hands'. Meanwhile, Mills astutely ensured that his star was given first choice for film theme songs and the Burt Bacharach/Hal David composition 'What's New Pussycat?' was a major US/UK hit. By 1966, however, Jones's chart fortunes were in decline and even the title track of a James Bond movie, *Thunderball*, fell outside the UK Top 30. Before long, the former chart topper was back playing working men's clubs and his period of stardom seemed spent. Mills took drastic action by regrooming his protege for an elder market. Out went the sexy clothes in favour of a more mature, tuxedoed image. By Christmas, 1966, Jones was effectively relaunched owing to the enormous success of 'Green Green Grass Of Home', which sold over a million copies in the UK alone and topped the charts for seven weeks. Jones retained the country flavour with a revival of Bobby Bare's 'Detriot City' and

'Funny Familiar Forgotten Feelings'. In the summer of 1966, he enjoyed one of his biggest UK hits with the intense 'I'll Never Fall In Love Again', which climbed to number 2. The hit run continued with the restrained 'I'm Coming Home', and the dramatic, swaggering 'Delilah', which added a sense of Victorian melodrama with its macabre line: 'I felt the knife in my hand, and she laughed no more'. In the summer of 1968, Jones again topped the **New Musical Express** charts with 'Help Yourself'.

As the 60s reached their close, Mills took his star to America where he hosted the highly-successful television show, *This Is Tom Jones*. Unlike similar series, Jones's show attracted some of the best and most critically acclaimed acts of the era. An unusual feature of the show saw Jones duetting with his guests. Some of the more startling vocal workouts occurred when Jones teamed-up with David Crosby during a Crosby, Stills And Nash segment, and on another occasion with Blood, Sweat And Tears' David Clayton-Thomas. Although Jones logged a handful of hits in the UK during the early 70s, he was now an American-based performer, whose future lay in the lucrative Las Vegas circuit. Jones became enormously wealthy during his supper club sojourn and had no reason to continue his recording career which petered out during the 70s. It was not until after the death of Mills, when his son Mark Woodward took over his management, that the star elected to return to recording. His recording of 'The Boy From Nowhere' (from the musical *Matador*) was perceived as a personal anthem and reached number 2 in the UK. It was followed by a re-release of 'It's Not Unusual' which also reached the Top 20. In 1988, a most peculiar collaboration occurred between Jones and the Art Of Noise on an appealing kitsch version of Prince's 'Kiss'. The song reached the UK Top 5 and Jones performed the number at the London Palladium. Soon after, he appeared with a number of other Welsh entertainers on a recording of Dylan Thomas's play for voices *Under Milk Wood*, produced by George Martin. Jones's continued credibility was emphasized once more when he was invited to record some songs written by the mercurial Van Morrison. After more than a decade on the Las Vegas circuit, Jones could hardly have hoped for a more rapturous welcome in the UK, both from old artists and the new elite.

Albums: *Along Came Jones* (1965), *A-Tom-Ic Jones* (1966), *From The Great* (1966), *Green, Green, Grass Of Home* (1967), *Live At The Talk Of The Town* (1967), *Delilah* (1968), *Help Yourself* (1968), *Tom Jones Live In Las Vegas* (1969), *This Is Tom Jones* (1969), *Tom* (1970), *I, Who Have Nothing* (1970), *Tom Jones Sings She's A Lady* (1971), *Tom Jones Live At Caeser's Palace, Las Vegas* (1971), *Close Up* (1972), *The Body And Soul Of Tom Jones* (1973), *Somethin' 'Bout You Baby I Like*

(1974), *Memories Don't Leave Like People* (1975), *Say You'll Stay Until Tomorrow* (1977), *Rescue Me* (1980), *Darlin'* (1981), *Matador - The Musical Life Of El Cordobes* (1987), *At This Moment* (1989), *After Dark* (1989). Compilations: *13 Smash Hits* (1967), *Tom Jones: Greatest Hits* (1973), *Tom Jones: 20 Greatest Hits* (1975), *The World Of Tom Jones* (1975), *Tom Jones Sings 24 Great Standards* (1976), *What A Night* (1978), *I'm Coming Home* (1978), *Super Disc Of Tom Jones* (1979), *Tom Jones Sings The Hits* (1979), *Do You Take This Man* (1979), *The Very Best Of Tom Jones* (1980), *Rescue Me* (1980), *The Golden Hits* (1980), *16 Love Songs* (1983), *The Tom Jones Album* (1983), *The Country Side Of Tom Jones* (1985), *The Soul Of Tom Jones* (1986), *Love Songs* (1986), *The Great Love Songs* (1987), *Tom Jones - The Greatest Hits* (1987), *It's Not Unusual - His Greatest Hits* (1987).

Joplin, Janis

b. 19 January 1941, Port Arthur, Texas, USA, d. 4 October 1970. Having made her performing debut in December 1961, this expressive singer subsequently enjoyed a tenure at Houston's Purple Onion club. Drawing inspiration from Bessie Smith and Odetta, Joplin developed a brash, uncompromising vocal style quite unlike accustomed folk madonnas Joan Baez and Judy Collins. The following year she joined the Waller Creek Boys, an Austin-based act which also featured Powell St. John, later of Mother Earth. In 1963 Janis moved to San Francisco where she became a regular attraction at the North Beach Coffee Gallery. This initial spell was blighted by her addiction to amphetamines and in 1965 Joplin returned to Texas in an effort to dry out. She resumed her university studies, but on recovery turned again to singing. The following year Janis was invited back to the Bay Area to front Big Brother And The Holding Company. This exceptional improvisational blues act was the ideal foil to her full-throated technique and although marred by poor production, their debut album fully captures an early optimism.

Janis's reputation blossomed following the Monterey Pop Festival, of which she was one of the star attractions. The attendant publicity exacerbated growing tensions within the line-up as critics openly declared that the group was holding the singer's potential in check. *Cheap Thrills*, a joyous celebration of true psychedelic soul, contained two Joplin 'standards', 'Piece Of My Heart' and 'Ball And Chain', but the sessions were fraught with difficulties and Janis left the group in November 1968. Electric Flag members Mike Bloomfield, Harvey Brooks and Nick Gravenites helped assemble a new act, initially known as Janis And The Joplinaires, but later as the Kozmic Blues Band. Former Big Brother Sam Andrew (guitar/vocals), plus Terry Clements (saxophone), Marcus Doubleday (trumpet), Bill King (organ), Brad Campbell (bass) and Roy Markowitz (drums) made up the unit's initial line-up which was then bedeviled by defections. A disastrous debut concert at the Stax/Volt convention in December 1968 was a portent of future problems, but although *I Got Dem Ol' Kozmic Blues Again Mama* was coolly received, the set nonetheless contained several excellent Joplin vocals, notably 'Try', 'Maybe' and 'Little Girl Blue'. However, live shows grew increasingly erratic as her addiction to drugs and alcohol deepened. When a restructured Kozmic Blues Band, also referred to as the Main Squeeze, proved equally uncomfortable, the singer dissolved the unit altogether, and undertook medical advice. A slimmed-down group, the Full Tilt Boogie Band, was unveiled in May 1970. Brad Campbell and late-comer John Till (guitar) were retained from the previous group, while the induction of Richard Bell (piano), Ken Pearson (organ) and Clark Pierson (drums) created a tighter, more intimate sound. In July they toured Canada with the Grateful Dead, before commencing work on a 'debut' album. The sessions were all but complete when, on 4 October 1970, the Joplin died of a heroin overdose at her Hollywood hotel.

The posthumous *Pearl* was thus charged with poignancy, yet it remains her most consistent work. Her love of 'uptown soul' is confirmed by the inclusion of three Jerry Ragavoy compositions, 'My Baby', 'Cry Baby' and the suddenly anthemic 'Get It While You Can', while 'Trust Me' and 'A Woman Left Lonely' shows an empathy with its southern counterpart. The highlight, however, is Kris Kristofferson's 'Me And Bobby McGee', which allowed Janis to be both vulnerable and assertive. The song deservedly topped the US chart when issued as a single and despite a plethora of interpretations, this remains the definitive version. Although a star at the time of her passing, Janis Joplin has not been accorded the retrospective acclaim afforded other deceased contemporaries. She was, like her idol Otis Redding, latterly regarded as one-dimensional, lacking in subtlety or nuance. Yet her impassioned approach was precisely her attraction - Janis knew few boundaries, artistic or personal - and her sadly brief catalogue is marked by bare-nerved honesty.

Albums: *I Got Dem Ol' Kozmic Blues Again Mama!* (1969), *Pearl* (1971), *Janis Joplin In Concert* (1972). Compilations: *Greatest Hits* (1973), film soundtrack including live and rare recordings *Janis* (1975), *Anthology* (1980), *Farewell Song* (1981). Further reading: *Buried Alive*, Myra Friedman. *Piece Of My Heart*, David Dalton.

Journeymen

This US folk trio comprising Scott McKenzie (guitar/vocals), Dick Weissman (b. Richard Weissman; banjo/guitar/vocals), and John Phillips (b. John Edmund Andrew Phillips, 30 August 1935, Parris Island, South Carolina, USA; guitar/vocals). The group were formed, like many others at the time, as a result of the folk revival of the late 50s and 60s, and featured strong harmonies and a commercial sound that made folk such a saleable commodity at the time. The Journeymen made their debut in 1961, at Gerde's Folk City, New York, and shortly after signed to Capitol Records, releasing *The Journeymen* later the same year. The group's popularity, and commerciality, waned after a relatively short life span, and the members went their separate ways. John attempted to revive the trio's fortunes with the New Journeymen, which featured his wife Michelle Phillips and Marshall Brickman. Phillips went on to form the Mamas And The Papas, while McKenzie found fame as the singer of the hit song 'San Francisco'. Weissman continued in the business, recording *The Things That Trouble My Mind* and *Dick Weissman Sings And Plays Songs Of Protest*. Albums: *The Journeymen* (1961), *Coming Attraction-Live* (1962), *New Directions* (1963).

Joystrings

'It's An Open Secret', which entered the UK Top 40 in February 1964, remains one of the most unlikely hits of the beat era. The song was written by Joy Webb, a captain in the Salvation Army. Her eight-piece group, the Joystrings, was drawn from the staff of the Army's Training College in London's Denmark Hill. The sole exception was drummer Wyncliffe Noble, an architect by trade. The octet was signed to EMI's Regal-Zonophone label, following a successful appearance on BBC television's *Tonight* programme, and in December they enjoyed another minor hit with 'A Starry Night'. Despite their seemingly transitory appeal, the Joystrings continued to record for several years, although their novelty aspect quickly waned. Albums: *Well Seasoned* (1966), *Carols Across The World* (1967).

Justice, Jimmy

b. 1940, Carlshalton, Surrey, England. Justice signed to Pye in 1960, owing partly to fellow stable-mate singer, Emile Ford, who had spotted Jimmy singing in a coffee-bar. When Justices's first two releases failed in the UK, he relocated to Sweden where his cover of the Jarmels' 'Little Lonely One' charted. In 1962 with the help of producer Tony Hatch, he strung together three UK Top 20 hits; the remarkably fresh cover of the Drifters US hit 'When My Little Girl Is Smiling', 'Ain't That Funny' - an original song penned by Johnny Worth and 'Spanish Harlem'. Jimmy spent 1962 commuting between England and

Sweden (where he had many previous bookings to honour) but managed, together with his group the Excheckers, to join a Larry Parnes' UK tour headed by Billy Fury and Joe Brown. This white singer who possessed a mature, soulful voice, was sometimes called 'Britain's Ben E. King', caused some controversy when he covered King's 'Spanish Harlem' with an uncannily similar vocal style. Justice also recorded on Decca in 1969, RCA in 1968 and B&C in 1972.

K

Kaleidoscope

Formed in 1966, this innovative group owed its origins to California's jugband and bluegrass milieu. Guitarists David Lindley and Chris Darrow were both former members of the Dry City Scat Band, while Solomon Feldthouse (vocals/oud/caz) had performed in the region's folk clubs. John Vidican (drums) and Charles Chester Crill - aka Connie Crill, Max Buda, Fenrus Epp or Templeton Parceley (violin/organ/harmonica/vocals) - completed the line-up which, having flirted with the name Bagdhad Blues Band, then settled on Kaleidoscope. *Side Trips* revealed a group of enthralling imagination, offering a music drawn from the individual members' disparate interests. Blues, jazz, folk and ethnic styles abounded as the quintet forged a fascinating collection, but although the album comprised short songs, Kaleidoscope's reputation as a superior live attraction was based on lengthy improvised pieces. The group tried to address this contrast with *A Beacon From Mars*, which contrasted six concise performances with two extended compositions, the neo-Eastern 'Taxim' and the feedback-laden title track. The album marked the end of this particular line-up as Darrow then opted to join the Nitty Gritty Dirt Band. Vidican also left the group, and thus newcomers Stuart Brotman (bass) and Paul Lagos (drums) were featured on *Incredible Kaleidoscope* which in turn offered a tougher, less acid-folk perspective. There were, nonetheless, several highlights, including the expanded 'Seven Ate Sweet' and propulsive 'Lie To Me', but the album was not a commercial success, despite the publicity generated by the group's sensational appearance at the 1968 Newport Folk Festival. Further changes in the line-up ensued with the departure of Brotman, who was fired during sessions for a prospective fourth album. His replacement, Ron Johnson, introduced a funk-

influenced element to the unit's sound, while a second newcomer, Jeff Kaplan, surprisingly took most of the lead vocals. Kaleidoscope's muse sadly failed to accommodate these changes, and *Bernice* was a marked disappointment. The late-period group did complete two excellent songs for the film soundtrack of *Zabriskie Point*, but the departures of Feldthouse and Crill in 1970 signalled their demise. Despite the addition of Richard Aplan to the line-up, Kaleidoscope folded later in the year in the wake of Kaplan's death from a drugs overdose. David Lindley subsequently embarked on a career as a session musician and solo artist, a path Chris Darrow also followed, albeit with less commercial success. The latter subsequently joined Feldthouse, Brotman, Lagos and Crill in the reformed unit completing *When Scopes Collide* which, although lacking the innovation of old, was nonetheless entertaining. The same line-up reconvened to complete the equally meritorious *Greetings From Kartoonistan...(We Ain't Dead Yet)*. Such sets simply enhanced the Kaleidoscope legend, which was considerably buoyed by a series of excellent compilations. They remain one of the era's most innovative acts.

Albums: *Side Trips* (1967), *A Beacon From Mars* (1968), *Incredible Kaleidoscope* (1969), *Bernice* (1970), *When Scopes Collide* (1976), *Greetings From Kartoonistna...(We Ain't Dead Yet)* (1991). Compilations: *Bacon From Mars* (1983), *Rampe Rampe* (1984), *Egyptian Candy* (1990).

Eden Kane, John Leyton and Adam Faith

Kane, Eden

b. Richard Sarstedt, 29 March 1942, Delhi, India. When his family returned from India to England during the mid-50s, Kane became involved in music, forming a skiffle group with his brothers. In 1960, he won a talent contest and came under the wing of managers Michael Barclay and Philip Waddilove. They changed his name to Eden Kane, inspired by the movie *Citizen Kane* and the biblical name Cain. Promoted by the chocolate firm, Cadbury's, Kane's first single was 'Hot Chocolate Crazy', which failed to chart. For the follow-up, Kane recorded the catchy, colloquial 'Well I Ask You', which took him to number 1 in the UK during the summer of 1961. Over the next year, three more Top 10 hits followed: 'Get Lost', 'Forget Me Not' and 'I Don't Know Why'. Kane's career suffered a serious setback early in 1963 when Barclay and Waddilove's company Audio Enterprises went into liquidation. The star's management was passed on to Vic Billings, who persuaded Fontana's influential A&R manager Jack Baverstock to sign him. In early 1964, Kane returned to the UK Top 10 with 'Boys Cry', which also proved a major hit in Australia. In the autumn of that year, Kane made the momentous decision to emigrate to Australia, later relocating to the USA. Although his chart days were over, his younger brothers Peter Sarstedt and Robin Sarstedt both enjoyed hits in their own right. The brothers combined their talents in 1973 for the album, *Worlds Apart Together*. Thereafter, Kane continued to play regularly on the revivalist circuit.

Albums: *Eden Kane* (1962), *It's Eden* (1964, reissued as *Smoke Gets In Your Eyes* in 1965), with the Sarstedt brothers *Worlds Apart Together* (1973).

Kasenetz-Katz Singing Orchestral Circus
The brainchild of bubblegum pop producers, Jerry Kasenetz and Jeff Katz, the Singing Orchestral Circus was a sprawling aggregation of eight groups on one record: the Ohio Express, the 1910 Fruitgum Company, Music Explosion, Lt. Garcia's Magic Music Box, Teri Nelson Group, Musical Marching Zoo, JCW Rat Finks and the St. Louis Invisible Marching Band. Together, they were responsible for one of bubblegum's more memorable moments with the international hit, 'Quick Joey Small' in 1968. With an attendant array of acrobats, clowns, fire-eaters and scantily-clad girls, the circus played a concert at Carnegie Hall with a repertoire which included such hits as 'Yesterday', 'We Can Work It Out', 'Hey Joe' and 'You've Lost That Lovin' Feelin''. The prestige of this event did not prevent them from taking their place as one-hit-wonders.

K-Doe, Ernie
b. Ernest Kador Jnr., 22 February 1936, New Orleans, Louisiana, USA. Previously a singer with touring gospel groups, K-Doe's earliest non-secular recordings were made in the mid-50s as a member of the Blue Diamonds. His first solo record, 'Do Baby Do', was released on Specialty in 1956. The singer's biggest hit came with the Allen Toussaint song, 'Mother-In-Law' (1961) which reached number 1 in the US pop charts. This pointed 'novelty' song was followed by 'Te-Ta-Te-Ta-Ta', and a strong double-sided release, 'I Have Cried My Last Tear'/'A Certain Girl'. The latter track proved popular in Britain

where it was covered by the Yardbirds and the Paramounts. Further K-Doe singles included 'Popeye Joe' and 'I'm The Boss', but it was not until 1967 that he returned to the R&B chart with two singles for the Duke label, 'Later For Tomorrow' and 'Until The Real Thing Comes Along'. He remains a popular, energetic performer and occasional recording artist in New Orleans.

Album: *Mother-In-Law* (1961). Compilation: *Burn, K-Doe, Burn!* (1989).

Keith

Keith
b. James Barry Keefer, 7 May 1949, Philadelphia, Pennsylvania, USA. Keith was best known for his Top 10 folk-rock single '98.6' in January 1967. Keefer started with a band called the Admirations in the early 60s, recording one single for Columbia Records, 'Caravan Of Lonely Men'. He was then discovered by journalist Kal Rudman, who took Keefer to Mercury Records executive Jerry Ross. Signed to that label, and renamed Keith, he recorded his first solo single, 'Ain't Gonna Lie', which just made the US Top 40. '98.6' followed and was his biggest hit, although Keith charted twice in 1967 with lesser hits, 'Tell Me To My Face' and 'Daylight Savin' Time'. He recorded a few more singles for Mercury and two albums, only the first of which made the charts. After spending time in the armed forces, he returned to change musical direction,

recording a single, 'In And Out Of Love', for Frank Zappa's Discreet label, and singing briefly with Zappa's band (he did not record with them). Keefer recorded one last album, for RCA Records, with no luck, and then left the music business until 1986, when an attempted comeback under his real name did not work out.

Albums: *98.6/Ain't Gonna Lie* (1967), *Out Of Crank* (1968), *The Adventures Of Keith* (1969).

Johnny Kidd

Kidd, Johnny, And The Pirates

Kidd (b. Frederick Heath, 23 December 1939, Willesden, London, England, d. 7 October 1966), is now rightly revered as an influential figure in the birth of British rock. Although his backing group would fluctuate, this enigmatic figure presided over several, seminal, pre-Beatles releases. Formed in January 1959, the original line-up consisted of two former members of the Five Nutters skiffle group, Kidd (lead vocals) and Alan Caddy (b. 2 February 1940, London, England; lead guitar), joined by Tony Docherty (rhythm guitar), Johnny Gordon (bass) and Ken McKay (drums), plus backing singers Mike West and Tom Brown. Their compulsive debut single, 'Please Don't Touch' barely scraped into the UK Top 20, but it remains one of the few authentic home-grown rock 'n' roll performances to emerge from the 50s. Its immediate successors were less original and although they featured session men, most of Kidd's

group were then dropped in favour of experienced hands.

By 1960, Kidd and Caddy were fronting a new rhythm section consisting of Brian Gregg (bass) and Clem Cattini (drums). Their first single, 'Shakin' All Over', was another remarkable achievement, marked by its radical stop/start tempo, Kidd's feverish delivery and an incisive lead guitar solo from session man Joe Moretti. The song deservedly topped the charts, but its inspiration to other musicians was equally vital. Defections resulted in the formation of a third line-up - Kidd, Johnny Spence (bass), Frank Farley (drums) and Johnny Patto (guitar) - although the last was replaced by Mick Green. Onstage, the group continued to wear full pirate regalia while the singer sported a distinctive eye-patch, but they were under increasing competition from the emergent Liverpool sound. Two 1963 hits, 'I'll Never Get Over You' and 'Hungry For Love', although memorable, owed a substantial debt to Merseybeat at the expense of the unit's own identity. The following year, Green left to join the Dakotas, precipitating a succession of replacements, and although he continued to record, a depressed leader talked openly of retirement. However, the singer re-emerged in 1966, fronting the New Pirates, but Kidd's renewed optimism ended in tragedy when, on 7 October, he was killed in a car crash. This pivotal figure is remembered both as an innovator and for the many musicians who passed through his ranks. John Weider (the Animals and Family), Nick Simper (Deep Purple) and Jon Morshead (Aynsley Dunbar Retaliation) are a few of those who donned the requisite costume, while the best-known line-up, Green, Spence and Farley, successfully re-established the Pirates' name during the late 70s.

Compilations: *Shakin' All Over* (1971), *The Best Of Johnny Kidd And The Pirates* (1987), *Rarities* (1987), *The Classics And The Rare* (1990).

King, Ben E.

b. Benjamin Earl Nelson, 28 September 1938, Henderson, North Carolina, USA. King began his career while still a high school student singing in a doo-wop group, the Four B's. He later joined the Five Crowns who, in 1959, assumed the name, the Drifters. King was the featured lead vocalist and occasional composer, on several of their recordings including 'There Goes My Baby' and 'Save The Last Dance For Me'. After leaving the group in 1960, he recorded the classic single, 'Spanish Harlem' (1961) which maintained the latin quality of the Drifters' work and deservedly reached the US Top 10. The follow-up, 'Stand By Me' (1961), was even more successful and was followed by further hits including 'Amor' (1961) and 'Don't Play That Song (You Lied)' (1962). Throughout this period, King's work was aimed increasingly at the pop audience. 'I (Who Have Nothing)' and 'I Could Have Danced All Night' (both 1963) suggested showbusiness rather than innovation, although Bert Berns's 'It's All Over' (1964) was a superb song. 'Seven Letters' and 'The Record (Baby I Love You)' (both 1965) prepared the way for the rhetorical 'What Is Soul?' (1967) which effectively placed King alongside such soul contemporaries as Otis Redding, Wilson Pickett and Joe Tex. Unfortunately, King's commercial standing declined towards the end of the 60s when he left the Atlantic/Atco group of labels. Unable to reclaim his former standing elsewhere, King later re-signed with his former company and secured a US Top 5 hit in 1975 with 'Supernatural Thing Part 1'. In 1977, a collaboration with the Average White Band resulted in two R&B chart entries and an excellent album, *Benny And Us*. However, King's later recordings, including *Music Trance* (1980) and *Street Tough* (1981), proved less successful. In 1986, 'Stand By Me' was included in a film of the same name and once more became an international hit, reaching the US Top 10 and number 1 in the UK, thereby briefly revitalizing the singer's autumnal career.

Albums: *Spanish Harlem* (1961), *Ben E. King Sings For Soulful Lovers* (1962), *Don't Play That Song* (1962), *Seven Letters* (1965), *What Is Soul* (1967), *Rough Edges* (1970), *Beginning Of It All* (1971), *Supernatural* (1975), *I Had A Love* (1976), with the Average White Band *Benny And Us* (1977), *Let Me Live In Your Life* (1978), *Music Trance* (1980), *Street Tough* (1981), *Save The Last Dance For Me* (1988). Compilations: *Greatest Hits* (1964), *Here Comes The Night* (1984), *Stand By Me (The Ultimate Collection)* (1987).

King, Carole

b. Carole Klein, 9 February 1942, Brooklyn, New York, USA. A proficient pianist from the age of four, King was a prolific songwriter by her early teens. When friend and neighbour Neil Sedaka embarked on his recording career, she followed him into the New York milieu, recording demos, singing back-up and even helping arrange occasional sessions. As a student at Queen's College, New York, she met future partner and husband Gerry Goffin whose lyrical gifts matched King's grasp of melody. She completed a handful of singles, including 'The Right Girl' (1958) and 'Baby Sittin'' (1959), prior to recording 'Oh Neil' (1960), a riposte to Sedaka's 'Oh Carol'. Although not a hit, her record impressed publishing magnate Don Kirshner, who signed the Goffin/King team to his Aldon Music empire. They scored notable early success with the Shirelles ('Will You Still Love Me Tomorrow'), Bobby Vee ('Take Good Care Of My Baby') and the Drifters ('Up On The Roof') and were later responsible for much of the early output on Dimension, the company's in-house label. The duo wrote, arranged and produced hits for Little Eva ('The Locomotion') and the Cookies ('Chains' and 'Don't Say Nothin' Bad About My Baby') while a song written with Bobby Vee in mind, 'It Might As Well Rain Until September', provided King with a solo hit in 1962. Although this memorable and highly evocative song barely reached the US Top 30, it climbed to number 3 in the UK. However, two follow-up singles fared less well. The Goffin/King oeuvre matured as the 60s progressed, resulting in several sophisticated, personalized compositions, including 'A Natural Woman' (Aretha Franklin), 'Goin' Back' (Dusty Springfield and the Byrds) and 'Pleasant Valley Sunday' (the Monkees). The couple also established the short-lived Tomorrow label, but their disintegrating marriage was chronicled on King's 1967 single, 'The Road To Nowhere', the year they dissolved their partnership.

King then moved to Los Angeles and having signed to Lou Adler's Ode label, formed the City with ex-Fugs duo Danny Kortchmar (guitar) and Charles Larkey (bass). (The latter was to become King's second husband.) The trio's lone album included the artist's versions of 'I Wasn't Born To Follow' and 'That Old Sweet Roll (Hi De Ho)', covered, respectively, by the Byrds and Blood, Sweat And Tears. King began a solo career in 1970 with *Writer*, before fully asserting her independence with *Tapestry*. This radiant selection contained several of the singer's most incisive compositions, notably 'You've Got A Friend', a US number 1 for James Taylor, 'It's Too Late', a US chart-topper for King, and 'So Far Away'. Unlike many of her former production-line contemporaries, King was able to shrug off teen preoccupations and use her skills to address adult doubts and emotions. *Tapestry* sold in excess of 10 million copies and established its creator as a major figure in the singer-songwriter movement. However, the delicate balance it struck between perception and self-delusion became blurred on *Music* and *Rhymes And Reasons*, which were regarded as relative disappointments. Each set nonetheless achieved gold disc status, as did *Fantasy*, *Wrap Around Joy* (which contained her second US number 1, 'Jazzman') and *Thoroughbred*. The last marked the end of King's tenure at Ode and she has since failed to reap the same commercial success. Her first release of the 80s, *Pearls*, comprised 'classic' Goffin/King songs, a release which many interpreted as an artistic impasse. Certainly King subsequently pursued a less frenetic professional life, largely restricting her live appearances to fund-raising concerns. Her recordings also became more measured and if *Speeding Time* or *City Streets* lacked the cultural synchronization *Tapestry* enjoyed with the post-Woodstock audience, her songwriting skills were still in evidence.

Albums: *Writer* (1970), *Tapestry* (1971), *Music* (1971),

Rhymes And Reasons (1972), *Fantasy* (1973), *Wrap Around Joy* (1974), *Really Rosie* (1975), *Thoroughbred* (1975), *Simple Things* (1977), *Welcome Home* (1978), *Touch The Sky* (1979), *Pearls (Songs Of Goffin And King)* (1980), *One To One* (1982), *Speeding Time* (1983), *City Streets* (1989). Compilation: *Her Greatest Hits* (1973).

King, Solomon

This US singer came to prominence in 1968 with the powerful hit ballad 'She Wears My Ring'. It was based on a classical piece of music called *Golandrina (The Swallow)*. King was signed by manager/entrepreneur Gordon Mills but failed to emulate the phenomenal success of his stablemates, Tom Jones and Engelbert Humperdinck. He continued to record well into the 70s, and his version of 'Say A Little Prayer' (1970) is a prized rarity among soul fans.
Album: *She Wears My Ring* (1968).

Kingsmen

Kingsmen

Jack Ely (vocals/guitar), Mike Mitchell (guitar) Bob Nordby (bass) and Lynn Easton (drums) began working as the Kingsmen in 1958. Based in Portland, Oregon, USA, they became a staple part of the region's thriving circuit prior to the arrival of Don Gallucci (keyboards) in 1962. The group's debut single, 'Louie Louie', was released the following year.

The song was composed and originally recorded by Richard Berry in 1956, and its primitive, churning rhythm was later adopted by several northwest state bands, including the Wailers and Paul Revere And The Raiders. However, it was the Kingsmen who popularized this endearing composition when it rose to number 2 in the US chart. Its classic C-F-G chord progression, as simple as it was effective, was absorbed by countless 'garage bands', and 'Louie Louie' has subsequently become one of rock's best-known and most influential creations. Indeed, a whole album's worth of recordings of the song by various artists, including the Kingsmen and Richard Berry, was issued by Rhino Records entitled, *The Best Of Louie Louie*. Relations between the individual Kingsmen were sundered on the single's success. Easton informed Ely that he now wished to sing lead, and furthered his argument by declaring himself the sole proprietor of the group's name, having judiciously registered the monicker at their inception. Ely and Norby walked out, although the former won a victory of sorts when a judgement declared that every pressing of the Kingsmen's greatest hit must include the words 'lead vocals by Jack Ely'. His former cohorts added Norm Sundholm (bass) and Gary Abbot (drums), but despite a succession of dance-related releases including 'The Climb', 'Little Latin Lupe Lu' and 'The Jolly Green Giant', the group was unable to maintain a long-term livelihood. Gallucci formed Don And The Goodtimes, Kerry Magnus and Dick Petersen replaced Sundholm and Abbot, but the crucial alteration came in 1967 when Easton left the group. Numerous half-hearted reincarnations aside, his departure brought the Kingsmen to an end.
Albums: *The Kingsmen In Person* (1963), *The Kingsmen, Volume 2 (More Great Sounds)* (1964), *The Kingsmen, Volume 3* (1965), *The Kingsmen On Campus* (1965), *How To Stuff A Wild Bikini* (1965, film soundtrack), *Up Up And Away* (1966). Compilations: *15 Great Hits* (1966), *The Kingsmen's Greatest Hits* (1967), *Louie Louie/Greatest Hits* (1986).

Kinks

It is ironic that one of Britain's most enduring and respected groups spawned from the beat boom of the early 60s has for the best part of two decades received success, adulation and financial reward in the USA. Today this most 'English' institution can still fill a vast stadium in any part of the USA, whilst in Britain, a few thousand devotees watch their heroes perform in a comparatively small club or hall. The Kinks is the continuing obsession of one of Britain's premier songwriting talents, Raymond Douglas Davies (b. 21 June 1944, Muswell Hill, London, England; vocals/guitar/piano). Originally known as the Ravens, the Kinks formed at the end of 1963 with a line-up comprising: Dave Davies (b. 3 February

1947, Muswell Hill, London; guitar/vocals) and Peter Quaife (b. 31 December 1943, Tavistock, Devon, England; bass), and were finally joined by Mick Avory (b. 15 February 1944, London; drums). Their first single 'Long Tall Sally' failed to sell (this record is sought by collectors), although they did receive a lot of publicity through the efforts of their shrewd managers Robert Wace, Grenville Collins and Larry Page. Their third single 'You Really Got Me', rocketed to the UK number 1 spot, boosted by an astonishing performance on the UK television show *Ready Steady Go*. This and its successor 'All Day And All Of The Night' arguably invented heavy-metal guitar, with the entrancing simple riffs supplied by the younger Davies. Over the next two years Ray Davies emerged as a songwriter of startling originality as his band were rarely out of the best-sellers list. Early in 1965, the group returned to number 1 with the languid 'Tired Of Waiting For You'. They enjoyed a further string of hits that year, including 'Everybody's Gonna Be Happy', 'Set Me Free', 'See My Friend' and 'Till The End Of The Day'. Although it failed to match the thrust of their early hits, 'See My Friend' was notable for its use of raga-inspired guitar and lyrical hints of homosexuality. Despite the humanity of his lyrics, Davies was occasionally a problematical character, renowned for his eccentric behaviour. The Kinks were equally tempestuous and frequently violent. Earlier in 1965, events had reached a head when the normally placid drummer, Mick Avory, attacked Dave Davies on stage with the hi-hat of his drum kit, having been goaded beyond endurance. Remarkably, the group survived such contretemps and soldiered on. A disastrous US tour saw them banned from that country, amid further disputes.

Throughout all the drama, Davies the songwriter remained supreme. He combined his own introspection with humour and pathos. He spelled out in his lyrics, the ordinary and the obvious, but in doing so he made people think. 'Dedicated Follower Of Fashion' brilliantly satirized the Carnaby Street narcissism while 'Sunny Afternoon' (another UK number 1) dealt with capitalism and class. 'Dead End Street' at the end of 1966 highlighted the plight of the working class poor: 'Out of work and got no money, a Sunday joint of bread and honey' while later in that same song Davies comments 'What are we living for, two-roomed apartment on the second floor, no money coming in, the rent collector knocks and tries to get in'. All these were sung with Davies' resigned laconic music hall style. Their albums, prior to *Face To Face* had contained a staple diet of R&B standards and comparatively harmless Davies originals. With *Face To Face* and *Something Else* however, he set about re-defining the English, with sparkling wit and steely nerve. One of Davies' greatest songs was the final track on the latter; 'Waterloo Sunset' was a

Kinks

simple but emotional *tour de force* with the melancholic singer observing two lovers (actor Terence Stamp and actress Julie Christie) meeting and crossing over Hungerford Bridge in London. It narrowly missed the top of the charts, as did the follow-up 'Autumn Almanac' with its gentle chorus, summing up the English working class of the 50s and 60s; 'I like my football on a Saturday, roast beef on Sunday is all right, I go to Blackpool for my holiday, sit in the autumn sunlight'.

Throughout this fertile period, Ray Davies, along with John Lennon/Paul McCartney and Pete Townshend, were Britain's finest writers. Then suddenly, in 1968 the Kinks fell from public grace in the UK, although still well-respected by the critics. Two superb concept albums, *The Kinks Are The Village Green Preservation Society* and *Arthur Or The Decline And Fall Of The British Empire*, failed to sell. This inexplicable quirk was all the harder to take as they contained some of Davies' finest songs. Both flops must have hurt him, although as concepts they are both remarkable in their unremarkableness. Writing honestly about everyday events no longer appealed to Davies' public. The former was likened to Dylan Thomas's *Under Milk Wood*, while *Arthur* had to compete with Pete Townshend's *Tommy*. Both were writing rock operas without each other's knowledge, but as Johnny Rogan stated in his biography of the Kinks: 'Davies' celebration of the mundane was far removed from the studious iconoclasm of *Tommy* and its successors'. Incredibly during this time the Kinks were more popular in Germany than anywhere else in the world; the Germans should be applauded for their grasp of such 'foreign' lyrics. The last hit single during this 'first' age of the Kinks was the glorious 'Days'. This lilting and timeless ballad is another of Davies' many classics and was a major hit for Kirsty MacColl in 1989.

Pete Quaife permanently departed in 1969 and was replaced by John Dalton. The Kinks returned to the UK best-sellers in July 1970 with 'Lola', an irresistible fable of transvestism, which marked the beginning of their breakthrough in the USA, by reaching the US Top 10. The resulting *Lola Vs Powerman And The Moneygoround Part One* was also a success in the USA. On this record Davies attacked the music industry and in one track, 'The Moneygoround' openly attacked his former managers and publishers, while alluding to the lengthy high court action in which he had been embroiled. The group now embarked on a series of mammoth US tours and rarely performed in Britain, although their business operation centre and recording studio, Konk, was based close to the Davies' childhood home in north London. Having signed a new contract with RCA in 1971 the band had now enlarged to incorporate a brass section, amalgamating with the Mike Cotton Sound. Following the interesting country-influenced *Muswell Hillbillies*, however, they suffered a barren period. Ray experienced drug and marital problems and their ragged half-hearted live performances showed a man who had lost his driving, creative enthusiasm. Throughout the early 70s, a series of average, over-ambitious concept albums appeared, as an outlet for Davies' prolific output. *Preservation Act I*, *Preservation Act II*, *Soap Opera* and *Schoolboys In Disgrace* were all thematic, and *Soap Opera* was adapted for British television as *Starmaker*.

At the end of 1976 John Dalton departed, as their unhappy and comparatively unsuccessful years with RCA ended. A new contract with Arista Records effected a remarkable change in fortunes. Both *Sleepwalker* (1977) and *Misfits* (1978) were excellent and successful albums; Ray had rediscovered the knack of writing short, punchy rock songs with quality lyrics. The musicianship of the band improved, in particular, Dave Davies, who after years in his elder brother's shadow, came into his own with a more fluid style.

Although still spending most of their time playing to vast audiences in the USA, the Kinks were adopted by the British new wave, and were cited by many punk bands as a major influence. Both the Jam ('David Watts') and the Pretenders ('Stop Your Sobbing') provided reminders of Davies' 60s songwriting skill. The British music press, then normally harsh on 60s dinosaurs, constantly praised the Kinks and helped to re-generate a market for them in Europe. Their following albums continued the pattern started with *Sleepwalker*, hard-rock numbers with sharp lyrics. Although continuing to be a huge attraction in the USA they have so far never re-appeared in the UK album charts, although they are regular victims of ruthless 'Greatest Hits' packages. As Ray Davies' stormy three-year relationship with Chrissie Hynde of the Pretenders drew to its close, so the Kinks appeared unexpectedly back in the UK singles chart with the charming 'Come Dancing'. The accompanying video and high publicity profile prompted the re-issue of their entire and considerable back catalogue. Towards the end of the 80s the band toured sporadically amidst rumours of a final break-up. In 1990 the band were inducted into the Rock 'n' Roll Hall of Fame, at the time they were only the fourth UK group to take the honour after the Beatles, Rolling Stones and the Who. During the ceremony both Pete Quaif and Mick Avory were present. Later that year they received the Ivor Novello award for 'outstanding services to British music'. After the comparative failure of *UK Jive* the band left London Records, and after being without a recording contract for some time signed with Sony in 1991. Whether or not this new label will produce further million selling albums is almost irrelevant, the band have already earned musical immortality. Raymond Douglas Davies has made his mark under the Kinks' banner as one of the most perceptive and prolific songwriters of our time and his catalogue of songs is one of the finest available.

Albums: *Kinks* (1964), *Kinda Kinks* (1965), *The Kink Kontroversy* (1965), *Face To Face* (1966), *Something Else* (1967), *Live At The Kelvin Hall* (1967), *The Kinks Are The Village Green Preservation Society* (1968), *Arthur Or The Decline And Fall Of The British Empire* (1969), *Lola Versus Powerman And The Moneygoround, Part One* (1970), *Percy* (1971, film soundtrack), *Muswell Hillbillies* (1971), *Everbody's In Showbiz, Everybody's A Star* (1972) *The Kinks Kronikles* (1972), *The Great Lost Kinks Album* (1973), *Preservation Act 1* (1973), *Preservation Act 2* (1974), *Soap Opera* (1975), *Schoolboys In Disgrace* (1975), *Sleepwalker* (1977), *Misfits* (1978), *Low Budget* (1979), *One For The Road* (1980), *Give The People What They Want* (1981), *State Of Confusion* (1983), *Word Of Mouth* (1984), *Think Visual* (1986), *The Road* (1988), *UK Jive* (1989). Compilations: *The Ultimate Collection* (1989), *The EP Collection* (1990), *Fab Forty: The Singles Collection, 1964-70* (1991), *The EP Collection* (1992).

Further reading: *The Kinks, The Sound And The Fury*, Johnny Rogan. *The Kinks, The Official Biography*, Jon Savage.

Knickerbockers

The Knickerbockers was formed in 1964 by Buddy Randell (saxophone), a former member of the Royal Teens and Jimmy Walker (drums/vocals). The line-up was completed by the Charles brothers, John (bass) and Beau (lead guitar). Originally known as the Castle Kings, the group took its name from an avenue in their hometown of Bergenfield, New Jersey, USA. Signed to the Challenge label, owned by singing cowboy Gene Autry, the quartet initially forged its reputation recording cover versions, but in 1965 they scored a US Top 20 hit with 'Lies', a ferocious rocker which many listeners assumed was the Beatles in disguise. However the Knickerbockers were more than mere copyists and later releases, which featured the instrumental muscle of experienced studio hands, established an energetic style which crossed folk-rock and the Four Seasons. The group broke up in 1968, unable to rekindle that first flame of success. Randell and Walker both attempted solo careers and for a short time the latter replaced Bill Medley in the Righteous Brothers.
Albums: *Sing And Sync-Along With Lloyd: Lloyd Thaxton Presents The Knickerbockers* (1965), *Jerk And Twine Time* (1966), *The Fabulous Knickerbockers* (1966), *Lies* (1966). Compilation: *The Fabulous Knickerbockers* (1988).

Knight, Gladys And The Pips

Gladys Knight (b. 28 May 1944, Atlanta, Georgia, USA), her brother Merald 'Bubba' (b. 4 September 1942, Atlanta, Georgia, USA), sister Brenda and cousins Elenor Guest and William Guest (b. 2 June 1941, Atlanta, Georgia, USA) formed their first vocal group in their native Atlanta in 1952. Calling themselves the Pips, the youngsters sang supper-club material in the week, and gospel music on Sundays. They first recorded for Brunswick in 1958, with another cousin to the Knights, Edward Patten (b. 2 August 1939) and Langston George making changes to the group line-up the following year when Brenda

and Elenor left to get married. Three years elapsed before their next sessions, which produced a version of Johnny Otis' 'Every Beat Of My Heart' for the small Huntom label. This song, which highlighted Knight's bluesy, compelling vocal style, was leased to VeeJay Records when it began attracting national attention, and went on to top the US R&B charts. By this time, the group, now credited as Gladys Knight And The Pips, had signed a long-term deal with Fury Records, where they issued a re-recording of 'Every Beat Of My Heart' which competed for sales with the original release. Subsequent singles such as 'Letter Full Of Tears' and 'Operator' sealed the group's R&B credentials, but a switch to the Maxx label in 1964 - where they worked with producer Van McCoy - brought their run of successes to a halt. Langston George retired from the group in the early 60s, leaving the quartet line-up which survived into the 80s.
In 1966, Gladys Knight and the Pips were signed to Motown's Soul subsidiary, where they were teamed up with producer/songwriter Norman Whitfield. Knight's tough vocals left them slightly out of the Motown mainstream, and throughout their stay with the label the group were regarded as a second-string act. In 1967, they had a major hit single with the original release of 'I Heard It Through The Grapevine', an uncompromisingly tough performance of a song that became a Motown standard in the hands of its author Marvin Gaye in 1969. 'The Nitty Gritty' (1968) and 'Friendship Train' (1969) proved equally successful, while the poignant 'If I Were Your Woman' was one of the label's biggest-selling releases of 1970. In the early 70s, the group slowly moved away from their original blues-influenced sound towards a more middle-of-the-road harmony blend. Their new approach brought them success in 1972 with 'Neither One Of Us (Wants To Say Goodbye)'. Later that year, Knight and The Pips elected to leave Motown for Buddah, unhappy at the label's shift of operations from Detroit to Hollywood. At Buddah, the group found immediate success with the US chart-topper 'Midnight Train To Georgia', an arresting soul ballad, while major hits like 'I've Got To Use My Imagination' and 'The Best Thing That Ever Happened To Me' mined a similar vein. In 1974, they performed Curtis Mayfield's soundtrack songs for the film *Claudine*; the following year, the title track of *I Feel A Song* gave them another soul number 1. Their smoother approach was epitomized by the medley of 'The Way We Were/Try To Remember' which was the centrepiece of *Second Anniversary* in 1975 - the same year that saw Gladys and the group host their own US television series.
Gladys made her acting debut in *Pipedream* in 1976, for which the group recorded a soundtrack album. Legal problems then dogged their career until the end

of the decade, forcing Knight and the Pips to record separately until they could sign a new deal with CBS. *About Love* in 1980 teamed them with the Ashford And Simpson writing/production partnership, and produced a strident piece of R&B social comment in 'Bourgie Bourgie'. Subsequent releases alternated between the group's R&B and MOR modes, and hits like 'Save The Overtime (For Me)' and 'You're Number One In My Book' (1983) and, after a move to MCA Records, 'Love Overboard' (1988), demonstrated that they could work equally well in either genre. The latter song earned them a Grammy award for the Best R&B performance in early 1989. Following this, Knight and the Pips split. Merald remained with Gladys as she achieved a UK Top 10 that year with the James Bond movie song, 'Licence To Kill'.

Albums: *Letter Full Of Tears* (1961), *Gladys Knight And The Pips* (1964), *Everybody Needs Love* (1967), *Feelin' Bluesy* (1968), *Silk 'N' Soul* (1968), *Nitty Gritty* (1969), *All In A Knight's Work* (1970), *If I Were Your Woman* (1971), *Standing Ovation* (1971), *Neither One Of Us* (1973), *All I Need Is Time* (1973), *Knight Time* (1974), *Imagination* (1973), *Knight Time* (1974), *Claudine* (1974), *I Feel A Song* (1974), *A Little Knight Music* (1975), *Second Anniversary* (1975), *Bless This House* (1976), *Pipe Dreams* (1976, film soundtrack), *Still Together* (1977), *The One And Only* (1978), *About Love* (1980), *Touch* (1981), *That Special Time Of Year* (1982), *Visions* (1983), *Life* (1985), *All Our Love* (1988). Compilations: *Greatest Hits* (1970), *Anthology* (1974), *Best Of* (1976), *30 Greatest* (1977), *The Collection - 20 Greatest Hits* (1984), *The Singles Album* (1989). Solo albums: Gladys Knight *Miss Gladys Knight* (1979). The Pips *At Last - The Pips* (1979), *Callin'* (1979).

Kooper, Al

b. 5 February 1944, Brooklyn, New York, USA. Kooper embarked upon a professional music career in 1959 as guitarist in the Royal Teens, who had enjoyed a novelty hit the previous year with 'Short Shorts'. He became a noted New York session musician and later forged a successful songwriting partnership with Bobby Brass and Irwin Levine. Their collaborations included 'This Diamond Ring', a chart-topper for Gary Lewis And The Playboys, 'I Must Be Seeing Things' (Gene Pitney) and 'The Water Is Over My Head' (the Rockin' Berries). In 1965, producer Tom Wilson asked Kooper to attend a Bob Dylan session. With Mike Bloomfield already installed on guitar, the eager musician opted for organ, an instrument with which he was barely conversant. Dylan nonetheless loved his instinctive touch which breathed fire into 'Like A Rolling Stone' and its attendant *Highway 61 Revisited* album. Kooper maintained his links with Dylan over the

years, guesting on *Blonde On Blonde* (1966), *New Morning* (1970) and *Under The Red Sky* (1990).

Kooper became involved in several electric folk sessions, notably for Tom Rush *(Take A Little Walk With Me)* and Peter, Paul And Mary *(Album)*. His solo version of 'I Can't Keep From Crying Sometimes' appeared on an Elektra label sampler, *What's Shakin'*, and his reading of 'Parchman Farm' was issued as a single in 1966. The organist was then invited to join the Blues Project, which became one of America's leading urban R&B acts. Kooper left the group in 1967 to found Blood, Sweat And Tears one of the originals of US jazz-rock, with whom he remained for one album before internal unrest resulted in his dismissal. He accepted a production post at Columbia Records, before recording the influential *Super Session* with Mike Bloomfield and Stephen Stills. This successful informal jam inspired several inferior imitations, not the least of which was the indulgent *Live Adventures Of Al Kooper And Mike Bloomfield*, which featured cameos by Elvin Bishop and the then relatively unknown Carlos Santana when Bloomfield was unable to finish the schedule. Kooper's solo career was effectively relaunched with *I Stand Alone*, but in keeping with many of his albums, this promising set was marred by inconsistency. A limited vocalist, his best work relied on his imaginative arrangements, which drew on the big band jazz of Maynard Ferguson and Don Ellis (whom he produced), and the strength of the supporting cast. *You Never Know Who Your Friends Are* and *New York City (You're A Woman)* were among his most popular releases. His double set *Easy Does It* contained a superb slowed down version of Ray Charles' 'I Got A Woman', resplendent with an exquisite jazz-piano solo introduction. Kooper, however, remained best-known for his role as a catalyst. He appeared on *Electric Ladyland* (Jimi Hendrix) and *Let It Bleed* (Rolling Stones) and produced the debut albums by Nils Lofgren and the Tubes. He established his own label, Sounds Of The South, in Atlanta, Georgia, and secured international success with early proteges Lynyrd Skynyrd.

During the 70s, Kooper became involved in several Blues Project reunions and the following decade he formed Sweet Magnolia, an *ad hoc* group comprising several studio musicians. In 1982, he completed *Championship Wrestling*, his first solo album for five years, which featured contributions from guitarist Jeff 'Skunk' Baxter (Steely Dan and Doobie Brothers). Al Kooper has since pursued an active career recording computerized soundtrack music, but in 1991 produced *Scapegoats* for Green On Red. Now happily living in Nashville, Kooper has been a major background personality in American rock for more than 30 years and has made a considerable contribution.

Albums: with Mike Bloomfield and Stephen Stills *Super Session* (1968), *The Live Adventures Of Al Kooper And Mike Bloomfield* (1969), *I Stand Alone* (1969), *You Never Know Who Your Friends Are* (1969), with Shuggie Otis *Kooper Session* (1970), *Easy Does It* (1970), *Landlord* (1971), *New York City (You're A Woman)* (1971), *A Possible Projection Of The Future/Childhood's End* (1972), *Naked Songs* (1973), *Act Like Nothing's Wrong* (1976), *Championship Wrestling* (1982). Compilation: *Al's Big Deal/Unclaimed Freight* (1975).
Further reading: *Backstage Pass*, Al Kooper.

Korner, Alexis

b. 19 April 1928, Paris, France, d. January 1984. An inspirational figure in British music circles, Korner was already versed in black music when he met Cyril Davies at the London Skiffle Club. Both musicians were frustrated by the limitations of the genre and transformed the venue into the London Blues And Barrelhouse Club where they not only performed together but also showcased visiting US bluesmen. When jazz trombonist Chris Barber introduced an R&B segment into his live repertoire, he employed Korner (guitar) and Davies (harmonica) to back singer Ottilie Patterson. Inspired, the pair formed Blues Incorporated in 1961 and the following year established the Ealing Rhythm And Blues Club in a basement beneath a local cinema. The group's early personnel included Charlie Watts (drums), Art Wood (vocals) and Keith Scott (piano), but later featured Long John Baldry, Jack Bruce, Graham Bond and Ginger Baker in its ever-changing line-up. Mick Jagger and Paul Jones were also briefly associated with Korner, whose continued advice and encouragement proved crucial to a generation of aspiring musicians. However, disagreements over direction led to Davies's defection following the release of *R&B From The Marquee*, leaving Korner free to pursue a jazz-based path. While former colleagues later found success with the Rolling Stones, Manfred Mann and Cream, Korner's excellent group was largely unnoticed by the general public, although he did enjoy a residency on a children's television show backed by his rhythm section of Danny Thompson (bass) and Terry Cox (drums). The name 'Blues Incorporated' was dropped when Korner embarked on a solo career, punctuated by the formation of several temporary groups, including Free At Last (1967), New Church (1969) and Snape (1972). While the supporting cast on such ventures remained fluid, including for a short time singer Robert Plant, the last two units featured Peter Thorup who also collaborated with Korner on CCS, a pop-based big band which scored notable hits with 'Whole Lotta Love' (1970), 'Walkin'' and 'Tap Turns On The Water' (both 1971). Korner also derived success from

his BBC Radio 1 show which extended a highly individual choice of material. He also broadcast on a long-running programme for the BBC World Service. Korner continued to perform live, often accompanied by former Back Door virtuoso bassist Colin Hodgkinson, and remained a highly respected figure in the music fraternity. He joined Charlie Watts, Ian Stewart, Jack Bruce and Dick Heckstall-Smith in the informal Rocket 88 and Korner's 50th birthday party, which featured appearances by Eric Clapton, Chris Farlowe and Zoot Money, was both filmed and recorded. In 1981, Korner began an ambitious 13-part television documentary on the history of rock, but his premature death from cancer in January 1984 left this and many other projects unfulfilled. However, Korner's stature as a vital catalyst in British R&B was already assured.
Albums: by Alexis Korner's Blues Incorporated *R&B From The Marquee* (1962), *Red Hot From Alex* aka *Alexis Korner's All Star Blues Incorporated* (1964), *At The Cavern* (1964), *Alexis Korner's Blues Incorporated* (1964), *Sky High* (1966), *Blues Incorporated (Wednesday Night Prayer Meeting)* (1967); by Alexis Korner *I Wonder Who* (1967), *A New Generation Of Blues* aka *What's That Sound I Hear* (1969), *Both Sides Of Alexis Korner* (1969), *Alexis* (1971), *Mr. Blues* (1974), *Alexis Korner* (1974), *Get Off My Cloud* (1975), *Just Easy* (1978), *Me* (1979), *The Party Album* (1980), *Juvenile Delinquent* (1984), *Live In Paris: Alexis Korner* (1988, archive recordings); by New Church *The New Church* (1970); by Snape *Accidentally Born In New Orleans* (1973), *Snape Live On Tour* (1974). Compilations: *Bootleg Him* (1972), *Profile* (1981), *Alexis 1957* (1984), *Testament* (1985), *Alexis Korner 1961-1972* (1986), *Hammer And Nails* (1987), *The Alexis Korner Collection* (1988).

Billy J Kramer And The Dakotas

Kramer, Billy J., (And The Dakotas)

b. William Howard Ashton, 19 August 1943, Bootle, Merseyside, England. Kramer originally fronted Merseybeat combo the Coasters, but was teamed with the Manchester-based Dakotas - Mike Maxfield (lead guitar), Robin McDonald (rhythm guitar), Ray Jones (bass) and Tony Maxfield (drums) - upon signing to Brian Epstein's management agency. Having topped the UK charts with the Beatles' 'Do You Want To Know A Secret' (1963), Kramer's UK chart success was maintained with a run of exclusive John Lennon/Paul McCartney songs, including the chart-topping 'Bad To Me', 'I'll Keep You Satisfied' (number 4) and 'From A Window' (number 10). 'Little Children' (1964), penned by US writers Mort Shuman and John McFarland, gave the group a third number 1 and their first taste of success in the USA, reaching number 7. This was quickly followed by the reissued 'Bad To Me' which also reached the Top 10. Their chart reign ended the following year with the Burt Bacharach-composed 'Trains And Boats And Planes' peaking at number 12 in the UK. Although subsequent efforts, most notably the lyrical 'Neon City', proved effective, Kramer's career was firmly in the descendent. He embarked on a solo career in January 1967, but having failed to find a new audience, sought solace on the cabaret and nostalgia circuit.

Albums: *Listen - To Billy J. Kramer* (1963), *Little Children* (1964), *I'll Keep You Satisfied* (1964), *Trains And Boats And Planes* (1965), *Kramer Versus Kramer* (1986). Compilations: *The Best Of Billy J. Kramer* (1984), *The EMI Years* (1991).

L

Lance, Major

b. 4 April 1941, Chicago, Illinois, USA. A former amateur boxer and a dancer on the Jim Lounsbury record-hop television show, Lance also sang with the Five Gospel Harmonaires and for brief period with Otis Leavill and Barbara Tyson in the Floats. His 1959 Mercury release, 'I Got A Girl', was written and produced by Curtis Mayfield, a high-school contemporary, but Major's career was not truly launched until he signed with the OKeh label three years later. 'Delilah' opened his account there, while a further Mayfield song, the stylish 'The Monkey Time' in 1963, gave the singer a US Top 10 hit. The partnership between singer and songwriter continued through 1963-64 with a string of US pop chart hits; 'Hey Little Girl', 'Um Um Um Um Um Um', 'The Matador' and 'Rhythm'. Although Lance's range was more limited than that of his associate, the texture and phrasing mirrored that of Mayfield's work with

his own group, the Impressions. 1965's 'Ain't That A Shame' marked a pause in their relationship as its commercial success waned. Although further vibrant singles followed, notably 'Investigate' and 'Ain't No Soul (In These Rock 'N' Roll Shoes)', Lance left OKeh for Dakar Records in 1968 where 'Follow The Leader' was a minor R&B hit. Two 1970 releases on Curtom, 'Stay Away From Me' and 'Must Be Love Coming Down', marked a reunion with Mayfield. From there the Major moved to Volt, Playboy and Osiris, the last of which he co-owned with Al Jackson a former member of Booker T. And The MGs. These spells were punctuated by a two-year stay in Britain (1972-74), during which Lance recorded for Contempo and Warner Brothers. Convicted of selling cocaine in 1978, the singer emerged from prison to find his OKeh recordings in demand as part of America's 'beach music' craze, where aficionados in Virginia and the Carolinas maintain a love of vintage soul.

Albums: *Monkey Time* (1963), *Major Lance's Greatest Hits - Recorded 'Live' At The Torch* (1973), *Now Arriving* (1978), *The Major's Back* (1983), *Live At Hinkley* (1986). Compilations: *Um Um Um Um Um - The Best Of Major Lance* (1964), *Major's Greatest Hits* (1965), *Monkey Time* (1983, 60s recording).

Lawrence, Steve

b. Stephen Leibowitz, 8 July 1935, Brooklyn, New York, USA. The son of a cantor in a Brooklyn synagogue, Lawrence was in the Glee club at Thomas Jefferson High School, where he began studying piano, saxophone, composition and arranging. He made his recording debut for King Records at the age of 16. The record, 'Mine And Mine Alone', based on 'Softly Awakes My Heart' from *Samson & Delilah*, revealed an amazingly mature voice and style. Influenced by Frank Sinatra, but never merely a copyist, he was an individual singer of great range and warmth. He got his first break on Steve Allen's *Tonight* television show, where he met, sang with and later married Eydie Gorme. During his US Army service (1958-60) he sang with military bands on recruiting drives and bond rallies. Back home he and Eydie embarked on a double act, making albums for CBS, ABC and United Artists, including *Steve & Eydie At The Movies*, *On Broadway*, *We Got Us*, *The Golden Hits* and *Our Love Is Here To Stay*, the latter a double album of great George Gershwin songs, which was the soundtrack of a well-received television special. Lawrence, on his own, had single hits with 'Portrait Of My Love' and 'Go Away Little Girl' in 1961/2, and enjoyed critical success with albums such as *Academy Award Losers* and *Portrait Of My Love*. As an actor he starred on Broadway in *What Makes Sammy Run?*, took the lead in *Pal Joey* in summer stock, and has acted in a crime series on US television.

Selected albums: *Here's Steve Lawrence* (1958), *Portrait Of My Love* (1961), *Winners* (1963), *Academy Award Losers* (1964), *Everybody Knows* (1964), *The Steve Lawrence Show* (1965), *Together On Broadway* (1967), *What It Was, Was Love* (1969), *Real True Lovin'* (1969), *We Got Us* (1984), *We're All Alone* (1985), *I Still Believe In Love* (1985). Compilation: *Best Of Steve And Eydie* (1977).

Lee, Brenda

b. Brenda Lee Tarpley, 11 December 1944, Lithonia, Georgia, USA. Even in early adolescence, she had an adult husk of a voice that could slip from anguished intimacy through sleepy insinuation to raucous lust even during 'Let's Jump The Broomstick', 'Speak To Me Pretty' and other jaunty classics that kept her in the hit parade from the mid-50s to 1965. Through local radio and, by 1956, wider exposure on Red Foley's Ozark Jubilee broadcasts, 'Little Brenda Lee' was ensured enough airplay for her first single, a revival of Hank Williams' 'Jambalaya', to crack the US country chart before her **Billboard** Hot 100 debut with 1957's 'One Step At A Time'. The novelty of her extreme youth facilitated bigger triumphs for 'Little Miss Dynamite' with the million-selling 'Rockin' Around The Christmas Tree' and later bouncy rockers before the next decade brought a greater proportion of heartbreak ballads such as 'I'm Sorry', 'Thanks A Lot' and 'Too Many Rivers' - plus an acting role in the children's fantasy movie, *The Two Little Bears*. 1963 was another successful year - especially in the UK with the title song of *All Alone Am I*, 'Losing You' (a French translation), 'I Wonder' and 'As Usual' each entering the Top 20. While 1964 finished well with 'Is It True' and 'Christmas Will Be Just Another Lonely Day', only minor hits followed. Though she may have weathered prevailing fads, family commitments caused Brenda to cut back on touring and record only intermittently after 1966's appositely-titled *Bye Bye Blues*.

Lee resurfaced in 1971 with a huge country hit in Kris Kristofferson's 'Nobody Wins' and later recordings that established her as a star of what was then one of the squarest seams of pop. When country gained a younger audience in the mid-80s, respect for its older practitioners found her guesting with Loretta Lynn and Kitty Wells on k.d. lang's *Shadowland*. - produced in 1988 by Owen Bradley (who had also supervised many early Lee records). In Europe, Brenda Lee remained mostly a memory - albeit a pleasing one as shown by Coast To Coast's hit revival of 'Let's Jump The Broomstick', a high UK placing for 1980's *Little Miss Dynamite* greatest hits collection and Mel Smith And Kim Wilde's 'Rockin' Around The Christmas Tree'. Lee is fortunate in having a large rock 'n' roll catalogue destined for immortality in addition to her now-high standing in the country music world.

Albums: *Grandma, What Great Songs You Sang* (1959), *Brenda Lee* (1960), *This Is. . . Brenda* (1960), *Emotions* (1961), *All The Way* (1961), *Sincerely* (1962), *Brenda, That's All* (1962), *The Show For Christmas Seals* (1962), *All Alone Am I* (1963), *Let Me Sing* (1963), *By Request* (1964), *Merry Christmas From Brenda Lee* (1964), *Top Teen Hits* (1965), *The Versatile Brenda Lee* (1965), *Too Many Rivers* (1965), *Bye Bye Blues* (1966), *Coming On Strong* (1966), with Pete Fountain *For The First Time* (1968), *Johnny One Time* (1969), *LA Sessions* (1977), *Even Better* (1980). Compilations: *10 Golden Years* (1966), *The Brenda Lee Story* (1974), *Little Miss Dynamite* (1980), *25th Anniversary* (1984), *The Golden Decade* (1985), *The Best Of Brenda Lee* (1986), *Love Songs* (1986),

Lee, Leapy

b. Lee Graham, 2 July 1942, Eastbourne, England. One of the troubled stars of British 60s pop, Lee's career took a surprise upswing when he moved from Kinks co-manager Robert Wace to the charismatic Gordon Mills. The latter produced the catchy 'Little Arrows', which narrowly failed to reach the UK number 1 spot. A minor hit with 'Good Morning' and a suitably broad showbusiness repertoire should have served Leapy well, but his waywardness proved his undoing. He began drinking with East End villains and befriended starlet Diana Dors and her husband Alan Lake. One evening at a pub in Sunnydale, Lake and Lee were involved in a fracas during which a publican was slashed across the wrist with a flick knife. Leapy was arrested, charged and suffered the indignity of a jail sentence which seriously put back his career, although Mills occasionally employed him as a producer. Lee eventually left the UK to sing in bars in Majorca, Spain.

Legrand, Michel

b. 24 February 1932, Paris, France. Legrand grew up in a musical environment - his father was an orchestra leader and film composer - and studied formally at the Paris Conservatoire. In the 50s he was an active pianist but was most successful as an arranger. Later in the decade he moved to New York and continued to arrange, but now with a strong orientation towards the contemporary jazz scene, for leading artists such as Miles Davis and John Coltrane. In France he had occasionally led his own bands and did so again in the USA. In these years he was also a prolific composer, writing material performed by Stan Getz, Phil Woods and others, and occasionally playing with jazzmen such as Shelly Manne. He had begun to compose music for French films in 1953, and, in the 60s, developed this area of his work on productions such

as *Lola*; *Cleo From 5 to 7* and *My Life To Live*. In 1964 he received the first of his many Academy Award nominations, for the score to *The Umbrellas Of Cherbourg*, which contained 'I Will Wait For You' and 'Watch What Happens' (English lyrics by Norman Gimbel). His second Oscar came for his work on the follow-up, *The Young Ladies Of Rochefort* (1968). In the late 60s he began to compose for US and British films. His score for one of the first of these, *The Thomas Crown Affair*, included 'The Windmills Of Your Mind' (lyric by Alan and Marilyn Bergman), which became popular for Noel Harrison (son of actor Rex) and Dusty Springfield, and won an Academy Award in 1968. Another collaboration with Alan and Marilyn Bergman produced 'What Are You Doing The Rest Of Your Life?', from *The Happy Ending* (1969). Throughout the 70s, Legrand continued to write prolifically for films such as *The Go-Between*, *Wuthering Heights*, *Summer Of 42* (another Oscar), *Lady Sings The Blues*, *One Is A Lonely Number* and *The Three Musketeers*. He teamed with the Bergmans yet again for Barbra Streisand's film *Yentl* (1983). Two of their 12 songs, 'Papa, Can You Hear Me?' and 'The Way He Makes Me Feel' were nominated, and the complete score won an Academy Award. Legrand's other film music included *Never Say Never Again*, Sean Connery's eagerly awaited return to the role of James Bond; *Secret Places* (title song written with Alan Jay Lerner); the amusing *Switching Channels* (theme written with Neil Diamond), starring Kathleen Turner, Burt Reynolds and Christopher Reve; *Fate* and *The Burning Shore*. In 1991 Legrand was back to his jazz roots for the score to *Dingo*, which he wrote with Miles Davis. Davis also gave an impressive performance in the movie. At his best with lyrical and sometimes sentimental themes, Legrand's writing for films remains his major contribution to popular music. Besides his feature film credits, Legrand also worked extensively in television, contributing music to *Brian's Song*, *The Adventures Of Don Quixote*, *It's Good To Be Alive*, *Cage Without A Key*, *A Woman Called Golda*, *The Jesse Owens Story*, *Promises To Keep*, *Sins* (mini-series), *Crossings*, *Casanova* and *Not A Penny More, Not A Penny Less* (1990).
Selected albums: *Legrand Jazz* (1958), *At Shelly's Manne Hole* (1968), *Michel Legrand Recorded Live At Jimmy's* (1973), *After The Rain* (1982).

Lemon Pipers

This New York-based quintet - Ivan Browne (vocals/rhythm guitar), Bill Bartlett (lead guitar), R.G. (Reg) Nave (organ), Steve Walmsley (bass) and Bill Albuagh (drums) - made its debut in 1967 with 'Turn Around And Take A Look'. Its rudimentary style was then replaced by the measured approach of aspiring songwriting/production team, Paul Leka and Shelly Pinz. Together they created a distinctive Lemon Pipers sound, a sparkling melange of sweeping strings and percussive vibraslaps exemplified on the group's million-selling hit, 'Green Tambourine'. The attendant album contained several songs - 'Rice Is Nice', 'Shoeshine Boy' - which were recorded in a similar style, but the set also contained the startling 'Through With You', an extended *tour de force* for Bartlett's rampaging guitarwork and a surprise for those anticipating easy-on-the-ear fare. Subsequent recordings failed to match their early success, and although a second album, *Jungle Marmalade*, offered several inventive moments, the Lemon Pipers were tarred as a bubblegum attraction on the strength of that first hit. The group broke up in 1969, although Bartlett later found success as a member of Ram Jam.
Albums: *Green Tambourine* (1967), *Jungle Marmalade* (1968). Compilation: *The Lemon Pipers* (1990).

Lester, Ketty

b. Revoyda Frierson, 16 August 1934, Hope, Arkansas, USA. Ketty Lester's began her singing career on completing a music course at San Francisco State College. A residency at the city's Purple Onion club was followed by a successful tour of Europe before she joined bandleader Cab Calloway's revue. Later domiciled in New York, Lester's popular nightclub act engendered a recording deal of which 'Love Letters' was the first fruit. The singer's cool-styled interpretation of this highly popular standard, originally recorded by Dick Haymes, reached the Top 5 in both the US and UK in 1962, eventually selling in excess of 1 million copies. The song has been covered many times with notable success for Elvis Presley and Alison Moyet. Its attractiveness was enhanced by a memorable piano figure but Lester was sadly unable to repeat the single's accomplished balance between song, interpretation and arrangement. She later abandoned singing in favour of a career as a film and television actress with appearances in *Marcus Welby MD*, *Little House On The Prairie*, *The Terminal Man* and *The Prisoner Of Second Avenue* to name but a few. She was later coaxed back into the studio, but only on her stipulation that it would be to perform sacred music only.
Albums: *Love Letters* (1962), *Soul Of Me* (1964), *Where Is Love* (1965), *When A Woman Loves A Man* (1967), *I Saw Him* (1985).

Lewis, Gary, And The Playboys

One of most commercially successful US pop groups of the mid-60s, the original Playboys comprised Gary Lewis (b. Gary Levital, 31 July 1946, New York, USA; vocals/drums), Alan Ramsey (b. 27 July 1943, New Jersey, USA; guitar), John West (b. 31 July 1939, Unrichville, Ohio, USA; guitar), David Costell

Gary Lewis

the time of his discharge in 1968, a set of Playboys were ready to return him to the charts with a remake of Brian Hyland's 'Sealed With A Kiss'. A revival of the Cascades' 'Rhythm Of The Rain' pointed to the fact that the group were running short of ideas while also indicating their future on the revivalist circuit. After disbanding the group at the end of the 60s, Lewis was unsuccessfully relaunched as a singer-songwriter but later assembled a new version of the Playboys for cabaret and festival dates.

Albums: *This Diamond Ring* (1965), *Everybody Loves A Clown* (1965), *Out Of Sight* (1966, film soundtrack), *She's Just My Style* (1966), *Gary Lewis Hits Again!* (1966), *You Don't Have To Paint Me A Picture* (1967), *New Directions* (1967), *Gary Lewis Now!* (1968), *Close Cover Before Playing* (1968), *Rhythm Of The Rain* (1969), *I'm On The Road Now* (1969). Compilations: *Golden Greats* (1966), *More Golden Greats* (1968), *Twenty Golden Greats* (1979), *Greatest Hits: Gary Lewis And The Playboys* (1986).

(b. 15 March 1944, Pittsburgh, Pennsylvania, USA; bass) and David Walker (b. 12 May 1943, Montgomery, Alabama, USA; keyboards). Group leader Gary Lewis was the son of comedian Jerry Lewis and had been playing drums since the age of 14. After appearing at selected Hollywood parties, the ensemble was offered a residency at the Disneyland Park and soon after were signed by Liberty Records and producer Leon Russell. Their debut single, 'This Diamond Ring' (co-written by Al Kooper and originally intended for former idol, Bobby Vee) topped the American charts in February 1965 and spearheaded an remarkable run of Top 10 hits that included 'Count Me In', 'Save Your Heart For Me', 'Everybody Loves A Clown', 'She's Just My Style', 'She's Gonna Miss Her' and 'Green Grass'. The latter, although written by UK composers Cook And Greenaway (alias David And Jonathan), predictably failed to make any impact in the UK market where the group remained virtually unknown. Undoubtedly the best-selling US group of the mid-60s without a UK hit to their name, they nevertheless enjoyed healthy record sales all over the world, appeared regularly on television and even participated in a couple of low budget movies, *A Swingin' Summer* and *Out Of Sight*. Their relative decline in 1967 probably had less to do with changing musical fashions than the induction of Gary Lewis to the US Armed Forces. By

Ramsey Lewis

Lewis, Ramsey

b. 27 May 1935, Chicago, Illinois, USA. Lewis started playing piano at the age of six. He graduated from school in 1948, after winning both the American Legion Award as an outstanding scholar and a special award for piano services at the Edward Jenner Elementary School. He began his career as an accompanist at the Zion Hill Baptist Church, an

experience of gospel that never left him. He later studied music at Chicago Music College with the idea of becoming a concert pianist, but left at the age of 18 to get married. He got a job working in a record shop and joined the Clefs, a seven-piece dance band. In 1956, he formed a jazz trio with the Clefs' rhythm section (whom he had known since high school): bassist Eldee Young and drummer Isaac 'Red' Holt. Lewis made his debut recordings with the Argo record label, which later became Chess. He also had record dates with prestigious names such as Sonny Stitt, Clark Terry and Max Roach. In 1959, he played at Birdland in New York City and at the Randall's Island Festival. In 1964, 'Something You Got' was a minor hit, but it was 'The In Crowd', an instrumental cover of Dobie Gray's hit, that made him famous, reaching number 5 in the US charts and selling over a million copies by the end of 1965. Lewis insisted on a live sound, complete with handclaps and exclamations, an infectious translation of a black church feel into pop. His follow-up, 'Hang On Sloopy' got to number 11 and sold another million. These hits set the agenda for his career. Earnings for club dates increased tenfold. His classic 'Wade In The Water' was a major hit in 1966, and became a long-standing encore number for Graham Bond. The rhythm section left, to resurface as a funk outfit in the mid-70s variously known as Redd Holt Unlimited and Young-Holt Unlimited. Lewis had an astute ear for hip, commercial sounds: his replacement drummer Maurice White left in 1971 to found the platinum mega-sellers Earth Wind And Fire. Lewis never recaptured this commercial peak, though he attempted to woo his audience by using synthesizers and disco rhythms, he continued with **Billboard** Top 100 hits well into the 70s. His album success was quite an achievement with over 30 of his albums making the *Billboard* Top 200 listings. *The In Crowd* stayed on the list for almost a year, narrowly missing the top spot. *Mother Nature's Son* was a tribute to the Beatles while the *Newly Recorded Hits* in 1973 was a dreadful mistake, the originals were far superior. By the 80s he was producing middle-of-the-road instrumental albums and accompanying singers, most notably Nancy Wilson. Nevertheless it is his 60s hits - simple, infectious and funky - that will long endure.
Albums: *Gentlemen Of Jazz* (1958), *Stretching Out* (1960), *Sound Of Christmas* (1962), *At The Bohemian Caverns* (1964), *Bach To The Blues* (1964), *The In Crowd* (1965), *Hang On Ramsey!* (1965), *Wade In The Water* (1966), *Goin' Latin* (1967), *The Movie Album* (1967), *Dancing In The Street* (1967), *Up Pops Ramsey Lewis* (1968), *Maiden Voyage* (1968), *Mother Nature's Son* (1969), *Another Voyage* (1969), *Ramsey Lewis: The Piano Player* (1970), *Them Changes* (1970), *Back To The Roots* (1971), *Upendo Ni Pamoja* (1972), *Funky*

Serenity (1973), *Sun Goddess* (1974), *Don't It Feel Good* (1975), *Salongo* (1976), *Love Notes* (1977), *Tequila Mockingbird* (1977), *Legacy* (1978), *Routes* (1980), *Three Piece Suite* (1981), *Live At The Savoy* (1982), *Les Fleurs* (1983), *Chance Encounter* (1983), with Nancy Wilson *The Two Of Us* (1984), *Renunion* (1984), *Fantasy* (1986), *Keys To The City* (1987), *Classic Encounter* (1989). Compilations: *Choice* (1965), *The Best Of Ramsey Lewis* (1970), *Newly Recorded All-Time Non-Stop Golden Hits* (1973), *The Greatest Hits Of Ramsey Lewis* (1990).

Leyton, John

b. 17 February 1939, Frinton-on-Sea, Essex, England. Originally a small-time actor in the television series *Biggles,* Leyton's good looks won him a recording contract with Top Rank Records. Backed by the strong management of Robert Stigwood and talented producer Joe Meek, he recorded 'Tell Laura I Love Her', but lost out to the chart-topping Ricky Valence. A second flop with 'Girl On The Floor Above' was followed by the timely intervention of songwriter Geoff Goddard with the haunting 'Johnny Remember Me'. Stigwood ensured that the song was incorporated into Leyton's latest television role as pop singer Johnny St. Cyr in *Harpers, West One*. The nationwide exposure focused attention on the record and its otherworldly ambience and elaborate production were enough to bring Leyton a UK number 1. The Goddard-composed follow-up 'Wild Wind' reached number 2, and there were further minor hits with 'Son This Is She', 'Lone Rider' and 'Lonely City'. Avoiding the ravages of the beat boom, Leyton continued his acting career in such films as *The Great Escape* (1963), *Von Ryan's Express* (1965) and *Krakatoa* (1968). After a 10-year recording hiatus, he made a brief comeback in 1974 with an album written entirely by Kenny Young. Thereafter, Leyton concentrated on television work and related business interests.
Albums: *The Two Sides Of John Leyton* (1961), *Always Yours* (1963), *John Leyton* (1974). Compilations: *Rarities* (1984), *The Best Of John Leyton* (1988).

Lind, Bob

b. 25 November 1942, Baltimore, Maryland, USA. Lind is best known for writing and recording the Top 5 folk-rock song 'Elusive Butterfly' in 1966. He moved around often with his family, and while settled in Denver, Colorado, he began singing folk music in clubs. He moved to the west coast and was signed to World Pacific Records, a division of the larger Liberty Records. Produced by Jack Nitzsche, Lind played guitar on his recordings for the label, while piano was handled by Leon Russell. His first single, 'Cheryl's Goin' Home', failed to catch on but was later covered by Cher and the Blues Project.

'Elusive Butterfly' was its b-side and became an international Top 10 hit. Lind was widely touted as 'the new Bob Dylan' and the latest spokesperson for youth during 1966. Despite his pop star looks and sensitive lyrics, however, his subsequent singles failed to reach the charts. *Don't Be Concerned* contained a number of sentimental, but attractive songs. His compositions continued to find interpreters, among them the Turtles, Noel Harrison, Nancy Sinatra and Bobby Sherman. Lind continued to record into the early 70s, switching to Capitol Records without a revival of his commercial fortunes. He was still performing in folk and country music circles in the early 80s.

Albums: *Don't Be Concerned* (1966), *The Elusive Bob Lind* (1966), *Photographs Of Feeling* (1966), *Since There Were Circles* (1971).

Little Anthony And The Imperials

Formed in Brooklyn, New York, USA in 1957 and originally called the Chesters, the group comprised 'Little' Anthony Gourdine (b. 8 January 1940, Brooklyn, New York, USA), Ernest Wright Jnr. (b. 24 August 1941, Brooklyn, New York, USA), Clarence Collins (b. 17 March 1941, Brooklyn, New York, USA), Tracy Lord and Glouster Rogers (b. 1940). A vital link between doo-wop and sweet soul, the Imperials were the prototype for the Delfonics and Stylistics. Gourdine first recorded in 1956 as a member of the Duponts. From there he helped form the Chesters, who became the Imperials on signing to the End label. The 'Little Anthony' prefix was subsequently added at the suggestion of the influential disc jockey Alan Freed. The group's first hit, the haunting 'Tears On My Pillow' (1958), encapsulated the essence of street-corner harmony. Further success came with 'So Much' (1959) and 'Shimmy Shimmy Ko-Ko-Bop' (1960), before Gourdine was persuaded to embark on an ill-fated solo career. In 1964, he formed a 'new' Imperials around Wright, Collins and Sammy Strain (b. 9 December 1940). Their first hit, 'I'm On The Outside (Looking In)' showcased Anthony's dazzling falsetto, a style continued on 'Goin' Out Of My Head' and 'Hurt So Bad' (both of which reached the US pop Top 10). Complementing these graceful releases were such uptempo offerings as 'Better Use Your Head' and 'Gonna Fix You Good' (both 1966). The line-up later drifted apart and in 1974 Sammy Strain replaced William Powell in the O'Jays. Three years later, Collins formed his own 'Imperials', touring Britain on the strength of two hit singles, a reissued 'Better Use Your Head', and a new recording, 'Who's Gonna Love Me'. In the 80s Gourdine released *Daylight* on the religious outlet, Songbird.

Albums: *We Are Little Anthony And The Imperials* (1959), *Shades Of The 40's* (1961), *I'm On The Outside Looking In* (1964), *Goin' Out Of My Head* (1965), *Paying Our Dues* (1967), *Reflections* (1967), *Movie Grabbers* (1968), *Out Of Sight, Out Of Mind* (1969), *On A New Street* (1974). Compilations: *Outside Looking In* (1984), *The Best Of Little Anthony And The Imperials* (1989). Solo album: Anthony Gourdine *Daylight* (1980).

Little Eva

Little Eva

b. Eva Narcissus Boyd, 29 June 1943, Bellhaven, North Carolina, USA. Discovered by songwriters Carole King and Gerry Goffin, Little Eva burst to fame in 1962 with the international hit, 'The Loco-Motion', a driving, dance-based song. Its ebullient, adolescent approach was muted on a follow-up single, 'Keep Your Hands Off My Baby', but although further releases from the following year, 'Let's Turkey Trot' and 'Old Smokey Locomotion', revived its novelty appeal, they lacked its basic excitement. Eva continued to record until 1965, but her only other substantial hit came with 'Swinging On A Star', a duet with Big Dee Irwin on which she was, unfortunately, uncredited. She made a UK chart comeback in 1972 with 'The Loco-Motion' re-issue peaking at number 11 and the song's lasting appeal was reaffirmed in 1988 when Kylie Minogue emulated Eva's original UK chart position.

Album: *Loco-Motion* (1962). Compilations: *Lil' Loco'Motion* (1982), *The Best Of Little Eva* (1988),

Back On Track (1989).

Liverpool Scene

The name 'Liverpool Scene' was derived from a poetry anthology which featured Roger McGough, Adrian Henri and Brian Patten. The writers subsequently appeared on UK television's *Look Of The Week*, where their readings were accompanied by guitarist Andy Roberts. McGough and Henri then recorded *The Incredible New Liverpool Scene*, which included definitive performances of their best-known work, including 'Let Me Die A Young Man's Death' (McGough) and 'Tonight At Noon' (Henri). While McGough pursued a career within Scaffold, Henri and Roberts added Mike Hart (guitar/vocals), Mike Evans (saxophone/vocals) Percy Jones (bass) and Brian Dodson (drums) to create an explicitly rock-based ensemble. UK disc jockey John Peel was an early patron and the group quickly found itself an integral part of music's underground circuit, culminating in their impressive appearance at the 1969 Isle Of Wight Festival. *The Amazing Adventures Of . . .* captured the sextet at their most potent, but successive albums, although worthwhile, failed to match the crucial balance between musical and lyrical content and the group broke up in 1970. Hart embarked on a solo career, but while Roberts initially found fame in Plainsong, he was later reunited with both Henri and McGough in Grimms.

Albums: *The Incredible New Liverpool Scene* (1967), *The Amazing Adventures Of . . .* (1968), *Bread On The Night* (1969), *Saint Adrian Co. Broadway And 3rd* (1970), *Heirloom* (1970). Compilation: *Recollections* (1972).

Lomax, Jackie

b. 10 May 1944, Wallasey, Merseyside, England. A former vocalist with the 60s beat group the Undertakers, Lomax began a new career in America when this respected Liverpool unit disbanded. Spells with two short-lived bands, the Mersey Lads and the Lost Souls, preceded a return to England where the singer worked with his own group, the Lomax Alliance, and as a solo act. Two strong, but unsuccessful, singles followed before he was signed to the fledgling Apple label but his opening release, 'Sour Milk Sea', written for him by George Harrison, was unfortunately overshadowed by hits for stablemates the Beatles and Mary Hopkin. Jackie's debut *Is This What You Want*, featured contributions from a host of star names including Harrison, Paul McCartney, Ringo Starr and Eric Clapton. The artist's stylish compositions and superb voice were equal to such esteemed company. Sadly, Apple's internal problems doomed his undoubted potential and following an interlude as part of the elusive Heavy Jelly, Lomax returned to America where he completed two more excellent albums, *Home Is In My Head* and *Three*. In 1973, the singer joined the British-based Badger, a group formed by ex-Yes organist, Tony Kaye. Lomax helped transform them from a progressive rock band into a more soulful aggregation, exemplified on *White Lady*, which was produced by Allen Toussaint and consisted solely of Jackie's songs. Badger then split into two factions, with Lomax and bassist Kim Gardner instigating an offshoot unit named after the album. Jackie subsequently resumed his solo career, but the releases which followed were disappointing and the ill-luck which had often dogged this worthwhile performer further undermined his career. Lomax did resurface in 1990 as one of several acts contributing to the 'tribute' album *True Voices* wherein he sang a version of Tim Buckley's 'Devil Eyes'.

Albums: *Is This What You Want* (1969), *Home Is In My Head* (1971), *Three* (1972), with Badger *White Lady* (1974), *Livin' For Lovin'* (1976), *Did You Ever* (1977).

Lopez, Trini

b. Trinidad Lopez III, 15 May 1937, Dallas, Texas, USA. Trini Lopez took folk songs and rocked them up into Latin rhythms, recording 14 chart albums and 13 chart singles between 1963 and 1968. Propelled by a strong R&B-influenced backbeat (usually provided by bassist Dave Shriver and drummer Gene Riggio) and his own incessantly rhythmic guitar, Lopez was at his best when playing live. A number of his nightclub performances were recorded and released as albums. Lopez listened to R&B music while growing up, and formed his first band in Wichita Falls, Texas at the age of 15. At the recommendation of Buddy Holly, Lopez went to the producer Norman Petty in Clovis, New Mexico, but Lopez did not record with him as Petty wanted to record only instrumental music. In 1958, however, Petty did secure Lopez and his group the Big Beats a deal with Columbia Records, which released the single 'Clark's Expedition'/'Big Boy', ironically an instrumental. Lopez made his first solo recording, his own composition 'The Right To Rock', for the Dallas-based Volk Records, and then signed with King Records in 1959, recording more than a dozen singles for that label, none of which charted. In late 1962, after the King deal expired, Lopez followed up on an offer by producer Snuff Garrett to join the post-Holly Crickets as vocalist. After a couple of weeks of auditions in Los Angeles that idea did not bear fruit and Lopez formed his own group.

He landed a steady engagement at the nightclub PJ's, where his audience soon grew. He was heard there by Frank Sinatra, who had started his own label, Reprise Records, and signed Lopez. He was placed with arranger/producer Don Costa, who wisely chose to record Lopez in concert at the club. His first album, *Trini Lopez At PJ's*, rose to number 2 in the summer of 1963 and stayed in the US charts for nearly two years. The first single from the album, an uptempo party-like version of Pete Seeger's 'If I Had A Hammer', reached number 3, (number 4 in the UK) out-performing Peter, Paul And Mary's more sedate rendering a year earlier. Lopez's subsequent recordings for Reprise displayed a musical eclecticism - he recorded a folk album, an R&B album, two Latin albums, country, in foreign languages (Spanish and German) and even Broadway show tunes, all in his infectiously simple sing-along style. Only one other Top 20 single resulted, 'Lemon Tree' in 1965, and he appeared in a number of films, including *The Dirty Dozen* and *Marriage On The Rocks*, but by the end of the 60s Lopez had largely disappeared from public view. He recorded sporadically in the 70s, including *Viva* and a number of singles for Capitol Records in 1971-72, and *Transformed By Time* for Roulette Records in 1978, and although he continued to sing in Las Vegas during the 80s little has been heard from Lopez since his heyday. There are numerous budget-label album releases of his music available, and several anthologies on European labels.

Selected albums: *Trini Lopez At PJ's* (1963), *More Trini Lopez At PJ's* (1963), *On The Move* (1964), *The Latin Album* (1964), *Live At Basin St. East* (1964), *The Folk Album* (1965), *The Love Album* (1965), *The Rhythm & Blues Album* (1965), *The Sing-Along World Of Trini Lopez* (1965), *Trini* (1966), *The Second Latin Album* (1966), *Trini Lopez In London* (1967), *Now!* (1967), *It's A Great Life* (1968), *Trini Country* (1968), *Viva* (1972), *Transformed By Time* (1978). Compilation: *Greatest Hits!* (1966), *La Bamba - 28 Greatest Hits* (1988).

Los Bravos

Originally known as Los Sonor, Mike Kogel (b. 25 April 1945, Beuliu, Germany; vocals), Antonio Martinez (b. 3 October 1945, Madrid, Spain; guitar), Manolo 'Manual' Fernandez (b. 29 September 1943, Seville, Spain; organ), Miguel Vicens Danus (b. 21 June 1944, Palma de Mallona, Spain; bass) and Pablo 'Gomez' Samllehi (b. 5 November 1943, Barcelona, Spain; drums) were voted Spain's top beat group following two Top 10 hits in their own country. They achieved international recognition in 1966 when 'Black Is Black', a song composed by two Englishmen, Tony Hayes and Steve Wadey, rose to number 2 in the UK charts in the wake of heavy promotion on pirate radio. The song's compulsive hookline proved equally popular in the USA where it reached number 4, but the quintet was sadly unable to repeat this success. Despite a series of superior pop performances, including an effervescent reading of an Easybeats' composition, 'Bring A Little Lovin''; 'I Don't Care' (1966) was the group's last UK Top 20 entry.

Albums: *Black Is Black* (1966), *Los Bravos* aka *Bring A Little Lovin'* (US) (1968).

Lothar And The Hand People

Although this splendidly-named quintet became fixtures of New York's underground circuit, they were formed in Denver, Colorado, USA in 1965. College drop-out John Arthur Emelin (vocals/theremin) was initially joined by Richard Lewis (rhythm guitar), Russell 'Rusty' Ford (bass) and Tom Lyle (drums), before William C. Wright (lead guitar) completed the line-up. Lewis and Wright were later replaced by Kim King (guitar) and Paul Conly (keyboards). Much attention to the group was given due to Emelin's use of the Theremin, an instrument capable of eerie electronic 'cries' similar to those used in horror movies and previously heard on the Beach Boys' 'Good Vibrations'. Lothar headed east at the behest of the Lovin' Spoonful whom they supported on a provincial tour. The new arrivals quickly secured a recording deal, but the apathy which greeted their first three singles delayed a debut album. *Presenting Lothar And The Hand People* was not issued until late 1968, although its simple, folksy atmosphere recalled a more innocent era. The album was produced by Robert Margouleff who went on to form the experimental Tonto's Expanding Headband. A second collection, *Space Hymn*, followed within a matter of months and showed a group embracing synthesized technology. The set maintained a love of melody, but despite positive reviews, the album was not a commercial success and Lothar And The Hand People broke up in 1971.

Albums: *Presenting Lothar And The Hand People* (1968), *Space Hymn* (1969). Compilation: *This Is It...Machines* (1986).

Loudermilk, John D.

b. 31 March 1934, Durham, North Carolina, USA. Loudermilk's first musical experience was banging a drum for the Salvation Army and he played various instruments as a child and appeared regularly on the radio from the age of 11. In 1956, George Hamilton IV recorded his song, 'A Rose And A Baby Ruth', which went from the local to the national charts, reaching number 6. A few months later Eddie Cochran made his debut in the US Top 20 with 'Sittin' In The Balcony', another Loudermilk song which he had recorded himself under the pseudonym, Johnny D.

When Loudermilk moved to Nashville, a stream of hits followed, the UK chart successes being 'Waterloo' (Stonewall Jackson, 1959); 'Angela Jones' (Michael Cox, 1960); 'Tobacco Road' (Nashville

Teens, 1964); 'Google Eye' (which was a catfish, Nashville Teens, 1964); 'This Little Bird' (Marianne Faithfull, 1965, and subsequently parodied by the Barron Knights); 'Then You Can Tell Me Goodbye' (Casinos, 1967, and a US country number 1 for Eddy Arnold); 'It's My Time' (the Everly Brothers, 1968); 'Indian Reservation (The Lament Of The Cherokee Reservation Indian)' (Don Fardon, 1970 and a US number 1 for the Raiders, 1971) and 'Sunglasses' (a revival of a Skeeter Davis record by Tracey Ullman, 1984). His controversial 'death' song, 'Ebony Eyes', was the b-side of the Everly Brothers' 1961 number 1, 'Walk Right Back'. Other successful b-sides include 'Weep No More My Baby' (Brenda Lee's 'Sweet Nuthins'); 'Stayin' In' (Bobby Vee's 'More Than I Can Say'); 'Heaven Fell Last Night' (the Browns' 'The Three Bells') and 'In A Matter Of Moments' (Louise Cordet's 'I'm Just A Baby'). Near misses include 'All Of This For Sally' (Mark Dinning), 'The Guitar Player (Him And Her)' for Jimmy Justice and 'To Hell With Love' for Adam Faith. He arranged an old song, 'Abilene', for George Hamilton IV, and it made the US charts in 1963 and became a country standard. His other country music successes include 'Talk Back Trembling Lips' (Ernest Ashworth and Johnny Tillotson); 'Bad News' (Johnny Cash and Boxcar Willie); 'Break My Mind' (George Hamilton IV, Gram Parsons and the Hillsiders); 'You're Ruinin' My Life' (Hank Williams Jnr.) and 'Half-Breed' (Marvin Rainwater). He wrote clever novelty songs for Bob Luman ('The Great Snowman' and 'The File') and for Sue Thompson ('Sad Movies (Make Me Cry)', 'Norman', 'James (Hold The Ladder Steady)' and 'Paper Tiger', all US Top 30 hits).

Loudermilk had his own hit with 'The Language Of Love', which made number 13 in the UK in 1962. He made several albums of his own material and they have been collected onto two Bear Family compilations, *Blue Train* and *It's My Time*, which contain two previously unreleased tracks in 'The Little Wind Up Doll' and 'Giving You All My Love'. He has often worked in the UK and performs his songs in a similar manner to Burl Ives. He produced Pete Sayers' best album, *Bogalusa Gumbo*, in 1979 but an album which he recorded at the same sessions has not been released. Sayers says of Loudermilk, 'His songs are so different that you can't really choose between them, but I like the virtually unknown ones like 'Ma Baker's Little Acre'. In concert, he's adding to his songs all the time, putting in riffs or telling a story in the middle of a song. His songs are like plants, growing all the time.'

Albums: *The Language Of Love* (1962), *Twelve Sides Of Loudermilk* (1962), *John D. Loudermilk Sings A Bizarre Collection Of Unusual Songs* (1965), *Suburban Attitudes In Country Verse* (1967), *Country Love Songs* (1968),

The Open Mind Of John D. Loudermilk (1969), *Elloree* (c.70s), *Just Passing Through* (1977). Compilations: *Blue Train* (1989), *It's My Time* (1989).

Love

For many, the doyens of Los Angeles progressive rock in the 60s, brilliantly erratic and producers of one of the finest rock albums ever made: *Forever Changes*. Love were formed in 1965 as the Grass Roots by Bryan Maclean (b. 1947 Los Angeles, California, USA; guitar/vocals), Arthur Lee (b. 1945, Memphis, Tennessee, USA; guitar/vocals), John Echols (b. 1945, Memphis, Tennessee, USA; lead guitar). Don Conka (drums) and Johnny Fleckenstein were soon replaced by Alban 'Snoopy' Pfisterer (b. 1947, Switzerland) and Ken Forssi (b. 1943, Cleveland, Ohio, USA). They become the first rock band to be signed by the expanding Elektra Records, just beating the Doors by a whisker. Their debut single was Burt Bacharach and Hal David's 'My Little Red Book', in a different form from the way the writers imagined it. Love were an instant sensation on the LA club scene, outrageous, loud, innovative and stoned. The furiously energetic '7 And 7 Is' was released in the summer of 1966 and became their second hit. Although 'The Castle' on *Da Capo* pointed to a new direction it was *Forever Changes* that put them in the history books. That album, 25 years later, is still found on most critics' recommended list and no comprehensive record collection should be without it. It is a superlative record, unassumingly brilliant, gentle, biting and full of surprises. It proved to be Arthur Lee's finest work and marked the end of the partnership with Bryan Maclean. A new Love featuring Lee, Frank Fayad (bass), Jay Donnellan (guitar) and the drumming pyrotechnics of George Suranovitch, proved to be the most stable line-up and lasted for two albums. Both records contained rare glimpses of *Forever Changes*, but ultimately they were bitter disappointments. *False Start* featured few memorable moments, one being a guitar solo from Jimi Hendrix. *Reel To Real* is a truly wretched affair. The long-held opinion that Arthur Lee had become a casualty of too many chemicals was strengthened throughout the 70s, 80s and 90s with various stories chronicling his erratic and eccentric behaviour. Many attempts to resurrect his career have faltered, although there are hopeful signs that his comeback in 1992 will be more lasting.

Albums: *Love* (1966), *Da Capo* (1967), *Forever Changes* (1967), *Four Sail* (1969), *Out Here* (1969), *False Start* (1970), *Reel To Real* (1974), *Love Live* (1982), *Love* (1982), as Arthur Lee And Love *Arthur Lee And Love* (1992). Compilations: *Love Revisited* (1970), *Love Masters* (1973), *Out There* (1988, a compilation culled from *Out Here* and *False Start*).

Love Affair

Originally formed in 1966, this London-based quintet comprised Steve Ellis (vocals), Morgan Fisher (keyboards), Rex Brayley (guitar), Mick Jackson (bass) and Maurice Bacon (drums). Although Ellis was barely 16 years old, the group performed frequently in clubs on a semi-professional basis. Fisher was briefly replaced by Lynton Guest and the following year Ellis, backed by session musicians, recorded a sparkling cover of Robert Knight's 'Everlasting Love' for CBS Records. By January 1968, the single unexpectedly hit number 1 in the UK and Love Affair became instant pop stars with Ellis' cherubic looks gracing teen magazines throughout the nation. With Mo Bacon's father Sid overseeing the management, the group resisted the solicitations of more powerful entrepreneurs, yet failed to exploit their potential. Four more hits followed, 'Rainbow Valley', 'A Day Without Love', 'One Road' and 'Bringing On Back The Good Times', but by the end of the 60s, the lead singer quit to form his own group, Ellis. Fisher reappeared in Mott The Hoople, Bacon became a music publisher and the group name was successively plundered for cabaret/revivalist bookings.

Compilation: *Greatest Hits* (1985).

Love Sculpture

Love Sculpture

Having recorded as the Human Beans, Dave Edmunds (b. 15 April 1944, Cardiff, South Glamorgan, Wales; guitar) and John Williams (bass) formed Love Sculpture in 1967 with Bob 'Congos' Jones (drums). This Cardiff-based trio enjoyed modest airplay with their debut single, 'River To Another Day', before a rousing interpretation of Aram Khachaturian's 'Sabre Dance', initially aired as a radio session by BBC disc jockey John Peel, became a surprising hit single. Its success bestowed a novelty tag on a group already hampered by a lack of musical direction and although their debut album offered worthy blues interpretations, the psychedelic tinges on a second set were somewhat anachronistic. This impasse led to a split in the original line-up and Mickey Gee (bass) and Terry Williams (drums, later of Man and Dire Straits) joined the guitarist for a final flourish. Edmunds then disbanded the group and embarked on a solo career.

Albums: *Blues Helping* (1968), *Forms And Feelings* (1969). Compilations: *The Classic Tracks 1968/72* (1974), *The Dave Edmunds And Love Sculpture Singles As And Bs* (1990).

Lovin' Spoonful

Lovin' Spoonful

Few American pop groups have gathered as much universal affection over the years as the brilliant and underrated Lovin' Spoonful. Their back catalogue of hits is constantly repackaged and reissued, as their stature increases. They were formed in 1965 by John Sebastian (b. 17 March 1944, New York, USA; vocal/guitar/harmonica/autoharp) and Zalman Yanovsky (b. 19 December 1944, Toronto, Canada; guitar/vocals) following their time together in the Mugwumps (as eulogized in the Mamas And The Papas hit 'Creeque Alley'). The band were completed by Steve Boone (b. 23 September 1943, Camp Lejeune, North Carolina, USA; bass) and Joe Butler (b. 19 January 1943, Long Island, New York, USA; drums/vocals). Their unique blend of jug-band, folk, blues and rock 'n' roll synthesized into what was termed as 'electric good-time music' kept them apart from every other American pop group at that time.

In two years they notched up 10 US Top 20 hits, all composed by John Sebastian. From the opening strum of Sebastian's autoharp on 'Do You Believe In Magic?' the party began; from the evocative 'You Didn't Have To Be So Nice', to the languid singalong 'Daydream'. From the punchy and lyrically outstanding 'Summer In The City'; 'Hot town summer in the city, back of my neck getting dirt and gritty', to the gentle romanticism of 'Rain On The Roof'; 'You and me and the rain on the roof, caught up in a summer shower, drying while it soaks the flowers, maybe we'll be caught for hours'. Their four regular albums were crammed full of other gems in addition to the hits. Additionally Sebastian wrote the music for two films; Woody Allen's *What's Up Tiger Lily* and Francis Ford Coppola's *You're A Big Boy Now*, the latter featuring the beautiful 'Darling Be Home Soon'. Sadly the non-stop party came to an end in 1968 following the departure of Yanovsky and the arrival, albeit briefly, of Jerry Yester. The quality of Sebastian's lyrics and melodies makes him one of the finest American songwriters. In 1991, Steve Boone, Joe Butler and the Yester brothers announced the reformation of the band for a tour - however, without Yanovsky and Sebastian, the 'magic' will not be there.

Albums: *Do You Believe In Magic* (1965), *Daydream* (1966), *What's Shakin'* (1966), *What's Up Tiger Lily* (1966, film soundtrack), *Hums Of The Lovin' Spoonful* (1966), *You're A Big Boy Now* (1967, film soundtrack), *Everything Playing* (1968), *Revelation: Revolution* (1968). Compilations: *The EP Collection* (1988), *Collection: Lovin' Spoonful, 20 Hits* (1988), *The Very Best Of The Lovin' Spoonful* (1988), *Go To The Movies* (1991).

Lulu

b. Marie MacDonald McLaughlin Lawrie, 3 November 1948, Lennox Castle, Glasgow, Scotland. Lulu was originally a beat group vocalist with her own backing group the Luvvers, who comprised, Ross Nelson (guitar), Jim Dewar (rhythm guitar), Alec Bell (keyboards), Jimmy Smith (saxophone), Tony Tierney (bass) and David Miller (drums). The 15-year-old singer first came to prominence with a rasping version of the Isley Brothers' 'Shout' in 1964. Under the tutelage of manager Marian Massey she survived a stormy couple of years during which only two of her eight singles charted. Abandoning the Luvvers along the way, she switched record labels from Decca to EMI/Columbia Records and found a new hitmaker in the form of Mickie Most. A cover of Neil Diamond's 'The Boat That I Row' saw an upsurge in her career during 1967, which was punctuated by an acting part in the movie *To Sir With Love*. The theme tune from the film gave her a million-selling US number 1, and in the UK it reached number 6, despite originally being relegated to b-side status. Further UK hits followed, notably 'Lets Pretend', 'Me, The Peaceful Heart', 'Boy' and 'I'm A Tiger'. Having established herself as an entertainer of wide appeal, Lulu was granted her own television series and later represented Britain in the Eurovision Song Contest. 'Boom-Bang-A-Bang' tied for first place and provided her highest UK chart placing at number 2. Her brief marriage to Maurice Gibb of the Bee Gees was followed by another switch of labels and musical styles when she worked with famed producer Jerry Wexler on two albums. A lean period of flop singles ended when David Bowie intervened to produce and arrange her hit version of 'The Man Who Sold The World'. During the 70s, she concentrated increasingly on stage work and developed her career as an all-round entertainer, a spin-off which was becoming the long-standing model/endorser for the Freeman's mail-order catalogue. Appearances in *Guys And Dolls, Song And Dance* and the television programme, *The Secret Diary Of Adrian Mole* distracted her from the studio but a disco re-recording of 'Shout', in 1986, repeated the Top 10 success of 22 years before.

Albums: *Something To Shout About* (1965), *Love Loves To Love Lulu* (1967), *Lulu's Album* (1969), *New Routes* (1970), *Melody Fair* (1971), *Don't Take Love For Granted* (1979), *Lulu* (1981), *Take Me To Your Heart Again* (1982). Compilations: *The Most Of Lulu* (1971), *Shout* (1983), *I'm A Tiger* (1989).

Lynch, Kenny

b. 18 March 1939, Stepney, London, England. Britain's best-known black all-round entertainer has been a television personality for three decades. The youngest of 13 children, he first appeared on stage at the age of 12 with his sister, singer Maxine Daniels. At 16 he joined Ed Nichol's Band and before going into the services in 1957 worked in a string of bands including Bob Miller's. He joined HMV Records and hit the UK Top 40 in 1960 with his debut single, a cover of 'Mountain Of Love'. He appeared in several films and hit his recording peak in 1963 with two successive Top 10 entries - a cover of 'Up On The Roof' and 'You Can Never Stop Me Loving You' (which made the US Top 20 when covered by Johnny Tillotson). Over the next 20 years he was one of the UK's busiest and most popular entertainers and was also awarded an OBE. He co-wrote the Small Faces number 1, 'Sha La La La Lee' and has recorded spasmodically since then on Columbia, Atlantic Records, Polydor, Laser, Towerbell and Spartan. In 1983, he had a surprise chart return with a Brit-funk track 'Half The Day's Gone And We Haven't Earned A Penny' on Satril.

Selected albums: *We Love Kenny* (1966), *Half The Day's Gone And We Haven't Earned A Penny* (1983).

M

McGuire, Barry

b. 15 October 1935, Oklahoma City, Oklahoma, USA. McGuire first came to prominence as a minor actor in *Route 66* before teaming up with singer Barry Kane as Barry And Barry. In 1962, he joined the New Christy Minstrels and appeared as lead singer on several of their hits, most notably, 'Green Green' and 'Saturday Night'. He also sang the lead on their comic but catchy 'Three Wheels On My Wagon'. While still a Minstrel, he composed the hit 'Greenback Dollar' for the Kingston Trio. After leaving the New Christy Minstrels, McGuire signed to Lou Adler's Dunhill Records and was assigned to staff writers P.F. Sloan and Steve Barri. At the peak of the folk-rock boom, they wrote the rabble-rousing protest 'Eve Of Destruction', which McGuire took to number 1 in the USA, surviving a blanket radio ban in the process.The anti-establishment nature of the lyric even provoked an answer record, 'Dawn Of Correction', written by John Madara and Dave White under the pseudonym the Spokesmen. Ironically, 'Eve Of Destruction' had originally been conceived as a flip-side and at one stage was offered to the Byrds, who turned it down. Coincidentally, both Barry McGuire and Byrds leader Jim (later Roger) McGuinn received a flattering namecheck on the Mamas And The Papas' hit 'Creeque Alley' ('McGuinn and McGuire were just a-getting higher in LA, you know where that's at'). McGuire, in fact, played a significant part in bringing the million-selling vocal quartet to Adler and they later offered their services as his backing singers.

McGuire attempted unsuccessfully to follow-up his worldwide hit with other Sloan material, including the excellent 'Upon A Painted Ocean'. He continued to pursue the protest route on the albums *Eve Of Destruction* and *This Precious Time*, but by 1967 he was branching out into acting. A part in *The President's Analyst* led to a Broadway appearance in the musical *Hair*. After the meagre sales of *The World's Last Private Citizen*, McGuire ceased recording until 1971, when he returned with former Mamas And The Papas sideman Eric Hord on *Barry McGuire And The Doctor*. The work featured backing from the cream of the 1965 school of folk-rock, including the Byrds' Chris Hillman and Michael Clarke. Soon afterwards, McGuire became a Christian evangelist and thereafter specialized in gospel albums.

Albums: *Eve Of Destruction* (1965), *This Precious Time* (1966), *The World's Last Private Citizen* (1967), *Barry McGuire And The Doctor* (1971), *Seeds* (1973), *Finer Than Gold* (1981), *Inside Out* (1982), *To The Bride* (1982), *Best Of Barry* (1982).

McKenzie, Scott

b. Philip Blondheim, 1 October 1944, Arlington, Virginia, USA. McKenzie began his professional career in the Journeymen, a clean-cut folk group. He later recorded some undistinguished solo material before fellow ex-member John Phillips, currently enjoying success with the Mamas And The Papas, invited the singer to join him in Los Angeles. Although the folk/rock-inspired 'No No No No No' failed to sell, the pairing flourished spectacularly on 'San Francisco (Be Sure To Wear Some Flowers In Your Hair)'. This altruistic hippie anthem, penned by Phillips, encapsulated the innocent wonderment felt by many onlookers of the era and the single, buoyed by an irresistible melody, reached number 4 in the US chart, but climbed to the dizzy heights of number 1 in the UK and throughout Europe. Meritorious follow-ups, 'Like An Old Time Movie' and 'Holy Man', failed to emulate such success, and although McKenzie briefly re-emerged with the low-key, country-influenced *Stained Glass Morning*, he remained out of the public eye until the 80s, when he joined Phillips in a rejuvenated Mamas And Papas.

Albums: *The Voice Of Scott McKenzie* (1967), *Stained Glass Morning* (1970).

Mamas And The Papas

Mamas And The Papas

Formed in Los Angeles in 1965, this enthralling harmony group embodied the city's astute blend of folk and pop. John Phillips (b. 30 August 1941, Parris Island, South Carolina, USA) had been a founder member of the popular Journeymen, before establishing this new attraction with his wife Michelle Phillips (b. Holly Michelle Gilliam, 6 April 1944, Long Beach, California, USA), and former Mugwumps' members Denny Doherty (b. 29 November 1941, Halifax, Nova Scotia, Canada) and Cass Elliot (b. Ellen Naimoi Cohen, 19 September 1943, Alexandria, Virginia, USA, d. 29 July 1974,

London, England). Although drawing inspiration from the flourishing milieu of New York's Greenwich Village, the quartet quickly moved to California, where they met producer Lou Adler through the interjection of mutual acquaintance Barry McGuire. The then unnamed Mamas And Papas contributed backing vocals to the latter's second album, which in turn inspired the group's own career. Their debut single, 'California Dreamin'', was originally recorded by McGuire, whose voice was simply erased and replaced by that of Doherty. Penned by Phillips and Gilliam, the song provided a vivid contrast between the cold New York winter and the warmth and security of life on the west coast and effectively established the group as arguably the finest vocal ensemble form their era working in the pop field. The group's bohemian image was reinforced by their compositional skill and distinctive individual personalities. Visually, they seemed eccentrically contrasting: John, a towering 6 foot 4 inches, thin as a rake, and cast in the role of group intellectual; Denny the 'good-looking Canadian' and master of the sarcastic one-liner; Cass, overweight, uproarious and charming; and Michelle, quiet, beautiful and 'angelic when she wants to be'. With 'California Dreamin'' they infiltrated the US Top 5 and the song became a standard, covered by many artists, most notably Jose Feliciano. The richly-harmonic follow-up, 'Monday Monday' reached number 1 in the US and also established the group in the UK. Further timeless hit singles followed, including the soaring 'I Saw Her Again' and a brilliant revival of the Shirelles 'Dedicated To The One I Love'. Michelle's sensual, semi-spoken introduction, backed by a solitary acoustic guitar remains one of the most classic and memorable openings to any pop recording.

The group's albums achieved gold status and while the first was sprinkled with cover versions, the second documented Phillip's development as a songwriter. He was involved in no less than 10 compositions, two of which ('No Salt On Her Tail' and 'Strange Young Girls') were particularly outstanding. Marital problems between John and Michelle eroded the stability of the group and she was fired in 1966 and briefly replaced by lookalike Jill Gibson. The group reconvened for *Deliver*, another strong album, which was followed by the autobiographical 'Creeque Alley', which humorously documented their rise to fame. During the summer of 1967 Phillips organized the Monterey Pop Festival and helped launch the career of former Journeymen Scott McKenzie by writing the chart-topping hippie anthem 'San Francisco'. In the winter of 1967, the group arrived in the UK for concerts at London's Royal Albert Hall. After docking at Southampton, Cass was arrested by police, charged with stealing blankets and

keys from the Royal Garden Hotel in Kensington on an earlier visit. The charges were dropped but the concerts were subsequently cancelled, amid break-up rumours. The unit managed to complete one last album, *The Papas And Mamas*, a superb work that highlighted Phillip's brilliance as a songwriter. 'Safe In My Garden', 'For The Love Of Ivy' and the sublime 'Twelve Thirty' were all minor classics, while 'Rooms' and 'Mansions' incisively documented the spiritual isolation that accompanied their rise to international stardom: 'Limousines and laughter, parties ever after/If you play the game you pay the price/purchasing our piece of paradise'. It was a fitting valediction.

After splitting up in 1968, the quartet embarked on solo careers, with varying success. Three years later, the group briefly reformed for *People Like Us*, but their individual contributions were taped separately and the results were disappointing. Cass enjoyed the greatest success as a solo artist but her career was tragically cut short by sudden death in July 1974. Michelle continued to pursue an acting career, while John plummeted into serious drug addiction, near-death and arrest. He subsequently recovered and in 1982 he and Denny reformed the Mamas And Papas. The new line-up featured Phillip's actress daughter Laura McKenzie (McKenzie Phillips) and Elaine 'Spanky' McFarlane of Spanky And Our Gang. Doherty left when the band began touring full-time, and was replaced by the aforementioned McKenzie for an attraction which steadfastly retains its popularity.

Albums: *If You Can Believe Your Eyes And Ears* (1966), *The Mamas And The Papas* aka *Cass, John, Michelle, Denny* (1966), *The Mamas And The Papas Deliver* (1967), *The Papas And The Mamas* (1968), *Monterey International Pop Festival* (1971), *People Like Us* (1971). Compilations: *Farewell To The First Golden Era* (1967), *Golden Era Volume 2* (1968), *16 Of Their Greatest Hits* (1969), *A Gathering Of Flowers* (1971), *20 Golden Hits* (1973), *The ABC Collection: Greatest Hits* (1976), *Creeque Alley: The History Of The Mamas And Papas* (1991).

Further reading: *Papa John*, John Phillips with Jim Jerome. *California Dreamin' - The True Story Of The Mamas And Papas*, Michelle Phillips.

Mancini, Henry

b. 16 April 1924, Cleveland, Ohio, USA. Prompted by his father, a steelworker who loved music, Mancini learned to play several musical instruments while still a small child. As a teenager he developed an interest in jazz and especially music of the big bands. He wrote some arrangements and sent them to Benny Goodman, from whom he received some encouragement. In 1942, he became a student at the Juilliard School of Music, but his career was

Henry Mancini

interrupted by military service during World War II. Immediately following the war he was hired as pianist and arranger by Tex Beneke, who was then leading the Glenn Miller orchestra. Later in the 40s Mancini began writing arrangements for studios, prompted initially by a contract to score for a recording date secured by his wife, singer Ginny O'Connor. He was also hired to work on films, and it was here that his interest in big band music paid off. He wrote the scores for two Hollywood bio-pics, *The Glenn Miller Story* (1954) and *The Benny Goodman Story* (1956). Mancini also contributed jazz-influenced scores for television, including those for the innovative *Peter Gunn* series and *Mr Lucky*. His film work continued with scores and songs for such films as *Breakfast At Tiffany's* (1961), from which came 'Moon River', (the Oscar winner that year), the title songs for *Days Of Wine And Roses* (1962), which again won an Oscar, and the title song from *Charade* (1963). His other film work includes 'Baby Elephant Walk' from *Hatari!* (1962), the theme from *The Pink Panther* (1964), 'Sweetheart Tree' from *The Great Race* (1965), and scores for *Wait Until Dark* (1967), *Darling Lili* (1970), *Mommie Dearest* (1980), *Victor/Victoria* (1982) and *That's Dancing* (1985). One of the most respected film and television composers, Mancini also regularly conducts orchestras in the USA and UK in concerts of his music, most of which stands comfortably on its own merits outside the context for which it was originally conceived.

Selected albums: *The Music From Peter Gunn* (1959), *Breakfast At Tiffany's* (1961), *Hatari* (1962), *The Concert Sound Of Henry Mancini* (1964), *The Latin Sound Of Henry Mancini* (1965), *Mancini '67* (1967), *A Warm Shade Of Ivory* (1969), *Mancini Country* (1970), *Mancini Plays Theme From Love Story* (1971), with Doc Severinsen *Brass, Ivory & Strings* (1973), *Mancini's Angels* (1977).

Further reading: *Henry Mancini*, Gene Lees.

Manfred Mann

During the UK beat boom of the early 60s, spearheaded by the Beatles, a number of R&B groups joined the tide with varying degrees of achievement. Of these, Manfred Mann had the most commercial success. The band was formed as the Mann-Hugg Blues Brothers by Manfred Mann (b. Manfred Lubowitz, 21 October 1940, Johannesburg, South Africa; keyboards) and Mike Hugg (b. 11 August 1942, Andover, Hampshire, England; drums/vibraphone). They became Manfred Mann shortly after adding Paul Jones (b. Paul Pond, 24 February 1942, Portsmouth, Hampshire, England; harmonica/vocals). The line-up was completed by Mike Vickers (b. 18 April 1941, Southampton, Hampshire, England; flute/guitar/saxophone) and Tom McGuinness (b. 2 December 1941, London, England; bass), following the departure of Dave Richmond. After being signed by a talent hungry HMV Records and following one unsuccessful instrumental, they made an impression with the catchy 'Cock-A-Hoop'. The prominent use of Jones' harmonica gave them a distinct sound and they soon became one of Britain's leading groups. No less than two of their singles were used as the theme music to the pioneering British television music programme, *Ready Steady Go*. '5-4-3-2-1' provided the breakthrough Top 10 hit in early 1964. By the summer, the group registered their first UK number 1 with the catchy 'Do Wah Diddy Diddy'. Over the next two years, they charted regularly with memorable hits such as 'Sha La La', 'Come Tomorrow', 'Oh No! Not My Baby' and Bob Dylan's 'If You Got To Go, Go Now'. In May 1966, they returned to number 1 with the sublime 'Pretty Flamingo'. It was to prove the last major hit on which Jones appeared. His departure for a solo career was a potential body blow to the group at a time when personnel changes were regarded as anathema by the pop media and fans. He was replaced by Michael D'Abo recruited from A Band Of Angels in preference to Rod Stewart, who failed the audition. Mike Vickers had previously departed for a lucrative career as a television composer. He was replaced by Jack Bruce on bass, allowing Tom McGuinness to move to lead guitar, a role he was happier with. Additionally, Henry Lowther (trumpet) and Lyn Dobson, (saxophone) enlarged the line-up for a time and Klaus Voorman replaced Bruce on bass. D'Abo's debut with the group was another hit rendering of a Dylan song, 'Just Like A Woman' their first for the Fontana label. He fitted in surprisingly well with the group, which surprised many critics by maintaining their hit formulae despite the departure of the charismatic Jones. Both 'Semi-Detached Surburban Mr. Jones' and 'Ha! Ha! Said The Clown' were formidable Top 5 hits in the classic Mann tradition. Along with America's Byrds, the group were generally regarded as the best interpreters of Dylan material, a view endorsed by the songwriter himself. This point was punctuated in 1968 when the group registered their third number 1 with the striking reading of his 'Mighty Quinn'. They ended the 60s with a final flurry of Top 10 hits, 'My Name Is Jack', 'Fox On The Run' and 'Raggamuffin Man' before abdicating their pop crown in favour of a heavier approach. Their albums had always been meatier and showed off their considerable dexterity as musicians working with jazz and blues-based numbers. Mann went on to form the jazz/rock unit Chapter Three and the highly successful Manfred Mann's Earth Band. Still highly respected, Manfred Mann remain one of the finest beat groups of the 60s.

Albums: *Five Faces Of Manfred Mann* (1964), *Mann Made* (1965), *Mann Made Hits* (1966), *As Is* (1966), *Soul Of Mann* (1967), *Up The Junction* (1967), *The Mighty Garvey* (1968), *The R&B Years* (1986). Compilations: *This Is Manfred Mann* (1971), *Semi-Detached Suburban* (1979), *The Singles Plus* (1987), *The EP Collection* (1989), *The Collection* (1990).

Manfred Mann

Mann, Barry

b. 9 February 1939, Brooklyn, New York, USA. One of the leading pop songwriters of his generation. Although trained as an architect, Mann began his career in music following a summer singing engagement in the Catskills resort. He initially composed material for Elvis Presley's publishers Hill & Range, before briefly collaborating with Howie Greenfield. In 1961, he enjoyed a Top 10 hit in his own right with 'Who Put The Bomp?', but thereafter it was as a composer that he dominated the Hot 100. During the same year as his solo hit, Mann had found a new songwriting partner in Cynthia Weil, whom he soon married. Their first success together was Tony Orlando's 'Bless You' (1961), a simple but effective love song, which endeared them to their new employer, bubblegum genius Don Kirschner, who housed a wealth of songwriting talent in the cubicles of his Brill Building offices. With intense competition from those other husband-and-wife teams Jeff Berry and Ellie Greenwich, and Gerry Goffin and Carole King, Mann and Weil responded with a wealth of classic songs which still sound fresh and impressive to this day. Like all great songwriters, they adapted well to different styles and themes, and this ensured that their compositions were recorded by a broad range of artists. There was the evocative urban romanticism of the Crystals' 'Uptown' (1962) and the Drifters' 'On Broadway' (1963), novelty teen fodder such as Eydie Gorme's 'Blame It On The Bossa Nova' (1963) and Paul Petersen's 'My Dad' (1963), the desolate neuroticism of Gene Pitney's 'I'm Gonna Be Strong' (1964) and the Righteous Brothers' 'You've Lost That Lovin' Feelin''(1964), and classic mid-60s protest songs courtesy of the Animals' 'We Gotta Get Out Of This Place', Jody Miller's 'Home Of The Brave', 'Only In America' (Jay And The Americans) and 'Kicks' (Paul Revere And The Raiders)

By the late 60s, Mann and Weil left Kirschner and moved to Hollywood. Throughout this period, they continued to enjoy hit success with Bobby Vinton's 'I Love How You Love Me' (1968), Jay And The Americans' 'Walking In The Rain' (1969) and B.J. Thomas' 'I Just Can't Help Believing' (1970). Changes in the pop marketplace subsequently reduced their hit output, but there were some notable successes such as Dan Hill's 'Sometimes When We Touch' (1977). Mann himself still craved recognition as a performer and won a recording contract, but his album work, most notably 1977's aptly titled *Survivor* failed to match the sales of his and his wife's much covered golden hits. *Survivor* was produced by Bruce Johnson and Terry Melcher, and was regarded as a leading example of the 70s' singer/songwriter oeuvre. Albums: *Who Put The Bomp* (1961), *Lay It All Out* (1971), *Survivor* (1975).

Marcels

The Marcels were one of several doo-wop influenced American vocal groups to score success in the early 60s, despite the passing of the genre's golden age. Cornelius 'Nini' Harp (lead singer), Ronald 'Bingo'

Mundy (tenor), Fred Johnson (bass), Gene Bricker (tenor) and Richard Knauss (baritone), all native to Pittsburg, Pennsylvania, USA, achieved fame for their distinctive version of Richard Rodgers/ Lorenz Hart's classic 'Blue Moon', previously a UK Top 10 hit for Elvis Presley in 1956, which topped both the US and UK charts in 1961. Johnson's distinctive bass introduction to the song has remained as one of most enduring vocal phrases of the time. The quartet scored a further US Top 10 hit that year with 'Heartaches', but its personnel was unstable, with Allen Johnson replacing Knauss and Walt Maddox replacing Bricker. Mundy walked out on the group during this same period, and this did nothing to prepare them for the ever-changing trends prevalent during the early 60s, and, eventually undermined the Marcels' long-term aspirations.
Album: *Blue Moon* (1961). Compilations: *Heartaches* (1987), *The Best Of The Marcels* (1990).

Mar-Keys

Formed in Memphis, Tennessee, USA, and originally known as the Royal Spades, their line-up comprised: Steve Cropper (b. 21 October 1941, Willow Spring, Missouri, USA; guitar), Donald 'Duck' Dunn (b. 24 November 1941, Memphis, Tennessee, USA; bass), Charles 'Packy' Axton (tenor saxophone), Don Nix (b. 27 September 1941, Memphis, Tennessee, USA; baritone saxophone), Wayne Jackson (trumpet), Charlie Freeman (b. Memphis, Tennessee, USA; guitar), Jerry Lee 'Smoochy' Smith (organ) and Terry Johnson (drums). Although their rhythmic instrumental style was not unique in Memphis, (Willie Mitchell followed a parallel path at Hi Records), the Mar-Keys were undoubted masters. Their debut hit, 'Last Night', reached number 3 in the US *Billboard* pop chart during the summer of 1961, establishing Satellite, its outlet, in the process. Within months, Satellite had altered its name to Stax and the Mar-Keys became the label's houseband. Initially all-white, two black musicians, Booker T. Jones (organ) and Al Jackson (drums), had replaced Smith and Johnson by 1962. The newcomers, along with Cropper and Dunn, also worked as Booker T. And The MGs. A turbulent group, the Mar-Keys underwent several changes. Freeman left prior to the recording of 'Last Night' (but would later return for live work), Nix and Axton also quit, while Joe Arnold and Bob Snyder joined on tenor and baritone saxophone. They in turn were replaced by Andrew Love and Floyd Newman, respectively. Although commercial success under their own name was limited, the group provided the backbone to sessions by Otis Redding, Sam And Dave, Wilson Pickett, Carla Thomas and many others, and were the pulsebeat to countless classic records. Axton, the son of Stax co-founder Estelle, later fronted the Packers,

who hit with 'Hole In The Wall' (1965). The single, released on Pure Soul, featured a not-inconspicuous MGs. Line-ups bearing the Mar-Keys' name continued to record despite the desertion of most of the original members. Nix later became part of the Delaney And Bonnie/Leon Russell axis while Charlie Freeman was later part of the Dixie Flyers, one of the last traditional housebands. Both he and Axton died in the early 70s, victims, respectively, of heroin and alcohol. Jackson, Love and Newman, meanwhile, continued the Mar-Keys legacy with releases on Stax and elsewhere, while simultaneously forging a parallel career as the Memphis Horns.
Albums: *Last Night* (1961), *Do The Popeye With The Mar-Keys* (1962), *The Great Memphis Sound* (1966), with Booker T. And The MGs *Back To Back* (1967), *Damifiknow* (1969), *Memphis Experience* (1971).

Marmalade

Originally known as Dean Ford And The Gaylords, this Glasgow-based quintet enjoyed considerable success on the Scottish club circuit between 1961 and 1967. Eventually, they were signed by agent/manager Peter Walsh and, after moving to London, changed their name to Marmalade. The line-up then comprised: Dean Ford (b. 5 September 1946, Coatbridge, Glasgow; lead singer), Graham Knight (b. 8 December 1946, Glasgow, Scotland; vocals/bass), Pat Fairley (b. 1 April 1946, Glasgow, Scotland; rhythm guitar), Willie Junior Campbell (b. 31 May 1947, Glasgow, Scotland; lead vocals) and Alan Whitehead (b. 24 July 1946, Oswestry, Shropshire, England; drums). Unpretentious and irresistibly commercial, the group reached the UK charts in May 1968 with 'Lovin' Things' and enjoyed a number 1 with an opportunist cover of John Lennon/Paul McCartney's 'Ob-La-Di, Ob-La-Da'. After several successes on CBS, Walsh negotiated a deal with Decca via Dick Rowe and Marmalade became the first *New Musical Express* UK chart toppers of the 70s by displacing Rolf Harris's 'Two Little Boys' with the moving 'Reflections Of My Life', a more serious work which ably displayed their underused compositional skills. In 1971, the group suffered a severe setback when Campbell, their producer and main songwriter, quit to attend the Royal College of Music. With replacement Hugh Nicolson (formerly of the Poets), they enjoyed several more hits, including 'Cousin Norman', 'Radancer' and 'Falling Apart At The Seams'. The latter proved a prophetic title, for the group were dogged by line-up changes during the 70s. Changes in the pop marketplace lessened their appeal, and a saucy 'sex on tour' story in the salacious Sunday papers caused them considerable embarrassment. With Knight and Whitehead surviving from the original line-up, Marmalade was resuscitated for cabaret purposes later in the decade.

Albums: *There's A Lot Of It* (1969), *Reflections Of My Life* (1970), *Songs* (1971), *Our House Is Rockin'* (1974), *Only Light On My Horizon* (1977), *Doing It All For You* (1979).

Martha And The Vandellas

Martha Reeves, Annette Sterling Beard, Gloria Williams and Rosalind Ashford formed the Del-Phis in 1960, one of the scores of female vocal groups then operating in Detroit, Michigan, USA. After Reeves began working as a secretary at Motown Records, they were offered a one-off single release on the label's Melody subsidiary, for which they were credited as the Vels. Gloria Williams left the group when the single flopped, but the remaining trio were allowed a second opportunity, recording 'I'll Have To Let Him Go' in late 1962, when the artist for whom it had been intended, Mary Wells, failed to turn up for the session. Renamed Martha And The Vandellas, the group divided their time between backing other Motown artists and recording in their own right. They were featured on Marvin Gaye's 1962 hit, 'Stubborn Kind Of Fellow', before the US Top 30 success of their own release, 'Come And Get These Memories', brought their career as second-string vocalists to an end. Their next single, the dynamic 'Heat Wave', was masterminded by the Holland/Dozier/Holland production team, and epitomized the confidence and verve of the Vandellas' finest work. 'Quick Sand' repeated the hit formula with a US Top 10 chart placing, while it was 'Dancing In The Street' which represented the pinnacle of their sound. The song, co-written by Marvin Gaye and William Stevenson, was an anthemic invitation to party, given added bite by the tense, political situation in the black ghettos. Holland/Dozier/Holland's production exploited all the potential of the music, using clunking chains to heighten the rhythmic feel, and a majestic horn riff to pull people to their feet. 'Dancing In The Street' was the most exciting record Motown had yet made, and it was a deserved number 2 hit in America.

Nothing the Vandellas recorded thereafter reached quite the same peak of excitement, though not for want of trying. 'Nowhere To Run' in 1965 was an irresistible dance hit, which again was given political connotations in some quarters. It introduced a new group member, former Velvelette Betty Kelly, who replaced Annette Sterling Beard. This line-up scored further Top 10 hits with 'I'm Ready For Love' and the infectious 'Jimmy Mack', and celebrated Motown's decision to give Martha Reeves individual credit in front of the group's name with another notable success, 'Honey Chile'. Reeves was taken seriously ill in 1968, and her absence forced the group to disband. By 1970, she was able to resume her

career, recruiting her sister Lois and another former Velvelette, Sandra Tilley, to form a new Vandellas' line-up. No major US hits were forthcoming, but in Britain they were able to capitalize on the belated 1969 success of 'Dancing In The Street', and racked up several Top 30 entries in the early 70s. When Motown moved their headquarters from Detroit to Hollywood in 1972, Reeves elected to stay behind. Disbanding the group once again, she fought a lengthy legal battle to have her recording contract annulled, and was eventually free to begin an abortive solo career. Her sister Lois joined Quiet Elegance, while Sandra Tilley retired from the record business, and died in 1982. Motown retained the rights to the Vandellas' name, but chose not to sully the memory of their early 60's hits by concocting a new version of the group without Martha Reeves.

Albums: *Come And Get These Memories* (1963), *Heat Wave* (1963), *Dance Party* (1965), *Watchout!* (1966), *Live!* (1967), *Ridin' High* (1968), *Sugar'n'Spice* (1969), *Natural Resources* (1970), *Black Magic* (1972). Compilations: *Greatest Hits* (1966), *Anthology* (1974).

Marvelettes

The Marvelettes' career epitomized the haphazard progress endured by many of the leading girl groups of the early 60s. Despite scoring several major USA hits, they were unable to sustain a consistent line-up, and their constant shift in personnel made it difficult to overcome their rather anonymous public image. The group was formed in the late 50s by five students at Inkster High School in Michigan, USA: Gladys Horton, Georgeanna Marie Tillman, Wanda Young, Katherine Anderson and Juanita Grant. They were spotted at a school talent show by Robert Bateman of the Satintones, who introduced them to Berry Gordy, head of the fledgling Motown organization. Bateman co-produced their early releases with Brian Holland, and the partnership found immediate success with 'Please Mr Postman' - a US number 1 in 1961, and Motown's biggest-selling record up to that point. This effervescent slice of pop-R&B captivated teenage audiences in the USA, and the song was introduced to an even wider public when the Beatles recorded a faithful cover version on their second album.

After a blatant attempt to repeat the winning formula with 'Twistin' Postman', the Marvelettes made the Top 20 again in 1962 with 'Playboy' and the chirpy 'Beechwood 4-5789'. The cycle of line-up changes was already underway, with Juanita Grant's departure reducing the group to a four-piece. The comparative failure of the next few singles also took its toll, and by 1965, Tillman had also left. The remaining trio, occasionally augmented by Florence Ballard of the Supremes, were paired with producer/writer Smokey Robinson. He tailored a series of ambitious hit singles for the group, the most successful of which was 'Don't Mess With Bill' in 1966 - though 'The Hunter Gets Captured By The Game' was arguably a more significant achievement. Gladys Horton, the Marvelettes' usual lead singer, left the group in 1967, to be replaced by Anne Bogan. They continued to notch up minor soul hits for the remainder of the decade, most notably 'When You're Young And In Love', before disintegrating in 1970. Wanda Young completed the group's recording commitments with an album, *The Return Of The Marvelettes*, which saw her supported by session vocalists. In 1989 original members Wanda Rogers and Gladys Horton, plus Echo Johnson and Jean McLain, recorded for Ian Levine's Motor City label issuing the disco-sounding 'Holding On With Both Hands' and *Now*. Johnson and McLain were replaced by Jackie and Regina Holleman for subsequent releases.

Albums: *Please Mr Postman* (1961), *The Marvelettes Sing* (1962), *Playboy* (1962), *The Marvellous Marvelettes* (1963), *Recorded Live: On Stage* (1963), *The Marvelettes* (1967), *Sophisticated Soul* (1968), *In Full Bloom* (1969), *The Return Of The Marvelettes* (1970), *Now* (1990).

Mayall, John

b. 29 November 1933, Macclesfield, Cheshire, England. The career of England's premier white blues exponent and father of British blues has now spanned five decades and much of that time has been spent unintentionally acting as a musical catalyst. Mayall formed his first band in 1955 while at college, and as the Powerhouse Four the group worked mostly locally. Soon after Mayall enlisted for National Service. He then became a commercial artist and finally moved to London to form his Blues Syndicate, the forerunner to his legendary Bluesbreakers. Along with Alexis Korner, Cyril Davis and Graham Bond, Mayall pioneered British R&B. The astonishing number of musicians who have passed through his bands reads like a who's-who. Even more remarkable is the number of names who have gone on to eclipse Mayall with either their own bands or as members of highly successful groups. Pete Frame author of *Rock Family Trees* has produced a detailed Mayall specimen, which is recommended. His roster of musicians included, John McVie, Hughie Flint, Mick Fleetwood, Roger Dean, Davey Graham, Eric Clapton, Jack Bruce, Aynsley Dunbar, Peter Green, Dick Heckstall-Smith, Keef Hartley, Mick Taylor, Henry Lowther, Tony Reeves, Chris Mercer, Jon Hiseman, Steve Thompson, Colin Allen, Jon Mark, Johnny Almond, Harvey Mandel, Larry Taylor, and Don 'Sugercane' Harris.

His 1965 debut, *John Mayall Plays John Mayall*, was a live album which, although badly recorded, captured the tremendous atmosphere of an R&B club. His first single, 'Crawling Up A Hill', is contained on this set

and it features Mayall's thin voice attempting to compete with an exciting, distorted harmonica and Hammond organ. *Bluesbreakers With Eric Clapton* is now a classic, and is highly recommended to all students of white blues. Clapton enabled his boss to reach a wider audience, as the crowds filled the clubs to get a glimpse of the guitar hero. *A Hard Road* featured some clean and sparing guitar from Peter Green, while *Crusade* offers a brassier, fuller sound. *The Blues Alone* showed a more relaxed style, and allowed Mayall to demonstrate his musical dexterity. *Diary Of A Band Vol. 1* and *Vol. 2* were released during 1968 and capture their live sound from the previous year; both feature excellent drumming from Keef Hartley, in addition to Mick Taylor on guitar. *Bare Wires*, arguably Mayall's finest work, shows a strong jazz leaning, with the addition of Jon Hiseman on drums and the experienced brass section of Lowther, Mercer and Heckstall-Smith. The album was an introspective journey and contained Mayall's most competent lyrics, notably the beautifully hymn-like 'I Know Now'. The similarly packaged *Blues From Laurel Canyon* (Mayall often produced his own artwork) was another strong album which was recorded in Los Angeles, where Mayall was domiciled. This marked the end of the Bluesbreakers name and, following the departure of Mick Taylor to the Rolling Stones, Mayall pioneered a drumless acoustic band featuring Jon Mark on acoustic guitar, Johnny Almond on tenor saxophone and flute, and Stephen Thompson on string bass. The subsequent live album, *The Turning Point*, proved to be his biggest-selling album and almost reached the UK Top 10. Notable tracks are the furious 'Room To Move', with Mayall's finest harmonica solo, and 'Thoughts About Roxanne' with some exquisite saxophone from Almond. The same line-up plus Larry Taylor produced *Empty Rooms*, which was more refined and less exciting.

The band that recorded *USA Union* consisted of Americans Harvey Mandel, 'Sugercane' Harris and Larry Taylor. It gave Mayall yet another success, although he struggled lyrically. Following the double reunion, *Back To The Roots*, Mayall's work lost its bite, and over the next few years his output was of poor quality. The halcyon days of name stars in his band had passed and Mayall had to suffer record company apathy. His last album to chart was *New Year, New Band, New Company* in 1975, featuring for the first time a female vocalist, Dee McKinnie, and future Fleetwood Mac guitarist Rick Vito. Following a run of albums which had little or no exposure, Mayall stopped recording, playing only infrequently close to his base in California. He toured Europe in 1988 to small but wildly enthusiastic audiences. That same year he signed to Island Records and released *Chicago Line*. Renewed activity and interest occurred in 1990 following the release of his finest album in many years, *A Sense Of Place*. Mayall was interviewed during a short visit to Britain and sounded positive, happy and unaffected by years in the commercial doldrums. As the sole survivor from the four 60s catalysts, Mayall is too important to be allowed to fade.

Albums: *John Mayall Plays John Mayall* (1965), *Bluesbreakers With Eric Clapton* (1966), *A Hard Road* (1967), *Crusade* (1967), *Blues Alone* (1967), *Diary Of A Band Vol.1* (1968), *Diary Of A Band Vol.2* (1968), *Bare Wires* (1968), *Blues From Laurel Canyon* (1968), *Looking Back* (1969), *Turning Point* (1969), *World Of John Mayall* (1970), *Empty Rooms* (1970), *USA Union* (1970), *World Of John Mayall Vol.2* (1971), *Back To The Roots* (1971), *Beyond The Turning Point* (1971), *Thru The Years* (1971), *Memories* (1971), *Jazz Blues Fusion* (1972), *Moving On* (1973), *Ten Years Are Gone* (1973), *Down The Line* (1973), *The Latest Edition* (1975), *New Year, New Band, New Company* (1975), *Time Expired, Notice To Appear* (1975), *John Mayall* (1976), *A Banquet Of Blues* (1976), *Lots Of People* (1977), *A Hard Core Package* (1977), *Blues Roots* (1978), *Bottom Line* (1979), *No More Interviews* (1979), *Last Of The British Blues* (1979), *Primal Solos* (1978), *Roadshow Blues* (1982), *The John Mayall Story Vol.1* (1983), *The John Mayall Story Vol.2* (1983), *Last Edition* (1983), *Behind the Iron Curtain* (1986), *Chicago Line* (1988), *A Sense Of Place* (1990).

Meek, Joe

b. 1929, Newent, Gloucestershire, England, d. 3 February 1967, London, England. Britain's premier independent record producer of the early 60s, Meek was equally renowned for his pioneering recording techniques and eccentric personality. His career began in 1954, when he joined IBC, the leading independent recording studio of the era. Originally an engineer, he worked on a number of hits, including Lonnie Donegan's 'Cumberland Gap', Frankie Vaughan's 'Green Door', Johnny Duncan's 'Last Train To San Fernando' and Humphrey Lyttelton's 'Bad Penny Blues'. He also turned his hand to songwriting, penning Tommy Steele's 'Put A Ring On Her Finger' in 1958.

By 1960, he had set up Lansdowne Studios in west London, where he worked with producer Denis Preston on recordings by various popular jazz artists. An ill-advised expansion policy encouraged Meek to launch Triumph Records, which enjoyed a hit with Michael Cox's 'Angela Jones' before rapidly winding down its activities. Thereafter, Meek concentrated on leasing tapes to major labels using the title, RGM Sound. He worked from a converted studio situated above a shop in Holloway Road, north London and it was here that he created the unusual sounds which were to become his hallmark. His first major hit as a producer was John Leyton's 'Johnny Remember Me', an atmospheric, eerily echo-laden affair which topped the UK charts in 1961. Leyton followed-up with other Meek-produced successes, including 'Wild Wind', 'Son, This Is She' and 'Lonely City'. With Geoff Goddard composing suitably ethereal material, Meek enjoyed further vicarious chart action with Mike Berry ('Tribute To Buddy Holly') and backing group the Outlaws ('Swingin' Low' and 'Ambush'). By 1962, the increasingly inventive producer had reached his apogee on the spacy instrumental 'Telstar', which took the Tornadoes to the top of the charts on both sides of the Atlantic. He was now hailed as a genuine original, with an innovative flair unmatched by any of his rivals. The accolades were to prove short-lived.

The mid-60s beat boom spearheaded by the Beatles seriously dented Meek's credibility and commercial standing. His work was increasingly regarded as novel, rather than important, and his love for gimmicks took precedence on recordings by Screaming Lord Sutch and others. Meek responded with the much publicized Heinz, who reached the Top 10 with the Eddie Cochran tribute, 'Just Like Eddie'. The swirling 'Have I The Right' provided a 1964 UK number 1 for the Honeycombs, but this was to be Meek's last major success. By 1965, he seemed something of an anachronism, and his production techniques seemed leaden and predictable rather than startling. The departure of songwriter Geoff Goddard weakened the supply of good material, and a motley series of flop records left record companies disenchanted. Meek's tempestuous personality and often violent behaviour alienated many old friends, while his homosexuality produced feelings of self-loathing and engendered a fear of imminent scandal. His mental instability worsened with successive personal and business problems, and on 3 February 1967, he was involved in a bizarre shooting incident in which he fatally shot his landlady before turning the gun on himself. It was the end of a sometimes brilliant but frustratingly erratic career.

Album: with the Blue Men *I Hear A New World* (1992), Compilation: *The Joe Meek Story Volume 1* (1992). Further reading: *The Legendary Joe Meek*, John Repsch.

Merseybeats

Originally called the Mavericks, this Liverpudlian quartet comprised Tony Crane (vocals/lead guitar), Billy Kinsley (vocals/bass), David Ellis (rhythm guitar) and Frank Sloan (drums). In 1962, long before the Beatles put Liverpool on the musical map, they rechristened themselves the Merseybeats. Early line-up changes saw Ellis and Sloan replaced by Aaron Williams and John Banks. By mid-1963, Beatlemania had engulfed the UK, and A&R representatives descended upon Liverpool in search of talent. The Merseybeats were scooped up by Fontana and initially signed by Brian Epstein, but left their new mentor within weeks, following an argument over image. Burt Bacharach and Hal David's 'It's Love That Really Counts' gave them a minor hit, but it was the relatively unknown songwriter Peter Lee Stirling (see Daniel Boone) who penned their biggest hit, 'I Think Of You'. Although essentially balladeers on single, the group's EPs had a grittier edge. The *On Stage* EP, with its use of monochrome photography, was extremely progressive in design terms as it did not feature the band on the cover, while their debut album included a variety of old musical standards. Pop star pressures prompted founding member Billy Kinsley to leave the group briefly, but he returned in time for their third major hit, 'Wishin' And Hopin''. Other members included Bob Garner, who was himself replaced by Johnny Gustafson from the Big Three.

The eclipse of the Mersey Sound eventually took its toll on the group, though a change of management to Kit Lambert brought two more minor hits, 'I Love You, Yes I Do' and 'I Stand Accused'. In January 1966, the group split, paving the way for hit duo, the Merseys. In later years, Tony Crane reactivated the group, which still performs regularly on the cabaret circuit.

Album: *The Merseybeats* (1964). Compilation: *The Merseybeats: Beat And Ballads* (1982).

Merseybeats

Migil Five

Red Lambert (guitar/vocals), Alan Watson (saxophone), Gil Lucas (piano), Lenny Blanche (bass) and Mike Felix (drums/lead vocals) achieved momentary fame when their 'Mockingbird Hill' single reached the UK Top 10 in 1964, on the strength of a fleeting bluebeat craze. Felix, Blanche and Lucas had previously worked as a jazz trio prior to embracing pop with the addition of Lambert. They recorded as the Migil Four before adding Watson at the suggestion of trumpeter Kenny Ball.

Despite inordinate press coverage, the group was unable to repeat this success. They later became stalwarts of the cabaret circuit before disintegrating when Felix began a solo career.

Album: *Mockingbird Hill* (1964).

Miller, Steve

b. 5 October 1943, Milwaukee, Wisconsin, USA. The young Miller was set on his musical path by having Les Paul as a family friend, and a father who openly encouraged music in the home. His first band, the Marksmen, was with school friend Boz Scaggs; also with Scaggs, he formed the college band, the Ardells, and at university they became the Fabulous Night Trains. He moved to Chicago in 1964, and became involved in the local blues scene with Barry Goldberg, resulting in the Goldberg Miller Blues Band. Miller eventually moved to San Francisco in 1966, after hearing about the growing hippie music scene, and formed the Miller Blues Band. Within a year he had built a considerable reputation and as the Steve Miller Band, he signed with Capitol Records for a then unprecedented $50,000, following his appearance at the 1967 Monterey Pop Festival. The band at that time included Boz Scaggs, Lonnie Turner, Jim Peterman and Tim Davis, and it was this line-up that was flown to London to record the Glyn Johns-produced *Children Of The Future*. The album was a critical success although sales were moderate, but it was *Sailor* later that same year which became his *pièce de résistance*. The clear production and memorable songs have lasted well and it remains a critics' favourite. Miller's silky-smooth voice and masterful guitar gave the album a touch of class that many of the other San Francisco rock albums lacked. The atmospheric instrumental 'Song For Our Ancestors' and well-crafted love songs like 'Dear Mary' and 'Quicksilver Girl' were just three of the many outstanding tracks. Scaggs and Peterman departed after this album, and Miller added the talented Nicky Hopkins on keyboards for *Brave New World*, which completed a trio of albums recorded in London with Johns. The blistering 'My Dark Hour' featured Paul McCartney (as Paul Ramon) on bass, while the epic 'Cow Cow' showed off Hopkins' sensitive piano.

The excellent *Your Saving Grace* maintained the quality of previous albums and repeated the success. Lonnie Turner and Hopkins left at the end of 1969, and Miller replaced Turner with Bobby Winkleman from local band Frumious Bandersnatch. *Number 5* completed a cycle of excellent albums which hovered around similar chart positions, indicating that while Miller was highly popular, he was not expanding his audience. He decided to change the format for *Rock Love*, by having half of the album live. Unfortunately, he chose to record a live set with arguably his weakest band; both Ros Valory and Jack King left within a year and the album sold poorly. Following a European tour, and in an attempt to reverse the trend of his last album, he released *Recall The Beginning . . . A Journey From Eden*, a perplexing album which showed Miller in a melancholic and lethargic mood; once again, Miller's fortunes declined further with poor sales.

After a gap of 18 months, Miller returned with the US chart-topping single 'The Joker', an easily contrived song over a simple riff in which Miller mentioned all references to his various self-titled aliases used in songs over the past years: 'Some people call me the Space Cowboy (*Brave New World*), some call me the Gangster Of Love (*Sailor*), some call me Maurice (*Recall The Beginning*) . . .'. The accompanying album was a similar success, stalling at number 2. His future had never looked brighter, but Miller chose to buy a farm and build a recording studio and he effectively vanished.

When he re-appeared on record three years later, only his loyal fans rated his commercial chances; however, the stunning *Fly Like An Eagle* became his best-selling album of all time and was a major breakthrough in the UK. This record, with its then state-of-the-art recording, won him many new fans, and finally put him in the major league as one of America's biggest acts. Almost as successful was the sister album *Book Of Dreams* (1977); they both gave him a number of major singles including the simplistic 'Rock 'N' Me' and the uplifting 'Jet Airliner'. Miller had now mastered and targeted his audience, with exactly the kind of songs he knew they wanted. Once again, he disappeared from the scene and a new album was not released for almost four years. The return this time was less spectacular. Although *Circle Of Love* contained one side of typical Miller - short, sharp, punchy melodic rock songs - side two was an over-long and self-indulgent epic, 'Macho City'. He once again corrected the fault by responding only six months later, with another US number 1, the catchy 'Abracadabra'. This gave him his second major hit in the UK, almost reaching the coveted top spot in 1982. In the USA, the album climbed near to the top and Miller was left with another million-plus sale. The momentum was lost over the following years, as a live album and *Italian X-Rays* were comparative failures. *Living In The 20th Century* contained a segment consisting of a tribute to Jimmy Reed, with whom Steve had played as a teenager. He opted out of the commercial market with the excellent *Born 2B Blue* in 1989. Together with his old colleague Ben Sidran, Miller paid homage to jazz and blues standards with some exquisite arrangements from Sidran. Songs like Billie Holiday's 'God Bless The Child' and 'Zip-A-Dee-Doo-Dah', were given lazy treatments with Miller's effortless voice. The record was only a moderate success.

In the autumn of 1990, while Miller bided his time with the luxury of deciding what to do next, over in Britain Levi's jeans had used 'The Joker' for one of their television advertisements. Capitol quickly released it, and astonishingly, Maurice, the space cowboy, the gangster of love, found himself with his first UK number 1.

Albums: *Children Of the Future* (1968), *Sailor* (1968), *Brave New World* (1969), *Your Saving Grace* (1969), *Revolution* (1969, film soundtrack featuring three Miller tracks), *Number 5* (1970), *Rock Love* (1971), *Recall The Beginning . . . A Journey From Eden* (1972), *The Joker* (1973), *Fly Like An Eagle* (1976), *Book Of Dreams* (1977), *Circle Of Love* (1981), *Abracadabra* (1982), *Steve Miller Band - Live!* (1983), *Italian X Rays* (1984), *Living In The 20th Century* (1987), *Born 2B Blue* (1988). Compilations: *Anthology* (1972), *Greatest Hits (1974-1978)* (1978), *A Decade Of American Music: Greatest Hits 1976-1986* (1987), *The Best Of 1968-1973* (1990), *Pegasus* (box set) (1992).

Millie

b. Millicent Small, 6 October 1942, Clarendon, Jamaica. After leaving home at the age of 13 to further her singing career in Kingston, Jamaica, Millie recorded several tracks with producer Coxsone Dodd, who teamed her up with Roy Panton. As Roy And Millie, they achieved local success with 'We'll Meet' and 'Oh, Shirley' and caught the attention of entrepreneur Chris Blackwell. On 22 June 1964, Millie accompanied Blackwell to the UK and recorded Harry Edwards' 'Don't You Know', before being presented with the catchy 'My Boy Lollipop', which became a transatlantic Top 5 hit. Such chart fame proved evanescent. A carbon copy follow-up, 'Sweet William', was only a minor hit, and thereafter she languished in relative obscurity. Even a brief tie-up with Jackie Edwards in Jackie And Millie, and a nude spread in a men's magazine failed to revitalize her career. Ultimately handicapped by her novelty hit, Millie's more serious work, such as the self-chosen *Millie Sings Fats Domino*, was sadly ignored.

Mindbenders

Originally a backing group for Wayne Fontana, the Mindbenders comprised Eric Stewart (b. 20 January 1945; guitar), Bob Lang (10 January 1946; bass) and Ric Rothwell (b. 11 March 1944; drums). In October 1965, they split with their leader and early the following year enjoyed a transatlantic number 2 hit with the Carole Bayer Sagar/Toni Wine composition, 'Groovy Kind Of Love'. The excellent follow-up, 'Can't Live With You, Can't Live Without You', failed to chart, while its successor 'Ashes To Ashes' was only a minor hit. A cameo appearance in the film *To Sir With Love* maintained the group's profile and they continued to record material by name writers such as Rod Argent and Robert Knight, but to no avail. A brave stab with an average cover of the Box Tops' 'The Letter' scraped into the Top 50s but shortly after the release of 'Uncle Joe The Ice Cream Man' in March 1968, the group dissolved. Eric Stewart and latter-day Mindbender Graham Gouldman went on to form Hotlegs and 10cc, while Bob Lang reappeared in Racing Cars.

Albums: *The Mindbenders* (1966), *With Woman In Mind* (1967).

Miracles

Of all the R&B vocal groups formed in Detroit, Michigan, USA, in the mid-50s, the Miracles proved to be the most successful. They were founded at the city's Northern High School in 1955 by Smokey Robinson (b. William Robinson, 19 February 1940, Detroit, Michigan, USA), Emerson Rogers, Bobby Rogers (b. 19 February 1940, Detroit, Michigan, USA), Ronnie White (b. 5 April 1939, Detroit, Michigan, USA) and Warren 'Pete' Moore (b. 19 November 1939, Detroit, Michigan, USA). Emerson Rogers left the following year, to be replaced by his sister Claudette, who in turn married Smokey Robinson in 1959. Known initially as the Matadors, the group became the Miracles in 1958, when they made their initial recordings with producer Berry Gordy.

He leased their debut, 'Got A Job' (an answer record to the Silhouettes' major hit 'Get A Job'), to End Records, produced a duet by Ron (White) And Bill (Robinson) for Argo, and licensed the classic doo-wop novelty, 'Bad Girl', to Chess in 1959. The following year, Gordy signed the Miracles directly to his fledgling Motown label. Recognizing the youthful composing talents of Smokey Robinson, he allowed the group virtual free rein in the studio, and was repaid when they issued 'Way Over There', a substantial local hit, and then 'Shop Around', which broke both the Miracles and Motown to a national audience. The song demonstrated the increasing sophistication of Robinson's writing, which provided an unbroken series of hits for the group over the next few years. Their raw, doo-wop sound was further refined on the Top 10 hit 'You Really Got A Hold On Me' in 1962, a soulful ballad which became a worldwide standard after the Beatles covered it in 1963. Robinson was now in demand by other Motown artists: Gordy used him as a one-man hit factory, to mastermind releases by the Temptations and Mary Wells, and the Miracles' own career suffered slightly as a result.

They continued to enjoy success in a variety of different styles, mixing dance-floor hits like 'Mickey's Monkey' and 'Going To A Go-Go' with some of Robinson's most durable ballads, like 'Oooh Baby Baby' and 'The Tracks Of My Tears'. Though Smokey sang lead on almost all the group's recordings, the rest of the group provided a unique harmony blend behind him, while guitarist Marv Tarplin - who co-wrote several of their hits - was incorporated as an unofficial Miracle from the mid-60s onwards. Claudette Robinson stopped touring with the group after 1965, although she was still featured on many of their subsequent releases. Exhausted by several years of constant work, Robinson scaled down his writing commitments for the group in the mid-60s, when they briefly worked with Holland/Dozier/Holland and other Motown producers. Robinson wrote their most ambitious and lasting songs, however, including 'The Tears Of A Clown' in 1966 (a belated hit in the UK and USA in 1970), and 'The Love I Saw In You Was Just A Mirage' and 'I Second That Emotion' in 1967. These tracks epitomized the strengths of Robinson's compositions, with witty, metaphor-filled lyrics tied to aching melody lines and catchy guitar figures, the latter often provided by Marv Tarplin. Like many of the veteran Motown acts, the Miracles went into a sales slump after 1967 - the year when Smokey Robinson was given individual credit on the group's records. Their slide was less noticeable in Britain, where Motown gained a Top 10 hit in 1969 with a reissue of 'The Tracks Of My Tears', which most listeners imagined was a contemporary record. The success of 'The Tears Of A Clown' prompted a revival in fortune after 1970. 'I'm The One You Need' became another reissue hit in Britain the following year, while 'I Don't Blame You At All', one of their strongest releases to date, scored chart success on both sides of the Atlantic.

In 1971, Robinson announced his intention of leaving the Miracles to concentrate on his position as vice-president of Motown Records. His decision belied the title of his final hit with the group, 'We've Come Too Far To End It Now' in 1972, and left the Miracles in the unenviable position of having to replace one of the most distinctive voices in popular music. Their choice was William 'Bill' Griffin (b. 15 August 1950, Detroit, Michigan, USA), who was introduced by Robinson to the group's audiences during a 1972 USA tour. The new line-up took time to settle, while Smokey Robinson launched a solo career to great acclaim in 1973. The group responded with *Renaissance*, which saw them working with Motown luminaries like Marvin Gaye and Willie Hutch. The following year, they re-established the Miracles as a hit-making force with 'Do It Baby' and 'Don'tcha Love It', dance-orientated singles which appealed strongly to the group's black audience. In 1975, 'Love Machine' became the Miracles' first US chart-topper, while the concept album *City Of Angels* was acclaimed as one of Motown's most progressive releases. This twin success proved to be the Miracles' last commercial gasp. Switching to Columbia in 1977, they lost Billy Griffin, who set out on a little-noticed solo career. Donald Griffin briefly joined the group in his place, but the Miracles ceased recording in 1978. Thereafter, Ronnie White and Bill Rogers steered the outfit into the new decade as a touring band, before the Miracles disbanded, without any fanfares only to be reformed by Bobby Rogers in 1982. He enlisted Dave Finlay and Carl Cotton as the new Miracles. Former members Billy Griffin and Claudette Robinson (ex-wife of Smokey) recorded solo tracks for Ian Levine's Motor City label during 1988-91. Griffin issued *Technicolour* in 1992. Another reformed group comprising Griffin,Robinson, Rogers, Donald Giffin, Cotton and Finlay also recorded for Levine remaking 'Love Machine' in 1990.

Albums: as the Miracles *Hi, We're The Miracles* (1961), *Cookin' With The Miracles* (1962), *I'll Try Something New* (1962), *The Fabulous Miracles* (1963), *Recorded Live: On Stage* (1963), *Christmas With The Miracles* (1963), *The Miracles Doin' 'Mickey's Monkey'* (1963), *Greatest Hits From The Beginning* (1965), *Going To A Go-Go* (1965), *Away We-A-Go-Go* (1966), *Renaissance* (1973), *Do It Baby* (1974), *Don'tcha Love It* (1975), *City Of Angels* (1975), *The Power Of Angels* (1976), *Love Crazy* (1977), *The Miracles* (1978), *Technicolour* (1992). As Smokey Robinson And The Miracles: *Make It Happen* (1967), *Greatest Hits Volume 2* (1968), *Special Occasion* (1968), *Live* (1969), *Time Out For Smokey Robinson And The Miracles* (1969), *Four In Blue* (1969), *What Love Has Joined Together* (1970), *A Pocketful Of Miracles* (1970), *The Season For Miracles* (1970), *One Dozen Roses* (1971), *Flying High Together* (1972), *1957-72* (1972).

Misunderstood

One of psychedelia's finest groups, the Misunderstood originated in Riverside, California, USA, and evolved from a local surfing group, the Blue Notes. Their first line-up - Greg Treadway (guitar), George Phelps (guitar) and Rick Moe (drums) - was augmented by Rick Brown (vocals) and Steve Whiting (bass), before adopting their new name in 1965. Phelps was then replaced by Glenn Ross 'Fernando' Campbell who played steel guitar. The quintet completed a single, 'You Don't Have To Go'/'Who's Been Talking?', before leaving for the UK on the suggestion of disc jockey John (Peel) Ravenscroft, then working in San Bernadino. Tredway was subsequently drafted, and his place was taken by Tony Hill (b. South Shields, Co. Durham, England). The group completed six masters during their London sojourn. 'I Can Take You To The

Sun', a hypnotic, atmospheric and ambitious performance, was their only contemporary release although the rousing 'Children Of The Sun' was issued, after their break-up, in 1968. Campbell later re-established the name with several British musicians. Their two blues-cum-progressive singles shared little with the early, trail-blazing unit, and the latterday version then evolved into Juicy Lucy.

Compilations: *Before The Dream Faded* (1982, six UK-recorded masters and several early demos), *Golden Glass* (1984, material by the group's second incarnation).

Moby Grape

Moby Grape

The legend that continues to grow around one of San Francisco's late 60s' groups is mainly based on their sparkling debut album, which fans vainly willed them to repeat. This iconoclastic band was formed in September 1966, with the seminal line-up of Alexander 'Skip' Spence (b. 18 April 1946, Windsor, Ontario, Canada; guitar/vocals), Jerry Miller (b. 10 July 1943, Tacoma, Washington, USA; guitar/vocals), Bob Mosley (b. 4 December 1942, Paradise Valley, California, USA; bass/vocals), Don Stevenson (b. 15 October 1942, Seattle, Washington, USA; drums) and Peter Lewis (b. 15 July 1945, Los Angeles, California, USA; guitar/vocals). With record companies queueing up to sign them, they decided to go with CBS and became marketing guinea pigs for an unprecedented campaign, whereupon 10 tracks (five singles plus b-sides) were released simultaneously. Not even the Beatles could have lived up to that kind of launch. Only one of the records dented the US chart: 'Omaha' reached a dismal number 88. Had the singles been released in normal sequence, they might have all been hits, as the quality of each song was outstanding. The band fell into immediate disarray, unable to cope with the pressure and hype. The resulting debut, *Moby Grape*, contained all these 10 tracks plus an additional three, and it deservedly reached the US Top 30 album charts. It is now recognized as a classic. The short, brilliantly structured, guitar-based rock songs with fine harmonies still sound fresh in the 90s.

Their follow-up was a similar success (yet a lesser work), and made the US Top 20 album chart. As with their debut, CBS continued with their ruthless marketing campaign, determined to see a return on their investment, as the Grape had originally held out for a considerable advance. *Wow* sported a beautiful surrealistic painting/collage by Bob Cato, depicting a huge bunch of grapes mixed with an 18th- century beach scene which came with a free album, *Grape Jam*. Additionally, one of the tracks was recorded at 78rpm, forcing the listener to get up and change the speed only to hear a spoof item played by Lou Waxman And His Orchestra. Amidst this spurious package were some of their finest songs, including Spence's 'Motorcycle Irene', Mosley's 'Murder In My Heart For The Judge' and arguably their best track, 'Can't Be So Bad'. Penned by Jerry Miller and featuring his exceptional guitar solo, this furious heavy rock item is suddenly sweetened by an outstanding four-part Mamas and The Papas-style harmony. The song failed to chart anywhere.

By now, Spence had departed with drug problems upon the release of *Moby Grape '69*, although his track 'Seeing' is one of the highlights of this apologetic and occasionally brilliant album (the previous hype is disclaimed by the sleeve notes). Notable tracks included Lewis's hymn-like 'I Am Not Willing' and the straightforward rocker 'Truck Driving Man'. A disastrous European tour was arranged, whereby the band was constantly overshadowed by the support band Group Therapy. Mosley left on their return to the USA, leaving the rest to fulfil their contract by making a fourth album. The poor-selling and lacklustre *Truly Fine Citizen* was badly received; the critics had already given up on them. The band then disintegrated, unable to use the name which was and still is owned by their manager, Matthew Katz. The remaining members have appeared as Maby Grope, Mosley Grape, the Grape and the Legendary Grape. During one of their many attempts at reformation, Mosley and Miller appeared on record as Fine Wine.

The original five reunited for one more undistinguished album in 1971. Out of the mire, only Mosley's 'Gypsy Wedding' showed some promise. Skip Spence delivered the quirky 'Chinese Song,' played on a koto, and the silk-voiced Lewis produced 'Horse Out In The Rain' with its unusual timing and extraordinary booming bass. A live album in 1978 delighted fans, but since then the ghost of Grape has been put to rest. Their influence has shown up in many bands over the past 20 years including the

Doobie Brothers, R.E.M. and the Smithereens.

Albums: *Moby Grape* (1967), *Wow* (1967), *Grape Jam* (1967), *Moby Grape '69* (1969), *Truly Fine Citizen* (1969), *20 Granite Creek* (1971), *Great Grape* (1973), *Live Grape* (1978). As Fine Wine *Fine Wine* (1976).

Mojos

Originally known as the Nomads, this Liverpool beat group was formed in 1962 by Stu James (vocals), Adrian Wilkinson (guitar), Keith Karlson (bass) and John Konrad (drums). They secured early minor fame by winning a songwriting contest which resulted in a recording deal. Pianist Terry O'Toole was added to the line-up prior to the release of the Mojos' debut single, and Nicky Crouch replaced Wilkinson before a follow-up, 'Everything's Alright', was recorded. This energetic 1964 single became a UK Top 10 hit, and the crafted excitement maintained throughout the performance assured its classic status. The group's later releases failed to match this quality, and although a revitalized line-up, consisting of James, Crouch, Lewis Collins (bass) and Aynsley Dunbar (drums) continued as Stu James and the Mojos, they broke up in December 1966. The singer then pursued a career in music publishing, while Dunbar joined John Mayall's Bluesbreakers and Collins pursued a acting career, later starring in the popular UK television series, *The Professionals*.

Album: *Working* (1982).

Money, Zoot

b. George Bruno Money, 17 July 1942, Bournemouth, Dorset, England. A veteran of his hometown's thriving music circuit, Money played in several local rock 'n' roll groups before forming the Big Roll Band in 1961. Its original line-up comprised Roger Collis (guitar), Kevin Drake (tenor saxophone), Johnny King (bass), Peter Brooks (drums) and Zoot on piano and vocals. By 1963, the singer was fronting an all-new unit of Andy Somers aka Andy Summers (guitar), Nick Newall (saxophone) and Colin Allen (drums), but he left the group for a temporary spot in Alexis Korner's Blues Incorporated. Zoot remained in London when his tenure ended, and his band subsequently joined him there. The Big Roll Band secured a residency at London's prestigious Flamingo Club, and added two new members, Paul Williams (bass/vocals) and Clive Burrows (saxophone), before recording their debut single, 'The Uncle Willie'. In 1965, the group released its first album, *It Should've Been Me*, a compendium of soul and R&B material which enhanced the band's growing reputation. A second album, *Zoot!*, recorded live at Klook's Kleek, introduced newcomer Johnny Almond, who replaced Burrows. This exciting set included a superb James Brown medley and confirmed the unit's undoubted strength. However, a devil-may-care attitude undermined their potential, and only one of their excellent singles, 'Big Time Operator' (1966), broached the UK Top 30. Money became famed as much for dropping his trousers onstage as for his undoubted vocal talent, and several of the line-up were notorious imbibers. Yet this lifestyle was reversed in 1967, when Money, Somers and Alan embraced the emergent 'flower-power' movement with Dantallion's Chariot. However, by the following year Zoot had resumed his erstwhile direction with *Transition*, a disappointing release which was pieced together from several sessions.

In 1968, both Money and Somers joined Eric Burdon in his American-based New Animals. Zoot's vocals were heard on a number of tracks with Burdon, notably a lengthy re-working of his Dantallion's Chariot showpiece, 'Madman'. Additionally, his spoken dialogue was featured on some of Burdon's more self-indulgent efforts on *Everyone Of Us*. The singer completed *Welcome To My Head* on the group's demise before returning to London for *Zoot Money*. He continued an itinerant path with Centipede, Grimms and Ellis, before joining Somers in the Kevin Coyne and Kevin Ayers bands. In 1980, Zoot released the low-key *Mr. Money*, since which he has played on numerous sessions and enjoyed a new career as a character actor in television drama and comedy.

Albums: *It Should've Been Me* (1965), *Zoot!* (1966), *Transition* (1968), *Welcome To My Head* (1969), *Zoot Money* (1970), *Mr. Money* (1980).

Monkees

Inspired by the burgeoning pop phenomena and armed with an advance from Columbia's Screen Gems subsidiary, US television producers Bob Rafelson and Bert Schneider began auditions for a show about a struggling pop group in 1965. When extant acts, including the Lovin' Spoonful, proved inappropriate, an advertisement in the *Daily Variety* solicited 437 applicants, including Stephen Stills, Danny Hutton (later Three Dog Night) and Paul Williams. Following suitably off-beat auditions, the final choice paired two musicians - Michael Nesmith (b. Robert Michael Nesmith, 30 December 1942, Houston, Texas, USA; guitar/vocals) and folksinger Peter Tork (b. Peter Halsten Thorkelson, 13 February 1944, Washington, D.C., USA; bass/vocals) - with two budding actors and former child stars - Davy Jones (b. 30 December 1945, Manchester, England; vocals) and ex-*Circus Boy* star Mickey Dolenz (b. George Michael Dolenz, 8 March 1945, Los Angeles, California, USA; drums/vocals). On 12 September 1966, the first episode of *The Monkees* was aired by NBC-TV and, despite low initial ratings, the show quickly became hugely popular, a feat mirrored

when it was launched in the UK. Attendant singles 'Last Train To Clarksville' (US number 1) and 'I'm A Believer' (US and UK number 1), and a million-selling debut album confirmed the group as the latest teenage phenomenon, drawing inevitable comparisons with the Beatles. However, news that the quartet did not play on their records fuelled an already simmering internal controversy. Early sessions had been completed by Tommy Boyce And Bobby Hart, authors of 'Last Train To Clarksville', and their backing group, the Candy Store Prophets, with the Monkees simply overdubbing vocals. Musical supervision was later handed to Screen Gems executive Don Kirshner, who in turn called in staff songwriters Gerry Goffin and Carole King, Neil Diamond and Jeff Barry to contribute material for the show. This infuriated the Monkees' two musicians, in particular Nesmith, who described the piecemeal *More Of The Monkees* as 'the worst album in the history of the world'.

Sales in excess of five million copies exacerbated tension, but the group won tacit approval from Schneider to complete several tracks under their own devices. An undeterred Kirshner coaxed Jones to sing on the already-completed backing track to 'A Little Bit Me, A Little Bit You' which was issued, without group approval, as their third single. The ensuing altercation saw Kirshner ousted, with the quartet gaining complete artistic freedom. Although not issued as a single in the USA, 'Alternate Title' (aka 'Randy Scouse Git'), Dolenz's ambitious paean to London, reached number 2 in Britain, while two further 1967 singles, 'Pleasant Valley Sunday' and 'Daydream Believer' (composed by John Stewart), achieved gold record status. *Headquarters*, the first Monkees album on which the group played, was a commercial and artistic success, consisting largely of self-penned material ranging from country-rock to vaudevillian pop. *Pisces, Aquarius, Capricorn And Jones Ltd* featured material drawn from associates Michael Murphy, Harry Nilsson and Chip Martin as the unyielding call on the group's talents continued. This creative drain was reflected in the disappointing *The Birds, The Bees And The Monkees* and its accompanying single, 'Valleri'. The track itself had been recorded in 1966, and was only issued when 'pirate' recordings, dubbed off-air from the television series, attracted considerable airplay. 'The Monkees are dead!', declared an enraged Nesmith, yet the song sold over a million copies, the group's last such success. The appeal of their series had waned as plots grew increasingly loose, and the final episode was screened in the USA on 25 March 1968. The quartet had meanwhile embarked on a feature film, *Head*, which contained many in-jokes about their artistic predicaments. Although baffling their one-time teenage audience, it failed to find favour with the underground circuit who still viewed the Monkees as bubblegum. However, *Head* has since been rightly lauded for its imagination and innovation. A dispirited Peter Tork left following its release, but although the remaining trio continued without him, their commercial decline was as spectacular as its ascendancy. Nesmith left for a solo career in 1969. and the following year the Monkees' name was dissolved in the wake of Dolenz/Jones recording *Changes*. However, in 1975, the latter-day duo joined their erstwhile songwriting team in *Dolenz, Jones, Boyce And Hart* which toured under the banner 'The Great Golden Hits Of The Monkees Show'. The project drew cursory interest, but the group's reputation was bolstered considerably during the 80s, when the independent Rhino Records label reissued the entire Monkees' back catalogue and the entire series was rescreened on MTV. Although Nesmith demured, Dolenz, Jones and Tork embarked on a highly successful, 20th-anniversary world tour which engendered a live album and a new studio set, *Pool It*. The group has since disbanded as members pursued contrasting interests, while attempts to create the New Monkees around Marty Roos, Larry Saltis, Jared Chandler and Dino Kovas in 1987 was aborted. Although reviled by many contemporary critics, the original group's work is now regarded as among the best American pop of its era.

Albums: *The Monkees* (1966), *More Of The Monkees* (1967), *Headquarters* (1967), *Pisces, Aquarius, Capricorn And Jones Ltd* (1967), *The Birds, The Bees And The Monkees* (1968), *Head* (1968, film soundtrack), *Instant Replay* (1969), *The Monkees Present...* (1969), *Changes* (1970), *Pool It* (1986), *20th Anniversary Concert Tour 1986* (1986). Compilations: *The Monkees Greatest Hits* (1969), *The Monkees Golden Hits* (1972), *The Monkees Greatest Hits* (1976), *Monkeemania* (1979), *The Monkees* (1981), *Monkee Business* (1982), *Monkee Flips* (1984), *The And Now...The Best Of The Monkees* (1986), *Missing Links* (1987), *The Monkees Live - 1967* (1987), *Hey! Hey! It's The Monkees Greatest Hits* (1989), *Missing Links Volume 2* (1990).

Monro, Matt

b. Terry Parsons, 1 December 1932, London, England, d. 7 February 1985. This velvet-voiced balladeer first played in bands under the pseudonym Al Jordan before adopting the name Monro, allegedly borrowed from Winifred Atwell's father. Between stints as a bus driver and singer on the UK Camay soap commercial, he recorded for a number of labels, but his choice of material was generally too predictable. His interpretation of 'Garden Of Eden', for example, had to compete with four other versions by hit artists Frankie Vaughan, Gary Miller, Dick James and Joe Valino. Monro's luck changed when producer George Martin asked him to contribute to a

Peter Sellers album, for this led to a contract with Parlophone and a Top 3 hit with 'Portrait Of My Love' (1960). For the next five years, Matt was a regular chart entrant, invariably specializing in big ballads. A cover of the James Bond movie theme 'From Russia With Love' and the emotive 'Walk Away' proved particularly successful, and the speedy release of a slick adaptation of the Beatles' 'Yesterday' underlined the sagacity of covering a song before your competitors.

A move to the USA in 1965 brought a decline in Monro's chart fortunes, but he sustained his career as an in-demand nightclub performer. The enduring commercial quality of his voice was recognised by Capitol Records with the Christmas release and television promotion of the compilation album, *Heartbreakers,* in 1980. Ill-health dogged the singer in the early 80s, and cancer finally took its toll in February 1985.

Selected albums: *Blue And Sentimental* (1957), *Portrait* (1961), *Love Is The Same Anywhere* (1961), *My Kind Of Girl* (1961, USA), *Matt Monro Sings Hoagy Carmichael* (1962), *I Have Dreamed* (1965), *Matt Monro And Don Rennie* (1965), *Walk Away* (1965, USA), *Hits Of Yesterday* (1965), *This Is The Life!* (1966), *Here's To My Lady* (1967), *Invitation To The Movies* (1967), *These Years* (1967), *The Late Late Show* (1968), *Invitation To Broadway* (1968), *Here And Now* (1969), *We're Gonna Change The World* (1970), *Let's Face The Music And Dance* (1972), *For The Present* (1973), *The Other Side Of The Stars* (1975), *The Long And Winding Road* (1975), *If I Never Hear Another Song* (1979), *Heartbreakers* (1980).

Monterey Pop Festival

16-18 June 1967. The burgeoning west coast American music scene was effectively launched at Monterey, California, USA in 1967. In a transition from 'pop music', performers and bands suddenly found that they were preaching their new music to a like-minded mass audience. The sounds became more adventurous as they explored other musical routes. Blues, jazz and folk became tinged with Eastern and African influences. This galvanization in turn made people more aware and tolerant of these ambitious and different styles. Nevertheless, the music was still labelled 'progressive pop' rather than rock. The festival was the brainchild of John Phillips, Alan Pariser, Paul Simon and Lou Adler, who assembled a board of artists to help stage the event. Derek Taylor the skilful former press officer of the Beatles and the Byrds was enrolled. Brian Wilson of the Beach Boys pulled out prior to the event. The Beatles were notably missing. The Rolling Stones, although absent, were there in spirit, with Brian Jones on the advisory board seen wandering in the crowd throughout the proceedings.

The three day festival was a forerunner to Woodstock, and history has subsequently shown that Monterey was more 'musically' important, although by today's standards it was a comparatively small affair with only 35,000 people present at any one time. The festival gave birth to a movement and introduced major new artists to the general public. It was at Monterey that Jimi Hendrix first attracted mass attention with the public burning of his guitar. Likewise it was Janis Joplin with her band, Big Brother And The Holding Company who grabbed the audience's imagination with her orgasmic and electrifying performance, as did a quasi-live album by the Mama And Papas. Otis Redding's accomplishment was memorable in that he brought together black soul and white rock music and became accepted by a predominantly white pop audience. His thrilling and frantic performance broke down all barriers, even though he wore a conservative blue suit instead of the regulation kaftan, beads and flowers. The first major pop music revolution since the Beatles was born at Monterey.

Among other artists who paraded their music at the festival were the Grateful Dead, Electric Flag (featuring the brilliant young Mike Bloomfield), Canned Heat, Buffalo Springfield, the Byrds, the Mamas And The Papas, Eric Burdon And The Animals, Hugh Masekela, Jefferson Airplane, Ravi Shankar, Booker T. And The MGs, the Who, Moby Grape, the Steve Miller Band, Country Joe And The Fish, Simon And Garfunkel, Beverly (Martyn), the Paupers, Lou Rawls, the Association, Johnny Rivers, Quicksilver Messenger Service, Laura Nyro, and the Blues Project. D.A. Pennebaker's 80 minute film *Monterey Pop* captured the event. No official album was ever released although a Jimi Hendrix/Otis Redding album included highlights of their performance. However, the show was broadcast on radio almost in its entirety in 1989 and further extracts from the festival have since been issued.

Montez, Chris

b. Christopher Montanez, 17 January 1943, Los Angeles, California, USA. Teenage vocalist Montez was discovered by impresario Jim Lee in 1961, and having joined the latter's Monogram label, enjoyed an international hit the following year with 'Let's Dance'. This exciting, Lee-penned single, redolent of the Hispanic 'latino-rock' style of Ritchie Valens sold over 1 million copies and climbed to number 2 in the UK. A follow-up, 'Some Kinda Fun', reached the UK Top 10 in 1963, but a three year hiatus ensued before the singer resurfaced on A&M in the US with a version of the much-covered 'Call Me'. The charmingly simple 'The More I See You', gave Montez a second UK Top 3 entry, while minor US successes followed with 'There Will Never Be

Another You' and 'Time After Time'. Re-released in the UK in 1972, 'Let's Dance' confirmed its timeless appeal by reaching the UK Top 10.

Albums: *Let's Dance And Have Some Kinda Fun!!!* (1963), *The More I See You/Call Me* (1966), *Time After Time* (1966), *Foolin' Around* (1967), *Watch What Happens* (1968).

Chris Montez and Tommy Roe

Moody Blues

The lengthy career of the Moody Blues has come in two distinct phases. The first from 1963-67, when they were a tough R&B-influenced unit, and the second from 1967 to the present, where they are regarded as rock dinosaurs performing a blend of pop utilizing symphonic themes which has been given many labels, among them pomp-rock, classical-rock and art-rock. The original band was formed in 1964 by Denny Laine (b. Brian Hines, 29 October 1944, Jersey; vocals/harmonica/guitar), Mike Pinder (b. 12 December 1942, Birmingham, England; piano/keyboards), Ray Thomas (b. 29 December 1942, Stourport on Severn, England; flute/vocals/harmonica), Graeme Edge (b. 30 March 1944, Rochester, Kent, England; drums) and Clint Warwick (b. 25 June 1940, Birmingham, England; bass). During their formative months they established a strong London club following, and soon received their big break, as so many others did, performing live on the influential television show *Ready Steady*

Go. A few months later their Bessie Banks cover, 'Go Now' topped the UK charts, complete with its striking piano introduction and solo. Although the single made the US Top 10, their commercial fortunes were on an immediate decline, although their following releases were impeccable.

Their splendid debut *The Magnificent Moodies* failed to sell as anticipated. Warwick and Laine departed in 1966 to be replaced by Justin Hayward (b. 14 October 1946, Swindon, Wiltshire, England) and John Lodge (b. 20 July 1945, Birmingham, England). So began phase two, which debuted with Hayward's classic, 'Nights In White Satin'. The accompanying *Days Of Future Passed* was an ambitious orchestral project with Peter Knight conducting the London Festival Orchestra and Tony Clark producing. The album was a massive success and started a run that continued through a further five albums, all involving Knight and Clark. The increased use of the mellotron gave an orchestrated feel to much of their work, and while they became phenomenally popular, they also received a great deal of criticism. During this period they founded Threshold Records, their own record label, and in 1973 reached the UK Top 10 with a re-entry for 'Nights In White Satin'.

The band parted company in 1974 to allow each member to indulge in spin-off projects. Hayward and Lodge became the Blue Jays, with great success, Thomas and Pinder each released solo albums, and Edge teamed with Adrian Gurvitz for *Kick Off Your Muddy Boots*. The group reunited for *Octave*, which became another huge hit, although shortly after its release Pinder decided to quit the business. Further discontent ensued when Clark resigned. Patrick Moraz from Yes and Refugee joined the band as Hayward's 'Forever Autumn' hit the charts. This track was taken from the Jeff Wayne epic, *The War Of The Worlds*. Each subsequent release has met with predictable glory both in Europe and America. The Moodies march on with the comforting knowledge that they will fill concert halls and sell vast amounts of records until the days of future have passed.

Albums: *The Magnificent Moodies* (1965), *Days Of Future Past* (1967), *In Search Of The Lost Chord* (1968), *On The Threshold Of A Dream* (1969), *To Our Children's Children* (1969), *A Question Of Balance* (1970), *Every Good Boy Deserves Favour* (1971), *Seventh Sojourn* (1972), *Caught Live + 5* (1977), *Octave* (1978), *Long Distance Voyager* (1981), *The Present* (1983), *The Other Side Of Life* (1986), *Sur La Mer* (1988), *Keys Of The Kingdom* (1991). Compilations: *This Is The Moody Blues* (1974), *Out Of This World* (1979), *Voices In The Sky - The Best Of The Moody Blues* (1985), *Greatest Hits* (1989). Solo: Justin Hayward and John Lodge *Blue Jays* (1975); Ray Thomas *From Mighty Oaks* (1975), *Hope Wishes And Dreams* (1976); Mike Pinder *The Promise* (1976); John

Lodge *Natural Avenue* (1977); Graeme Edge Band *Kick Off Your Muddy Boots* (1975), *Paradise Ballroom* (1977); Justin Hayward *Songwriter* (1977), *Night Flight* (1980), *Moving Mountains* (1985), *Classic Blue* (1989); Denny Laine *Japanese Tears* (1980), *Hometown Girls* (1985), *Weep For Love* (1985), *Wings On My Feet* (1987), *Lonely Road* (1988), *Master Suite* (1988), *Holly Days* (c.80s).

Morgan, Derrick

b. March 1940, Stewarton, Jamaica. Morgan's recording career stretches back to the birth of the Jamaican record industry, c.1959-60. An imposing figure invariably topped with an almost brimless pork-pie hat, his cool, hip and rhythmic voice, enlivened by the occasional excited yelp, applied itself successfully to a variety of styles in those formative years, such as the Latin beat of 'Fat Man' (1960), the gospel fervour of 'I Pray For You' (1961) and the shuffling R&B of his Jamaican Independence anthem 'Forward March' (1962). He duetted with female singer Patsy on a series of Shirley And Lee-styled numbers, that duo being currently popular in Jamaica, before settling into a ska style with 'Shake A Leg' (1962) and other recordings for Prince Buster. His split from Buster to join the Chinese-owned Beverley's Records led to an entertaining, and successful, exchange of insults on singles like Morgan's 'Blazing Fire' and Buster's unequivocal 'Blackhead Chinese Man'. Morgan recorded prolifically throughout the 60s and into the 70s, recording rock steady such as 'Greedy Gal' (1967) and a definitive flying-cymbals reggae version of Max Romeo's 'Wet Dream' (1975). About this time his sight, always impaired, deteriorated to the extent where he could see only 'light and clouds' and he is now musically less active, though as recently as 1990 he travelled to London for a ska revival concert.

Albums: *Forward March* (1963), *Seven Letters* i (1969), *Seven Letters* ii (1970), *Moon Hop* (1970), *In The Mood* (1973), *Development* (1975).

Morrison, Van

b. George Ivan Morrison, 31 August 1945, Belfast, Northern Ireland. The son of a noted collector of jazz and blues records, Morrison at the age of 12 joined Deannie Sands And The Javelins, an aspiring skiffle group, but within two years was an integral part of the Monarchs, a showband which, by 1963, was embracing R&B and soul. Tours of Scotland and England were undertaken before the group travelled to Germany where they completed a lone single for CBS, 'Bozoo Hully Gully'/'Twingy Baby', before disbanding. The experience Morrison garnered - he took up vocals, saxophone and harmonica - proved invaluable upon his return to Belfast and a subsequent merger with members of local attraction the

Gamblers in a new act, Them. This exciting group scored two notable hit singles with 'Baby Please Don't Go' and 'Here Comes The Night' (both 1965), while the former's b-side 'Gloria', a snarling Morrison original, is revered as a classic of the garage-band genre. The group's progress was hampered by instability and Morrison's reluctance to court the pop marketplace - a feature continued throughout his career - but their albums showed the early blossoming of an original stylist. His reading of Bob Dylan's 'It's All Over Now, Baby Blue' (*Them Again*) is rightly regarded as one of the finest interpretations in a much-covered catalogue. Them was dissolved in 1966 following an arduous USA tour, but within months the singer had returned to New York at the prompting of producer Bert Berns. Their partnership resulted in 'Brown-Eyed Girl', an ebullient celebration of love in a style redolent of classic black harmony groups. The single deservedly reached the US Top 10, in turn inspiring the hurriedly-issued *Blowin' Your Mind*. Morrison later claimed the set was culled from sessions for projected singles and, although inconsistent, contained the cathartic 'T.B. Sheets', on which Van first introduced the stream-of-consciousness imagery re-occurring in later work. Berns' premature death brought this period to a sudden end, and for the ensuing 12 months Morrison punctuated live performances by preparing his next release.

Astral Weeks showed the benefit of such seclusion, as here an ambition to create without pop's constraints was fully realized. Drawing support from a stellar backing group which included Miles Davis' bassist Richard Davis and Modern Jazz Quartet drummer Connie Kay, Morrison created an ever-shifting musical tapestry, inspired by blues, soul and gospel, yet without ever aping their sound. His vocal performance was both assured and highly emotional and the resultant collection is justifiably lauded as one of rock's landmark releases. On *Moondance* the artist returned to a more conventional sense of discipline, on which tighter, punchier, jazzier arrangements formed the platform for the singer's still-soaring inflections. 'Caravan', 'Into The Mystic' and the title track itself (reminiscent of Kenny Burrell's 'Midnight Blue'), became a staple part of Van's subsequent career, offering an optimistic spirit prevalent in the artist's immediate recordings. Both *Van Morrison, His Band And The Street Choir* and *Tupelo Honey* suggested a newfound peace of mind, as a now-married Morrison celebrated the idyll of his sylvan surroundings. 'Domino' and 'Wild Night' were the album's respective US hit singles, both of which invoked the punch of classic Stax-era soul, and if the former set offered a greater debt to R&B, its counterpart showed an infatuation with country styles. Both preoccupations were maintained on *St.*

Dominic's Preview, one of Morrison's most enigmatic releases. Having opened the set with 'Jackie Wilson Said', an effervescent tribute to the great soul singer later covered by Dexy's Midnight Runners, Van wove a path through rock and late-night jazz culminating in two lengthy compositions, both laced with chiming acoustic 12-string guitar, 'Listen To The Lion' and 'Almost Independence Day'. Here he resumed vocal improvisation and by alternately whispering, pleading, shouting and extolling, created two intoxicating and hypnotic performances.

Morrison's next release, *Hard Nose The Highway*, proved disappointing as the artist enhanced an ever-widening palette with contributions by the Oakland Symphony Chamber Chorus and such disparate inclusions as 'Green', culled from the educational children's show, *Sesame Street*, and the folk standard 'Wild Mountain Thyme', herein retitled 'Purple Heather'. Despite the presence of 'Wild Love' and 'The Great Deception', the album is generally regarded as inconsistent. However, Morrison reclaimed his iconoclast position with the enthralling *It's Too Late To Stop Now*, an in-concert selection on which he was backed by the Caledonia Soul Orchestra. Van not only restated his own impressive catalogue, but acknowledged his mentors with a series of tight and outstanding recreations, notably of Sonny Boy Williamson ('Take Your Hand Out Of Your Pocket'), Ray Charles ('I Believe To My Soul') and Bobby Bland ('Ain't Nothing You Can Do'). The result was a seamless tribute to R&B and one of rock's definitive live albums. It was succeeded by the pastoral

Veedon Fleece a set inspired by a sabbatical in Ireland during 1973. Its sense of spirituality - a keynote of Morrison's later work - is best captured on 'You Don't Pull No Punches But You Don't Push The River', but 'The Streets Of Arklow' and 'County Fair' are equally evocative. The judicious use of uillean pipes and woodwind enhanced the rural atmosphere of a collection which, although received with mixed reviews, is, in retrospect, a lynchpin in the artist's subsequent development. A three-year hiatus ended with the release of *A Period Of Transition*, a largely undistinguished set on which the singer collaborated actively with Dr. John. *Wavelength*, which featured former Them organist Peter Bardens, was welcomed as a marked improvement and if lacking the triumphs of earlier work, contained none of its pitfalls and instead offered a mature musical consistency. Similar qualities abounded on *Into The Music* which included the noticeably buoyant 'Bright Side Of The Road', Van's first solo, albeit minor, UK chart entry. It also featured 'And The Healing Has Begun', wherein Morrison celebrated his past in order to address his future, and the shamelessly nostalgic 'It's All In The

Game', a cover version of Tommy Sands' 1957 hit single. Although a general penchant for punchy soul suggested part of a continuing affinity, it instead marked the end of a stylistic era. On *Common One* Morrison resumed his introspective path and, on the expansive 'Somewhere In England', referred to the works of Wordsworth, Coleridge and T.S. Eliot in a piece whose gruff, improvisatory nature polarized critics proclaiming it either mesmerising or self-indulgent.

A greater sense of discipline on *Beautiful Vision* resulted in another much lauded classic. Although noted for 'Cleaning Windows', a joyous celebration of the singer's formative Belfast years, the album contained several rich, meditative compositions, notably 'Dweller On The Threshold' and 'Across The Bridge Where Angels Dwell'.

Inarticulate Speech Of The Heart and *A Sense Of Wonder* continued in a similar vein, the former boasting the compulsive 'Rave On John Donne', wherein Van again places his work on a strictly literary pantheon, while the latter opened with the equally evocative 'Tore Down A La Rimbaud'. The title track of the latter set the style for many beautifully wandering and spiritually uplifting songs of the next fertile period. *Live At The Grand Opera House, Belfast* was an insubstantial resume, failing to capture the sense of occasion demonstrably apparent in person, but Morrison confirmed his artistic rebirth with *No Guru, No Method, No Teacher*. Here he openly acknowledged his musical past - the set included the punningly titled 'Here Comes The Knight' - as well as offering a searing riposte to those perceived as imitators on 'A Town Called Paradise'. 'Tir Na Nog' and 'One Irish Rover' continued his long-running affair with Celtic themes, a feature equally relevant on *Poetic Champions Compose*. The wedding of love and religion, another integral part of the artist's 80s' work, was enhanced by the sumptuous 'Sometimes I Feel Like A Motherless Child', on which the singer's contemplative delivery was truly inspirational. Morrison, many years into his career, was now producing an astonishingly high standard of work. His albums during this period were events, not mere releases.

Irish Heartbeat, a festive collaboration with traditional act the Chieftains, offered a joyous but less intensive perspective. Although the title song and 'Celtic Ray' were exhumed from Van's own catalogue, its highlights included moving renditions of 'She Moved Through The Fair' and 'Carrickfergus'. By this time (1988) Morrison was resettled in London and had invited R&B vocalist/organist Georgie Fame to join his touring revue. *Avalon Sunset* enhanced the singer's commercial ascendancy when 'Whenever God Shines His Light On Me', a duet with Cliff Richard, became a UK Top 20 single, Morrison's first since Them's

halcyon days. The album had once again a strong spiritual feel combined with childhood memories. Morrison, however, was also able to compose and deliver quite immaculate love songs, including a cover of 'Have I Told You Lately That I Love You'. *Enlightenment* thus engendered considerable interest although Morrison, as oblivious to pop's trappings as always, simply maintained his peerless progress. The mixture was as before, from the pulsating opening track, 'Real Real Gone', itself once considered for *Common One*, through gospel and the biographical, where 'Days Before Rock 'N' Roll' recalls the singer's discovery, by radio, of Ray Charles and Little Richard. 1991 witnessed another unlikely collaboration when Morrison recorded several songs with Tom Jones, one of which, 'Carrying A Torch', was remade for *Hymns To The Silence*. This expansive double set confirmed the artist's prolific nature, yet reviews lauding its sense of grandeur also queried its self-obsession. Morrison, whose disdain for the press is legendary, will doubtlessly remain unmoved, yet the paradox of a man capable of sumptuous music and a barking temper is indeed intriguing. It is a tribute that such aberrations can be set aside in order to enjoy his enthralling catalogue. Taken as a whole, this body of work is arguably one the most necessary, complete and important collections in rock music, and it is still growing.

Albums: *Blowin' Your Mind* (1967), *Astral Weeks* (1968), *Moondance* (1970), *Van Morrison, His Band And The Street Choir* (1970), *Tupelo Honey* (1971), *St. Dominic's Preview* (1972), *Hard Nose The Highway* (1973), *It's Too Late To Stop Now* (1974), *Veedon Fleece* (1974), *A Period Of Transition* (1977), *Wavelength* (1978), *Into The Music* (1979), *Common One* (1980), *Beautiful Vision* (1982), *Inarticulate Speech Of The Heart* (1983), *Live At The Grand Opera House, Belfast* (1984), *A Sense Of Wonder* (1984), *No Guru, No Method, No Teacher* (1986), *Poetic Champions Compose* (1987), with the Chieftains *Irish Heartbeat* (1988), *Avalon Sunset* (1989), *Enlightenment* (1990), *Hymns To The Silence* (1991). Compilations: *The Best Of Van Morrison* (1971), *T.B. Sheets* (1973), *This Is Where I Came In* (1977), *The Very Best Of Van Morrison* (1990), *Bang Masters* (1991).

Further reading: *Van Morrison: A Portrait Of The Artist*, Johnny Rogan.

Mother Earth

Formed in Texas in 1966, Mother Earth was one of several American groups to move to the more liberal San Francisco during the west coast beat boom of the late 60s. The original line-up featured three former members of the Wigs, John 'Toad' Andrews (guitar), Bob Arthur (bass) and George Rains (drums), as well as songwriter R. Powell St. John, who composed several songs for the 13th Floor Elevators. Blues singer Tracy Nelson (b. 27 December 1944, Madison, Wisconsin, USA), was Mother Earth's featured vocalist, while the group was latterly augmented by Mark Naftalin (keyboards) and Martin Fierro (horns). The ensemble made its tentative debut on the soundtrack of the film *Revolution*, before completing a promising debut album in 1968. Nelson's powerful voice enhanced its blues-based foundation, while admirable cameos from guitarist Mike Bloomfield and fiddler Spencer Perkin added to the informal atmosphere. The following year Mother Earth moved to a farm on the outskirts of Nashville. Their music became increasingly country-orientated and by the release of a fourth album, *Satisfied*, only Nelson and Andrews remained from the group's first release. In 1973 they took the name Tracy Nelson/Mother Earth, but the group was dissolved when the singer's self-titled solo album won critical and commercial plaudits.

Albums: *Living With The Animals* (1968), *Make A Joyful Noise* (1969), *Presents Tracy Nelson Country* (1969), *Satisfied* (1970), *Bring Me Home* (1971), *Mother Earth* (1972), *Poor Man's Paradise* (1973).

Mothers Of Invention

This celebrated group was formed in 1965 when guitarist Frank Zappa (b. 21 December 1940, Baltimore, Maryland, USA) replaced Ray Hunt in the Soul Giants, a struggling R&B-based bar band. Ray Collins (vocals), Dave Coronado (saxophone), Roy Estrada (bass) and Jimmy Carl Black (drums) completed their early line-up, but Coronado abandoned the group when the newcomer unveiled his musical strategy. Now renamed the Mothers, the quartet was relocated from Orange County to Los Angeles where they were briefly augmented by several individuals, including Alice Stuart, James Guercio and Henry Vestine, later guitarist in Canned Heat. These temporary additions found Zappa's vision daunting as the Mothers embarked on a disarming melange of 50s pop, Chicago R&B and *avant garde* music. They were embraced by the city's nascent Underground before an appearance at the famed Whiskey A Go-Go resulted in a recording deal when producer Tom Wilson caught the end of one of their sets.

Now dubbed the Mothers Of Invention, owing to pressure from the record company, the group added guitarist Elliott Ingber (Winged Eel Fingerling) before commencing *Freak Out*, rock music's first double album. This revolutionary set featured several exceptional pieces including 'Trouble Every Day', 'Hungry Freaks, Daddy' and 'The Return Of The Son Of Monster Magnet', each of which showed different facets of Zappa's evolving tableau. The Mothers second album, *Absolutely Free*, featured a radically reshaped line-up. Ingber was fired at the end

of 1966 while Zappa added a second drummer, Billy Mundi, plus Don Preston (keyboards), Bunk Gardner (horns) and Jim 'Motorhead' Sherwood (saxophone) to the original group nucleus. A six-month residency at New York's Garrick Theater combined spirited interplay with excellent material and the set showed growing confidence. Satire flourished on 'Plastic People', 'America Drinks & Goes Home' and 'Brown Shoes Don't Make It', much of which was inspired by the 'cocktail-bar' drudgery the group suffered in its earliest incarnation. However, Zappa's ire was more fully flexed on *We're Only In It For The Money*, which featured several barbed attacks on the trappings of 'flower-power'. Housed in a sleeve which cleverly mocked the Beatles' *Sgt. Pepper's Lonely Hearts Club Band*, the set included 'The Idiot Bastard Son' ('The father's a Nazi in Congress today, the mother's a hooker somewhere in LA') and 'Who Needs The Peace Corps' ('I'll stay a week and get the crabs and take a bus back home') and indicated Zappa's growing fascination with technology. The album also introduced new member Ian Underwood (saxophone/keyboards), who became an integral part of the group's future work. *Cruising With Ruben And The Jets* was, to quote the liner notes; 'an album of greasy love songs and cretin simplicity'. Despite such cynicism, the group displayed an obvious affection for the 50s doo-wop material on offer, all of which was self-penned and included re-recordings of three songs, 'How Could I Be Such A Fool', 'Any Way The Wind Blows' and 'You Didn't Try To Call Me', first aired on *Freak Out*. However, the album was the last wholly new set committed by the 'original' line-up. Later releases, *Uncle Meat* (a soundtrack to the then unmade film), *Burnt Weeny Sandwich* and *Weasels Ripped My Flesh*, were all compiled from existing live and studio tapes as tension within the group pulled it apart. The musicians enjoyed mixed fortunes; Estrada joined newcomer Lowell George in Little Feat, third drummer Arthur Dyre Tripp III switched allegiance to Captain Beefheart, while Jimmy Carl Black formed Geronimo Black with brothers Buzz and Bunk Gardner.

A new Mothers was formed in 1970 from the musicians contributing to Zappa's third solo album, *Chunga's Revenge*, and the scatalogical 'on the road' documentary, *200 Motels*. Three former Turtles, Mark Volman, Howard Kaylan (both vocals) and Jim Pons (bass) joined Aynsley Dunbar (drums) and longstanding affiliates Ian Underwood and Don Preston in the group responsible for *Fillmore East - June 1971*. Here, however, the early pot-pourri of Stravinsky, John Coltrane, doo-wop and 'Louie Louie' gave way to condescending innuendo as Zappa threatened to become the person once the subject of his ire. Paradoxically, it became the group's best-selling album to date, setting the tone for future releases and reinforcing the guitarist's jaundiced view of his audience. This period was brought to a sudden end at London's Rainbow Theatre. A 'jealous' member of the audience attacked the hapless Zappa onstage, pushing him into the orchestra pit where he sustained multiple back injuries and a compound leg fracture. His slow recuperation was undermined when the entire new Mothers, bar Underwood, quit *en masse* to form what became known as Flo And Eddie. Confined to the studio, Zappa compiled *Just Another Band From L.A.* and used the Mothers epithet for the jazz big band on *The Grand Wazoo*. Reverting to rock music, the Mothers' name was re-established with a new, tighter line-up in 1973. However subsequent albums, *Over-Nite Sensation*, *Roxy And Elsewhere* and *One Size Fits All*, are indistinguishable from projects bearing Zappa's name and this now superfluous title was abandoned in 1975, following the release *Bongo Fury*, a collaboration with Captain Beefheart. Zappa's career has progressed to such a high-level that his entire catalogue has been remastered and re-issued with the advent of the compact disc. The quality of those early Mothers Of Invention recordings are by today's standards quite outstanding.

Albums: *Freak Out* (1966), *Absolutely Free* (1967), *We're Only In It For The Money* (1968), *Cruising With Ruben And The Jets* (1968), *Uncle Meat* (1969), *Burnt Weeny Sandwich* (1969), *Weasels Ripped My Flesh* (1970), *Fillmore East - June 1971* (1971), *200 Motels* (1971, film soundtrack), *Just Another Band From L.A.* (1972), *The Grand Wazoo* (1972), *Over-Nite Sensation* (1973), *Roxy And Elsewhere* (1974), *One Size Fits All* (1975), with Captain Beefheart *Bongo Fury* (1975). Compilations: *Mothermania* (1969), *The XXXX Of The Mothers Of Invention* (1969), *The Worst Of The Mothers* (1971).

Further reading: *No Commercial Potential*, David Walley. *Zappalog*, Norbert Obermanns. *The Real Frank Zappa Book*, Frank Zappa and Peter Occhigrosso.

Motown Records

The history of Motown Records remains a paradigm of success for independent record labels, and for black-owned industry in the USA. The corporation was formed in 1959 by Berry Gordy, a successful R&B songwriter who required an outlet for his initial forays into production. He used an $800 loan to finance the release of singles by Marv Johnson and Eddie Holland on his Tamla label, one of a series of individual trademarks which he eventually included beneath the Motown umbrella. Enjoying limited local success, Gordy widened his roster, signing acts like the Temptations and Marvelettes in 1960. That year, the Miracles' 'Shop Around' gave the company its first major US. hit, followed in 1961 by their first

number 1, the Marvelettes' 'Please Mr Postman'. Gordy coined the phrase 'The Sound Of Young America' to describe Motown's output, and the apparent arrogance of his claim quickly proved well-founded. By 1964, Motown were scoring regular hits via the Supremes and the Four Tops, while Mary Wells' 'My Guy' helped the label become established outside the USA. The label's vibrant brand of soul music, marked by a pounding rhythm and a lightness of touch which appealed to both pop and R&B fans, provided America's strongest response to the massive impact of the British beat group invasion in 1964 and 1965. At the same time, Gordy realized the importance of widening his commercial bases; in 1965, he overtly wooed the middle-of-the-road audience by giving the Supremes a residency at the plush Copa nightclub in New York - the first of many such ventures into traditional showbiz territory. The distance between Motown's original fans and their new surroundings led to accusations that the company had betrayed its black heritage, though consistent chart success helped cushion the blow.

In 1966, Motown took three steps to widen its empire, snapping up groups like the Isley Brothers and Gladys Knight And The Pips from rival labels, opening a Hollywood office to double its promotional capabilities, and snuffing out its strongest opposition in Detroit by buying the Golden World and Ric-Tic group of R&B companies. Throughout these years, Gordy maintained a vice-like grip over Motown's affairs; even the most successful staff writers and producers had to submit their work to a weekly quality control meeting, and faced the threat of having their latest creations summarily rejected. Gradually dissent rose within the ranks, and in 1967 Gordy lost the services of his A&R controller, Mickey Stevenson, and his premier writing/production team, Holland/Dozier/Holland. Two years of comparative failure followed before Motown regained its supremacy in the pop market by launching the career of the phenomenally successful Jackson Five in 1969. Gordy made a bold but ultimately unsuccessful attempt to break into the rock market in 1970, with his Rare Earth label, one of a variety of spin-off companies launched in the early part of the decade. This was a period of some uncertainty for the company: several major acts either split up or chose to seek artistic freedom elsewhere, and the decision to concentrate the company's activities in its California office in 1973 represented a dramatic break from its roots. At the same time, Gordy masterminded the birth of Motown's film division, with the award-winning biopic about Billie Holiday, *Lady Sings The Blues*. The burgeoning artistic and commercial success of Stevie Wonder kept the record division on course, though outsiders noted a distinct lack of young talent to replace the company's original stalwarts.

The mid-70s proved to be Motown's least successful period for over a decade; only the emergence of the Commodores maintained the label as a contemporary musical force. Motown increasingly relied on the strength of its back catalogue, with only occasional releases, like the Commodores' 'Three Times A Lady' and Smokey Robinson's 'Being With You', rivalling the triumphs of old. The departure of Marvin Gaye and Diana Ross in the early 80s proved a massive psychological blow, as despite the prominence of Commodores leader Lionel Richie, the company failed to keep pace with the fast-moving developments in black music. From 1986, there were increasing rumours that Berry Gordy was ready to sell the label: these were confirmed in 1988, when Motown was bought by MCA, with Gordy retaining some measure of artistic control over subsequent releases. After more than a decade of disappointing financial returns, Motown remains a record industry legend on the strength of its remarkable hit-making capacities in the 60s.

Move

Formed in late 1965 from the ashes of several Birmingham groups, the original Move comprised Roy Wood (vocals/guitar), Carl Wayne (vocals), Chris 'Ace' Kefford (bass), Trevor Burton (guitar) and Bev Bevan (drums). Under the guidance of Tony Secunda, they moved to London, signed to Decca's hit subsidiary Deram, and rapidly established themselves as one of the most inventive and accomplished pop groups on the live circuit. Their first two hit singles, the classically-inspired 'Night Of Fear' and upbeat psychedelic 'I Can Hear The Grass Grow' sounded fresh and abrasive and benefitted from a series of publicity stunts masterminded by Secunda. Like the Who, the Move specialized in 'auto-destruction', smashing television sets and cars onstage and burning effigies of Adolf Hitler, Ian Smith and Dr Veerwoord. In 1967, they signed to the reactivated Regal Zonophone label which was launched with the fashionably titled 'Flowers In The Rain', the first record played on BBC Radio 1. The mischievous Secunda attempted to promote the disc with a saucy postcard depicting Harold Wilson. The Prime Minister promptly sued for libel, thereby diverting Roy Wood's royalties to charity.

In February 1968, the group returned as strong as ever with the high energy, 50's inspired, 'Fire Brigade'. Soon afterwards, Ace Kefford suffered a nervous breakdown and left the group which continued as a quartet, with Burton switching to bass. The catchy but chaotic 'Wild Tiger Woman' fared less well than expected, as did their bizarrely eclectic EP *Something Else*. Management switches from Tony Secunda to Don Arden and Peter Walsh brought

further complications, but the maestro Wood responded well with the evocative 'Blackberry Way', a number 1 in some UK charts. A softening of their once violent image with 'Curly' coincided with Burton's departure and saw Carl Wayne recklessly steering them on to the cabaret circuit. Increasing friction within their ranks culminated in Wayne's departure for a solo career, leaving the Move to carry on as a trio. The heavy rock sound of 'Brontosaurus' and 'When Alice Comes Down To The Farm' supplemented their diverse hit repertoire, and further changes were ahead. The recruitment of Jeff Lynne from the Idle Race encouraged them to experiment with cellos and oboes while simultaneously pursuing their career as an increasingly straightforward pop act. The final flurry of Move hits ('Tonight', 'Chinatown' and 'California Man') were bereft of the old invention, which was henceforth to be discovered in their grand offshoots, the Electric Light Orchestra (ELO) and Wizzard.

Albums: *The Move* (1968), *Shazam* (1970), *Looking On* (1970), *Message From The Country* (1971).

Mystery Trend

An early but minor group in the San Francisco scene of the 60s, the Mystery Trend took its name after misunderstanding a line in Bob Dylan's 'Like A Rolling Stone' which referred to a 'mystery tramp'. The group consisted of Ron Nagle (vocals), Bob Cuff (guitar), Larry Bennett (bass), Larry West (lead guitar) and John Luby (drums). They performed many concerts in the San Francisco ballrooms of the era, but released only one single, 'Johnny Was A Good Boy'/'A House On The Hill' on Verve, in early 1967, at which time West departed. Cuff left the band in the summer of 1967 and was replaced by John Gregory, who went on to join Seatrain. The Mystery Trend split up in 1968. Nagle recorded a solo album, *Bad Rice*, in 1970 and produced albums by Paul Kantner (of Jefferson Airplane) and John Hiatt. Nagle also formed a unit called Durocs during the 70s.

Napoleon XIV

The pseudonym of songwriter/performer/recording engineer Jerry Samuels, Napoleon XIV burst into the US/UK Top 10 in the summer of 1966 with the bizarre 'They're Coming To Take Me Away, Ha-

Haaa!' Although clearly a novelty song, its subject matter, mental illness (brought on by the loss of the singer's dog), prompted a ban on many American radio stations. An attempted follow-up, 'I'm In Love With My Little Red Tricycle' failed to capture the public's imagination and Napoleon's credibility was further dented when it was revealed that the performer undertaking personal appearances to promote the record was not Samuels but a certain Richard Stern. The presence of Napoleon imitator Kim Fowley hardly helped matters. An album based round the hit with lyrics by comedy writer Jim Lehrer was rushed out but in spite of such amusing titles as 'Photogenic, Schizophrenic You', 'The Nuts In My Family Tree' and 'Bats In My Belfry', it failed to sell in vast quantities. Its final track was not even by Napoleon but instead featured the strains of Josephine XV warbling the acerbic 'I'm Happy They Took You Away, Ha-Haaa!'. In 1990, Napoleon's finest moment was given a fresh airing courtesy of former Dead Kennedys vocalist Jello Biafra whose new group Lard cut a startling version of the hit.
Album: *They're Coming To Take Me Away, Ha-Haaa!* (1966).

Nash, Johnny

b. 9 August 1940, Houston, Texas, USA. John Lester Nash Jnr.'s vocational path was defined early on when he balanced bit-parts in movies with singing lead soprano in a gospel choir. With his voice broken, he starred in such films as 1958's *Take A Giant Step* - with a Caribbean location - and *Key Witness* (1960), while his regular singing spots on a New York television variety series kept him in moderate Hot 100 strikes both as a soloist and, to a lesser degree, as one of the *ad hoc* Teen Commandments with Paul Anka and George Hamilton IV. His liking for Sam Cooke's light soul was made evident in 1965 with an R&B smash, 'Let's Move And Groove Together' but he left a more idiosyncratic mark on Britain with a pop-reggae hybrid that caught on when 'Hold Me Tight', 'You Got Soul' and a version of Cooke's 'Cupid' each made 1969's Top 10. All were produced by Byron Lee in Jamaica. Further refinement of this style was suspended by acting commitments; however, on a set in Sweden Nash met Bob Marley whose 'Stir It Up' put him back in the UK charts in 1971, paving the way for 'I Can See Clearly Now' (perhaps his best-loved single), 'There Are More Questions Than Answers' and, in the USA, 'Guava Jelly'. After a string of flops, a 1975 song written by Ernie Smith, 'Tears On My Pillow' became Nash's only UK number 1. When another Cooke opus, 'What A Wonderful World', struggled into the Top 30 in 1976, Nash chose to devote more energy to films and his West Indian recording complex. In 1991 'Stir It Up' soundtracked an ITV coffee commercial.
Albums: *Hold Me Tight* (1968), *Let's Go Dancing* (1969), *I Can See Clearly Now* (1972), *My Merry-Go-Round* (1973), *What A Wonderful World* (1977), *Stir It Up* (1981), *Johnny Nash* (1985), *Here Again* (1986), *Tears On My Pillow* (1987). Compilations: *Greatest Hits* (1974), *The Johnny Nash Collection* (1977).

Nashville Teens

Formed in Weybridge, Surrey in 1962, the Nashville Teens initially comprised vocalists Arthur 'Art' Sharp (b. 26 May 1941, Woking, Surrey, England) and Ray Phillips (b. Ramon John Phillips, 16 January 1944, Tiger Bay, Cardiff, Wales), Michael Dunford (guitar), John Hawken (b. 9 May 1940, Bournemouth, Dorset, England; piano), Pete Shannon (b. Peter Shannon Harris, 23 August 1941, Antrim, Northern Ireland; bass) and Roger Groom (drums). Dunford and Groom left the line-up the following year and the group was completed by John Allen (b. John Samuel Allen, 23 April, 1945, St. Albans, Hertfordshire, England; guitar), Barrie Jenkins (b. 22 December 1944, Leicester, England; drums) and third vocalist Terry Crow for a protracted tenure in Hamburg, Germany. This period is chronicled on *Jerry Lee Lewis; Live At The Star Club* on which the septet backed the veteran rock 'n' roll star. In 1964, and with Crow now absent, the Teens were aligned with producer Mickie Most for a pounding version of 'Tobacco Road', which deservedly climbed to number 6 in the UK. The similarly-styled 'Google Eye' also proved popular, reaching the Top 10, but a split with Most ended this brief ascendancy. Collaborations with Andrew Loog Oldham ('This Little Bird') and Shel Talmy ('The Hard Way') were minor hits, but at the expense of the unit's undeniable grasp of R&B. Groom rejoined the line-up in 1966 when Jenkins left for the Animals, but despite excellent versions of Randy Newman's 'The Biggest Night Of Her Life' and Bob Dylan's 'All Along The Watchtower', the Nashville Teens were unable to rekindle former success. A spate of defections - John Hawken later found fame with Renaissance - left Phillips the sole remaining original member. He continues to front this act and concurrently performs with the British Invasion All-Stars, which features musicians drawn from the Downliners Sect, Creation and the Pretty Things.
Album: *Live At The Red House* (1984).

Nazz

Formed in Philadelphia, USA in 1967, the Nazz comprised of Todd Rundgren (guitar/vocals), Carson Van Osten (bass/vocals), both ex-members of bar-band Woody's Truck Stop, Stewkey (lead vocals/keyboards) and Thom Mooney (drums). Although the quartet made its live debut supporting the Doors, manager John Kurland deliberately cultivated an air of exclusivity which ultimately hampered progress. A lucrative recording deal with publishers Screen Gems resulted in *Nazz*, a synthesis of British and US pop invoking the Who, Jimi Hendrix, Buffalo Springfield and Small Faces. However, the unit's anglophilia and mod affectations proved unfashionable in the face of acid-rock which, when coupled with growing internal disharmony, sowed the seeds of their demise. *Nazz Nazz* emphasized the positive elements of its predecessor and although the same influences were still apparent, a sense of individuality was also present. Rundgren's departure for a solo career in 1970 brought the Nazz to an end, and *Nazz III*, compiled from material from the *Nazz Nazz* sessions, was issued posthumously. Stewkey and Mooney were later joined by Rick Neilsen and Tom Petersson (later of Cheap Trick) in a group which took a variety of names, but only Rundgren achieved lasting success outside the Nazz. Despite negligible commercial gain, his former group's work was later lauded as the precursor to a generation of British-influenced US bands, notably the Raspberries, Stories and Sparks.

Albums: *Nazz* (1968), *Nazz Nazz* (1969), *Nazz III* (1970). Compilation: *Best Of The Nazz* (1983).

Neil, Fred

b. 1937, St. Petersburg, Florida, USA. An important figure in America's folk renaissance, Neil's talent first emerged in 1956 when he co-wrote an early Buddy Holly single, 'Modern Don Juan'. By the following decade he was a fixture of the Greenwich Village circuit, both as a solo act and in partnership with fellow singer Vince Martin. The duo embarked on separate careers following the release of *Tear Down The Walls*. Neil's subsequent solo *Bleecker And MacDougal* was an influential collection and contained the original version of 'The Other Side Of This Life', later covered by the Youngbloods, Lovin' Spoonful and the Jefferson Airplane. The singer's deep, resonant voice was equally effective, inspiring the languid tones of Tim Buckley and Tim Hardin. A reticent individual, Neil waited two years before completing *Fred Neil*, a compulsive selection which featured two of the artist's most famous compositions, 'The Dolphins' and 'Everybody's Talkin''. The latter was adopted as the theme song to *Midnight Cowboy*, a highly-successful film, although it was a version by Harry Nilsson which became the hit single. Such temporary trappings were of little note to Neil, who preferred the anonymity of his secluded Florida base, from where he rarely ventured. An appearance at the Los Angeles club, the Bitter End, provided the material for *The Other Side Of This Life*, Neil's last album to date and an effective resume of his career. This informal performance also contained other

favoured material, including 'You Don't Miss Your Water', which featured assistance from country singer Gram Parsons. A major, if self-effacing talent, Fred Neil has now withdrawn from music altogether.

Albums: *Hootenanny Live At The Bitter End* (1964), *World Of Folk Music* (1964), with Vince Martin *Tear Down The Walls* (1964), *Bleecker And MacDougal* aka *Little Bit Of Rain* (1964), *Fred Neil* aka *Everybody's Talkin'* (1966), *Sessions* (1968), *The Other Side Of This Life* (1971). Compilation: *The Very Best Of Fred Neil* (1986).

Nelson, Rick

b. Eric Hilliard Nelson, 8 May 1940, Teaneck, New Jersey, USA, d. 31 December 1985, De Kalb, Texas, USA. Nelson came from a showbusiness family and his parents had sung in bands during the 30s and 40s. They had their own US radio show, *The Adventures Of Ozzie And Harriet*, soon transferred to television, in which Ricky and his brother David appeared. By 1957 Nelson embarked on a recording career, with the million selling, double-sided 'I'm Walkin''/'A Teenager's Romance'. A third hit soon followed with 'You're My One And Only Love'. A switch from the label Verve to Imperial saw Nelson enjoy further success with the rockabilly 'Be-Bop Baby'. In 1958 Nelson formed a full-time group for live work and recordings, which included James Burton (guitar), James Kirkland (later replaced by Joe Osborn) (bass), Gene Garf (piano) and Richie Frost (drums). Early that year Nelson enjoyed his first transatlantic hit with 'Stood Up' and registered his first US chart topper with 'Poor Little Fool'. His early broadcasting experience was put to useful effect when he starred in the Howard Hawks movie western, *Rio Bravo* (1959), alongside John Wayne and Dean Martin. Nelson's singles continued to chart regularly and it says much for the quality of his work that the b-sides were often as well known as the a-sides. Songs such as 'Believe What You Say', 'Never Be Anyone Else But You', 'It's Late', 'Sweeter Than You', 'Just A Little Too Much' and 'I Wanna Be Loved' showed that Nelson was equally adept at singing ballads and uptempo material. One of his greatest moments as a pop singer occurred in the spring of 1961 when he issued the million-selling 'Travelin' Man' backed with the exuberant Gene Pitney composition 'Hello Mary Lou'. Shortly after the single topped the US charts, Nelson celebrated his 21st birthday and announced that he was changing his performing name from Ricky to Rick.

Several more pop hits followed, most notably 'Young World', 'Teenage Idol', 'It's Up To You', 'String Along' (his first for his new label, Decca), 'Fools Rush In' and 'For You'. With the emergence of the beat boom, Nelson's clean-cut pop was less in demand and in 1966 he switched to country music.

His early albums in this vein featured compositions from such artists as Willie Nelson, Glen Campbell, Tim Hardin, Harry Nilsson and Randy Newman.

In 1969 Nelson formed a new outfit the Stone Canyon Band featuring former Poco member Randy Meisner (bass), Allen Kemp (guitar), Tom Brumley (steel guitar) and Pat Shanahan (drums). A version of Bob Dylan's 'She Belongs To Me' brought Nelson back into the US charts and a series of strong, often underrated albums followed. A performance at Madison Square Garden in late 1971 underlined Nelson's difficulties at the time. Although he had recently issued the accomplished *Rick Sings Nelson*, on which he wrote every track, the audience were clearly more interested in hearing his early 60s hits. Nelson responded by composing the sarcastic 'Garden Party', which reaffirmed his determination to go his own way. The single, ironically, went on to sell a million and was his last hit record. After parting with the Stone Canyon Band in 1974, Nelson's recorded output declined, but he continued to tour extensively. On 31 December 1985, a chartered plane carrying him to a concert date in Dallas caught fire and crashed near De Kalb, Texas. Nelson's work deserves a place in rock history as he was one of the few 'good looking kids' from the early 60s who had a strong voice which, coupled with exemplary material, remains durable.

Albums: *Teen Time* (1957), *Ricky* (1957), *Ricky Nelson* (1958), *Ricky Sings Again* (1959), *Songs By Ricky* (1959), *More Songs By Ricky* (1960), *Rick Is 21* (1961), *Album Seven By Rick* (1962), *A Long Vacation* (1963), *For Your Sweet Love* (1963), *Ricky Sings For You* (1964), *The Very Thought Of You* (1964), *Spotlight On Rick* (1965), *Best Always* (1965), *Love And Kisses* (1966), *Bright Lights And Country Music* (1966), *Country Fever* (1967), *On The Flip-Side* (1967, film soundtrack), *Another Side Of Rick* (1969), *In Concert* (1970), *Rick Sings Nelson* (1970), *Rudy The Fifth* (1971), *Garden Party* (1972), *Windfall* (1974), *Intakes* (1977), *Playing To Win* (1981). Compilations: *It's Up To You* (1963), *Million Sellers* (1964), *The Very Best Of Rick Nelson* (1970), *Legendary Masters* (1972), *The Singles Album 1963-1976* (1977), *The Singles Album 1957-63* (1979), *Rockin' With Ricky* (1984), *String Along With Rick* (1984), *The Best Of Ricky Nelson* (1985), *All The Best* (1986).

Further reading: *Ricky Nelson*, Joel Selvin.

Nelson, Sandy

b. Sander L. Nelson, 1 December 1938, Santa Monica, California, USA. Drummer Nelson began his career as a member of the Kip Tyler Band. Appearances in live rock 'n' roll shows led to his becoming an in-demand session musician, where he joined an *ad hoc* group of young aspirants including Bruce Johnston and Phil Spector. Nelson played on 'To Know Him Is To Love Him', a million-selling single written and produced by the latter for his vocal group, the Teddy Bears. Johnston meanwhile assisted the drummer on an early demo of 'Teen Beat', a powerful instrumental which achieved gold status in 1959 on reaching the Top 10 in both the US and UK. Two years later, Nelson secured another gold disc for 'Let There Be Drums', co-composed with Richie Podolor, who became a successful producer with Three Dog Night and Steppenwolf. The pattern was now set for a plethora of releases on Imperial, each of which combined a simple guitar melody with Nelson's explosive percussion breaks, a style echoing that of the concurrent surf craze. Its appeal quickly waned and 'Teen Beat '65' (1964) - recorded in the artist's garage studio - was his last chart entry. Guitarists Glen Campbell and Jerry McGee, later of the Ventures, as well as bassist Carole Kaye were among the musicians contributing to his sessions, but these lessened dramatically towards the end of the decade. During the 70s Nelson was featured in one of impresario Richard Nader's *Rock 'N' Roll Revival* shows, but he retired following the disappointing disco-influenced *Bang Bang Rhythm*. Despite being tempted into occasional, informal recordings, Nelson has remained largely inactive in professional music since 1978, although instrumental aficionados still marvel at the drummer's extensive catalogue.

Albums: *Teen Beat* (1960), *He's A Drummer Boy* aka *Happy Drums* (1960), *Let There Be Drums* (1961), *Drums Are My Beat!* (1962), *Drummin' Up A Storm* (1962), *Golden Hits* (retitled *Sandy Nelson Plays Fats Domino*) (1962), *On The Wild Side* aka *Country Style* (1962), *Compelling Percussion* aka *And Then There Were Drums* (1962), *Teen Age House Party* (1963), *The Best Of The Beats* (1963), *Be True To Your School* (1963), *Live! In Las Vegas* (1964), *Teen Beat '65* (1965), *Drum Discotheque* (1965), *Drums A Go-Go* (1965), *Boss Beat* (1966), *'In' Beat* (1966), *Superdrums* (1966), *Beat That #!!&** *Drum* (1966), *Cheetah Beat* (1967), *The Beat Goes On* (1967), *Souldrums* (1968), *Boogaloo Beat* (1968), *Rock 'N' Roll Revival* (1968), *Golden Pops* (1968), *Rebirth Of The Beat* (1969), *Manhattan Spiritual* (1969), *Groovy!* (1969), *Rock Drum Golden Disc* (1972), *Keep On Rockin'* (1972), *Roll Over Beethoven* aka *Hocus Pocus* (1973), *Let The Good Times Rock* (1974), *Bang Bang Rhythm* (1975). Compilations: *Beat That Drum* (1963), *Sandy Nelson Plays* (1963), *The Very Best Of Sandy Nelson* (1978), *20 Rock 'N' Roll Hits: Sandy Nelson* (1983).

Newbeats

This distinctive pop trio featured falsetto Larry Henley (b. 30 June 1941, Arp, Texas, USA) with brothers Marcus 'Marc' Mathis (b. 9 February 1942; bass) and Lewis 'Dean' Mathis (b. 17 March 1939, Hahira, Georgia, USA). Dean had joined Paul

Howard's Western Swing Band in 1956 as a pianist and later moved to Dale Hopkin's Band, with Marc joining shortly afterwards. The Mathis brothers then performed and recorded as Dean And Marc; their version of 'Tell Him No' narrowly missed the US Top 40 in 1959. Henley briefly joined the act before they went their separate ways. After recording as the Brothers on Checker and Argo they also had releases on Check Mate and May before joining Hickory Records, where Henley had been recording fruitlessly as a soloist. Since neither act was successful they decided to record together as the Newbeats. Their first single, 'Bread And Butter', became their biggest hit, shooting to number 2 in the US charts and into the UK Top 20 in 1964. In the USA the shrill-sounding trio kept the Top 40 hits rolling with 'Everything's Alright' in 1964, 'Break Away (From That Boy)' and 'Run Baby Run' (a belated UK Top 10 hit in 1971), the last two in 1965. After a decade on Hickory the trio went to Buddah Records in 1973 and then in 1974 to Playboy. The trio split up that year, with Henley then recording without chart success for Capricorn and later for Atco and Epic. He then turned his attention to songwriting, and has been very successful since. His best known song was Bette Midler's version of a 1983 country hit 'Wind Beneath My Wings'.

Albums: *Bread & Butter* (1964), *Big Beat Sounds By The Newbeats* (1965), *Run Baby Run* (1966).

New Christy Minstrels

Randy Sparks (b. 29 July 1933, Leavenworth, Kansas, USA), formed this commercialized folk group in 1961. Determined to create a unit that was 'a compromise between the Norman Luboff Choir and the Kingston Trio', he added a popular Oregon quartet, the Fairmount Singers, to his own Randy Sparks Three. A third unit, the Inn Group, which featured Jerry Yester, was absorbed into the line-up, while other Los Angeles-based performers embellished these core acts. Fourteen singers made up the original New Christy Minstrels but although the ensemble was viewed as supplementary to the participants' other careers, interest in the unit's debut *Presenting The New Christy Minstrels*, led to it becoming a full-time venture. Most of these early recruits, including the entire Inn Group, abandoned Sparks' creation at this point, creating the need for further, wholesale changes. New enlistments, including Barry McGuire, Barry Kane and Larry Ramos, joined the Minstrels whose next release, *In Person*, documented a successful appearance at the famed Troubador club. The following year (1963) the group secured its first hit single with 'Green Green' which established the ensemble as a leading popular attraction. The group, however, remained volatile as members continued to come and go. Gene

Clark disbanded his Kansas-based trio, the Surf Riders, in order to join the Minstrels, but left after a matter of months, frustrated at the rather conservative material the ensemble recorded. He later formed the Byrds with (Jim) Roger McGuinn and David Crosby. Randy Sparks ended his relationship with the Minstrels in the summer of 1964. Maligned for creating their MOR image, his departure did not result in the more daring direction several members wished to pursue. McGuire, who was increasingly unhappy with such material as 'Three Wheels On My Wagon' and 'Chim Chim Cheree', left the group after seeing several British groups perform during the Minstrels European tour that year. His gravelly rasp was soon heard on his solo international protest hit, 'Eve Of Destruction'. In 1966 Larry Ramos accepted an invitation to join the Association and although several excellent new vocalists, including Kim Carnes and Kenny Rodgers, had been absorbed into the Minstrels, their influential days were over. Longstanding members Mike Settle and Terry Williams left when their new ideas were constantly rejected. They formed the First Edition with the equally ambitious Rodgers, and subsequently enjoyed the kind of success the parent group previously experienced. Although the New Christy Minstrels continued to exist in some form into the 80s, singing early hits, show tunes and standards, their halcyon days ended during the mid-60s.

Albums: *Presenting The New Christy Minstrels* (1962), *The New Christy Minstrels In Person* (1962), *The New Christy Minstrels Tell Tall Tales, Legends And Nonsense* (1963), *Ramblin' (Featuring Green, Green)* (1963), *Merry Christmas!* (1963), *Today* (1964), *Land Of Giants* (1964), *The Quiet Side Of The New Christy Minstrels* (1964), *The New Christy Minstrels Sing And Play Cowboys And Indians* (1965), *The Academy Award Winner - Chim Chim Cheree* (1965), *The Wandering Minstrels* (1965), *In Italy...In Italian* (1966), *New Kick!* (1966), *Christmas With The Christies* (1966), *On Tour Through Motortown* (1968), *Big Hits From Chitty Chitty Bang Bang* (1968), *You Need Someone To Love* (1970), *The Great Soap Opera Themes* (1976). Compilation: *Greatest Hits* (1966).

Newley, Anthony

b. 24 September 1931, London, England. After attending the Italia Conti Stage School Newley worked as a child actor in several films, including *The Little Ballerina*, *Vice Versa*, and in 1948 played the Artful Dodger in David Lean's successful version of *Oliver Twist*. He made his London theatrical debut in John Cranko's revue, *Cranks* in 1955, and had character parts in well over 20 films before he was cast as rock 'n' roll star Jeep Jackson in *Idle On Parade* in 1959. Newley's four-track vocal EP, and his version of the film's hit ballad, Jerry Lordan's 'I've

Waited So Long', started a three-year UK chart run which included 'Personality', 'If She Should Come To You', 'And The Heavens Cried', the novelty numbers 'Pop Goes The Weasel' and 'Strawberry Fair' and two UK number 1 hits, 'Why' and Lionel Bart's, 'Do You Mind'. Newley also made the album charts in 1960 with his set of old standards, *Love Is A Now And Then Thing*. He made later appearances in the charts with *Tony* (1961), and the comedy album *Fool Britannia* (1963), on which he was joined by his wife, Joan Collins and Peter Sellers. In 1961 Newley collaborated with Leslie Bricusse (b. 29 January 1931, London) on the off-beat stage musical, *Stop The World - I Want To Get Off*. Newley also directed, and played Littlechap, the small man who fights the system. The show, which was later filmed in 1966, produced several hit songs, including 'What Kind Of Fool Am I', 'Once In A Lifetime' and 'Gonna Build A Mountain'.

In 1964 Bricusse and Newley wrote the lyric to John Barry's music for Shirley Bassey to sing over the titles of the James Bond movie, *Goldfinger*. The team's next musical show in 1965, *The Roar Of The Greasepaint - The Smell Of The Crowd*, with comedian Norman Wisdom in the lead, toured the north of England but did not make the West End. When it went to Broadway Newley took over (co-starring with Cyril Richard), and 'Who Can I Turn To?', 'A Wonderful Day Like Today' and 'This Dream' was added to the show. It was a smash hit. In 1967 Newley appeared with Rex Harrison and Richard Attenborough in the film musical *Doctor Doolittle*, with script and songs by Bricusse. Despite winning an Oscar for 'Talk To The Animals', the film was considered an expensive flop, as was Newley's own movie project in 1969, a pseudo-autobigraphical sex-fantasy entitled *Can Heironymus Merkin Ever Forget Mercy Humppe And Find True Happiness?* Far more successful, in 1971, was *Willy Wonka And The Chocolate Factory*, a Roald Dahl story with music and lyrics by Bricusse and Newley. Sammy Davis Jnr. had a million-selling record with one of the songs, 'The Candy Man'. They also wrote several songs for the 1971 NBC television musical adaptation of *Peter Pan*, starring Mia Farrow and Danny Kaye. Bricusse and Newley's last authentic stage musical, *The Good Old Bad Old Days*, opened in London in 1972 and had a run of 309 performances. Newley sang some of the songs, including 'The People Tree', on his own *Ain't It Funny*. He has lived in California for some years, one of several British singers to become hugely successful in the USA. In his cabaret act he bemoaned the fact that he has not had a hit with one of his own songs. A major 1989 London revival of *Stop The World - I Want To Get Off* directed by Newley, and in which he also appeared, closed after five weeks. Newley also wrote the book, music and lyrics for the London stage musical,

Sherlock Holmes, in 1989.

His collaborator, Leslie Bricusse, won Ivor Novello awards for his songs, 'Out Of Town' (from the 1956 Max Bygraves film, *Charlie Moon*), 'My Kind Of Girl' (a hit for Matt Monro in 1960), and 'If I Ruled The World', from the 1963 musical, *Pickwick*, and a Top 20 entry for its star, Harry Secombe. He has also contributed to movie musicals such as *Goodbye Mr Chips,* for which he wrote the lyrics and *Scrooge* and worked with Henry Mancini.

Albums: *Love Is A Now And Then Thing* (1960), *Tony* (1961), *Stop The World - I Want To Get Off* (1962, US stageshow soundtrack), with Peter Sellers and Joan Collins *Fool Britannia* (1963), *The Roar Of The Greasepaint - The Smell Of The Crowd* (1965, US stageshow soundtrack). Compilations: *The Romantic World Of Anthony Newley* (1970), *The Lonely World Of Anthony Newley* (1972), *The Singer And His Songs* (1978), *Anthony Newley: Mr. Personality* (1985). Compilation: *Greatest Hits* (1991).

Nice

Nice

Originally the back-up band to soul singer P.P. Arnold, the Nice became one of the true originators of what has variously been described as pomp-rock, art-rock and classical-rock. The band comprised Keith Emerson (b. 1 November 1944, Todmorden, Yorkshire, England; keyboards), Brian 'Blinky' Davison (b. 25 May 1942, Leicester, England; drums), Lee Jackson (b. 8 January 1943, Newcastle-Upon-Tyne, England; bass/vocals) and David O'List (b. 13 December 1948, Chiswick, London, England; guitar). After leaving Arnold in October 1967 the Nice quickly built a reputation as one of the most visually exciting bands. Emerson's stage act involved, in true circus style, throwing knives into his Hammond Organ, which would emit outrageous sounds, much to the delight of the audience. Their debut, *The Thoughts Of Emerlist Davjack*, while competent, came nowhere near reproducing their exciting live sound. By the time of the release of its follow-up, *Ars Longa Vita Brevis*, O'List had departed, being unable to compete with Emerson's showmanship and subsequently joined Roxy Music. The album contained their notorious single, 'America', from *West Side Story*. During one performance at London's Royal Albert Hall, they burnt the American flag on stage and were severely lambasted, not only by the Albert Hall authorities, but also by the song's composer, Leonard Bernstein. The band continued their remaining life as a trio, producing their most satisfying and successful work. Both *Nice* and *Five Bridges Suite* narrowly missed the top of the UK charts, although they were unable to break through in the USA. The former contained an excellent reading of Tim Hardin's 'Hang On To A Dream', with exquisite piano from Emerson. The latter was a bold semi-orchestral suite about working-class life in Newcastle-upon-Tyne. One of their other showpieces was an elongated version of Bob Dylan's 'She Belongs To Me'. *Five Bridges* also contained versions of 'Intermezzo From The Karelia Suite' by Sibelius and Tchaikovsky's 'Pathetique'. Their brave attempt at fusing classical music and rock together with the Sinfonia of London was admirable, and much of what Emerson later achieved with the huge success of Emerson, Lake And Palmer should be credited to the brief but valuable career of the Nice. With Emerson's departure, Jackson floundered with Jackson Heights, while Davison was unsuccessful with his own band, Every Which Way. Jackson and Davison teamed up again in 1974 to form the ill-fated Refugee.

Albums: *The Thoughts Of Emerlist Davjack* (1967), *Ars Longa Vita Brevis* (1968), *Nice* (1969), *Five Bridges* (1970), *Elegy* (1971). Compilations: *Autumn 76-Spring 68* (1972), *20th Anniversary Release* (1987).

Nina And Frederick

This Danish singing duo was popular in the late 50s and early 60s. Nina had married the wealthy Danish aristocrat Baron Frederick Von Pallandt in 1954, and teamed up with her husband to record a string of duo hits, including 'Mary's Boy Child' (1959), 'Little Donkey' (1960) and 'Sucu Sucu' (1961). They separated in 1969 largely because he wanted to retire and she did not. Afterwards the Baron became a virtual recluse on a farm in Ibiza; they divorced in 1976. Nina, meanwhile, ventured into cabaret and acting, making her film debut in Robert Altman's *The Long Goodbye* in 1973, co-starring with Elliot Gould. She was later implicated in a minor scandal in the early 70s when she went on holiday with Clifford Irving, the fraudulent biographer of Howard Hughes, who was later jailed. In 1980 she appeared briefly in *American Gigolo*.

Selected albums: *Nina And Frederick* i (1960), *Nina And Frederick* ii (1961), *An Evening With Nina And Frederick At The Royal Albert Hall* (1966), *Dawn* (1967). Solo album: Nina (compilation) *Golden Hour Presents Nina* (1978).

1910 Fruitgum Company

The aptly-named Fruitgum Company were at the forefront of a brief wave of bubblegum-pop in the late 60s. Bubblegum was a form that offered solid dance beats, infantile lyrics and catchy choruses built around instantly-hummable melody lines. The Super K production team of Jeff Katz and Jerry Kasenetz were masters of the form and specialized in studio in-house creations such as the Fruitgum Company. Writer Joey Levine was the voice behind the hits which began with the nursery game anthem 'Simon Says' in 1968 and continued with '1, 2, 3, Red Light', 'Goody Goody Gumdrops', 'Indian Giver' and 'Special Delivery'. A touring troupe headed by Levine was hastily assembled and kept this manufactured group alive until they became expendable at the end of the decade.

Albums: *Simon Says* (1968), *1, 2, 3, Red Light* (1968), *Indian Giver* (1969), *1910 Fruitgum Company And Ohio Express* (1969).

Nyro, Laura

b. Laura Nigro, 18 October 1947, The Bronx, New York City, USA. The daughter of an accomplished jazz trumpeter, Nyro was introduced to music at an early age, reputedly completing her first composition when she was only eight years old. Her main influences ranged from Bob Dylan to John Coltrane, but the artist's debut *More Than A New Discovery* (aka *The First Songs*) revealed a talent akin to Brill Building songwriters Carole King and Ellie Greenwich. Nyro's empathy for soul and R&B enhanced her individuality, although she later disowned the set, claiming its stilted arrangements were completed against her wishes. The set nonetheless contained several songs adapted by other artists, notably 'Stoney End' (Barbara Streisand), 'And When I Die' (Blood, Sweat And Tears) and 'Wedding Bell Blues' (Fifth Dimension). *Eli And The Thirteenth Confession* complied more closely to Nyro's wishes; while containing the highly popular 'Stone Souled Picnic', it revealed the growing sense of introspection that flourished on the following year's *New York Tendaberry*. Here the singer's dramatic intonation, capable of sweeping from a whisper to anguished vibrato within a phrase, emphasized a bare emotional nerve exposed on 'You Don't Love Me When I Cry' and 'Sweet Lovin' Baby'. Her frequent jumps in tempo irked certain critics, but the majority applauded its audacious ambition and peerless fusion of gospel and white soul. The extraordinary *Christmas And The Beads Of Sweat*, which included the startling 'Christmas Is My Soul', offered a similar passion while *Gonna Take A Miracle*, a collaboration with producers Kenny Gamble and Leon Huff, acknowledged the music which provided much of the artist's inspiration. Backed by the Sigma Sound Studio houseband and singing trio Labelle, Nyro completed enthralling versions of uptown R&B and Motown favourites. She then retired from music altogther, but re-emerged in 1975 upon the disintegration of her marriage. *Smile* showed the singer's talent had remained intact and included the powerful 'I Am The Blues', while an attendant promotional tour spawned *Season Of Lights*. *Nested* was, however, less impressive and a further domestically-inspired hiatus followed. *Mother's Spiritual* reflected Nyro's reactions to both parenthood and ageing; her comeback was confirmed in 1988 when she embarked on her first concert tour in over a decade. Laura Nyro remains a singularly impressive performer while her intonation has proved influential on several other women singers, notably Rickie Lee Jones.

Albums: *More Than A New Discovery* aka *The First Songs* (1967), *Eli And The Thirteenth Confession* (1968), *New York Tendaberry* (1969), *Christmas And The Beads Of Sweat* (1970), *Gonna Take A Miracle* (1971), *Smile* (1976), *Season Of Lights* (1978), *Nested* (1979), *Mother's Spiritual* (1985), *Live At The Bottom Line* (1990). Compilation: *Impressions* (1980).

O

Peter Asher, Ricky Nelson and Phil Ochs

Ochs, Phil

b. 19 December 1940, El Paso, Texas, d. 7 April 1976. A superior singer/songwriter, particularly adept at the topical song, Phil Ochs began his career at Ohio State University. He initially performed in a folksinging duo, the Sundowners, before moving to New York, where he joined the radical Greenwich Village enclave. Ochs' early work was inspired by Woody Guthrie, Bob Gibson and Tom Paxton, and its political nature led to his involvement with the *Broadside* magazine movement. The singer was signed to the prestigious Elektra Records label, and through his initial work was hailed as a major new talent. He achieved popular acclaim when Joan Baez took one of his compositions, 'There But For Fortune', into the pop charts. Ochs' own version later appeared on his *In Concert*, the artist's best-selling set which also featured the evocative 'When I'm Gone' and the wry 'Love Me I'm A Liberal'. Ochs' move to A&M Records in 1967 signalled a new phase in his career. *Pleasures Of The Harbour*, which included the ambitious 'Crucifixion', emphasized a greater use of orchestration, as well as an increasingly rock-based perspective. He remained a lyrical songwriter; his sense of melody was undiminished, but as the decade's causes grew increasingly blurred, so the singer became disillusioned. Although *Rehearsals For Retirement* documented the political travails of a bitter 1968, the sardonically-titled *Phil Ochs Greatest Hits* showed an imaginative performer bereft of focus. He donned a gold-lamé suit in a misguided effort to 'wed Elvis Presley to the politics of Che Guevara', but his in-concert rock 'n' roll medleys were roundly booed by an audience expecting overt social comment. This period is documented on the controversial *Gunfight At Carnegie Hall*. Ochs' later years were marked by tragedy. He was attacked during a tour of Africa and an attempted strangulation permanently impaired his singing voice. Beset by a chronic songwriting block, Phil sought solace in alcohol and although a rally/concert in aid of Chile, *An Evening With Salvador Allende*, succeeded through his considerable entreaties, he later succumbed to schizophrenia. Phil Ochs' was found hanged at his sister's home on 7 April 1976. One of the finest performers of his generation, he was considered, at least for a short time, Bob Dylan's greatest rival.

Albums: *All The News That's Fit To Sing* (1964), *I Ain't Marching Anymore* (1965), *Phil Ochs In Concert* (1966), *The Pleasures Of The Harbour* (1967), *Tape From California* (1968), *Rehearsals For Retirement* (1968), *Phil Ochs Greatest Hits* (1970), *Gunfight At Carnegie Hall* (1975). Compilations: *Phil Ochs - Chords Of Fame* (1976), *Phil Ochs - Songs For Broadside* (1976), *Broadside Tapes* (1976), *A Toast To Those Who Are Gone* (1987), *There But For Fortune* (1989). Further reading: *Phil Ochs: Death Of A Rebel*, Marc Elliott.

Ofarim, Esther And Abi

Esther Ofarim (b. Esther Zaled, 13 June 1943, Safed,

Israel) and Abraham Reichstadt (b. 5 October 1939, Tel Aviv, Israel) were a husband and wife team who shot to fame in their homeland during the early 60s. With a keen eye for the international market, Esther had represented Switzerland in the 1963 Eurovision Song Contest while the duo extended their appeal on the Continent via concert performances and foreign language recordings. An appearance on the high-rating *Eamonn Andrews Show* on UK television, in which Esther and Abi sang a novelty love duet, proved so popular that the song became an overnight smash. 'Cinderella Rockefella' (composed by Mason Williams) topped the British charts for three weeks in early 1968 and although the duo seemed likely one-hit-wonders they managed a successful follow-up with 'One More Dance'. The partnership subsequently broke up when their marriage was dissolved.
Albums: *2 In 3* (1968), *Ofarim Concert - Live '69* (1969).

Ohio Express

Key players in the bubblegum trend of the late 60s, the Ohio Express evolved from the Mansfield, Ohio, USA-based group Rare Breed in 1967. The group consisted of Joey Levine (lead vocals), Dale Powers (lead guitar), Doug Grassel (rhythm guitar), Jim Pflayer (keyboards), Dean Krastan (bass) and Tim Corwin (drums). Their first single, 'Beg, Borrow And Steal', had originally been recorded by the group under its old monicker in 1966 before it was reissued the following year by Cameo Records. There the group teamed up with producers Jerry Kasenetz and Jeff Katz, and reached number 29 in the autumn of 1967. A second Cameo single to chart was 'Try It', a song penned by Levine which was later covered by the Standells. In 1968 the Ohio Express signed with Neil Bogart's Buddah Records and released the bubblegum 'Yummy Yummy Yummy', which became their biggest hit, reaching the Top 5 on both sides of the Atlantic. By the end of 1969 they would chart on six more occasions, the final time with 'Sausalito (Is The Place To Go)', sung by Graham Gouldman, later of 10cc fame. The Ohio Express released six albums, of which only *Ohio Express* and *Chewy Chewy* made any real impact on the US charts. The group carried on until 1972; Levine formed Reunion in 1974.
Albums: *Beg, Borrow And Steal* (1968), *Ohio Express* (1968), *Salt Water Taffy* (1968), *Chewy Chewy* (1969), *Mercy* (1969). Compilation: *Very Best Of The Ohio Express* (1970).

O'Rahilly, Ronan

The inspirational figure behind UK pirate radio's classic era, O'Rahilly initially worked as a song plugger for the renowned Rik Gunnell Agency.

When the BBC refused to entertain a Georgie Fame release he was touting, Ronan looked to Radio Veronica, a pirate radio ship anchored off the Dutch coast, and hatched plans for his own similar operation. He secured the requisite backing to purchase and refit the *Frederica*, a Danish passenger ferry, which began broadcasting as Radio Caroline on 28 March 1964. The station's name was taken from the daughter of the late US President, John F. Kennedy. Within four months O'Rahilly had absorbed an early rival, Radio Atlanta, into his organization. The original ship was relocated off the Isle of Man while the new acquisition, the *Mi Amigo*, was anchored off the east coast of England as Caroline South. Several more stations followed in the wake of Ronan's vision, including Radio London and Radio City. Much of station's freewheeling style was curbed when the idealistic O'Rahilly went into partnership with the businessman Phil Solomon. Although beloved by loyal audiences, the 1967 Marine Offences Bill came into effect on 15 August 1967, effectively closing the pirates' heyday. O'Rahilly was the only proprietor to defy the law and the *Mi Amigo* continued broadcasting, albeit intermittently, until 1973, when the entrepreneur leased the ship to the Radio Veronica consortium. Ronan's pursuance of alternative careers also included a role as executive producer on the Marianne Faithfull film, *Girl On A Motor Cycle*, and an unfulfilled plan to operate a pirate television service.

Orbison, Roy

b. 23 April 1936, Vernon, Texas, USA, d. 7 December 1988. Critical acclaim came too late for one of the leading singers of the 60s. He became the master of the epic ballad of doom-laden despair. Orbison possessed a voice of remarkable range and power, often finding it more comfortable to stay in the high register. The former reluctant rockabilly singer, who worked with Norman Petty and Sam Phillips in the 50s, moved to Nashville and became a staff writer for Acuff-Rose Music. He used his royalties from the success of 'Claudette', recorded by the Everly Brothers, and written for his first wife, to buy himself out of his contract with Sun Records. He signed with the small Monument label. Although his main intention was to be a songwriter, Orbison found himself glancing the US chart with 'Up Town' in 1960. A few months later his song 'Only The Lonely' was rejected by Elvis Presley and the Everly Brothers. Orbison then decided to record it himself. The result was a sensation. The song topped the UK charts and narrowly missed the top spot in the USA. The trite opening of 'dum dum dum dummy doo wah, yea yea yea yea yeah', leads into one of the most distinctive pop songs ever recorded. It climaxes with a glass-shattering falsetto, and is destined to remain a modern classic.

The shy and quietly-spoken Roy donned a pair of dark-tinted glasses to cover up his chronic astigmatism, although early publicity photos had already sneaked out. Over the next five years he enjoyed unprecedented success in Britain and America, repeating his formula with further stylish but doom-laden ballads, including 'Blue Angel', 'Running Scared', 'Crying', 'Dream Baby', 'Blue Bayou' and 'In Dreams'. Even during the take-over of America by the Beatles' (with whom he became good friends), Roy was one of the few American artists to retain his ground commercially. During the Beatles peak chart year he scored two UK number 1 singles, the powerful 'It's Over' and the hypnotic 'Oh Pretty Woman'. The latter has an incredibly simple instrumental introduction with acoustic guitar and snare drum, and it is recognized today by millions. It was subsequently used for the late 80s blockbuster film *Pretty Woman*. Such was the art of Orbison, having the advantage of crafting his own songs to suit his voice and temperament. Although he continued to have hits throughout the 60s, none except 'It's Too Soon To Know' reached former heights; he regularly toured Britain, which he regarded as his second home. He experienced appalling tragedy when in 1966 his wife, Claudette, was killed as she fell from the back of his motorcycle, and in 1968 a fire destroyed his home, also taking the lives of his two sons. In 1967 he starred as a singing cowboy in *The Fastest Guitar Alive,* but demonstrated that he was no actor. By the end of the decade Roy's musical direction had faltered and he resorted to writing average MOR songs like the unremarkable 'Penny Arcade'.

The 70s were barren times for his career, although a 1976 compilation topped the UK charts. By the end of the decade he underwent open heart surgery. He bounced back in 1980, winning a Grammy for his duet with Emmylou Harris on 'That Lovin' You Feelin' Again' from the film *Roadie*. David Lynch used 'In Dreams' to haunting effect in his chilling film *Blue Velvet* in 1986. The following year Orbison was inducted into the Rock 'n' Roll Hall of Fame; at the ceremony he sang 'Oh Pretty Woman' with Bruce Springsteen. With Orbison once again in favour, Virgin Records signed him, and he recorded an album of his old songs using today's hi-tech production techniques. The result was predictably disappointing; it was the sound and production of those classics that had made them great. The video *A Black And White Night*, showed Roy being courted by numerous stars, including Tom Waits, Springsteen and Elvis Costello. This high profile led him to join George Harrison, Bob Dylan, Tom Petty and Jeff Lynne as the Traveling Wilburys. Their splendid debut album owed much to Orbison's major input.

Less than a month after its critically acclaimed release, Roy suffered a fatal heart attack in Nashville. The posthumously released *Mystery Girl* in 1989 was the most successful album of his entire career, and not merely because of morbid sympathy. The record contained a collection of songs that indicated a man feeling happy and relaxed; his voice had never sounded better. The uplifting 'You Got It' and the mellow 'She's A Mystery To Me' were impressive epitaphs to the legendary Big 'O'.

Albums: *Lonely And Blue* (1961), *Crying* (1962), *In Dreams* (1963), *Exciting Sounds Of Roy Orbison (Roy Orbison At The Rockhouse)* (1964), *Oh Pretty Woman* (1964), *There Is Only One Roy Orbison* (1965), *The Orbison Way* (1966), *The Fastest Guitar Alive* (1967, film soundtrack), *The Classic Roy Orbison* (1966), *Orbisongs* (1966), *Roy Orbison Sings Don Williams* (1967), *Cry Softly, Lonely One* (1967), *The Fastest Guitar Alive* (1968), *Early Orbison* (1968), *Roy Orbison's Many Moods* (1969), *The Big O* (1970), *Hank Williams: The Roy Orbison Way* (1971), *Roy Orbison Sings* (1972), *Memphis* (1973), *Milestones* (1974), *I'm Still In Love With You* (1976), *Regeneration* (1977), *Laminar Flow* (1979), *Big O Country* (1983), *Problem Child* (1984), *In Dreams* (1987), *For The Lonely* (1988), *Mystery Girl* (1989), *Best Love Standards* (1989), *Our Love Song* (1989), *Rare Orbison* (1989), *A Black And White Night* (1989). Compilations: *Roy Orbison's Greatest Hits* (1967), *Golden Days* (1981), *The Sun Years* (1980, early recordings), *In Dreams: The Greatest Hits* (1987), *The Legendary Roy Orbison* (1988), *The Greatest Hits* (1988),

Further reading: *Dark Star*, Ellis Amburn. *Only The Lonely*, Alan Clayson.

Orlando, Tony

b. 4 April 1944, New York, USA. An engaging, commercially-minded singer, Orlando's early success came in 1961 when he scored two US Top 40 entries with 'Halfway To Paradise' and 'Bless You'. The former, a superb Gerry Goffin/Carole King composition, was later successfully covered by Billy Fury, but Orlando enjoyed an emphatic UK hit when the latter reached number 5. Subsequent releases, including 'Happy Times' (1961) and 'Chills' (1962) were less impressive and Orlando began forging a backroom career in the music business, eventually rising to general manager of Columbia Records's April/Blackwood publishing division. In 1970 he was tempted back into recording when he formed the highly popular Dawn. A later solo album was recorded on the Elektra label.

Album: *Bless You (And 11 Other Great Hits)* (1961), *Tony Orlando* (1978). Compilation: *Before Dawn* (1976).

Orlons

A mixture of school friends and neighbours, this Philadelphia-based group was formed by Shirley Brickley (b. 9 December 1944), Steve Caldwell (b. 22 November 1942), Rosetta Hightower (b. 23 June 1944) and Marlena Davis (b. 4 October 1944). Introduced to Cameo Records by the lead singer of the Dovells, Len Barry, the Orlons' first hits, 'The Wah Watusi', 'Don't Hang Up' and 'South Street', cleverly exploited the male/female aspect of the group. Each of these releases reached the US Top 5, but their potential was undermined when 'Cross Fire!' (1963) and 'Rules Of Love' (1964) were only minor hits. Any lingering impetus was lost when Davis and Caldwell left the line-up, but although Audrey Brickley took their place, the Orlons broke up in 1968 when Rosetta Hightower moved to the UK to become a session singer.
Albums: *The Wah-Watusi* (1962), *All The Hits* (1963), *South Street* (1963), *Not Me* (1964), *Down Memory Lane* (1964). Compilations: *Biggest Hits* (1963), *Golden Hits Of The Orlons And The Dovells* (1963).

Overlanders

This UK vocal trio - Paul Arnold (aka Paul Friswell), Laurie Mason and Peter Bartholemew - initially pursued a folk-based career, but scored a surprise, if minor, US hit in 1964 with their version of 'Yesterday's Gone'. Buoyed by the addition of Terry Widlake (bass) and David Walsh (drums), they enjoyed a UK number 1 the following year with an opportunistic version of the Beatles' 'Michelle', but the reshaped group was unable to shake off a somewhat anachronistic image. A strong follow-up to their chart-topper, 'My Life', unfortunately failed to chart. Arnold left for a solo career in 1966, but despite the arrival of Ian Griffiths, the Overlanders failed to reap reward from their early success.
Album: *The Overlanders* (1966).

P

Pacific Gas And Electric

Formed in Los Angeles, California, USA in 1968, Pacific Gas And Electric was a quintet which merged blues, gospel, soul, jazz and rock. The members were Charlie Allen (vocals), Glen Schwartz (lead guitar), Thomas Marshall (rhythm guitar), Brent Black (bass) and Frank Cook (drums), the latter an alumnus of Canned Heat. The group's first album, *Get It On*, was initially issued on the small Bright Orange label and then reissued on the band's own Power Records, scraping into the charts at number 159. An appearance at the Miami Pop Festival in December 1968 was considered a highlight of that event and the group came to the attention of Columbia Records, who subsequently signed them. A self-titled album was released on Columbia in August 1969 and fared somewhat better, reaching number 91. The group's third album, *Are You Ready*, did not fare as well, reaching only to number 101, but it did yield their only hit single in the title track, a gospel-influenced rocker which climbed to number 14 in mid-1970. One other album and a couple of further singles were issued but by 1971 the group was in disarray. Various personnel changes, including the addition of a horn section, left Allen the only original member by 1973, when the group's final album was issued on Dunhill Records.
Albums: *Get It On* (1968), *Pacific Gas And Electric* (1969), *Are You Ready* (1970), *PG&E* (1971), *Pacific Gas And Electric, Starring Charlie Allen* (1973). Compilation: *The Best Of* (1985).

Paddy, Klaus And Gibson

Formed in 1965, this Liverpool-based 'supergroup' featured Paddy Chambers (lead guitar; ex-Big Three and Escorts), Klaus Voorman (bass) and Gibson Kemp (drums; ex-Kingsize Taylor And The Dominoes). Their three singles included a version of Marvin Gaye's 'No Good Without You Baby' and the theme song to British television's *Quick Before They Catch Us*, but despite the patronage of Beatles' manager Brian Epstein, the trio failed to secure commercial success. Plans by Pete Townshend to amalgamate the group with part of the Who fell apart when tribulations within the latter act were settled. Paddy, Klaus And Gibson embarked on separate careers late in 1966 with Voorman securing subsequent fame as the illustrator of the Beatles' *Revolver* album cover and also as a member of Manfred Mann and the Plastic Ono Band.

Paramor, Norrie

b. 1913, London, England, d. 9 September 1979. The most prolific producer of UK pop chart-toppers was a mild, bespectacled gentleman who had studied piano prior to servitude in metropolitan dance bands. He was well into his thirties before earning minor celebrity as a songwriter, after which he was appointed A&R manager of Columbia, an EMI subsidiary. In 1954, he produced the first of two UK number 1 hits for Eddie Calvert and another for Ruby Murray the following year. Although too critically blinkered to see rock 'n' roll being more than 'an American phenomenon - and they do it best', he still provided Columbia with such an act in

Tony Crombie's Rockets but had better luck with the mainstream efforts of Michael Holliday and the Mudlarks - both backed by the Ken Jones Orchestra. Then, in 1958, a demo tape by Cliff Richard And The Drifters arrived on his desk. With no rock 'n' roller currently on his books, he contracted Cliff intending to play it safe with a US cover with the Jones band until persuaded to stick with the Drifters (soon renamed the Shadows) and push a group original ('Move It') as the a-side. Partly through newspaper publicity engineered by Paramor, 'Move It' was a smash, and a consequent policy was instigated of Richard recording singles of untried numbers - among them, at Paramor's insistence, Lionel Bart's 'Living Doll'. Columbia was successful too with the Shadows - even if Paramor wished initially to issue 'Apache' - their first smash - as a b-side. Later, he offended Shadows purists by augmenting the quartet on disc with horn sections and his trademark lush string arrangements.

Other Paramor signings were not allowed to develop to the same idiosyncratic extent as Richard and his associates. Ricky Valance scored his sole chart-topper with a US cover while Helen Shapiro was visualized as a vague 'answer' to Brenda Lee; Paramor even booking and supervising some Shapiro sessions in Nashville in 1963. Paramor's greatest success during this period, however, was with Frank Ifield, who dominated the early 60s UK pop scene with three formidable number 1 hits. With the advent of self-contained beat groups, Paramor came to be regarded as a throwback to the outmoded Tin Pan Alley epoch. However, as late as 1968, he racked up another number 1 with Scaffold's 'Lily The Pink'. By 1970, he was semi-retired - but he continued to dabble in independent production for such as the Excaliburs, and his publishing company was still finding material for Cliff in the 70s. Paramor remains one of the most underrated figures in the history of UK pop and a posthumous reappraisal of his work is overdue.

Selected albums: *In London, In Love . . .* (1956), *The Zodiac* (1957), *Lovers In Latin* (1959), *Staged For Stereo* (1961), *Lovers In London* (1964), with Patricia Clark *Lovers In Tokio* (1964), *Warm And Willing* (1965), *Shadows In Latin* (1966), *Norrie Paramor Plays The Hits Of Cliff Richard* (1967), *Soul Coaxing* (1968), *BBC Top Tunes* (1974), *Radio 2 Top Tunes, Volume 1* (1974), *Radio 2 Top Tunes, Volume 2 and 3* (both 1975), *Love* (1975), *My Personal Choice* (1976), *Silver Serenade* (1977), *Norrie Paramor Remembers . . . 40 Years Of TV Themes* (1976), *Temptation* (1978), *Rags And Tatters* aka *Ragtime* (1978), *Classical Rhythm* (1979). Compilations: *Paramagic Pianos* (1977), *The Best Of Norrie Paramor* (1984), *Ragtime* (1985).

Paramounts

Formed in Southend, Essex, England in 1961, the Paramounts evolved out of local beat attraction the Raiders. Comprising Gary Brooker (b. 29 May 1945, Southend, Essex, England; keyboards/vocals), Robin Trower (b. 9 March 1945, Southend, Essex, England; guitar), Chris Copping (b. 29 August 1945, Southend, Essex, England; bass) and Mick Brownlee (drums), the latter replaced by Barrie (B.J.) Wilson (b. 18 March 1947, Southend, Essex, England) in 1963. The group became one of the region's most popular R&B acts and by 1963 had secured a prestigious deal with EMI Records. Diz Derrick replaced the college-bound Copping prior to recording 'Poison Ivy', the quartet's debut single and sole UK Top 40 entry. Subsequent releases included material drawn from the Coasters, Jackie DeShannon and P.F. Sloan, but despite considerable acclaim, the Paramounts failed to achieve due commercial success. Later reduced to backing Sandie Shaw and Chris Andrews, they split up in October 1966. Brooker then formed a songwriting team with lyricist Keith Reid which in turn inspired the formation of Procol Harum. By 1969, and in the wake of numerous defections, this attraction contained the same line-up as that of the original Paramounts. Trower and Brooker pursued subsequent solo careers, while the latter also worked with Joe Cocker and Eric Clapton.
Compilation: *Whiter Shades Of R&B* (1983).

Parker, Bobby

R&B singer Parker is best recalled for 'Watch Your Step', a frantic, exciting performance released in 1961. This self-penned single was a minor US hit, peaking at number 51, but nonetheless secured a British release on the renowned London label. Although never a chart entry, the song proved highly popular and was a staple part of many groups' repertoires. Tony Jackson and the Spencer Davis Group were among those recording sympathetic interpretations and such interest inspired Sue Records to reissue the original version. Another Parker composition, 'Steal Your Heart Away', completed the coupling, and this impassioned ballad, based on Ray Charles' 'I Believe To My Soul', was also the subject of several interpretations, notably by the Moody Blues and Cliff Bennett And The Rebel Rousers. In 1969, the singer recorded a single, 'It's Hard But It's Fair'/'I Couldn't Quit My Baby', for the UK specialist outlet Blue Horizon. Such approbation, sadly, did not help further Parker's own career, and he is now viewed as a one-hit wonder, albeit of a superior nature.

Partridge, Don

b. 1945, Bournemouth, Dorset, England. Self-styled 'King of the Street Singers', Partridge was discovered

busking in London's Berwick Street market by former Viscount Don Paul, who in turn became his manager. 'Rosie', the singer's self-penned debut single, was reputedly recorded for the sum of £8, but became a surprise UK Top 5 hit in 1968. The artist's unconventional lifestyle and penchant for straight-talking resulted in good copy, and engendered greater publicity than his novelty status might otherwise suggest. 'Blue Eyes', Partridge's follow-up single, reached number 3, yet the song is less well recalled than its ebullient predecessor. The singer later supervised *The Buskers*, a various-artists compilation, and enjoyed one further chart entry with 'Breakfast On Pluto' in 1969. After this brief flirtation with fame, Partridge returned to busking roots and continued to perform into the 90s.
Album: *Don Partridge* (1968).

Paul And Paula

Paul (b. Ray Hildebrand, 21 December 1940, Joshua, Texas, USA) and Paula (b. Jill Jackson, 20 May 1942, McCaney, Texas, USA) were college students prior to singing together on a local radio's cancer fund appeal. In November 1962 they auditioned a Hildebrand composition, 'Hey Paula', for Fort Worth producer Major Bill Smith, and within weeks the song topped the US chart. 'Hey Paula' captured a 'puppy-love' naivety beloved by middle-America in the immediate pre-Beatles era. 'Hey, hey, hey Paula, I wanna marry you', and the continuing simplistic call and answer lyric found a receptive audience. 'Young Lovers', which recounted the eve of the duo's wedding, provided another hit, but although subsequent releases, including 'Our First Quarrel', continued the storyline, Paul And Paula were unable to repeat the success of their million-selling debut and ended up sounding overly cloying.
Albums: *Paul And Paula Sing For Young Lovers* (1963), *We Go Together* (1963), *Holiday For Teens* (1963).

Pavone, Rita

b. 23 August 1945, Turin, Italy. This freckled, diminutive daughter of a Fiat factory mechanic shone in an 'Unknowns Festival' organized in 1962 at Ariccia by freelance record producer Teddy Reno. Signed to RCA Italia, her first single, 'La Partita Di Pallone' ('The Football Song') sold a million. Her popularity was further strengthened with regular appearances on *Studio 1*, Italian television's top variety showcase. After 'Come To Non C'E' Nessumo' became the country's best-selling single of 1963, she branched out with foreign language recordings, earning chart placings in Spain, South America, Japan, Germany - and Britain where BBC and ITV slots in autumn 1966 reactivated the three-year-old 'Cuore', a Barry Mann-Cynthia Weill melody with Italian lyrics. Translated as 'Heart', this

Luis Enriquez production (with an apt throbbing rhythm) jumped into the UK Top 30 over Christmas. It was also the apex of her career in terms of record sales but she continued to develop as an entertainer, even making slight headway in the USA with a spot on *The Ed Sullivan Show*, and making her silver screen debut in 1966's *Rita The Mosquito*.
Selected album: *Rita Pavone* (1964).

Paxton, Tom

b. 31 October 1937, Chicago, Illinois, USA. Paxton's interest in folk music developed as a student at the University of Oklahoma. In 1960 he moved to New York and became one of several aspiring performers to frequent the city's Greenwich Village coffee-house circuit. Paxton made his professional debut at the Gaslight, the renowned folk haunt which also issued the singer's first album. Two topical song publications, *Sing Out!* and *Broadside*, began publishing his original compositions which bore a debt to the traditional approach of Pete Seeger and Bob Gibson. Tom also auditioned to join the Chad Mitchell Trio, but although he failed, the group enjoyed a 1963 hit with 'The Marvellous Toy', one of his early songs. The following year Paxton was signed to the Elektra label for whom he recorded his best known work. *Ramblin' Boy* indicated the diversity which marked his recorded career and contained several highly-popular performances including 'The Last Thing On My Mind', 'Goin' To The Zoo' and 'I Can't Help But Wonder Where I'm Bound'. Subsequent releases continued this mixture of romanticism, protest and children's songs, while 'Lyndon Johnson Told The Nation' (*Ain't That News*) and 'Talkin' Vietnam Pot Luck Blues' (*Morning Again*) revealed a talent for satire and social comment. *The Things I Notice Now* and *Tom Paxton 6* enhanced Paxton's reputation as a mature and complex songwriter, yet he remained better known for such simpler compositions as 'Jennifer's Rabbit' and 'Leaving London'. Paxton left Elektra during the early 70s and although subsequent recordings proved less popular, he commanded a loyal following, particularly in the UK, where he was briefly domiciled. *How Come The Sun* (1971) was the first of three albums recorded during this period and although his work became less prolific, Paxton was still capable of incisive, evocative songwriting, such as 'The Hostage', which chronicled the massacre at Attica State Prison. This powerful composition was also recorded by Judy Collins. Although Paxton was never fêted in the manner of his early contemporaries Bob Dylan, Phil Ochs and Eric Anderson, his work reveals a thoughtful, perceptive craftsmanship.
Albums: *Live At The Gaslight* (early 60s), *Ramblin' Boy* (1964), *Ain't That News* (1965), *Outward Bound* (1966), *Morning Again* (1968), *The Things I Notice*

Now (1969), Tom Paxton 6 (1970), The Compleat Tom Paxton (1971), How Come The Sun (1971), Peace Will Come (1972), New Songs Old Friends (1973), Children's Song Book (1974), Something In My Life (1975), Saturday Night (1976), New Songs From The Briar Patch (1977), Heroes (1978), Up And Up (1980), The Paxton Report (1981), The Marvellous Toy And Other Gallimaufry (1984), In The Orchard (1985), One Million Lawyers And Other Disasters (1985), Even A Gray Day (1986), The Marvellous Toy (1980), And Loving You (1988), Politics-Live (1989). Compilations: The Very Best Of Tom Paxton (1988), Storyteller (1989).

Peaches And Herb

Herb Fame (b. Herbert Feemster, 1942) and Francine Barker (b. Francine Hurd, 1947). These two Washington-based singers were signed separately to the same record label, Date, and met on a promotional tour. Producer Dave Kapralik put the couple together, and their easy, if unexceptional, voices took 'Close Your Eyes' into the US Top 10 in 1967. The duo continued to figure in the charts as 'United' (1968) and 'When He Touches Me (Nothing Else Matters)' (1969). However, although Barker was featured on these records, she had been replaced for live performances by former session singer Marlene Mack, (b. 1945, Virginia, USA). The 'sweethearts of soul' were ostensibly disbanded in July 1970 when a disillusioned Fame left music in favour of the Police Department, although a 'bogus' duo hurriedly stepped in to fill the gap. Herb resumed recording in 1976 with a new 'Peaches', Linda Greene (b. Washington, DC, USA). Following a brief spell at MCA Records, the reconstituted couple moved to Polydor where they scored a major hit with 'Shake Your Groove Thing' (1978). The following year 'Reunited' reached number 1 in the US and number 4 in the UK. They continued to enjoy success into the 80s, but such releases lacked the charm of their early work.
Albums: Let's Fall In Love (1967), For Your Love (1967), Golden Duets (1967), Peaches And Herb (1977), 2 Hot! (1978), Twice The Fire (1979), Worth The Wait (1980). Compilation: Peaches And Herb's Greatest Hits (1968).

Peanut Butter Conspiracy

Originally known as the Ashes, this Los Angeles quintet assumed the above name in 1966. The group, comprising Sandi Robinson (vocals), John Merrill (guitar), Lance Fent (guitar), Al Brackett (bass) and Jim Voigt (drums) made their debut with 'Time Is After You' for the locally-based Vault label, before securing a major deal with Columbia/CBS the following year. Here they were united with producer Gary Usher, who sculpted a harmonious sound redolent of the Mamas And The Papas, Jefferson

Airplane and Spanky And Our Gang. The Peanut Butter Conspiracy Is Spreading included their anthem-like single, 'It's A Happening Thing' and the haunting 'Then Came Love', but the album failed to make a significant commercial breakthrough. Fent was replaced by Bill Wolff for The Great Conspiracy wherein the group showed a greater emphasis on instrumental prowess. 'Turn On A Friend' and 'Time Is After You' confirmed the unit's undoubted potential, but they were dropped from the label following the failure of 'I'm A Fool'/'It's So Hard', a non-album single. A reshaped line-up emerged to complete For Children Of All Ages on the Challenge label, but this lacklustre set was a great disappointment and the group then folded. Lance Fent subsequently worked with Randy Meisner while late-period member Ralph Shuckett (ex-Clear Light) reappeared in Jo Mama.
Albums: The Peanut Butter Conspiracy Is Spreading (1967), The Great Conspiracy (1968), For Children Of All Ages (1968). Compilation: Turn On A Friend (1989).

Pentangle

Formed in 1967, the Pentangle was inspired by Bert And John, a collaborative album by folk musicians Bert Jansch (b. 3 November 1943, Glasgow, Scotland) and John Renbourn. Vocalist Jacqui McShee, an established figure on the traditional circuit, joined Danny Thompson (b. April 1939; bass) and Terry Cox (drums), both of Alexis Korner's Blues Incorporated, in a quintet which would also embrace blues and jazz forms. Their respective talents were expertly captured on The Pentangle, where the delicate acoustic interplay between Jansch and Renbourn was brilliantly underscored by Thompson's sympathetic support and McShee's soaring intonation. Stylish original material balanced songs pulled from folk's heritage ('Let No Man Steal Your Thyme', 'Brunton Town'), while the inclusion of the Staple Singers 'Hear My Call' confirmed the group's eclectism. This feature was expanded on the double-set Sweet Child, which included two compositions by jazz bassist Charles Mingus, 'Haitian Fight Song' and 'Goodbye Pork Pie Hat'. The unit enjoyed considerable commercial success with Basket Of Light, which included 'Light Flight', the theme song to the UK television series, Take Three Girls. However, despite an undoubted dexterity and the introduction of muted electric instruments, subsequent releases were marred by a sense of sterility, and lacked the passion of concurrent releases undertaken by the two guitarists. Pentangle was disbanded in 1972, following which Thompson began a partnership with John Martyn. Cox undertook a lucrative session career before backing French singer Charles Aznavour, and while Jansch continued his solo career, McShee fronted the John Renbourn Band between 1974-81. The original Pentangle reconvened the following year for a European tour and *Open The Door*, although defections owing to outside commitments led to considerable changes. McShee and Jansch were joined by Nigel Portman-Smith (bass) and Mike Piggott for *In The Round*, but by 1991 the latter had departed and Peter Kirtly (guitar) and Gerry Conway (drums) were now featured in the group. The future of this particular line-up was then jeopardized by plans to reunite the founding quintet.

Albums: *The Pentangle* (1968), *Sweet Child* (1968), *Basket Of Light* (1969), *Cruel Sister* (1970), *Solomon's Seal* (1972), *Open The Door* (1982), *In The Round* (1988), *So Early In The Spring* (1989). Compilations: *Reflections* (1971), *History Book* (1971), *Pentangling* (1973), *The Pentangle Collection* (1975), *Anthology* (1978), *The Essential Pentangle Volume 1* (1987), *The Essential Pentangle Volume 2* (1987).

Peter And Gordon

Both the sons of doctors and former pupils of the prestigious English public school Westminster Boys, this privileged pair were signed by producer Norman Newell, following a residency at London's Piccadilly Club. Peter Asher (b. 2 June 1944, London, England) and Gordon Waller (b. 4 June 1945, Braemar, Grampian, Scotland), had a crucial advantage over their contemporaries - the priceless patronage of Paul McCartney, who was then dating Peter's sister, Jane. The perfectly enunciated 'A World Without Love' quickly became a transatlantic chart topper and two more 1964 McCartney compositions, 'Nobody I Know' and 'I Don't Want To See You Again', brought further success. The Beatle connection was again evident on 'Woman', which McCartney composed under the pseudonym Bernard Webb. In the meantime, the duo had switched to successful revivals of 50s material, including Buddy Holly's 'True Love Ways' and the Teddy Bears' retitled 'To Know You Is To Love You'. Peter and Gordon's wholesome image was somewhat belied by Waller's appearances in the salacious British Sunday press, but this did little to affect their popularity in the USA. Although the partnership was strained by late 1966, the saucy 'Lady Godiva' provided a new direction and was followed by the similarly-quaint novelty numbers 'Knight In Rusty Armour' and 'Sunday For Tea'. One year later, they split. Waller subsequently pursued an unsuccessful solo career while Asher emerged as a formidable producer and manager.

Albums: *Peter And Gordon* (1964), *A World Without Love* (1964), *In Touch With Peter And Gordon* (1964), *I Don't Want To See You Again* (1965), *I Go To Pieces* (1965), *True Love Ways* (1965), *Hurtin' 'N' Lovin'* (1965), *The Hits Of Nashville* (1966), *Woman* (1966), *Somewhere* (1966), *Lady Godiva* (1967), *A Knight In*

Rusty Armour (1967), *In London For Tea* (1967), *Hot, Cold And Custard* (1968). Compilations: *Peter And Gordon's Greatest Hits* (1966), *The Best Of Peter And Gordon* (1983), *Hits And More* (1986).

Peter, Paul And Mary

Peter Yarrow (b. 31 May 1938, New York City, New York, USA), Noel Paul Stookey (b. Paul Stookey, 30 November 1937, Baltimore, Maryland, USA) and Mary Allin Travers (b. 7 November 1937, Louisville, Kentucky, USA) began performing together in the spring of 1961. They were brought together by Albert Grossman, one of folk music's successful entrepreneurs, in an attempt to create a contemporary Kingston Trio. The three singers were already acquainted through the close-knit coffee-house circuit, although Dave Van Ronk was briefly considered as a possible member. The group popularized several topical songs, including 'If I Had A Hammer' and were notable early interpreters of Bob Dylan compositions. In 1963 their version of 'Blowin' In The Wind' reached number 2 in the US chart while a follow-up reading of 'Don't Think Twice, It's Alright' also broached the Top 10. They were also renowned for singing children's songs, the most memorable of which was the timeless 'Puff The Magic Dragon'. The trio became synonymous with folk's liberal traditions, but were increasingly perceived as old-fashioned as the 60s progressed. Nonetheless a 1966 selection, *Album*, included material by Laura Nyro and featured assistance from Paul Butterfield, Mike Bloomfield and Al Kooper, while the following year's 'I Dig Rock 'N' Roll Music' became their fifth US Top 10 hit. Peter, Paul And Mary enjoyed their greatest success in 1969 with 'Leaving On A Jet Plane'. This melodramatic John Denver song reached number 1 in the US and number 2 in the UK, but by then the individual members were branching out in different directions. Yarrow had been the primary force behind *You Are What You Eat*, an eccentric hippie film which also featured Tiny Tim and John Simon, and in 1970 he, Travers and Stookey announced their formal dissolution. The three performers embarked on solo careers but were ultimately unable to escape the legacy of their former group. They reunited briefly in 1972 for a George McGovern Democratic Party rally, and again in 1978. They have since continued to perform material reminiscent of their golden era. Although criticized for a smooth and wholesome delivery, Peter, Paul and Mary was one of the era's most distinctive acts and played a crucial bridging role between two contrasting generations of folk music.

Albums: *Peter, Paul And Mary* (1962), *Peter, Paul And Mary - Moving* (1963), *In The Wind* (1963), *Peter, Paul And Mary In Concert* (1964), *A Song Will Rise* (1965), *See What Tomorrow Brings* (1965), *Peter, Paul And*

Mary Album (1966), *Album 1700* (1967), *Late Again* (1968), *Peter, Paul And Mommy* (1969), *Reunion* (1978), *Such Is Love* (1982), *No Easy Walk To Freedom* (1988). Compilations: *10 Years Together/The Best Of Peter, Paul And Mary* (1970), *Most Beautiful Songs* (1973), *Collection* (1982). Solo albums: Peter Yarrow *Peter* (1972), *That's Enough For Me* (1973), *Hard Times* (1975); Paul Stookey *Paul And* (1971), *Band And Body Works* (1980); Mary Travers *Mary* (1971), *Morning Glory* (1972), *All My Choices* (1973), *Circles* (1974), *It's In Everyone Of Us* (1978).

Pickett, Bobby 'Boris'

b. 11 February 1940, in Somerville, Massachusetts, USA. Bobby 'Boris' Pickett (And The Crypt-Kickers) recorded the US number 1 'Monster Mash' in 1962, a song which has remained alive for decades due to perennial radio airplay each Halloween. Pickett moved to Los Angeles in 1961, upon his release from military service, hoping to become an actor. Instead, he joined a singing group called the Cordials. Pickett, an avowed fan of actor Boris Karloff, worked an impression of the horror film star into some of the group's songs and he and the Cordials' Leonard Capizzi wrote 'Monster Mash' to cash in on the dance craze launched by Dee Dee Sharp's 'Mashed Potato Time' hit of 1962. Pickett was signed to Gary S. Paxton's Garpax label and 'Monster Mash' worked its way to the top of the charts in time for Halloween 1962. The record later returned to the US charts twice, this time on Parrot Records, reaching number 91 in 1970 and then hitting the Top 10 for a second time three years later. It was not until 1973 that the song made any significant impact upon the UK chart, when it reached number 3 in September. It was also successfully covered by the UK unit the Bonzo Bog Doo-Dah Band. Pickett had two other minor US chart singles in 1962-63, including the Top 30 'Monster's Holiday', but he is indelibly linked with the classic novelty number.
Albums: *The Original Monster Mash* (1962), *The Original Monster Mash* (1973, reissue of the previous title, minus four tracks).

Pickett, Wilson

b. 18 March 1941, Prattville, Alabama, USA. Raised in Detroit, Pickett sang in several of the city's R&B groups. He later joined the Falcons, an act already established by the million-selling 'You're So Fine'. Pickett wrote and sang lead on their 1962 hit, 'I Found A Love', after which he launched his solo career. A false start at Correctone was overturned by two powerful singles, 'If You Need Me' and 'It's Too Late', recorded for Lloyd Price's Double L outlet. The former track's potential was undermined by Solomon Burke's opportunistic cover version on Atlantic Records, the irony of which was compounded when Pickett moved to that same label in 1964. An inspired partnership with guitarist Steve Cropper produced the classic standard, 'In The Midnight Hour', as well as, 'Don't Fight It' (both 1965), '634-5789 (Soulsville, USA)', 'Land Of A 1,000 Dances', 'Mustang Sally' (all 1966) and 'Funky Broadway' (1967). The singer's other collaborators included erstwhile Falcon Eddie Floyd and former Valentino, Bobby Womack. The latter partnership proved increasingly important as the 60s progressed. A 1968 album, *The Midnight Mover*, contained six songs featuring Womack's involvement. Deprived of the Stax houseband due to their break with Atlantic, Pickett next recorded at Fame's Muscle Shoals studio. A remarkable version of 'Hey Jude', with Duane Allman on guitar, was the highlight of this period. A further experiment, this time with producers Gamble And Huff, resulted in two hits, 'Engine Number 9' (1970) and 'Don't Let The Green Grass Fool You' (1971), while a trip to Miami provided 'Don't Knock My Love', his last Top 20 hit for Atlantic. Wilson switched to RCA in 1972, but the previous success was hard to regain. A mercurial talent, Pickett returned to Muscle Shoals for *Funky Situation* (1978), issued on his own Wicked label. More recently he worked alongside Joe Tex, Don Covay, Ben E. King and Solomon Burke in a revamped Soul Clan. Pickett was the invisible figure and role model in the award-winning soul music film *The Commitments* in 1991.
Albums: *It's Too Late* (1963), *In The Midnight Hour* (1965), *The Exciting Wilson Pickett* (1966), *The Wicked Pickett* (1966), *The Sound Of Wilson Pickett* (1967), *I'm In Love* (1968), *The Midnight Mover* (1968), *Hey Jude* (1969), *Right On* (1970), *Wilson Pickett In Philadelphia* (1970), *Don't Knock My Love* (1971), *Mr. Magic Man* (1973), *Miz Lena's Boy* (1973), *Tonight I'm My Biggest Audience* (1974), *Live In Japan* (1974), *Pickett In Pocket* (1974), *Join Me & Let's Be Free* (1975), *A Funky Situation* (1978), *I Want You* (1979), *The Right Track* (1981), *American Soul Man* (1987). Compilations: *The Best Of Wilson Pickett* (1967), *The Best Of Wilson Pickett Vol.2* (1971), *Greatest Hits* (1987).

Piltdown Men

It is not unusual for session musicians to jam together in the studio while waiting for a recording to start and that is exactly how the Piltdown Men were born. A team of seven regular Los Angeles-based Capitol Records musicians, including noted arranger Lincoln Mayorga and Ed Cobb from the Four Preps, were playing around with the children's nursery rhyme 'Old MacDonald' and the result was the saxophone-laden instrumental track known as 'MacDonald's Cave'. Mayorga quickly penned another track, 'Brontosaurus Stomp', and Capitol rushed a single out under a group name that suited the stone-age styled titles. To their surprise 'MacDonald's Cave' was a UK Top 20 hit in 1960 and the b-side made the lower reaches of the US Top 100. Interest in the anonymous group quickly faded in their homeland but they continued to make rockin' instrumental records for the UK market and had two more Top 20 hits with 'Piltdown Rides Again' and 'Goodnight Mrs. Flintstone', which were again based on well-known traditional songs. After a couple of non-chart singles the Piltdown Men vanished into pre-history.

Pinkerton's Assorted Colours

Originally known as the Liberators, this Rugby-based quintet comprised: Samuel 'Pinkerton' Kemp (vocals/autoharp), Tony Newman (guitar), Tom Long (guitar), Barrie Bernard (bass) and Dave Holland (drums). One of the lesser known British pop groups of the period, they came under the wing of Fortunes manager Reg Calvert, who encouraged them to change their name and to each don a different pastel shade suit. This unusual stress on colour was reflected in various publicity stunts such as polluting the fountains of Trafalgar Square with red dye. The gimmicky use of a kazoo and autoharp, aided by extensive plugging on the pirate radio stations Radio City and Radio Caroline, proved sufficient to break their Decca debut single, 'Mirror Mirror'. A minor dispute between their manager and rival Phil Solomon over the ownership of various group names brought them even more publicity than their next single, 'Don't Stop Loving Me Baby', which barely scraped into the Top 50. Stuart Colman replaced Bernard in the line-up, but by that time the group were losing momentum and their prospects were further blighted by the tragic death of their manager. After a lean patch, the group abbreviated their name to Pinkerton's Colours, then Pinkerton and finally evolved into the Flying Machine. That last incarnation brought a happier ending for, in the summer of 1969, the spin-off group achieved a US Top 5 hit with 'Smile A Little Smile For Me'.

Pink Floyd

One of the most predominant and celebrated rock bands of all time, Pink Floyd came to prominence in London during the hallucinogenic summer of 1967. The original quartet comprised: Syd Barrett (b. Roger Barrett, 6 January 1946, Cambridge, England; vocals), Roger Waters (b. 9 September 1944, Cambridge, England; vocals/bass), Nick Mason (b. 27 January 1945, Birmingham, England; drums) and Rick Wright (b. 28 July 1945, London, England; keyboards). Their legendary extended sets, complete with psychedelic light show at London's UFO club, spearheaded the British underground music movement. Surprisingly their hit singles were totally different to their live act and featured the wonderfully

quirky lyrics of Syd Barrett. 'Arnold Layne' is a tale of a transvestite who steals ladies' clothes from washing lines; this infectious pop song escaped a BBC ban and rose into the UK Top 20. 'See Emily Play', another Barrett tale, made number 6. Astonishingly it was 12 years before they appeared in the singles chart again. By the end of a marijuana-soaked year, Barrett had imbibed more than most, and was often comatose on stage and incoherent with interviewers. His colleagues, seeing his condition could destroy the band, brought in Syd's old friend David Gilmour (b. 6 March 1944, Cambridge, England; guitar/vocals) and after a brief period as a quintet, gently cajoled him to leave. From that point on the band explored and enlarged their instrumental prowess with older numbers like 'Astronomy Domine' and 'Set The Controls For The Heart Of The Sun'.

The double set *Ummagumma* demonstrated this to its fullest. By today's standards the album appears self-indulgent and dated, but at the time it was a vanguard of progressive space-rock. That same year (1969) they released a soundtrack to the film *More*. This underrated and often forgotten collection contains the gentle 'Cirrus Minor' and the hard rock 'Nile Song', which has an uncanny similarity to music on *The Wall*. At the same time the Floyd were establishing themselves as a major concert attraction and drew 100,000 to their free concert in London's Hyde Park the following year. *Atom Heart Mother* started a series of impressive photographic album covers by the Hipgnosis studio, none of which featured the band; this gave the members a faceless image as most people recognized the group by their album covers and not by their faces. The seemingly abstract sleeve of *Meddle*, for example, is in fact a macro lens shot of an ear. The music within contained some classic pieces, notably 'One Of These Days' and the epic 'Echoes'.

Their festering talent finally exploded in 1973 with *Dark Side Of The Moon*. This marked the arrival of Waters as an important lyricist and Gilmour as a guitar hero. The album has subsequently become one of the biggest selling records of all time, currently in excess of 25 million copies. Its astonishing run on the *Billboard* chart lasted over 10 years.

The following two albums suffered from an acute inferiority complex and only managed sales of several million! The brilliant eulogy to Syd Barrett, 'Shine On You Crazy Diamond' was one of the highpoints of *Wish You Were Here*, while *Animals* featured a scathing attack on the 'clean-up television' campaigner Mary Whitehouse. By now the band was one of the most successful in the world. While they were criticized for being anathema to the punk movement in 1977, they kept a low profile amidst rumours of a break-up. At the end of that year, almost as a backlash, Nick Mason produced the Damned's *Music For Pleasure*. Wright and Gilmour both released solo albums in 1978 and it was now assumed that the band had disintegrated. *The Wall* came in 1979; this Waters-dominated epic has now become second only to *Dark Side Of The Moon* in sales. The album contained the anti-educational system 'Another Brick In The Wall', whch not only restored the group to the UK charts, but ended the 70s with a massive number 1 hit. *The Wall* was a subtly screened semi-autobiographical journey; a troubled Waters poured out anger and scorn. The film appeared in 1982, starred Bob Geldof and featured the ground-breaking animation of Gerald Scarfe. The historic live extravaganza was performed by the remains of the Berlin Wall in 1990. *The Final Cut* came in 1983 and is essentially a Waters solo album. On this he continued to vent anger and bitterness. In retrospect it was a stark album that showed no warmth as it displayed a fragmented band. One single, 'Not Now John' made the UK Top 30, but by the end of the year the knives were drawn as an acrimonious parting occurred. The following year both Waters and Gilmour released solo albums and both found similar success, although Gilmour retained a much higher profile as a session musician and appeared with Bryan Ferry at the Live Aid concert in 1984.

In 1987 Mason and Gilmour decided to work together again and use the Pink Floyd banner; Rick Wright also returned, albeit as a salaried member. Waters instigated an injunction, which was overturned, allowing temporary use of the name. The cryptically titled *A Momentary Lapse Of Reason* was released and moved steadily towards the top of the charts. It sounded like a Pink Floyd album much to the relief of fans, critics and Gilmour, Wright and Mason. A massive world tour began in September that year and finished 12 months and over 150 concerts later.

Albums: *The Piper At The Gates Of Dawn* (1967), *A Saucerful Of Secrets* (1968), *More* (1969, film soundtrack), *Ummagumma* (1969), *Atom Heart Mother* (1970), *Meddle* (1971), *Obscured By Clouds* (1972, film soundtrack), *Dark Side Of The Moon* (1973), *Wish You Were Here* (1975), *Animals* (1977), *The Wall* (1979), *The Final Cut* (1983), *A Momentary Lapse Of Reason* (1987), *Delicate Sound Of Thunder* (1988). Compilations: *Relics* (1971), *First Eleven* (1977, 11 album box-set), *A Collection Of Great Dance Songs* (1981), *Works* (1983).

Pioneers

A Jamaican vocal group, the original Pioneers, formed in 1962, consist of the brothers Sydney and Derrick Crooks, and Glen Adams. The latter later enjoyed a career as vocalist and studio musician, playing organ as a member of Lee Perry's Upsetters. The Pioneers' debut, 'Sometime', was recorded for Leslie Kong's Beverleys label during 1965. By late 1967 they were recording for the Caltone label, owned by Ken Lack, former road manager of the Skatalites. In 1968, Sidney teamed up with Jackie Robinson to record a series of local hits for producer Joe Gibbs, hitting number 1 in the Jamaican chart with their first attempt, 'Gimme Little Loving'. They followed up with another number 1, 'Long Shot', a song celebrating the victories of a famous Jamaican racehorse. Further successes for Gibbs included 'Dem A Laugh', 'No Dope Me Pony', 'Me Nah Go A Bellevue', 'Catch The Beat', and 'Mama Look Deh', which the Maytals used as the basis for their huge local hit of 1968, 'Monkey Man'. Sidney and Jackie then teamed up with Desmond Dekker's brother George, and returned to record for Leslie Kong, initially releasing another local hit 'Nana' under the group name of the Slickers. Subsequent records for Kong were recorded under the name of the Pioneers, including their famous continuation of the racehorse saga, 'Long Shot Kick De Bucket', which tells how Long Shot and a horse named Combat died in a race at Caymanas Park track in Kingston. Other local hits for Kong included the Jamaican chart-topper 'Easy Come Easy Go', the frenetic 'Samfie Man', about a confidence trickster, and 'Mother Rittie'. After their sojourn at Beverleys, they took up residence in England, where 'Long Shot Kick De Bucket' had reached the UK chart, peaking at number 21 in early 1970. They toured Egypt and the Lebanon later that year, returning in 1971 to record in a much more lightweight 'pop' reggae style. Their greatest success came with the Jimmy Cliff-penned 'Let Your Yeah Be Yeah' which got to number 5 in the autumn of 1971. Smaller success came with the cover versions '100 lbs Of Clay' and 'A Little Bit Of Soap'. Since 1973, George has pursued a singing and composing career, Jackie has been a solo vocalist, while Sidney Crooks has concentrated on production, since the late 80s operating his own studio in Luton, Bedfordshire, England. Their best records remain those they recorded for Joe Gibbs and Leslie Kong during 1968-70.

Albums: *Greetings From The Pioneers* (1968), *Long Shot* (1969), *Battle Of The Giants* (1970), *Let Your Yeah Be Yeah* (1972), *I Believe In Love* (1973), *Freedom Feeling* (1973), *Roll On Muddy River* (1974), *I'm Gonna Knock On Your Door* (1974), *Pusher Man* (1974). Compilation: *Greatest Hits* (1975).

Pirate Radio

Although UK pop was flourishing in the wake of the Beatles and the Rolling Stones, the means of greatest access - radio - was sorely constrained. The problem of limited air-time was made particularly apparent to record plugger Ronan O'Rahilly as he tried in vain to secure plays for a single by his client Georgie

Fame. Inspired by Radio Veronica, anchored off the Dutch coast since 1960, O'Rahilly secured the financial backing to purchase and refit the *Frederica*, a 1930 Danish passenger ferry. Renamed the *Caroline* after the daughter of US President John F. Kennedy, the ship sailed from Greenore in the Irish Republic and was anchored off Felixstowe, Suffolk on 27 March 1964. Following a brief test transmission around midnight that evening, Radio Caroline began regular broadcasts at noon the next day, opening with the Beatles' 'Can't Buy Me Love'. The reaction was quick and positive. The BBC was taken completely by surprise and their bland formula of popular music was immediately ignored as millions turned over to 'Caroline on 199 your all-day music station'. Within months several other stations had appeared, broadcasting sometimes contrasting music in often uncomfortable, even farcical, circumstances.

In July 1964 Radio Caroline acquired an early rival - Radio Atlanta. The original ship was relocated off the Isle Of Man while the Atlanta vessel, the *Mi Amigo*, now christened Caroline South, was sited off Frinton, Essex. Its main competitor was established the following December when a former minesweeper, the *Galaxy*, anchored off Walton-on-the-Naze, Essex, began broadcasts as Radio London. Recalled by many as the genre's exemplary station, its imaginative playlist, powerful transmitter and memorable jingles combined to create a unique character. Its staff included John Peel, Kenny Everett, Tommy Vance and Tony Blackburn, a contrast which ensured the station's balance. The Carolines also boasted their share of future celebrities. Blackburn and Vance spent time on the *Mi Amigo*, alongside Simon Dee, Emperor Roscoe, Mike Ahearn and Dave Lee Travis. Life on board any of the vessels was usually gruelling, yet despite cramped conditions, storms and seasickness, a spirit of adventure and camaraderie bonded the disc jockey and audience.

The pirates constructed their own charts, loosely based on those of the music press, but punctuated with singles peculiar to individual ships. It resulted in a curious double standard; record companies could not court them officially, yet the pirates were crucial in pushing material, particularly original American versions, which might not otherwise have been hits. 'You've Lost That Lovin' Feelin'' (the Righteous Brothers) and 'Elusive Butterfly' (Bob Lind) were two prime examples of the pirates' influence and the stations were also less apprehensive of controversial material, including death discs and protest songs. However, loyalty to a particular release was not simply borne out of altruism, and the Caroline organization later admitted that records could be bought into their chart. When Phil Solomon took over the programming of the station he mercilessly plugged the recordings of his own acts on the Major Minor label, such as the Dubliners and David McWilliams. Radio London's publishing house, Pall Mall Limited, owned the rights to a succession of b-sides, fuelling rumours that this would guarantee airtime to the partnership. Despite the pervasive influence of the two major stations, many others were peppered around Britain's coastline. Radio Scotland, initially anchored off Dunbar in East Lothian, inspired a fierce loyalty, maintaining onshore links through its Clan Balls, which featured national and local groups. Its nominal counterpart, Radio England, provided the UK with its most overtly American system, based on a fast-moving, non-stop format. Johnny Walker, later of Caroline, began his career there.

Nearby was Radio 355, also known as Britain Radio while further north, off Scarborough, lay Britain 270. Ships, however, were not the only source and several stations were sited on the disused army and navy watch-towers embedded in the Thames Estuary. Radio Essex, later BBMS (Britain's Better Music Station) was based on Fort Knock John; Radio 390, recalled with affection for Mike Raven's R&B Show, broadcast from the sprawling Red Sands' edifice; while between the two, on Shivering Sands, lay Radio City. The station had begun life in May 1964 when the platform was seized by singer Screaming Lord Sutch who proclaimed it Radio Sutch. The novelty quickly palled; records and valves were in short supply and provisions appeared in exchange for free advertising, and by September control had passed to pop group manager Reg Calvert, who renamed it Radio City. Although the new owner initially announced that the venture was a success, he made an aborted attempt to sell the station to Caroline at the end of 1965. Six months later Calvert approached Radio London, but problems arose over ownership of City's transmitter. Major Oliver Smedley claimed it was his, then raided the complex, leaving behind him a posse of riggers who, it is said, were about to retrieve his property. On 21 June 1966, Calvert arrived at Smedley's home following a heated meeting earlier in the day. A scuffle broke out during which the Major fired a shotgun, killing Calvert instantly. Although his widow, Dorothy, tried to keep the station on air, it closed prematurely in February 1967 when the Rochford, Essex magistrate ruled that Shivering Sands lay within British territorial waters and was thus under the scope of the Wireless Telegraphy Act. The scandal, coupled with the tragic drowning of an engineer, a disc jockey and the co-proprietor of the short-lived Radio Invicta, fuelled the ire of an already seething establishment. Time was already running out; a 1965 Council of Europe declared all offshore broadcasting illegal and one by one the member states introduced laws forbidding their ports to be used as a base.

On 15 August 1967, the Marine Offences Act came into effect resulting, overnight, in the closure of every station, barring the irrepressible Radio Caroline. As midnight passed, renegade disc jockeys Johnnie Walker and Robbie Dale kept the flag flying. Excluded from British patronage, the owners looked to the Continent, but support from this source grew equally problematical. Caroline nonetheless remained a *cause célèbre* for many years, broadcasting for several months before disappearing again, only to resume transmission when all hope seemed lost. Its legacy was also maintained onshore with the proliferation of minority or community-based stations which sprang up during the 80s. These pirates viewed Radio 1 and its commercial counterparts as restrictive as O'Rahilly had viewed the old BBC Light Programme. Caroline's tempestuous story ended in 1989 in the wake of new British laws. In the most punitive action to date, the ship was holed below the waterline during a combined raid by British and Dutch authorities and all equipment put 'out of action'. With this act the legacy of Britain's offshore pirate radio would appear to be over. Their influence on the UK popular music was colossal: they alone defined how pop radio should be delivered, and much of their legacy still exists in modern radio presentation.

Len Barry and Gene Pitney

Pitney, Gene

b. 17 February 1941, Hartford, Connecticut, USA. Although Pitney began recording in 1959 ('Classical Rock 'N' Roll' was recorded with Ginny Mazarro as Jamie And Jane), his initial success came as a songwriter, providing the Kalin Twins with 'Loneliness', Roy Orbison with 'Today's Teardrops' and Bobby Vee with 'Rubber Ball'. His solo recording career took off in 1961 with the multi-tracked 'I Wanna Love My Life Away' and the dramatic film themes 'Town Without Pity' and 'The Man Who Shot Liberty Valance'. Throughout this period, he was still writing for other artists, creating big hits for Ricky Nelson ('Hello Mary Lou') and the

Crystals ('He's A Rebel'). In 1963, Pitney toured Britain where his 'Twenty Four Hours From Tulsa' reached the Top 10. After meeting the Rolling Stones, he recorded Mick Jagger and Keith Richards' 'That Girl Belongs To Yesterday'. Despite the onslaught of the beat groups, Pitney's extraordinarily impassioned big ballads remained popular in the USA and especially in the UK. Among his hits from this era were Barry Mann and Cynthia Weill's 'I'm Gonna Be Strong' (1964), 'I Must Be Seeing Things' (1965), 'Looking Through The Eyes Of Love' (1965), 'Princess In Rags' (1965), 'Backstage' (1966), Randy Newman's 'Nobody Needs Your Love' (1966), 'Just One Smile' (1966) and 'Something's Gotten Hold Of My Heart' (1967). The controversial 'Somewhere In The Country' (about an unmarried mother) was less successful. In addition, Pitney recorded albums in Italian and Spanish, with one of his songs, 'Nessuno Mi Puo Guidicare' coming second in the 1966 San Remo Song Festival. There were also country music albums with George Jones and Melba Montgomery. By the late 60s, his popularity in America had waned but he continued to tour in Europe, having the occasional hit like 'Maria Elena' (1969), 'Shady Lady' (1970) and 'Blue Angel' (1974). In 1988 he had unexpected success when he sang on a revival of 'Something's Gotten Hold Of My Heart' with Marc Almond, which topped the UK charts.

Albums: *The Many Sides Of Gene Pitney* (1962), *Only Love Can Break A Heart* (1963), *Pitney Sings Just For You* (1963), *Blue Gene* (1964), *Gene Pitney Meets The Fair Young Ladies Of Folkland* (1964), *I'm Gonna Be Strong* (1965), *George Jones And Gene Pitney* (1965), *Nobody Needs Your Love* (1966), *Looking Through The Eyes Of Love* (1966), *Young Warm And Wonderful* (1967), *Just One Smile* (1967), *Pitney Today* (1968), *Pitney '75* (1975), *Walkin' In The Sun* (1979). Compilations: *Big Sixteen* (1967), *Best Of Gene Pitney* (1969), *His 20 Greatest Hits* (1976).

Plastic Penny

This immensely talented UK quartet came together in 1968 when three former members of the Universals, Brian Keith (vocals), Paul Raymond (keyboards) and Tony Murray (bass), joined Mick Grabham (lead guitar) and Nigel Olsson (drums) to record for Larry Page's recently launched Page One record label. Their debut was the refreshing and melodic 'Everything I Am', originally recorded by the Box Tops. It became a UK Top 10 hit, but after the failure of the Bill Martin/Phil Coulter composition 'Nobody Knows If', the group drifted into other recording ventures. Singer Brian Keith was the first to quit, leaving before the completion of the group's sole album. One-hit-wonders on paper, Plastic Penny nevertheless established themselves as an excellent musicians' training ground. Grabham founded Cochise and later joined Procol Harum, Murray teamed up with the Troggs, Paul Raymond had spells with Chicken Shack and Savoy Brown, and Olsson collaborated with the Spencer Davis Group and Elton John.

Album: *Two Sides Of A Penny* (1968).

Plastic Penny

Poets

Formed in Glasgow, Scotland in 1961, the Poets were one of Britain's more adventurous acts. Although obliged to play contemporary hits, the group - George Gallagher (vocals), Hume Paton (guitar), Tony Myles (guitar), John Dawson (bass) and Alan Weir (drums) - brought original songs and R&B favourites into their early sets. By 1964 they had become a leading attraction, resplendent in frilled shirts and matching velvet suits. Rolling Stones' manager Andrew Loog Oldham signed the quintet to his management and production company, attracted by their image and self-composed material. The Poets' debut single 'Now We're Thru', reached number 31 in the UK charts. Its ethereal drone and echoed 12-string guitars enhanced Gallagher's nasal delivery and the performance was the template for subsequent releases. Although the group would not secure another hit, their versatile recordings included ballads and uptempo R&B, imbued with their unique approach. The Poets' line-up fragmented and by 1967 none of the original group remained. Andi Mulvey (vocals), Fraser Watson (guitar), Ian McMillan (guitar), Norrie Maclean (bass) and Raymond Duffy (drums - on loan from Dean Ford And The Gaylords) completed 'Wooden Spoon', the unit's last official single. Further fragmentation ensued, but the name was retained until the early 70s. The core of the group subsequently joined Longdancer, while McMillan formed Blue with late-period member Hughie Nicholson.

Poole, Brian, And The Tremeloes

Formed in the late 50s and fronted by vocalist Brian

Poole (b. 2 November 1941, Barking, Essex, England), this UK pop group were initially known as Brian Poole and the Tremilos when they made their debut at the Ilford Palais in 1960. Poole was originally known as a Buddy Holly imitator and even went as far as wearing spectacles filled with plain glass. After his backing musicians reverted to the title Tremeloes, the entire ensemble successfully auditioned for Decca Records on 1 January 1962 and were signed in favour of the Beatles. A cover of the Isley Brothers' 'Twist And Shout' brought them a UK Top 10 hit the following year. The follow-up, a reading of the Contours' 'Do You Love Me?' hit number 1 in the UK and 15 other countries. American success, however, remained frustratingly elusive. Appropriately, the group's manager Peter Walsh recruited Buddy Holly's former mentor Norman Petty to play piano on two further UK smashes, the wistful 'Someone Someone' and mawkish 'The Three Bells'. Thereafter, the group's popularity waned and they seemed increasingly dated in comparison to the more aggressive R&B-based UK pop outfits that emerged in 1964-65. Sensing a crisis, Poole elected to leave the group and branch out into the world of big ballads. He subsequently moved into cabaret, retired to the family butcher business, and later resurfaced with a record and publishing company. Against the odds, it was his backing group, the Tremeloes, that went on to achieve enormous chart success under their own name. In the 90s Poole and most of his original Tremeloes are back ploughing the rich vein of 60s nostalgia tours.

Albums: *Twist And Shout With Brian Poole And The Tremeloes* (1963), *It's About Time* (1965). Compilation: *Remembering Brian Poole And The Tremeloes* (1977).

Posey, Sandy

b. Martha Sharp, 1945, Jasper, Alabama, USA. As a teenager Posey moved to west Memphis where she embarked on a career as a studio session singer. Her contributions to innumerable records impressed producer Chips Moman, who encouraged the artist as both a songwriter and performer. Posey's debut single, 'Born A Woman', reached number 12 in the US charts in 1966, while its pithy lyric - 'If you're born a woman, you're born to be hurt' - brought a new maturity to the often-maudlin approach common to female country singers. 'Single Girl', its equally accomplished follow-up, scaled the UK and US Top 20s, before 'What A Woman In Love Won't Do', 'I Take It Back' and 'Are You Never Coming Home' (all 1967) continued her run of success. Posey was one of several singers backing Elvis Presley when he undertook sessions at Moman's American studios. She was featured on 'Mama Liked The Roses', and also appeared with the singer during his first Las Vegas engagement (1969). However, while retaining a popularity within the country market, Sandy's distinctive approach as a solo act latterly proved too specialized for pop.

Albums: *Born A Woman* (1966), *I Take It Back* (1967). Compilations: *Very Best Of Sandy Posey* (1974).

Presley, Elvis

b. Elvis Aaron Presley, 8 January 1935, Tupelo, Mississippi, USA, d. 16 August 1977, Memphis, Tennessee. The most celebrated popular music phenomenenon of his era and, for many, the purest embodiment of rock 'n' roll, Elvis's life and career have become part of rock legend. The elder of twins, his younger brother, Jesse Garon, was stillborn, a tragedy which partly contributed to the maternal solicitude that affected his childhood and teenage years. Presley's first significant step towards a musical career took place at the age of eight when he won $5.00 in a local song contest performing the lachrymose Red Foley ballad, 'Old Shep'. His earliest musical influence came from attending the Pentecostal Church and listening to the psalms and gospel songs. He also had a strong grounding in country and blues and it was the combination of these different styles that was to provide his unique musical identity.

By the age of 13, Presley had moved with his family to Memphis and during his later school years began cultivating an outsider image with long hair, spidery sideburns and ostentatious clothes. After leaving school he took a job as a truck driver, a role in keeping with his unconventional appearance. In spite of his rebel posturing, Elvis remained studiously polite to his elders and was devoted to his mother. Indeed, it was his filial affection that first prompted him to visit Sun Records, whose studios offered the sophisticated equivalent of a fairground recording booth service. As a birthday present to his mother, Gladys, Elvis cut a version of the Ink Spots' 'My Happiness', backed with the Raskin/Brown/Fisher standard 'That's When Your Heartaches Begin'. The studio manager, Marion Keisker, noted Presley's unusual but distinctive vocal style and informed Sun's owner/producer Sam Phillips of his potential. Phillips nurtured the boy for almost a year before putting him together with country guitarist Scotty Moore and bassist Bill Black. Their early sessions showed considerable promise, especially when Presley began alternating his unorthodox low-key delivery with a high-pitched whine. The amplified guitars of Moore and Black contributed strongly to the effect and convinced Phillips that the singer was startlingly original. In Presley, Sam saw something that he had long dreamed of discovering: a white boy who sang like a negro.

Presley's debut disc on Sun was the extraordinary 'That's All Right (Mama)', a showcase for his rich, multi-textured vocal dexterity, with sharp, solid backing from his compatriots. The b-side, 'Blue Moon Of Kentucky', was a country song but the arrangement showed that Presley was threatening to slip into an entirely different genre, closer to R&B. Local response to these strange-sounding performances was encouraging and Phillips eventually shifted 20,000 copies of the disc. For his second single, Presley cut Roy Brown's 'Good Rockin' Tonight' backed by the zingy 'I Don't Care If The Sun Don't Shine'. The more roots-influenced 'Milkcow Blues Boogie' followed, while the b-side 'You're A Heartbreaker' had some strong tempo changes which neatly complemented Presley's quirky vocal. 'Baby Let's Play House'/'I'm Left, You're Right, She's Gone' continued the momentum and led to Presley performing on the *Grand Old Opry* and *Louisiana Hayride* radio programmes. A series of live dates commenced in 1955 with drummer D.J. Fontana added to the ranks. Presley toured clubs in Arkansas, Louisiana and Texas billed as 'The King Of Western Bop' and 'The Hillbilly Cat'. Audience reaction verged on the fanatical, which was hardly surprising given Presley's semi-erotic performances. His hip-swivelling routine, in which he cascaded across the stage and plunged to his knees at dramatic moments in a song, was remarkable for the period and prompted near-riotous fan mania. The final Sun single, a cover of Junior Parker's 'Mystery Train', was later acclaimed by many as the definitive rock 'n' roll single with its chugging rhythm, soaring vocal and enticing lead guitar breaks. It established Presley as an artist worthy of national attention and ushered in the next phase of his career, which was dominated by the imposing figure of Colonel Tom Parker.

The Colonel was a former fairground huckster who managed several country artists including Hank Snow and Eddy Arnold. After relieving disc jockey Bob Neal of Presley's managership, Parker persuaded Sam Phillips that his financial interests would be better served by releasing the boy to a major label. RCA Records had already noted the commercial potential of the phenomenon under offer and agreed to pay Sun Records a release fee of $35,000, an incredible sum for the period. The sheer diversity of Presley's musical heritage and his remarkable ability as a vocalist and interpreter of material enabled him to escape the cultural parochialism of his R&B-influenced predecessors. The attendant rock 'n' roll explosion, in which Presley was both a creator and participant, ensured that he could reach a mass audience, many of them newly-affluent teenagers.

It was on 10 January 1956, a mere two days after his 21st birthday, that Elvis entered RCA's studios in Nashville to record his first tracks for a major label.

His debut session produced the epochal 'Heartbreak Hotel', one of the most striking pop records ever released. Co-composed by Hoyt Axton's mother Mae, the song evoked nothing less than a vision of absolute funereal despair. There was nothing in the pop charts of the period that even hinted at the degree of desolation described in the song. Presley's reading was extraordinarily mature and moving, with a determined avoidance of any histrionics in favour of a pained and resigned acceptance of loneliness as death. The economical yet acutely emphatic piano work of Floyd Cramer enhanced the stark mood of the piece, which was frozen in a suitably minimalist production. The startling originality and intensity of 'Heartbreak Hotel' entranced the American public and pushed the single to number 1 for an astonishing eight weeks. Whatever else he achieved, Presley was already assured a place in pop history for one of the greatest major label debut records ever released. During the same month that 'Heartbreak Hotel' was recorded, Presley made his national television debut displaying his sexually-enticing gyrations before a bewildered adult audience whose alleged outrage subsequently persuaded producers to film the star exclusively from the waist upwards. Having outsold his former Sun colleague Carl Perkins with 'Blue Suede Shoes', Presley released a debut album which contained several of the songs he had previously cut with Sam Phillips, including Little Richard's 'Tutti Fruitti', the R&B classic 'I Got A Woman' and an eerie, wailing version of Richard Rodgers/Lorenz Hart's 'Blue Moon', which emphasized his remarkable vocal range.

Since hitting number 2 in the UK lists with 'Heartbreak Hotel', Presley had been virtually guaranteed European success and his profile was increased via a regular series of releases as RCA took full advantage of their bulging back catalogue. Although there was a danger of overkill, Presley's talent, reputation and immensely strong fan base vindicated the intense release schedule and the quality of the material ensured that the public was not disappointed. After hitting number 1 for the second time with the slight ballad 'I Want You, I Need You, I Love You', Presley released what was to become the most commercially successful double-sided single in pop history, 'Hound Dog'/'Don't Be Cruel'. The former was composed by the immortal rock 'n' roll songwriting team of Leiber And Stoller, and presented Presley at his upbeat best with a novel lyric, complete with a striking guitar solo and spirited handclapping from his backing group the Jordanaires. Otis Blackwell's 'Don't Be Cruel' was equally effective with a striking melody line and some clever and amusing vocal gymnastics from the hiccuping King of Western Bop, who also received a co-writing credit. The single remained at number 1 in the USA

for a staggering 11 weeks and both sides of the record were massive hits in the UK.

Celluloid fame for Presley next beckoned with *Love Me Tender*, produced by David Weisbert, who had previously worked on James Dean's *Rebel Without A Cause*. Elvis's movie debut received mixed reviews but was a box office smash, while the smouldering, perfectly-enunciated title track topped the US charts for five weeks. The spate of Presley singles continued in earnest through 1957 and one of the biggest was another Otis Blackwell composition, 'All Shook Up' which the singer used as a cheekily oblique comment on his by now legendary dance movements. By late 1956 it was rumoured that Presley would be drafted into the US Army and, as if to compensate for that irksome eventuality, RCA, Twentieth Century Fox and the Colonel stepped up the work-rate and release schedules. Incredibly, three major films were completed in the next two-and-a-half years. *Loving You* boasted a quasi-autobiographical script with Presley playing a truck driver who becomes a pop star. The title track became the b-side of '(Let Me Be Your) Teddy Bear' which reigned at number 1 for seven weeks. The third movie, *Jailhouse Rock*, was Elvis's most successful to date with an excellent soundtrack and some inspired choreography. The Leiber and Stoller title track was an instant classic which again topped the US charts for seven weeks and made pop history by entering the UK listings at number 1. The fourth celluloid outing, *King Creole* (adapted from the Harold Robbins' novel, *A Stone For Danny Fisher*) is regarded by many as Presley's finest film of all and a firm indicator of his sadly unfulfilled potential as a serious actor. Once more the soundtrack album featured some surprisingly strong material such as the haunting 'Crawfish' and the vibrant 'Dixieland Rock'.

By the time *King Creole* was released in 1958, Elvis had already been inducted into the US Forces. A publicity photograph of the singer having his hair shorn symbolically commented on his approaching musical emasculation. Although rock 'n' roll purists mourned the passing of the old Elvis, it seemed inevitable in the context of the 50s that he would move towards a broader base appeal and tone down his rebellious image. From 1958-60, Presley served in the US Armed Forces, spending much of his time in Germany where he was regarded as a model soldier. It was during this period that he first met 14-year-old Priscilla Beaulieu, whom he would later marry in 1967. Back in America, the Colonel kept his absent star's reputation intact via a series of films, record releases and extensive merchandising. Hits such as 'Wear My Ring Around Your Neck', 'Hard Headed Woman', 'One Night', 'I Got Stung', 'A Fool Such As I' and 'A Big Hunk O' Love' filled the long two-year gap and by the time Elvis reappeared, he was ready to assume the mantle of an all-round entertainer. The change was immediately evident in the series of number 1 hits that he enjoyed in the early 60s. The enormously successful 'It's Now Or Never', based on the Italian melody 'O Sole Mio', revealed the King as an operatic crooner, far removed from his earlier raucous recordings. 'Are You Lonesome Tonight?', originally recorded by Al Jolson as early as 1927, allowed Presley to quote some Shakespeare in the spoken-word middle section as well as showing his ham-acting ability with an overwrought vocal. The new clean-cut Presley was presented on celluloid in *GI Blues*. The movie played upon his recent Army exploits and saw him serenading a puppet on the charming chart-topper 'Wooden Heart', which also allowed Elvis to show off his knowledge of German. The grandiose 'Surrender' completed this phase of big ballads in the old-fashioned style. For the next few years Presley concentrated on an undemanding spree of films including *Flaming Star*, *Wild In The Country*, *Blue Hawaii*, *Kid Galahad*, *Girls! Girls! Girls!*, *Follow That Dream*, *Fun In Acapulco*, *It Happened At The World's Fair*, *Kissin' Cousins*, *Viva Las Vegas*, *Roustabout*, *Girl Happy*, *Tickle Me*, *Harem Scarem*, *Frankie And Johnny*, *Paradise Hawaiian Style* and *Spinout*. Not surprisingly, most of his album recordings were hastily completed soundtracks with unadventurous commissioned songs. For his singles he relied increasingly on the formidable Doc Pomus/Mort Shuman team who composed such hits as 'Mess Of Blues', 'Little Sister' and 'His Latest Flame'. More and more, however, the hits were adapted from films and their chart positions suffered accordingly. After the 1963 number 1 'Devil In Disguise', a bleak period followed in which such minor songs as 'Bossa Nova Baby', 'Kiss Me Quick', 'Ain't That Lovin' You Baby' and 'Blue Christmas' became the rule rather than the exception. Significantly, his biggest success of the mid-60s, 'Crying In The Chapel', had been recorded five years before, and part of its appeal came from the realization that it represented something ineffably lost. In the wake of the Beatles' rise to fame and the beat boom explosion Presley seemed a figure out of time. Yet, in spite of the dated nature of many of his recordings, he could still invest power and emotion into classic songs. The sassy 'Frankie And Johnny' was expertly sung by Elvis as was his moving reading of Ketty Lester's 'Love Letters'. His other significant 1966 release, 'If Everyday Was Like Christmas', was a beautiful festive song unlike anything else in the charts of the period. By 1967, however, it was clear to critics and even a large proportion of his devoted following that Presley had seriously lost his way. He continued to grind out pointless movies such as *Double Trouble*, *Speedway*, *Clambake* and *Live A Little, Love A Little*, even though the box office returns were increasingly poor. His capacity to register instant hits, irrespective of the material was also wearing thin as such lowly-placed singles as 'You Gotta Stop' and 'Long Legged Woman' demonstrated all too alarmingly. However, just as Elvis's career had reached its all-time nadir he seemed to wake up, take stock, and break free from the artistic malaise in which he found himself.

Two songs written by country guitarist Jerry Reed, 'Guitar Man' and 'US Male', proved a spectacular return to form for Elvis in 1968, such was Presley's conviction that the compositions almost seemed to be written specifically for him. During the same year Colonel Tom Parker had approached NBC-TV about the possibility of recording a Presley Christmas special in which the singer would perform a selection of religious songs similar in feel to his early 60s album *His Hand In Mine*. However, the executive producers of the show vetoed that concept in favour of a one-hour spectacular designed to capture Elvis at his rock 'n' rollin' best. It was a remarkable challenge for the singer, seemingly in the autumn of his career, and he responded to the idea with unexpected enthusiasm. The *Elvis TV Special* was broadcast in America on 3 December 1968 and has since gone down as one of the most celebrated moments in pop broadcasting history. The show was not merely good but an absolute revelation, with the King emerging as if he had been frozen in time for 10 years. His determination to recapture past glories oozed from every movement and was discernible in every aside. With his leather jacket and acoustic guitar strung casually round his neck, he resembled nothing less than the consummate pop idol of the 50s who had entranced a generation. To add authenticity to the proceedings he was accompanied by his old sidekicks Scotty Moore and D.J. Fontana. There was no sense of self-parody in the show as Presley joked about his famous surly curled-lip movement and even heaped passing ridicule on his endless stream of bad movies. The music concentrated heavily on his 50s classics but, significantly, there was a startling finale courtesy of the passionate 'If I Can Dream' in which he seemed to sum up the frustration of a decade in a few short lines.

The critical plaudits heaped upon Elvis in the wake of his television special prompted the singer to undertake his most significant recordings in years. With producer Chips Moman overseeing the sessions in January 1969, Presley recorded enough material to cover two highly-praised albums, *From Elvis In Memphis* and *From Memphis To Vegas/From Vegas To Memphis*. The former was particularly strong with such distinctive tracks as the eerie 'Long Black Limousine' and the engagingly melodic 'Any Day Now'. On the singles front, Presley was back in top form and finally coming to terms with contemporary issues, most notably on the socially aware 'In The Ghetto' which hit number 2 in the UK and number 3 in the USA. The glorious 'Suspicious Minds', a wonderful song of marital jealously with cascading tempo changes and an exceptional vocal arrangement, gave him his first US chart-topper since 'Good Luck Charm' back in 1962. Subsequent hits such as the maudlin 'Don't Cry Daddy', which dealt with the death of a marriage, ably demonstrated Elvis's ability to read a song. Even his final few films seemed less disastrous than expected. In 1969's *Charro*, he grew a beard for the first time in his portrayal of a moody cowboy, while *A Change Of Habit* dealt with more serious matter than usual. More importantly, Presley returned as a live performer at Las Vegas with a strong backing group including guitarist James Burton and pianist Glen D. Hardin. In common with John Lennon, who also returned to the stage that same year with the Plastic Ono Band, Presley opened his set with Carl Perkins' 'Blue Suede Shoes'. His comeback was well-received and one of the live songs, 'The Wonder Of You', stayed at number 1 in Britain for six weeks during the summer of 1970. There was also a revealing documentary film of the tour Elvis - *That's The Way It Is* and a companion album which included contemporary cover songs such as Tony Joe White's 'Polk Salad Annie', Creedence Clearwater Revival's 'Proud Mary' and Neil Diamond's 'Sweet Caroline'.

During the early 70s Presley continued his live performances, but soon fell victim to the same artistic atrophy that had bedevilled his celluloid career. Rather than re-entering the studio to record fresh material he relied on a slew of patchy live albums which saturated the marketplace. What had been innovative and exciting in 1969 swiftly became a tedious routine and an exercise in misdirected potential. The backdrop to Presley's final years was a sordid slump into drug dependency, reinforced by the pervasive unreality of a pampered lifestyle in his fantasy home, Gracelands. The dissolution of his marriage in 1973 coincided with a further decline and an alarming tendency to put on weight. Remarkably, he continued to undertake live appearances, covering up his bloated frame with brightly coloured jump suits and an enormous, ostentatiously-jewelled belt. He collapsed onstage on a couple of occasions and finally on 16 August 1977 his tired, burnt-out body expired. The official cause of death was a heart attack, no doubt brought on by barbiturate usage over a long period. In the weeks following his demise, his record sales predictably rocketed and 'Way Down' proved a fittingly final UK number 1.

The importance of Presley in the history of rock 'n' roll and popular music remains incalculable. In spite of his iconographic status, the Elvis image was never captured in a single moment of time like that of Bill Haley, Buddy Holly or even Chuck Berry. Presley, in spite of his apparent creative inertia, was not a one-dimensional artist clinging to history but a multi-faceted performer whose career spanned several decades and phases. For purists and rockabilly enthusiasts it is the early Elvis who remains of greatest importance and there is no doubting that his personal fusion of black and white musical influences, incorporating R&B and country, produced some of the finest and most durable recordings of the century. Beyond Elvis 'The Hillbilly Cat', however, there was the face that launched a thousand imitators, that black-haired, smiling or smouldering presence who stared from the front covers of numerous EPs, albums and film posters of the late 50s and early 60s. It was that well-groomed, immaculate pop star who inspired a generation of performers and second-rate imitators in the 60s. There was also Elvis the Las Vegas performer, vibrant and vulgar, yet still distant and increasingly appealing to a later generation brought up on the excesses of 70s rock and glam ephemera. Finally, there was the bloated Presley who bestrode the stage in the last months of his career. For many, he has come to symbolize the decadence and loss of dignity that is all too often heir to pop idolatry. It is no wonder that Presley's remarkable career so sharply divides those who testify to his ultimate greatness and those who bemoan the gifts that he seemingly squandered along the way. In a sense, the contrasting images of Elvis have come to represent everything positive and everything destructive about the music industry.

Albums: *Rock 'N' Roll* (1956), *Rock 'N' Roll No. 2* (1957), *Loving You* (1957), *Elvis' Christmas Album* (1957), *King Creole* (1958), *Elvis' Golden Records, Volume 1* (1958), *Elvis* (1959), *A Date With Elvis* (1959), *Elvis' Golden Records, Volume 2* (1960), *Elvis Is Back!* (1960), *G.I. Blues* (1960), *His Hand In Mine* (1961), *Something For Everybody* (1961), *Blue Hawaii* (1961), *Pot Luck* (1962), *Girls! Girls! Girls!* (1963), *It Happened At The World's Fair* (1963), *Fun In Acapulco* (1963), *Elvis' Golden Records, Volume 3* (1964), *Kissin' Cousins* (1964), *Roustabout* (1964), *Girl Happy* (1965), *Flaming Star And Summer Kisses* (1965), *Elvis For Everyone* (1965), *Harem Holiday* (1965), *Frankie And Johnny* (1966), *Paradise, Hawaiian Style* (1966), *California Holiday* (1966), *How Great Thou Art* (1967), *Double Trouble* (1967), *Clambake* (1968), *Elvis' Golden Records, Volume 4* (1968), *Speedway* (1968), *Elvis - TV Special* (1968), *From Elvis In Memphis* (1970), *On Stage February 1970* (1970), *That's The Way It Is* (1971), *I'm 10,000 Years Old - Elvis Country* (1971), *Love Letters From Elvis* (1971), *Elvis Sings The Wonderful World Of Christmas* (1971), *Elvis Now* (1972), *He Touched Me* (1972), *Elvis As Recorded At Madison Square Garden* (1972), *Aloha From Hawaii Via Satellite* (1973), *Elvis* (1973), *Raised On Rock* (1973), *A*

Legendary Performer, Volume 1 (1974), Good Times (1974), Elvis Recorded On Stage In Memphis (1974), Hits Of The 70s (1974), Promised Land (1975), Having Fun With Elvis On Stage (1975), Today (1975), The Elvis Presley Sun Collection (1975), From Elvis Presley Boulevard, Memphis, Tennessee (1976), Welcome To My World (1977), A Legendary Performer (1977), He Walks Beside Me (1978), The '56 Sessions, Vol. 1 (1978), Elvis's 40 Greatest (1978), Elvis - A Legendary Performer, Volume 3 (1979), Our Memories Of Elvis (1979), The '56 Sessions, Vol. 2 (1979), Elvis Presley Sings Leiber And Stoller (1980), Elvis Aaron Presley (1979), Elvis Sings The Wonderful World Of Christmas (1979), The First Year (1979), The King . . . Elvis (1980), This Is Elvis (1981), Guitar Man (1981), Elvis Answers Back (1981), The Ultimate Performance (1981), Personally Elvis (1982), The Sound Of Your Cry (1982), Jailhouse Rock/Love In Las Vegas (1983), The First Live Recordings (1984), A Golden Celebration (1984), Rare Elvis (1985), Essential Elvis (1986).
Further reading: Elvis: A Biography, Jerry Hopkins. Elvis: The Final Years, Jerry Hopkins. Elvis '56: In The Beginning, Alfred Wertheimer And Gregory Martinelli. Elvis, Albert Goldman. Up And Down With Elvis Presley, Marge Crumbaker. Elvis, Dave Marsh. Elvis: The Complete Illustrated Record, Roy Carr And Mick Farren. Elvis And Gladys: The Genesis Of The King, Elaine Dundy.

Preston, Johnny

b. John Preston Courville, 18 August 1939, Port Arthur, Texas, USA. This pop ballad and rock singer first performed in the Lamar University (Beaumont, Texas) group the Shades, in 1957, and was brought to the attention of Mercury Records by disc jockey and singer, the Big Bopper (Jape Richardson). Amongst the tracks Richardson wrote and produced for him was the novelty 'Running Bear', a sad tale of Red Indian love gone wrong. The record took four months to chart Stateside but it then went on to became a chart-topper in the US and UK (after Richardson's tragic death in the plane crash with Buddy Holly). Despite a disastrous UK tour (cut three weeks short due to poor houses), he had transatlantic Top 20 successes with the follow-ups 'Cradle Of Love' and a revival of Shirley And Lee's 'Feel So Fine'. He later recorded for Imperial, TCF Hall (including 'Running Bear '65'), ABC and Hallway, but never graced the charts again.
Album: Johnny Preston Sings (1960).

Pretty Things

One of England's seminal R&B bands, the Pretty Things were formed at Sidcup Art College, Kent, England, in September 1963. The original line-up featured a founder member of the Rolling Stones, Dick Taylor (b. 28 January 1943, Dartford, Kent,

England; guitar), plus Phil May (b. 9 November 1944, Dartford, Kent, England; vocals), Brian Pendleton (b. 13 April 1944, Wolverhampton, West Midlands, England; rhythm guitar), John Stax (b. 6 April 1944, Crayford, Kent, England; bass) and Peter Kitley (drums), although the latter was quickly replaced by Viv Andrews. The group secured a recording deal within months of their inception. Their label then insisted that the luckless Andrews be removed in favour of Viv Prince, an experienced musician and ex-member of Carter-Lewis And The Southerners. The Pretty Things' debut single, 'Rosalyn', scraped into the UK Top 50, but its unfettered power, coupled with the group's controversial, unkempt appearance, ensured maximum publicity. Their brash, almost destructive, approach to R&B flourished with two exciting UK Top 20 singles, 'Don't Bring Me Down' and 'Honey I Need'. The unit's exuberant first album offered much of the same. Skip Alan (b. Alan Skipper, 11 June 1948, London, England) replaced the erratic Prince in November 1965. Although the Pretty Things' commercial standing had declined, subsequent singles, 'Midnight To Six Man' and 'Come See Me', were arguably their finest work, combining power with purpose. However, first Pendleton, then Stax, abandoned the group and sessions for a third album, Emotions, were completed with two former members of the Fenmen, Wally Allen (bass/vocals) and John Povey (b. 20 August 1944, London, England; keyboards/vocals). Initially hired on a temporary basis, the duo proved crucial to the Pretty Things' subsequent development.
By late 1967 the quintet was immersed in the emergent underground scene. Their music combined harmonies with experimentation, and two exceptional singles, 'Defecting Grey' and 'Talking About The Good Times', are definitive examples of English 'flower-power' pop. The group's newfound confidence flourished on S.F. Sorrow, an ambitious concept album which reportedly influenced the Who's Tommy. The set was not a commercial success, and a recurring instability - Skip Alan was replaced by former Tomorrow drummer John 'Twink' Alder - only to rejoin again, also proved detrimental. Dick Taylor's departure in November 1969 was highly damaging, and although the group's subsequent album, Parachute, was lauded in Rolling Stone magazine, his distinctive guitar sound was notably absent. The Pretty Things collapsed in 1971, but reformed under a core of May, Povey and Skip Alan to complete Freeway Madness. This trio remained central through the group's subsequent changes until May embarked on a solo career in 1976. Two years later the Emotions line-up - May, Taylor, Povey, Allen and Alan - was reunited. The same quintet, plus guitarist Peter Tolson (b. 10 September 1951,

Bishops Stortford, Hertfordshire, England), completed a studio album, *Cross Talk* in 1980, and since then the group has been revived on numerous occasions, notably with May and Taylor at the helm. In 1990 a revitalized unit released a rousing version of Barry McGuire's 1965 US number 1 'Eve Of Destruction'.

Albums: *The Pretty Things* (1965), *Get The Picture* (1965), *Emotions* (1967), *S.F. Sorrow* (1968), *Parachute* (1970), *Freeway Madness* (1972), *Silk Torpedo* (1974), *Savage Eye* (1976), *Live '78* (1978), *Cross Talk* (1980), *Live At The Heartbreak Hotel* (1984), *Out Of The Island* (1988). The group also completed several albums of background music suitable for films: *Electric Banana* (1967), *More Electric Banana* (1968), *Even More Electric Banana* (1969), *Hot Licks* (1973), *Return Of The Electric Banana* (1978). Compilations: *We'll Be Together* (1966), *Greatest Hits 64-67* (1975), *The Vintage Years* (1976), *Attention* (1976), *Attention Volume 2* (1976), *Singles A's And B's* (1977), *Cried From The Midnight Circus* (1986), *Let Me Hear The Choir Sing* (1986), *Closed Restaurant Blues* (1987).

Alan Price, Georgie Fame and Dave Berry

Price, Alan

b. 19 April 1941, Fatfield, Co. Durham, England. From the age of eight Price taught himself the piano, guitar and bass and lost no time in playing with local bands, usually containing various members of the as yet unformed Animals. His first major band was variously known as the Kansas City Five, (or Seven or Nine), the Kontours, the Pagans and finally the Alan Price Rhythm And Blues Combo. The late Graham Bond recommended the combo to his manager Ronan O'Rahilly and the name was changed as the band prepared to infiltrate the London R&B scene. As the most musically talented member of the Animals, Price eventually found the constant high-profile and touring too much. Always an introvert and having a more sophisticated and broader musical palette than the rest of the band, it was only a matter of time before the mentally exhausted Price left the Animals. Fear of flying was given as the

official reason in May 1965, although leaving the band at the peak of their success was seen as tantamount to professional suicide. That year he appeared in the classic D.A. Pennebaker movie *Don't Look Back* as one of Bob Dylan's entourage. Within a very short time he had assembled the Alan Price Set, who debuted in August that year with 'Any Day Now'. Although not a hit, the record showed great promise. This was confirmed with their second release, a stirring version of Screamin' Jay Hawkins' 'I Put A Spell On You'. While the record featured Price's distinctive fast arpeggio organ sound, the public were happy to discover that he could also sing well.

He followed with further singles which showed an unashamedly pop bias. In 1967 he had two major hits written by Randy Newman; 'Simon Smith And His Amazing Dancing Bear' and 'The House That Jack Built'. In 1970 he teamed up with Georgie Fame as Fame And Price Together and had a hit with the MOR-sounding 'Rosetta'. That same year he wrote the score for two musicals, *Home*, written by Lindsay Anderson, and his own *The Brass Band Man*. Price was then commissioned to write the music for Anderson's film, *O Lucky Man!* in 1973, for which he won a BAFTA award. His apparent serious nature and 'straight' appearance kept him apart from the hipper music scene, of which his former colleague Eric Burdon was one of the leading lights. His vaudeville-tinged playing effectively allied him with an older audience. In 1974 Price once again went against the grain and hit the charts with 'Jarrow Song', having been bought up in the town famous for its workers' march of 1936. Price's social conscience was stirred, and he produced the excellent autobiographical album *Between Today And Yesterday*. The critical success of the album garnered him a BBC television documentary.

Price starred in *Alfie Darling* in 1975, winning the Most Promising New British Actor award. In 1978 and 1979 he dented the charts with 'Just For You', some copies of which were pressed in heart-shaped red vinyl. He enjoys a fruitful career, often appears on television and is always able to fill a concert hall, in addition to continuing to write stage musicals like *Andy Capp* and *Who's A Lucky Boy?* Price took part in two abortive Animals reunions in 1977 and 1983.

Albums: *The Price To Play* (1966), *The Price On His Head* (1967), *Fame And Price, Price And Fame Together* (1971), *O Lucky Man!* (1973, film soundtrack), *Between Today And Yesterday* (1974), *Metropolitan Man* (1974), *Performing Price* (1975), *Shouts Across The Street* (1976), *Rainbows End* (1977), *Alan Price* (1977), *England My England* (1978), *Rising Sun* (1980), *A Rock And Roll Night At The Royal Court* (1981), *Geordie Roots And Branches* (1983), *Travellin' Man* (1986), *Liberty* (1989).

Further reading: *Wild Animals*, Andy Blackford.

Prince Buster

b. Cecil Bustamante Campbell, 28 May 1938, Kingston, Jamaica. Buster was named after Alexandra Bustamante, the leader of the Jamaican Labour Party, and began his career as a boxer, but soon found his pugilistic talents being put to use as a bouncer/strong arm man and minder for Coxsone Dodd's Down Beat Sound System. Competition was fierce in those early days, with fights often breaking out between the suporters of rival sounds with wires (and people) being cut regularly, and Buster still carries the scars (literally). He claims, like so many others, to have personally invented the ska sound and he was certainly involved from the very early stages - at first with his work for Coxsone and after they had parted company with his own Voice Of The People Sound System, record label and shop. His very first recording session produced one of the all-time classics of Jamaican music 'Oh Carolina' with vocals by the Folks Brothers and musical accompaniment from Count Ossie. Inventive and innovative at the time, the record still sounds every bit as exciting now as it did then. Buster released countless records both by himself and other top acts on his Wild Bells, Voice Of The People and Buster's Record Shack labels, which were subsequently released in the UK on the Blue Beat label. They proved as popular there as they had been in Jamaica, firstly with the Jamaican community and secondly with the mods, who took the Prince to their hearts with songs such as 'Al Capone' and 'Madness'. He toured the UK in the mid-60s to ecstatic crowds and appeared on the hugely popular *Ready, Steady, Go* television show.

He recorded in many different styles but his talking records were the most popular, including the hilarious 'Judge Dread' where he admonishes rude boys and sentences them to 400 years; the wildly misogynist 'Ten Commandments'; the evocative 'Ghost Dance' - a look back at his early Kingston dance hall days; the confused and confusing 'Johnny Cool'; and the not so well known but equally wonderful 'Shepherd Beng Beng'. He also claims to have taught Georgie Fame to do the ska and he influenced other white pop acts - Madness named themselves after his song (debuting with a tribute, 'The Prince') and inspired doorman/bouncer Alex Hughes to adopt the name Judge Dread and have UK chart hits with variations on Prince Buster's lewd original 'Big Five'. Buster had tended towards 'slack' or rude records towards the end of the 60s which were only mildly risqué compared with what was to follow but caused a sensation at the time. He wisely invested his money in record shops and juke box operations throughout the Caribbean and, in the early 70s, took to recording many of the current top names including Big Youth, Dennis Alcapone, John Holt, Dennis Brown and Alton Ellis with varying degrees of success, but he soon realized that his older recordings would outsell his newer efforts every time and he turned to re-pressing his extensive back catalogue on single and releasing his old albums both in Jamaica and the UK. He also put together some brilliant compilations where the superb sleeve notes written by the Prince himself attack in no uncertain terms the music of the day: 'They have used guns to spoil the fun and force tasteless and meaningless music upon the land.'

Throughout the rest of the 70s and on into the 80s he lived on his shops, his juke boxes and his past glories but he returned to live work in the latter half of the 80s. He has become a crowd puller again for, as he says: 'The people know my songs and loved them.' He has even started, for the first time in years, to record new music again (1992). While it is impossible to forecast if this will prove successful or not one cannot ever take away the fact that Prince Buster's music has already inspired generations of performers. He is respected abroad - probably more than in his native Jamaica - but he will always have his place as one of the few Jamaican artists to reach directly to the international audience. Many more have played their part indirectly but his name was known both through his own recordings ('Al Capone' reached the lower regions of the UK national charts) and his work with other people. It is unlikely that any other Jamaican artist (apart from Bob Marley) still has his records regularly played and known in clubs and dances throughout the world.

Selected albums: *Judge Dread Rock Steady* (1967), *Big Five* (1972), *Wreck A Pum Pum* (1976), *She Was A Rough Rider* (1978, reissued 1988), *On Tour* (1988 - reissue date), *Judge Dread* (1991 - reissue date). Compilations: *Prince Buster's Fabulous Greatest Hits* (1980), *Fabulous Greatest Hits* (1991).

Proby, P.J.

b. James Marcus Smith, 6 November 1938, Houston, Texas, USA. This iconoclastic singer spent his early career in Hollywood, recording demos for song publishing houses. Several low-key singles ensued, credited to Jett Powers and a number of bit parts as an actor ensued, before the Proby appellation surfaced on 'So Do I' (1963). 'Powers' had already demonstrated a songwriting talent, his most notable composition being 'Clown Shoes' for Johnny Burnette in 1962. The artist came to Britain the following year, at the behest of producer Jack Good, to appear on the *Around The Beatles* television special. An ebullient revival of 'Hold Me', originally a gentle ballad, brought Proby a UK Top 3 hit, while the similarly raucous 'Together' reached number 8. Proby completely changed direction following a

P. J. Proby

continued to court publicity for erratic behaviour. In 1985 he completed two suitably eccentric versions of 'Tainted Love', previously a hit for Soft Cell which became the first of a series of contentious singles for a Manchester-based independent label. Recreations of songs by Joy Division ('Love Will Tear Us Apart') and David Bowie ('Heroes') followed, but further releases were marred by poor production and the artist's often incoherent intonation. Although years of apparent self-abuse has robbed the singer of his powers of old, he retains the ability to enthral and infuriate.

Albums: *I Am P.J. Proby* (1964), *P.J. Proby* (1965), *P.J. Proby In Twon* (1965), *Enigma* (1966), *Phenomenon* (1967), *Believe It Or Not* (1968), *Three Week Hero* (1969), *I'm Yours* (1973), *The Hero* (1981), *Clown Shoes* (1987). Compilations: as Jet Powers *California License* (1969), *Somewhere* (1975), *The Legendary P.J. Proby At His Very Best* (1986), *The Legendary P.J. Proby At His Very Best, Volume 2* (1987).

Procol Harum

Procol Harum

This UK group was formed in Essex, England following the demise of the R&B pop unit, the Paramounts, Procol Harum comprised: Gary Brooker (b. 29 May 1945, Southend, Essex, England; piano/vocals), Matthew Fisher (b. 7 March 1946, London, England; organ), Bobby Harrison (b. 28 June 1943, East Ham, London, England; drums), Ray Royer (b. 8 October 1945; guitar) and Dave Knights (b. 28 June 1945, Islington, London, England; bass). Their debut with the ethereal 'A Whiter Shade Of Pale' made them one of the biggest successes of 1967. The record has now achieved classic status with continuing sales, which now run to many millions. The long haunting Bach-influenced introduction takes the listener through a sequence of completely surreal lyrics, which epitomized the 'Summer Of Love'. 'We skipped the light fandango, turned cartwheels across the floor, I was feeling kind of seasick, the crowd called out for more'. It was followed by the impressive Top 10 hit 'Homburg'. By the time of

move to Liberty Records and, again, reached the UK Top 10 with a memorable version of 'Somewhere' from *West Side Story*. This record started a series of epic ballads featuring Proby's strong but affected vocal. Both 'I Apologise' (complete with Billy Eckstine paraphrasing) and 'Maria' (again from *West Side Story*) were big hits. Proby's biggest hit, however, was with the popular UK press. Following a 'split trousers' incident, Proby was accused of obscenity. He then made an act of regularly splitting his crushed blue velvet jumpsuit. He completed his attire during the mid-60s with a Tom Jones wig and black bow tie and baggy nightshirts. His chart career floundered with John Lennon and Paul McCartney's 'That Means A Lot', and although further immaculate productions followed with 'To Make A Big Man Cry' and the Righteous Brothers' sounding 'I Can't Make It Alone', Proby was relegated to the cabaret circuit. Although he continued to record, the press were more interested in his tax problems and subsequent bankruptcy. *Three Week Hero* won retrospective acclaim when the singer's backing group achieved fame as Led Zeppelin. In 1970, Proby took the role of Iago in *Catch My Soul*, former mentor Good's rock adaptation of *Othello*. Proby's subsequent work was more sporadic; he appeared on the UK nightclub circuit, played Elvis Presley in the stage production *Elvis On Stage* until he was sacked, and the hastily thrown together album, (only recorded in mono), the band were falling apart. Harrison and Royer departed to be replaced with Brooker's former colleagues Barrie 'B.J.' Wilson (b. 18 March 1947, Southend, Essex, England) and Robin Trower (b. 9 March 1945, London, England) respectively. The other unofficial member of the band was lyricist Keith Reid (b. 10 October 1946), whose penchant for imaginary tales of seafaring appeared on numerous albums. The particularly strong *A Salty Dog*, with its classic John Player cigarette pack cover, was released to critical acclaim.

Fisher and Knights departed and the circle was completed when Chris Copping (b. 29 August 1945, Southend, Essex, England; organ/bass) became the last remaining ex-Paramount to join. On *Broken Barricades*, in particular, Trower's Jimi Hendrix-influenced guitar patterns began to give the band a heavier image which was not compatible with Reid's introspective fantasy sagas. This was resolved by Trower's departure, to join Frankie Miller in Jude, and following the recruitment of Dave Ball (b. 30 March 1950) and the addition of Alan Cartwright (bass), the band pursued a more symphonic direction. The success of *Live In Concert With The Edmonton Symphony Orchestra* was unexpected. It marked a surge in popularity, not seen since the early days. The album contained strong versions of 'Conquistador' and 'A Salty Dog', and was a Top 5, million-selling album in the USA. Further line-up changes ensued with Ball departing and Mick Grabham (ex-Plastic Penny and Cochise) joining in 1972. This line-up became their most stable and they enjoyed a successful and busy four years during which time they released three albums. *Grand Hotel* was the most rewarding, although both the following had strong moments. 'Nothing But The Truth' and 'The Idol' were high points of *Exotic Birds And Fruit*; the latter showed traces of Keith Reid's epic work. 'Pandora's Box' was the jewel in *Procol's Ninth*, giving them another surprise hit single. By the time their final album was released in 1977 the musical climate had dramatically changed and Procol Harum were one of the first casualties of the punk and new wave movement. Having had a successful innings Gary Brooker initiated a farewell tour and Procol quietly disappeared. In the words of Keith Reid; 'they fired the gun and burnt the mast'. During 1991 the band re-formed, and unlike many reformed 'dinosaurs' the result was a well-received, album *The Prodigal Stranger*.

Albums: *Procol Harum* (1967), *Shine On Brightly* (1968), *A Salty Dog* (1969), *Home* (1970), *Broken Barricades* (1971), *In Concert With The Edmonton Symphony Orchestra* (1972), *Grand Hotel* (1973), *Exotic Birds And Fruit* (1974), *Procol's Ninth* (1975), *Something Magic* (1977), *The Prodigal Stranger* (1991).

Compilations: *The Best Of Procol Harum* (1973), *Platinum Collection* (1981), *Collection: Procol Harum* (1986).

Puckett, Gary, And The Union Gap

Originally known as the Outcasts, a San Diego act renowned for cover versions, this popular group took the name Union Gap in January 1967. Although burdened by a *passé* image - they dressed in American Civil War uniforms - 'General' Gary Puckett (b. 17 October 1942, Hibbing, Minnesota, USA; vocals), 'Sergeant' Dwight Benett (b. December 1945, San Diego, California, USA; tenor saxophone), 'Corporal' Kerry Chater (b. 7 August 1945, Vancouver, British Columbia, Canada; bass), 'Private' Gary 'Mutha' Withem (b. 22 August 1946, San Diego, California, USA; woodwind/piano) and 'Private' Paul Whitbread (b. 8 February 1946, San Diego, California, USA; drums) enjoyed considerable success through their relationship with songwriter/producer Jerry Fuller. 'Woman Woman' achieved gold status in 1967, and the following year the quintet scored three more million-sellers with 'Young Girl', a chart-topper in the US and UK, 'Lady Willpower' and 'Over You', each of which were marked by Puckett's soaring vocal line. However, the formula appeal of their highly-polished sound gradually waned and the unit disbanded in 1971.

Albums: *Woman Woman* (1968), *Young Girl* (1968), *Incredible* (1968), *The New Gary Puckett And The Union Gap Album* (1970). Solo album: *The Gary Puckett Album* (1971). Compilation: *Gary Puckett And The Union Gap's Greatest Hits* (1970).

Purify, James And Bobby

Formed in 1965, this high-powered soul duo consisted of James Purify (b. 12 May 1944, Pensacola, Florida, USA) and Robert Lee Dickey (b. 2 September 1939, Tallahassee, Florida, USA). Unfairly tarnished as a surrogate Sam And Dave, the duo's less frenetic style was nonetheless captivating. During the early 60s Dickey worked as a singer/guitarist in the Dothan Sextet, a group fronted by Mighty Sam McClain. When Florida disc jockey 'Papa' Don Schroeder offered Sam a solo career, Dickey introduced his cousin, James Purify, as a replacement. Their onstage duets became so popular that Schroeder added them to his fast-growing roster. Their first single, 'I'm Your Puppet', was recorded at Fame in Muscle Shoals and released on Bell. Written by Dan Penn and Spooner Oldham, this simple, poignant ballad became the duo's only US Top 10 hit in September 1966. Rather than follow their own path, the cousins were tempted towards cover versions including 'Shake A Tail Feather' and 'I Take What I Want'. In spite of the undoubted quality of

these releases, many critics dubbed them 'contrived'. In 1967 'Let Love Come Between Us' became their last US Top 30 hit, although several strong records followed. When Dickey retired in 1970 James found another 'Bobby' in Ben Moore and it was this new combination which secured a 1976 British hit with a remake of 'I'm Your Puppet'. Unable to sustain this rejuvenation, the duo parted, although Moore resurfaced in 1979 with a solo album, *Purified*. The pick of the original duo's Bell recordings can be found on *100% Purified Soul*.
Albums: *James And Bobby Purify* (1967), *The Pure Sound Of The Purifys* (1968), *James And Bobby Purify* (1976), *You And Me Together Forever* (1978). Compilation: *100% Purified Soul* (1988).

Purple Gang

Formed in Manchester, England, the original line-up comprised of Lucifer (b. Peter Walker; vocals/kazoo), Deejay Robinson (harmonica/mandolin), Ank Langley (jug), Geoff Bourjer (piano/washboard) and James 'Joe' Beard (guitar). All were students at Stockport College of Art. The Purple Gang achieved notoriety when 'Granny Takes A Trip', their debut single, was adopted by the English 'underground' as an unofficial anthem. Although a gentle, happy, jugband song, the 'trip' reference was taken to be about LSD, despite fervent claims by the group that this was not their intention. Joe Beard (12-string guitar), Gerry Robinson (mandolin), Geoff Bowyer (keyboards) and Lucifer completed an attendant album in the space of two days, but had split up by the time of its release. Continued interest in their anthemic single inspired a reformation in 1969, but with George Janken (bass) and Irish Alex (washboard/drums) replacing Lucifer. However, the heavy style embraced by the new unit lacked the charm of earlier acoustic, goodtime music and failed to generate interest.
Album: *The Purple Gang Strikes* (1968).

Pyramids

The Pyramids were a seven-piece, UK-based ska/rock steady band consisting of Josh Roberts, Ray Knight, Roy Barrington, Monty Naismith, Ray Ellis, Mick Thomas and Frank Pitter. A popular live attraction in Britain in the late 60s, they hit with 'Train Tour To Rainbow City', an appropriately chugging piece written and produced by Eddy Grant and bearing a close resemblance to Prince Buster's 'Train To Girls Town'. As rock steady gave way to reggae, elements of the band, including Ellis, Naismith and Thomas, resurfaced in 1969 as Symarip with 'Skinhead Moon Stomp', based on Derrick Morgan's 'Moon Hop' hit, which was one of the anthems of the skinhead era but which had to wait until its 1980 re-issue to gain a chart placing.

Albums: *Pyramids* (1968), as Symarip *Skinkead Moon Stomp* (1970).

? And The Mysterians

Formed 1963 in Texas, USA as XYZ, ? and the Mysterians entered rock 'n' roll immortality as the band which first popularized the punk-rock classic '96 Tears' in 1966. ? (Question Mark) was vocalist Rudy Martinez (b. 1945, Mexico) and, after numerous line-up changes, the Mysterians became Frankie Rodriguez, Jnr. (b. 9 March 1951, Crystal City, Texas, USA; keyboards), Robert Lee 'Bobby' Balderrama (b. 1950, Mexico; lead guitar), Francisco Hernandez 'Frank' Lugo (b. 15 March 1947, Welasco, Texas, USA; bass) and Eduardo Delgardo 'Eddie' Serrato (b. 1947, Mexico; drums). '96 Tears' was initially intended as the b-side of their debut single, first issued on the tiny Pa-Go-Go label. However, disc jockeys in Michigan, where the group had now settled, turned it over and began playing the three-chord rocker with the now-infamous lead organ line (played on a Vox, not Farfisa as legend dictates). The record was sold to the Cameo label and re-released, whereupon it became a number 1 single. The group's name invited further publicity, with ? (Martinez had changed his name legally) refusing to divulge his true identity and opaque sunglasses shielding him from recognition. The group charted with three more Cameo singles of which only 'I Need Somebody', in 1966, made any significant impact, reaching number 22 in the US charts. That single is notable in that the b-side, '8-Teen' was later a hit for Alice Cooper in 1971 after undergoing a slight title change to 'Eighteen'. Despite success with their singles and their first album, ? And The Mysterians never again came close to recapturing their brief moment of fame. '96 Tears' was incorporated into the live sets of countless 'garage bands' during the 60s, and was later revived by such artists as Eddie And The Hot Rods (1976), Garland Jeffreys (1981) and the Stranglers (1990).
Albums: *96 Tears* (1966), *Action* (1967). Compilation: *96 Tears Forever* (1985).

Quickly, Tommy

b. 7 July c.1943, Liverpool, England. A popular singer in his native Liverpool, Quickly started performing in The Challengers, a band formed with his sister. He joined Brian Epstein's management stable in 1963. A highly-publicized launch ensued, including a prestigious slot on the Beatles concurrent package tour, while his debut single, 'Tip Of My Tongue', was an exclusive, if undistinguished, John Lennon/Paul McCartney song. Quickly was subsequently teamed with the Remo Four, but although 'Kiss Me Now' echoed the chirpy pop of Gerry And The Pacemakers, the singer was unable to repeat their success. A 1964 release, 'The Wild Side Of Life', reached the Top 40, but the artist's recording career was brought to an end when the follow-up, 'Humpty Dumpty', failed to chart. During the mid-60s he became involved in drugs and developed a strong dependency. Some years ago Quickly fell from a ladder and suffered serious head injuries, causing brain damage which has severely restricted his life.

Tommy Quickly

Quicksilver Messenger Service

Of all the bands that came out of the San Francisco area during the late 60s Quicksilver typified most, the style, attitude and the sound. The original band in 1964 comprised: Dino Valenti (b. 7 November 1943, New York City, USA; vocals), John Cipollina (b. 24 August 1943, Berkeley, California, USA, d. 29 May 1989; guitar), David Freiberg (b. 24 August 1938, Boston, Massachusetts, USA; bass/vocals), Jim Murray (vocals/harmonica), Casey Sonoban (drums) and, very briefly, Alexander 'Skip' Spence (b. 18 April 1946, Windsor, Ontario, Canada; guitar/vocals), before being whisked off to join the Jefferson Airplane as drummer. Another problem which would prove to be significant in Quicksilver's development was the almost immediate arrest and imprisonment of Valenti for a drugs offence. He did not rejoin the band until late 1969. In 1965 the line-up was strengthened by the arrival of Gary Duncan (b. Gary Grubb, 4 September 1946, San Diego, California, USA; guitar) and, replacing Sonoban, Greg Elmore (b. 4 September 1946, San Diego, California, USA). Murray departed soon after their

well-received appearance at the Monterey Pop Festival in 1967. The quartet of Cipollina, Duncan, Elmore and Freiberg recorded the first two albums; both are important in the development of San Francisco rock music, as the twin lead guitars of Cipollina and Duncan made them almost unique. The second collection *Happy Trails* is now regarded as a classic. George Hunter and his Globe Propaganda company were responsible for some of the finest album covers of the 60s and *Happy Trails* is probably their greatest work. Likewise the live music within showed a spontaneity that the band were never able to recapture on subsequent recordings. The side-long suite of Bo Diddley's 'Who Do You Love' has some incredible dynamics and extraordinary interplay between the twin guitarists. Duncan departed soon after and was replaced by UK session pianist and ex-Steve Miller Band member, Nicky Hopkins. His contributions breathed some life into the disappointing *Shady Grove*, notably with the frantic 'Edward, The Mad Shirt Grinder'. *Just For Love* shows a further decline, with Valenti, now back with the band, becoming overpowering and self-indulgent. 'Fresh Air' gave them a Top 50 US hit in 1970. Cipollina departed, as did Freiberg following his arrest in 1971 for drug possession (he found a lucrative career later with Jefferson Starship). Various incarnations have appeared over the years with little or no success. As recently as 1987, Gary Duncan recorded an album carrying the Quicksilver name, but by then old Quicksilver fans were more content to purchase copies of the first two albums on compact disc.

Albums: *Quicksilver Messenger Service* (1968), *Happy Trails* (1969), *Shady Grove* (1969), *Just For Love* (1970), *What About Me* (1971), *Quicksilver* (1971), *Comin' Thru* (1972), *Solid Silver* (1975), *Maiden Of The Cancer Moon* (1983), *Peace By Piece* (1987). Compilations: *Anthology* (1973), *Sons Of Mercury* (1991).

(Young) Rascals

This expressive act, one of America's finest pop/soul ensembles, made its debut in a New Jersey club, the Choo Choo in February 1965. Felix Cavaliere (b. 29 November 1943, Pelham, New York, USA; organ/vocals), Eddie Brigati (b. 22 October 1946, New York City, USA; vocals/percussion) and Dino

Danelli (b. 23 July 1945, New York City, USA; drums) were each established musicians on the city's R&B circuit, serving time in several popular attractions, including Joey Dee And The Starlighters. It was here the trio encountered Gene Cornish (b. 14 May 1946, Ottawa, Canada; vocals/guitar), who became the fourth member of a breakaway group, initially dubbed Felix And The Escorts, but later known as the Young Rascals. The quartet enjoyed a minor hit with 'I Ain't Gonna Eat Out My Heart Anymore' before securing a US number 1 with the energetic 'Good Lovin''. Despite a somewhat encumbering early image - knickerbockers and choir-boy shirts - the group's soulful performances endeared them to critics and peers, earning them a 'group's group' sobriquet. Now established as one of the east coast's most influential attractions, spawning a host of imitators from the Vagrants to Vanilla Fudge, the Young Rascals secured their biggest hit with 'Groovin''. This melancholic performance became an international hit, signalling a lighter, more introspective approach, and although Brigati was featured on the haunting 'How Can I Be Sure', a US Top 5 entry, Cavaliere gradually became the group's focal point. In 1968 the group dropped its 'Young' prefix and enjoyed a third US number 1 with 'People Got To Be Free'. An announcement that every Rascals' live appearance must also include a black act enforced the group's commitment to civil rights, but effectively banned them from southern states. The quartet later began exploring jazz-based compositions, and although remaining respected, lost much of their commercial momentum. Brigati and Cornish left the group in 1971, and although newcomers Buzzy Feiten (guitar), Ann Sutton (vocals) and Robert Popwell (drums) contributed to final albums, Peaceful World and Island Of Real, the Rascals were clearly losing momentum and broke up the following year. Felix Cavaliere then enjoyed a moderate solo career while Danelli and Cornish formed Bulldog and Fotomaker. The three musicians were reunited in 1988 for an extensive US tour.
Albums: The Young Rascals (1966), Collections (1966), Groovin' (1967), Once Upon A Dream (1968), Freedom Suite (1969), Search And Nearness (1969), See (1970), Peaceful World (1971), Island Of Real (1972). Selected compilations: Timepeace - The Rascals' Greatest Hits (1968), Star Collection (1973), Searching For Ecstasy - The Rest Of The Rascals 1969-1972 (1988).

Rawls, Lou

b. 1 December 1935, Chicago, Illinois, USA. Briefly a member of the acclaimed gospel group, the Pilgrim Travellers, this distinctive singer began forging a secular career following his move to California in 1958. An association with Sam Cooke culminated in 'Bring It On Home To Me', where the Rawls'

throaty counterpoint punctuated his colleague's sweet lead vocal. Lou's own recordings showed him comfortable with either small jazz combos or cultured soul, while an earthier perspective was shown on his 1965 release, Live!. He scored two Top 20 singles with 'Love Is A Hurtin' Thing' (1966) and 'Dead End Street' (1967), and enjoyed further success with a 1969 reading of Mabel John's 'Your Good Thing (Is About To End)'. Several attempts were made to mould Rawls into an all-round entertainer, but while his early 70s work was generally less compulsive, the singer's arrival at Philadelphia International signalled a dramatic rebirth. 'You'll Never Find Another Love Like Mine', an international hit in 1976, matched the classic Philly sound with Rawl's almost plumby delivery and prepared the way for a series of exemplary releases including 'See You When I Git There' (1977) and 'Let Me Be Good To You' (1979). The singer maintained his association with producers Gamble And Huff into the next decade. His last chart entry, 'I Wish You Belonged to Me', came in 1987 on the duo's self-named label, since when he has recorded for the jazz outlet, Blue Note. Rawls has also pursued an acting career and provided the voice for several Budweiser beer commercials.
Albums: Lou Rawls Sings, Les McCann Ltd Plays Stormy Monday (1962), Black And Blue (1963), Tobacco Road (1963), Nobody But Lou Rawls (1965), Lou Rawls And Strings (1965), Live! (1966), Soulin' (1966), Merry Christmas Ho! Ho! (1965), Carryin' On (1966), Too Much! (1967), That's Lou (1967), Merry Christmas Ho! Ho! Ho! (1967), Feeling Good (1968), You're Good For Me (1968), The Way It Was - The Way It Is (1969), Your Good Thing (1969), You Made Me So Very Happy (1970), Bring It On Home To Me (1970) Natural Man (1971), Silk And Soul (1972), All Things In Time (1976), Unmistakably Lou (1977), When You Hear Lou, You've Heard It All (1977), Live (1978), Let Me Be Good To You (1979), Sit Down And Talk To Me (1980), Shades Of Blue (1981), Now Is The Time (1982), When The Night Comes (1983), Close Company (1984), Love All Your Blues Away (1986), At Last (1989). There are also several compilations, including: 'Live' The Best Of Lou Rawls (1968), Soul Serenade (1985), Stormy Monday (1985), Classic Soul (1986).

Redding, Otis

b. 9 September 1941, Dawson, Georgia, USA, d. 10 December 1967. The son of a Baptist minister, Redding assimilated gospel music during his childhood and soon became interested in jump blues and R&B. After resettling in Macon, he became infatuated with local luminary, Little Richard, and began singing on a full-time basis. A high-school friend and booking agent, Phil Walden, then became his manager. Through Walden's contacts Redding joined Johnny Jenkins And The Pinetoppers as a sometime singer and occasional driver. Redding also began recording for sundry local independents and his debut single, 'She's Alright', credited to Otis And The Shooters, was quickly followed by 'Shout Bamalama'. Both performances were firmly in the Little Richard mould. The singer's fortunes blossomed when one of his own songs, 'These Arms Of Mine', was picked up for the Stax subsidiary, Volt. Recorded at the tail end of a Johnny Jenkins session, this aching ballad crept into the American Hot 100 in May 1963. Further poignant releases, 'Pain In My Heart', 'That's How Strong My Love Is' and 'I've Been Loving You Too Long', were balanced by brassy, uptempo performances including 'Mr. Pitiful', 'Respect' and 'Fa Fa Fa Fa Fa Fa (Sad Song)'. He remained something of a cult figure until 1965 and the release of the magnificent *Otis Blue* in which original material nestled beside the Rolling Stones' 'Satisfaction' and two songs by a further mentor, Sam Cooke. Redding's version of the Temptations' 'My Girl' then became a UK hit, while the singer's popularity was further enhanced by the visit of the *Hit The Road Stax* revue in 1967. 'Tramp', a duet with Carla Thomas, also provided success while Redding's production company, Jotis, was responsible for launching Arthur Conley. A triumphant appearance at the Monterey Pop Festival suggested that Redding was about to attract an even wider following but tragedy struck on 10 December 1967. The light aircraft in which he was travelling plunged into Lake Monona, Madison, Wisconsin, killing the singer, his valet, the pilot and four members of the Bar-Kays. The wistful '(Sittin' On) The Dock Of The Bay', a song Redding recorded just three days earlier, became his only million-seller and US pop number 1. The single's seeming serenity, as well as several posthumous album tracks, suggested a sadly unfulfilled maturity. Although many now point to Redding's limited range, his emotional drive remains compelling, while the songs he wrote, often with guitarist Steve Cropper, stand among soul's most lasting moments. Redding is rightly regarded as a giant of soul music.

Albums: *Pain In My Heart* (1964), *The Great Otis Redding Sings Soul Ballads* (1965), *Otis Blue/Otis Redding Sings Soul* (1965), *The Soul Album* (1966), *Complete And Unbelievable ... The Otis Redding Dictionary Of Soul* (1966), *Live In Europe* (1966), with Carla Thomas *The King & Queen* (1967), *Here Comes Some Soul From Otis Redding And Little Joe Curtis* (1967, pre-1962 recordings), *The Dock Of The Bay* (1968), *The Immortal Otis Redding* (1968), *Otis Redding In Person At The Whiskey A Go Go* (1968), *Love Man* (1969), *Tell The Truth* (1970), *Monterey International Pop Festival* (1970), *Live Otis Redding* (1982). Selected compilations: shared with Jimi Hendrix *The History Of Otis Redding* (1967), *The Best*

Of Otis Redding (1972), *Pure Otis* (1979), *Come To Me* (1984), *Dock Of The Bay - The Definitive Collection* (1987), *The Otis Redding Story* (1989, 4 album box-set).

Otis Redding

Reeves, Martha

b. Martha Reeves, 18 July 1941, Alabama, USA. Reeves was schooled in both gospel and classical music, but it was vocal group R&B that caught her imagination. She began performing in the late 50s under the name Martha Lavaille, briefly joining the Fascinations and then the Del-Phis. In 1961 she joined the fledgling Motown organization in Detroit, where she served as secretary to William Stevenson in the A&R department. Her other duties included supervizing Little Stevie Wonder during office hours, and singing occasional backing vocals on recording sessions. Impressed by the power and flexibility of her voice, Berry Gordy offered her the chance to record for the label. She reassembled the Del-Phis quartet as the Vels for a single in 1962, and later that year she led the group on their debut release under a new name, Martha And The Vandellas. From 1963 onwards, they became one of Motown's most successful recording outfits, and Reeves' strident vocals were showcased on classic hits like 'Heat Wave', 'Dancing In The Street' and 'Nowhere To Run'. She was given individual credit in front of the group from 1967 onwards, but their career was interrupted the following year when she was taken seriously ill, and had to retire from performing. Fully recovered, Reeves emerged in 1970 with a new line-up of Vandellas. After two years of episodic success, she reacted bitterly to Motown's decision to relocate from Detroit to Hollywood, and fought a legal battle to be released from her contract. The eventual settlement entailed that she lost the use of the Vandellas' name, but left her free to sign a solo contract with MCA in 1973. Her debut album was the result of lengthy recording sessions with producer Richard Perry. It gained much critical acclaim but was commercially disappointing, failing to satisfy either rock or soul fans with its hybrid style. Moving to Arista Records in 1977, she was submerged by the late 70s disco boom on a series of albums that allowed her little room to display her talents. Her subsequent recording deals have been unproductive, and since the early 80s she has found consistent work on package tours featuring former Motown artists. During the late 80s she toured with a 'fake' Vandellas before being reunited with the original group (Annette Sterling and Rosalind Holmes) on Ian Levine's Motor City label. They released 'Step Into My Shoes' in 1989 while ex-Vandella Lois Reeves also recorded for Levine's label.

Albums: *Martha Reeves* (1974), *The Rest Of My Life* (1977), *We Meet Again* (1978), *Gotta Keep Moving* (1980).

Reparata And The Delrons

Schoolfriends Mary Aiese, Nanette Licari, Anne Fitzgerald and Regina Gallagher began performing together in 1962. Dubbed the Del-Rons in honour of the Dell-Vikings and Del-Satins, they appeared at dances in their Brooklyn neighbourhood before Mary realigned the group around Carol Drobinicki, Sheila Reille, Kathy Romeo and Margi McGuire. The last was asked to leave when the unit acquired a recording deal which in turn engendered 'Whenever A Teenager Cries'. This light, but plaintive offering topped the local New York chart, but although it only rose to number 60 nationally, the single - credited to Reparata And The Delrons - nonetheless secured the trio's reputation. With Mary taking the lead spot, the group underwent further alterations when original member Licari and newcomer Lorraine Mazzola replaced Reille and Romeo. Although commercial success eluded them, the revitalized trio recorded a series of excellent singles, including the Jeff Barry-penned 'I'm Nobody's Baby Now' and 'I Can Hear The Rain', which featured Melba Moore on backing vocals. Despite continued apathy at home the trio enjoyed a major UK hit when the excellent 'Captain Of Your Ship' reached number 13 in 1968. Paradoxically the vocal line featured Mazzola, who assumed the name Reparata when Mary Aiese retired in 1970. Mazzola, Licari and newcomer Cookie Sirico completed the concept album, *1970 Rock 'N' Roll Revolution*, which contained various 'girl-group' classics, before disbanding in 1973. Mazzola later appeared in Lady Flash, the backing group to Barry Manilow, but her continued use of the name Reparata was challenged by Aiese who reclaimed the appellation for a series of solo singles, of which 'Shoes' reached the UK Top 50 in 1975.

Albums: *Whenever A Teenager Cries* (1965), *1970 Rock 'N' Roll Revolution* (1970).

Paul Revere And The Raiders

Revere, Paul, And The Raiders

Formed in Portland, Oregon, USA in 1961, when pianist Revere added Mark Lindsay (vocals/saxophone) to the line-up of his club band, the Downbeats. Drake Levin (guitar), Mike Holliday (bass) and Michael Smith (drums) completed a group later known as Paul Revere And The Nightriders, before settling on their Raiders appellation. Several locally-issued singles ensued, including 'Beatnik Sticks' and 'Like Long Hair', the latter of which rose into the US Top 40. Group manager and disc jockey Roger Hart then financed a demonstration tape which in turn engendered a prestigious recording deal with CBS/Columbia. Their version of bar-band favourite 'Louie Louie' was issued in 1963, but although highly successful regionally, was outsold by local rivals the Kingsmen who secured the national hit. A year passed before the Raiders recorded a new single, during which time Phil Volk had replaced Holliday. 'Louie Go Home' showed their confidence remained undiminished, but it was 1965 before the Raiders hit their commercial stride with the punky 'Steppin' Out'. By this point the group was the resident act on *Where The Action Is*, Dick Clark's networked, daily television show. The attendant exposure resulted in a series of classic pop singles, including 'Just Like Me' (1965) 'Kicks', 'Hungry', 'Good Things' (all 1966) and 'Him Or Me - What's It Gonna Be' (1967), each of which were impeccably produced by Terry Melcher. However, the Raiders' slick stage routines and Revolutionary War garb - replete with thigh-boots, tights, frilled shirts and three-cornered hats - was frowned upon by the emergent underground audience. The departures of Smith, Levin and Volk made little difference to the Raiders' overall sound, enhancing suspicion that session musicians were responsible for the excellent studio sound. Later members Freddie Weller (guitar), Keith Allison (bass) and Joe (Correro) Jnr. (drums) were nonetheless accomplished musicians, and thus enhanced the professional approach marking *Hard &*

Heavy (With Marshmallow) and *Collage*. Despite inconsistent chart places, the group maintained a high television profile as hosts of *Happening 68*. In 1969 Lindsay embarked on a concurrent solo career, but although 'Arizona' sold over 1 million copies, later releases proved less successful. Two years later the Raiders scored an unexpected US chart-topper with 'Indian Reservation', previously a UK hit for Don Fardon, but it proved their final Top 20 hit. Although Weller forged a new career in country music, Revere and Lindsay struggled to keep the group afloat, particularly when dropped by their longstanding label. The former eventually became the act's custodian, presiding over occasional releases for independent outlets. The Raiders flourished briefly during the US Bicentennial celebrations, before emerging again in 1983 mixing old favourites and new songs on their Raiders America label. This regeneration proved short-lived, although Revere still fronts a version of the group for the nostalgia circuit.

Albums: *Paul Revere And The Raiders* aka *In The Beginning* (1961), *Like, Long Hair* (1961), *Here They Come* (1965), *Just Like Us* (1965), *Midnight Ride* (1966), *The Spirit Of 67* aka *Good Thing* (1967), *Revolution* (1967), *A Christmas Present....And Past* (1967), *Goin' To Memphis* (1968), *Something Happening* (1968), *Hard And Heavy (With Marshmallow)* (1969), *Alias Pink Puzz* (1969), *Collage* (1970), *Indian Reservation* (1971), *Country Wine* (1972). Compilations: *Greatest Hits* (1967), *Greatest Hits Volume 2* (c.60s), *All-Time Greatest Hits* (c.70s), *Kicks* (1982).

Rhinoceros

A rock band that promised more than it was able to deliver, Rhinoceros was an Elektra Records' signing of the late 60s. The group looked a formidable line-up on paper with Michael Fonfara, ex-Electric Flag (keyboards), Billy Mundi, ex-Mothers Of Invention (drums), Doug Hastings, ex-Buffalo Springfield (guitar), Danny Weis, ex-Iron Butterfly (guitar) and John Finlay (vocals). The spectacular fold out cover artwork on their debut by G. Sazaferin showed a brightly colourful, beaded Rhinoceros. Unfortunately the music was disappointing, only the Buddy Miles influenced 'You're My Girl (I Don't Want To Discuss It)' and their 'greatest hit' the instrumental 'Apricot Brandy' stood out. The BBC adopted the latter as a Radio 1 theme. Two more albums followed, but by now the ponderous Rhinoceros had turned into a dodo.

Albums: *Rhinoceros* (1968), *Satin Chickens* (1969), *Better Times Are Coming* (1970).

Richard, Cliff

b. Harry Roger Webb, 14 October 1940, Lucklow, India. One of the most popular and enduring talents

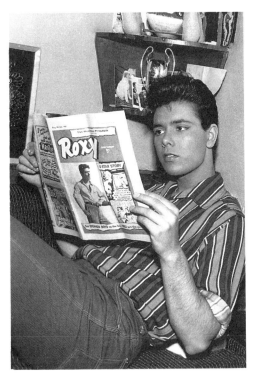

Cliff Richard

in the history of UK showbusiness, Richard began his career as a rock 'n' roll performer in 1957. His fascination for Elvis Presley encouraged him to join a skiffle group and several months later he teamed up with drummer Terry Smart and guitarist Ken Payne to form the Drifters. They played at various clubs in the Cheshunt/Hoddesdon area of Hertfordshire before descending on the famous 2Is coffee bar in London's Old Compton Street. There they were approached by lead guitarist Ian Samwell and developed their act as a quartet. In 1958, they secured their big break in the unlikely setting of a Saturday morning talent show at the Gaumont cinema in Shepherd's Bush. It was there that the senatorial theatrical agent George Ganyou recognized Cliff's sexual appeal and singing abilities and duly financed the recording of a demonstration tape of 'Breathless' and 'Lawdy Miss Clawdy'. A copy reached the hands of EMI producer Norrie Paramor who was impressed enough to grant the ensemble an audition. Initially, he intended to record Richard as a solo artist backed by an orchestra, but the persuasive performer insisted upon retaining his own backing group. With the assistance of a couple of session musicians, the unit recorded the American teen ballad 'Schoolboy Crush' as a projected first single. An acetate of the recording was paraded around Tin Pan Alley and came to the attention of the influential television producer Jack

Good. It was not the juvenile 'Schoolboy Crush' which captured his attention, however, but the Ian Samwell b-side 'Move It'. Good reacted with characteristically manic enthusiasm when he heard the disc, rightly recognizing that it sounded like nothing else in the history of UK pop. The distinctive riff and unaffected vocal seemed authentically American, completely at odds with the mannered material that usually emanated from British recording studios. With Good's ceaseless promotion, which included a full-page review in the music paper *Disc*, Cliff's debut was eagerly anticipated and swiftly rose to number 2 in the UK charts. Meanwhile, the star made his debut on Good's television showcase *Oh Boy!*, and rapidly replaced Marty Wilde as Britain's premier rock 'n' roll talent. The low-key role offered to the Drifters persuaded Samwell to leave the group to become a professional songwriter, and by the end of 1958 a new line-up emerged featuring Hank B. Marvin and Bruce Welch. Before long, they changed their name to the Shadows, in order to avoid confusion with the black American R&B group, the Drifters.

Meanwhile, Richard consolidated his position in the rock 'n' roll pantheon, even outraging critics in true Elvis Presley fashion. The *New Musical Express* denounced his 'violent, hip-swinging' and 'crude exhibitionism' and pontificated: 'Tommy Steele became Britain's teenage idol without resorting to this form of indecent, short-sighted vulgarity'. Critical mortification had little effect on the screaming female fans who responded to the singer's boyish sexuality with increasing intensity.

1959 was a decisive year for Richard and a firm indicator of his longevity as a performer. With management shake-ups, shifts in national musical taste and some distinctly average singles his career could easily have been curtailed, but instead he matured and transcended his Presley-like beginnings. A recording of Lionel Bart's 'Living Doll' provided him with a massive UK number 1 and three months later he returned to the top with the plaintive 'Travellin' Light'. He also starred in two films, within 12 months. *Serious Charge*, a non-musical drama, was banned in some areas as it dealt with the controversial subject of homosexual blackmail. The Wolf Mankowitz directed *Expresso Bongo*, in which Richard played the delightfully named Bongo Herbert, was a cinematic pop landmark, brilliantly evoking the rapacious world of Tin Pan Alley. It remains one of the most revealing and humorous films ever made on the music business and proved an interesting vehicle for Richard's varied talents.

From 1960 onwards Richard's career progressed along more traditional lines leading to acceptance as a middle-of-the-road entertainer. Varied hits such as the breezy, chart-topping 'Please Don't Tease', the

rock 'n' rolling 'Nine Times Out Of Ten' and reflective 'Theme For A Dream' demonstrated his range, and in 1962 he hit a new peak with 'The Young Ones'. A glorious pop anthem to youth, with some striking guitar work from Hank Marvin, the song proved one of his most memorable number 1 hits. The film of the same name was a charming period piece, with a strong cast and fine score. It broke box office records and spawned a series of similar movies from its star, who was clearly following Elvis Presley's cinematic excursions as a means of extending his audience. Unlike the King, however, Richard supplemented his frequent movie commitments with tours, summer seasons, regular television slots and even pantomime appearances. The run of UK Top 10 hits continued uninterrupted until as late as mid-1965. Although the showbiz glitz had brought a certain aural homogeneity to the material, the catchiness of songs like 'Bachelor Boy', 'Summer Holiday', 'On The Beach' and 'I Could Easily Fall' was undeniable. These were neatly, if predictably, complemented by ballad releases such as 'Constantly', 'The Twelfth Of Never' and 'The Minute You're Gone'.

The formula looked likely to be rendered redundant by the British beat boom, but Richard expertly rode that wave, even improving his selection of material along the way. He bravely, though relatively unsuccessfully, covered a Rolling Stones song, 'Blue Turns To Grey', before again hitting top form with the beautifully melodic 'Visions'. During 1966, he had almost retired after converting to fundamentalist Christianity, but elected to use his singing career as a positive expression of his faith. The sparking 'In The Country' and gorgeously evocative 'The Day I Met Marie' displayed the old strengths to the full, but in the swiftly changing cultural climate of the late 60s, Richard's hold on the pop charts could no longer be guaranteed. The 1968 Eurovision Song Contest offered him a chance of further glory, but the jury placed him a close second with the 'oom-pah-pah'-sounding 'Congratulations'. The song was nevertheless a consummate Eurovision performance and proved one of the biggest UK number 1s of the year. Immediately thereafter, Cliff's chart progress declined and his choice of material proved at best desultory. Although there were a couple of solid entries, Raymond Froggatt's 'Big Ship' and a superb duet with Hank Marvin 'Throw Down A Line', Richard seemed a likely contender for Variety as the decade closed.

The first half of the 70s saw him in a musical rut. The chirpy but insubstantial 'Goodbye Sam, Hello Samantha' was a Top 10 hit in 1970 and heralded a notable decline. A second shot at the Eurovision Song Contest with 'Power To All Our Friends' brought his only other Top 10 success of the period and it was widely assumed that his chart career was spent. However, in 1976 there was a surprise resurgence in his career when Bruce Welch of the Shadows was assigned to produce his colleague. The sessions resulted in the best-selling album *I'm Nearly Famous*, which included two major hits 'Miss You Nights' and 'Devil Woman'. The latter was notable for its decidedly un-Christian imagery and the fact that it gave Richard a rare US chart success. Although Welch remained at the controls for two more albums, time again looked as though it would kill off Richard's perennial chart success. A string of meagre singles culminated in the dull 'Green Light' which stalled at number 57, his lowest chart placing since he started singing. Coincidentally, his backing musicians, Terry Britten and Alan Tarney, had moved into songwriting and production at this point and encouraged him to adopt a more contemporary sound on the album *Rock 'N' Roll Juvenile*. The most startling breakthrough however was the attendant single 'We Don't Talk Anymore', written by Tarney and produced by Welch. An exceptional pop record, which gave the singer his first UK number 1 hit in over a decade and also reached the Top 10 in the US. The 'new' Richard sound, so refreshing after some of his staid offerings in the late 70s, brought further well arranged hits, such as 'Carrie' and 'Wired For Sound', and ensured that he was a chart regular throughout the 80s.

Although he resisted the temptation to try anything radical, there were subtle changes in his musical approach. One feature of his talent that emerged during the 80s was a remarkable facility as a duettist. Collaborations with Olivia Newton-John, Phil Everly, Sarah Brightman, Sheila Walsh, Elton John and Van Morrison added a completely new dimension to his career. It was something of a belated shock to realize that Richard may be one of the finest harmony singers working in the field of popular music. His perfectly enunciated vocals and the smooth texture of his voice have the power to complement work that he might not usually tackle alone.

The possibility of his collaborating with an artist even further from his sphere than Van Morrison remains a tantalizing challenge. Throughout his three decades in the pop charts, Cliff has displayed a valiant longevity. He parodied one of his earliest hits with comedy quartet the Young Ones and registered yet another number 1; he appeared in the stage musical *Time*; he sang religious songs on gospel tours; he sued the *New Musical Express* for an appallingly libellous review far more vicious than their acerbic comments back in 1958; he was decorated by the Queen; and he celebrated his 50th birthday with a move into social commentary with the anti-war hit 'From A Distance'. And so he goes on. Richard has outlasted every

musical trend of the past four decades with a sincerity and commitment that may well be unmatched in his field. He is British pop's most celebrated survivor.

Selected albums: *Cliff* (1959), *Cliff Sings* (1959), *Me And My Shadows* (1960), *Listen To Cliff* (1961), *21 Today* (1961), *The Young Ones* (1961), *32 Minutes And 17 Seconds With Cliff Richard* (1962), *Summer Holiday* (1963), *Cliff's Hit Album* (1963), *When In Spain* (1963), *Wonderful Life* (1964), *Aladdin And His Wonderful Lamp* (1964), *Cliff Richard* (1965), *More Hits By Cliff* (1965), *When In Rome* (1965), *Love Is Forever* (1965), *Kinda Latin* (1966), *Finders Keepers* (1966), *Cinderella* (1967), *Don't Stop Me Now* (1967), *Good News* (1967), *Cliff In Japan* (1968), *Two A Penny* (1968), *Established 1958* (1968), *The Best Of Cliff* (1969), *Sincerely Cliff* (1969), *It'll Be Me* (1969), *Cliff 'Live' At The Talk Of The Town* (1970), *All My Love* (1970), *About That Man* (1970), *Tracks 'N' Grooves* (1970), *His Land* (1970), *Cliff's Hit Album* (1971), *The Cliff Richard Story* (1972), *The Best Of Cliff Volume 2* (1972), *Take Me High* (1973), *Help It Along* (1974), *The 31st Of February Street* (1974), *Everybody Needs Somebody* (1975), *I'm Nearly Famous* (1976), *Cliff Live* (1976), *Every Face Tells A Story* (1977), *Small Corners* (1977), *Green Light* (1978), *Thank You Very Much* (1979), *Rock 'N' Roll Juvenile* (1979), *40 Golden Greats* (1979), *Rock On With Cliff* (1980), *The Cliff Richard Songbook* (1980), *Listen To Cliff* (1980), *I'm No Hero* (1980), *Love Songs* (1981), *Wired For Sound* (1981), *Now You See Me, Now You Don't* (1982), *Dressed For The Occasion* (1983), *Silver* (1983), *Cliff In The 60s* (1984), *Cliff And The Shadows* (1984), *Walking In The Light* (1984), *The Rock Connection* (1984), *Time* (1986), *Hymns And Inspirational Songs* (1986), *Always Guaranteed* (1987), *Private Collection* (1988).

Richards, Ron

From a UK music publishing background, Richards entered the realm of record production in the 50s as George Martin's A&R lieutenant at Parlophone. Although the label specialized in variety and comedy, Richards and his boss strove to transform it into a viable pop label. Among discoveries given specifically to Richards were Shane Fenton And The Fentones, Judd Proctor, Paul Raven (later, Gary Glitter) and the Clyde Valley Stompers. Some of these artists had hits, but a bigger feather in Richards' cap during this period was overseeing an Ella Fitzgerald session. Plus, a fact not greatly appreciated at the time, taking charge of the Beatles recording debut for EMI, until an intrigued Martin assumed responsibility. Entirely Richards' doing was the 1963 signing to Parlophone of the Hollies who, under his aegis, survived Merseybeat's collapse as the most distinguished northern group (other than the Beatles) - and the vehicle on 1965's 'I'm Alive'. That year, he also produced P.J. Proby and, while remaining a stalwart of EMI's Abbey Road complex, left the firm to join Martin's Associated Independent Recording (AIR) company, with whom CBS's New Seekers emerged as his most renowned clients as, gradually, he came to work more as an administrator than a studio functionary.

Righteous Brothers

Despite their professional appellation, Bill Medley (b. 19 September 1940, Santa Anna, California, USA) and Bobby Hatfield (b. 10 August 1940, Beaver Dam, Wisconsin, USA) were not related. They met in 1962 at California's Black Derby club, where they won the approbation of its mixed-race clientele. By blending Medley's sonorous baritone to Hatfield's soaring high tenor, this white duo's vocal style invoked that of classic R&B, and a series of excellent singles, notably 'Little Latin Lupe Lu', followed. They achieved national fame in 1964 following several appearances on US television's highly-popular *Shindig*. Renowned producer Phil Spector then signed the act to his Philles label and proceeded to mould his 'Wagerian' sound to their dramatic intonation. 'You've Lost That Lovin' Feelin'' justifiably topped the US and UK charts and is rightly lauded as one the greatest pop singles of all time. A similar passion was extolled on 'Just Once In My Life' and 'Ebb Tide', but the relationship between performer and mentor rapidly soured. The Righteous Brothers moved outlets in

1966, but despite gaining a gold disc for '(You're My) Soul And Inspiration', a performance modelled on their work with Spector, the duo was unable to sustain the same success. They split in 1968, with Medley beginning a solo career and Hatfield retaining the name with new partner Jimmy Walker, formerly of the Knickerbockers. This short-lived collaboration ended soon afterwards, but the original pair were reunited in 1974 for an appearance on *The Sonny And Cher* Comedy Hour. They scored a US Top 3 hit that year with the maudlin 'Rock 'n' Roll Heaven', but were unable to regain former glories and have subsequently separated and reformed on several occasions. In 1987 Medley enjoyed an international smash with '(I've Had) The Time Of My Life', a duet with Jennifer Warnes taken from the film *Dirty Dancing*, while a reissue of 'Unchained Melody', a hit for the Righteous Brothers in 1965, topped the UK chart in 1990 when culled from the soundtrack of the film *Ghost*.

Albums: *The Righteous Brothers - Right Now* (1963), *Blue-Eyed Soul* (1965), *This Is New* (1965), *You've Lost That Lovin' Feelin'* (1965), *Just Once In My Life* (1965), *Back To Back* (1966), *Go Ahead And Cry* (1966), *Soul And Inspiration* (1966), *Sayin' Somethin'* (1967), *Souled Out* (1967), *Standards* (1967), *One For The Road* (1968), *Rebirth* (1970), *Kingston Rock* (1974), *Give It To The People* (1974), *Sons Of Mrs Righteous* (1975). Compilations: *The Best Of The Righteous Brothers* (1965), *In Action* (1966), *Greatest Hits* (1967), *Greatest Hits Volume 2* (c.70s), *2 By 2* (1973), *Best Of The Righteous Brothers* (1987).

Rip Chords

One of the first rock groups signed to Columbia Records in the USA, the Rip Chords were best known for a 'hot rod' hit in early 1964, 'Hey Little Cobra', which reached the Top 5 just as the Beatles broke through in the USA. The group's records were actually the work of singer/producer Terry Melcher, and singer Bruce Johnston, later of the Beach Boys. However, that duo did not represent the Rip Chords in concerts; a completely different set of musicians was sent out on the road. The Rip Chords were an already-existing group in 1963, including Phil Stewart, Ernie Bringas, Arnie Marcus and Rich Rotkin. Stewart and Bringas approached Melcher, a staff producer at Columbia, and were signed to the label. Their first single, 'Here I Stand', was a minor chart hit in 1963, as was 'Gone', written by Melcher and Johnston and featuring the latter on background vocals. Melcher and Johnston heard 'Hey Little Cobra', written by former Teddy Bears member Annette Kleinbard under the name Carol Connors, and recorded it themselves. Although the pair had planned to record under the name Bruce and Terry, they decided to release the record under the Rip

Righteous Brothers

Chords' name, since that group already had appeared in the charts. The single shot to number 4. *Hey Little Cobra And Other Hot Rod Hits*, was recorded in 1964, featuring Melcher and Johnston singing on nearly half the tracks. Another car-orientated single, 'Three Window Coupe', by Jan Berry of Jan And Dean and Roger Christian, was a Top 30 hit in the summer of 1964 and was followed with an album of the same name, which also featured Melcher and Johnston on most of the tracks. After one final chart single, 'One Piece Topless Bathing Suit', Melcher turned down the Brian Wilson composition 'Help Me Rhonda' for the Rip Chords and took on more production for Columbia, most notably for Paul Revere And The Raiders and the Byrds. From that point on the Rip Chords ceased to exist.
Albums: *Hey Little Cobra And Other Hot Rod Hits* (1964), *Three Window Coupe* (1964).

Robinson, Smokey

b. William Robinson, 19 February 1940, Detroit, USA. A founding member of the Miracles at Northern High School, Detroit, in 1955, Robinson became one of the leading figures in the local music scene by the end of the decade. His flexible tenor voice, which swooped easily into falsetto, made him the group's obvious lead vocalist, and by 1957 he was composing his own variations on the R&B hits of the day. That year he met Berry Gordy, who was writing songs for R&B star Jackie Wilson, and looking for local acts to produce. Vastly impressed by Robinson's affable personality and promising writing talent, Gordy took the teenager under his wing. He produced a series of Miracles singles in 1958 and 1959, all of which featured Smokey as composer and lead singer, and leased them to prominent R&B labels. In 1960 he signed the Miracles to his Motown stable, and began to groom Robinson as his second-in-command. In Motown's early days, Robinson was involved in every facet of the company's operations, writing, producing and making his own records, helping in the business of promotion and auditioning many of the scores of young hopefuls who were attracted by Gordy's growing reputation as an entrepreneur. Robinson had begun his career as a producer by overseeing the recording of the Miracles' 'Way Over There', and soon afterwards he was charged with developing the talents of Mary Wells and the Supremes. Wells soon became Robinson's most successful protegee: Smokey wrote and produced a sophisticated series of hit singles for her between 1962 and 1964. These records, like 'You Beat Me To The Punch', 'Two Lovers' and 'My Guy', demonstrated his growing confidence as a writer, able to use paradox and metaphor to transcend the usual banalities of the teenage popular song. A measure of Robinson's influence over Wells' career is

the fact that she was unable to repeat her chart success after she elected to leave Motown, and Robinson, in 1964.
Although Robinson was unable to turn the Supremes into a hit-making act, he experienced no such failure in his relationship with Motown's leading male group of the mid-60s, the Temptations. Between 1964 and 1965, Smokey was responsible for the records that established their reputation, writing lyrical and rhythmic songs of a calibre which few writers in pop music have equalled since. 'The Way You Do The Things You Do' set the hit sequence in motion, followed by the classic ballad 'My Girl' (later equally popular in the hands of Otis Redding), the dance number 'Get Ready', 'Since I Lost My Baby' and the remarkable 'It's Growing', which boasted a complex lyric hinged around a series of metaphorical images. During the same period, Robinson helped to create two of Marvin Gaye's most enduring early hits, 'Ain't That Peculiar' and 'I'll Be Doggone'. Throughout the 60s, Smokey Robinson combined this production and A&R work with his own career as leader of the Miracles. He married fellow group member Claudette Rogers in 1959, and she provided the inspiration for Miracles hits like 'You've Really Got A Hold On Me' and 'Oooh Baby Baby'. During the mid-60s, Robinson was apparently able to turn out high-quality songs to order, working with a variety of collaborators including fellow Miracle Ronnie White, and Motown guitarist Marv Tarplin. As the decade progressed, Bob Dylan referred to Robinson apparently without irony, as 'America's greatest living poet': as if to justify this assertion, Robinson's lyric writing scaled new heights on complex ballads like 'The Love I Saw In You Was Just A Mirage' and 'I Second That Emotion'. From 1967 onwards, Robinson was given individual credit on the Miracles' releases. For the next two years, their commercial fortunes went into a slide, which was righted when their 1965 recording of 'The Tracks Of My Tears' became a major hit in Britain in 1969, and the four-year-old 'The Tears Of A Clown' achieved similar success on both sides of the Atlantic in 1970. At the end of the decade, Smokey briefly resumed his career as a producer and writer for other acts, collaborating with the Marvelettes on 'The Hunter Gets Captured By The Game', and the Four Tops on 'Still Water'. Business concerns were occupying an increasing proportion of his time, however, and in 1971 he announced that he would be leaving the Miracles the following year, to concentrate on his role of Vice-President of the Motown corporation. A year after the split, Smokey launched his solo career, scoring a hit single with 'Sweet Harmony', an affectionate tribute to his former group, and issuing the excellent *Smokey*. The album included the epic 'Just My Soul Responding', a biting piece of social

comment about the USA's treatment of blacks and American Indians.

Robinson maintained a regular release schedule through the mid-70s, with one new album arriving every year. Low-key and for the most part lushly produced, they made little impact on the market, though Robinson's songwriting was every bit as consistent as it had been in the 60s. He continued to break new lyrical ground, striking the banner for non-macho male behaviour on 1974's 'Virgin Man', and giving name to a new style of soft soul on 1975's *A Quiet Storm*. Singles like 'Baby That's Backatcha' and 'The Agony And The Ecstasy' sold well on the black market, but failed to achieve national airplay in the States, while in Britain Robinson was recorded as a left-over from the classic era of Motown. His first film soundtrack project, *Big Time* in 1977, won little praise, and it appeared as if his creative peak was past. Instead, he hit back in 1979 with 'Cruisin'', his biggest chart success since 'The Tears Of A Clown' nine years earlier. A sensuous ballad in the musical tradition of his 60s work, the record introduced a new eroticism into his writing, and restored faith in his stature as a contemporary performer. Two years later, he scored his first UK number 1 with 'Being With You', a touching love song which came close to equalling that achievement in the States. 'Tell Me Tomorrow' enjoyed more Stateside success in 1982, and Robinson settled into another relaxed release schedule, which saw him ride out the 80s on a pattern of regular small hits and consistent album sales. Smokey was contributing significantly less new material, however, and his 1988 autobiography, *Smokey*, revealed that he had been battling against cocaine addiction for much of the decade. Although his marriage to Claudette failed, he returned to full health and creativity, and enjoyed two big hits in 1987, 'Just To See Her' and 'One Heartbeat'. Voted into the Rock And Roll Hall Of Fame in 1988, Smokey Robinson is now one of the senior figures in popular music, a writer and producer still best remembered for his outstanding work in the 60s, but who has seldom betrayed the responsibility of that legacy since then.

Albums: *Smokey* (1973), *Pure Smokey* (1974), *A Quiet Storm* (1975), *Smokey's Family Robinson* (1976), *Deep In My Soul* (1977), *Big Time* (1977), *Love Breeze* (1978), *Smokin'* (1978), *Where There's Smoke?* (1979), *Warm Thoughts* (1980), *Being With You* (1981), *Yes It's You Lady* (1982), *Touch The Sky* (1983), *Blame It On Love* (1984), *Essar* (1984), *Smoke Signals* (1985), *One Heartbeat* (1987), *Love, Smokey* (1990).

Further reading: *Smokey*, Smokey Robinson with David Ritz.

Rock Steady

The rock steady era ran from approximately 1965-68,

although it is almost impossible to pinpoint when ska actually became rock steady in the frantic, frenetic atmosphere of Jamaican music, and certain records such as Peter Tosh's 'I'm The Toughest', the Wailers' 'Rasta Put It On' and Alton Ellis And The Flames' 'Cry Tough' were rock steady records but made before the genre was defined as such. Far slower and less urgent than ska it actually allowed vocalists to show what they could really do and consequently singers (and their songs) became far more important than they had been previously. The best of Duke Reid's output for the rock steady period serves as a definition of all that the music was capable of. The Treasure Isle's house band Tommy McCook And The Supersonics set the standard for others to follow and while many other producers made excellent rock steady records none were able to match the Duke's consistency and popularity although Coxsone Dodd often came close. The shift of emphasis away from costly horn sections meant that many more people could now afford to become involved in record production, and many new producers began to make their mark. When the melodic prominence gave way to the electric (as opposed to the stand up) bass the direction that the music would take for the next 25 years was very clearly defined.

Albums: Alton Ellis *Hottest Hits Volume One*, *Hottest Hits Volume Two*, *Mr Soul Of Jamaica*, various artists *Rock Steady Coxsone Style*, *Get Ready Rock Steady*.

Rockin' Berries

This early 60s UK pop quintet comprised Clive Lea (b. 16 February 1942, Birmingham, England; vocals), Geoffrey Turton (b. 11 March 1944, Birmingham, England; guitar), Bryan Charles 'Chuck' Botfield (b. 11 November 1943, Birmingham, England; guitar), Roy Austin (b. 27 December 1943, Birmingham, England; guitar) and Terry Bond (b. 22 March 1943, Birmingham, England; drums). After beginning as an R&B cover group, they fell under the spell of visiting American Kim Fowley, who suggested they cover the Tokens' US hit 'He's In Town'. The song hit the Top 5 in late 1964 and was followed by two other hits, 'What In The World's Come Over You' (not the Jack Scott song of the same name) and an excellent reading of the Reflections' 'Poor Man's Son', with Lea and Turton on counter vocals. Like several of their contemporaries, the Berries quickly laid the foundations for a career in cabaret by including comedy sketches and parodic impressions of other artists into their act. A minor hit with 'The Water Is Over My Head' in July 1966 concluded their chart run. By 1968 Turton had embarked on a solo career as Jefferson, while the group continued on the timeless supper club circuit.

Album: *In Town* (1965). Compilation: *Bowl Of Rockin' Berries* (1988).

Roe, Tommy

b. 9 May 1942, Atlanta, Georgia, USA. Vocalist Roe began his career with high school act, the Satins. The group performed several of his compositions, notably 'Sheila', which they recorded in 1960. The single was unsuccessful, but Roe revived the song two years later upon securing a solo deal. This Buddy Holly-influenced rocker topped the US chart, and reached the Top 3 in Britain where the artist enjoyed considerable popularity. Roe scored two Top 10 hits in 1963 with 'The Folk Singer' and 'Everybody' and, although not a major chart entry, 'Sweet Pea' garnered considerable airplay through the auspices of pirate radio. The song reached the US Top 10, as did its follow-up, 'Hooray For Hazel', but Roe's biggest hit came in 1969 when 'Dizzy' topped the charts on both sides of the Atlantic. The singer enjoyed further success with 'Heather Honey' and 'Jam Up Jelly Tight', but for much of the 70s he opted to pursue a low-key career in his home state. Roe did attempt a 'comeback' with *Energy* and *Full Bloom*, but subsequently plied the nostalgia circuit. Memories of his past success were resurrected when 'Dizzy' returned to the top of the UK charts in 1992 in a version by the Wonder Stuff and Vic Reeves.
Albums: *Sheila* (1963), *Something For Everybody* (1963), *Sweet Pea* (1966), *It's Now A Winter's Day* (1967), *Phantasia* (1967), *Dizzy* (1969), *We Can Make Music* (1970), *Energy* (1976), *Full Bloom* (1977). Compilations: *12 In A Roe* (1970), *Greatest Hits* (1970), *Beginnings* (1971), *16 Greatest Hits* (1976).

Rogers, Julie

b. Julie Rolls, 6 April 1943, London, England. She left her Bermondsey secondary school in 1959 for a long working holiday as a dancer in Spain. Next, she worked as a secretary and then a ship's stewardess before becoming singer with a middle-of-the-road band led by Teddy Foster with whom she would later function in a cabaret duo, and, under a new stage surname, made a radio debut in 1962 on the BBC Light Programme's *Music With A Beat*. Following an audition for Philips A & R manager Johnny Franz, she recorded her first single 'It's Magic', in 1963. Her recording career touched its zenith the following year when 'The Wedding' - an orchestrated translation of a song (by Argentinian Joaquin Prieto) which she had first heard in Spain - rose to a UK number 3, triggered by an initial plug on the ITV television regional magazine, *Day By Day*. As well as generating huge sheet music sales, it also disturbed the US Top Ten, despite two previous hit versions in 1961 by Anita Bryant and Malcolm Vaughan. The yuletide follow-up, 'Like A Child' and 1965's 'Hawaiian Wedding Song' were only minor hits, but Rogers remained in demand on the variety circuit for the rest of the decade.

Rolling Stone

Former student Jann Wenner founded *Rolling Stone* in partnership with Ralph J. Gleason, a seasoned jazz and rock columnist and a writer of beautiful prose. First published in San Francisco in 1967, the magazine drew its early inspiration from the city's considerable underground movement which encompassed both musical and visual arts. However, Wenner shrewdly avoided ephemeral trappings and, although chronicling the counter culture, his publication maintained an editorial distance bordering on ambivalence. *Rolling Stone* was also expertly designed and its conventional layout, mirroring that of the 'establishment' press, ascribed it an air of authority. It also demonstrated that hippies could actually deliver (the typography, notably its use of dropped capitals was quite brilliant). The magazine also exploited a niche in America's publishing market and while the UK boasted **New Musical Express** and **Melody Maker,** the US had no comparable outlet for pop and rock journalism. Wenner thus attracted a generation of writers, including Greil Marcus, Ed Ward and Lester Bangs, whose passion for music was matched by their literacy. *Rolling Stone* was uniquely informative, its record reviews were studious and well-argued, while the *Rolling Stone* Interview became a byword for lengthy, detailed examinations of musicians, their work and overall philosophies. Two interviews with John Lennon, wherein he demolished the sanctity surrounding the Beatles, established the format as a vehicle for controversial subjects and while helping generate wider interest in the publication, marked the end of its wholehearted dalliance with music. Being featured on the cover was as important as being on the front of *Time* or *Newsweek* and Dr Hook brilliantly capitalized on this with the amusing 'Cover Of The *Rolling Stone*' which reached the US Top 3. Not surprisingly they were featured a few weeks afterwards! Other facets, notably politics, began to encroach on its editorial space, particularly those surrounding the ill-fated McGovern presidential campaign of 1972, and the magazine drew plaudits for several sterling examples of brave reportage, notably its dogged pursuit of the truth surrounding the death of nuclear worker Karen Silkwood (1974).
Although readers welcomed the amphetamine-paced writings of Hunter S. Thompson, long-time critics bemoaned an increasingly perfunctory coverage of rock - film stars and media figures began attracting a greater percentage of covers - but the flaccid state of US 70s music did little to inspire strong journalism. *Rolling Stone*'s relocation to New York in 1977 provided the final break with the past and while Wenner's brainchild had long-since achieved a respectability, the magazine had become merely a cypher rather than a kernel. By the 80s its most

popular issues were devoted to single topics; fashion, live concerts, the 100 best albums. Its days of controversy ended.

Further reading: *The Rolling Stone Story*, Robert Draper.

Rolling Stones

Originally billed as the Rollin' Stones, the first line-up of this immemorial English 60s group was a nucleus of Mick Jagger (b. Michael Philip Jagger, 26 July 1943, Dartford, Kent, England; vocals), Keith Richard (b. Keith Richards, 18 December 1943, Dartford, Kent, England; guitar), Brian Jones (b. Lewis Brian Hopkin-Jones, 26 February 1942, Cheltenham, Gloucestershire, England, d. 3 July 1969; rhythm guitar) and Ian Stewart (b. 1938, d. 12 December 1985; piano). Jagger and Richard were primary school friends who resumed their camaraderie in their closing teenage years after finding they had a mutual love for R&B and particularly the music of Chuck Berry, Muddy Waters and Bo Diddley. Initially, they were teamed with bassist Dick Taylor (later of the Pretty Things) and before long their ranks extended to include Jones, Stewart and occasional drummer Tony Chapman. Their patron at this point was the renowned musician Alexis Korner, who had arranged their debut gig at London's Marquee club on 21 July 1962. In their first few months the group met some opposition from jazz and blues aficionados for their alleged lack of musical 'purity' and the line-up remained unsettled for several months.

In late 1962 bassist Bill Wyman (b. William Perks, 24 October 1936, Plumstead, London, England) replaced Dick Taylor while drummers came and went including Carlo Little (from Screaming Lord Sutch's Savages) and Mick Avory (later of the Kinks, who was billed as appearing at their debut gig, but didn't play). It was not until as late as January 1963 that Charlie Watts reluctantly surrendered his day job and committed himself to the group. After securing a residency at Giorgio Gomelsky's Crawdaddy Club in Richmond, the Stones' live reputation spread rapidly through London's hip cognoscenti. One evening, the flamboyant Andrew Loog Oldham appeared at the club and was so entranced by the commercial prospects of Jagger's sexuality that he wrested them away from Gomelsky and, backed by the financial and business clout of agent Eric Easton, became their manager. Within weeks, Oldham had produced their first couple of official recordings at IBC Studios. By this time, record company scouts were on the prowl with Decca's Dick Rowe leading the march and successfully signing the group. After re-purchasing the IBC demos, Oldham selected Chuck Berry's 'Come On' as their debut. The record was promoted on the prestigious UK television pop programme

Thank Your Lucky Stars and the Stones were featured sporting matching hounds-tooth jackets with velvet collars. This was to be one of Oldham's few concessions to propriety for he would soon be pushing the boys as unregenerate rebels. Unfortunately, pianist Ian Stewart was not deemed sufficiently pop star-like for Oldham's purpose and was unceremoniously removed from the line-up, although he remained road manager and occasional pianist. After supporting the Everly Brothers, Little Richard, Gene Vincent and Bo Diddley on a Don Arden UK package tour, the Stones released their second single, a gift from John Lennon and Paul McCartney entitled 'I Wanna Be Your Man'. The disc fared better than its predecessor climbing into the Top 10 in January 1964. That same month the group enjoyed their first bill-topping tour supported by the Ronettes.

The early months of 1964 saw the Stones catapulted to fame amid outrage and controversy about the surliness of their demeanour and the length of their hair. This was still a world in which the older members of the community were barely coming to terms with the Beatles neatly-groomed mop tops. While newspapers asked 'Would you let your daughter marry a Rolling Stone?', the quintet engaged in a flurry of recording activity which saw the release of an EP and an album both titled *The Rolling Stones*. The discs consisted almost exclusively of extraneous material and captured the group at their most derivative stage. Already, however, there were strong signs of an ability to combine different styles. The third single, 'Not Fade Away', saw them fuse Buddy Holly's quaint original with a chunky Bo Diddley beat that highlighted Jagger's vocal to considerable effect. The presence of Phil Spector and Gene Pitney at these sessions underlined how hip the Stones had already become in the music business after such a short time. With the momentum increasing by the month, Oldham characteristically over-reached himself by organizing a US tour which proved premature and disappointing. After returning to the UK, the Stones released a decisive cover of the Valentinos' 'It's All Over Now', which gave them their first number 1. A best-selling EP, *Five By Five*, cemented their growing reputation, while a national tour escalated into a series of near riots with scenes of hysteria wherever they played. There was an ugly strain to the Stones' appeal which easily translated into violence. At the Winter Gardens Blackpool the group hosted the most astonishing rock riot yet witnessed on British soil. Frenzied fans displayed their feelings for the group by smashing chandeliers and demolishing a Steinway grand piano. By the end of the evening over 50 people were escorted to hospital for treatment. Other concerts were terminated within minutes of the group appearing on-stage and the hysteria continued throughout Europe. A return to the USA saw them disrupt the stagey *Ed Sullivan Show* prompting the presenter to ban rock 'n' roll groups in temporary retaliation. In spite of all the chaos at home and abroad, America remained resistant to their appeal, although that situation would change dramatically in the New Year.

In November 1964, 'Little Red Rooster' was released and entered the *New Musical Express* chart at number 1, a feat more usually associated with the Beatles and, previously, Elvis Presley. The Stones now had a formidable fan base and their records were becoming more accomplished and ambitious with each successive release. Jagger's accentuated phrasing and posturing stage persona made 'Little Red Rooster' sound surprisingly fresh while Brian Jones's use of slide guitar was imperative to the single's success. Up until this point, the group had recorded cover versions as a-sides, but manager Andrew Oldham was determined that they should emulate the example of Lennon/McCartney and locked them in a room until they emerged with satisfactory material. Their early efforts, 'It Should Have Been You' and 'Will You Be My Lover Tonight?' (both recorded by the late George Bean) were bland, but Gene Pitney scored a hit with the emphatic 'That Girl Belongs To Yesterday' and Jagger's girlfriend Marianne Faithfull became a teenage recording star with the moving 'As Tears Go By'. 1965 proved the year of the international breakthrough and three extraordinary self-penned number 1 singles. 'The Last Time' saw them emerge with their own distinctive rhythmic style and underlined an ability to fuse R&B and pop in an enticing fashion. America finally succumbed to their spell with '(I Can't Get No) Satisfaction', a quintessential pop lyric with the still youthful Jagger sounding like a jaundiced roué. Released in the UK during the 'summer of protest songs', the single encapsulated the restless weariness of a group already old before its time. The distinctive riff, which Keith Richard invented with almost casual dismissal, became one of the most famous hook lines in the entire glossary of pop and was picked up and imitated by a generation of garage groups thereafter. The 1965 trilogy of hits was completed with the engagingly surreal 'Get Off Of My Cloud' in which Jagger's surly persona seemed at its most pronounced to date. As well as the number 1 hits of 1965, there was also a celebrated live EP, *Got Live If You Want It* which reached the Top 10 and, *The Rolling Stones No. 2* that continued the innovative idea of not including the group's name on the front of the sleeve. There was also some well documented bad boy controversy when Jagger, Jones and Wyman were arrested and charged with urinating on the wall of an East London petrol station. Such scandalous behaviour merely reinforced the public's already ingrained view of the Stones as juvenile degenerates.

With the notorious Allen Klein replacing Eric Easton as Oldham's co-manager, the Stones consolidated their success by renegotiating their Decca contract. Their single output in the USA simultaneously increased with the release of a couple of tracks unavailable in single form in the UK. The sardonic put-down of suburban valium abuse, 'Mother's Little Helper' and the Elizabethan-styled 'Lady Jane', complete with atmospheric dulcimer, displayed their contrasting styles to considerable effect. Both these songs were included on their fourth album, *Aftermath*. A breakthrough work in a crucial year, the recording revealed the Stones as accomplished rockers and balladeers, while their writing potential was emphasized by Chris Farlowe's chart-topping cover of 'Out Of Time'. There were also signs of the Stones' inveterate misogyny particularly on the cocky 'Under My Thumb' and an acerbic 'Stupid Girl'. Back in the singles chart, the group's triumphant run continued with the startlingly chaotic '19th Nervous Breakdown' in which frustration, impatience and chauvinism were brilliantly mixed with scale-sliding descending guitar lines. 'Paint It Black' was even stronger, a raga-influenced piece with a lyric so doom-laden and defeatist in its imagery that it is a wonder that the angry performance sounded so passionate and urgent. The Stones' nihilism reached its peak on the extraordinary 'Have You Seen Your Mother Baby, Standing In The Shadow?', a scabrous-sounding solicitation taken at breathtaking pace with Jagger spitting out a diatribe of barely coherent abuse. It was probably the group's most adventurous production to date, but its acerbic sound, lengthy title and obscure theme contributed to rob the song of sufficient commercial potential to continue the chart-topping run. Ever outrageous, the group promoted the record with a photo session in which they appeared in drag, thereby adding a clever, sexual ambivalence to their already iconoclastic public image.

1967 saw the Stones' anti-climactic escapades confront an establishment crackdown. The year began with an accomplished double a-sided single, 'Let's Spend The Night Together'/'Ruby Tuesday' which, like the Beatles' 'Penny Lane'/'Strawberry Fields Forever', narrowly failed to reach number 1 in their home country. The accompanying album, *Between The Buttons*, trod water and also represented Oldham's final production. Increasingly alienated by the Stones' bohemianism, he would move further away from them in the ensuing months and surrender the management reins to his partner Klein later in the year. On 12 February, Jagger and Richard were arrested at the latter's West Wittering home 'Redlands' and charged with drugs offences. Three months later, increasingly unstable Brian Jones was raided and charged with similar offences. The Jagger/Richard trial in June was a cause célèbre which culminated in the notorious duo receiving heavy fines and a salutary prison sentence. Judicial outrage was tempered by public clemency, most effectively voiced by *The Times*' editor William Rees-Mogg who, borrowing a phrase from Pope, offered an eloquent plea in their defence under the leader title, 'Who Breaks A Butterfly On A Wheel?' Another unexpected ally was rival group the Who, who rallied to the Stones' cause by releasing a single coupling 'Under My Thumb' and 'The Last Time'. The sentences were duly quashed on appeal in July, with Jagger receiving a conditional discharge for possession of amphetamines. Three months later, Brian Jones tasted judicial wrath with a nine-month sentence and suffered a nervous breakdown before seeing his imprisonment rescinded at the end of the year.

The flurry of drug busts, court cases, appeals and constant media attention had a marked effect on the Stones' recording career which was severely curtailed. During their summer of impending imprisonment, they released the fey 'We Love You', complete with slamming prison cell doors in the background. It was a weak, flaccid statement rather than a rebellious rallying cry. The image of the cultural anarchists cowering in defeat was not particularly palatable to their fans and even with all the publicity, the single barely scraped into the Top 10. The eventful year ended with the Stones' apparent answer to *Sgt Pepper's Lonely Hearts Club Band* — the extravagantly-titled *Their Satanic Majesties Request*. Beneath the exotic 3-D cover was an album of psychedelic/cosmic experimentation bereft of the R&B grit that had previously been synonymous with the Stones' sound. Although the album had some strong moments, it had the same inexplicably placid inertia of 'We Love You', minus notable melodies or a convincing direction. The overall impression conveyed was that in trying to compete with the Beatles' experimentation, the Stones had somehow lost the plot. Their drug use had channelled them into laudable experimentation but simultaneously left them open to accusations of having 'gone soft'. The revitalization of the Stones was demonstrated in the early summer of 1968 with 'Jumpin' Jack Flash', a single that rivalled the best of their previous output. The succeeding album, *Beggars Banquet*, produced by Jimmy Miller, was also a return to strength and included the socio-political 'Street Fighting Man' and the brilliantly macabre 'Sympathy For The Devil', in which Jagger's seductive vocal was backed by hypnotic Afro-rhythms and dervish yelps.

While the Stones were re-establishing themselves, Brian Jones was falling deeper into drug abuse. A conviction in late 1968 prompted doubts about his availability for US tours and in the succeeding months he contributed less and less to recordings and became increasingly jealous of Jagger's leading role in the group. Richard's wooing and impregnation of Jones' girlfriend Anita Pallenberg merely increased the tension. Matters reached a crisis point in June 1969 when Jones officially left the group. The following month he was found dead in the swimming pool of the Sussex house that had once belonged to writer A.A. Milne. The official verdict was 'death by misadventure'. A free concert at London's Hyde Park two days after his death was attended by a crowd of 250,000 and became a symbolic wake for the tragic youth. Jagger released thousands of butterfly's and narrated a poem by Shelley for Brian. Three days later, Jagger's former love Marianne Faithfull attempted suicide. This was truly the end of the first era of the Rolling Stones.

The group played out the last months of the 60s with a mixture of vinyl triumph and further tragedy. The sublime 'Honky Tonk Women' kept them at number 1 for most of the summer and few would have guessed that this was to be their last UK chart topper. The new album, *Let It Bleed* (a parody of the Beatles' *Let It Be*) was an exceptional work spearheaded by the anthemic 'Gimme Shelter' and revealing strong country influences ('Country Honk'), startling orchestration ('You Can't Always Get What You Want') and menacing blues ('Midnight Rambler'). It was a promising debut from John Mayall's former guitarist Mick Taylor, who had replaced Jones only a matter of weeks before his death. Even while *Let It Bleed* was heading for the top of the album charts, however, the Stones were singing out the 60s to the backdrop of a Hells Angels' killing of a black man at the Altamont Festival in California. The tragedy was captured on film in the grisly *Gimme Shelter* movie released the following year. After the events of 1969, it was not surprising that the group had a relatively quiet 1970. Jagger's contrasting thespian outings reached the screen in the form of *Performance* and *Ned Kelly* while Jean-Luc Goddard's tedious portrait of the group in the studio was delivered on *One Plus One*. For a group who had once claimed to make more challenging and gripping films than the Beatles and yet combine artistic credibility with mass appeal, it all seemed a long time coming.

After concluding their Decca contract with a bootleg-deterring live album, *Get Yer Ya-Ya's Out*, the Stones established their own self-titled label. The first release was a three track single, 'Brown Sugar'/'Bitch'/'Let It Rock', which contained some of their best work, but narrowly failed to reach number 1 in the UK. The lead track contained a quintessential Stones riff: insistent, undemonstrative and stunning, with the emphatic brass work of Bobby Keyes embellishing Jagger's vocal power. The new album, *Sticky Fingers* was as consistent as it was accomplished, encompassing the bluesy 'You Gotta Move', the thrilling 'Moonlight Mile', the wistful 'Wild Horses' and the chilling 'Sister Morphine', one the most despairing drug songs ever written. The entire album was permeated by images of sex and death, yet the tone of the work was neither self-indulgent nor maudlin. The group's playful fascination with sex was further demonstrated on the elaborately designed Andy Warhol sleeve which featured a waist-view shot of a figure clad in denim, with a real zip fastener which opened to display the lips and tongue motif that was shortly to become their corporate image. Within a year of *Sticky Fingers*, the group returned with a double album, *Exile On Main Street*. With Keith Richard firmly in control, the group were rocking-out on a series of quick-fire songs. The album was severely criticized at the time of its release for its uneven quality but was subsequently re-evaluated favourably, particularly in contrast to their later work.

The Stones' soporific slide into the 70s mainstream probably began during 1973 when their jet-setting was threatening to upstage their musical endeavours. Jagger's marriage and Richard's confrontations with the law took centre stage while increasingly average albums came and went. *Goat's Head Soup* was decidedly patchy but offered some strong moments and brought a deserved US number 1 with the imploring 'Angie'. 1974's 'It's Only Rock 'n' Roll' proved a better song title than a single, while the undistinguished album of the same name saw the group reverting to Tamla Motown for the Temptations' 'Ain't Too Proud To Beg'.

The departure of Mick Taylor at the end of 1974 was followed by a protracted period in which the group sought a suitable replacement. By the time of their next release, *Black And Blue*, former *Faces* guitarist Ronnie Wood was confirmed as Taylor's successor. The album showed the group seeking a possible new direction playing variants on white reggae, but the results were less than impressive.

By the second half of the 70s the gaps in the Stones' recording and touring schedules were becoming wider. The days when they specially recorded for the singles market were long past and considerable impetus had been lost. Even big rallying points, such as the celebrated concert at Knebworth in 1976, lacked a major album to promote the show and served mainly as a greatest hits package.

By 1977, the British music press had taken punk to its heart and the Stones were dismissed as champagne-swilling old men, who had completely lost touch with their audience. The Clash effectively summed up the mood of the time with their slogan 'No Elvis, Beatles, Stones' in '1977'.

Against the odds, the Stones responded to the challenge of their younger critics with a comeback album of remarkable power. *Some Girls* was their most consistent work in years, with some exceptional high-energy workouts, not least the breathtaking 'Shattered'. The disco groove of 'Miss You' brought them another US number 1 and showed that they could invigorate their repertoire with new ideas that worked. Jagger's wonderful pastiche of an American preacher on the mock country 'Far Away Eyes' was another unexpected highlight. There was even an attendant controversy thanks to some multi-racist chauvinism on the title track, not to mention 'When The Whip Comes Down' and 'Beast Of Burden'. Even the cover jacket had to be re-shot because it featured unauthorized photos of the famous, most notably actresses Lucille Ball, Farrah Fawcett and Raquel Welch. To conclude a remarkable year, Keith Richard escaped what seemed an almost certain jail sentence in Toronto for drugs offences and was merely fined and ordered to play a couple of charity concerts. As if in celebration of his release and reconciliation with his father, he reverted to his original family name Richards. In the wake of Richards' reformation and Jagger's much-publicized and extremely expensive divorce from his model wife Bianca, the Stones reconvened in 1980 for *Emotional Rescue*, a rather lightweight album dominated by Jagger's falsetto and over-use of disco rhythms. Nevertheless, the album gave the Stones their first UK number 1 since 1973 and the title track was a Top 10 hit on both sides of the Atlantic. Early the following year a major US tour (highlights of which were included on *Still Life*) garnered enthusiastic reviews, while a host of repackaged albums reinforced the group's legacy. 1981's *Tattoo You* was essentially a crop of old outtakes but the material was anything but stale. On the contrary, the album was surprisingly strong and the concomitant single 'Start Me Up' was a reminder of the Stones at their 60s best, a time when they were capable of producing classic singles at will. One of the Stones' cleverest devices throughout the 80s was their ability to compensate for average work by occasional flashes of excellence. The workmanlike *Undercover*, for example, not only boasted a brilliantly menacing title track ('Undercover Of The Night') but one of the best promotional videos of the period. While critics continually questioned the group's relevance, the Stones were still releasing worthwhile work, albeit in smaller doses.

A three-year silence on record was broken by *Dirty Work* in 1986, which saw the Stones sign to CBS Records and team up with producer Steve Lillywhite. Surprisingly, it was not a Stones original that produced the expected offshoot single hit, but a cover of Bob And Earl's 'Harlem Shuffle'. A major record label signing often coincides with a flurry of new work, but the Stones were clearly moving away from each other creatively and concentrating more and more on individual projects. Wyman had already tasted some chart success in 1983 with the biggest solo success from a Stones' number, 'Je Suis Un Rock Star' and it came as little surprise when Jagger issued his own solo album, *She's The Boss*, in 1985. A much publicized-feud with Keith Richards led to speculation that the Rolling Stones story had come to an anti-climactic end, a view reinforced by the appearance of a second Jagger album, *Primitive Cool*, in 1987. When Richards himself released the first solo work of his career in 1988, the Stones' obituary had virtually been written. As if to confound the obituarists, however, the Stones reconvened in 1989 and announced that they would be working on a new album and commencing a world tour. Later that year the hastily-recorded *Steel Wheels* appeared and the critical reception was generally good. 'Mixed Emotions' and 'Rock And A Hard Place' were radio hits while 'Continental Drift' included contributions from the master musicians of Joujouka, previously immortalized on vinyl by the late Brian Jones. After nearly 30 years in existence, the Rolling Stones began the 90s with the biggest grossing international tour of all time, and ended speculation about their future by reiterating their intention of playing on indefinitely. The world's greatest rock band is a title that is likely to stick.

Albums: *The Rolling Stones* (1964), *The Rolling Stones* (1965), *Out Of Our Heads* (1965), *Aftermath* (1966), *Between The Buttons* (1967), *Their Satanic Majesties Request* (1967), *Beggars Banquet* (1968), *Let It Bleed* (1969), *Get Yer Ya-Ya's Out!* (1970), *Sticky Fingers* (1971), *Exile On Main Street* (1972), *Goat's Head Soup* (1973), *It's Only Rock 'N' Roll* (1974), *Black And Blue* (1976), *Love You Live* (1977), *Some Girls* (1978), *Emotional Rescue* (1980), *Tattoo You* (1981), *Still Life (American Concerts 1981)* (1982), *Undercover* (1983), *Dirty Work* (1986), *Steel Wheels* (1989). Additional US albums include: *December's Children (And Everybody's)* (1965), *Got Live If You Want It!* (1966). Various compilation and archive albums have also been issued.

Further reading: *Stones Touring Party*, Robert Greenfield. *Up And Down With The Rolling Stones*, Tony Sanchez. *The Rolling Stones - The First Twenty Years*, David Dalton. *The Stones*, Philip Norman. *The True Adventures Of The Rolling Stones*, Stanley Booth.

Ronettes

Veronica 'Ronnie' Bennett (b. 10 August 1943, New York, USA), her sister Estelle (b. 22 July 1944, New York, USA) and cousin Nedra Talley (b. 17 January 1946, New York, USA) began their career as a dance act the Dolly Sisters. By 1961 they had become the resident dance troupe at the famed Peppermint Lounge, home of the twist craze, and having taken tuition in harmony singing, later secured a recording deal. The trio's first single, 'I Want A Boy', was credited to Ronnie And The Relatives, but when 'Silhouettes' followed in 1962, the Ronettes appellation was in place. They recorded four singles for the Colpix/May group and appeared on disc jockey Murray The K's *Live From The Brooklyn Fox* before a chance telephone call resulted in their signing with producer Phil Spector. Their first collaboration, the majestic 'Be My Baby' defined the girl-group sound as Spector constructed a cavernous accompaniment around Ronnie's plaintive, nasal voice. The single reached the Top 5 in the US and UK before being succeeded by the equally worthwhile 'Baby I Love You', another Top 20 entrant in both countries. The producer's infatuation with Ronnie - the couple were later married - resulted in some of his finest work being reserved for her and although ensuing singles, including 'The Best Part of Breaking Up', 'Walking In The Rain' (both 1964) and 'Is This What I Get For Loving You' (1965), failed to emulate the Ronettes' early success, they are among the finest pop singles of all time. The group's career was shelved during Spector's mid-60s 'retirement', but they re-emerged in 1969 with 'You Came, You Saw You Conquered'. Credited to 'The Ronettes Featuring The Voice Of Veronica', this excellent single was nonetheless commercially moribund and Ronnie's aspirations were again sublimated. She separated from Spector in 1973 and joined Buddah Records, founding a new group with vocalists Denise Edwards and Chip Fields. Ronnie And The Ronettes made their debut that year with 'Lover Lover', before changing their name to Ronnie Spector and the Ronettes for 'I Wish I Never Saw The Sunshine', an impassioned remake of a song recorded by the original line-up, but which remained unissued until 1976. The unit's name was then dropped as its lead singer pursued her solo ambitions.

Albums: *Presenting The Fabulous Ronettes Featuring Veronica* (1964), *The Ronettes Featuring Veronica* (1965). Compilations: *The Ronettes Sing Their Greatest Hits* (1975), *The Colpix Years 1961-63* (1987).

Rooftop Singers

Cashing in on the folk music revival of the early 60s, the Rooftop Singers were a trio specifically assembled for the purpose of recording a single song, 'Walk Right In', originally recorded in 1930 by Gus Cannon And The Jugstompers. The Rooftop Singers consisted of Erik Darling (b. 25 September 1933, Baltimore, Maryland, USA), Bill Svanoe and former Benny Goodman band vocalist, Lynne Taylor. Darling had played in folk groups called the Tune Tellers and the Tarriers, the latter including future actor Alan Arkin, and replaced Pete Seeger in the

Weavers in 1958, remaining with them for four years. In 1962 he heard 'Walk Right In' and adapted the lyrics for a more modern sound, utilizing two 12-string guitars and an irresistible rhythm; he then assembled the trio and signed with Vanguard Records. 'Walk Right In' became that label's, and the group's, only number 1 record. The Rooftop Singers placed one album and two other folk songs in the US charts: 'Tom Cat' and 'Mama Don't Allow'. The group disbanded in 1967 and Taylor died the same year; Darling and Svanoe subsequently retired from the music business.

Albums: *Walk Right In!* (1963), *Goodtime* (1964), *Rainy River* (1965).

Rose, Tim

b. September 1940. A one-time student priest and navigator for the USAF Strategic Air Command, Rose began his professional music career playing guitar with the Journeymen, a folk group active in the early 60s which featured John Phillips and Scott McKenzie. He subsequently joined Cass Elliott and James Hendricks in another formative attraction, the Big Three. Although initially based in Chicago, the trio later moved to New York, where Rose forged a career as a solo singer on the group's disintegration in 1964. A gruff stylist and individual, he was turned down by Elektra and Mercury before securing a deal with Columbia. A series of majestic singles then followed, including 'Hey Joe' (1966) and 'Morning Dew' (1967). Rose's slow, brooding version of the former was the inspiration for that of Jimi Hendrix, while the latter, written by Rose and folksinger Bonnie Dobson, was the subject of cover versions by, among others, Jeff Beck and the Grateful Dead. *Tim Rose* was assembled from several different sessions, but the presence of several crack session musicians - Felix Pappalardi (bass/piano), Bernard Purdie (drums) and Hugh McCracken (guitar) - provided a continuity. The set included a dramatic reading of 'I'm Gonna Be Strong', previously associated with Gene Pitney, and the haunting anti-war anthem 'Come Away Melinda', already recorded by the Big Three, on which Rose's blues-soaked, gritty voice was particularly effective. The singer's next release, 'Long Haired Boys', was recorded in the UK under the aegis of producer Al Kooper, before Rose returned to the USA to complete *Through Rose Coloured Eyes* (1969). This disappointing album lacked the strength of its predecessor and the artist was never again to scale the heights of his early work. He switched outlets to Capitol for *Love, A Kind Of Hate Story*, before the disillusioned performer abandoned major outlets in favour of the Playboy label where his manager's brother was employed. The promise of artistic freedom was fulfilled when Gary Wright of Spooky Tooth, a group Rose revered, produced the ensuing sessions. The album, also entitled *Tim Rose*, contained a version of the Beatles' 'You've Got To Hide Your Love Away' performed at a snail's pace. It was not a commercial success and the singer again left for the UK where he believed audiences were more receptive. Resident in London, Rose undertook a series of live concerts with fellow exile Tim Hardin, but this ill-fated partnership quickly collapsed. *The Musician*, released in 1975, revealed a voice which retained its distinctive power, but an artist without definite direction. Little has been heard from Rose for many years.

Albums: *Tim Rose* (1967), *Through Rose Coloured Eyes* (1969), *Love, A Kind Of Hate Story* (1970), *Tim Rose* (1972), *The Musician* (1975).

Rotary Connection

Formed in 1967, Rotary Connection was a Chicago, USA-based group mixing art-rock and soul. The group was assembled by Marshall Chess, son of Chess Records founder Leonard Chess. Looking to update the company's image, Marshall Chess chose several hip-looking singers and musicians, intending to keep the group's membership revolving with each new recording. The original Rotary Connection included pianist/arranger Charles Stepney, who co-produced with Chess, guitarist/vocalist Bobby Simms, bassist/vocalist Mitch Aliotta, drummer Kenny Venegas, and three vocalists: Sid Barnes, Judy Hauff and Minnie Riperton. Chess placed the group on his Cadet/Concept label and recorded a debut album largely consisting of covers of recent hits, re-done in a progressive/psychedelic style. Subsequent albums consisted of original material. The group, which underwent several personnel changes in its lifetime, ultimately recorded six albums up to 1971 but experienced only minor chart success. Riperton left in 1970 to pursue a solo career, but the group disbanded in the mid-70s and the others retreated into obscurity.

Albums: *Rotary Connection* (1967), *Aladdin* (1968), *Peace* (1968), *Songs* (1969), *Dinner Music* (1970), *Hey Love* (1971).

Routers

A USA instrumental group formed in the early 60s in the Los Angeles area, the original Routers were not the same musicians that eventually secured its only hit in 1962 with 'Let's Go (Pony)'. The original group consisted of musicians Mike Gordon, Al Kait, Bill Moody, Lynn Frazier and a fifth musician (unknown). Signed to Warner Brothers Records, the group was assigned to producer Joe Saraceno, who then proceeded to use studio musicians and not the actual group on the recording of 'Let's Go (Pony)'. The single reached the US charts number 19 and *Let's Go With The Routers*, was released, but it too was apparently recorded by session musicians such as Hal Blaine and Plas Johnson. Warner Brothers continued to issue singles under the name Routers, one of which, 'Sting Ray', reached the charts in 1963. There were three other Warner albums, followed by later Routers singles on RCA Records and Mercury Records (which also released an album) as late as 1973, after which the name was apparently shelved and the remaining members disbanded.

Albums: *Let's Go With The Routers* (1963), *The Routers Play 1963's Great Instrumental Hits* (1963), *Charge!* (1964), *Go Go Go With The Chuck Berry Songbook* (1965), *Superbird* (1973).

Royal Guardsmen

As if to prove just about any topic could become a hit song, the Royal Guardsmen made a career in the mid-60s out of writing about Snoopy, the dog in the *Peanuts* comic strip. The group formed in 1966 in Ocala, Florida, USA and consisted of Chris Nunley (vocals), Tom Richards (lead guitar), Barry Winslow (rhythm guitar/vocals), Bill Balogh (guitar), Billy Taylor (organ) and John Burdette (drums). That same year, under the management of Phil Gernhard, the group signed to Laurie Records and recorded a novelty tune, 'Snoopy Vs. The Red Baron', which ultimately peaked at number 2 in the US chart in January 1967 and eventually reached number 8 in the UK chart that same year. Capitalizing on the debut's success, they recorded further Snoopy songs - 'The Return Of The Red Baron', 'Snoopy's Christmas' and 'Snoopy For President' - as well as other novelty songs. One 1967 single, 'Airplane Song (My Airplane)', was written by Michael Martin Murphey, who had his own US number 3 hit in 1975 with 'Wildfire'. The Royal Guardsmen disbanded in 1968.

Albums: *Snoopy Vs. The Red Baron* (1967), *Return Of The Red Baron* (1967), *Snoopy And His Friends* (1967), *Snoopy For President* (1968).

Ruby And The Romantics

Edward Roberts (first tenor), George Lee (second tenor), Ronald Mosley (baritone) and Leroy Fann (bass) had been working as the Supremes prior to the arrival of Ruby Nash Curtis (b. 12 November 1939, New York City, New York, USA) in 1962. Ruby had met the group in Akron, Ohio and took on the role as their lead singer. They subsequently secured a contract with the New York label Kapp and at the suggestion of the company, changed their name to Ruby And The Romantics. By the following year they had taken the evocative 'Our Day Will Come' to the top of the US pop chart, earning them a gold disc. Over the next 12 months the group scored a further six hits including the original version of 'Hey There Lonely Boy' which, with a change of gender, was later revived by Eddie Holman. After three years

at Kapp, the group signed to the ABC label. In 1965 'Does He Really Care For Me', the Romantics' last chart entry, preceded a wholesale line-up change. Ruby brought in a new backing group; Richard Pryor, Vincent McLeod, Robert Lewis, Ronald Jackson and Bill Evans, but in 1968 the forthright Curtis replaced this version with Denise Lewis and Cheryl Thomas.

Albums: *Our Day Will Come* (1963), *Till Then* (1963), *Ruby And The Romantics* (1967), *More Than Yesterday* (1968). Compilation: *Greatest Hits Album* (1966).

Ruffin, Jimmy

b. 7 May 1939, Collinsville, Mississippi, USA. The son of a minister, Ruffin was born into a musical family: his brother, David Ruffin, and cousin, Melvin Franklin, both became mainstays of the Temptations. Ruffin abandoned his gospel background to become a session singer in the early 60s, joining the Motown stable in 1961 for a one-off single before he was drafted for national service. After leaving the US Army, he returned to Motown, turning down the opportunity to join the Temptations and instead recommending his brother for the job. His commercial breakthrough came in 1966 with the major US and UK hit 'What Becomes Of The Broken-Hearted', which displayed his emotional, if rather static, vocals. After three smaller hits, Ruffin found success in the USA hard to sustain, concentrating instead on the British market. 'I'll Say Forever My Love' and 'It's Wonderful' consolidated his position in the UK, and in 1970 he was voted the world's top singer in one British poll. Ruffin left Motown in the early 70s after an unsuccessful collaboration with his brother, and achieved minor success with singles on Polydor and Chess. Despite his popularity as a live performer in Britain, he enjoyed no significant hits until 1980, when 'Hold On To My Love', written and produced by Robin Gibb of the Bee Gees, brought him his first USA Top 30 hit for 14 years. A duet with Maxine Nightingale, 'Turn To Me', was a big seller in 1982, while Ruffin's only other success of note in the 80s was the British chart-contender 'There Will Never Be Another You' in 1985. He joined Ian Levine's Motor City label in 1988 and recorded two singles with Brenda Holloway.

Albums: *Top Ten* (1967), *Ruff'n'Ready* (1969), *The Groove Governor* (1970), with David Ruffin *I Am My Brother's Keeper* (1970), *Jimmy Ruffin* (1973), *Love Is All We Need* (1975), *Sunrise* (1980).

Rush, Tom

b. 8 February, 1941, Portsmouth, New Hampshire, USA. Tom Rush began performing in 1961 while a student at Harvard University. Although he appeared at clubs in New York and Philadelphia, he became a pivotal figure of the Boston/New England circuit and such haunts as the Cafe Yana and the Club 47. *Live At The Unicorn*, culled from two sets recorded at another of the region's fabled coffee houses, was poorly distributed but its competent mixture of traditional songs, blues and Woody Guthrie compositions was sufficient to interest the renowned Prestige label. *Got A Mind To Ramble* and *Blues Songs And Ballads*, completed over three days, showcased an intuitive interpreter. Rush's exemplary versions of 'Barb'ry Allen' and 'Alabama Bound' were enough to confirm his place alongside Dave Van Ronk and Eric Von Schmidt, the latter of whom was an important influence on the younger musician. *Tom Rush*, his first release on the Elektra label, was one of the era's finest folk/blues sets. The artist had developed an accomplished bottleneck guitar style which was portrayed to perfection on 'Panama Limited', an 8-minute compendium comprising several different songs by Bukka White. *Take A Little Walk With Me* contained the similarly excellent 'Galveston Flood', but its high points were six electric selections drawn from songs by Bo Diddley, Chuck Berry and Buddy Holly. Arranged by Al Kooper, these performances featured musicians from Bob Dylan's ground-breaking sessions and helped transform Rush from traditional to popular performer. This change culminated in *The Circle Game*, which contained material by Joni Mitchell, James Taylor and Jackson Browne, each of whom had yet to record in their own right. The recording also included the poignant 'No Regrets', the singer's own composition, which has since become a pop classic through hit versions by the Walker Brothers (1976) and Midge Ure (1982).

Tom Rush, the artist's first release for Columbia/CBS, introduced his long-standing partnership with guitarist Trevor Veitch. Once again material by Jackson Browne and James Taylor was to the fore, but the album also contained compositions by Fred Neil and Murray McLaughlin's beautiful song of leaving home, 'Child's Song', confirming Rush as having immaculate taste in choice of material. However two subsequent releases, *Wrong End Of The Rainbow* and *Merrimack County*, saw an increased emphasis on material Rush either wrote alone, or with Veitch. By contrast a new version of 'No Regrets' was the sole original on *Ladies Love Outlaws*, a collection which marked a pause in Rush's recording career. It was 1982 before a new set, *New Year*, was released. Recorded live, it celebrated the artist's 20th anniversary while a second live album, *Late Night Radio*, featured cameos from Steve Goodman and Mimi Farina. Both were issued on Rush's Night Light label on which he also repackaged his 1962 debut. In 1990 his New Hampshire home and recording studio were totally destroyed by fire, and this cultured artist has since moved to Wyoming.

Albums: *Live At The Unicorn* (1962), *Got A Mind To Ramble* (later known as *Mind Rambling*) (1963), *Blues Songs And Ballads* (1964), *Tom Rush* (1965), *Take A Little Walk With Me* aka *The New Album* (1966), *The Circle Game* (1968), *Tom Rush* (1970), *Wrong End Of The Rainbow* (1970), *Merrimack County* (1972), *Ladies Love Outlaws* (1974), *New Year* (1982), *Late Night Radio* (1984). Compilations: *Classic Rush* (1970), *The Best Of Tom Rush* (1975).

Ryan, Paul And Barry

b. Paul and Barry Sapherson, 24 October 1948, Leeds, England. The twin sons of popular singer Marion Ryan (married to impresario Harold Davidson), Paul and Barry were launched as clean-cut act to attendant showbusiness publicity. Their debut single, 'Don't Bring Me Your Heartaches' reached the UK Top 20 in 1965, and over the ensuing months the siblings enjoyed respectable, if unspectacular, chart placings with 'Have Pity On The Boy' and 'I Love Her'. The Ryans shifted away from their tailored image with 'Have You Ever Loved Somebody' (1966) and 'Keep It Out Of Sight' (1967), penned, respectively, by the Hollies and Cat Stevens, but such releases were less successful. They split amicably in 1968 with Paul embarking on a songwriting career while Barry recorded as a solo act. Together they created 'Eloise', the latter's impressive number 2 hit and subsequent million seller, but ensuing singles failed to emulate its popularity. Paul's compositions included 'I Will Drink The Wine', which was recorded by Frank Sinatra, but neither brother was able to sustain initial impetus.

Album: *The Ryans* (1967). Barry Ryan: *Barry Ryan Sings Paul Ryan* (1968). Paul Ryan: *Scorpio Rising* (1976).

Rydell, Bobby

b. Robert Ridarelli, 26 April 1942, Philadelphia, Pennsylvania, USA. Probably the most musically talented of the late 50s Philadelphia school of clean-cut teen idols, Rydell first performed in public as a drummer at the age of seven. At nine he debuted on Paul Whiteman's *Teen Club* amateur television show and was the show's regular drummer for three years. He attended the same boys club as Fabian and Frankie Avalon, formed a duo with Avalon in 1954 and shortly after they both joined local group Rocco And The Saints. After several rejections from labels, he recorded his first solo single 'Fatty Fatty' for his manager's Veko label. In 1958 he joined Cameo and his fourth release for that label 'Kissin' Time' (which owed something to 'Sweet Little Sixteen') became the first of his 18 US Top 40 hits over the next four years. The photogenic pop/rock singer's best-known transatlantic hits are 'Wild One', 'Sway' and 'Volare' (only two years after the song first topped the charts) all in 1960 and 'Forget Him', a number written and produced in Britain by Tony Hatch in 1963. Rydell, whose ambition was always to be an all-round entertainer, starred in the movie *Bye Bye Birdie* and quickly, and initially successfully, moved into the cabaret circuit. The arrival of the British groups in 1964 was the final nail in his chart coffin. He later recorded without success for Capitol, Reprise, RCA, Perception and Pickwick International. Rydell has continued to work the club and oldies circuit and had some recognition for his role in rock when the high school in the 70s musical *Grease* was named after him. Selected albums: *Bobby's Biggest Hits* (1961), *Rydell At The Copa* (1961), *Rydell/Chubby Checker* (1961), *All The Hits* (1962), *Biggest Hits Vol. 2* (1962), *Top Hits Of 1963* (1964), *Forget Him* (1964).

Ryder, Mitch (And The Detroit Wheels)

b. William Levise Jnr., 26 February 1945, Detroit, Michigan, USA. An impassioned singer, bearing an aural debt to Little Richard, Levise spent his formative years frequenting the clubs on Woodward Avenue, watching many of Tamla/Motown's star attractions. Having outgrown two high school bands, he formed Billy Lee And The Rivieras in 1963. Jim McCarty (lead guitar; later of Buddy Miles Express and Cactus), Joe Cubert (rhythm guitar), Earl Elliott (bass) and 'Little' John Badanjek (drums) completed the group's early line-up, which recorded two singles for local labels prior to their 'discovery' by producer Bob Crewe. The quintet was then given a shaper name - Mitch Ryder And The Detroit Wheels - and in 1965 secured their biggest hit with the frenzied 'Jenny Take A Ride'. Uninhibited at a time of increasing sophistication, Ryder successfully captured the power of his black inspirations. Subsequent releases showed a similar verve, but the group reached its zenith with the exceptional medley of 'Devil With A Blue Dress On' and 'Good Golly Miss Molly'. From there, however, the formula became predictable and more studied recreations failed to emulate its fire. The Wheels were summarily fired in 1967 as the singer was coaxed towards safer fare. He and Crewe split up in rancorous circumstances but a union with guitarist Steve Cropper resulted in the excellent *Detroit/Memphis Experiment*. In 1971 Ryder formed Detroit, a hard-edged rock band of great promise which disintegrated prematurely. The singer then abandoned music, nursing a throat ailment which threatened his one-time livelihood. He resumed performing in the late 70s and although later releases lack the overall passion of those initial recordings, there are moments when that erstwhile strength occurs. In the 90s Ryder is still a major concert attraction. A primary influence on Bruce Springsteen, the architect of Detroit's 'high-energy'

performers, the MC5 and the Stooges, Mitch Ryder's talent should not be under-estimated.
Selected albums: with the Detroit Wheels *Take A Ride* (1966), *Breakout...!!!* (1966), *Sock It To Me!* (1967); Mitch Ryder solo: *What Now My Love* (1967), *All The Heavy Hits* (1967), *Mitch Ryder Sings The Hits* (1968), *The Detroit-Memphis Experiment* (1969), *How I Spent My Vacation* (1978), *Naked But Not Dead* (1979), *Got Change For A Million* (1981), *Live Talkies* (1982), *Smart Ass* (1982), *Never Kick A Sleeping Dog* (1983), *In The China Shop* (1986), *Red Blood And White Mink* (1989), *La Gash* (1992). Compilations: *All Mitch Ryder Hits!* (1967), *Mitch Ryder And The Detroit Wheels' Greatest Hits* (1972), *Wheels Of Steel* (1983), *Rev Up* (1990), *The Beautiful Toulang Sunset* (1990), *The Very Best Of* (1992).

S

Sadler, Barry, Staff Sgt.

b. 1941, New Mexico, USA. While stationed at Fort San Houston, Texas, Staff Sgt. Barry Sadler spent his spare time composing a number of songs and, after serving in Vietnam, decided to complete a lyric dedicated to his regiment. The result was submitted to a publisher who passed the composition on to author Robin Moore whose book, *The Green Berets*, was a best-seller. Together, Sadler and Moore refashioned the song into 'The Ballad Of The Green Berets' which, following its release on RCA Records surprisingly dominated the USA number 1 position for an astonishing five weeks. Sadler's repertoire was limited, but he managed to complete a follow-up, 'The A Team' and a best-selling album. His career thereafter was stormy and controversial. After re-enlisting in the Army and briefly pursuing an acting career, he was charged and acquitted of the murder of Nashville songwriter Lee Emerson Bellamy. Three years later, in 1981, he was found not guilty of a charge of shooting his former business partner. It was an extraordinary denouement to the career of one of the most unlikely chart-topping artists of all time.
Albums: *Ballads Of The Green Berets* (1966), *The 'A' Team* (1966).

St. Louis Union

Initially based in Manchester, the St. Louis Union - Tony Cassiday (vocals), Keith Miller (guitar), Alex Kirby (tenor saxophone), David Tomlinson (organ), John Nichols (bass) and Dave Webb (drums) -

attracted attention as winners of the 1965 *Melody Maker* beat group contest. Their prize was a recording contract with Decca Records, the first fruits of which was a version of 'Girl', plucked from the Beatles' album *Rubber Soul*. The sextet took the song into the UK Top 30, despite competition from the Truth. They later enjoyed a role in *The Ghost Goes Gear*, a film which also featured the Spencer Davis Group. However, the chart failure of subsequent singles, 'Behind The Door' and 'East Side Story', brought their brief career to an end.

St Peters, Crispian

b. Robin Peter Smith, 5 April 1943, Swanley, Kent, England. Originally a member of UK pop group the Beat Formula Three, Smith was plucked from obscurity by manager Dave Nicolson, rechristened Crispian St Peters and signed to a 10 year management and production contract. After two unsuccessful singles for Decca ('At This Moment' and 'No No No') Nicolson persuaded him to cover We Five's US hit 'You Were On My Mind'. Although the single was almost buried in the pre-Christmas sales rush of 1965, it continued to sell into the New Year and took Crispian into the UK Top 10. Under Nicolson's tutelage, the shy star was momentarily transformed into arrogance incarnate and astonished the conservative music press of the period by his suggestion that he'd written 80 songs of better quality than those of the Beatles. Other stars were also waved aside as Crispian announced that he was better than Elvis Presley: 'I'm going to make Presley look like the Statue of Liberty . . . I am sexier than Dave Berry and more exciting than Tom Jones . . . and the Beatles are past it'. Outraged readers denounced him in letters columns, but St Peters returned stronger than ever with the sprightly 'Pied Piper', a Top 10 hit on both sides of the Atlantic. Thereafter he was remembered more for his idle boasts than his music. After successive chart failures, he switched to country, a form that better suited his singing style. Serious psychological problems hampered his remote chances of a serious comeback and he fell into obscurity, reappearing irregularly on the flickering revivalist circuit. Serious psychological problems prevented his making an emphatic comeback.
Album: *Simply . . . Crispian St Peters* (1970).

Sainte-Marie, Buffy

b. 20 February 1941, Piapot Reserve, Saskatchewan, Canada. An honours graduate from the University of Massachusetts, Buffy eschewed a teaching career in favour of a folksinger. She was signed to the Vanguard label in 1964, following her successful performances at Gerde's Folk City. Her debut *It's My Way*, introduced a remarkable compositional and performing talent. Sainte-Marie's impassioned plea for

Indian rights, 'Now That The Buffalo's Gone', reflected her native- American parentage and was one of several standout tracks, along with 'Cod'ine' and 'The Universal Soldier'. The latter was recorded, successfully, by Donovan, which helped introduce Buffy to a wider audience. Her second selection included 'Until It's Time For You To Go', a haunting love song which was later recorded by Elvis Presley. However, Sainte-Marie was also a capable interpreter of other writer's material, as her versions of songs by Bukka White, Joni Mitchell and Leonard Cohen showed. Her versatility was also apparent on a superb C&W collection, *I'm Gonna Be A Country Girl Again*, and on *Illuminations*, which featured an electronic score on several tracks. A campaigner for Indian rights, Sainte-Marie secured an international hit in 1971 with the theme song to the film, *Soldier Blue*, but subsequent releases failed to capitalize on this success. Temporarily bereft of direction, Buffy returned to the Indian theme with *Sweet America*, but with the collapse of the ABC labels, she retired to raise her family and concentrate on her work for children's foundations. She composed the 1982 Joe Cocker/Jennifer Warnes' hit, 'Up Where We Belong' which featured in the film *An Officer And A Gentleman*. Her welcome return in 1991, following her signing with Chrysalis Records, produced the warmly-received *Coincidence And Likely Stories*.
Albums: *It's My Way* (1964), *Many A Mile* (1965), *Little Wheel Spin And Spin* (1966), *Fire, Fleet And Candlelight* (1967), *I'm Gonna Be A Country Girl Again* (1968), *Illuminations* (1970), *She Used To Wanna Be A Ballerina* (1971), *Moonshot* (1972), *Quiet Places* (1973), *Buffy* (1974), *Changing Woman* (1975), *Sweet America* (1976), *Coincidence And Likely Stories* (1992). Compilations: *The Best Of Buffy Sainte-Marie* (1970), *Native North American Child: An Odyssey* (1974), *The Best Of Buffy Sainte-Marie, Volume 2* (1974).

Sakamoto, Kyu

b. 1941, Kawasaki, Japan, d. 12 August 1985. The original singer with the Paradise Kings, he signed to Toshiba Records in 1959 after being discovered singing in the tea rooms of his home town. He had a succession of hits in Japan, but his only major worldwide hit was 'Sukiyaki', in 1963. The reason for its international success was due to Louis Benjamin of Pye Records in England, who brought home a copy from Japan for popular trad-jazz clarinettist Kenny Ball. At this stage the record (written in 1962 by pianist Hachidai Nakamura and lyricist Rokusuke Ei) was called 'Ueo Muite Aruko' ('Walk With Your Chin Up'). This duly changed to 'Sukiyaki'. Ball's version reached the Top 10 in the UK and interest was stirred in the original which repeated the feat a few months later. Sakamoto never managed to duplicate his initial world-wide success (although the

follow up ,'China Nights', was a minor US hit), but continued to be a star in his native country, appearing in many films and on television programmes. His career came to an abrupt end in 1985 when he was among the 524 passengers killed when a Japanese Boeing 747 civil aircraft crashed outside Tokyo.
Selected album: *Sukiyaki And Other Japanese Hits* (1963).

Sam And Dave

Samuel David Moore (b. 12 October 1935, Miami, Florida, USA) and David Prater (b. 9 May 1937, Ocilla, Georgia, USA, d. 11 April 1988). Sam And Dave first performed together in 1961 at Miami's King Of Hearts club. Moore originally sang in his father's Baptist church before joining the Melonaires, while Prater, who had worked with the Sensational Hummingbirds, was also gospel-trained. Club-owner John Lomelo became the duo's manager and was instrumental in securing their contract with Roulette. Five singles and one album subsequently appeared between 1962-64, produced by R&B veteran Henry Glover, but it was not until Jerry Wexler signed Sam And Dave to Atlantic Records that their true potential blossomed. For political reasons their records appeared on Stax; they used the Memphis-based houseband while many of their strongest moments came from the Isaac Hayes/David Porter staff writing team. 'You Don't Know Like I Know', 'Hold On I'm Comin' (both 1966), 'Soul Man' (1967) and 'I Thank You' (1968), featuring Prater's gritty delivery and Moore's higher interjections, were amongst the genre's finest. When Stax and Atlantic parted in 1968, Sam And Dave reverted to the parent company, but a disintegrating personal relationship seemed to mirror their now decaying fortune. The amazing 'Soul Sister, Brown Sugar' (1969) delayed the slide, but the duo split briefly the next year when Sam Moore began his own career. Three solo singles followed, but the pair were reunited by a deal with United Artists. A renewed profile, on the strength of the Blues Brothers' success with 'Soul Man', faltered when the gulf between the two men proved irreconcilable. By 1981, Moore was again pursuing an independent direction
 but his sole chart success came when he was joined by Lou Reed for a remake of 'Soul Man' six years later. Prater found a new foil in the 'Sam' of Sam & Bill, but before they were able to consolidate this new partnership, Prater died in a car crash on 11 April 1988. Arguably soul's definitive duo, Sam And Dave released records that combined urgency with an unbridled passion.
Albums: *Sam And Dave* (1962), *Hold On, I'm Comin'* (1966), *Double Trouble* (1966), *Double Dynamite* (1967), *Soul Men* (1967), *I Thank You* (1968), *Back At 'Cha* (1976), *Sweet And Funky Gold* (1978).

Compilations: *The Best Of Sam And Dave* (1969), *Can't Stand Up For Falling Down* (1984), *Wonderful World* (1987), *Sweet Funky Gold* (1988).

Sam The Sham And The Pharaohs

Sam The Sham (And The Pharaohs)
b. Domingo Samudio aka Sam Samudio, Dallas, Texas, USA. Although drawing inspiration from the Tex-Mex tradition, Sam's initial releases were made for Memphis-based outlets. Backed by the Pharaohs, which comprised Ray Stinnet (guitar), Butch Gibson (saxophone), David Martin (bass) and Jerry Patterson (drums) - he scored a US chart-topper in 1965 with 'Wooly Bully', a pulsating novelty-dance song which achieved immortality as a staple part of aspiring bar band repertoires. The single became the act's sole UK Top 20 hit, but they enjoyed further success in the USA with 'Lil' Red Riding Hood', which reached number 2 the following year. The group later mutated into the Sam The Sham Revue, but the singer dissolved the venture in 1970 to embark on a solo career under his own name. Although *Hard And Heavy* featured support from guitarist Duane Allman, the set was marred by inconsistency and failed to establish its proponent's talent. Domingo subsequently contributed to the soundtrack of the motion picture *The Border* (1982) and remains a popular talent in his native state.
Albums: *Sam The Sham And Wooly Bully* (1965), *Their Second Album* (1965), *When The Boys Meet The Girls* (1965, film soundtrack), *Sam The Sham And The Pharaohs On Tour* (1966), *Lil' Red Riding Hood* (1966), *The Sam The Sham Revue/Nefertiti* (1967), *Ten Of Pentacles* (1968). Compilation: *The Best Of Sam The Sham And The Pharaohs* (1967). As Sam Domingo *Hard And Heavy* (1970).

Savoy Brown
Formed in 1966 as the Savoy Brown Blues Band, this institution continues to be led by founding guitarist Kim Simmonds. The original line-up comprising Simmonds, Brice Portius (vocals), Ray Chappell (bass), John O'Leary (harmonica), Bob Hall (piano)

and Leo Mannings (drums), were featured on early sessions for producer Mike Vernon's Purdah label, before a second guitarist, Martin Stone, joined in place of O'Leary. The re-shaped sextet then secured a recording deal with Decca. Their debut *Shake Down*, was a competent appraisal of blues favourites, featuring material by Freddie King, Albert King and Willie Dixon. Unhappy with this reverential approach, Simmonds pulled the group apart, retaining Hall on an auxiliary basis and adding Chris Youlden (vocals), Dave Peverett (guitar/vocals), Rivers Jobe (bass) and Roger Earl (drums). The new line-up completed 'Getting To The Point' before Jobe was replaced by Tone Stevens. The restructured unit was an integral part of the British blues boom. In Youlden they possessed a striking frontman, resplendent in bowler hat and monacle, whose confident, mature delivery added panache to the group's repertoire. Their original songs matched those they chose to cover, while the Simmonds/Peverett interplay added fire to Savoy Brown's live performances. 'Train To Nowhere', from *Blue Matter*, has since become one of the genre's best-loved recordings. Youlden left the group following *Raw Sienna*, but the inner turbulence afflicting the group culminated at the end of 1970 when Peverett, Stevens and Earl walked out to form Foghat. Simmonds meanwhile toured America with a restructured line-up - Dave Walker (vocals), Paul Raymond (keyboards), Andy Pyle (bass) and Dave Bidwell (drums) - setting a precedent for Savoy Brown's subsequent development. Having honed a simple, blues-boogie style, the guitarist now seemed content to repeat it and the group's ensuing releases are of decreasing interest. Simmonds later settled in America, undertaking gruelling tours with musicians who become available, his determination both undeterred and admirable.

Albums: *Shake Down* (1967), *Getting To The Point* (1968), *Blue Matter* (1969), *A Step Further* (1969), *Raw Sienna* (1970), *Looking In* (1970), *Street Corner Talking* (1971), *Hellbound Train* (1972), *Lion's Share* (1972), *Jack The Toad* (1973), *Boogie Brothers* (1974), *Wire Fire* (1975), *Skin 'N' Bone* (1976), *Savage Return* (1978), *Rock 'N' Roll Warriors* (1981), *Just Live* (1981), *A Hard Way To Go* (1985), *Make Me Sweat* (1988). Compilations: *The Best Of Savoy Brown* (1977), *Blues Roots* (1978), *Highway Blues* (1985).

Scaffold

Formed in Liverpool, England in 1962, the Scaffold was the unlikely confluence of two concurrent 'booms' - satire and Merseybeat. Poet Roger McGough (b. 9 November 1937) and humorist John Gorman (b. 4 January 1937) joined Mike McGear (b. Michael McCartney, 7 January 1944), younger brother of Paul McCartney, to create an act not solely reliant on pop for success. They contributed material

to *Gazteet*, a late-night programme on ABC-Television and following an acclaimed residency at London's Establishment club, took their 'Birds, Marriages and Deaths' revue to the 1964 Edinburgh Festival, where they would return on several occasions. Although the trio enjoyed major hits with 'Thank U Very Much' (1967) and 'Lily The Pink' (1968) - the latter of which was a massive Christmas UK number 1 - these tongue-in-cheek releases contrasted the group's in-concert revues and albums. Here McGough's poetry and Gorman's comedy routines were of equal importance and their versatility was confirmed on *The Scaffold* and *L The P*. The schoolboy-ish 'Gin Gan Goolie' gave the group a minor chart entry in 1969, before the unit was absorbed by Grimms, a larger, if similarly constituted, act which also featured members of the Liverpool Scene. On its demise McGear recorded *Woman*, before agreeing to resurrect Scaffold for *Fresh Liver* on which Zoot Money (keyboards) and Ollie Halsall (guitar) joined the Average White Band horn section to help bring a rock-based perspective to the trio's work. The haunting 'Liverpool Lou' provided another UK Top 10 hit in 1974, but the founder members embarked on separate paths following *Sold Out*. McGear resumed his solo career, and became a credible photographer, while McGough returned to writing poetry. Gorman pursued a career in television, principally on the cult UK television children's show *Tiswas* and was back in the UK charts alongside Sally James, Chris Tarrant and Lenny Henry as the Four Bucketeers with 'The Bucket Of Water Song' in 1980.

Albums: *The Scaffold* (1967), *L The P* (1968), *Lily The Pink* (1969), *Fresh Liver* (1973), *Sold Out* (1974). Compilation: *The Singles A's And B's* (1984).

Searchers

One of the premier groups from the mid-60s Merseybeat explosion, the Searchers comprised: Chris Curtis (b. Christopher Crummey, 26 August 1941, Oldham, Lancashire, England; drums), Mike Pender (b. Michael John Prendergast, 3 March 1942, Liverpool, England; lead guitar), Tony Jackson (b. 16 July 1940, Liverpool, England; vocals/bass) and John McNally (b. 30 August 1941, Liverpool, England; rhythm guitar). Having previously backed Liverpool singer Johnny Sandon, they broke away and took their new name from the 1956 John Ford western, *The Searchers*. During 1962, they appeared in Hamburg and after sending a demo tape to A&R representative Tony Hatch were signed to Pye Records the following year. Their Doc Pomus/Mort Shuman debut 'Sweets For My Sweet' was a memorable tune with strong harmonies and a professional production. By the summer of 1963, it climbed to number 1 establishing the Searchers as rivals to Brian Epstein's celebrated stable of Liverpool groups. *Meet The Searchers*, was swiftly issued and revealed the group's R&B pedigree on such standards as 'Farmer John' and 'Love Potion Number 9'. Meanwhile, Tony Hatch composed a catchy follow-up single, 'Sugar And Spice', which just failed to reach number 1. It was their third single, however, that won them international acclaim. The Jack Nitzsche/Sonny Bono composition 'Needles And Pins' was a superb melody, brilliantly arranged by the group and a striking chart-topper of its era. It also reached the US Top 20 in March 1964.

Earlier that year the band released their atmospheric cover of the Orlons' 'Don't Throw Your Love Away', which gave the group their third UK number 1 single. The pop world was shocked by the abrupt departure of Jackson whose falsetto vocals had contributed as much to the group's early sound and identity. He was replaced in the autumn by Frank Allen (b. Francis Renaud McNeice, 14 December 1943, Hayes, Middlesex, England), a former member of Cliff Bennett And The Rebel Rousers. A strident reading of Jackie De Shannon's 'When You Walk In The Room' was another highlight of 1964 which showed their rich Rickenbacker guitar work to notable effect. The Malvina Reynolds' protest song, 'What Have They Done To The Rain?' indicated their folk-rock potential, but its melancholic tune and slower pace was reflected in a lower chart placing. A return to the 'old' Searchers sound with the plaintive 'Goodbye My Love', took them back into the UK Top 5 in early 1965, but the number 1 days were over. For a time, it seemed that the Searchers might not slide so inexorably as rivals Billy J. Kramer And The Dakotas and Gerry And The Pacemakers. They enjoyed further US success where their cover of the Clovers' 'Love Potion Number 9' was a Top 10 hit at the end of 1964 and on into 1965. This continued with 'Bumble Bee (US number 21), 'Goodbye My Lover Goodbye' (US number 52). The Curtis/Pender hit, 'He's Got No Love' (US number 79, UK number 12) showed that they could write their own hit material but this run could not be sustained. The release of P.F. Sloan's 'Take Me For What I'm Worth' (US number 76, UK number 20) suggested that they might become linked with the Bob Dylan-inspired folk-rock boom. Instead, their commercial fortunes rapidly declined and after Curtis left in 1966, they were finally dropped by Pye. Cabaret stints followed but the Searchers continued playing and in the circumstances underwent minimal line-up changes. They threatened a serious resurgence in 1979 when Sire issued a promising comeback album. The attempt to reach a new wave audience was ultimately unsuccessful, however, and after the less well received *Play For Today* (titled *Love's Melodies* in the USA), the group stoically returned to the cabaret circuit.

Selected albums: *Meet The Searchers* (1963), *Sugar And Spice* (1963), *Hear! Hear!* (1964, US release, live at the Star Club, Hamburg), *It's The Searchers* (1964), *This Is Us* (1964, US release), *The New Searchers LP* (1965, US release), *The Searchers No. 4* (1965, US release), *Sounds Like Searchers* (1965), *Take Me For What I'm Worth* (1965), *Second Take* (1972), *Needles And Pins* (1974), *The Searchers* (1979), *Play For Today* (1981), *100 Minutes Of The Searchers* (1982), *The Searchers Hit Collection* (1987), *The EP Collection* (1989), *30th Anniversary Collection* (1992).

Sebastian, John

b. 17 March 1944, New York, USA. The son of the famous classical harmonica player John Sebastian. John Jnr. is best known for being a member of the much-loved Lovin' Spoonful in the 60s, which established him as one of the finest American songwriters of the century. When the Spoonful disbanded Sebastian started a solo career that was briefly threatened when he was asked to become the fourth member of Crosby, Stills And Nash, but he declined when it was found that Stephen Stills wanted him to play drums. In 1969 his performance was one of the highlights of the Woodstock Festival, singing his warm material to a deliriously happy audience. His tie-dye jacket and jeans appearance, warm rapport, and acoustic set (aided by copious amounts of LSD) elevated him to a star. Sebastian debuted in 1970 with a solo work *John B Sebastian*, containing much of the spirit of Woodstock. Notable tracks like the autobiographical 'Red Eye Express' and the evocative 'How Have You Been', were bound together with one of his finest songs, 'She's A Lady'. Less than two minutes long, this love song was perfect for the times, and was a lyrical triumph with lines like 'She's a lady, and I chance to see her in my shuffling daze, she's a lady, hypnotised me there that day, I came to play in my usual way, hey'. Simply accompanied by Stills' and Crosby's mellow Gretsch guitar, it remains a modern classic. Sebastian faltered with the uneven *Four Of Us*, a travelogue of hippie ideology but followed a few months later with the engaging, *Real Live,* recorded at four gigs in California. At that time Sebastian was performing at a punishing rate throughout Europe and America. *Tarzana Kid* sold poorly, but later grew in stature with critics.

At this time Sebastian was working with the late Lowell George, and a strong Little Feat influence is shown. The album's high point is a Sebastian/George classic, the beautiful 'Face Of Appalachia'. Two years later John was asked to write the theme song for a US comedy television series, *Welcome Back Kotter*. The result was a number 1 hit, 'Welcome Back'. Astonishingly, since then, no new album had appeared until 1992, when a Japanese label released his most recent songs. Throughout that time, however, Sebastian never stopped working. He accompanied Sha Na Na and NRBQ on many lengthy tours, appeared as a television presenter, wrote a children's book and among other commissions he composed the music for the *Care Bears* television series. Severe problems with his throat threatened his singing career at one point. He declined to be part of the 1992 reformed Lovin' Spoonful. Sebastian was, is and always will be the heart and soul of that band.

Albums: *John B. Sebastian* (1970), *The Four Of Us* (1971), *Real Live* (1971), *Tarzana Kid* (1974), *Welcome Back* (1976).

Sedaka, Neil

b. 13 March 1939, Brooklyn, New York, USA. Pianist Sedaka began his songwriting career with lyricist Howard Greenfield in the early 50s. During this high school period, Sedaka dated Carol Klein (later known as Carole King). For a brief period, Sedaka joined the Tokens, then won a scholarship to New York's Juilliard School of Music. In 1958, the pianist joined Don Kirshner's Brill Building school of instant songwriters. Sedaka's first major hit success came with 'Stupid Cupid', which was an international smash for Connie Francis. The following year, Sedaka signed to RCA as a recording artist and enjoyed a minor US hit with 'The Diary'. The frantic follow-up 'I Go Ape' was a strong novelty record, which helped establish Sedaka. This was followed by one of his most famous songs, 'Oh Carol', a lament directed at his former girlfriend Carole King, who replied in kind with the less successful 'Oh Neil'. Sedaka's solid voice and memorable melodies resulted in a string of early 60s hits, including 'Stairway To Heaven', 'Calendar Girl', 'Little Devil', 'King Of Clowns', 'Happy Birthday Sweet Sixteen' and 'Breaking Up Is Hard To Do'. These songs summed up the nature of Sedaka's lyrical appeal. The material subtly dramatized the trials and rewards of teenage life and the emotional upheavals resulting from birthdays, break-ups and incessant speculation on the qualities of a loved one. Such songs of neurotic love had their distinct time in the early 60s, and with the decline of the clean-cut teen balladeer and the emergence of groups, there was an inevitable lull in Sedaka's fortunes. He abandoned the pop star role but continued writing a fair share of hits over the next 10 years, including 'Working On A Groovy Thing' (Fifth Dimension), 'Puppet Man' (Tom Jones) and 'Is This The Way To Amarillo?' (Tony Christie). In 1972, Sedaka effectively relaunched his solo career with *Emergence* and relocated to the UK. By 1973, he was back in the British charts with 'That's When The Music Takes

Me' from *Solitaire*. The third album of the comeback, *The Tra-La Days Are Over*, was highly regarded and included 'Our Last Song Together', dedicated to Howard Greenfield. With *Laughter In The Rain*, Sedaka extended his appeal to his homeland. The title track topped the US charts in 1975, completing a remarkable international comeback. That same year, the Captain And Tennille took Sedaka's 'Love Will Keep Us Together' to the US number 1 spot and the songwriter followed suit soon after with 'Bad Blood'. The year ended with an excellent reworking of 'Breaking Up Is Hard To Do' in a completely different arrangement which provided another worldwide smash. He enjoyed his last major hit during 1980 in the company of his daughter Dara on 'Should've Never Let You Go'. Sedaka continues to tour regularly.

Albums: *Rock With Sedaka* (1959), *Emergence* (1972), *Solitaire* (1972), *The Tra-La Days Are Over* (1973), *Laughter In The Rain* (1974), *Live At The Royal Festival Hall* (1974), *Overnight Success* (1975), *The Hungry Years* (1975), *Steppin' Out* (1976), *A Song* (1977), *In The Pocket* (1980), *Come See About Me* (1984), *Love Will keep Us Together: The Singer And His Songs* (1992). Compilations: *Neil Sedaka Sings His Greatest Hits* (1963), *Sedaka's Back* (1975), *Laughter And Tears: The Best Of Neil Sedaka Today* (1976), *Neil Sedaka's Greatest Hits* (1977), *Timeless* (1991), *Originals: The Greatest Hits* (1992).

Further reading: *Breaking Up Is Hard To Do*, Neil Sedaka.

Seekers

Founded in Australia in 1963, the original Seekers comprised Athol Guy (b. 5 January 1940, Victoria, Australia, vocals/double bass), Keith Potger (b. 2 March 1941, Columbo, Sri Lanka, vocals/guitar), Bruce Woodley (b. 25 July 1942, Melbourne, Australia, vocals/guitar) and Ken Ray (lead vocals/guitar). After a year with the above line-up, Athol Guy recruited Judith Durham (b. 3 July 1943, Melbourne, Australia) as the new lead singer and it was this formation which won international success. Following a visit to London in 1964, the group were signed to the Grade Agency and secured a prestigious guest spot on the televised *Sunday Night At The London Palladium*. Tom Springfield, of the recently-defunct Springfields, soon realized that the Seekers could fill the gap left by his former group and offered his services as songwriter/producer. Although 1965 was one of the most competitive years in pop, the Seekers strongly challenged the Beatles and the Rolling Stones as the top chart act of the year. A trilogy of folk/pop smashes: 'I'll Never Find Another You', 'A World Of Our Own' and 'The Carnival Is Over' widened their appeal, leading to lucrative supper club dates and frequent television appearances

Apart from Tom Springfield's compositions, they also scored a massive chart hit with Malvina Reynolds' 'Mornington Ride' and gave Paul Simon his first UK success with a bouncy adaptation of 'Someday One Day'. Meanwhile, Bruce Woodley teamed up with Simon to write some songs, including the Cyrkle hit 'Red Rubber Ball'. In early 1967, the breezy 'Georgy Girl' (written by Tom Springfield and Jim Dale) was a transatlantic Top 10 hit but thereafter the group were no longer chart regulars. Two years later, they bowed out in a televised farewell performance. Judith Durham subsequently went solo, while Keith Potger oversaw the formation of the New Seekers. In 1975, the old Seekers briefly reformed with teenage Dutch singer Louisa Wisseling replacing Judith Durham. They enjoyed a final moment of chart glory when 'The Sparrow Song' topped the Australian charts.

Albums: *The Seekers* (1965), *A World Of Our Own* (1965), *The New Seekers* (1965, US release), *Come The Day* (1966), *Seen In Green* (1967), *Georgy Girl* (1967, US release), *Live At The Talk Of The Town* (1968), *Four And Only Seekers* (1969), *The Seekers* (1975). Compilations: *The Best Of The Seekers* (1967), *The Very Best Of The Seekers* (1974), *An Hour Of The Seekers* (1988), *The Seekers Greatest Hits* (1988).

Serendipity Singers

This nine piece group was formed at the University of Colorado in the wake of the success of the New Christy Minstrels. The line-up was based around Mike Brovsky (vocals), Brooks Hatch (vocals), and Bryan Sennett (vocals). To these were added Jon Arbenz (guitar), John Madden (guitar), Bob Young (bass), Diane Decker (vocals), Tommy Tieman (vocals) and Lynne Weintraub (vocals). Their material, though not strictly folk, encompassed a range of songs from traditional through to pop music. From performing on college campuses, they moved outside of the confines of university and sang at the Bitter End in New York. As a result, the group were offered a recording deal with Philips and a spot on the influential *Hottenanny* television show. *The Serendipity Singers* contained the group's one big hit, 'Don't Let The Rain Come Down (Crooked Little Man)', which reached the US Top 10 in 1964. The album scaled the US Top 20 the same year. A follow-up 'Beans In My Ears' made the US Top 30, but despite regularly touring at home, mainly on the college circuit, and touring abroad, the group never repeated their earlier success.

Albums: *The Serendipity Singers* (1964), *The Many Sides Of The Serendipity Singers* (1964), *Take Your Shoes Off With The Serendipity Singers* (1965), *We Belong Together* (1966).

Shades Of Blue

This vocal group came from Detroit, Michigan, USA. 'Oh How Happy', with its sing-a-long simplicity and good cheer zoomed up the US chart in 1966 reaching number 12. The Shades Of Blue was discovered and produced by soul singer Edwin Starr, who was looking for a white group to record 'Oh How Happy', a song he had written years earlier. After the group were turned down by another Detroit company, Starr took them to Harry Balk's small Impact operation, and with 'Oh How Happy' Impact they broke through. The group could not give Balk another big record, as their two subsequent records in 1966 , 'Lonely Summer' and 'Happiness',stalled on the lower reaches of the charts. Album: *Happiness Is The Shades of Blue* (1966).

Shadows

The UK's premier instrumental group, the Shadows evolved from the Five Chestnuts to become Cliff Richard's backing group, the Drifters. By late 1958 the line-up had settled and under their new name the Shadows, the group comprised: Hank B Marvin (b. Brian Robson Rankin, 28 October 1941, Newcastle-upon-Tyne, England; lead guitar), Bruce Welch (b. 2 November 1941, Bognor Regis, Sussex, England; rhythm guitar), Jet Harris (b. Terence Hawkins, 6 July 1939, London, England; bass) and Tony Meehan (b. Daniel Meehan, 2 March 1943, London, England; drums). Soon after backing Cliff Richard on his first single, they were signed as a group by EMI Columbia's A&R manager Norrie Paramor. After two singles under their old name, the Drifters, they issued the vocal 'Saturday Dance', which failed to sell. An abrupt change of fortune came in 1960 when they met singer/songwriter Jerry Lordan, who presented them with 'Apache'. Their instrumental was one of the finest of its era and dominated the UK number 1 position for six weeks, as well as being voted single of the year in several music papers. It was duly noted that they had knocked their singer's 'Please Don't Tease' off the top of the charts and, in doing so, firmly established themselves as important artists in their own right. The Shadows' influence on the new generation of groups that followed was immense. Marvin was revered as a guitarist, and although the group were firmly part of the British show-business establishment, their musical credibility was beyond question. A wealth of evocative instrumentals followed, including 'FBI', 'The Frightened City', 'The Savage' and 'Guitar Tango'. These Top 10 singles were interspersed with four formidable UK number 1 hits: 'Kon Tiki', 'Wonderful Land', 'Dance On' and 'Foot Tapper'. Despite such successes, the group underwent personnel shifts. Both Tony Meehan and Jet Harris left the group to be replaced by drummer Brian Bennett (b. 9 February 1940, London, England) and bassist Brian Locking. Ironically, the Shadows soon found themselves competing against the combined forces of Jet Harris And Tony Meehan, who recorded some startling instrumentals in their own right, including the chart-topping 'Diamonds'.

The Shadows continued to chart consistently during 1963-64 with 'Atlantis', 'Shindig', 'Geronimo', 'Theme For Young Lovers' and 'The Rise And Fall Of Flingel Bunt', but it was clear that the Mersey beat boom had lessened their appeal. Throughout this period, they continued to appear in films with Cliff Richard and undertook acting and musical roles in *Aladdin And His Wonderful Lamp* at the London Palladium, which spawned the hit 'Genie With The Light Brown Lamp'. An attempted change of direction was notable in 1965 with the minor vocal hits, 'The Next Time I See Mary Ann' and 'Don't Make My Baby Blue'. Further movie and pantomime appearances followed, amid a decline in chart fortunes. At the end of 1968, the group announced that they intended to split up. In late 1969, a streamlined Shadows featuring Marvin, Rostill, Bennett and pianist Alan Hawkshaw toured Japan. Marvin then pursued some solo activities before reuniting with Welch for the Crosby, Stills & Nash-influenced Marvin, Welch & Farrar. The early 70s coincided with numerous personal dramas. Marvin became a Jehovah's Witness, Welch had a tempestuous relationship with singer Olivia Newton-John and Rostill was fatally electrocuted while playing his guitar. In 1974, the Shadows reconvened for *Rockin' With Curly Leads*, on which they were joined by bassist/producer Alan Tarney. Several live performances followed and the group were then offered the opportunity to represent the United Kingdom in the Eurovision Song Contest. They achieved second place with 'Let Me Be The One', which also provided them with their first UK Top 20 hit in 10 years. The stupendous success of an accompanying *20 Golden Greats* compilation effectively revitalized their career. By 1978, they were back in the UK Top 10 for the first time since 1965 with an instrumental reading of 'Don't Cry For Me Argentina'. That feat was repeated several months later with 'Theme From The Deer Hunter (Cavatina)'. Regular tours and compilations followed and in 1983, the group received an Ivor Novello Award from the British Academy of Songwriters, Composers and Authors to celebrate their 25th anniversary. Long regarded as one of the great institutions of British pop music, the Shadows have survived a generation of musical and cultural changes in fashion yet continue to please audiences with their instrumental abilities.

Albums: *The Shadows* (1961), *Out Of The Shadows* (1962), *Dance With The Shadows* (1964), *The Sound Of The Shadows* (1965), *Shadow Music* (1966), *Jigsaw* (1967), *From Hank, Bruce, Brian And John* (1967), *Established 1958* (1968), *Shades Of Rock* (1970), *Rockin' With Curly Leads* (1974), *Specs Appeal* (1975), *Live At The Paris Olympia* (1975), *Tasty* (1977), *Thank You Very Much* (1978), *Change Of Address* (1980), *Hits Right Up Your Street* (1981), *Life In The Jungle/Live At Abbey Road* (1982), *XXV* (1983), *Guardian Angel* (1984), *Moonlight Shadows* (1986), *Simply Shadows* (1987), *Stepping To The Shadows* (1989), *Reflections* (1991). Compilations: *The Shadows Greatest Hits* (1963), *More Hits* (1965), *Somethin' Else* (1969), *20 Golden Greats* (1977), *String Of Hits* (1980), *Another String Of Hot Hits* (1980), *At Their Very Best* (1989), *Themes And Dreams* (1991) .

Shadows Of Knight

Formed in Chicago in 1965, the original line-up comprised of Jim Sohns (vocals), Warren Rogers (lead guitar), Jerry McGeorge (rhythm guitar), Norm Gotsch (bass) and Tom Schiffour (drums). As the houseband at the city's Cellar club, the Shadows were already highly popular when they secured a recording contract. Their debut single, a cover version of the classic Them track, 'Gloria', was the climax to the quintet's stage act, but when the group toned down its mildly-risqué lyric, they were rewarded with a US Top 10 hit. By this point Gotsch had been replaced, with Rogers switching to lead to accommodate new guitarist Joe Kelly. Their best-known line-up now established, the Shadows enjoyed another minor chart entry with 'Oh Yeah', before completing their debut album. *Gloria* comprised of several Chicago R&B standards which, paradoxically, were patterned on British interpretations of the same material. Two excellent group originals, 'Light Bulb Blues' and 'It Happens That Way', revealed an emergent, but sadly under-used, talent. *Back Door Men* offered a slightly wider perspective with versions of 'Hey Joe' and 'Tomorrow's Gonna Be Another Day' (also recorded by the Monkees), but the highlight was an inspired interpretation of 'Bad Little Woman', originally recorded by Irish group the Wheels. Dave 'The Hawk' Wolinski replaced Warren Rogers when the latter was drafted in late 1966. This was the prelude to wholesale changes when, on 4 July 1967, Sohns fired the entire group. The singer subsequently reappeared fronting a new line-up - John Fisher, Dan Baughman, Woody Woodfuff and Kenny Turkin - and a new recording deal with the bubblegum Super K label. 'Shake' gave the group a final US Top 50 entry, but its unashamed pop approach owed little to the heritage of the 'old'. Further releases for the same outlet proved equally disappointing, while an attempt at recreating the past with 'Gloria 69' was unsuccessful. Sohns has led several versions of his group over the ensuing years, McGeorge found fleeting notoriety as a member of H.P. Lovecraft, while Wolinski found fame as a member of Rufus and his work with Michael Jackson.

Albums: *Gloria* (1966), *Back Door Men* (1967), *The Shadows Of Knight* (1969). Compilations: *Gloria* (1979), *Gee-El-O-Are-I-Ay* (1985).

Shangri-Las

Late entrants in the early 60's school of 'girl groups', the Shangri-Las comprised two pairs of sisters, Mary-Ann and Margie Ganser and Betty and Mary Weiss. During 1963 they were discovered by George 'Shadow' Morton and recorded two singles under the name Bon Bons before signing to the newly formed Red Bird label. Relaunched as the Shangri-Las, they secured a worldwide hit with 'Remember (Walkin' In The Sand)', a delightful arrangement complete with the sound of crashing waves and crying seagulls. It was the sound-effect of a reving motorbike engine which opened their distinctive follow-up, 'Leader Of The Pack', which was even more successful and a prime candidate for the 'death disc' genre with its narrative of teenage love cut short because of a motorcycle accident. By 1966, Margie Ganser had left the group, though this had little effect on their popularity or output. They had already found a perfect niche, specializing in the doomed romanticism of American teenage life and unfolding a landscape filled with misunderstood adolescents, rebel boyfriends, disapproving parents, the foreboding threat of pregnancy and, inevitably, tragic death. This hit formula occasionally wore thin but Shadow Morton could always be relied upon to engineer a gripping production. During their closing hit phase in 1966/67, the group recorded two songs, 'I Can Never Go Home Anymore' and 'Past Present And Future' which saw the old teenage angst transmogrified into an almost tragic, sexual neuroticism. The enduring commercial quality of their best work was underlined by consistent repackaging and the successive chart reappearances of the biker anthem, 'Leader Of The Pack'.

Albums: *Leader Of The Pack* (1965), *'65* (1965). Compilation: *Golden Hits* (1984).

Further reading: *Girl Groups: The Story Of A Sound*, Alan Betrock.

Shannon, Del

b. Charles Westover, 30 December 1934, Coopersville, Michigan, USA, d. 8 February 1990. From the plethora of clean, American, post doo-wop male vocalists to find enormous success in the early 60s, only a small handful retained musical credibility. Shannon was undoubtedly from this pedigree. More than 30 years after his chart debut, Shannon's work is still regularly played. His early musical interests took him under the country influence of the legendary Hank Williams. Shannon's first record release however was pure gutsy pop; the infectious melody

Del Shannon

was written by accident while rehearsing in the local Hi-Lo club with keyboard player Max Crook (Maximillian). The song was 'Runaway', a spectacular debut that reached the top of the charts in the USA and UK, and was subsequently recorded by dozens of admiring artists. The single, with its shrill sounding Musitron (an instrument created by Crook) together with Shannon's falsetto, was irresistible. Shannon succeeded where others failed, due to his talent as a composer and his apparent maturity, appealing to the public with a clear youthful strident voice. This paradox was cleared up many years later, when it was discovered that he was five years older than stated. Had this come out in 1961, it is debatable whether he would have competed successfully alongside his fresh-faced contemporaries. His teenage tales of loneliness, despair, broken hearts, failed relationships, infidelity and ultimate doom, found a receptive audience. Shannon would rarely use the word 'love' in his lyrics. Even the plaintive, almost happy, 1962 hit 'Swiss Maid' combined his trademark falsetto with yodelling, ending with the heroine dying, forlorn and unhappy. Over the next three years Shannon continued to produce and write his own material with great success, especially in Britain, where his run of 10 consecutive hits ended with 'Sue's Gotta Be Mine' in October 1963. In the interim, he had produced several memorable Top 10 successes, including the bitingly acerbic 'Hats Off To Larry' and 'Little Town Flirt', which betrayed an almost misogynistic contempt. The re-worked themes of his songs were now beginning to pale, and together with the growth of Merseybeat, Shannon's former regular appearances in the charts became sporadic, even though he was the first American artist to record a Beatles' song, 'From Me To You'.

Shannon worked steadily for the next 25 years, enjoying a few more hit singles including a cover version of Bobby Freeman's 'Do You Wanna Dance', followed by 'Handy Man', formerly a hit for Jimmy Jones, from whom he 'borrowed' his famous falsetto. In 1965 'Keep Searchin'' was Shannon's last major success The song had an elegiac feel, recalling an era of innocence already passed. Throughout the 60s and 70s Shannon was a regular visitor to Britain where he found a smaller but more appreciative audience. He acquired many professional admirers over the years including Jeff Lynne, Tom Petty and Dave Edmunds, who variously helped him rise above his sad decline into a nether world of alcohol and pills. The 1981 Petty produced *Drop Down And Get Me* was critically well-received but sold poorly. Ironically, he received a belated hit in America with 'Sea Of Love', which found favour in 1982. This led to a brief renaissance for him in the USA. Although Shannon was financially secure through wise property investment, he still performed regularly. Ultimately however, he was branded to rock 'n' roll revival tours which finally took their toll on 8 February 1990, when a severely depressed Shannon pointed a .22 calibre rifle to his head and pulled the trigger, ending the misery echoed in his catalogue of hits.

Albums: *Runaway With Del Shannon* (1961), *Hats Off To Del Shannon* (1963), *Little Town Flirt* (1963), *Handy Man* (1964), *Del Shannon Sings Hank Williams* (1965), *1,661 Seconds With Del Shannon* (1965), *This Is My Bag* (1966), *Total Commitment* (1966), *The Further Adventures Of Charles Westover* (1968), *Live In England* (1972), *Drop Down And Get Me* (1981), *Rock On* (1991). Compilations: *The Best Of Del Shannon* (1967), *The Vintage Years* (1979), *Runaway Hits* (1990), *I Go To Pieces* (1990), *Looking Back, His Biggest Hits* (1991).

Shapiro, Helen

b. 28 September 1946, Bethnal Green, London, England. Helen Shapiro drew considerable attention when, as a 14 year old schoolgirl, she scored a UK Top 3 hit with 'Don't Treat Me Like A Child'. A deep intonation belied her youth and by the end of 1961 the singer had scored two chart-topping singles with 'You Don't Know' and 'Walkin' Back To Happiness'. This success was maintained the following year with 'Tell Me What He Said' (number 2) and 'Little Miss Lonely' (number 8), as Helen won

concurrent polls as 'Best British Female Singer' and was voted 'Best Newcomer' by the Variety Club of Great Britain. However, having recorded the original version of 'It's My Party' during an artistically fruitful session in Nashville, Helen was disappointed when an acetate reached Lesley Gore, who enjoyed a massive international hit using a similar arrangement. Shapiro's producer, Norrie Paramor, also vetoed the opportunity to record 'Misery', composed with Helen in mind by John Lennon and Paul McCartney. Indeed the advent of the Beatles helped undermine the singer's career. Despite being younger than many beat group members, Shapiro was perceived as belonging to a now-outmoded era and despite a series of excellent singles, was eclipsed by 'newcomers' Cilla Black and Dusty Springfield. The late 60s proved fallower still and, barring one pseudonymous release, Helen did not record at all between 1970-75. A Russ Ballard song, 'Can't Break The Habit' became a minor hit in Europe during 1977 and in turn engendered *All For The Love Of The Music*, a set sadly denied a UK release. Six years later Shapiro resurfaced on writer Charlie Gillett's Oval label. *Straighten Up And Fly Right* showed the singer had lost none of her early power and this excellent collection of standards was rightly acclaimed. An equally confident collaboration with jazz musician Humphrey Lyttelton ensued, since which Helen Shapiro has maintained a high profile through radio, television and live appearances, singing jazz-influenced big band material.

Albums: *Tops With Me* (1962), *Helen's Sixteen* (1963), *Helen In Nashville* (1963), *Helen Hits Out* (1964), *All For The Love Of The Music* (1977), *Straighten Up And Fly Right* (1983), *Echoes Of The Duke* (1985), *The Quality Of Mercer* (1987). Compilations: *Twelve Hits And A Miss Shapiro* (1967), *The Very Best Of Helen Shapiro* (1974), *The 25th Anniversary Album* (1986), *The EP Collection* (1989).

Helen Shapiro

Sharp, Dee Dee

b. Dione LaRue, 9 September 1945, Philadelphia,

Pennsylvania, USA. A backing vocalist for the Cameo-Parkway labels, Dee Dee Sharp was the uncredited voice on Chubby Checker's 'Slow Twistin'' single. Her own debut, 'Mashed Potato Time', was recorded at the same session and thanks to the power of Dick Clark's *American Bandstand* television show this energetic, excited song became an immediate success. Cameo sadly chose to milk its dance-based appeal and releases such as 'Gravy (For My Mashed Potatoes)' and 'Do The Bird' packaged her as a temporary novelty act at the expense of an untapped potential. Dee Dee resurfaced in the 70s on the TSOP/Philadelphia International labels. Married to producer Kenny Gamble, she scored two minor soul hits with 'I'm Not In Love' (1976 - a cover of the 10cc hit) and 'I Love You Anyway' (1981).

Albums: *It's Mashed Potato Time* (1962), *Down To Earth* (1962), *Do The Bird* (1963), *All The Hits* (1963), *Down Memory Lane* (1963), *What Color Is Love* (1978). Compilation: *18 Golden Hits* (mid-60s).

Shaw, Sandie

Sandi Shaw

b. Sandra Goodrich, 26 February 1947, Dagenham, Essex, England. Discovered by singer Adam Faith, Shaw was taken under the imperious wing of his manager Eve Taylor and launched as a teenage pop star in 1964. Her first single, 'As Long As You're Happy', proved unsuccessful but the follow-up, an excellent reading of Burt Bacharach and Hal David's

'(There's) Always Something There To Remind Me' reached number 1 in the UK. A striking performer, known for her imposing height, model looks and bare feet, Shaw's star shone for the next three years with a series of hits, mainly composed by her songwriter/producer Chris Andrews. His style, specializing in abrupt, jerky, oom-pah rhythms and plaintive ballads, served Sandie well, especially on the calypso-inspired 'Long Live Love', which provided her second UK number 1 in 1965. By the following year, Shaw's chart placings were slipping and Taylor was keen to influence her towards cabaret. Chosen to represent Britain in the 1967 Eurovision Song Contest, Shaw emerged triumphant with the Bill Martin/Phil Coulter composed 'Puppet On A String', which gave her a third UK number 1. After one further Martin/Coulter hit, 'Tonight In Tokyo', she returned to Andrews with only limited success. By 1969 she was back on the novelty trail with Peter Callender's translation of the French 'Monsieur Dupont'. Attempts to launch Shaw as a family entertainer were hampered by salacious newspaper reports and during the 70s, troubled by a failed marriage to fashion entrepreneur Jeff Banks, she effectively retired. In the early 80s she was rediscovered by Heaven 17 offshoots BEF, and recorded a middling version of 'Anyone Who Had A Heart', previously a number 1 for her old rival Cilla Black. The Shaw resurgence was completed when she was heavily promoted by Smiths' vocalist Morrissey, one of whose compositions, 'Heaven Knows I'm Miserable Now' was clearly inspired by the title of Shaw's failed 60s single, 'Heaven Knows I'm Missing You Now'. With instrumental backing from the Smiths, Shaw enjoyed a brief chart comeback with 'Hand In Glove' in 1984. In 1986, she reached the lower regions of the UK chart with a cover of Lloyd Cole's 'Are You Ready To Be Heartbroken?'. Her comeback album, on Rough Trade, featured songs by Morrissey, the Smiths and Jesus And Mary Chain.

Albums: *Sandie* (1965), *Me* (1965), *Puppet On A String* (1967), *Love Me, Please Love Me* (1967), *Reviewing The Situation* (1969), *Hello Angel* (1988). Compilations: *A Golden Hour Of Sandie Shaw - Greatest Hits* (1974), *20 Golden Pieces* (1986), *The Sandie Shaw Golden CD Collection* (1989), *The EP Collection* (1991). Further reading: *The World At My Feet*, Sandie Shaw.

Sherman, Allan

b. Allan Copelon, 30 November 1924, Chicago, Illinois, USA, d. 21 November 1973. Allan Sherman enjoyed a lucrative career during the 60s with his self-penned parodies of popular and folk songs. After his parents' 1930 divorce, Sherman lived with his mother and attended 21 different schools in Chicago, Los Angeles, New York and Miami. After attending

college in the early 40s and serving in the army, he began writing. One of his first works was a musical parody in which the Jewish Sherman starred himself as Adolf Hitler. In 1947 he began working in the fledgling television medium, writing jokes for variety programmes. He joined the popular US *I've Got A Secret* show in 1951, with which he stayed for seven years. Sherman then wrote for the Steve Allen programme but in 1960 found himself unemployed. His career took an upswing when he entertained guests at neighbour Harpo Marx's party with witty send-ups of show tunes. Talent scout Bullets Durgom, who had nurtured the success of Jackie Gleason, took an interest and convinced Warner Brothers Records to sign Sherman. Originally the label wanted him to record his show tune parodies but decided on folk songs instead, as folk was the music of the moment. Sherman's *My Son, The Folk Singer*, was issued in October 1962 and became the fastest-selling album in Warners' history at that time. The rotund Sherman capitalized on Jewish suburban humour by turning folk songs such as Harry Belafonte's 'Matilda' into 'My Zelda', and the folk song 'The Streets Of Laredo' into 'The Streets Of Miami'. The French standard 'Frere Jacques' became 'Sarah Jackman' and the USA patriotic number 'The Battle Hymn Of The Republic' was turned into 'The Ballad Of Harry Lewis', the story of a garment salesman. The debut and the following two albums all reached number 1 in the US album charts, this record, for a comedian, is unlikely to be beaten. Sherman's success was immediate, with numerous appearances on major USA television programmes and a headlining concert at Carnegie Hall. The formula of the first album was repeated on the subsequent *My Son, The Celebrity* and *My Son, The Nut*. The third album also produced a number 2 single, 'Hello Muddah, Hello Fadduh! (A Letter From Camp)', based on Ponchielli's 'Dance Of The Hours'. By 1964 the phenomenal novelty had diminished although Sherman continued to record for Warner Brothers until 1967, hosted television specials, acted on the stage and even wrote humour books, but never regained that initial blast of fame. He died in Los Angeles, due to respiratory illness caused by his obesity.
Albums: *My Son, The Folk Singer* (1962), *My Son, The Celebrity* (1963), *My Son, The Nut* (1963), *Allan In Wonderland* (1964), with Arthur Fiedler And The Boston Pops *Peter And The Commissar* (1964), *For Swingin' Livers Only* (1964), *My Name Is Allan* (1965), *Live! (Hoping You Are The Same)* (1966), *Togetherness* (1967). Compilations: *Best Of Allan Sherman* (1979), *A Gift Of Laughter (Best Of Volume II)* (1986).

Shirelles

Formed in Passaic, New Jersey, USA, the Shirelles are arguably the archetypal 'girl-group'; Shirley Owens (b. 10 June 1941), Beverley Lee (b. 3 August 1941), Doris Kenner (b. 2 August 1941) and Addie 'Micki' Harris (b. 22 January 1940, d. 10 June 1982) were initially known as the uncomfortably named Poquellos. School-friends for whom singing was simply a pastime, the quartet embarked on professional career when a classmate, Mary Jane Greenberg, recommended them to her mother. Florence Greenberg, an aspiring entrepreneur, signed them to her Tiara label, on which the resultant single, 'I Met Him On A Sunday', was a minor hit. This inspired the inauguration of a second outlet, Scepter, where the Shirelles secured pop immortality with 'Will You Love Me Tomorrow'. Here Alston's tender, aching vocal not only posed the ultimate question, but implied she already had decided 'yes' to her personal dilemma. One of pop's most treasured recordings, it was followed by a series of exceptional singles, 'Mama Said' (1961), 'Baby It's You' (1962) and 'Foolish Little Girl' (1963), which confirmed their exemplary position. The Shirelles' effect on other groups, including those in Britain, is incalculable, and the Beatles, the Merseybeats, and Manfred Mann are among those who covered their work. The quartet's progress was dealt a crucial setback when producer and arranger Luther Dixon left to take up another post. Newer Scepter acts, including Dionne Warwick, assumed the quartet's one-time prime position while a punitive record contract kept the group tied to the label. By the time the Shirelles were free to move elsewhere, it was too late to enjoy a contemporary career and the group was confined to the 'oldies' circuit. Sadly, Micki Harris died aged 42, on 10 June 1982. By combining sweetening strings with elements of church music, the group provided a pivotal influence on the direction of popular music.
Albums: *Trumpets And Strings* (1963), *Baby It's You* (1962), *Twist Party* (1962), *Foolish Little Girl* (1963). Solo albums: Shirley Alston (Owens) *With A Little Help From My Friends* (1975), *Lady Rose* (1977). Compilations: *Soulfully Yours* (1985), *Sha La La* (1985), *Lost And Found* (1987), *Greatest Hits* (1987), *The Collection* (1990).
Further reading: *Girl Groups: The Story Of A Sound*, Alan Betrock.

Simon, John

b. 11 August 1941, Norwalk, Connecticut, USA. Having studied music at college, Simon joined Columbia Records where he intially worked on documentary material. He switched to pop in 1966 and produced 'Red Rubber Ball', a US Top 3 hit for the Cyrkle. This led to involvement with other acts, including Simon And Garfunkel and Leonard Cohen, and his score for the off-beat movie, *You Are What*

You Eat. One of Simon's songs from the film, 'My Name Is Jack', became a major hit for Manfred Mann. The artist's relationship with the Band was especially fruitful. He not only produced the group's first two albums but also acted as an auxiliary member on piano, tuba and horns. Simon's first solo album featured reciprocal help from several Band members and included 'Davy's On The Road Again', a song he composed with Robbie Robertson. However, despite successful work with Gordon Lightfoot, Bobby Charles and Seals And Crofts, John Simon later drifted out of favour as both producer and performer.

Albums: *You Are What You Eat* (1968, film soundtrack), *The John Simon Album* (1971), *The Journey* (1972).

Simon And Garfunkel

This highly successful vocal duo first played together during their early years in New York. Paul Simon (b. 13 October 1941, Newark, New Jersey, USA) and Art Garfunkel (b. Arthur Garfunkel, 5 November 1941, Forest Hills, New York, USA) were initially inspired by the Everly Brothers and under the name Tom And Jerry enjoyed a US hit with the rock 'n' roll styled 'Hey Schoolgirl'. They also completed an album which was later reissued after their rise to international prominence in the 60s. Garfunkel subsequently returned to college and Simon pursued a solo career before the duo reunited in 1964 for *Wednesday Morning 3AM*. A strong, harmonic work, which included an acoustic reading of 'The Sound Of Silence', the album did not sell well enough to encourage the group to stay together. While Simon was in England the folk rock-boom was in the ascendant and producer Tom Wilson made the presumptuous but prescient decision to overdub 'Sound Of Silence' with electric instrumentation. Within weeks, the song was number 1 in the US charts, and Simon and Garfunkel were hastily reunited.

An album titled after their million-selling single was rush-released early in 1966 and proved a commendable work. Among its major achievements was 'Homeward Bound', an evocative and moving portrayal of life on the road, which went on to become a transatlantic hit. The solipsistic 'I Am A Rock' was another international success with such angst-ridden lines as, 'I have no need of friendship, friendship causes pain'. In keeping with the social commentary that permeated their mid-60s' work, the group included two songs whose theme was suicide: 'A Most Peculiar Man' and 'Richard Cory'. Embraced by a vast following, especially among the student population, the duo certainly looked the part with their college scarves, duffle coats and cerebral demeanour. Their next single, 'The Dangling Conversation', was their most ambitious lyric to date and far too esoteric for the Top 20. Nevertheless, the work testified to their artistic courage and boded well for the release of a second album within a year: *Parsley, Sage, Rosemary And Thyme*. The album took its title from a repeated line in 'Scarborough Fair', which was their excellent harmonic weaving of that traditional song and another, 'Canticle'. An accomplished work, the album had a varied mood from the grandly serious 'For Emily, Whenever I May Find Her' to the bouncy '59th Street Bridge Song (Feelin' Groovy)' (subsequently a hit for Harpers Bizarre). After two strong but uncommercial singles, 'At The Zoo' and 'Fakin' It', the duo contributed to the soundtrack of the 1968 film, *The Graduate*. The key song in the film was 'Mrs Robinson' which provided the group with one of their biggest international sellers. That same year saw the release of *Bookends*, a superbly-crafted work, ranging from the serene 'Save The Life Of My Child' to the personal odyssey 'America' and the vivid imagery of 'Old Friends'. *Bookends* is still felt by many to be their finest work.

In 1969 the duo released 'The Boxer', a long single that nevertheless found commercial success on both sides of the Atlantic. This classic single reappeared on the group's next album, the celebrated *Bridge Over Troubled Water*. One of the best-selling albums of all time (303 weeks on the UK chart), the work's title track became a standard with its lush, orchestral arrangement and contrasting tempo. Heavily gospel-influenced, the album included several well-covered songs such as 'Keep The Customer Satisfied', 'Cecilia' and 'El Condor Pasa'. While at the peak of their commercial success, with an album that dominated the top of the chart listings for months, the duo became irascible and their partnership abruptly ceased.

The release of a *Greatest Hits* package in 1972 included four previously unissued live tracks and during the same year the duo performed together at a benefit concert for Senator George McGovern. After a long break, a further duet occurred on the hit single 'My Little Town' in 1975. In 1981 they again reunited. The results were captured on *The Concert In Central Park*. Although another studio album was undertaken, the sessions broke down and Simon transferred the planned material to his 1983 solo *Hearts And Bones*.

Albums: *Wednesday Morning 3AM* (1968), *The Sound Of Silence* (1966), *Parsley, Sage, Rosemary And Thyme* (1966), *The Graduate* (1968, film soundtrack), *Bookends* (1968), *Bridge Over Troubled Water* (1970), *The Concert In Central Park* (1981). Compilations: *Simon And Garfunkel's Greatest Hits* (1972), *The Simon And Garfunkel Collection* (1981), *The Definitive Simon And Garfunkel* (1992).

Sinatra, Nancy

b. 8 June 1940, Jersey City, New Jersey, USA. Determined not to rest on the laurels of famous father Frank Sinatra, Nancy spent several years taking lessons in music, dance and drama. She made an impressive appearance on the Sinatra/Elvis Presley television special (1959) and two years later made her recording debut with 'Cuff Links And A Tie Pin'. Further releases vied with a budding acting career until 1966 when, having teamed with producer/songwriter Lee Hazelwood, Nancy enjoyed an international smash with the sultry number 1 'These Boots Are Made For Walkin''. It's descending bass line on every verse made it one of the most recognisable hits of 1966. Further success with 'How Does That Grab You Darlin'' and 'Sugar Town' ensued, before 'Something Stupid', a duet with her father, gave the singer a second UK chart topper. Nancy maintained thespian ambitions with roles in The Wild Angels and Elvis Presley's Speedway before performing the theme song to the James Bond film You Only Live Twice. She and Hazelwood scored further success with two country-influenced duets, 'Jackson' (1967) and 'Did You Ever' (1971), but her interest in singing gradually declined. Sinatra later completed a biography of her father.

Albums: Boots (1966), How Does That Grab You Darlin' (1966), Nancy In London (1966), Sugar (1967), Country My Way (1967), Movin' With Nancy (1968), with Lee Hazelwood Nancy And Lee (1968), Nancy (1969), Woman (1970), This Is Nancy Sinatra (1971), with Hazelwood Did You Ever (1972). Compilations: Nancy's Greatest Hits (1970), All-Time Hits (1988), Lightning's Girl (198?), The Very Best Of Nancy Sinatra (1988).

Singing Nun

Christened Janine Deckers in 1928, d. 1985. but better known as Sister Luc-Gabrielle of the Fichermont convent in Brussels, this guitar-playing vocalist came to prominence after signing to Philips Records in 1961. Their Belgium branch issued her album Soeur Sourire ('Sister Smile'), which sold well on the Continent. One of the songs, the French sung 'Dominique', a breezy tribute to the founder of the Dominican order, captured the imagination of the international record-buying public and became a worldwide hit, reaching number 1 in the USA during the Christmas of 1963. Her album also reached the top of the US charts in the same month and she received the Grammy Award for 'Best Gospel or Religious Recording' of 1963. Revenue for the sales of her work was contributed to foreign missions. Although the Singing Nun appeared on the prestigious Ed Sullivan Show, she failed to secure a hit follow-up. However, Debbie Reynolds starred in a 1966 film of the nun's life and the movie was advertised with a shot of Sister Sourire riding a scooter and playing an acoustic guitar. Worldly trappings eventually enticed Deckers from the convent in October 1966 and she later recorded the controversial 'Glory Be To God For The Golden Pill'. Deckers committed suicide in Belgium in 1985. Albums: Soeur Sourire (1962), The Singing Nun (1963).

Sir Douglas Quintet

Formed in 1964, the quintet was fashioned by a Houston-based producer, Huey P. Meaux and former teenage prodigy, Doug Sahm (b. 6 November 1941, San Antonio, Texas, USA). The name, Sir Douglas Quintet, first used on 'Sugar Bee' (1964), was fashioned to suggest Anglo credentials in the midst of the British Invasion, but Sahm's southern accent soon put paid to such attempted deception. Augie Meyer (b. 31 May 1940; organ), Francisco (Frank) Morin (b. 13 August 1946; horns), Harvey Kagan (b. 18 April 1946; bass) and John Perez (b. 8 November 1942; drums) completed the line-up which scored an international hit with 'She's About A Mover', an infectious blend of Texas pop and the Beatles' 'She's A Woman', underscored by Meyer's simple, insistent keyboards. This charming style continued on several further singles and the band's debut album, prematurely entitled The Best Of The Sir Douglas Quintet. In keeping with several Texans, including Janis Joplin and the Thirteenth Floor Elevators, the Quintet sought the relaxed clime of San Francisco following an arrest on drugs charges in 1966. However, it was two years before the band resumed recording with Honky Blues, although only Sahm and Morin were retained from the earlier unit which was bolstered by other Lone Star state exiles Wayne Talbert (piano), Martin Fierro (horns) and George Rains (drums).

The original Quintet was reconstituted for Mendocino. This superb selection remains their finest offering and includes the atmospheric 'At The Crossroads', a fiery remake of 'She's About a Mover' and the compulsive title track, which became the group's sole million-seller when released as a single. This commercial peak was not sustained and despite delivering several other excellent albums, the unit broke up in 1972 when Sahm embarked on a solo career. It was, however, a temporary respite and since reforming in 1976 the group has been resurrected on several occasions, in part to tour and capitalise on a continued European popularity.

Albums: The Best Of The Sir Douglas Quintet (1965), Sir Douglas Quintet + 2 - Honkey Blues (1968), Mendocino (1969), 1+1+1 = 4 (1970), The Return Of Doug Salanda (1971), Rough Edges (1973), Quintessence (1982), Border Wave (1983), Rio Medina (1984), Very Much Alive/Love Ya, Europe (1988), Midnight Sun (1988). Compilations: The Sir Douglas Quintet

Collection (1986), *Sir Doug's Recording Trip* (1988).

Ska

Until the 50s the indigenous folk music of Jamaica was mento - similar to calypso in some ways but with its own style and content. However, with the influence of R&B radio stations from Southern American cities such as Miami, Nashville and New Orleans beaming into Jamaica a totally new style evolved - ska. The popularity of R&B in Jamaica prompted enterprising locals to start their own Sound Systems - precursors of the travelling disco - but with the type of amplification equipment that guaranteed that the audience actually felt the music rather than merely listened to it. Sound System operators such as Sir Coxsone (Dodd) The Downbeat, Duke Reid The Trojan and Tom The Great Sebastian became hugely popular figures and their regular weekend dances would draw capacity crowds. Top sounds would often play against each other and the competition was cut throat (and often violent) so the sounds worked hard to obtain the latest (and most exclusive) records. Small fortunes were spent on record-buying sprees to America and label details would be scratched out or obscured to prevent a rival discovering the names of real crowd-pleasing tunes. Towards the end of the decade the source of hard-rocking R&B began to dry up as the black American audience moved towards a smoother style of music which cut no ice at all in Jamaica. There had been little or no recording industry in Jamaica up until this time but the Sound System men now started to make their own R&B tunes that they would play on dubs (acetate discs) to their followers. Initially, the audiences were not let in on the secret that these were Jamaican recordings but to the surprise of people like Duke Reid and Coxsone the public actually liked their tunes enough to want to buy copies and they began to release them on vinyl to satisfy the demand. The emphasis in these Jamaican R&B recordings was always firmly placed on the off-beat and coupled with the mento influence and the free-blowing jazz musicians employed a specifically new style which became known as ska. The origins of the word are unclear and there are many different explanations (all purporting to the right one) but it is probably onomatopoeic and based on the sounds their disc jockeys would make live on the set (and later on record) to spur the dancers on. Many claim to be the first to record ska but the most influential Sound System man turned record producer was Coxsone Dodd who together with Duke Reid virtually controlled the music business in Jamaica throughout the 60s.

Instrumental records proved the most popular with Don Drummond, Tommy McCook, Rico Rodriquez, Clue J Drumbago becoming household names in Jamaica. Vocalists came through to a lesser extent - ska's frantic pace and 'noisiness' did not really lend itself to subtle singing styles but Laurel Aitken, Owen Gray and Higgs & Wilson amongst countless others became Jamaica's first home grown stars.

The popularity of the music extended beyond the confines of the Western Kingston and it achieved a cult following in the UK among the mods (in London especially) during the early 60s, where records released on the Island and Blue Beat labels initially for the expatriate Jamaicans found favour with the young white crowd. In fact the music was known as Blue Beat after the record label while Prince Buster appeared on national television on *Ready Steady Go* and Millie Small scaled the UK national charts with her ska based rendition of Barbie Gaye's R&B hit 'My Boy Lollipop'. Ska reigned supreme until 1966 when the music began to slow down, the electric bass (rather than the stand up bass) came to the fore and rock steady was born. Ska's influence and legacy are out of all proportion to its humble origins and apart from being the beginning of what is now known as reggae music, its basic feel and sounds have been revived time after time throughout the world most notably in the late 70s when the English 2/Tone movement used ska as its starting point and frame of musical reference. It is hardly surprising that people discovering ska for the first time now still find it as fresh, exciting and innovative as it sounded in those Western Kingston dance halls over 30 years ago.

Albums: With Don Drummond *Greatest Hits*, with various artists *Intensified* (Vols, 1 & 2), *King Edwards Presents Ska-volution*, *Oldies But Goodies* (Vols. 1 & 21), with the Skatalites *Ska Authentic*, with various artists *Ska Bonanza*, *Ska Au Go Go, The Birth Of Ska*.

Skatalites

The Skatalites were formed in June 1964, drawing from the ranks of session musicians then recording in the studios of Kingston, Jamaica. The personnel included Don Drummond (trombone), Roland Alphonso (tenor sax), Tommy McCook (tenor sax), Johnny 'Dizzy' Moore (trumpet), Lester Sterling (alto Sax), Jerome 'Jah Jerry Hines (guitar), Jackie Mittoo (piano), Lloyd Brevett (bass), and Lloyd Knibbs (drums). The band name was a Tommy McCook pun on the Soviet space satellite of 1963. The Skatalites' music, reputedly named after the characteristic 'ska' sound made by the guitar when playing the after beat, was a powerful synthesis; combining elements of R&B and swing jazz in arrangements and solos, underpinned by the uniquely Jamaican-stressed after beat, as opposed to the 'down beat' of R&B. Many of the musicians had learnt music at Alpha Boys' School in Kingston, then honing their talent in the Jamaican swing bands of the

40s and early 50s, and in numerous 'hotel bands' playing for the tourist trade. Most of the musicians thereby developed recognizable individual styles. Repertoire was drawn from many sources, including adaptations of Latin tunes, movie themes and updated mento, a Jamaican folk song form. Perhaps their most famous and typical tune is 'Guns Of Navarone' recorded in 1965 and a big club hit in the UK in the mid-60s. They recorded hundreds of superb instrumentals for various producers, either under the group name or as bands led by the particular musician who had arranged the session. Under the Skatalite name they made important music for Clement Dodd and Duke Reid, as well as for Justin and Philip Yap's Top Deck record label. They stayed together for just over two years until August 1965, when a combination of financial, organizational and personal problems caused the break-up of the band after their last gig, a police dance at the Runaway Bay Hotel. Of the main protagonists, Jackie Mittoo and Roland Alphonso were persuaded by Clement Dodd to form the Soul Brothers band, who would make many instrumentals and supply backing tracks at Studio One until 1967. Tommy McCook worked principally for Duke Reid, where he formed the studio band known as the Supersonics, and was musical co-director for Reid's Treasure Isle label with alto saxophonist Herman Marques. The tragically wayward Don Drummond suffered from severe depression and died on 6 May 1969 in Bellevue Asylum, Kingston. The Skatalites had backed virtually every singer of note in the studios, at the same time laying the musical foundation for subsequent developments in Jamaican music. They released a reunion album in 1975; not ska, but high quality instrumental reggae. In 1984 the band played the Jamaican and London 'Sunsplash' concerts to rapturous acclaim. The reformed group also toured Japan with vocalists Prince Buster and Lord Tanamo in 1989, recording live and in the studio.
Albums: *Ska Authentic* (1967), *The Skatalites* (1975), *Return Of The Big Guns* (1984), *Skatalites At Sunsplash* (1985), *Stretching Out* (1987), *Celebration Time* (1988). Compilation: *Best Of The Skatalites* (1974).

Skip Bifferty

John Turnbull (guitar/vocals), Mickey Gallagher (keyboards), Colin Gibson (bass) and Tommy Jackman (drums) were all members of the Chosen Few, a popular beat group initially based in Newcastle-upon-Tyne, England. Vocalist Graham Bell was added to the line-up which assumed the name Skip Bifferty in the spring of 1966. The quintet made their energetic debut in August the following year with the excellent 'On Love', a song from their previous incarnation's repertoire. It was followed by two memorable examples of pop psychedelia, the last

of which, 'Man In Black' was produced by the Small Faces' team of Steve Marriott and Ronnie Lane. Skip Bifferty's first album continued the melodic craftsmanship of those singles. Bell's assured voice soared over a rich tapestry of sound, resulting in one of the late 60s' most rewarding collections. The group's potential withered under business entanglements and an astonishing conflict with their proprietorial manager Don Arden. Although they tried to forge an alternative career as Heavy Jelly, litigation over the rights to the name brought about their demise. Bell, Turnbull and Gallagher were later reunited in Bell And Arc, but while the singer then embarked on an ill-fated solo career, his former colleagues found success in Ian Dury's Blockheads. The band have subsequently become a cult item for UK record collectors.
Album: *Skip Bifferty* (1968).

Sledge, Percy

b. 25 November 1941, Leighton, Alabama, USA. An informal, intimate singer, Sledge led a popular campus attraction, the Esquires Combo, prior to his recording debut. Recommended to Quin Ivy, owner of the Norala Sound studio, Percy arrived with a rudimentary draft of 'When A Man Loves A Woman'. A timeless single, its simple arrangement hinged on Spooner Oldham's organ sound and the singer's homely, nasal intonation. Released in 1966, it was a huge international hit, setting the tone for Percy's subsequent path. A series of emotional, poignant ballads followed, poised between country and soul, but none would achieve the same commercial profile. 'It Tears Me Up', 'Out Of Left Field' (both 1967) and 'Take Time To Know Her' (1968) nonetheless stand amongst southern soul's finest achievements. Having abandoned Atlantic Records, Sledge re-emerged on Capricorn in 1974 where *I'll Be Your Everything* continued this chosen direction. Two 80s collections, *Percy* and *Wanted Again*, offer similar fare, and confirm the singer's intimate yet unassuming delivery. Released in Britain following the runaway success of a resurrected 'When A Man Loves A Woman', they are not diminished by comparison.
Albums: *When A Man Loves A Woman* (1966), *Warm And Tender Soul* (1966), *The Percy Sledge Way* (1967), *Take Time To Know Her* (1968), *I'll Be Your Everything* (1974), *If Loving You Is Wrong* (1986), *Percy* (1987), *Wanted Again* (1989). Compilations *The Best Of Percy Sledge* (1969), *Any Day Now* (1984), *When A Man Loves A Woman (The Ultimate Collection)* (1987).

Sloan, P.F.

b. Philip Sloan, 1946, Los Angeles, California, USA. Signed by entrepreneur Lou Adler in 1964 as a songwriter for Dunhill Records, Sloan, in conjunction with Steve Barri, first enjoyed success writing surfing hits. The emergence of folk-rock in 1965 brought Sloan to the fore as a serious singer/songwriter thanks to the catch-all protest number 'Eve Of Destruction'. Originally offered to the Byrds, the song was finally released by the gruff-voiced Barry McGuire and climbed to number 1 in the USA, despite an extensive radio ban. Sloan was criticized in purist folk circles for his apparent opportunism, but was embraced by many as the voice of youth and spokesman of his generation. His poetic lyrics and love of simile in such songs as 'Upon A Painted Ocean' brought premature comparisons with Bob Dylan. During his 1965 peak, Sloan himself branched out into solo work with such social commentaries as 'Songs Of Our Times' and 'Sins Of A Family'. His compositions continued to be covered by such artists as the Searchers, Turtles and Herman's Hermits, and he also produced US hit group the Grass Roots. During the late 60s, Sloan was still writing protest material with some success, most notably on *Measure Of Pleasure*. After splitting with long-term partner Steve Barri, he attempted to take on the mantle of the introspective singer-songwriter in *Raised On Records*, but the work was not well received. Without a contract, Sloan wound down his music business commitments, prompting no less a personage than Jimmy Webb to mourn the absence of the great protester with the tribute 'P.F. Sloan' from the 1977 album *El Mirage*.

Albums: *Measure Of Pleasure* (1968), *Raised On Records* (1972).

Sly And The Family Stone

This US group was formed in San Francisco, California in 1967. Sly Stone (b. Sylvester Stewart, 15 March 1944, Dallas, Texas, USA), Freddie Stone (b. 5 June 1946, Dallas, Texas, USA; guitar), Rosie Stone (b. 21 March 1945, Vallejo, California, USA; piano), Cynthia Robinson (b. 12 January 1946, Sacramento, California, USA; trumpet), Jerry Martini (b. 1 October 1943, Colorado, USA; saxophone), Larry Graham (b. 14 August 1946, Beaumont, Texas, USA; bass), Greg Errico (b. 1 September 1946, San Francisco, California, USA; drums). Sly Stone's recording career began in 1948. A child prodigy, he drummed and added guitar to 'On The Battlefield For My Lord', a single released by his family's group, the Stewart Four. At high school he sang harmony with the Vicanes, but by the early 60s he was working the bars and clubs on San Francisco's North Beach enclave. Sly learned his trade with several bands, including Joe Piazza And The Continentals, but he occasionally fronted his own. 'Long Time Away', a single credited to Sylvester Stewart, dates from this period. He also worked as a disc jockey at stations KSOL and KDIA. Sly joined Autumn

Records as a songwriter/house-producer, and secured a 1964 success with Bobby Freeman's 'C'mon And Swim'. His own opportunistic single, 'I Just Learned How To Swim', was less fortunate, a fate which also befell 'Buttermilk Pts 1 & 2'. Stone's production work, however, was exemplary; the Beau Brummels, the Tikis and the Mojo Men enjoyed a polished, individual sound. In 1966 Sly formed the Stoners, a short-lived group which included Cynthia Robinson. The following year Sly And The Family Stone made its debut on the local Loadstone label with 'I Ain't Got Nobody'. The group was then signed to Epic, where their first album proclaimed itself *A Whole New Thing*. However, it was 1968 before 'Dance To The Music' became a Top 10 single in the US and UK. 'Everyday People' topped the US chart early the following year, but Sly's talent was not fully established until a fourth album, *Stand!*, was released. Two million copies were sold, while tracks including the title song, 'I Want To Take You Higher' and 'Sex Machine', transformed black music forever. Rhythmically inventive, the whole band pulsated with a crazed enthusiasm which pitted doo-wop, soul, the San Francisco sound, and more, one upon the other. Contemporaries, from Miles Davis to George Clinton and the Temptations, showed traces of Sly's remarkable vision.

A sensational appearance at the Woodstock Festival reinforced his popularity. The new decade began with a double-sided hit, 'Thank You (Falettinme Be Mice Elf Agin)'/'Everybody Is A Star', an R&B and pop number 1, but the optimism suddenly clouded. Sly began missing concerts, those he did perform were often disappointing and when *There's A Riot Goin' On* did appear in 1971, it was dark, mysterious and brooding. This introverted set nonetheless provided reached number 1 in the US chart, and three successful singles, 'Family Affair' (another US R&B and pop number 1), 'Running Away' and 'Smilin'', but the joyful noise of the 60s was now over. *Fresh* (1973) lacked Sly's erstwhile focus while successive releases, *Small Talk* and *High On You*, reflected a waning power. The Family Stone was also crumbling, Larry Graham left to form Graham Central Station, while Andy Newmark replaced Greg Errico. Yet the real undermining factor was the leader's drug dependency, a constant stumbling block to Sly's recurrent 'comebacks'. A 1979 release, *Back On The Right Track*, featured several original members, but later tours were dogged by Stone's addiction problem. Jailed for possession of cocaine in 1987, this innovative artist closed the decade fighting further extradition charges.

Albums: *Whole New Thing* (1967), *Dance To The Music* (1968), *Life* (1968), *M'Lady* (1968), *Stand!* (1969), *There's A Riot Going On* (1971), *Fresh* (1973), *Small Talk* (1974), *High Energy* (1975), *High On You*

(1975), *Heard You Missed Me, Well I'm Back* (1976), *Back On The Right Track* (1979), *Ain't But The One Way* (1983). Compilations: *Greatest Hits* (1970), *Ten Years Too Soon* (1979, a collection of re-mixes), *Anthology* (1981, compiles the group's Epic singles up to 1973), *The Best Of* (1992).

Small Faces

Formed in London during 1965, this mod-influenced group initially comprised: Steve Marriott (b. 30 January 1947, Bow, London, England, d. 20 April 1991; vocals/guitar), Ronnie 'Plonk' Lane (b. 1 April 1946, Plaistow, London, England; bass), Jimmy Winston (b. James Langwith, 20 April 1945, Stratford, London, England; organ) and Kenny Jones (b. 16 September 1948, Stepney, London, England; drums). Fronted by former child actor Marriott, the group were signed to Don Arden's Contemporary Records management and production and their product was licensed to Decca. Their debut, 'Whatcha Gonna Do About It', an in-house composition/production by Ian Samwell (formerly of Cliff Richard's Drifters) was a vibrant piece of Solomon Burke-influenced R&B that brought them into the UK Top 20. Within weeks of their chart entry, organist Smith was replaced by Ian McLagan (b. 12 May 1945, London, England), a former member of Boz And The Boz People. While their first release had been heavily hyped, the second, 'I Got Mine', failed to chart. Arden responded to this setback by recruiting hit songwriters Kenny Lynch and Mort Shuman, whose catchy 'Sha-La-La-La-Lee' gave the group a UK Top 3 hit. The Marriott/Lane composed 'Hey Girl' reinforced their chart credibility, which reached its apogee with the striking, Arden produced 'All Or Nothing'. The latter was their most raucous single to date; its strident chords and impassioned vocal ensuring the disc classic status in the annals of mid-60s UK white soul. The festive 'My Mind's Eye' brought a change of style, which coincided with disagreements with their record company.

By early 1967, the group were in litigation with their manager and found themselves banned from the prestigious television programme *Top Of The Pops* after Marriott insulted its producer. A final two singles for Decca, 'I Can't Make It' and 'Patterns' proved unsuccessful. Meanwhile, the group underwent a series of short term management agreements with Harold Davison, Robert Wace and Andrew Oldham. The Rolling Stones' manager signed them to his label Immediate and this coincided with their metamorphosis into a quasi-psychedelic ensemble. The drug influenced 'Here Comes The Nice' was followed by the experimental and slightly parodic 'Itchycoo Park'. With their Top 10 status reaffirmed, the group returned to their blues style

with the powerful 'Tin Soldier', which featured P.P. Arnold on backing vocals. For 'Lazy Sunday' the group combined their cockney charm with an alluring paean to hippie indolence; it was a strange combination of magnificent music hall wit and drug influenced mind expansion. Those same uneasy elements were at work on their chart-topping *Ogden's Nut Gone Flake*, which won several design awards for its innovative round cover in the shape of a tobacco tin. For their final single, the group bowed out with the chaotic 'The Universal' and the posthumous hit 'Afterglow Of Your Love'. By February 1969, Marriott decided to join Peter Frampton of the Herd in a new group, which emerged as Humble Pie. The Small Faces then disbanded only to re-emerge as the Faces. Successful reissues of 'Itchycoo Park' and 'Lazy Sunday' in the mid-70s persuaded Marriott, Jones, McLagan and new boy Rick Wills to revive the Small Faces name for a series of albums, none of which were well received. Subsequently, Jones joined the Who, Wills teamed up with Foreigner, McLagan played live with the Rolling Stones and Marriott reverted to playing small pubs in London. In 1989, Marriott recorded *30 Seconds To Midnight*, but was unable to forge a fully successful solo career. He perished in a fire in his Essex home in 1991.

Albums: *The Small Faces* (1966), *Small Faces* (1967), *There Are But Four Faces* (1968), *Ogden's Nut Gone Flake* (1968). Compilations: *From The Beginning* (1967), *The Autumn Stone* (1969), *Early Faces* (1972), *Playmates* (1977), *78 In The Shade* (1978), *For Your Delight* (1980).

Smoke

Mick Rowley (vocals), Mal Luker (lead guitar), Phil Peacock (rhythm guitar), John 'Zeke' Lund (bass) and Geoff Gill (drums) were initially known as the Shots. This Yorkshire, England, group was groomed for success by Alan Brush, a gravel pit owner and self-made millionaire who harboured dreams of pop management. His ambitions faltered when the Shots' lone single, 'Keep A Hold Of What You Got', failed to sell. Phil Peacock then dropped out of the line-up, but within months the remaining quartet approached producer Monty Babson with several new demos. The most promising song, 'My Friend Jack', was released in February 1967 under the group's new name, the Smoke. Although irresistibly commercial, problems arose when the line 'my friend Jack eats sugar lumps' was construed as celebrating drug abuse. The record was banned in Britain, but became a massive hit on the continent and on the pirate radio ships, inspiring a release for the group's only album, *It's Smoke Time*. Later singles continued their quirky-styled pop, but they failed to garner a significant breakthrough. Having toyed with yet another appellation, Chords Five; Lund, Luker and Gill began work as resident musicians at Babson's Morgan Sound studios. Several more singles, credited to the Smoke, appeared on various labels during the late 60s/early 70s. These often throwaway efforts featured sundry variations on the above triumvirate, accompanied by any other backroom staff present.

Album: *It's Smoke Time* (1967). Compilation: *My Friend Jack* (1988).

Smoke

Soft Machine

Founded in 1966, the original line-up was Robert Wyatt, Kevin Ayers, Daevid Allen, Mike Ratledge and, very briefly, guitarist Larry Nolan. By autumn 1967 the classic line-up of the Softs' art-rock period (Ayers, Wyatt and Ratledge) had settled in. They toured with Jimi Hendrix, who, along with his producer, ex-Animals member Chas Chandler, encouraged them and facilitated the recording of their first album. (There had been earlier demos for Giorgio Gomelesky's Marmalade label, but these were not issued until later, and then kept re-appearing in different configurations under various titles.) From the end of 1968, when Ayers left, until February 1970, the personnel was in a state of flux (Lyn Dobson, Marc Charig and Nick Evans were members for a while), and the music was evolving into a distinctive brand jazz-rock. Arguably, *Volume Two* and *Third* contain their most intriguing and

exciting performances. Highlighted by Wyatt's very English spoken/sung vocals, the group had still managed to inject some humour into their work. The finest example is Wyatt's mercurial 'Moon In June'. By mid-1970 the second definitive line-up (Ratledge, Wyatt, Hugh Hopper and Elton Dean) was finally in place. It was this band that Tim Souster showcased when he was allowed a free hand to organise a late-night Promenade Concert in August 1970. In autumn 1971, Wyatt left to form Matching Mole (a clever pun on the French translation of Soft Machine; Machine Molle), and Phil Howard came in on drums until John Marshall became the permanent drummer. For the next few years, through a number of personnel changes (farewell Dean and Hopper, welcome Roy Babbington, Karl Jenkins) the Soft Machine were, for many listeners, the standard against which all jazz-rock fusions, including most of the big American names, had to be measured. However, with Ratledge's departure in January 1976 the group began to sound like a legion of other guitar-led fusion bands, competent and craftsmanlike, but, despite the virtuosity of Allan Holdsworth and John Etheridge, without the edge of earlier incarnations, and certainly without the dadaist elements of Wyatt's time. In 1984, Jenkins and Marshall brought together a new edition of the band (featuring Dave Macrae, Ray Warleigh and a number of new Jenkins compositions) for a season at Ronnie Scott's club. It is their first three albums which contain the best of their work which clearly shows they were one of the most adventurous and important progressive bands of the late 60s.

Albums: *Soft Machine* (1968), *Soft Machine Volume Two* (1969), *Third* (1970), *Fourth* (1971), *Fifth* (1972), *Six* (1973), *Seven* (1973), *Bundles* (1975), *Softs* (1976), *Triple Echo* (1977, a 3-LP set, mainly a compilation but including some previously unissued material), *Live At The Proms 1970* (1988), *The Peel Sessions* (1990), *The Untouchable* (1990), *As If . . .*(1991).

Soft Machine

Sonny And Cher

Sonny And Cher

Although touted as the misunderstood young lovers of 1965 folk rock Sonny Bono and Cher were not as fresh and naive as their image suggested. Salvatore Bono (b. 16 February 1935, Detroit, Michigan) already had a chequered history in the music business stretching back to the late 50s when he wrote and produced records by such artists as Larry Williams, Wynona Carr and Don And Dewey. Bono also recorded for several small labels under an array of aliases such as Don Christy, Sonny Christy and Ronny Sommers. With arranger Jack Nitzsche, he co-wrote 'Needles And Pins', a UK number 1 for the Searchers in 1964. That same year, Sonny married Cherilyn Sarkasian La Pier (b. 20 May 1946, El Centro, California) whom he had met while recording with the renowned producer Phil Spector. Although the duo recorded a couple of singles under the exotic name Caeser And Cleo, it was as Sonny and Cher that they found fame with the transatlantic number 1 'I Got You Babe'. Arranged by the underrated Harold Battiste, the single was a majestic example of romanticized folk rock and one of the best produced discs of its time. Bono's carefree, bohemian image obscured the workings of a music business veteran and it was no coincidence that he took full advantage of the pair's high profile. During late 1965, they dominated the charts as both a duo

and soloists with such hits was 'Baby Don't Go', 'All I Really Want To Do', 'Laugh At Me', 'Just You' and 'But You're Mine'. Although their excessive output resulted in diminishing returns, their lean periods were still punctuated by further hits, most notably 'Little Man' and 'The Beat Goes On'. By the late 60s, they had fallen from critical grace, but starred in a couple of low budget movies, *Good Times* and *Chastity*. A brief resurgence as MOR entertainers in the 70s brought them their own television series, although by that time they had divorced. Eventually, extra-curricular acting activities ended their long-standing musical partnership. Cher went on to achieve a phenomenally successful acting and singing career.
Albums: *Look At Us* (1965), *The Wondrous World Of Sonny And Cher* (1966), *In Case You're In Love* (1967), *Good Times* (1967), *Sonny And Cher Live* (1971), *All Ever Need Is You* (1972), *Mama Was A Rock And Roll Singer - Papa Used To Write All Her Songs* (1974), *Live In Las Vegas, Vol. 2* (1974). Compilations: *Baby Don't Go* (1965, early recordings), *The Best Of Sonny And Cher* (1967), *Greatest Hits* (1974), *The Sonny And Cher Collection: An Anthology Of Their Hits Alone And Together* (1991).

Sorrows

Formed in Coventry, England in 1963, the Sorrows consisted of Don Maughn (vocals), Pip Whitcher (lead guitar), Wez Price (rhythm guitar), Philip Packham (bass) and Bruce Finley (drums). They achieved minor fame with 'Take A Heart', a pulsating, brooding performance wherein a rolling drum pattern and throbbing bass create a truly atmospheric single. Their fusion of R&B and mod-pop continued on several ensuing releases, but the quintet was unable to secure a consistent success. Maughn, who was later known as Don Fardon, left the group for a solo career in 1967. A restructured Sorrows, Price, Packham, Finley and Chris Fryers (vocals/organ/guitar), then moved to Italy, where 'Take A Heart' had become a substantial hit. The group completed several further recordings exclusive to that country, before breaking up at the end of the decade.
Albums: *Take A Heart* (1965), *Old Songs New Songs* (1968). Compilation: *Pink Purple Yellow And Red* (1987 - compiles all of the original group's singles).

Soul, Jimmy

b. James McCleese, 24 August 1942, Weldon, North Carolina, USA, d. 25 June 1988. A former boy preacher, McCleese acquired his 'Soul' epithet from his congregations. He subsequently toured southern US states as a member of several gospel groups, including the famed Nightingales, wherein Jimmy was billed as 'The Wonder Boy', before discovering a

forte for pop and R&B. He became a popular attraction around the Norfolk area of Virginia where he was introduced to songwriter/producer Frank Guida, who guided the career of Gary 'U.S.' Bonds. Soul joined Guida's S.P.Q.R label and scored a Top 20 US R&B hit with his debut single, 'Twistin' Matilda', before striking gold with his second release, 'If You Wanna Be Happy', which topped the US pop chart in 1963. Both songs were remakes of popular calypso tunes, reflecting Guida's passion for West Indian music. The song also became a minor hit in Britain, and was latterly covered by the Peter B's, a group which included Peter Bardens, Peter Green and Mick Fleetwood. It sadly proved Soul's final chart entry although he nonetheless remained a popular entertainer. Jimmy Soul died in June 1988.
Albums: *If You Wanna Be Happy* (1963), *Jimmy Soul And The Belmonts* (1963).

Sounds Nice

When Decca Records' A&R representative Tony Hall heard Jane Birkin and Serge Gainsbourg's 'Je T'Aime ... Moi Non Plus' at the Antibes festival in the South of France, he immediately recognized the potential of an instrumental version. When the song was duly banned in Britain in 1969 this newly formed and as yet unnamed group recorded a non-sexy version retitled 'Love At First Sight' which later became a Top 20 hit. After the recording session, Hall played a finished tape to Paul McCartney who casually remarked, 'sounds nice', thereby giving the group a name. Although the hit duo never charted again, their line-up was particularly interesting. Tim Mycroft, after stints with the Freewheelers, the Third Ear Band and Gun had decided to concentrate on writing and teamed-up with arranger Paul Buckmaster. The third man behind the hit was producer Gus Dudgeon, who had recently enjoyed hits with David Bowie, Locomotive and the Bonzo Dog Doo-Dah Band. Following their pledge to create 'instrumentals with a difference' Buckmaster and Dudgeon went on to work successfully with Elton John.

Sounds Orchestral

Led by pianist John Pearson (b. 18 June 1925, London, England), Sounds Orchestral was a conglomeration of session musicians who included in their ranks Kenny Clare (ex-drummer with Johnny Dankworth) and bass player/producer Tony Reeves (ex-Colosseum). The orchestral concept was conceived by renowned producer John Schroeder. 'People are looking for a change from the incessant beat and I intend Sounds to fulfil that demand', he told the pop press in early 1965. The group went someway towards fulfilling that ambition with their cover of the Vince Guaraldi Trio's 1960 recording 'Cast Your Fate To The Wind'. With its melodic arrangement and subtle jazz rhythm, the song took the UK charts by storm in January 1965, climbing into the Top 3. Surprisingly, this unlikely pop hit also reached the US Top 10, paving the way for a number of instrumental hits during 1965, courtesy of artists ranging from Horst Jankowski to Marcello Minerebi and Nini Rosso.
Selected albums: *Cast Your Fate To The Wind* (1970), *Dreams* (1983), *Sleepy Shores* (1985). Compilation: *Golden Hour Of Sounds Orchestral* (1973).

Spanky And Our Gang

The original line-up of this engaging US harmony group - Elaine 'Spanky' McFarlane (lead vocals/tambourine/ washboard), Nigel Pickering (12-string guitar) and Oz Bach (stand-up bass/kazoo) - began performing together in Chicago's folk clubs. Within months they were joined by Malcolm Hale (guitar/vocals) and John George Seiter (drums) and this restructured line-up scored a US Top 10 hit with its debut release, 'Sunday Will Never Be The Same'. This evocative song bore traces of the Mamas And The Papas and the more conservative Seekers, a style maintained on its follow-up, 'Lazy Day'. Bach was then replaced by Geoffrey Myers, who in turn made way for Kenny Hodges. Sixth member Lefty Baker (vocals/guitar) expanded the group's harmonic range, but while the haunting 'Like To Get To Know You' suggested a more mature direction, Spanky And Our Gang seemed more content with a bubbly, good-time, but rather lightweight approach. The premature death of Malcolm Hale in 1968 undermined the group's inner confidence, and any lingering momentum faltered when 'Give A Damn', a campaign song for the Urban Coalition League, incurred an airplay ban in several states. The remaining quintet broke up in 1969 although McFarlane and Pickering retained the name for the country-influenced *Change*. In 1981 the former joined a rejuvenated Mamas And The Papas, before touring with an all-new Spanky And Our Gang.
Albums: *Spanky And Our Gang* (1967), *Like To Get To Know You* (1968), *Anything You Choose/Without Rhyme Or Reason* (1969), *Spanky And Our Gang Live* (1970), *Change* (1975). Compilations: *Spanky's Greatest Hits* (1969), *The Best Of Spanky And Our Gang* (1986).

Spector, Phil

b. Harvey Phillip Spector, 26 December 1940, Bronx, New York, USA. Arguably pop's most distinctive record producer. Spector became involved in music upon moving to Fairfax, California in 1953. While there, he joined a loosely-knit community of young aspirants, including Lou Adler, Bruce Johnson and Sandy Nelson, the latter of whom played drums on Spector's debut recording, 'To Know Him Is To Love Him'. This million-selling single for the Teddy Bears - Spector, Annette Kleibard and Marshall Leib - topped the US chart in 1958, but further releases by the group proved less successful. The artist's next project, the Spectors Three, was undertaken under the aegis of local entrepreneurs Lee Hazelwood and Lester Sill, but when it too reaped little commercial rewards, the latter recommended Phil's talents to New York production team Leiber And Stoller. In later years Spector made extravagant claims about his work from this period which have been rebuffed equally forcibly by his one-time mentors. He did contribute greatly as a composer, co-writing 'Spanish Harlem' and 'Young Boy Blues' for Ben E. King, while adding a notable guitar obligato to the Drifters' 'On Broadway'. His productions, although less conspicuous, included releases by LaVern Baker, Ruth Brown and Billy Storm, as well as the Top Notes' original version of the seminal 'Twist And Shout'. Spector's first major success as a producer came with Ray Petersen's version of 'Corrina Corrina', a US Top 10 in 1960, and Curtis Lee's 'Pretty Little Angel Eyes', which reached number 7 the following year. Work for the Paris Sisters not only engendered a Top 5 hit, ('I Love How You Love Me') but rekindled an association with Lester Sill, with whom Spector formed Philles Records in 1961.

Within months he bought his partner out to become sole owner, and this autocratic behaviour would mark all subsequent endeavours. It nonetheless resulted in a string of classic recordings for the Crystals and Ronettes including 'He's A Rebel' (1962), 'Then He Kissed Me', 'Be My Baby' and 'Baby I Love You' (all 1963) which were not only substantial international hits, but defined the entire 'girl-group' genre. Imitative releases supervised by David Gates, Bob Crewe and Sonny Bono, although excellent in their own right, failed to recapture Spector's dense production technique, later dubbed the 'wall of sound', which relied on lavish orchestration, layers of percussion and swathes of echo. Recordings were undertaken at the Gold Star studio in Los Angeles where arranger Jack Nitzsche and engineer Larry Levine worked with a team of exemplary session musicians, including Tommy Tedeso (guitar), Larry Knechtal (piano, bass), Harold Battiste, Leon Russell (keyboards) and Hal Blaine (drums). Although ostensibly geared to producing singles, Phil did undertake the ambitious A Christmas Gift To You, on which his label's premier acts performed old and new seasonal favourites. Although not a contemporary success - its bonhomie was made redundant following the assassination of President Kennedy - the set is now rightly regarded as a classic. Spector's releases also featured some of the era's finest songwriting teams - Goffin And King, Barry And Greenwich and Barry Mann and Cynthia Weil - the latter of which composed 'You've Lost That Lovin' Feelin" for the Righteous Brothers, the producer's stylistic apogee. Several critics also cite 'River Deep Mountain High', a 1966 single by Ike And Tina Turner as Spector's greatest moment. It represented Spector's most ambitious production, but although his efforts were rewarded with a UK Top 3 hit, this impressive release barely scraped the US Hot 100 and a dispirited Spector folded his label and retired from music for several years.

He re-emerged in 1969 with a series of releases for A&M which included 'Black Pearl' a US Top 20 hit entry for Sonny Charles And The Checkmates. Controversy then dogged his contribution to the Beatles' Let It Be album. Spector assembled the set from incomplete tapes, but his use of melancholic orchestration on 'The Long And Winding Road' infuriated the song's composer, Paul McCartney, who cited this intrusion during the group's rancorous break-up. Spector nonetheless became installed at their Apple label, where he produced albums by John Lennon (The Plastic Ono Band, Imagine, Sometime In New York City), George Harrison (All Things Must Pass and the commemorative Concert For Bangla Desh). However, his behaviour grew increasingly erratic following the break-up of his marriage to former Ronette Ronnie Spector and his relationship with Lennon was severed during sessions for the nostalgic Rock 'N' Roll album (1974). In the meantime Phil had established the Warner-Spector outlet which undertook new recordings with, among others, Cher and Nilsson, as well as several judicious re-releases. A similar relationship with UK Polydor led to the formation of Phil Spector International, on which contemporary singles by Dion, Darlene Love and Jerri Bo Keno vied with 60s' recordings and archive material. As the 70s progressed so Spector became a recluse, although he emerged to produce albums by Leonard Cohen (Death Of Ladies Man - 1977) and the Ramones (End Of The Century - 1980), the latter of which included a revival of 'Baby I Love You', the group's sole UK Top 10 hit. Despite undertaking abortive sessions with the Flamin' Groovies, Phil remained largely detached from music throughout the 80s, although litigation against Leiber and Stoller and biographer Mark Ribowsky kept his name in the news. Spector was inducted into the Rock 'n' Roll Hall Of Fame in 1989, and having adopted Allen Klein as representative, completed negotiations with EMI for the rights to his extensive catalogue. The interest generated by this acquisition is a tribute to the respect afforded this producer whose major achievements were contained within a brief, three-year, period.

Compilations: A Christmas Gift To You (1963), Phil

Spector Wall Of Sound, Volume 1: The Ronettes (1975), *Phil Spector Wall Of Sound, Volume 2: Bob B. Soxx And The Blue Jeans* (1975), *Phil Spector Wall Of Sound, Volume 3: The Crystals* (1975), *Phil Spector Wall Of Sound, Volume 4: Yesterday's Hits Today* (1976), *Phil Spector Wall Of Sound, Volume 5: Rare Masters* (1976), *Phil Spector Wall Of Sound, Volume 6: Rare Masters Volume 2* (1976), *The Phil Spector Story* (1976), *Echoes Of The Sixties* (1977), *Phil Spector 1974-1979* (1979), *Wall Of Sound* (1981), *Phil Spector: The Early Productions 1958-1961* (1984), *Twist And Shout: Twelve Atlantic Tracks Produced By Phil Spector* (1989).
Further reading: *Out Of His Head*, Richard Williams, London, 1972. *The Phil Spector Story*, Rob Finnis, London, 1975. *He's A Rebel: The Truth About Phil Spector, Rock 'N' Roll's Legendary Madman*, Mark Ribowsky, New York, 1989.

Spirit

'Out of Topanga Canyon, from the Time Coast' stated the CBS publicity blurb for one of their finest acts of the late 60s. The rock band with a hint of jazz arrived with their self-titled debut album. Formerly Spirits Rebellious, the new band comprised: Randy California (b. Randolph Wolfe, 20 February 1951, Los Angeles, California, USA; guitar), Ed 'Mr Skin' Cassidy (b. 4 May 1931, Chicago, Illinois, USA; drums), John Locke (b. 25 September 1943, Los Angeles, California, USA; keyboards), Jay Ferguson (b. 10 May 1947, Burbank, California, USA; vocals) and Mark Andes (b. 19 February 1948, Philadelphia, Pennsylvania, USA; bass). Media interest was assured when it was found out that not only had the band a shaven-headed drummer who had played with many jazz giants including, Gerry Mulligan, Cannonball Adderley and Thelonious Monk, but that he was also the guitarist's father (later amended to step-father). The quality of the music however needed no hype. The album's tasteful use of strings mixed with Locke's stunning electric piano blended well with California's mature hard-edged guitar. Ferguson's lyrics were quirky and brilliant. 'Fresh Garbage', for example, contained the lines; 'Well look beneath your lid some morning, see the things you didn't quite consume, the world's a can for your fresh garbage.' The album reached number 31 in the US chart and stayed for over seven months. The following year's *The Family That Plays Together* in 1969, was a greater success and spawned a US Top 30 hit single 'I Got A Line On You'. Ferguson had to share the songwriting credits with the fast-developing California. The Lou Adler-produced set flowed with perfect continuity and almost 25 years later, the album sounds fresh. *Clear Spirit* contained Locke's instrumental music for the film *The Model Shop*, including the beautifully atmospheric 'Ice'. As a touring band they were most impressive, with Cassidy's massive drum kit

sometimes dwarfing the stage. California would often use a clear perspex Stratocaster, while tinkering with his echoplex device which emitted the most colourful sound. Ferguson meanwhile, would keep the female fans happy, bare chested, west-coast sun tanned and handsome; he was a natural sex-symbol. The band's fourth collection, *The Twelve Dreams Of Dr Sardonicus* was arguably their finest work with Ferguson and California's songwriting reaching a peak. Although it was their lowest charting album to date (failing to make the Top 50 in the USA), it has subsequently and deservedly become their best-selling record. Randy's awareness for environmental and ecological issues was cleverly linked into his song 'Nature's Way', while Ferguson put in strong contributions including 'Animal Zoo'. At this time Spirit had their legendary album *Potatoland* rejected (it was eventually released after active petitioning from the UK rock magazine, *Dark Star*). The tensions within the band were mounting and Ferguson and Andes left to form Jo Jo Gunne. Surprisingly, California also departed to be replaced by Al and Christian Staehely. The John Locke dominated *Feedback* was not a commercial or critical success. The remains of Spirit disintegrated, while Jo Jo Gunne prospered and Randy attempted a solo career.

In 1976 Spirit returned with a new recording contract and a rejuvenated California. During the recent past it was found that Randy had jumped off London's Waterloo Bridge into the polluted River Thames and was miraculously rescued. The new nucleus of California, Cassidy and bassist Larry Knight toured regularly and built up a loyal following in Britain and Germany. The albums, whilst delighting the fans, sold poorly and the band became despondent. Nevertheless, there were some spectacular highlights, most notably the stunning yet perplexing double album *Spirit of '76*. While Ferguson was enjoying great success as a solo artist, Mark Andes was with Firefall. A depressed California interviewed in London in 1978-79 stated that Spirit would not rise and that he would *never* play with Ed Cassidy again. Fortunately California was wrong as the original five were back together in 1984 for *The Thirteenth Dream*. They attempted re-workings of vintage Spirit numbers and sadly the album failed. California still keeps the Spirit name alive with various assorted line-ups, usually together with the fatherly hand of Ed Cassidy.
Albums: *Spirit* (1968), *The Family That Plays Together* (1969), *Clear Spirit* (1969), *The Twelve Dreams Of Dr. Sardonicus* (1970), *Feedback* (1972), *Spirit Of '76* (1975), *Son Of Spirit* (1976), *Farther Along* (1976), *Future Games (A Magical Kahuana Dream)* (1977), *Live* (1978), *Journey To Potatoland* (1981), (1984), *The Thirteenth Dream (Spirit Of '84)* (1984), *Rapture In The Chamber* (1989), *Tent Of Miracles* (1990).

Compilations: *The Best Of Spirit* (1973). *Chronicles* (1991), *Time Circle* (1991), *Spirit - The Collection* (1991).

Spotniks

Spotnicks

A Swedish instrumental group of the late 50s and early 60s, their career actually continued well into the 80s. Originally they consisted of Bo Winberg (b. 27 March 1939, Gothenburg, Sweden), Bob Lander (b. Bo Starander, 11 March 1942, Sweden), Bjorn Thelin (b. 11 June 1942, Sweden) and Ole Johannsson (b. Sweden). They were assembled by Winberg in 1957 as the Frazers, with Lander on guitar and vocals, Thelin on bass, Johannsson on drums, with Winberg himself playing lead guitar and building most of the bands equipment; including a guitar transmitter that allowed primitive flex-free playing. Spotted by Roland F. Fernedorg in 1960 they became the Spotnicks in 1961 and had several hit singles in their homeland. They were signed to Oriole in the UK in 1962 and toured the country, gaining instant notoriety for their gimmick of wearing spacesuits on stage. They played a mixture of instrumentals and Lander vocals, and first hit with 'Orange Blossom Special' in 1962. That same year they toured Russia and were introduced to Cosmonaut Yuri Gagarin.

They had further UK hits with 'Rocket Man', 'Hava Nagila' and 'Just Listen To My Heart' during 1962-

63. In 1963 they made their cinematic debut in the pop film *Just For Fun*. A cover of the Tornados' 'Telstar' was released in Sweden under the pseudonym the Shy Ones. Johansson left in 1963 to become a priest and was replaced by Derek Skinner (b. 5 March 1944, London, England). In 1965 they added organist Peter Winsens to the line-up and in September Skinner left to be replaced by Jimmy Nicol. Nicol was the drummer famed for having deputized for Ringo Starr on a 1964 World Tour when he was hospitalized after having collapsed with tonsillitis. Nicol had also played with the Blue Flames and his own band the Shubdubs. After much touring Nicol left in early 1967 and was replaced by Tommy Tausis (b. 22 March 1946). In October Thelin was called up for National Service and replaced by Magnus Hellsberg. Several further line-up changes occurred over the following years as the band continued to tour and record prolifically in Europe. Winberg was the only constant member although Lander was normally in the band until he left to form the Viking Truckers. The band were still active as of the mid-80s.

Selected albums: *Out-A-Space* (1963), *The Spotnicks In Paris* (1964), *The Very Best Of The Spotnicks* (1982), *In The Middle Of The Universe* (1984), *Music For The Millions* (1985), *Highway Boogie* (1986), *Love Is Blue* (1988).

Springfield, Dusty

b. Mary O'Brien, 16 April 1939, London, England. A long-standing critical favourite but sadly neglected by the public from the early 70s until the end of the 80s, the career of Britain's finest white soul singer has been a turbulent one. Formerly referred to as 'the White Negress', Dusty began as a member of the cloying pop trio the Lana Sisters in the 50s, and moved (with her brother Tom) into the Springfields, one of Britain's top pop/folk acts of the early 60s. During the Merseybeat boom Dusty made a bold move and went solo. Her 1963 debut with 'I Only Want To Be With You' removed any doubts the previously shy convent girl may have had; this jaunty, endearing song is now a classic of 60s' pop. She joined the swinging London club scene and became a familiar icon for teenage girls with her famous beehive blonde hairstyle and her dark 'panda' eye make-up. Over the next three years Dusty was constantly in the best-selling singles chart and consistently won the top female singer award, beating off stiff opposition from Lulu, Cilla Black and Sandie Shaw. During this time she campaigned unselfishly on behalf of the then little known American soul and Motown artists; her mature taste in music made her different from many of her contemporaries. Springfield's early albums were strong sellers, although they now appear to have been rushed

Dusty Springfield and Dave Clark

what was underground and hip, and what was pop and unhip, got under way. Dusty, well aware that she could be doomed to the variety club circuit in Britain, moved to Memphis, one of the music capitals of the world, and immediately succeeded in recording her finest work, *Dusty In Memphis*. The production team of Tom Dowd, Jerry Wexler and Arif Mardin were the first people to recognize and allow her natural soul voice to be placed up-front, rather than competing with the arrangement. The album remains a classic and one of the finest records of the 60s. The single 'Son Of A Preacher Man' became a major hit, but the album failed in Britain and reached a derisory number 99 in the US chart. Following this bitter blow Dusty retreated and kept a lower profile, although her second album for Atlantic, *A Brand New Me*, was a moderate success. Released in the UK as *From Dusty With Love,* the Thom Bell/Kenny Gamble credited production boosted her failing popularity in Britain, where she still resided. *Cameo,* from 1973, exuded class and a superlative cover of Van Morrison's 'Tupelo Honey', but produced no hit singles.

Dusty had disappeared from the charts, and following a veiled admission in an interview in the London *Evening Standard* in 1975 that she was bisexual, she moved to Los Angeles. For the next few years she recorded sporadically, preferring to spend her time with tennis players like Billie Jean King and to campaign for animal rights (she is an obsessive cat lover). Following the release of the inappropriately titled *It Begins Again*, she was propelled towards a comeback, which failed. The strong disco-influenced *White Heat* in 1982 was her best album during these musical barren times. A further attempt to put her in the public eye was orchestrated by club owner Peter Stringfellow, but after one single 'Just Like Butterflies' she flew off again.

Her phoenix-like return at the end of the 80s was due entirely to Neil Tennant and Chris Lowe of the Pet Shop Boys who persuaded her to duet with them on their hit single 'What Have I Done To Deserve This?'. They then wrote the theme for the film *Scandal*, which Dusty took into the best-sellers. Now recording and living back in Britain, she is less insecure, older and wiser. Springfield still retains a singing voice that can chill the spine and warm the heart, and with modern recording techniques she can now be heard to greater effect.

works. Her pioneering choice of material by great songwriters such as Burt Bacharach, Hal David, Randy Newman and Carole King was exemplary. The orchestral arrangements of Ivor Raymonde and Johnny Franz drowned Dusty's voice at times, and her vocals appeared thin and strained. She made superb cover versions of classics such as 'Mockingbird', 'Anyone Who Had A Heart', 'Wishin' And Hopin'', 'La Bamba', 'Who Can I Turn To' and 'Sunny'. Her worldwide success came, when her friend Vicki Wickham, and Simon Napier-Bell added English words to the Italian hit 'Io Che Non Vivo (Senzate)' and created 'You Don't Have To Say You Love Me'; this million selling opus proved her sole UK chart topper in 1966. By the end of the following year she was becoming disillusioned with the show business carousel on which she found herself trapped. Her comparatively progressive *Where Am I Going* was an artistic success but it flopped, and the following year a similar fate awaited the excellent *Dusty . . . Definitely*. Her exquisite choice of songs was no longer getting through to the fans. On this album she executed a fine version of Herb Alpert's 'This Girl's In Love', and the definitive interpretation of Randy Newman's 'I Think It's Going To Rain Today'.

In 1968, as Britain was bathed in the progressive music revolution, the uncomfortable split between

Albums: *A Girl Called Dusty* (1964), *Everything Is Coming Up Dusty* (1965), *Where Am I Going* (1967), *Dusty . . . Definitely* (1968), *Dusty In Memphis* (1969), *A Brand New Me (From Dusty With Love)* (1970), *See All Her Faces* (1972), *Cameo* (1973), *Dusty Sings Burt Bacharach And Carole King* (1975), *It Begins Again* (1978), *Living Without Your Love* (1979), *White Heat* (1982), *Reputation* (1990). Compilations: *Golden Hits*

(1966), *Greatest Hits* (1981), *The Silver Collection* (1988).
Further reading: *Dusty*, Lucy O'Brien.

Springfields

Formed in 1960, this popular UK folk-based attraction was based around singer/songwriter Tom O'Brien (b. 2 July 1934, Hampstead, London, England) and his sister Mary (b. 16 April 1939, Hampstead, London, England), who accompanied him on guitar. Better known as Tom and Dusty Springfield, the duo was later joined by the former's partner, Tim Field, and the following year the revitalized unit became one of Britain's top vocal groups. The trio enjoyed UK Top 5 singles with 'Island Of Dreams' (1962) and 'Say I Won't Be There' (1963), by which time Field had been replaced by Mike Longhurst-Pickworth, who took the less-cumbersome professional name Mike Hurst. The Springfields enjoyed success in America with 'Silver Threads And Golden Needles', a country standard which paradoxically failed to chart in Britain. However, although the single went on to sell in excess of one million copies, it was the group's only substantial US hit. The group split up in 1963 with each member then pursuing solo ventures. Dusty Springfield became one of the Britain's leading female singers, brother Tom continued his songwriting career while Hurst established himself as a leading pop producer through work with Cat Stevens.
Albums: *Silver Threads And Golden Needles* (1962), *Folk Songs From The Hills* (1963), *Kinda Folksy* (1963).
Compilations: *The Springfields Story* (mid-60s).

Standells

Tony Valentino (guitar/vocals) and Larry Tamblyn (organ) formed the Standells in 1962. The early line-up included drummer Gary Leeds, who later found fame in the Walker Brothers. Gary Lane (bass) and former Mousketeer, Dick Dodd (drums). The quartet became a leading teen-based attraction in plush Los Angeles night-spots. This conformist image was shattered on their association with producer Ed Cobb who fashioned a series of angst-cum-protest punk anthems in 'Sometimes Good Guys Don't Wear White', 'Why Pick On Me' and the exceptional 'Dirty Water', a US number 11 hit in 1966. In 1966 Gary Lane left the group during a tour of Florida. He was initially succeeded by Dave Burke who in turn was replaced the following year by John Fleck (nee Fleckenstein). The latter, who co-wrote 'Can't Explain' on Love's debut album, has since become a leading cinematographer. The Standells also appeared in the exploitation film, *Riot On Sunset Strip* (1967), but by this time their career was waning. Unfashionable in the face of San Francisco's acid-rock, the group's career was confined to the cabaret circuit as original members drifted away. Lowell George, later of Frank Zappa's Mothers Of Invention and Little Feat, briefly joined their ranks, but by 1970 the Standells had become an oldies attraction.
Albums: *The Standells Live At PJs* (1964), *Live And Out Of Sight* (1964), *Dirty Water* (1966), *Why Pick On Me* (1966), *The Hot Ones* (1966), *Try It* (1967).
Compilation: *The Best Of The Standells* (1984).

Staple Singers

This well-known US family gospel group consisted of Roebuck 'Pops' Staples (b. 28 December 1915, Winona, Mississippi, USA) and four of his children, Mavis Staples (b. 1940, Chicago, Illinois, USA), Pervis Staples (b. 1935), Cleotha Staples (b. 1934) and Yvonne Staples (b. 1939). The quintet fused an original presentation of sacred music, offsetting Mavis Staples' striking voice against her father's lighter tenor, rather than follow the accustomed 'jubilee' or 'quartet' formations, prevalent in the genre. Pops' striking guitar work, reminiscent of delta-blues, added to their inherent individuality. Singles such as 'Uncloudy Day', 'Will The Circle Be Unbroken' and 'I'm Coming Home', proved especially popular, while an original song, 'This May Be The Last time' provided the inspiration for the Rolling Stones' hit 'The Last Time'.
During the early half of the 60s, the group tried to broaden its scope. Two singles produced by Larry Williams, 'Why (Am I Treated So Bad)' and 'For What It's Worth', a Stephen Stills' composition, anticipated the direction the Staples would take on signing with Stax in 1967. Here they began recording material contributed by the label's established songwriters, including Homer Banks and Bettye Crutcher, which embraced a moral focus, rather than a specifically religious one. Reduced to a quartet following the departure of Pervis, a bubbling version of Bobby Bloom's 'Heavy Makes You Happy' (1970) gave the group their first R&B hit. This newfound appeal flourished with 'Respect Yourself' (1971) and 'I'll Take You There' (1972 - a US pop number 1), both of which expressed the group's growing confidence. Their popularity was confirmed with 'If You're Ready (Come Go With Me)' (1973), 'City In The Sky' (1974), and by appearances in two films, *Wattstax* and *Soul To Soul*. The Staple Singers later moved to the Curtom label where they had an immediate success with two songs from a Curtis Mayfield-penned film soundtrack, 'Let's Do It Again' (another US pop number 1) and 'New Orleans'. These recordings were the group's last major hits although a series of minor R&B chart places between 1984-85 continued the Staples' long-established ability to be both populist and inspirational.
Albums: *Gospel Program* (1961), *Hammers And Nails* (1962), *Great Day* (1963), *25th Day Of December*

(1962), *Spirituals* (1965), *Amen* (1965), *Freedom Highway* (1965), *Why* (1966), *This Little Light* (1966), *For What It's Worth* (1967), *Staple Singers* (1968), *Pray On* (1968), *Soul Folk In Action* (1968), *We'll Get Over* (1970), *I Had A Dream* (1970), *Heavy Makes You Happy* (1971), *The Staple Swingers* (1971), *Bealtitude: Respect Yourself* (1972), *Be What You Are* (1973), *Use What You Got* (1973), *City In The Sky* (1974), *Let's Do It Again* (1975), *Pass It On* (1976), *Family Tree* (1977), *Unlock Your Mind* (1978), *Hold On To Your Dream* (1981), *Turning Point* (1984). *The Staple Singers* (1985). Compilations: *Swing Low* (1961, early recordings), *Uncloudy Day* (1961, early recordings), *Tell It Like It Is* (1972, early recordings), *Great Day* (1975, early recordings), *Stand By Me* (1977, early recordings), *Respect Yourself: The Best Of The Staple Singers* (1988), *Freedom Highway* (1991). Solo album: Pop Staples (with Steve Cropper and Albert King) *Jammed Together* (1970), *Peace To The Neighborhood* (1992).

Starr, Edwin

b. Charles Hatcher, 21 January 1942, Nashville, Tennessee, USA. The brother of soul singers Roger and Willie Hatcher, Edwin Starr was raised in Cleveland, where he formed the Future Tones vocal group in 1957. They recorded one single for Tress, before Starr was drafted into the US Army for three years. After completing his service, he toured for two years with the Bill Doggett Combo, and was then offered a solo contract with the Ric Tic label in 1965. His first single, 'Agent Double-O-Soul', was a US Top 30 hit and Starr, exploited its popularity by appearing in a short promotional film with actor Sean Connery, best-known for his role as James Bond. 'Stop Her On Sight (SOS)' repeated this success, and brought Starr a cult following in Britain, where his strident, gutsy style proved popular in specialist soul clubs. When Motown Records took over the Ric Tic catalogue in 1967, Starr was initially overlooked by the label's hierarchy. He re-emerged in 1969 with '25 Miles', a Top 10 hit which owed much to the dominant soul style of the Stax label. An album of duets with Blinky brought some critical acclaim, before Starr resumed his solo career with the strident politically-outspoken, 'War', a US number 1 in 1970. Teamed with writer/producer Norman Whitfield, Starr was allowed to record material which had been earmarked for the Temptations, who covered both of his subsequent Motown hits, 'Stop The War Now' and 'Funky Music Sho Nuff Turns Me On'.

Starr's own credentials as a writer had been demonstrated on 'Oh How Happy', which had become a soul standard since he first recorded it in the late 60s. He was given room to blossom on the 1974 soundtrack *Hell Up In Harlem*, which fitted into the 'blaxploitation' mould established by Curtis Mayfield and Isaac Hayes. Tantalized by this breath of artistic freedom, Starr left the confines of Motown in 1975, recording for small labels in Britain and America before striking a new commercial seam in 1979 with two major disco hits, 'Contact' and 'HAPPY Radio'. In the 80s, Starr was based in the UK, where he collaborated with the Style Council on a record in support of striking coalminers, and enjoyed a run of club hits on the Hippodrome label, most notably 'It Ain't Fair' in 1985. Between 1989 and 1991 Starr worked with Ian Levine's Motor City Records, recording a re-make of '25 Miles' in a modern style and releasing *Where Is The Sound*.
Albums: *Soul Master* (1968), *25 Miles* (1969), with Blinky *Just We Two* (1969), *War And Peace* (1970), *Involved* (1971), *Hell Up In Harlem* (1974), *Free To Be Myself* (1975), *Edwin Starr* (1977), *Afternoon Sunshine* (1977), *Clean* (1978), *HAPPY Radio* (1979), *Stronger Than You Think I Am* (1980), *Where Is The Sound* (1991). Compilation: *20 Greatest Motown Hits* (1986).

Steppenwolf

Although based in southern California, Steppenwolf evolved out of a Toronto act, the Sparrow(s). John Kay (b. Joachim F. Krauledat, 12 April 1944, Tilsit, Germany; vocals), Michael Monarch (b. 5 July 1950, Los Angeles, California, USA; lead guitar), Goldy McJohn (b. 2 May 1945; keyboards), Rushton Moreve (bass) and Jerry Edmonton (b. 24 October 1946, Canada; drums) assumed their new name in 1967, inspired by the novel of cult author Herman Hesse. John Morgan replaced Moreve prior to recording. The group's exemplary debut album included 'Born To Be Wild' which reached number 2 in the US charts. This rebellious anthem was written by Dennis Edmonton (Mars Bonfire), guitarist in Sparrow and brother of drummer Jerry. It was featured in the famous opening sequence of the film *Easy Rider* and has since acquired classic status. Steppenwolf actively cultivated a menacing, hard-rock image, and successive collections mixed this heavy style with blues. 'Magic Carpet Ride' and 'Rock Me' were also US Top 10 singles yet the group deflected any criticism such temporal success attracted by addressing such contemporary issues as politics, drugs and racial prejudice.

Newcomers Larry Byrom (guitar) and Nick St. Nicholas (b. 28 September 1943, Hamburg, Germany; bass), former members of Time, were featured on *Monster*, Steppenwolf's most cohesive set. A concept album based on Kay's jaundiced view of contemporary (1970) America, it was a benchmark in the fortunes of the group. Further changes undermined their cohesion, and later versions seemed content to further a spurious biker image, rather than enlarge on earlier achievements. John Kay dissolved the band in 1972, but his solo career proved inconclusive and within two years he was leading a reconstituted Steppenwolf. The singer has left and reformed his creation several times over the ensuing years, but has been unable to repeat former glories.

Albums: *Steppenwolf* (1968), *The Second* (1968), *Steppenwolf At Your Birthday Party* (1969), *Early Steppenwolf* (1969 - Sparrow recordings from 1967), *Monster* (1969), *Steppenwolf 'Live'* (1970), *Steppenwolf 7* (1970), *For Ladies Only* (1971), *Rest In Peace* (1972), *Slow Flux* (1974), *Hour Of The Wolf* (1975), *Skullduggery* (1976), *Reborn To Be Wild* (1977), *Wolf Tracks* (1982), *Rise And Shine* (1990). Compilations: *Steppenwolf Gold* (1971), *16 Greatest Hits* (1973), *Masters Of Rock* (1975), *The Best Of Steppenwolf* (1979), *Golden Greats: Steppenwolf* (1985).

Cat Stevens

Stevens, Cat

b. Steven Georgiou, 21 July 1947, London, England. For Yusuf Islam, the constant search for the meaning of life that littered his lyrics and arose in interviews, seems to have arrived. Those who criticized his sometimes trite espousing, now accept that his conversion to the Islamic faith and his retirement from a music world of 'sin and greed' was a committed move that will not be reversed. His legacy as Cat Stevens is a considerable catalogue of timeless songs, many destined to become classics. In 1966, producer Mike Hurst spotted Cat performing at the Hammersmith College, London; he was so impressed that he arranged to record him and his song, 'I Love My Dog'. Tony Hall at Decca Records was similarly impressed and Stevens became the first artist on the new Deram label. The record and its b-side 'Portobello Road' showed great promise and over the next two years Stevens delivered many perfect pop songs. Some were recorded by himself but many other artists queued up for material from this precociously talented teenager. His own hits; 'Matthew And Son', 'I'm Gonna Get Me A Gun' and 'Bad Night' were equalled by the quality of his songs for others. The soulful 'First Cut Is The Deepest' by P.P. Arnold and the addictive 'Here Comes My

Baby'; the Tremeloes'. His two Decca albums were packed full of short, infectious songs, although they suffered from dated accompaniments. Stevens contracted tuberculosis and was absent for some time. During his convalescence he took stock of his life. Over the next eight years and 11 albums, the astute listener can detect a troubled soul.

Mona Bone Jakon was the first in the series of albums known as bedsitter music. It was followed by two hugely successful works: *Tea For The Tillerman* and *Teaser And The Firecat*. These showed the solitary songwriter, letting the listener into his private thoughts, aspirations and desires. Stevens was the master of this genre and produced a wealth of simplistic, yet beautiful songs. Anthems like 'Wild World', 'Peace Train' and 'Moon Shadow', love songs including 'Lady D'Arbanville', 'Hard Headed Woman' and 'Can't Keep It In', are all faultless and memorable compositions. Stevens was at his sharpest with his posing numbers that hinted of dubiety, religion and scepticism. Two of his finest songs are 'Father And Son' and 'Sitting'. The first is a dialogue between father and son, and gives the listener an insight into his lonely childhood in Soho. The line 'How can I try to explain, when I do he turns away again, its always been the same, same old story' the child continues with 'from the moment I could talk, I was ordered to listen, now there's a way that I know, that I have to go, away, I know I have to go'. The song is astonishingly powerful in relating Stevens' own turmoil to virtually every person that has ever heard the song. 'Sitting' is similarly powerful, although it is a song of great hope. It opens confidently, 'Ooh I'm on my way I know I am, somewhere not so far from here, all I know is all I feel right now, I feel the power growing in my hair'. Few were unmoved by these two songs. In his time Stevens had eight consecutive gold albums and 10 hit singles in the UK and 14 in the USA. In recent years he has been very active teaching and spreading the word of Islam; in 1991 prior to the Gulf War he travelled to Baghdad to seek the freedom of hostages. We should not selfishly carp that he gave up music, but instead we should be grateful for his outstanding catalogue extant.

Albums: *Matthew & Son* (1967), *New Masters* (1968), *Mona Bone Jakon* (1970), *Tea For The Tillerman* (1970), *Teaser & The Firecat* (1971), *Very Young And Early Songs* (1972), *Catch Bull At Four* (1972), *Foreigner* (1973), *Buddha And The Chocolate Box* (1974), *View From The Top* (1974), *Numbers* (1975), *Izitso* (1977), *Back To Earth* (1978). Compilations: *Greatest Hits* (1975), *Footsteps In The Dark* (1984), *The Very Best Of Cat Stevens* (1990).

Stevens, Connie

b. Concetta Ann Ingolia, 8 August 1938, Brooklyn,

New York, USA. Stevens was an actress and singer, whose antecedents are said to have been Italian, Irish, English and Mohican. Stevens entered show-business at the age of 16 and, in 1959, after making several appearances on the Warner Brothers' hit television series *77 Sunset Strip*, had a chart hit with the novelty, 'Kookie, Kookie, (Lend Me Your Comb)', in collaboration with one of the show's stars, Edd Byrnes. The record sold over a million copies, as did Stevens' first and only solo hit, 'Sixteen Reasons' (1960). Her other 60s releases included 'Why'd You Wanna Make Me Cry?', 'Mr. Songwriter' and 'Now That You've Gone', *Connie Stevens* and *Sings The Hank Williams Songbook*. Stevens' other television work included the drama, *The Littlest Angel*, with Fred Gwynne, E.G. Marshall and Cab Calloway; and *Wendy And Me*, a series in which she co-starred with comedian, George Burns, shortly after his wife, Gracie, retired. From 1959-62, Stevens starred with Robert Conrad, Anthony Eisley and Grant Williams in another Warner 'episodic/action' series, *Hawaiian Eye*. She also appeared in the theatre, and shortly after starring on Broadway with Tony Perkins in Neil Simon's play, *Star Spangled Girl*, she followed Debbie Reynolds and Elizabeth Taylor, and became singer Eddie Fisher's third wife - they later divorced. After making her big screen debut in 1959 with *Eighteen And Anxious*, she appeared with Jerry Lewis and Marilyn Maxwell in *Rock-A-Bye-Baby*, with songs by the unusual combination of Harry Warren and Sammy Cahn. Her other movies included a couple of 1961 soap operas, *Parrish* and *Susan Slade*; the ghostly *Two On A Guillotine* (1965); a film version of the hit Broadway play, *Never Too Late* (1965); a re-make of the 1948 UK film, *No Orchids For Miss Blandish*; and television movies, such as *Mr. Jericho*, and *The Sex Symbol*. The latter project was plagued by legal action because of its similarity to Marilyn Monroe's life story. Stevens' other television projects, in the 80s and early 90s, included an appearance on *Bob Hope's Christmas Show* from the Persian Gulf (1988); *Bring Me The Head Of Dobie Gillies; Tape Heads*; and *Murder She Wrote*. In 1987 she was reunited with Edd Byrnes, this time on the big screen, in *Back To The Beach*, a nostalgic look back at the surf/beach-type movies of the 60s, with several of the original stars, such as Frankie Avalon and Annette Funicello.
Albums: *Conchetta* (1958), *Hawaiian Eye* (1959, television soundtrack), *Connie Stevens From 'Hawaiian Eye'* (1960), *Connie* (1961), *The Hank Williams Songbook* (1962), *Palm Springs Weekend* (1963, film soundtrack), *The Littlest Angel* (1969, television soundtrack).

Stewart, Al

b. 3 September 1945, Glasgow, Scotland. Stewart first came to prominence during the folk boom of the mid-60s. His musical career began in Bournemouth, where he playing guitar, backing Tony Blackburn in the Sabres. In 1965, he moved to London, played at various folk clubs and shared lodgings with Jackson C. Frank, Sandy Denny and Paul Simon. Stewart was signed to Decca in 1966 and released one unsuccessful single, 'The Elf', featuring Jimmy Page on lead guitar. The following year, he joined CBS and released the acoustic, string-accompanied, introspective *Bedsitter Images*. The succeeding *Love Chronicles*, a diary of Stewart's romantic life, was most notable for the lengthy title track and the fact that it used a contentious word ('fucking') in an allegedly artistic context. The singer's interest in acoustic folk continued on *Zero She Flies*, which featured the historical narrative 'Manuscript'. Stewart's interest in the confessional love song reached its conclusion on *Orange*, with the impressive 'Night Of The 4th Of May'. This was followed by his most ambitious work to date, *Past, Present And Future*. Pursuing his interest in historical themes, Stewart presented some of his best acoustic workouts in the impressive 'Roads To Moscow' and epic 'Nostradamus'. A considerable gap ensued before the release of *Modern Times*, which saw Stewart making inroads into the American market for the first time.
After leaving CBS and signing to RCA, he relocated to California and surprised many by the commercial power of his celebrated *Year Of The Cat*, which reached the US Top 10. The title track also gave Stewart his first US hit. Another switch of label to Arista preceded *Time Passages*, which suffered by comparison with its predecessor. The underrated *24 P Carrots* was succeeded by a part studio/part live album, which merely consolidated his position. With *Russians And Americans*, Stewart embraced a more noticeable political stance, but the sales were disappointing. Legal and contractual problems effectively deterred him from recording for four years until the welcome, if portentous, *The Last Days Of The Century*. During that time he had re-located to France and set about expanding his impressive cellar of vintage wines. Stewart remains one of the more underrated performers, despite his commercial breakthrough in the 70s.
Albums: *Bedsitter Images* (1967), *Love Chronicles* (1969), *Zero She Flies* (1970), *The First Album (Bedsitter Images)* (1970), *Orange* (1972), *Past, Present And Future* (1973), *Modern Times* (1975), *Year Of The Cat* (1976), *Time Passages* (1978), *24 P/Carrots* (1980), *Indian Summer/Live* (1981), *Russians And Americans* (1984), *Last Days Of The Century* (1988), *Rhymes In Rooms - Al Stewart Live Featuring Peter White* (1992). Compilations: *The Early Years* (1978), *Best Of Al Stewart* (1985), *Chronicles ... The Best Of Al Stewart* (1991).

Stewart, Billy

b. 24 March 1937, Washington, DC, USA, d. 17 January 1970. Introduced to music by his family's Stewart Gospel Singers, Billy embraced a more secular direction with the Rainbows, a group which also included Don Covay and Marvin Gaye. From there Stewart joined Bo Diddley's band on piano. His solo debut, 'Billy's Blues', was released on Chess in 1956, after which he worked with the Marquees. A second single, 'Billy's Heartaches' (1957), appeared on the OKeh label, but a return to Chess in the early 60's proved decisive. A succession of melodic songs, including 'I Do Love You' and 'Sitting In The Park' (both 1965), established a crafted style which blended R&B jazz and the singer's distinctive vocal delivery. These elements were prevalent in his radical interpretation of George Gershwin and DuBose Heyward's 'Summertime', a Top 10 US hit in 1966. Stewart's subsequent releases were less successful although he remained a popular live attraction. In January 1970, while touring in North Carolina, Billy's car plunged into the River Neuse, killing him and three of his musicians.
Albums: *I Do Love You* (1965), *Unbelievable* (1966). Compilation: *One More Time* (1990).

Stooges

Purveyors, with the MC5, of classic, high-energy American rock, the Stooges' influence on successive generations is considerable. They were led by the enigmatic James Jewel Osterberg (aka Iggy Stooge and Iggy Pop, b. 21 April 1947, Ann Arbor, Michigan, USA) who assumed his unusual sobriquet in deference to the Iguanas, a high-school band in which he drummed. Iggy formed the Psychedelic Stooges with guitarist Ron Asheton. Scott Asheton (drums) and Dave Alexander (bass) completed the line-up which quickly became a fixture of Detroit's thriving underground circuit. By September 1967, the group had dropped its adjectival prefix and had achieved a notoriety through the onstage behaviour of its uninhibited frontman. The Stooges' first album was produced by John Cale although the group's initial choice was veteran soul svengali, Jerry Ragavoy. This exciting debut matched its malevolent, garage-band sneer with the air of nihilism prevalent in the immediate post-summer of love era. Iggy's exaggerated, Mick Jagger-influenced swagger swept over the group's three-chord maelstrom to create an enthralling and compulsive sound. The band were augmented by saxophonist Steven Mackay for *Funhouse*. This exceptional release documented a contemporary live set, opening with the forthright 'Down On The Street' and closing with the anarchic, almost free-form 'LA Blues'. This uncompromising collection proved uncommercial and the Stooges were then dropped by their record label. A second

guitarist, Bill Cheatham joined in August 1970, while over the next few months two bassists, Zeke Zettner and Jimmy Recca, passed through the ranks as replacements for Dave Alexander. Cheatham was then ousted in favour of James Williamson, who made a significant contribution to the ensuing Stooges' period. Long-time Iggy fan, David Bowie, brought the group to the Mainman management stable and the singer was also responsible for mixing *Raw Power*. Although it lacked the purpose of its predecessors, the set became the Stooges' most successful release and contained two of their best-known performances, 'Gimme Danger' and 'Search And Destroy'. However, the quartet - Iggy, Williamson and the Asheton brothers - were dropped from Mainman for alleged drug dependence. In 1973, Scott Thurston (keyboards) was added to the line-up, but their impetus was waning. The Stooges made their final live appearance on 9 February, 1974 at Detroit's Michigan Palace. This tawdry performance ended with a battle between the group and a local biker gang, the results of which were captured on *Metallic KO*. Within days a drained Iggy Pop announced the formal end of the Stooges.
Albums: *The Stooges* (1969), *Funhouse* (1970), as Iggy And The Stooges *Raw Power* (1973), *Metallic KO* (1976), *Rubber Legs* (1988, rare recordings from 1973/4). Compilations: as Iggy Pop and James Williamson *Kill City* (1977), *No Fun* (1980), as Iggy And The Stooges *I'm Sick Of You* (1981), *I Gotta Right* (1983).

Storm, Rory

b. 1940, Liverpool, England. Vocalist Alan Caldwell began performing as a member of the Texan Skiffle Group, before forming one of the city's first beat groups with Johnny Byrne (alias Johnny Guitar), Lou Walters, Ty Brian and Ritchie Starkey, later known as Ringo Starr. The quintet employed several names - the Raving Texans, Al Caldwell And His Jazzmen - before becoming Rory Storm And The Hurricanes in 1960, with Caldwell assuming the lead persona. They enjoyed a fervent local popularity, in part because of the singer's showmanship, and were placed third behind the Beatles and Gerry And The Pacemakers in a poll undertaken by the *Mersey Beat* newspaper in 1962. Ringo's switch to the Beatles in August that year precipitated a recurrent drumming problem, and a stand-in was required on the Hurricanes' contributions to *This Is Merseybeat*. Spirited but unoriginal, the three tracks they completed revealed a barely adequate vocalist, while a later version of 'America', produced by Brian Epstein, failed to capture an in-concert fire. The premature death of Ty Brian and the departure of Lou Walters ended any lingering potential, and the Hurricanes were disbanded in 1966 following their appearance at the last night of the famed Cavern club. Rory then pursued a career as a disc jockey but, increasingly prone to ill-heath, he died in 1972 following an accidental overdose of alcohol and medication. His grief-stricken mother comitted suicide on discovering his body.

Strangeloves

Formed in 1964 in New York City, the Strangeloves consisted of songwriters and record producers Bob Feldman, Jerry Goldstein and Richard Gottehrer. Although they left their mark under the name Strangeloves with only four singles and one album, their fascinating story extends both before and beyond the group's brief tenure. Feldman and Goldstein had been childhood friends in Brooklyn, New York and sang in street corner doo-wop groups. They began writing songs together and had their first success with 'Big Beat', which disc jockey Alan Freed used as the theme song of his television show. By 1960 they had recorded some unsuccessful singles as Bob and Jerry when they met Bronx native Gottehrer, who was also writing songs. Before long the trio's compositions were being recorded by such major artists as Dion, Pat Boone, Freddy Cannon, Bobby Vee and the Jive Five. Their greatest success came in 1963 when Feldman, Goldstein and Gottehrer wrote and produced 'My Boyfriend's Back', which became a number 1 hit for the Angels. By the following year, however, the landscape of pop music had changed with the arrival of the Beatles, and the trio had to rethink its approach. They created the Strangeloves (taking their name from the Stanley Kubrick/Peter Sellers' film, *Dr. Strangelove*) and a mythical story to go with them. Wearing bizarre costumes, they said they were from the Australian outback and put on phony accents. Their names became Niles, Miles and Giles Strange.

In 1965, they released their first single, 'Love Love Love', on Swan Records, which failed to chart. They then signed to Bang Records and released 'I Want Candy', a Bo Diddley-like rocker that reached number 11. Three further singles charted: 'Cara-Lin' (number 39 in 1965), 'Night Time' (number 30 in 1966) and 'Hand Jive' (number 100 in 1966). Their only album also made the charts.

In addition to their recordings as the Strangeloves, Goldstein and Feldman recorded as the Kittens, as Rome and Paris, as Bobby and the Beaus and as Ezra and the Iveys. The trio produced the McCoys' hit 'Hang On Sloopy' and recorded as the Sheep.

Following the break-up of the Strangeloves, Goldstein worked for Uni Records, and later produced the group War. Feldman continued to write music and produce, working with artists such as Jay and the Americans, Johnny Mathis, Freddy Cannon and Link Wray. Gottehrer became a partner

in Sire Records and a successful record producer during the punk era, producing the first two albums by the Go-Go's, the debut album by Blondie and many others. Feldman recently formed a new Strangeloves group.
Album: *I Want Candy* (1965).

Strawberry Alarm Clock

Based in California and originally known as the Sixpence, the Strawberry Alarm Clock enjoyed a US number 1 in 1967 with the memorable 'Incense And Peppermints'. This euphoric slice of 'flower-power' bubblegum was initially intended as a b-side and the featured voice was that of a friend, on hand during the session, rather than an official member. The group - Mark Weitz (organ), Ed King (lead guitar), Lee Freeman (rhythm guitar), Gary Lovetro (bass) and Randy Seol (drums) - added a second bassist, George Bunnell, prior to recording a debut album. The new arrival was also an accomplished songwriter, and his contributions enhanced a set which coupled hippie trappings with enchanting melodies and some imaginative instrumentation. Such features were maintained on successive Strawberry Alarm Clock albums, while 'Tomorrow' and 'Sit With The Guru' continued their reign as chart contenders. The group supplied much of the music for the film *Psyche-Out*, in which they also appeared. Gary Lovetro left the line-up prior to *Wake Up It's Tomorrow*, and several subsequent changes undermined the band's direction. *Good Morning Starshine*, released in 1969, introduced a reshaped unit where Jimmy Pitman (guitar) and Gene Gunnels (drums) joined Weitz and King, the latter of whom was relegated to bass. Although undoubtedly professional, this particular quartet lacked the innovation of its predecessor and although they remained together until 1971, the Strawberry Alarm Clock was unable to regain its early profile. Ed King later joined Lynyrd Skynyrd, while several of his erstwhile colleagues were reunited during the 80s for a succession of 'summer of love revisited' tours.
Albums: *Incense And Peppermints* (1967), *Wake Up It's Tomorrow* (1967), *The World In A Seashell* (1968), *Good Morning Starshine* (1969). Compilations: *The Best Of The Strawberry Alarm Clock* (1970), *Changes* (1971), *Strawberries Mean Love* (1987).

Strawbs

This versatile unit was formed in 1967 by guitarists Dave Cousins (b. 7 January 1945; guitar/banjo/piano/recorder) and Tony Hooper. They initially worked as a bluegrass group, the Strawberry Hill Boys, with mandolinist Arthur Phillips, but later pursued a folk-based direction. Truncating their name to the Strawbs, the founding duo added Ron Chesterman on bass prior to the arrival of singer Sandy Denny whose short spell in the line-up is documented in *All Our Own Work*. This endearing collection, released in the wake of Denny's success with Fairport Convention, features an early version of her exemplary composition, 'Who Knows Where The Time Goes'. Cousins, Hooper and Chesterman released their official debut, *Strawbs*, in 1968. This excellent selection featured several of the group's finest compositions, including 'Oh How She Changed' and 'The Battle', and was acclaimed by both folk and rock audiences. *Dragonfly*, was less well-received, prompting a realignment in the band. The original duo was joined by former Velvet Opera members John Ford (b. 1 July 1948, Fulham, London, England; bass/acoustic guitar) and Richard Hudson (b. Richard William Stafford Hudson, 9 May 1948, London, England; drums/guitar/sitar), plus Rick Wakeman (keyboards), a graduate of the Royal Academy of Music. The Strawbs embraced electric rock with *Just A Collection Of Antiques And Curios*, although critical analysis concentrated on Wakeman's contribution.

Such plaudits continued on *From The Witchwood* but the pianist grew frustrated within the group's framework and left to join Yes. He was replaced by Blue Weaver (b. 11 March 1947, Cardiff, South Glamorgan, Wales; guitar/autoharp/piano) from Amen Corner. Despite the commercial success generated by the outstanding *Grave New World*, tension within the Strawbs mounted, and in 1972, Hooper was replaced by Dave Lambert (b. 8 March 1949, Hounslow, Middlesex, England). Relations between Cousins and Hudson and Ford were also deteriorating and although 'Lay Down' gave the band its first UK Top 20 single, the jocular 'Part Of The Union', written by the bassist and drummer, became the Strawbs' most successful release. The group split following an acrimonious US tour. The departing rhythm section formed their own unit, Hudson-Ford while Cousins and Lambert brought in pianist John Hawken (ex-Nashville Teens and Renaissance), Chas Cronk (bass) and former Stealers Wheel drummer Rod Coombes. However, a series of poorly-received albums suggested the Strawbs had lost both direction and inspiration. Cousins nonetheless presided over several fluctuating line-ups and continued to record into the 80s despite a shrinking popularity. In 1989, the group reunited, including the trio of Cousins, Hooper And Hudson, for the *Don't Say Goodbye*.

Albums: *Strawbs* (1969), *Dragonfly* (1970), *Just A Collection Of Antiques And Curios* (1970), *From The Witchwood* (1971), *Grave New World* (1972), *All Our Own Work* (1973 - as Sandy Denny And The Strawbs), *Bursting At The Seams* (1973), *Hero And Heroine* (1974), *Ghosts* (1975), *Nomadness* (1976), *Deep Cuts* (1976), *Burning For You* (1977), *Dead Lines* (1978), *Don't Say Goodbye* (1988). Compilations: *Strawbs By Choice* (1974), *Best Of The Strawbs* (1978).

String-a-Longs

Keith McCormack (vocals/guitar), Richard Stevens (guitar), James Torres (guitar), Aubrey Lee de Cordova (bass) and Don Allen (drums) were a Texan high school group with a bias towards instrumentals. Encouraged by audience reaction to their act at local dances and parties, they auditioned for Norman Petty in his studio in Clovis, New Mexico. Impressed, Petty collaborated with Stephens and Torres on the writing of 1961's 'Wheels', the String-a-Longs first single and only hit. Inconsequential but maddeningly catchy, it entered international Top 10s, but lack of further similar success brought the group back to parochial engagements and impending disbandment within two years.

Sullivan, Big Jim

b. c1940, London, England, he worked in a sheet-metal factory before joining a skiffle group as a guitarist. Sullivan was soon hired by Marty Wilde as a member of his backing group, the Wildcats. In 1959, the group backed Eddie Cochran on his final UK tour, anbd later recorded the instrumentals 'Trambone' and 'Samovar' as the Krew Kats. After that group split up, Sullivan became a session musician and teacher, giving lessons to young hopefuls like Ritchie Blackmore and Jimmy Page. During the 60s he played on thousands of recordings, backing such artists as Michael Cox, the Kinks, Small Faces, Jonathan King, Donovan, the Rolling Stones, Nancy Wilson and Sarah Vaughan. In 1969 he accompanied Tom Jones on a world tour. Sullivan made occasional records under his own name at this time. 'You Don't Know What You've Got' (1961) was a cover version of Ral Donner's hit while 'She Walks Through The Fair' was a traditional Irish tune. Sullivan also studied Indian music with Ustad Vilayat Khan and in 1968 made a sitar album for Mercury. Two years later, he played with Blackmore and Albert Lee as Green Bullfrog, a studio group reproduced by Derek Lawrence. In 1974 he made a rare vocal album for Lawrence's Retreat label, following this by forming Tiger with Dave Macrae (keyboards), Phil Curtis (bass) and Billy Rankin (drums). The band made albums for Retreat and EMI (*Going Down Laughing*, 1976). During the 80s, Sullivan remained in demand for session work and made more solo recordings, among which was *Test Of Time* produced by Mike Vernon.

Albums: *Sitar Beat* (1968), *Jim Sullivan* (1972), *Big Jim's Back* (1974), *Sullivan Plays O'Sullivan* (1977), *Rock 'n' Roll Wrecks* (1983), *Test Of Time* (1983).

Sullivan, Ed

b. 28 September 1902, New York City, New York, USA, d. 13 October 1974. Sullivan hosted the most popular variety programme on US television during the 50s and 60s. He presented hundreds of the most important musical acts of the era to a wide audience; it was on *The Ed Sullivan Show* that most of America first saw Elvis Presley and the Beatles. Guest musical acts nearly always performed live, some backed by Sullivan's orchestra, led by Ray Bloch. Sullivan was one of seven children, and grew up in New York's Harlem section until the age of five, when his family moved to the suburb of Port Chester, New York, north of the city. He had no particular desire to be an entertainer and took a job as a sportswriter with a Port Chester newspaper as a teenager. In the early 20s he was hired by the *New York Evening Graphic* newspaper in the city, and then by the larger *New York Daily News* in 1932. While at that paper he began hosting vaudeville shows, which led, in 1947, to an offer by CBS Television to host a new programme (at that time *all* television programmes were new, the medium having opened up at the close of World War II) called *Toast of The Town*. It debuted on 20 June 1948; he held on to his newspaper column as well. On 25 September 1955 the programme's name was changed to *The Ed Sullivan Show*. On his show, Sullivan featured any kind of entertainment he thought would grab a portion of the viewing audience, from opera singers to jugglers, dancing chimps to pop groups. The programme became one of the highest-rated on American television, and was a Sunday night ritual for millions of Americans. Sullivan became a celebrity himself while his mannerisms and way of speaking became fodder for many comedians and impressionists. Among the hundreds of musical artists to have appeared on the show, in addition to Presley and the Beatles, were Louis Armstrong, Judy Garland, Liberace, the Rolling Stones, the Doors and Ella Fitzgerald. (In 1990, the audio and video rights to some of those performances were leased, and compilation albums featuring music from *The Ed Sullivan Show* began to appear in the USA.) The programme was broadcast for the last time on 6 June 1971.

Supremes

America's most successful female vocal group of all time was formed by four Detroit schoolgirls in the late 50s. Diana Ross (b. 26 March 1944, Detroit, USA), Betty Hutton, Florence Ballard (b. 30 June 1943, Detroit, USA) and Mary Wilson (b. 4 March 1944, Detroit, USA) named themselves the Primettes in tribute to the local male group, the Primes - who themselves found fame in the 60s as the Temptations. Having issued a solitary single on a small local label, the Primettes were signed to Berry Gordy's Motown stable, where they initially found public acceptance hard to find. For more than two years, they issued a succession of flop singles, despite the best efforts of top Motown writer/producer Smokey Robinson to find them a suitable vehicle for their unsophisticated talents. Only when Diana Ross supplanted Florence Ballard as the group's regular lead vocalist, at Gordy's suggestion, did the Supremes break into the US charts. The dynamic 'When The Lovelight Starts Shining In His Eyes', modelled on the production style of Phil Spector, was the group's first hit in 1963. The follow-up single flopped, so Gordy handed the group over to the newly-formed Holland/Dozier/Holland writing and production team. They concocted the slight, but effervescent, 'Where Did Our Love Go' for the Supremes, which topped the US charts and was also a major hit in Britain. This achievement inaugurated a remarkable run of success for the group and their producers, as their next four releases - 'Baby Love', 'Come See About Me', 'Stop! In The Name Of Love' and 'Back In My Arms Again' - all topped the US singles charts, while 'Baby Love' became the only record by an American group to reach number 1 in Britain during the beat-dominated year of 1964. All these singles were hinged around insistent, very danceable rhythms with repetitive lyrics and melodies, which placed no great strain on Ross's fragile voice. With their girl-next-door looks and endearingly unsophisticated demeanour, the Supremes became role models for young black Americans and their name was used to promote a range of merchandising, even (ironically) a brand of white bread.

The rather perfunctory 'Nothing But Heartaches' broke the chart-topping sequence, which was immediately restored by the more ambitious 'I Hear A Symphony'. As Holland/Dozier/Holland moved into their prime, and Ross increased in confidence, the group's repertoire grew more mature. They recorded albums of Broadway standards, played residencies at expensive night-clubs, and were expertly groomed by Motown staff as all-round entertainers. Meanwhile, the hits kept coming, with four more US number 1 hits in the shape of 'You Can't Hurry Love', 'You Keep Me Hanging On', 'Love Is Here And Now You're Gone' and 'The Happening' - the last of which was a blatant attempt to cash in on the psychedelic movement. Behind the scenes, the group's future was in some jeopardy: Florence Ballard had grown increasingly unhappy in the supporting role into which Berry Gordy had forced her, and her occasionally erratic and troublesome behaviour was ultimately used as an excuse to force her out of the group. Without fanfare, Ballard was ousted in mid-1967, and replaced by Cindy Birdsong; most fans simply did not notice. At the same time, Diana Ross's prime position in the group's hierarchy was confirmed in public, when she was given individual credit on the group's records, a move which prompted a flurry of similar demands from the lead singers of other Motown groups.

'Reflections', an eerie, gripping song that was one of Motown's most adventurous productions to date, introduced the new era. Motown's loss of Holland/Dozier/Holland slowed the group's progress in 1968, before they bounced back with two controversial slices of overt social commentary, 'Love Child' and 'I'm Livin' In Shame', the first of which was yet another US number 1. The Supremes also formed a successful recording partnership with the Temptations, exemplified by the hit single 'I'm Gonna Make You Love Me'.

During 1969, there were persistent rumours that Berry Gordy was about to launch Diana Ross on a solo career. These were confirmed at the end of the year, when the Supremes staged a farewell performance, and Ross bade goodbye to the group with the elegiac 'Someday We'll Be Together' - a US chart-topper on which, ironically, she was the only member of the Supremes to appear. Ross was replaced by Jean Terrell, sister of heavyweight boxer Ernie Terrell. The new line-up, with Terrell and Mary Wilson alternating lead vocal duties, found immediate success with 'Up The Ladder To The Roof' in early 1970, while 'Stoned Love', the group's biggest UK hit for four years, revived memories of their early successes with its rhythmic base and repetitive hook. The Supremes also tried to revive the atmosphere of their earlier recordings with the Temptations on a series of albums with the Four Tops. Gradually, their momentum was lost, and as Motown shifted its centre of activity from Detroit to California, the Supremes were left behind. Lynda Laurence replaced Cindy Birdsong in the line-up in 1972; Birdsong returned in 1974 when Laurence became pregnant. The latter move coincided with the departure of Jean Terrell, whose place was taken by Scherrie Payne. With the group recording rarely, Birdsong quit again, leaving Mary Wilson - at last established as the unchallenged leader - to recruit Susaye Greene in her place. This trio recorded the self-explanatory *Mary, Scherrie And Susaye* in 1976, before disbanding the following year. Mary Wilson attempted to assemble a new set of Supremes for recording purposes, and actually toured Britain in 1978 with Karen Rowland and Karen Jackson in the line-up. The termination of her Motown contract stymied this move, however, and since then the use of the Supremes' name has legally resided with Motown. They have chosen not to sully the memory of their most famous group by concocting an ersatz Supremes to cash in on their heritage. Jean Terrell, Scherrie Payne and Lynda Lawrence won the rights to use the Supremes' name in the UK. Payne began recording disco material with producer Ian Levine in 1989, for the Nightmare and Motor City labels. Levine also signed Lawrence, Wilson and ex-

Supreme Susaye Greene to solo deals and recorded Terrell, Lawrence and Greene for a remake of 'Stoned Love'. Bouncing Back was due in 1992 together with a single recorded with the Originals. The career of Mary Wilson has also continued with a starring role in the Toronto, Canada production of the stage musical *The Beehive* in 1989 and the publication of the second volume of her autobiography in 1990.

Albums: as the Supremes *Meet The Supremes* (1963), *Where Did Our Love Go?* (1964), *A Bit Of Liverpool* (1964), *The Supremes Sing Country, Western And Pop* (1964), *We Remember Sam Cooke* (1965), *More Hits By The Supremes* (1965), *Merry Christmas* (1965), *The Supremes At The Copa* (1965), *I Hear A Symphony* (1966), *Supremes A-Go-Go* (1966), *The Supremes Sing Holland, Dozier, Holland* (1967), *Right On* (1970), with the Four Tops *The Magnificent Seven* (1970), *New Ways But Love Stays* (1970), with the Four Tops *The Return Of The Magnificent Seven* (1971), *Touch* (1971), with the Four Tops *Dynamite* (1971), *Floy Joy* (1972), *The Supremes* (1972), *The Supremes* (1975), *High Energy* (1976), *Mary, Scherrie And Susaye* (1976).

Albums: as Diana Ross & the Supremes *Diana Ross And The Supremes Sing Rodgers And Hart* (1967), *Reflections* (1968), *Diana Ross And The Supremes Sing And Perform 'Funny Girl'* (1968), *Diana Ross And The Supremes Live At London's Talk Of The Town* (1968), with the Temptations *Diana Ross And The Supremes Join The Temptations* (1968), *Love Child* (1968), with the Temptations *TCB* (1968), *Let The Sunshine In* (1969), with the Temptations *Together* (1969), *Cream Of The Crop* (1969), *Diana Ross And The Supremes On Broadway* (1969), *Farewell* (1970).

Further reading: *Dreamgirl: My Life As A Supreme*, Mary Wilson. *Girl Groups: The Story Of A Sound*, Alan Betrock. *Supreme Faith: Someday We'll Be Together*, Mary Wilson and Patricia Romanowski.

Surfaris

Formed in Glendale, California in 1962, the Surfaris - Jim Fuller (b. 1947; lead guitar), Jim Pash (b. 1949; guitar), Bob Berryhill (b. 1947; guitar), Pat Connolly (b. 1947; bass) and Ron Wilson (b. 1945; drums) - achieved international success the following year with 'Wipe Out'. This frantic yet simplistic instrumental, originally envisaged as a throwaway b-side, is recognized as one of the definitive surfing anthems, although some of its lustre has been removed in the wake of a protracted allegation of plagiarism. Merrell Fankhauser, former guitarist with the Impacts, successfully claimed the piece infringed his composition of the same title. Further controversy arose when the Surfaris discovered that the music gracing their debut album was, in fact, played by a rival group, the Challengers. However, despite their understandable anger, such backroom machinations remained rife throughout the quintet's career. Their third album, *Hit City '64*, introduced a partnership with producer Gary Usher, who employed a team of experienced session musicians on ensuing Surfaris' releases.

In 1965 the group abandoned beach and hot-rod themes for folk rock. Wilson had developed into an accomplished lead singer and with Ken Forssi replacing Connolly on bass, the Surfaris completed the promising *It Ain't Me Babe*. However, Usher then severed his relationship with the band and they broke up when the last remaining original member, Jim Pash, left the line-up. Wilson died in 1989 from a brain haemorrhage. Newcomer Forssi then joined Love, and although no other member achieved similar success, Berryhill resurrected the Surfaris' name in 1981.

Albums: *Wipe Out* (1963), *The Surfaris Play Wipe Out And Others* (1963), *Hit City '64* (1964), *Fun City, USA* (1964), *Hit City '65* (1965), *It Ain't Me Babe* (1965), *Surfaris Live* (1983). Compilations: *Yesterday's Pop Scene* (1973), *Surfers Rule* (1976), *Gone With The Wave* (1977).

Sutch, Screaming Lord

b. 10 November 1940, Middlesex, England. David Sutch rose to prominence in 1960 as the first long-haired pop star, with tresses in excess of 18 inches. His recording career peaked with such early releases as 'Til The Following Night', 'Jack The Ripper' and 'I'm A Hog For You Baby', all produced by the late Joe Meek. Although never registering a chart entry, Sutch boasted one of the most accomplished live acts of the era in the Savages, whose ranks included such luminaries as Ritchie Blackmore, Nicky Hopkins and Paul Nicholas. For 30 years, Sutch has sustained his flagging recording career with a plethora of publicity stunts ranging from dramatic marriage proposals to standing for Parliament and founding his own radio station. In 1970, he enjoyed some minor success in the US album charts with *Lord Sutch And Heavy Friends*, which featured Blackmore, Jimmy Page, Jeff Beck, Keith Moon, Nicky Hopkins, Noel Redding and John Bonham. He now combines club work with the presidency of the Monster Raving Loony Party.

Albums: *Lord Sutch And Heavy Friends* (1970), *Hands Of Jack The Ripper* (1972), *Rock And Horror* (1982), *Alive And Well* (1982).

Swinging Blue Jeans

Determined to concentrate on rock 'n' roll, several leading figures in Liverpool's skiffle scene founded the Bluegenes in 1958. They were singer and lead guitarist Ray Ennis (b. 26 May 1942), rhythm guitarist Ray Ellis (b 8 March 1942), bass-player Les Braid (b 15 September 1941), drummer Norman Kuhlke (b 17 June 1942) and Paul Moss (banjo). All were born in Liverpool. Minus Moss, the group became one of the leading attractions in the Merseyside beat group scene and also played in Hamburg. Following the Beatles' first successes, the Swinging Blues Jeans (as they had been renamed) signed a recording deal with EMI's HMV label. The Beatles'-sounding 'It's Too Late Now', was a minor hit the following year, but it was the group's third single, 'Hippy Hippy Shake', which provided their biggest success when it reached number 2. This rasping rendition of a Chan Romero song remains one of the era's finest performances, invoking a power the Blue Jeans never quite recaptured. Their version of 'Good Golly Miss Molly' nonetheless peaked at number 11, while the reflective rendition of Betty Everett's soul ballad 'You're No Good' reached number 3. An excellent reading of Dionne Warwick's hit 'Don't Make Me Over' stalled outside the Top 30. It was, however, the quartet's last substantial hit despite a series of highly-polished other singles, including 'Promise You'll Tell Her' (1964), 'Crazy 'Bout My Baby' (1965). The Blue Jeans were unfairly dubbed anachronistic. Several personel changes also ensued, including the induction of two former Escorts, Terry Sylvester and Mike Gregory, but neither this, nor a brief change of name to Music Motor, made any difference to their fortunes. In 1968, the band was briefly renamed Ray Ennis and the Blue Jeans but when Sylvester was chosen to replace Graham Nash in the Hollies, the remaining members decided to split up. However, the revival of interest in 60s music persuaded Ennis to re-form the Swinging Blue Jeans in 1973. He re-recorded 'Hippy Hippy Shake' for an album on Dart Records and continued leading the band on the UK scampi-and-chips revival circuit for the next two decades. A 1992 reissue album included nine previous unreleased tracks among them were versions of Little Richard's 'Ready Teddy' and & 'Three Little Fishes', the novelty song first recorded in 1939 by US bandleader Kay Kyser.

Albums: *Blue Jeans A' Swinging* aka *Swinging Blue Jeans* aka *Tutti Frutti* (1964), *The Swinging Blue Jeans: La Voce Del Padrone* (1966), *Hippy Hippy Shake* (1973), *Brand New And Faded* (1974), *Dancin'* (1985). Compilations: *Hippy Hippy Shake* (1964), *Shake: The Best Of The Swinging Blue Jeans* (1986).

Syndicate Of Sound

Formed in San Jose, California, USA in 1964, the Syndicate Of Sound were known for one classic garage-band/punk single, 'Little Girl', a US Top 10 hit on Bell Records in 1966. The group consisted of Don Baskin (b. 9 October 1946, Honolulu, Hawaii, USA; vocals/saxophone), John Sharkey (b. 8 June 1946, Los Angeles, California, USA;

guitar/keyboards), Jim Sawyers (lead guitar), Bob Gonzales (bass) and John Duckworth (b. 18 November 1946, Springfield, Missouri, USA; drums). After an unsuccessful single for the Scarlet label, they recorded 'Little Girl' for the local Hush Records. It was a regional hit and picked up for national distribution by Bell, for which the group also recorded an album. The group placed two other minor singles on the charts, one later that year for Bell and another in 1970 on Buddah. They also recorded unsuccessfully for Capitol and disbanded in 1970.

Album: *Little Girl* (1966).

T

Tanega, Norma

b. 30 January 1939, Vallejo, California, USA. Her Filipino parents actively encouraged their daughter's interest in music and art, both of which she studied. Although classically-trained, Tanega quickly showed a preference for guitar. She moved to New York to work as a graphic artist, but quickly became immersed in the city's folk enclave. She drew encouragement from Bob Dylan and Tom Paxton and her prolific songwriting resulted in a recording deal. Tanega's debut single, 'Walkin' My Cat Named Dog' (1966), reached number 22 both in the US and UK charts, and she was optimistically categorized alongside other lyrical artists, including Janis Ian and Bob Lind. Sadly, Tanega's hit proved to be her strongest composition; further releases were unsuccessful and the first phase of the singer's career ended almost as quickly as it had begun. She briefly re-emerged in 1977 with an album recorded for RCA Records.

Albums: *Walkin' My Cat Named Dog* (1966), *I Don't Think It Will Hurt* (1977).

Taste

A popular blues-rock attraction, Taste was formed in Cork, Eire in 1966 when Eric Kittringham (bass) and Norman Damery (drums) joined Rory Gallagher (b. 2 March 1949, Ballyshannon, Co. Donegal, Eire), erstwhile guitarist with the Impact Showband. The new group became a leading attraction in Ireland and in Germany, but in 1968 Gallagher replaced the original rhythm section with Charlie McCracken (bass) and John Wilson (ex-Them) on drums. The new line-up then became a part of London's burgeoning blues and progressive circuit. Their debut, *Taste*, was one of the era's most popular releases, and featured several in-concert favourites, including 'Same Old Story' and 'Sugar Mama'. *On The Boards* was another commercial success, and the group seemed poised to inherit the power-trio mantle vacated by Cream. However, the unit broke up in October 1970 following a rancorous split between Gallagher and his colleagues. The guitarist then began a fruitful solo career.

Albums: *Taste* (1969), *On The Boards* (1970), *Live Taste* (1971), *Live At The Isle Of Wight* (1972). Compilation: *The Greatest Rock Sensation* (1978).

Taylor, Kingsize, And The Dominoes

Vocalist Taylor led one of the most exciting Liverpool beat groups during the early 60s, but approbation in their homeland was undermined by an almost perpetual residency in German clubs. Originally signed to Philips, they completed several singles not issued in the UK before compounding this anonymity by agreeing to record for Polydor as the Shakers. *Let's Do The Slop, Twist, Madison, Hully Gully With The Shakers* was a worthwhile resume of R&B/soul staples, but the unit's complex series of recordings is best exemplified in their rendition of Solomon Burke's 'Stupidity'. This compulsive release, credited to Taylor and the Dominoes, was one of the finest of the genre, but the band ceased recording later that year following a live EP culled from a set at Hamburg's Star Club. Taylor achieved notoriety during the 70s when his reel-to-reel tape of a Beatles' performance at the same venue formed the basis for several archive packages. A Dominoes' set on the same spool - the prime reason for its initial recording - did not generate the same interest although their version of 'Hully Gully' has erroneously crept into several aforementioned Beatles' releases.

Album: *Let's Do The Slop, Twist, Madison, Hully Gully With The Shakers* (1963).

Taylor, R. Dean

Toronto-born R. Dean Taylor remains the most successful white artist to emerge from the Motown Records stable. The protege of writer/producer Brian Holland, he worked on many of the mid-60s hits produced by the Holland/Dozier/Holland partnership, and later claimed to have helped compose several songs credited to them. He began his recording career in 1965, with 'Let's Go Somewhere', but found more success with two of his compositions for the Supremes, 'Love Child' and 'I'm Living In Shame', both of which brought a new realism into the group's work. In 1967, he recorded the classic soul number 'There's A Ghost In My House', which enjoyed cult status in Britain. A year later he released the evocative 'Gotta See Jane', which also charted in the UK that summer. His most memorable single was 'Indiana Wants Me', an effect-laden melodrama which climbed high in both the UK and US charts in 1970. Despite his popularity in Britain, where a revival of 'There's A Ghost In My House' reached the Top 3 in 1974, Taylor was unable to repeat this success with his subsequent recordings, either on his own Jane label in 1973, or with Polydor from 1974.

Albums: *I Think Therefore I Am* (1970), *Indiana Wants Me* (1971), *LA Sunset* (1975).

T-Bones

This studio instrumental group came from Los Angeles, California. The group was conceived in 1964 by Liberty Records to record albums of surf instrumentals, and the company hired Joe Saraceno (b. 16 May 1937, Utica, New York, USA) to produce the group because of his previous experience with another studio instrumental hitmaker, the Routers (of 'Let's Go' fame). By its very nature the T-Bones's personnel changed from session to session. Their only Top 10 hit, 'No Matter What Shape (Your Stomach's In)' (US number 3), in 1965 was based on a jingle of an Alka Seltzer commercial. It yielded the group's fourth album, *No Matter What Shape* (1966), and its personnel included guitarist Danny Robert Hamilton (b. Spokane, Washington, USA), bassist Frank Carollo (b. Leland, Mississippi, USA), and drummer Tommy Clark Reynolds (b. New York, New York, USA). The group's follow-up, 'Slippin' 'N' Chippin'' (number 62) in 1966, was based on a jingle from a Nabisco Sip 'N' Chip commercial, and produced an album of the same name. After one more album the T-Bones emerged as a vocal/instrumental group Hamilton, Joe Frank & Reynolds, hitting most notably with 'Fallin' In Love' in 1975.

Albums: *Boss Drag* (1964), *Boss Drag At The Beach* (1964), *Doin' The Jerk* (1965), *No Matter What Shape* (1966), *Slippin' And Chippin'* (1966), *Everyone's Gone To The Moon* (1966).

Tea And Symphony

Formed in Birmingham, England, this adventurous ensemble was part of the city's Big Bear management stable. Although Tea And Symphony originally consisted of James Langston (vocals/guitar), Jeff Daw (guitar) and Nigel Phillips (drums/'exotic' instruments), they were often augmented by musicians from the agency including Bob Lamb and Mick Hincks from the group Locomotive. Tea And Symphony's debut *An Asylum For The Musically Insane*, was an enchanting, if self-indulgent collection, but its period-piece madness was sadly jettisoned for the more formal follow-up, *Jo Sago*. Guitarists Bob Wilson and Dave Carroll were now part of the group's fluid line-up, but the ensemble broke up in 1971 when both of these artists, and drummer Bob Lamb, joined the Idle Race. The three individuals remained with their newfound outlet when it became known as the Steve Gibbons Band.

Albums: *An Asylum For The Musically Insane* (1969), *Jo Sago* (1970).

Tempo, Nino, and April Stevens

Nino Tempo, (b. 6 January 1935, Niagara Falls, New York, USA) forged a career as session musician and arranger/composer for Rosemary Clooney and Steve Lawrence, before forming a duo with sister April Stevens (b. 29 April, Niagara Falls, New York, USA). The latter had already enjoyed minor success as a solo act with 'Teach Me Tiger', but the siblings scored a major hit in 1963 when their revival of 'Deep Purple' which topped the US charts and secured a Grammy award as that year's 'Best Rock 'N' Roll Recording'. They also held the record for many years with the longest title, the b-side of 'Deep Purple' was 'I've Been Carrying A Torch For You For So Long That It's Burned A Great Big Hole In My Heart'. Reworkings of 'Whispering' and 'Stardust' also reached the best-sellers but Tempo achieved a more contemporary outlook following backroom and compositional work with Phil Spector. He and April embraced a folk-rock/girl group direction with 'All Strung Out' and 'I Can't Go On Living (Without You Baby)' which the former co-wrote with Jerry Riopelle. An excellent attendant album contained compositions by David Gates and Warren Zevon, but the couple's *passe* image hindered potential interest. They later embarked on separate paths with Tempo resuming his association with Spector during the 70s, particularly with new protege Jerri Bo Keno.

Albums: *Deep Purple* (1963), *Nino & April Sing The Great Songs* (1964), *Hey Baby* (1966), *Nino Tempo, April Stevens Programme* (60s), *All Strung Out* (1967).

Temptations

Temptations

The most successful group in black music history was

formed in 1961 in Detroit, Michigan, USA, by former members of two local R&B outfits. Eddie Kendricks (b. 17 December 1939, Union Springs, Alabama, USA) and Paul Williams (b. 1939, Birmingham, Alabama, USA, d. 17 August 1973) both sang with the Primes; Melvin Franklin (b. 1942, Montgomery, Alabama, USA), Eldridge Bryant and Otis Williams (b. 1941, Texarkana, Texas, USA) came from the Distants. Initially known as the Elgins, the quintet were renamed the Temptations by Berry Gordy when he signed them to Motown in 1961. After issuing three singles on the Motown subsidiary Miracle Records, one of them under the pseudonym of the Pirates, the group moved to the Gordy label. 'Dream Come Home' provided their first brief taste of chart status in 1962, though it was only when they were teamed with writer/producer/performer Smokey Robinson that the Temptations achieved consistent success. The group's classic line-up was established in 1963, when Eldridge Bryant was replaced by David Ruffin (b. 18 January 1941, Meridian, Mississippi, USA). His gruff baritone provided the perfect counterpoint to Kendricks' wispy tenor and falsetto, a contrast which Smokey Robinson exploited to the full. Over the next two years, he fashioned a series of hits in both ballad and dance styles, carefully arranging complex vocal harmonies which hinted at the group's doo-wop heritage. 'The Way You Do The Things You Do' was the Temptations' first major hit, a stunningly simple rhythm number featuring a typically cunning series of lyrical images. 'My Girl' in 1965, the group's first US number 1, demonstrated Robinson's graceful command of the ballad idiom, and brought Ruffin's vocals to the fore for the first time. This track, featured in the movie 'My Girl', was reissued in 1992 and was once again a hit.
'It's Growing', 'Since I Lost My Baby', 'My Baby' and 'Get Ready' continued the run of success into 1966, establishing the Temptations as the leaders of the Motown sound. 'It's Growing' brought a fresh layer of subtlety into Robinson's lyric writing, while 'Get Ready' embodied all the excitement of the Motown rhythm factory, blending an irresistible melody with a stunning vocal arrangement. Norman Whitfield succeeded Robinson as the Temptations' producer in 1966 - a role he continued to occupy for almost a decade. He introduced a new rawness into their sound, spotlighting David Ruffin as an impassioned lead vocalist, and creating a series of R&B records that rivalled the output of Stax and Atlantic for toughness and power. 'Ain't Too Proud To Beg' introduced the Whitfield approach, and while the Top 3 hit 'Beauty Is Only Skin Deep' represented a throwback to the Robinson era, 'I'm Losing You' and 'You're My Everything' confirmed the new direction.

The peak of Whitfield's initial phase with the group was 'I Wish It Would Rain', a dramatic ballad which the producer heightened with delicate use of sound effects. The record was another major hit, and gave the Temptations their sixth R&B number 1 in three years. It also marked the end of an era, as David Ruffin first requested individual credit before the group's name, and when this was refused, elected to leave for a solo career. He was replaced by ex-Contour Dennis Edwards, whose strident vocals fitted perfectly into the Temptations' harmonic blend. Whitfield chose this moment to inaugurate a new production style. Conscious of the psychedelic shift in the rock mainstream, and the inventive soul music being created by Sly And The Family Stone, he joined forces with lyricist Barrett Strong to pull Motown brutally into the modern world. The result was 'Cloud Nine', a record which reflected the increasing use of illegal drugs among young people, and shocked some listeners with its lyrical ambiguity. Whitfield created the music to match, breaking down the traditional barriers between lead and backing singers and giving each of the Temptations a recognizable role in the group. Over the next four years, Whitfield and the Temptations pioneered the concept of psychedelic soul, stretching the Motown formula to the limit, introducing a new vein of social and political comment, and utilizing many of rock's experimental production techniques to hammer home the message. 'Runaway Child, Running Wild' examined the problems of teenage rebellion; 'I Can't Get Next To You' reflected the fragmentation of personal relationships (and topped the US charts with the group's second number 1 hit); and 'Ball Of Confusion' bemoaned the disintegrating fabric of American society. These lyrical tracts were set to harsh, uncompromising rhythm tracks, seeped in wah-wah guitar and soaked in layers of harmony and counterpoint. The Temptations were greeted as representatives of the counter-culture, a trend which climaxed when they recorded Whitfield's outspoken protest against the Vietnam War, 'Stop The War Now'. The new direction alarmed Eddie Kendricks, who felt more at home on the series of collaborations with the Supremes which the group also taped in the late 60s. He left for a solo career in 1971, after recording another US number 1, the evocative ballad 'Just My Imagination'. He was replaced first by Richard Owens, then later in 1971 by Damon Harris. This line-up recorded the 1972 number 1, 'Papa Was A Rolling Stone', a production *tour de force* which remains one of Motown's finest achievements, belatedly winning the label its first Grammy award. After that, everything was an anti-climax. Paul Williams left the group in 1973, to be replaced by another former Distant member, Richard Street; Williams shot himself in 1973, after years of depression and drug abuse. Whitfield's partnership with Strong was broken the same year, and although he continued to rework the 'Papa Was A Rolling Stone' formula, the commercial and artistic returns were smaller. The Temptations still scored hits, and 'Masterpiece', 'Let Your Hair Down' (both 1973) and 'Happy People' (1975) all topped the soul charts, but they were no longer a leading force in black music.

Whitfield left Motown in 1975; at the same time, Glenn Leonard replaced Damon Harris in the group. After struggling on for another year, the Temptations moved to Atlantic for two albums, which saw Louis Price taking the place of Dennis Edwards. When the Atlantic deal brought no change of fortunes, the group returned to Motown, and to Dennis Edwards. 'Power' in 1980 restored them to the charts, before Rick James engineered a brief reunion with David Ruffin and Eddie Kendricks for a tour, an album, and a hit single, 'Standing On The Top'. Ruffin and Kendricks then left to form a duo, Ron Tyson replaced Glenn Leonard, and Ali-Ollie Woodson took over the role of lead vocalist from Edwards. Woodson brought with him a song called 'Treat Her Like A Lady', which became their biggest UK hit in a decade. Subsequent releases confirmed the quality of the current line-up, though without a strong guiding hand they are unlikely to rival the achievements of the late 60s and early 70's line-ups, the culmination of Motown's classic era.

Albums: *Meet The Temptations* (1964), *The Temptations Sing Smokey* (1965), *The Temptin' Temptations* (1965), *Gettin' Ready* (1966), *Live!* (1967), *With A Lot O' Soul* (1967), *In A Mellow Mood* (1967), *Wish It Would Rain* (1968), *Diana Ross And The Supremes Join The Temptations* (1968), with Diana Ross And The Supremes *TCB* (1968), *Live At The Copa* (1968), *Cloud Nine* (1969), *The Temptations' Show* (1969), *Puzzle People* (1969), with Diana Ross And The Supremes *Together* (1969), with Diana Ross And The Supremes *On Broadway* (1969), *Psychedelic Shack* (1970), *Live At London's Talk Of The Town* (1970), *Christmas Card* (1970), *Sky's The Limit* (1971), *Solid Rock* (1972), *All Directions* (1972), *Masterpiece* (1973), *1990* (1973), *A Song For You* (1975), *House Party* (1975), *Wings Of Love* (1976), *The Temptations Do The Temptations* (1976), *Hear To Tempt You* (1977), *Bare Back* (1978), *Power* (1980), *The Temptations* (1981), with Jimmy Ruffin and Eddie Kendricks *Reunion* (1982), *Surface Thrills* (1983), *Back To Basics* (1984), *Truly For You* (1984), *Touch Me* (1985), *To Be Continued . . .* (1986), *Together Again* (1987), *Special* (1989), *Milestone* (1991). Compilations: *Greatest Hits* (1966), *Greatest Hits, Volume 2* (1970), *Anthology* (1973), *25 Anniversary* (1986), *Compact Command Perfomances* (1989).

Ten Years After

Formed in Nottingham, England as the Jaybirds in 1965 they abandoned their pedestrian title for a name which slotted in with the booming underground progressive music scene. The quartet of Alvin Lee (b. 19 December 1944, Nottingham, England; guitar/vocals), Chick Churchill (b. 2 January 1949, Mold, Flint/Clwyd, Wales; keyboards), Ric Lee (b. 20 October 1945, Cannock, Staffordshire, England; drums) and Leo Lyons (b. 30 November 1943, Bedford, England; bass) played a mixture of rock 'n' roll and blues which kept them apart from the mainstream blues *cognoscenti* of Fleetwood Mac, Chicken Shack and Savoy Brown. Their debut album was largely ignored and it took months of gruelling club work to establish their claim. The superb live *Undead*, recorded at Klooks Kleek club, spread the word that Alvin Lee was not only an outstanding guitarist, but he was the fastest by a mile. Unfortunately for the other three members, Alvin overshadowed them to the extent that they became merely backing musicians in what was described as the Alvin Lee show. The band began a series of US tours which gave them the record of more US tours than any other UK band. Lee's furious performance of 'Goin' Home' at the Woodstock Festival was one of the highlights, although that song became a millstone for them. Over the next two years they delivered four solid albums, which all charted in the UK and the USA. *Ssssh*, with its Graham Nash cover photography, was the strongest. 'Stoned Woman' epitomized their sound and style although it was 'Love Like A Man' from *Cricklewood Green* that gave them their only UK hit. *A Space In Time* saw them briefly relinquish guitar-based pieces in favour of electronics. By the time of *Rock 'N' Roll To The World* the band were jaded and they rested from touring to work on solo projects. This resulted in Alvin's *On The Road To Freedom* with gospel singer Mylon Le Fevre and a dull album from Chick Churchill, *You And Me*. When they reconvened, their spark and will had all but gone and remaining albums were poor. After months of rumour, Lee admitted that the band had broken up. In 1978 Lee formed the trio Ten Years Later, with little reaction, and in 1989 the original band reformed and released *About Time,* but only their most loyal fans were interested. The band was still active in the early 90s.

Albums: *Ten Years After* (1967), *Undead* (1968), *Stonedhenge* (1969), *Ssssh* (1969), *Cricklewood Green* (1970), *Watt* (1970), *A Space In Time* (1971), *Rock 'N' Roll Music To The World* (1972), *Recorded Live* (1973), *Positive Vibrations* (1974), *About Time* (1989). Compilations: *Alvin Lee & Company* (1972), *Goin' Home! - Their Greatest Hits* (1975), *Original Recordings Vol. 1* (1987).

Terrell, Tammi

b. Thomasina Montgomery, 29 April 1945, Philadelphia, Pennsylvania, USA, d. 16 March 1970. Tammi Terrell began recording for Scepter/Wand Records at the age of 15, before touring with the James Brown Revue for a year. In 1965, she married heavyweight boxer Ernie Terrell, the brother of future Supreme Jean Terrell. Tammi's warm, sensuous vocals won her a contract with Motown later that year, and in 1966 she enjoyed a series of R&B hits, among them a soulful rendition of 'This Old Heart Of Mine'. In 1967, she was selected to replace Kim Weston as Marvin Gaye's recording partner. This inspired teaming produced Gaye's most successful duets, and the pair issued a stream of hit singles between 1967 and 1969. 'Ain't No Mountain High Enough' and 'You're All I Need To Get By' epitomized their style, as Marvin and Tammi weaved around each other's voices, creating an aura of romance and eroticism which led to persistent rumours that they were lovers.

From the beginning, their partnership was tinged with unhappiness, Terrell collapsing in Gaye's arms during a performance in 1967. She was diagnosed as suffering from a brain tumour, and despite a series of major operations over the next three years, her health steadily weakened. By 1969, she was unable to perform in public, and on several of the duo's final recordings, their producer, Valerie Simpson, controversially claims to have taken her place. Ironically, one of these tracks, 'The Onion Song', proved to be the most successful of the Gaye/Terrell singles in the UK. Tammi Terrell died on 16 March 1970, her burial service attracting thousands of mourners, including many of her Motown colleagues. Her death has been the subject of much speculation, centred on rumours that her brain disorders were triggered by beatings administered by a member of the Motown hierarchy. These accusations were given voice in *Number One With A Bullet*, a novel by former Gaye aide Elaine Jesmer, which included a character clearly based on Terrell.

Albums: *Early Show* (1969), *Irresistible* (1969). With Marvin Gaye: *United* (1968), *You're All I Need* (1968), *Easy* (1969).

Tex, Joe

b. Joseph Arrington Jnr., 8 August 1933, Rogers, Texas, USA, d. 13 August 1982. The professional career of this popular singer began onstage at the Apollo. He won first place in a 1954 talent contest and duly secured a record deal. Releases on King, Ace and the Anna labels were derivative and disappointing, but Tex meanwhile honed his songwriting talent. James Brown's version of 'Baby You're Right' (1962) became a US R&B number 2, after which Tex was signed by Buddy Killen, a Nashville song publisher, who in turn established Dial as a recording outlet. Although early releases showed promise, it was not until 1965 that Tex prospered. Recorded at Fame and distributed by Atlantic, 'Hold On To What You've Got' was a US Top 5 hit. The first of several preaching singles, its homely values were maintained on 'A Woman Can Change A Man' and 'The Love You Save (May Be Your Own)'. However, Joe was equally comfortable on uptempo songs, as 'S.Y.S.L.J.F.M. (The Letter Song)' (1966) and 'Show Me' (1967) proved. Later releases were less successful and although 'Skinny Legs And All' and 'Men Are Gettin' Scarce' showed him still capable of major hits, the singer seemed unsure of his direction. A fallow period ended with 'I Gotcha' (1972), an irresistibly cheeky song, but Tex chose this moment to retire. A convert to the Muslim faith since 1966, he changed his name to Yusuf Hazziez, and toured as a spiritual lecturer. He returned to music in 1975. Two years later he enjoyed a 'comeback' hit with the irrepressible 'Ain't Gonna Bump No More (With No Big Fat Woman)'. By the 80s, however, Joe had withdrawn again from full-time performing. He devoted himself to Islam, his Texas ranch and the Houston Oilers football team. He was tempted into a Soul Clan reunion in 1981, but in August 1982 he died following a heart attack.

Albums: *Hold What You've Got* (1965), *The New Boss* (1965), *The Love You Save* (1966), *I've Got To Do A Little Better* (1966), *Live And Lively* (1968), *Soul Country* (1968), *Happy Soul* (1969), *You Better Get It* (1969), *Buying A Book* (1969), *With Strings And Things* (1970), *From The Roots Came The Rapper* (1972), *I Gotcha* (1972), *Joe Tex Spills The Beans* (early 70s), *Another Man's Woman* (early 70s), *Bumps And Bruises* (1977), *Rub Down* (1978), *He Who Is Without Funk Cast The First Stone* (1979). Compilations: *The Very Best Of Joe Tex* (1988), *The Very Best Of Joe Tex - Real Country Soul . . . Scarce As Hen's Teeth* (1988), *Different Strokes* (1989), *Stone Soul Country* (1989).

Them

Formed in Belfast, Northern Ireland in 1963, Them's tempestuous career spawned some of the finest records of their era. The original line-up - Van Morrison (b. 31 August 1945, Belfast, Northern Ireland; vocals/harmonica), Billy Harrison (guitar), Eric Wrixen (keyboards), Alan Henderson (bass) and Ronnie Millings (drums) - were stalwarts of the city's Maritime Hotel, where they forged a fiery, uncompromising brand of R&B. A demo tape featuring a lengthy version of 'Lovelight' engendered a management deal with the imposing Phil Solomon, who persuaded Dick Rowe to sign the group to Decca Records. The group then moved to London and issued their debut single, 'Don't Start Crying Now' which flopped. Brothers Patrick and Jackie

McAuley had replaced Wrixen and Millings by the time Them's second single, 'Baby Please Don't Go', was released. Although aided by session musicians, the quintet's performance was remarkable, and this urgent, exciting single - which briefly served as the theme song to the influential UK television pop programme *Ready Steady Go* - deservedly reached the UK Top 10. It was backed by the Morrison-penned 'Gloria', a paean to teenage lust hinged to a hypnotic riff, later adopted by aspiring bar bands. The follow-up 'Here Comes The Night', was written and produced by R&B veteran Bert Berns. It peaked at number 2, and although it implied a long career, Them's internal disharmony undermined progress. Peter Bardens replaced Jackie McAuley for the group's debut album which matched brooding original songs, notably the frantic 'Mystic Eyes' and 'You Just Can't Win', with sympathetic covers. Further defections ensued when subsequent singles failed to emulate early success and by the release of *Them Again*, the unit had been recast around Morrison, Henderson, Jim Armstrong (guitar), Ray Elliott (saxophone/keyboards) and John Wilson (drums). This piecemeal set nonetheless boasted several highlights, including the vocalist's impassioned reading of the Bob Dylan composition, 'It's All Over Now, Baby Blue'. Dave Harvey then replaced Wilson, but this version of Them disintegrated in 1966 following a gruelling US tour and dispute with Solomon. Posthumous releases included the extraordinary 'The Story Of Them' documenting the group's early days at the Maritime in Belfast. Morrison then began a highly prolific solo career, leaving behind a period of confusion which saw the McAuley brothers re-emerge with a rival group known variously as 'Them', 'Them Belfast Gypsies', the 'Freaks Of Nature', or simply the 'Belfast Gypsies'. Meanwhile ex-Mad Lads singer Kenny McDowell joined Henderson, Armstrong, Elliott and Harvey in a reconstituted Them who moved to Los Angeles following the intervention of producer Ray Ruff. *Now And Them* combined garage R&B with the *de rigueur* west coast sound exemplified by the lengthy 'Square Room', but the new line-up found it hard to escape the legacy of its predecessors. Elliott left the group in 1967, but the remaining quartet completed the psychedelic *Time Out, Time In For Them* as a quartet before McDowell and Armstrong returned to Belfast to form Sk'Boo. Henderson then maintained the Them name for two disappointing albums, on which he was supported by anonymous session musicians, before joining Ruff for a religious rock-opera, *Truth Of Truths*. He subsequently retired from music altogether, but renewed interest in his old group's heritage prompted a reunion of sorts in 1979 when the bassist recruited Billy Harrison, Eric Wrixen, Mel Austin (vocals) and Billy Bell (drums)

for *Shut Your Mouth*. True to form both Harrison and Wrixen were fired prior to a tour of Germany; after which the Them appellation was again laid to rest.

Albums: *Them* aka *The Angry Young Them* (1965), *Them Again* (1966), *Now And Them* (1967), *Time Out, Time In For Them* (1968), *Them* (1970), *In Reality* (1971), *Shut Your Mouth* (1979). Compilations: *Here Comes The Night* (1965), *The World Of Them* (1969), *Them Featuring Van Morrison* (1973), *Backtrackin' With Them* (70s), *Rock Roots: Them* (1976), *Collection: Them* (1986), *The Singles* (1987).

Further reading: *Van Morrison: A Portrait Of The Artist*, Johnny Rogan.

Them

Thomas, Carla

b. 21 December 1942, Memphis, Tennessee, USA. The daughter of Rufus Thomas, Carla first performed with the Teen Town Singers. ''Cause I Love You', a duet with her father, was released on Satellite (later Stax) in 1960, but the following year she established herself as a solo act with 'Gee Whiz (Look At His Eyes)'. Leased to Atlantic, the song became a US Top 10 hit. 'I'll Bring It On Home To You' (1962), (an answer to Sam Cooke), 'What A Fool I've Been' (1963) and 'Let Me Good To You' (1965) then followed. 'B-A-B-Y', written by Isaac Hayes and David Porter, reached the US R&B Top 3, before a series of duets with Otis Redding proclaimed her 'Queen of Soul'. An excellent version of Lowell Fulson's 'Tramp' introduced the partnership. 'Knock On Wood' and 'Lovey Dovey' followed before Redding's premature death. Carla's own career was eclipsed as Aretha Franklin assumed her regal mantle. Singles with William Bell and Johnnie Taylor failed to recapture past glories, although the singer stayed with Stax until its bankruptcy in 1975. Since then Carla has not recorded, although she does tour occasionally with the Stax revival shows.

Albums: *Gee Whiz* (1961), *Comfort Me* (1966), *Carla* (1966), with Otis Redding *King And Queen* (1967), *The Queen Alone* (1967), *Memphis Queen* (1969), *Love Means Carla Thomas* (1971). Compilation: *The Best Of*

Carla Thomas (1969).

Thomas, Irma

b. Irma Lee, 18 February 1941, Ponchatoula, Louisiana, USA. The 'Soul Queen Of New Orleans' was discovered in 1958 by bandleader Tommy Ridgley. Her early records were popular locally, but an R&B hit came in 1960 with '(You Can Have My Husband But Please) Don't Mess With My Man'. The following year Thomas rejoined producer/writer Allen Toussaint, with whom she had worked on her first recordings. This reunion resulted in two of Irma's finest singles, 'It's Raining' and 'Ruler Of My Heart' (1962), the latter a prototype for Otis Redding's 'Pain In My Heart'. After signing with the Imperial label in 1963 she recorded 'Wish Someone Would Care' (1964), which reached the US Top 20, while the follow-up, 'Anyone Who Knows What Love Is (Will Understand)', also entered the national chart. This single is better recalled for its b-side, 'Time Is On My Side', which was successfully covered by the Rolling Stones. Thomas continued to record excellent singles without achieving due commercial success. Her final hit was a magnificent interpretation of 'Good To Me' (1968), recorded at Muscle Shoals and issued on Chess. She then moved to Canyon, Roker and Cotillion, before appearing on Swamp Dogg's short-lived Fungus label with *In Between Tears* (1973). Irma has continued to record fine albums and remains a highly popular live attraction.
Albums: *Wish Someone Would Care* (1964), *Take A Look* (1968), *In Between Tears* (1973), *Irma Thomas Live* (1977), *Soul Queen Of New Orleans* (1978), *Safe With Me* (1979), *Hip Shakin' Mama* (1981), *The New Rules* (1986), *The Way I Feel* (1988), *Simply The Best* (1991). Compilations: *Time Is On My Side* (1983), *Best Of: Breakaway* (1986), *Something Good: The Muscle Shoals Sessions* (1989), *Ruler Of Hearts* (1989).

Thomas, Rufus

b. 26 March 1917, Cayce, Mississippi, USA. A singer, dancer and entertainer, Thomas learned his trade as a member of the Rabbit's Foot Minstrels, a vaudeville-inspired touring group. By the late 40s he was performing in several Memphis nightclubs and organizing local talent shows. B.B. King, Bobby 'Blue' Bland and Little Junior Parker were discovered in this way. When King's career subsequently blossomed, Thomas replaced him as a disc jockey at WDIA and remained there until 1974. He also began recording and several releases appeared on Star Talent, Chess and Meteor before 'Bear Cat' became a Top 3 US R&B hit. An answer to Willie Mae Thornton's 'Hound Dog', it was released on Sun in 1953. Rufus remained a local celebrity until 1960 when he recorded with his daughter, Carla Thomas.

Their duet, "Cause I Love You" was issued on the fledgling Satellite (later Stax) label where it became a regional hit. Thomas secured his reputation with a series of infectious singles. 'Walking The Dog' (1963) was a US Top 10 entry while several of his other recordings, notably 'Jump Back' and 'All Night Worker' (both in 1964) were beloved by aspiring British groups. His later success with novelty numbers – 'Do The Funky Chicken' (1970), '(Do The) Push And Pull, Part 1' (1970) and 'Do The Funky Penguin' (1971) – has obscured the merits of less brazen recordings. 'Sophisticated Sissy' (1967) and 'Memphis Train' (1968) are prime 60s' R&B. Rufus stayed with Stax until its 1975 collapse, from where he moved to AVI. His releases there included *If There Were No Music* and *I Ain't Getting Older, I'm Gettin' Better*. In 1980 Thomas re-recorded several of his older songs for a self-named collection on Gusto. The 80s saw him putting aside R&B and recording rap with *Rappin' Rufus*, on the Inchiban label and tackling blues with *That Woman Is Poison* on the Alligator label.
Albums: *Walking The Dog* (1964), *Do The Funky Chicken* (1970), *Doing The Push And Pull Live At PJs* (1971), *Did You Hear Me* (1973), *Crown Prince Of Dance* (1973), *Blues In The Basement* (1975), *If There Were No Music* (1977), *I Ain't Gettin' Older, I'm Gettin' Better* (1977), *Rufus Thomas* (1980), *Rappin' Rufus* (1986), *That Woman Is Poison* (1988). Compilation: *Jump Back - A 1963-67 Retrospective* (1984).

Three Dog Night

This highly successful US harmony rock trio formed in 1968 with a line-up comprising Danny Hutton (b. 10 September 1942, Buncrana, Eire), Cory Wells (b. 5 February 1942, Buffalo, New York, USA) and Chuck Negron (b. Charles Negron, 8 June 1942, New York, USA). The three lead singers were backed by Jim Greenspoon (b. 7 February 1948, Los Angeles, California, USA; organ), Joe Schermie (b. 12 February, Madison, Wisconsin, USA; bass), Mike Allsup (b. 8 March 1947, Modesto, California, USA; guitar) and Floyd Sneed (b. 22 November 1943, Calgary, Alberta, USA; drums). With their distinctive and sometimes extraordinary harmonic blend, the group registered an impressive 21 **Billboard** Top 40 hits between 1969-75. Their startling version of Lennon/McCartney's 'It's For You' typified the group at their best, but it was their original arrangements of the work of less well-known writers that brought welcome exposure and considerable royalties to fresh talent. Both Nilsson and Laura Nyro first glimpsed the Top 10 courtesy of Three Dog Night's covers of 'One' and 'Eli's Coming', respectively. The risque 'Mama Told Me Not To Come' provided the same service for Randy

Newman while also giving the group their first number 1 in 1970. During the next two years they registered two further US chart toppers, 'Joy To The World' (composed by Hoyt Axton) and 'Black And White' (a UK hit for reggae group Greyhound). Always ready to record promising material and adapt it to their distinctive harmonic blend, they brought vicarious US chart success to Russ Ballard's 'Liar' and Leo Sayer's UK number 1 'The Show Must Go On'. By the early 70s, there were gradual changes in the trio's back-up musicians, with several members of Rufus joining during 1976. The departure of Danny Hutton (replaced by Jay Gruska) proved a body blow, however, and precipitated the group's decline and disbandment. During 1981, they reunited briefly with Hutton but failed to retrieve past chart glories. The strength of Three Dog Night lay in the power of their harmonies and the strength of the material they adapted. In the age of the singer/songwriter, they were seldom applauded by critics but their inventive arrangements struck a chord with the public to the tune of 10 million selling records. Three Dog Night brought a fresh approach to the art of covering seemingly uncommercial material and demonstrated how a strong song can be translated into something approaching a standard.
Albums: *Three Dog Night* (1969), *Suitable For Framing* (1969), *Captured Live At The Forum* (1969), *It Ain't Easy* (1970), *Naturally* (1970), *Golden Bisquits* (1971), *Harmony* (1971), *Seven Separate Fools* (1972), *Around The World With Three Dog Night* (1973), *Cyan* (1973), *Hard Labor* (1974), *Coming Down Your Way* (1975), *American Pastime* (1976). Compilation: *Joy To The World - Their Greatest Hits* (1975).

Tiny Tim

b. Herbert Khaury, 12 April 1925, New York, USA. Eccentric entertainer Tiny Tim played regularly on the New York Greenwich Village circuit during the early/mid-60s. With his warbling voice, long scraggly hair and camp mannerisms, he specialized in show tunes dating back to the musicals of the 20s. Following an appearance in the film *You Are What You Eat*, he secured a regular spot on the highly rated *Rowan And Martin's Laugh-In* comedy series. The comic incongruity of this middle-aged man, who sang in a cracked falsetto and played the ukulele proved novel enough to warrant a Top 20 US hit with 'Tiptoe Through The Tulips'. Several albums and tours followed and at the height of his media fame he attracted a mass audience for his live television marriage on Johnny Carson's *The Tonight Show* to the young girl he called 'Miss Vicky' (Victoria May Budinger). His professed celibacy and highly moral sexual standpoint created instant copy and the controversial marriage was well chronicled, from the birth of baby Tulip, to the divorce court. By

the early 70s the Tiny Tim fad had passed, and having lost his contract with Reprise he continued to issue singles on small independent labels, to little success. Nearly 20 years later he reappeared on the revival circuit with the old act intact and in 1989 his version of AC/DC's 'Highway To Hell' was released to modest sales.
Albums: *God Bless Tiny Tim* (1968), *Tiny Tim's Second Album* (1969), *For All My Friends* (1969).

Tokens

Formed in 1955 in Brooklyn, New York, USA, the Tokens were one of the most successful white harmony groups of the early 60s, best known for their 1961 number 1 single 'The Lion Sleeps Tonight' (number 11 in the UK). The group was originally called the Linc-Tones (taken from Lincoln High School, which the original members all attended) and consisted of tenor vocalist Hank Medress (b. 19 November 1938, Brooklyn), Neil Sedaka (b. 13 March 1939, Brooklyn), Eddie Rabkin and Cynthia Zolitin. The following year Rabkin left and was replaced by Jay Siegel (b. 20 October 1939, Brooklyn). With that line-up the group recorded 'I Love My Baby' for the Melba label, with no success. The next change came in 1958 when Sedaka departed for a hugely successful solo career as a performer and songwriter. Zolitin also left in 1958 and the remaining duo carried on for a year with other singers as Darrell And The Oxfords, recording two singles for Roulette Records.
Twelve-year-old Mitch Margo (b. 25 May 1947, Brooklyn) and his brother Phil (b. 1 April 1942, Brooklyn) joined Medress and Siegel in December 1959 and the group changed its name to the Tokens. This was the most successful and stable line-up of the Tokens. Their first recording as such was the 1961 self-penned 'Tonight I Fell In Love', which the Tokens sold to the small Warwick Records. Following the record's rise to number 15 in the USA, the Tokens forged a creative partnership with producers and songwriters Hugo Peretti and Luigi Creatore at RCA Records.
That pair, along with songwriter George Weiss, reworked the folk song 'Wimoweh', itself reworked by the folk group the Weavers from a 30s South African song called 'Mbube', into 'The Lion Sleeps Tonight'. After the single peaked at the top of the US charts (number 11 in the UK), the quartet took on another vocalist, Joseph Venneri, for live performances (he later appeared on recordings, and was replaced in the mid-60s by Brute Force, whose real name was Stephen Friedland and who went on to record solo two albums under the Brute Force pseudonym after leaving the Tokens in 1970). In early 1962 the Tokens began branching out from recording under their own name by signing a

production deal with Capitol Records and establishing Big Time Productions in New York. During 1962, they attempted to repeat the success of their number 1 record by reworking other songs, including another African folk song, 'B'wa Nina (Pretty Girl)', and the Ritchie Valens hit 'La Bomba' (with a slight spelling change), itself an old Mexican folk song. The Tokens never recaptured the success they enjoyed with 'The Lion Sleeps Tonight', although they appeared on the US singles chart regularly until the beginning of the 70s on a succession of record labels, including their own B.T. Puppy Records, which they formed in 1964 (the label's greatest success was with the group the Happenings, who released two Top 5 singles on the label, produced by the Tokens). Among their other notable releases were 'He's In Town' in 1964, 'I Hear Trumpets Blow' in 1966 and 'Portrait Of My Love' in 1967.

Meanwhile, their production career took off in 1963 with the success of 'He's So Fine', a number 1 single by the girl group the Chiffons. Members of the Tokens also sang on many sessions for other artists at this time, including Bob Dylan (*Highway 61 Revisited*) and the Blues Project. In 1967 the Tokens signed with Warner Brothers Records (which refused to release a concept album they had recorded, titled *Intercourse*, which the group released itself in 1971) and two years later switched over to Buddah Records. By then their reign as hitmakers was long over, and the group began splintering. Mitch Margo spent 1969-71 in the Army and Medress departed the group in October 1970 to produce. His most successful venture was as co-producer of Tony Orlando and Dawn, one of the best-selling pop groups of the 70s. Medress also produced a 1972 remake of 'The Lion Sleeps Tonight' by Robert John, which reached number 3 in the USA, and produced records by singer Dan Hill and New York rocker/cabaret singer Buster Poindexter, a pseudonym for ex-New York Dolls singer David Johansen. The Tokens carried on without Medress until 1973, when the remaining trio changed its name to Cross Country and signed to Atco Records. As such they placed one single on the US chart, a remake of the Wilson Pickett hit 'In The Midnight Hour' which reached number 30 in 1973. The group finally split in 1974, although they cut a single together, 'A Tribute To The Beach Boys '76', in 1976. A reunion concert in New York in 1981 featured the Margo brothers, Siegel and Medress. Some of the group members, particularly Mitch Margo, attempted to keep the Tokens name alive by forming new groups into the 80s, and one even re-recorded 'The Lion Sleeps Tonight' in 1988 for the small Downtown label. Phil Margo went on to become a manager of rock bands. Jay Siegel became owner/manager of a recording studio in New York. Selected albums: *The Lion Sleeps Tonight* (1961), *We, The Tokens, Sing Folk* (1962), *Wheels* (1964), *Again* (1966), *I Hear Trumpets Blow* (1966), with the Happenings *Back To Back* (1967), *It's A Happening World* (1967), *Life Is Groovy* (1970), *Tokens Of Gold* (1969), *December 5th* (1971), *Both Sides Now* (1971), *Intercourse* (1971), *Cross Country* (1973). Compilations: *Greatest Moments* (1970), *Very Best Of The Tokens* (1971).

Tornados

The only serious challengers to the Shadows as Britain's top instrumental unit, the Tornados merely lasted as long as their console svengali, independent record producer Joe Meek. In 1961, he assembled the quintet initially as house band at his Holloway, London studio, to back solo performers such as Don Charles, John Leyton and Billy Fury who was namechecked in the title of their debut 'Love And Fury'. From Colin Hicks and his Cabin Boys, Meek had drawn Alan Caddy (b. 2 February 1940, London, England; guitar) and drummer Clem Cattini. Guitarist George Bellamy (b. 8 October 1941, Sunderland, England; guitar) and Roger Lavern (b. Roger Jackson, 11 November 1938, Kidderminster, England; keyboards) were session players while Heinz Burt on bass was one of Meek's own proteges.

In their own right, the Tornados made the big time with a second single, the otherworldly 'Telstar'. Composed by Meek with his creative confrére Geoff Goddard deputizing for Lavern on clavioline, this quintessential 60s instrumental anticipated many of the electronic ventures of a subsequent and less innocent pop generation. Moreover in 1962 it topped the domestic hit parade and unbelievably did likewise in the USA where no UK group, not even the Shadows, had made much headway. Though a capitalizing tour of North America was unwisely cancelled, Meek's boys played 'Eric the Red' to Britain's invasion of US charts two years later. 1963 was another good year for the Tornados with 'Globetrotter', 'Robot' and 'The Ice Cream Man' - all with catchy juxtapositions of outer space aetheria and funfair vulgarity - cracking the UK Top 20. Flattering too were those myriad copyist combos in their artistic debt, notably the Volcanos with 'Polaris'. Danger, however, became apparent in the comparative failure of 'Dragonfly' shortly after the exit of Burt. The absence of his blond Norse radiance onstage coupled with the levelling blow of the beat boom and its emphasis on vocals had rendered the Tornados *passé*. Worse, new ideas were thin on the ground. The 'Robot' b-side, 'Life On Venus', for instance, almost repeated the 'Telstar' melody while 'Early Bird' and 1965's 'Stingray' harked back to its million-selling sound. Following the departure of

Cattini, the last original Tornado, there came further desperate strategies until the penniless Meek's 1967 suicide and the outfit's interrelated disbandment. In the mid-70s, Bellamy, Burt, Cattini and Lavern - as 'The Original Tornados' - managed some nostalgia revues and a re-make of 'Telstar' before going their separate ways. Nevertheless, with a new Tornados, Cattini tried again in 1989. While this line-up features a female singer, the loudest cheers are reserved for the ancient instrumentals, especially Meek's eerie US number 1.

Albums: *Away From It All* (1964). Compilations: *Remembering* (1976).

Toys

Three high-school friends, Barbara Harris (b. 18 August 1945, Elizabeth City, North Carolina, USA), Barbara Parritt (b. 1 October 1944, Wilmington, North Carolina, USA) and June Montiero (b. 1 July 1946, New York City, USA) formed the Toys in Jamaica, New York. The group is best recalled for their 1965 hit 'A Lover's Concerto', a Supremes-influenced performance adapted from Bach's 'Minuet In G'. 'Attack', another piece appropriated from a classical theme, also reached the US and UK charts but further releases, 'May My Heart Be Cast To Stone' and 'Baby Toys' were only minor US pop hits. Although a 1968 single, 'Sealed With A Kiss' returned them to the US soul Top 50, the trio split up soon afterwards.

Albums: *The Toys Sing 'A Lover's Concerto' And 'Attack'* (1966).

Traffic

Traffic

Formed in 1967 this stellar UK group comprised Steve Winwood (b. 12 May 1948, Birmingham, England; keyboards/guitar/bass/vocals), Chris Wood (b. 24 June 1944, Birmingham, England, d. 12 July 1983; saxophone/flute), Jim Capaldi (b. 24 August 1944, Evesham, Worcestershire, England; drums/percussion/vocals) and Dave Mason (b. 10 May 1947, Worcester, England; guitar/vocals).

Winwood had conceived, plotted and formed Traffic just prior to his departure from the Spencer Davis Group. Traffic were archetypes of psychedelic Britain in 1967 in dress, attitude and music. They were the originators of the 'getting it together in the country cottage' syndrome, which found so many followers. Their pot-pourri of musical styles was innovative and daring, created in the communal atmosphere of their cottage in Berkshire. Their first single 'Paper Sun' with its infectious sitar opening was an instant hit, closely followed by 'Hole In My Shoe' (parodied in a 1984 number 2 UK hit by Neil the hippie, from BBC television's *The Young Ones*) and the film theme 'Here We Go Round The Mulberry Bush'. Mason left at the end of an eventful year, just as the first album, *Mr Fantasy* was released. From then on Traffic ceased to be a singles band, and built up a large following, especially in the USA. Their second album *Traffic*, showed refinement and further progression. Dave Mason had returned briefly and two of his songs were particularly memorable, 'You Can All Join In' and 'Feelin' Alright' (later covered by Joe Cocker). In 'Who Knows What Tomorrow Might Bring?', Winwood sings, 'We are not like all the rest, you can see us any day of the week, come around, sit down, take a sniff, fall asleep, baby you don't have to speak'. This lyric perfectly encapsulated the hippie lifestyle of the late 60s. Another outstanding song, 'Forty Thousand Headmen' combined a lyrical tale of pure fantasy with lilting flute and jazz tempo.

Their third album *Last Exit*, was a fragmented affair and during its recording Mason departed once more. The second side consisted of just two tracks recorded live with the band as a trio. Winwood bravely attempts to hold the ensemble together by singing and playing Hammond organ in addition to using the bass pedals to compensate for the lack of a bass guitar. At this point the band disintegrated leaving Winwood to wander into Blind Faith. The others teamed up once again with Dave Mason to form the short-lived Mason, Capaldi, Wood and Frog. The Frog was Mick Weaver (aka Wynder K. Frog). Neither band lasted; the former made one highly successful album and the latter were never committed to vinyl.

Following a brief spell as a member of Ginger Baker's Airforce, Winwood embarked on a solo project, to be called Mad Shadows. He enlisted the help of Wood and Capaldi, and to the delight of the music press this became Traffic once again. The resulting album was the well received *John Barleycorn Must Die*. Rick Grech formerly of Family, Blind Faith and Airforce also joined the band. In 1971 *Welcome To The Canteen* appeared with Dave Mason rejoining for a third time. This disappointing live album contained an overlong version of 'Gimme Some Lovin'' from Winwood's days in the Spencer Davis Group. Ironically it was Mason who shone, with two tracks from his superb *Alone Together* album.

Drummer Jim Gordon (from Derek And The Dominos) and Reebop Kwaku Baah joined in 1971, allowing Capaldi to take the role as frontman. The superb *Low Spark Of The High Heeled Boys* (1971) was followed by *Shoot Out At The Fantasy Factory* in 1973. The latter had the substitution of David Hood and Roger Hawkins for Grech and Gordon. Both albums were to achieve gold status in the USA. Throughout their turbulent career Traffic were never able to reproduce their inventive arrangements on stage. Witnesses would concur that Traffic were erratic when playing live. This meandering trait was highlighted on their penultimate album, *On The Road*.

The final record was *When The Eagle Flies* in 1974, another fine collection with Rosko Gee on bass and 'Gentleman' Jim Capaldi back behind the drum kit. Traffic did not so much break up as fizzle out. They left an indelible mark as creators of inventive and sometimes glorious music.

Albums: *Mr Fantasy* (1967), *Traffic* (1968), *Last Exit* (1969), *John Barleycorn Must Die* (1970), *Welcome To The Canteen* (1971), *Low Spark Of The High Heeled Boys* (1971), *Shoot Out At The Fantasy Factory* (1973), *On The Road* (1973), *When The Eagle Flies* (1974). Compilations: *Best Of Traffic* (1970), *Heavy Traffic* (1975), *More Heavy Traffic* (1975), *Smiling Phases* (1991)

Further reading: *Keep On Running: The Steve Winwood Story*, Chris Welch. *Back In The High Life: A Biography Of Steve Winwood*, Alan Clayson.

Trashmen

This surf rock quartet from Minneapolis, Minnesota, USA comprised three guitarists: Dal Winslow (b. 1942), Tony Andreason (b. 1943), Bob Reed (b. 1942) and drummer Steve Wahrer (b. 1942). Formed in 1962 the group quickly became a very popular live act in the upper midwest. Their first and biggest hit was the novelty garage rock epic 'Surfin' Bird', complete with Winslow's unbelievable gravelly vocal, which went into the US Top 5. Their follow-up 'Bird Dance Beat' also made the US Top 40 and their debut album *Surfin' Bird* nearly graced the Top 40 too. Both hit songs borrowed heavily from soul group the Rivingtons' compositions 'Papa-Oom-Mow-Mow' and 'The Bird's The Word', and after legal battles the Rivingtons received their rightful royalties from the Trashmen's records. The distinctive group, whose name is thought by many to describe aptly their music, later recorded on Argo, Tribe and Bear without success. Wahrer died of throat cancer at the age of 47 in 1989.

Album: *Surfin' Bird* (1964).

Tremeloes

When UK chart-toppers Brian Poole And The Tremeloes parted company in 1966 few would have wagered that the backing group would outdo the lead singer. Remarkably, however, the relaunched Tremeloes would eclipse not only Poole, but the orginal hit-making group. At the time of their reconvening in 1966, the line-up comprised Rick West (b. Richard Westwood, 7 May 1943, Dagenham, Essex, England; guitar), Alan Blakely (b. 1 April 1942, Dagenham, Essex, England; rhythm guitar), Dave Munden (b. 2 December 1943, Dagenham, Essex, England; drums) and Alan Howard (b. 17 October 1941, Dagenham, Essex, England; bass). In May of 1966 Howard was replaced by Mike Clark; however a mere three months later his spot was taken by Len 'Chip' Hawkes (b. 11 November 1946, London, England), whose lead vocals and boyish looks gave the group a stronger visual identity. In order to keep up with the times, the group abandoned their stage suits in favour of Carnaby Street garb and fashionably longer hair. Their second generation debut was a cover of Paul Simon's 'Blessed', which proved unsuccessful. Seeking more commercial material they next covered 'Good Day Sunshine' from the Beatles' *Revolver*. In spite of radio play it too failed to chart but their third release 'Here Comes My Baby' (a Cat Stevens composition) smashed into the Top 10 on both sides of the Atlantic. An astute follow-up with 'Silence Is Golden', previously the flip-side of the Four Seasons' 'Rag Doll', proved a perfect vehicle for the Tremeloes' soft harmonic style and gave them their only number 1. Having established themselves as a hit act, they notched up an impressive run of hits during the late 60s including 'Even The Bad Times Are Good', 'Suddenly You Love Me', 'Helule Helule' and 'My Little Lady'. At the end of the decade, the group seemed weary of their role in the pop world and broke away from their usual Tin Pan Alley songsmiths to write their own material. Their first attempt, '(Call Me) Number One', was an impressive achievement, arguably superior to the material that they had recorded since 1967. When it reached number 2 in the charts, the group convinced themselves that a more ambitious approach would bring even greater rewards. Over-reacting to their dream start as hit writers, they announced that they were 'going heavy' and suicidally alienated their pop audience by dismissing their earlier record-buying fans as 'morons'. Their brief progressive phase was encapsulated in the album *Master*, which won no new fans but provided a final Top 20 single, 'Me And My Life'. Thereafter, they turned increasingly to cabaret where their strong live performances were well appreciated. In 1974 Chip Hawkes went to Nashville, USA to pursue an unsuccessful solo career.

Albums: *Here Comes The Tremeloes* (1967), *The Tremeloes: Chip, Rick, Alan And Dave* (1967), *Here Comes My Baby* (USA 1967), *1958/68 World Explosion* (1968), *The Tremeloes 'Live' In Cabaret* (1969), *Master* (1970), *Shiner* (1974), *Don't Let The Music Die* (1976).

Trent, Jackie

b. Jacqueline Trent, 6 September 1940, Newcastle-Under-Lyme, Staffordshire, England. This singer and lyricist achieved most of her success in collaboration with her husband, Tony Hatch. After performing in amateur productions from an early age, Trent started singing with local bands at the age of 13, and turned professional when she was 17. She toured parts of Europe and the Middle East, and played in cabaret in London, and traditional seaside shows. In the early 60s she recorded for the Oriole label before successfully auditioning for Pye Records producer, Tony Hatch in 1964. Hatch had already written several successful compositions, including the theme to the television UK soap opera, *Crossroads*. Together, they wrote the melodic 'Where Are You Now', which Trent took to number 1 in the UK charts in 1965. During the late 60s they composed several major hits for Petula Clark, including 'Don't Sleep In The Subway', 'The Other Man's Grass', 'I Couldn't Live Without Your Love', 'Colour My World', 'My Love' and 'Call Me'. Scott Walker also made the charts with their 'Joanna' in 1968. For their wedding day in 1967, Pye issued 'The Two Of Us', an incidental item they had recorded months before. Its success, particularly in Australia, caused them to form a double act for cabaret, and make frequent trips to the Antipodes. In 1970 Trent starred as Nell Gwynne in the regional musical *Nell!*, with Hatch as co-producer and musical director. Two years later the couple wrote the score for Cameron Mackintosh's first West End production *The Card*, a musical adaptation of Arnold Bennett's novel, which starred Jim Dale, Marti Webb, Eleanor Bron and Millicent Martin. The songs included 'I Could Be The One', 'That's The Way The Money Goes' and 'Opposite Your Smile'. Another project, *Rock Nativity* (1974), proved to be 'one biblical musical too many'. Around the same time they released *Two For The Show*. From 1982 onwards, Hatch and Trent spent the majority of each year living and working in Australia and in 1986 they wrote the theme song for *Neighbours*, a television soap, set in Melbourne. Its success spread to the UK, and it was even introduced into the USA in 1991. They composed several other UK television themes, including *Mr & Mrs*. Hatch and Trent's most successful stage project *The Card*, was scheduled for a major UK revival in 1992.

Albums: *The Magic Of Jackie Trent* (late 60s), *The Night, The Music And...* (1979), with Tony Hatch

Our World Of Music (1980). Compilations: *The Best Of Jackie Trent* (1973), *Golden Hour Of Jackie Trent And Tony Hatch* (1976).

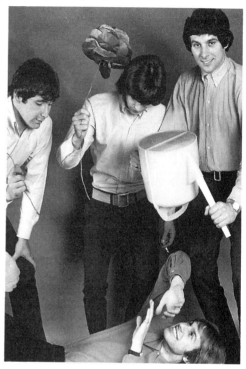

Troggs

Troggs

The original Troggs were an ill-starred early 60s group from Andover, Hampshire, England who suddenly found themselves reduced to two members: vocalist Dave Wright and bassist Reginald Ball (b. 12 June 1943, Andover, England). Another local group, Ten Foot Five, were suffering similar personnel upheavals with bassist Peter Staples (b. 3 May 1944, Andover, England) and guitarist Chris Britton (b. 21 January 1945, Watford, Hertfordshire, England) surviving the purge. At the suggestion of their respective managers, the two groups amalgamated, with Ball surprisingly emerging as the new lead vocalist. On the advice of **New Musical Express** journalist Keith Altham, Ball later changed his name to Reg Presley in the hope of attracting some attention from Elvis fans. Wright, meanwhile, had moved on to another Hampshire group, the Loot, while the revitalized Troggs found a drummer, Ronnie Bond (b. Ronald Bullis, 4 May 1943, Andover, England). After signing with producer/manager Larry Page, the group recorded a one-off single for CBS, 'Lost Girl'. Their debut flopped but after switching to Larry's new label Page One (distributed by Fontana), they found success with a cover of Chip Taylor's 'Wild Thing', which reached number 2 in the UK in May 1966. The follow-up, 'With A Girl Like You', went one better, establishing the Troggs as one of the most popular groups in the country. Stateside success was equally impressive with 'Wild Thing' topping the charts. Unfortunately, due to a misunderstanding with Sonny And Cher's managers Charlie Greene and Brian Stone (who had organized a re-recording of the disc), 'Wild Thing' was released on two different labels, Atco and Mercury. To make matters worse, the flip-side of the Atco version was the scheduled follow-up, 'With A Girl Like You'.

While their prospects in America waned, the group enjoyed an affectionate notoriety at home where their provincial politeness and inane naiveté contrasted markedly with the forced sexiness of songs such as 'I Can't Control Myself' and 'Anyway That You Want Me'. Although the group boasted three songwriters and potential solo artists whose work was covered by others, they were never taken seriously by the press or pop elite. While clearly at home with basic rockers like 'Give It To Me', the group also tinkered with counter culture subject matter on 'Night Of The Long Grass' and 'Love Is All Around', and their albums also occasionally veered towards the psychedelic market.

Any hopes of sustaining their hit career were lost when they fell out with Larry Page in a High Court action that made case law. Thereafter they became predominantly a touring group, with Presley infrequently abetted by Britton, Bond and Tony Murray (from Plastic Penny). During the 70s they achieved a certain cult status thanks to the hilarious 'Troggs Tapes', a notorious bootleg recording of an abortive session, consisting mainly of a stream of swear words. Later that decade they reunited with Page for an odd reworking of the Beach Boys' 'Good Vibrations' and recorded a live album at Max's Kansas City. Two-and-a-half decades on, the band still perform with their credibility growing rather than shrinking. Their R.E.M. linked *Athens Andover* took people by surprise. The band had utilized Presley songs (and one from Chip Taylor), and blended the raw Troggs sound with R.E.M.'s Peter Buck and Mike Mills. The album was a clear indication that after being the butt of jokes for many years the Troggs are one of the finest ever 60s pop bands.

Albums: *From Nowhere The Troggs* (1966), *Trogglodynamite* (1967), *Cellophane* (1967), *Mixed Bag* (1968), *Trogglomania* (1969), *Contrasts* (1976), *The Original Trogg Tapes* (1976), *Live At Max's Kansas City* (1981), *Black Bottom* (1983), *Rock It Baby* (1984), *Rock It Up* (1985) *Wild Things* (1987), *Au* (1990), *Athens Andover* (1992). Compilations: *Best Of The Troggs* (1988), *14 Greatest Hits* (1988).

Troy, Doris

b. Doris Payne, 6 January 1937, New York City, USA. The daughter of a Baptist preacher, Doris abandoned her gospel beginnings in favour of a jazz group, the Halos. She recorded as half of Jay And Dee before signing with Atlantic in 1963. An accomplished writer, her shuffling 'Just One Look' was a US Top 10 hit that same year, and covered the following year by the Hollies, reached the UK number 2 slot. Other releases included the equally insistent 'What'cha Gonna Do About It?', which reached the UK Top 40 in 1964, but failed to succeed in her home country. Later singles for Capitol and Calla were equally under-rated. After settling in London in 1969, she recorded a self-titled album for the Beatles' label Apple, with the help of George Harrison and Eric Clapton. Doris also recorded for People and Polydor and later worked as a session singer, contributing to a number of albums including Pink Floyd's *Dark Side Of The Moon*. From 1980-1986, Troy performed in an off-Broadway musical, *Mama I Want To Sing*, which produced a live album.

Albums: *Just One Look* (1963), *Doris Troy* (1970), *Rainbow Testament* (1972), *Stretching Out* (1974), *Mama I Want To Sing* (1986).

Truth

Truth

Hairdresser Steven Gold met future singing partner

Francis Aiello while cutting the latter's hair. Taking their name from a favourite Ray Charles' song, 'Tell The Truth', the duo scored a UK Top 30 hit in 1966 with their debut single, an opportunistic cover of 'Girl' from the Beatles' *Rubber Soul* album. Although the Truth drew plaudits for 'I Go To Sleep', written by Ray Davies of the Kinks, it emphasized the Truth's inability to acquire exclusive material. Subsequent singles included 'Walk Away Renee' and 'Sueno', originally recorded, respectively, by the Left Banke and Rascals, but when such releases failed to chart the duo abandoned their brief pop career. Album: *Truth* (1975).

Tucker, Tommy
b. Robert Higginbotham, 5 March 1933, Springfield, Ohio, USA, d. 22 January 1982. Renowned as an R&B performer, Tucker began his career as a jazz musician playing piano and clarinet for the Bob Woods Orchestra. He led his own group, the Dusters, and worked with saxophonist Roland Kirk prior to recording 'Hi-Heel Sneakers' in 1964. This simple, but compulsive 12-bar blues song established the singer's reputation when it was consistently covered by other acts. This one song contained a pot-pourri of references, the bizarre 'hi-heel sneakers' and 'wig hats on her head.' The casually understated delivery of the line 'You better wear some boxing gloves, in case some fool might want to fight', gave the song great subtle humour. Further excellent singles in a similar style, including 'Long Tall Shorty', were less successful and forced Tucker to revert to club work. He visited Britain during the 70s as part of the *Blues Legends* package and, inspired by an enthusiastic response, began recording again. This irrepressible performer, sadly, died from poisoning in January 1982.
Albums: *Hi-Heel Sneakers* (1964), *Mother Tucker* (1974), *Rocks Is My Pillow, Cold Ground Is My Bed* (1982), *Memphis Badboy* (1987), *1933 Tommy Tucker* (1988), *1942 Tommy Tucker* (1988).

Turner, Ike And Tina
Ike Turner (b. 5 November 1931, Clarkdale, Mississippi, USA) and Tina Turner (b. Anna Mae Bullock, 26 November 1938, Brownsville, Tennessee, USA). The commercial rebirth of singer Tina Turner, coupled with revelations about her ex-husband's unsavoury private life, has obscured the important role Ike Turner played in the development of R&B. A former piano-player with Sonny Boy Williamson and Robert Nighthawk, Ike formed his Kings Of Rhythm during the late 40s. This influential group was responsible for 'Rocket 88', a 1950 release often named as the first rock 'n' roll recording but confusingly credited to its vocalist, Jackie Brenston. Turner then became a talent scout for Modern

Ike and Tina Turner

Records where he helped develop the careers of Bobby 'Blue' Bland, B.B. King and Howlin' Wolf. Now based in St. Louis, his Kings Of Rhythm were later augmented by a former gospel singer, Annie Mae Bullock. Originally billed as 'Little Ann', she gradually became the core of the act, particularly following her marriage to Ike in 1958. Their debut release as Ike And Tina Turner came two years later. 'A Fool In Love', a tough, uncompromising release featuring Tina's already-powerful delivery, preceded several excellent singles, the most successful of which was 'It's Gonna Work Out Fine' (1961). Highlighted by Ike's wry interjections, this superior performance defined the duo's early recordings.

Although their revue was one of the leading black music touring shows, the Turners were curiously unable to translate this popularity into record sales. They recorded for several labels, including Sue, Kent and Loma, but a brief spell with Philles was to prove the most controversial. Here producer Phil Spector constructed his 'wall-of sound' around Tina's impassioned voice but the resultant single, 'River Deep Mountain High', was an unaccountable miss in the US, although in the UK charts it soared to the Top 3. Its failure was to have a devastating effect on Spector. Ike, unhappy at relinquishing the reins, took the duo elsewhere when further releases were less successful. A support slot on the Rolling Stones 1969 North American tour introduced the Turners to a wider, generally white, audience. Their version of John Fogerty's 'Proud Mary' was a gold disc in 1971, while the autobiographical 'Nutbush City Limits' (1973) was also an international hit. The group continued to be a major in-concert attraction, although Tina's brazen sexuality and the show's tried formula ultimately paled. The Turners became increasingly estranged as Ike's character darkened; Tina left the group in the middle of a tour and the couple were finally divorced in 1976. Beset by problems, chemical or otherwise, Ike is now in prison, a stark contrast to his ex-wife's very public profile.

Albums: *The Soul Of Ike And Tina Turner* (1960), *Dance With The Kings Of Rhythm* (1960), *The Sound Of Ike And Tina Turner* (1961), *Dance With Ike And Tina Turner* (1962), *Festival Of Live Performances* (1962), *Dynamite* (1963), *Don't Play Me Cheap* (1963), *It's Gonna Work Out Fine* (1963), *Please Please Please* (1964), *The Soul Of Ike And Tina Turner* (1964), *The Ike And Tina Turner Show Live* (1965), *Ike And Tina Turner Revue Live* (1965), *River Deep - Mountain High* (1966), *So Fine* (1968), *Cussin', Cryin' And Carrying On* (1969), *Get It Together!* (1969), *River Deep - Mountain High* (1969), *Her Man, His Woman* (1969), *A Black Man's Soul* (1969), *Outta Season* (1969), *In Person* (1969), *The Hunter* (1969), *Come Together* (1970), *Working Together* (1970), *Live In Paris* (1971), *Live At Carnegie Hall - What You Hear Is What You Get* (1971), *Bad Dreams* (1971), *'Nuff Said* (1971), *Feel Good* (1972), *Let Me Touch Your Mind* (1973), *Nutbush City Limits* (1973), *Strange Fruit* (1974), *Sweet Island Rhode Red* (1974), *Delilah's Power* (1977), *Airwaves* (1978), *Love Explosion* (1978).

Compilations: *Ike And Tina Turner's Greatest Hits* (1972), *Tough Enough* (1984), *The Ike And Tina Turner Sessions* (1987), *The Best Of Ike And Tina Turner* (1987), *Fingerpoppin' -The Warner Brothers Years* (1988), *Best Of Ike And Tina Turner* (1991). Ike Turner also recorded several solo albums including: *Blues Roots* (1972), *I'm Tore Up* (1978). Ike's early work with the Kings Of Rhythm and as a talent scout is represented on *Hey Hey* (1984), *Rockin' Blues* (1986), *Ike Turner And His Kings Of Rhythm Volumes 1 & 2* (1988), *Talent Scout Blues* (1988).

Further reading: *I Tina*, Tina Turner with Kurt Loder.

Turtles

Having begun their career playing in college-based surf instrumental groups, the Nightriders and the Crossfires, this Los Angeles sextet abruptly switched to beat music during 1964 in imitation of the Beatles. The line-up consisted of Howard Kaylan (b. Howard Kaplan, 22 June 1947, New York, USA; vocals/saxophone) and Mark Volman (b. 19 April 1947, Los Angeles, California, USA; vocals/saxophone), backed by Al Nichol (b. 31 March 1945, North Carolina, USA; piano/guitar), Jim Tucker (b. 17 October 1946, Los Angeles, California, USA; guitar), Chuck Portz (b. 28 March 1945, Santa Monica, California, USA; bass) and Don Murray (b. 8 November 1945, Los Angeles, California, USA; drums). By the summer of 1965 they found themselves caught up in the folk rock boom and, impressed by the success of local rivals the Byrds, elected to call themselves the Tyrtles. That idea was soon dropped but as the Turtles they slavishly followed the Byrds blueprint, covering a Bob Dylan song, 'It Ain't Me Babe' to considerable effect. After rejecting 'Eve Of Destruction' as a possible follow-up, they used the services of its composer, the new 'king of protest' P.F. Sloan. His pen provided a further two major US hits, 'Let Me Be' and 'You Baby' before their commercial appeal wilted. The psychedelic boom of 1967 saw a change in the group's image and coincided with line-up fluctuations resulting in the induction of drummer John Barbata and successive bassists Chip Douglas and Jim Pons.

The exuberant 'Happy Together' revitalized their chart fortunes, reaching number 1 in the US and also charting in the UK. That song has now achieved classic status and is a perennial turntable hit. The follow-up 'She'd Rather Be With Me' was another zestful singalong establishing the group as expert pop craftsmen. The mid-tempo 'You Know What I Mean' and 'Elenore' were also impressive, with the usual sprinkling of affectionate parody that worked against the odds. The Turtles hardly looked like pop stars but sang delightfully anachronistic teen ballads and ended their hit career by returning to their folk-rock roots, courtesy of 'You Showed Me', first recorded by the Byrds in 1964. With a final touch of irony their record company issued the once rejected 'Eve Of Destruction' as the group's final single. After the group dissolved, Kaylan and Volman (with Pons) joined the Mothers Of Invention and later emerged as Flo And Eddie, offering their services as producers and backing singers to a number of prominent artists.

Albums: *It Ain't Me Babe* (1965), *You Baby* (1966), *Happy Together* (1967), *The Battle Of The Bands* (1968), *Turtle Soup* (1969). Various compilations have also been issued.

Twinkle

b. Lynn Annette Ripley, 15 July 1947, Surbiton, Surrey, UK. Unlike her mid-60s female contemporaries, Twinkle actually wrote her own hits, a feat that should not be underestimated. After traipsing around Denmark Street, the Tin Pan Alley of British pop, the 17-year-old was auditioned by producer Tommy Scott and placed in the hands of manager Phil Solomon. Like most of the Solomon stable she was signed to Decca by Dick Rowe and her records were arranged by Phil Coulter. 'Terry', a biker anthem similar in theme to the contemporaneous Shangri-Las' hit 'Leader Of The Pack', was a Top 3 smash in early 1965. The teenager soon made her first public appearance supporting Jerry Lee Lewis at Brighton and prepared her next release, the charming 'Golden Lights', which proved only a minor hit. Although she wrote several other songs, including 'Boy That I Once Knew', 'Saturday Nights' and 'Unhappy Boy', no further success was forthcoming. Her main frailty was a lack of vocal power which prevented her building a following on the live circuit. After retiring to become a housewife, she returned briefly in 1972 with a cover of the Monkees' 'I'm A Believer'. More recently, her work was introduced to a younger audience thanks to the Smiths' cover of 'Golden Lights'.

Twist

Probably the most popular dance of the rock era, the twist first came to the attention of the general public in 1960 with Chubby Checker's recording of the same name. However, that song was written two years earlier by Hank Ballard and the dance actually had roots as far back as 1956. According to Cal Green, Ballard's guitarist at the time, the song originated with a gospel group called the Sensational Nightingales. Joe Cook of the group Little Joe And The Thrillers ('Peanuts', 1957) agrees, having said that he was offered a dance song in 1956 with the lyrics 'Come on baby, let's do the twist' by the gospel group.

A member of the Nightingales, Joseph Wallace, confirmed this in 1988, stating that he had written the original version of the song based on a dance his younger sister and her friends were doing. Since that group was not allowed to record secular material, Cal Green has said, they offered the song to Ballard in 1957. It was first written as a 12-bar blues and speeded up to dance tempo by Ballard. The original song's tune was replaced to match a song Ballard had recorded in 1957, 'Is Your Love For Real'. When 'The Twist' was finally recorded by Ballard, it was issued as a b-side and failed to cause any significant reaction. Ballard's name was listed as the sole author of the song, and Cal Green has said that it was Checker who came up with the dance that became known as the twist; it bore little relation to the original dance that Wallace had witnessed. Checker's recording of 'The Twist', on Parkway Records, became a US number 1 in the summer of 1960 and sparked a sensation among teenagers that permeated through to Europe.

A year and a half later, the dance had become a national craze also practised by adults. The single again topped the charts, becoming the only record of the rock era to return to the number 1 position after an absence of more than a year. Meanwhile, Hank Ballard signed over his performing rights of the song to entrepreneur Morris Levy in 1975. A plethora of twisting songs have been released, including: 'Twist And Shout' (Isley Brothers, Beatles and Brian Poole And The Tremeloes), 'Twist Polka' (Ray Henry), 'The Twist' and 'Let's Twist Again' (Chubby Checker), 'Twisting The Night Away' (Sam Cooke/Devine), 'The Twist' (Ray Anthony And The Bookends), 'Twist Twist Senora' (Gary 'U.S.' Bonds), 'Twistin' Matilda' (Jimmy Soul), 'Twistin' U.S.A.', and 'Twistin' All Night Long' (Danny And The Juniors), 'Twistin' Postman' (the Marvelettes), 'Twistin' Bells' (Santo And Johnny), 'Twisting By The Pool' (Dire Straits), 'Hey Let's Twist' and 'Peppermint Twist' (Joey Dee And The Starlighters). There were even twisting albums released, including *Twisting With The Cadillacs*, *Twistin' With Duane Eddy*, *Twist With Bobby Darin* and *Twist With The Ventures*.

Tyrannosaurus Rex

Formed in 1967 by singer/guitarist Marc Bolan, Tyrannosaurus Rex was originally envisioned as an electric sextet until a hire purchase company repossessed their equipment. Bolan was then joined by percussionist Steve 'Peregrine' Took in an acoustic-based venture which combined his love of classic rock 'n' roll with an affection for faerie mythology. Marc's unusual quivering vocal style rendered most of his lyrics incomprehensible, but the effect was genuinely enchanting and the duo were quickly adopted by the emergent 'underground'. BBC Disc jockey John Peel became a tireless promoter of the group which shared billings on his roadshow and was featured heavily on his radio programme *Top Gear*. Tyrannosaurus Rex enjoyed three minor hit singles with 'Debora', 'One Inch Rock' and 'King Of The Rumbling Spires', and achieved notable success with their albums, of which *My People Were Fair And Had Sky In Their Hair But Now They're Content To Wear Stars On Their Brows* and *Unicorn* reached the UK Top 20. The latter set showed a marked departure from previous stark accompaniment, adding harmonium, bass and piano to their lexicon. Their partnership was sundered in 1969 following an acrimonious US tour and Bolan was joined by Mickey Finn, late of Hapshash And The Coloured Coat for *A Beard Of Stars*. Here the unit's transformation was complete and this electric set, although still encompassing chimerical fables, was the natural stepping-stone for Bolan's transformation into a fully-fledged pop idol with T. Rex.

Albums: *My People Were Fair And Had Sky In Their Hair But Now They're Content To Wear Stars On Their Brows* (1968), *Prophets, Seers, Sages, The Angels Of The Ages* (1968), *Unicorn* (1969), *A Beard Of Stars* (1970). Compilation: *The Best Of T.Rex* (1971).

U

Undertakers

Formed in Wallasey, Merseyside in 1961, the Undertakers were initially known as the Vegas Five, but assumed their new sobriquet when a printer's error advertised them as such in a local newspaper. Their original line-up featured Jimmy McManus (vocals), Chris Huston (lead guitar), Geoff Nugent (guitar, vocals), Brian 'Boots' Jones (saxophone, vocals), Dave 'Mushy' Cooper (bass) and Bob Evans (drums), but within 18 months the core of Jones, Huston and Nugent had been joined by Jackie Lomax (bass, vocals) and Bugs Pemberton (drums). The quintet completed four singles between 1963-64, including versions of material by the Shirelles ('Everybody Loves A Lover'), Solomon Burke ('Stupidity') and Roscoe Gordon ('Just A Little Bit'). Adequate rather than urgent, these releases lacked the passion of corresponding live performances where, bedecked in black frock coats, the Undertakers added a strong visual approach to their brand of driving R&B. An album entitled *Undertakers* was recorded for Pye in 1964, but never released. The group attempted to update their image by truncating their name to the 'Takers, but split up in 1965 following a chaotic spell domiciled in New York. Jackie Lomax then pursed an intermittently successful career both as a solo and as a session vocalist.

United States Of America

Formed in 1967 by New York-born electronics composer, Joseph Byrd. The rest of the line-up comprised University of California Los Angeles students Dorothy Moskowitz (vocals), Gordon Marron (electric violin), Rand Forbes (bass) and Craig Woodson (drums). The quintet's lone, self-titled album, a biting satire on contemporary America, featured several haunting compositions including 'Love Song For The Dead Che' and 'The Garden Of Earthly Delights'. At times reminiscent of Jefferson Airplane, the innovative use of electronic effects gave the collection its chilling factor and it remains one of era's more lasting works. Byrd was also responsible for arranging Phil Ochs' powerful composition 'Pleasures Of The Harbour' and later formed a new group, the Field Hippies. However, the resultant *The American Metaphysical Circus*, lacked the discipline of his first release. Moscovitz subsequently re-emerged in Country Joe McDonald's All Star Band while Byrd was responsible for producing Ry Cooder's 1978 release, *Jazz*, and recording two quirky, synthesizer solo albums.

Album: *The United States Of America* (1968). Solo albums: Joseph Byrd *Joe Byrd And The Field Hippies* (1969), *Yankee Trancendoodle* (1975), *Xmas Yet To Come* (1980).

Unit Four Plus Two

Formed in Hertfordshire, England, this aptly named 60s pop sextet comprised: Buster Meikle (b. David Meikle, 1 March 1942, vocals, guitar), Tommy Moeller (b. 23 February 1945; vocals, tambourine, piano, guitar), Peter Moules (b. 14 October 1944; vocals, autoharp, guitar, banjo), Rodney Garwood (b. 27 March 1944; bass) and Hugh Halliday (b. 12 December 1944; drums). Originally Unit Four, a folk quartet, they extended their ranks to six in January 1962. The folk element remained in their repertoire with such standards as 'Cottonfields' and 'La Bamba', while their first two Decca singles, 'Green Fields' and 'Sorrow And Rain' were out of keeping with the prevalent beat scene. With the assistance of Russ Ballard and Bob Henrit of the Roulettes (who would later join the group), they recorded the rhythmic 'Concrete And Clay', which brought them to number 1 in the UK in 1965. The follow-up, 'You've Never Been In Love Like This Before', reached the Top 20, but after a couple of further minor hits with 'Baby Never Say Goodbye' and 'Hark!', their lightweight pop style proved insufficient for chart success. In 1969, with the beat boom long forgotten, they disbanded.

Album: *Unit Four Plus Two - First Album* (1965). Compilation: *Remembering* (1977).

V

Valance, Ricky

b. David Spencer, c.1939, Ynytsdou, South Wales. After singing in local clubs for a couple of years, Valance was discovered by an A&R representative from EMI Records and placed in the hands of producer Norrie Paramor. At the first recording session, Ricky was given the chance of covering Ray Peterson's US hit, 'Tell Laura I Love Her'. A wonderfully-enunciated reading was rewarded with a number 1 hit in September 1960, thanks to airplay on Radio Luxembourg, but none of Valance's follow-ups even reached the Top 50. He continued playing the clubs, however, and still regularly appears on the revival circuit.

Valentinos

Formed in the 1950s and originally known as the Womack Brothers, the group's line-up featured Bobby Womack (b. 4 March 1944, Cleveland, Ohio, USA), Friendly Womack Jnr. (b. 1941, Cleveland, Ohio, USA), Harry Womack (b. 1946, Cleveland, Ohio, USA), Curtis Womack (b. 1943, Cleveland, Ohio, USA), Cecil Womack (b. 1941, Cleveland, Ohio, USA). They were also known briefly as the Lovers. Part of a large religious family, their father, Friendly Snr., led his own gospel group, the Voices Of Love. The Womack Brothers also sang spiritual material and were signed to singer Sam Cooke's Sar label following a Cleveland concert. They were later renamed the Valentinos. One of Bobby's songs, 'Couldn't Hear Nobody Pray', was reshaped by Cooke's manager into the secular 'Looking For A Love', a Top 10 R&B single in 1962. Another original, 'Somewhere There's A God', became 'Somewhere There's A Girl', but the Valentinos' next chart entry came in 1964 with the bubbling 'It's All Over Now'. Their own version was overshadowed by that of the Rolling Stone; their fate was impeded further by Cooke's death. The group subsequently recorded for several labels, including Checker, although little was ever released. Disillusioned, the brothers drifted apart and Bobby Womack began his solo career. However, the Valentinos did briefly reunite for two 70s' singles, 'I Can Understand It' and 'Raise Your Hand In Anger'. The family's personal history has been remarkably complex. Cecil married and managed singer Mary Wells, but the couple were later divorced. Mary then married Curtis Womack. Cecil meanwhile married Sam Cooke's daughter, Linda, inaugurating the successful Womack And Womack duo. In 1986 Friendly Jnr and Curtis formed the Brothers Womack with singer Lewis Williams. The remaining brother, Harry, was stabbed to death by his wife. *Double Barrelled Soul* (1968) offers six Valentinos' Sar masters alongside six by the Simms twins. *Bobby Womack And The Valentinos* (1984) divides itself between group recordings and solo material recorded for Checker.
Selected albums: *Double Barrelled Soul* (1968, one side only), *Bobby Womack And The Valentinos* (1984).

Van Der Graaf Generator

This UK band's name was suggested by its first drummer Chris Judge-Smith who, with Nick Peame (keyboards) and singer lyricist Peter Hammill teamed up at Manchester University, England, in 1967. With the enlistment of Keith Ellis (ex-Koobas) on bass, and the substitution of Smith for Guy Evans, and Peame by electronics boffin and ex-church organist Hugh Banton, the band recorded a single, 'People You Were Going To', before breaking up. However, as Hammill was not yet ready to function outside the context of a group, his intended album, *The Aerosol Grey Machine*, evolved into a band effort. By then Hammill had developed a manic, but clear vocal style and a fatalistic line as a wordsmith that demonstrated both his B.Sc. studies and a liking for artists such as Leonard Cohen and David Ackles. This self-expression was framed in 'progressive' fashion replete with much extrapolation, dynamic shifts and tempo refinements.

In 1969 Ellis was replaced by Nic Potter-ex-Misunderstood (like Evans)-and David Jackson (woodwinds), who were added as a second album tiptoed into the UK charts. However, the band remained more popular in Europe. At home, the next offering was promoted via a tour (minus Potter) with Lindisfarne, and a well-received set at 70s Plumpton Blues Festival, in which Hammill was almost upstaged by the inventive Jackson, who was also conspicuous in the epic 'A Plague Of Lighthouse Keepers' on *Pawn Hearts*. With another disbandment imminent by 1971, Hammill inaugurated a solo career which continued over five albums until the group reformed, initially for a French tour in 1975. A more raw sound pervaded their albums, thanks to the recruitment of String-Driven Thing's violinist Graham Smith when Banton and Jackson departed in 1976. With Potter and Evans, the two embarked on a series of instrumental projects (*The Long Hello Volumes 1-4*) while Hammill continued as a soloist when, unable to expand commercially beyond a loyal cult market, they finally broke up after 1978's in-concert double, *Vital*.
Albums: *The Aerosol Grey Machine* (1968), *The Least We Can Do Is Wave To Each Other* (1969), *H to He Who Am The Only One* (1970), *Pawn Hearts* (1971), *Godbluff* (1975), *Still Life* (1976), *World Record* (1976), *The Quiet Zone* (1977), *Vital* (1978) Compilations: *Repeat Performance* (1980), *Time Vaults* (1985, rare recordings).

Van Ronk, Dave

b. 30 June 1936, Brooklyn, New York, USA. Van Ronk learned to play guitar and later played in jazz groups in New York. He also learned to play the banjo. His first love was New Orleans jazz, and his initial involvement with folk music did not come about until 1957, when he worked with Odetta. From this, his interest in blues grew, inspired by Josh White. Van Ronk's reputation for playing blues, together with his distinctive gruff voice, grew until he was signed by Folkways Records in 1959. His first album, however, appeared during the same year on the Lyrichord label. After a couple of releases he moved to Prestige in 1962, and from the mid-60s concentrated more on jazz and jugband music. He formed a band called the Ragtime Jug Stompers, and in 1964 signed to Mercury Records. He continued playing concerts both in the USA and abroad and in 1965 played the Carnegie Hall as part of the New York Folk Festival. Van Ronk worked a lot less during the 70s. However, many of his earlier works were still available well into the 80s. In 1974 Dave took the stage with Bob Dylan and Phil Ochs for *An Evening With Salvador Allende*, for a closing version of Dylan's 'Blowin' In The Wind'. *Dave Van Ronk*, on Fantasy Records, was a re-issue of his first two Prestige albums.

Albums: *Sings Ballads, Blues And Spirituals* (1959), *Fo'csle Songs And Shanties* (1959), *The Unfortunate Rake* (1960), *Inside* (1962), *Dave Van Ronk, Folksinger* (1963), with the Red Onion Jazz Band *In The Tradition* (1963), *The Genius Of Dave Van Ronk* (1964), *Ragtime Jug Stompers* (1964), *Just Dave Van Ronk* (1964), *Gambler's Blues* (1965), *No Dirty Names* (1966), *Dave Van Ronk And The Hudson Dusters* (1967), *Van Ronk* (1969), *Sunday Street* (1976), *Black Mountain Blues* (70s), *Dave Van Ronk Sings Earthy Ballads And Blues* (70s). Compilation: *Hesitation Blues* (1988).

Vanilla Fudge

This US rock group were formed in 1967 and comprised Mark Stein (b. 11 March 1947, New Jersey, USA; organ), Vince Martell (b. 11 November 1945, New York City, New York, USA; guitar), Tim Bogert (b. 27 August 1944, Richfield, New Jersey, USA; bass) and Joey Brennan (drums). All were previously members of the Pigeons, a New York-based group modelled on the (Young) Rascals. Brennan was latterly replaced by Carmine Appice (b. 15 December 1946, New York, USA), and having established a style in which contemporary songs were imaginatively rearranged, the unit was introduced to producer Shadow Morton, who had a reputation for melodramatic pop with the Shangri-Las. Dubbed Vanilla Fudge by their record label, the quartet scored an immediate success with an atmospheric revival of the Supremes' hit, 'You Keep Me Hanging On'. The slowed tempo, studious playing and mock-gospel harmonies set a precedent for the group's debut album which featured similarly operatic versions of the Impressions' 'People Get Ready', Sonny And Cher's 'Bang Bang' and the Beatles' 'Eleanor Rigby' and 'Ticket To Ride'. The audacity of this first selection was impossible to repeat. A flawed concept album, *The Beat Goes On*, proved overambitious, while further selections showed a group unable to create original material of the calibre of the first album. Subsequent records relied on simpler, hard-edged rock. When Vanilla Fudge split in 1970, the bassist and drummer remained together in Cactus before abandoning their creation in favour of Beck, Bogert And Appice. Stein worked with Tommy Bolin and Alice Cooper before forging a new career

composing advertising jingles, while Martell later appeared in the Good Rats, a popular Long Island bar-band. The group briefly reformed in 1983, releasing *Mystery* which failed to make any impact.
Albums: *Vanilla Fudge* (1967), *The Beat Goes On* (1968), *Renaissance* (1968), *Near The Beginning* (1969), *Rock And Roll* (1970), *Mystery* (1984).

Vaughan, Frankie

b. Frank Abelson, 3 February 1928, Liverpool, England. While studying at Leeds College of Art, Vaughan's vocal performance at a college revue earned him a week's trial at the music hall, Kingston Empire. Warmly received, he went on to play the UK variety circuit, developing a stylish act with trademarks which included a top hat and cane, a particularly athletic side kick, and his theme song 'Give Me The Moonlight'. From 'That Old Piano Roll Blues' in 1950 through to the late 60s, with 'There Must Be A Way' in 1967, he was consistently high in the UK charts with songs such as 'Green Door', 'Garden Of Eden', 'Kisses Sweeter Than Wine', 'Kewpie Doll', 'The Heart Of A Man', 'Tower Of Strength' and 'Loop-De-Loop'.
His film debut in 1956 as Elmer in the Arthur Askey comedy *Ramsbottom Rides Again*, was followed by a straight role in *These Dangerous Years*, and a musical frolic with the normally staid Anna Neagle in *The Lady Is A Square*. In 1961, following his role in *Let's Make Love* with Marilyn Monroe and Yves Montand, his disaffection for Hollywood ensured that a US film career was not pursued. At home, however, he had become an extremely well-established performer, headlining at the London Palladium and enjoying lucrative summer season work, appealing consistently to mainly family audiences. In 1985 he was an unexpected choice to replace James Laurenson as the belligerent Broadway producer Julian Marsh in the West End hit musical *42nd Street*. A one-year run in the show ended with ill-health and some acrimony. His career-long efforts for the benefit of young people, mainly through the assignment of record royalties to bodies such as the National Association of Boys' Clubs, was recognized by an OBE in 1965.
Selected albums: *Frankie Vaughan Showcase* (1958), *Frankie Vaughan At The London Palladium* (1959), *Frankie Vaughan Songbook* (1967), *There Must Be A Way* (1967), *Double Exposure* (1971), *Frankie* (1973), *Frankie Vaughan's Sing Song* (1973), *Sincerely Yours, Frankie Vaughan* (1975), *Sings* (1975), *Seasons For Lovers* (1977), *Time After Time* (1986). Compilations: *Spotlight On Frankie Vaughan* (1975), *100 Golden Greats* (1977), *Golden Hour Presents Frankie Vaughan* (1978), *Greatest Hits* (1983), *Love Hits And High Kicks* (1985), *Music Maestro Please* (1986).

Vee, Bobby

b. Robert Thomas Velline, 30 April 1943, Fargo, North Dakota, USA. Vee's first exposure to the rock 'n' roll scene occurred in macabre circumstances when his group, the Shadows, were deputized for Buddy Holly after the singer was killed in an air crash. Soon after, Vee's group were discovered by famed producer Tommy 'Snuff' Garrett and saw their record 'Suzie Baby' released on a major label, Liberty. Vee rapidly became a solo artist in his own right. One of his first recordings was a cover of Adam Faith's 'What Do You Want', which failed to emulate the British artist's UK chart-topping success. Vee was subsequently groomed as a soloist; his college-boy looks and boy-next-door persona combined cleverly with a canon of teenage anthems provided by Brill Building songwriters. After charting with a revival of the Clovers' 1956 hit 'Devil Or Angel', Vee found transatlantic success via the infectious, if lyrically innocuous 'Rubber Ball'. Between 1961 and 1962, he peaked with a series of infectious hits including 'More Than I Can Say', 'How Many Tears', 'Take Good Care Of My Baby' (a US number 1), 'Run To Him', 'Please Don't Ask About Barbara', 'Sharing You' and 'A Forever Kind Of Love'. The imaginatively-titled 'The Night Has A Thousand Eyes' proved his most enduring song. Like many American teen-orientated artists, Vee's appeal waned following the arrival of the Beatles and the beat group explosion.

He did manage a couple of film appearances (*Play It Cool* and *Just For Fun*) before the hit bubble burst. Whilst Beatlemania raged, he reverted to the work of his original inspiration, Buddy Holly. Both *Bobby Vee Meets The Crickets* and *Bobby Vee Meets The Ventures* were promoted by touring. In 1967 Vee returned to the US Top 10 with 'Come Back When You Grow Up'. An attempt to fashion a more serious image prompted Vee to revert to his real name for *Nothing Like A Sunny Day*. The experiment was short-lived, however, and Vee later contented himself with regular appearances at rock 'n' roll revival shows.

Albums: *Bobby Vee Sings Your Favorites* (1960), *Bobby Vee* (1961), *Bobby Vee With Strings And Things* (1961), *Bobby Vee Sings Hits Of The Rockin' '50s* (1961), *Take Good Care Of My Baby* (1961), *Bobby Vee Meets The Crickets* (1962), *A Bobby Vee Recording Session* (1962), *Merry Christmas From Bobby Vee* (1962), *The Night Has A Thousand Eyes* (1963), *Bobby Vee Meets The Ventures* (1963), *I Remember Buddy Holly* (1963), *Bobby Vee Sings The New Sound From England!* (1964), *30 Big Hits From The 60s* (1964), *C'Mon Let's Live A Little* (1966, film soundtrack), *Come Back When You Grow Up* (1967), *Just Today* (1968), *Do What You Gotta Do* (1968), *Gates, Grills And Railings* (1969), *Nothing Like A Sunny Day* (1972). Compilations: *Bobby Vee's Golden Greats* (1962), *Bobby Vee's Golden Greats,* *Volume Two* (1966), *The Bobby Vee Singles Album* (1980).

Velvelettes

Two pairs of sisters, Millie and Cal Gill, and Bertha and Norma Barbee, formed the original Velvelettes' line-up in 1961 at Western Michigan State University. After recording a one-off single, 'There He Goes', for IPG Records in 1963, they were signed to Motown, where they were placed in the hands of fledgling producer Norman Whitfield. This partnership spawned three classic singles, 'Needle In A Haystack', 'He Was Really Sayin' Something' and 'These Things Will Keep Me Lovin' You', which epitomized Motown's approach to the all girl-group sound. A flurry of personnel changes effectively halted the Velvelettes' progress in 1965: Millie Gill and the Barbee sisters left, to be replaced briefly by two future members of Martha And The Vandellas, Sandra Tilley and Betty Kelly, and Annette McMullen. This line-up also dissolved after a few months. In 1970, 'These Things Will Keep Me Loving You' became a belated UK hit, confirming the Velvelettes' cult status among British soul fans. The original line-up re-grouped in 1984 to play revival shows, and re-recorded their hits for Nightmare Records. The original line-up of Carolyn Gill-Street, Bertha Barbee-McNeal, Norma Barbee-Fairhurst and Millie Gill-Arbour recorded a disco version of 'Needle In A Haystack' for Ian Levine's label in 1987 and continue recording to the present time. *One Door Closes* contained half of old hits and half of new material, recorded in an updated Motown style.

Album: *One Door Closes* (1990).

Velvet Opera

This popular UK act, which adeptly mixed soul and psychedelic/progressive styles, evolved from Jaymes Fenda And The Vulcans, one of several groups to secure a recording deal following their appearance in the televised contest, *Ready Steady Win*. Former Vulcan songwriter John Ford (b. 1 July 1948, Fulham, London, England; bass) was subsequently joined by Elmer Gantry (vocals), Colin Forster (guitar) and Richard Hudson (b. Richard William Stafford Hudson, 9 May 1948, London, England; drums) in a group initially dubbed Elmer Gantry's Velvet Opera. Their excellent debut album included the pulsating 'Flames' which, despite regular appearances on BBC Radio 1's *Top Gear*, failed to become a hit. In 1968 Forster was replaced by Paul Brett who then left to join Fire. Gantry also abandoned the group, which then truncated their name to Velvet Opera. Colin Forster rejoined Ford, Hudson and new vocalist John Joyce for *Ride The Hustler's Dream*, but this lacked the purpose of its predecessor save for the excellent 'Anna Dance Square'. The quartet fell apart when Hudson and Ford joined the Strawbs, with whom they remained until 1973. Having written several of the group's most commercial offerings, the duo then left to pursue their own career as Hudson-Ford. By 1974, Gantry was fronting a band which, until checked by litigation, accepted illicit bookings as 'Fleetwood Mac' while the genuine article were off the road. A year later, Gantry emerged once more as singer on Stretch's solitary UK chart entry, 'Why Did You Do It'.

Albums: *Elmer Gantry's Velvet Opera* (1967), *Ride The Hustler's Dream* (1969).

Velvet Underground

The antithesis of late-60s west coast love and peace, New York's Velvet Underground portrayed a darker side of that era's hedonism. Their pulsating drive married intellectual precision and resulted in one of rock's most innovative and lasting catalogues. Lou Reed (b. 2 March 1942, Freeport, Long Island, New York, USA; guitar/vocal) and John Cale (b. 5 December 1940, Crynant, West Glamorgan, Wales; viola/bass/organ) provided a contrast in personality and approach which ensured the group's early notoriety. Reed was a contract songwriter/performer at Pickwick Records, responsible for a series of budget-priced recordings issued under several names, the best-known of which was the Primitives. Cale, a classically-trained child prodigy, had secured a scholarship to study in America, but was drawn into the group's nascent circle when he contributed a viola passage to Reed's anti-dance composition, 'The Ostrich'. A third Primitive, Walter De Maria, was quickly replaced by Sterling Morrison (b. 29 August 1942, East Meadow, Long Island, New York, USA; guitar), who had studied creative writing with Reed at Syracuse University. The reshaped unit was completed by drummer Angus MacLise who suggested they adopt the name 'Velvet Underground', the title of a contemporary pulp paperback. MacLise was also instrumental in securing the group's first gigs at multi-media events and happenings, but left when the Velvets began accepting fees. He was replaced by Maureen 'Mo' Tucker (b. 1945, New Jersey, USA), sister to a friend of Sterling Morrison. The group met pop-art celebrity Andy Warhol in 1965 following an appearance at the Cafe Bizarre. He invited them to join the Exploding Plastic Inevitable, a theatrical mixture of music, films, light-shows and dancing, and also suggested adding actress/singer Nico (Christa Paffgen, b. 16 October 1938, Cologne,Germany) to the Velvet's line-up.

The group recorded their debut album in the spring of 1966 but the completed master was rejected by several major companies, fearful of both its controversial content and lengthy tracks. *The Velvet Underground And Nico* was eventually issued by MGM/Verve the following year. Infamous for Warhol's prominent involvement - he designed the distinctive peel-off banana screenprint featured on its sleeve and is credited as producer - this powerful collection introduced Reed's decidedly urban infatuations, a fascination for street culture and amorality bordering on voyeurism. Reed's talent, however, was greater than mere opportunism. His finely-honed understanding of R&B enhanced a graphic lyricism whereby songs about drugs ('I'm Waiting For The Man'/'Heroin'), sado-masochism ('Venus In Furs') or sublimation ('I'll Be Your Mirror') were not only memorable for their subjects, but also as vibrant pop compositions. Such skills were intensified by Cale's haunting, graphic viola work, Nico's gothic intonation and the group's combined sense of dynamism which blended Tucker's relentless pulse with some of rock's most inspired sonic experimentation. Now rightly regarded as a musical milestone, *The Velvet Underground And Nico* was generally reviled on release. Contemporary radio shunned its stark ugliness and subject matter, while the disparate counter-cultures of Los Angeles and San Francisco abhorred the dank underbelly this uncompromising group posed to challenge their floral dreams.

Nico left for a solo career in 1967 and the remaining quartet then parted from Warhol's patronage. Sessions for a second album, *White Light/White Heat*, exacerbated other internal conflicts and its six compositions were marked by a raging intensity. While the title track and the relentless 'I Heard Her Call My Name' suggested an affinity to 'I'm Waiting For The Man', two extended pieces, 'The Gift' and 'Sister Ray', caught the group at its most radical. The latter performance, a grinding, remorseless, sexual cacophony, was recorded live in the studio at maximum volume, and although Reed later suggested he was trying to approximate the free-jazz of Ornette Coleman, this 17-minute *tour de force* offers some of John Cale's most inspired atonal instrumental work. This pivotal figure was then removed from the group and replaced by an orthodox bassist, former Glass Menagerie member, Doug Yule. A third album, entitled simply *The Velvet Underground*, unveiled a pastoral approach, gentler and more subtle, retaining the chilling, disquieting aura of previous releases. Now firmly within Reed's grasp, the quartet were implicit rather than direct, although moments of their previous fury were apparent on several interludes.

Loaded, an album of considerable commercial promise, emphasized their newfound perspective. Released in 1970, this unfettered collection contained one of Reed's most popular compositions, 'Sweet

Jane', and in celebrating pop's rich heritage, offered an optimism rarely heard in previous work. Paradoxically, by the time *Loaded* was issued, Lou Reed had abandoned the group he had created and Yule, who had encouraged the commercial aspect of the album, now took control, leading several variations on the Velvet Underground name. A poorly-received album, *Squeeze*, confirmed that the definitive unit ended with Reed's departure, so much so that the album is not generally perceived to be part of the Velvet's discography.

Despite the tribulations endured during its brief lifespan, the Velvets have since become one of rock's most influential groups, particularly during the 80s when a new generation of performers, from Joy Division to Jesus And Mary Chain, declared their indebtedness. A series of archive releases, including *1969 - The Velvet Underground Live*, *VU* and *Another View*, add further fuel to the talent and insight which lay within the Velvet Underground and enhance their legendary status.

Albums: *The Velvet Underground and Nico* (1967), *White Light/White Heat* (1967), *The Velvet Underground* (1969), *Loaded* (1970), *Live At Max's Kansas City* (1972), *Squeeze* (1972), *1969 - The Velvet Underground Live* (1974), *VU* (1985), *Another View* (1986). Compilations: *Andy Warhol's Velvet Underground* (1971), *Velvet Underground* (1986- five album box set), *The Best Of The Velvet Underground* (1989).

Further reading: *Up-Tight, The Velvet Underground Story*, Victor Bockris/Gerard Malanga.

Ventures

This pivotal instrumental group was formed in Tacoma, Washington, USA in 1959 when workmates Don Watson (rhythm guitar) and Bob Bogle (lead guitar) discovered a mutual interest in music. They began performing together as the Impacts, using a pick-up rhythm section, before Nokie Edwards (bass) and Skip Moore (drums) completed a line-up redubbed the Ventures. The quartet made its debut with 'Cookies And Coke', released on their own Blue Horizon label, before discovering 'Walk Don't Run' on Chet Atkins' *HiFi In Focus* album. Initially a jazz instrumental, it nonetheless lent itself to a simplified chord structure and by emphasizing its beat, the Ventures constructed a powerful, compulsive sound which not only became their trademark, but was echoed in the concurrent surfing style. The single reached number 2 in the US charts (number 8 UK) with sales in excess of 1 million copies, a distinction matched by its follow-up, 'Perfidia'. At this point Moore had been replaced by Howie Johnson, who in turn retired following a major car accident. Drummer Mel Taylor was then added to the group.

Other notable Ventures' singles included '2000 Pound Bee' (1962), which featured the then-revolutionary fuzz-guitar, 'The Savage' (1963), originally recorded by the Shadows, and 'Diamond Head' (1965), later immortalized by the Beach Boys. The Venture's continued appeal lay in an ability to embrace contemporary fashion, as evinced on *The Ventures (Batman)* (1966), *Super Psychedelics* (1967) or *Underground Fire* (1968), without straying too far from their established format. They also survived several personnel changes; Nokie traded roles with Bogle in 1963 before leaving altogether four years later. He was replaced by session guitarist Jerry McGee, whose numerous credits include Elvis Presley, the Monkees and Kris Kristofferson, and organist Sandy Lee, although the latter was in turn supplanted by Johnny Durrill, formerly of the Five Americans. In 1969 the Ventures scored their last major US hit when 'Hawaii Five-O', the theme tune to a popular detective series, reached number 4. They remained a popular attraction, particularly in Japan, where the group were the subject of almost fanatical reverence. Annual tours throughout the 70s were supplemented by many exclusive recordings, and several tracks were hits twice: once as instrumentals and again with lyrics courtesy of local composers and singers. The group withstood the loss of Taylor, McGee and Durrill; the remaining trio added new drummer Jo Barile, and buoyed by a succession of keyboard players and vocalists, they continued their highly-lucrative career. Musically, the Ventures continued to court contemporary trends, including disco and reggae, while assuming greater artistic control with the founding of their Tridex label. Mel Taylor rejoined Bogle, Wilson and Edwards in 1979 as the unit attempted to rekindle their reputation at home. The Ventures remain one of the world's most respected instrumental units.

Selected Albums: *Walk Don't Run* (1960), *The Ventures* (1961), *Another Smash!!!* (1961), *The Colorful Ventures* (1961), *Twist With The Ventures* aka *The Ventures - Dance* (1962), *The Ventures' Twist Party* aka *Dance With The Ventures* (1962), *Mashed Potatoes And Gravy* aka *The Ventures' Beach Party* (1962), *Going To The Ventures' Dance Party* (1962), *The Ventures Play Telstar, The Lonely Bull* (1963), *The Ventures Surfing* (1963), *Bobby Vee Meets The Ventures* (1963), *The Ventures Play The Country Classics* aka *I Walk The Line* (1963), *Let's Go!* (1963), *The Ventures In Space* (1964), *Walk Don't Run Volume Two* (1964), *The Ventures Knock Me Out* (1965), *Play Guitar With The Ventures* (1965), *The Ventures In Japan* (1965), *The Ventures On Stage* (1965), *The Ventures A-Go-Go* (1965), *The Ventures Christmas Album* (1965), *Where The Action Is* (1966), *All About The Ventures* (1966), *The Ventures (Batman)* (1966), (1966), *Go With The Ventures* (1966), *Wild Things* (1966), *Guitar Freakout* aka

Revolving Sounds (1967), *The Ventures On Stage Encore* (1967), *Pops In Japan* (1967), *Super Psychedelics* aka *Changing Times* (1967), *$1,000,000 Weekend* (1967), *Flights Of Fantasy* (1968), *The Ventures Live Again* (1968), *Pops In Japan* (1968), *The Horse* aka *The Ventures On The Scene* (1968), *The Ventures In Tokyo '68* (1968), *Underground Fire* (1968), *Hawaii Five-O* (1969), *Swamp Rock* (1969), *The Ventures 10th Anniversary Album* (1970), *Live! The Ventures* (1970), *Golden Pops* (1970), *New Testament* (1971), *Theme From Shaft* (1971), *Pops In Japan '71* (1971), *Joy - The Ventures Play The Classics* (1972), *Rock'n'Roll Forever* (1972), *The Ventures On Stage '72* (1972), *The Ventures On Stage '73* (1973), *Pops In Japan '73* (1973), *The Ventures On Stage '74* (1974), *The Jim Croce Songbook* (1974), *The Ventures Play The Carpenters* (1974), *Hollywood Yuya Meets The Ventures* (1976), *The Ventures On Stage '76* (1976), *Rocky Road* (1976), *TV Themes* (1977), *Live In Japan '77* (1977), *The Ventures On Stage '78* (1978), *Latin Album* (1978), *The Ventures Original Four* (1980), *Chameleon* (1980), *Super Live '80* (1980), *The Ventures* (1981), *60's Pops* (1981), *Tokyo Callin' 60s Pops Of Japan* (1981), *Pops In Japan '81* (1981), *St Louis Memory* (1982), *The Ventures Today* (1983). Compilations: *Running Strong* (1966), *The Versatile Ventures* (1966), *Golden Greats By The Ventures* (1967), *Supergroup* (1969), *More Golden Greats* (1970), *A Decade With The Ventures* (1971), *The Ventures* (1971), *Only Hits* (1973), *Legendary Masters* (1974), *15th Anniversary Album: 15 Years Of Japanese Pops* (1975), *The Very Best Of The Ventures* (1975), *Now Playing* (1975), *The Early Sounds Of The Ventures* (1976), *Ventures' Rare Collections For Great Collectors Only* (1980), *Best 10 Volume Two* (1980), *The Ventures Greatest Hits* (1981), *The Last Album On Liberty* (1982), *Twenty Rock 'N' Roll Hits: The Ventures* (1983), *Collection: The Ventures* (1986), *The Best Of The Ventures* (1987), *Walk Don't Run - The Best Of The Ventures* (1990).

Vinton, Bobby

b. Stanley Robert Vinton, 16 April 1935, Canonsburg, Pennsylvania, USA. Born of Polish extraction, Vinton was one of the more enduring boy-next-door pop idols who sprang up in the early 60s. He began as a trumpeter before agreeing to front his high school band as featured vocalist. A tape of one such performance reached Epic Records which signed him in 1960. Composed by Al Byron and Paul Evans, 'Roses Are Red' was Vinton's first national smash but it was overtaken in Britain by Ronnie Carroll's Top 10 cover. Despite a much-publicized arrival in London for his cameo in the teen-exploitation film *Just For Fun*, a second US number 1, 'Blue Velvet', was initially ignored in the UK, though another American smash, a revival of Vaughn Monroe's 'There I've Said It Again', made number

34 in 1963. Vinton continued playing in supper clubs until 1968, when a policy of revamping hits by old rivals put his arrangements of Jimmy Crawford's 'I Love How You Love Me', Bobby Vee's 'Take Good Care Of My Baby and the Teddy Bears' retitled 'To Know Her Is To Love Her' high up the Hot 100. This formula worked again in 1972 with Brian Hyland's 'Sealed With A Kiss' but it was 1974's 'My Melody Of Love', a new song co-written by Vinton himself, that gave him one more US chart-topper. His version of 'Blue Moon' was heard on the soundtrack of *An American Werewolf In London* in 1981 but it was the use of 'Blue Velvet' in both the 1989 film of the same name and a television commercial that brought about a huge 1991 windfall in Britain, where the pragmatic Vinton became omnipresent until its fall from the chart and the failure of 'Roses Are Red', which was reissued as the follow-up.

Albums: *Roses Are Red* (1962), *Bobby Vinton Sings The Big Ones* (1962), *Blue Velvet* (1963), *There! I've Said It Again* (1964), *My Heart Belongs To Only You* (1964), *Tell Me Why* (1964), *Mr. Lonely* (1964), *Bobby Vinton Sings For Lonely Nights* (1965), *Laughing On The Outside (Crying On The Inside)* (1965), *Great Motion Picture Themes* (1966), *Satin Pillows And Careless* (1966), *Please Love Me Forever* (1967), *Take Good Care Of My Baby* (1968), *I Love How You Love Me* (1968), *Vinton* (1969), *My Elusive Dreams* (1970), *Ev'ry Day Of My Life* (1972), *Sealed With A Kiss* (1972), *Melodies Of Love* (1974), *With Love* (1974), *Heart Of Hearts* (1975), *The Bobby Vinton Show* (1975), *The Name Is Love* (1977). Compilations: *Bobby Vinton's Greatest Hits* (1964), *Bobby Vinton's Greatest Hits Of Love* (1969), *Bobby Vinton's All-Time Greatest Hits* (1972), *With Love* (1974), *Bobby Vinton Sings The Golden Decade Of Love - Songs Of The 50s* (1975).

Vogues

This US vocal group were formed in Turtle Creek, near Pittsburgh, Pennsylvania by school friends Bill Burkette (lead baritone), Don Miller (baritone), Hugh Geyer (first tenor) and Chuck Blasko (second tenor). They began singing, as the Val-Aires, in 1960, but took the above name prior to signing with the tiny Co & Ce label. In 1965 the Vogues scored two US Top 5 singles with 'You're The One' and 'Five O'Clock World', the latter of which was a majestic slice of east coast harmony pop, reminiscent of Jay And The Americans or the Four Seasons at their best. The quartet continued to enjoy minor success, but it was not until they joined Reprise Records that the group enjoyed another significant hit. 'Turn Around, Look At Me' was the Vogues only million-selling release and the prelude to a decidedly MOR direction when they took the 1957 Bobby Helms hit, 'My Special Angel' to the Top 10. Their later work lacked the earthy enthusiasm of those early offerings, although its professionalism secured a place with adult audiences.

Albums: *Meet The Vogues* (1965), *You're The One* (1966), *Five O'Clock World* (1966), *Turn Around, Look At Me* (1968), *Till* (1969), *Memories* (1969). Compilation: *The Vogues' Greatest Hits* (1969).

W

Walker, Junior, And The All Stars

b. Autry DeWalt II, 1942, Blythesville, Arkansas, USA. Walker was inspired to take up the saxophone by the jump blues and R&B bands he heard in the early 50s. In his mid-teens, he formed his first instrumental combo, the Jumping Jacks, adopting the stage name Junior Walker after a childhood nickname. By 1961 he had achieved a prominent local reputation, which reached the ear of label owner and former Moonglow, Harvey Fuqua. He signed Walker to his Harvey label, allowing him free rein to record a series of raw saxophone-led instrumentals. In 1964 Walker followed Fuqua to Motown, where he perfected a blend of raunchy R&B and Detroit soul typified by his 1965 hit, 'Shotgun'. With its repeated saxophone riffs and call-and-response vocals, it established Walker as the label's prime exponent of traditional R&B, a reputation that was confirmed by later hits like 'Shake And Fingerpop' and 'Road Runner'. The latter was produced by Holland/Dozier/Holland, who also encouraged Walker to record instrumental versions of hits they had written for other Motown artists. Walker's style became progressively more lyrical in the late 60s, a development that reached its peak on the 1969 US Top 5 hit, 'What Does It Take (To Win Your Love)?'. This also marked the pinnacle of his commercial success, as subsequent attempts to repeat the winning formula were met with growing public indifference, and from 1972 onwards the All Stars recorded only sporadically. *Hot Shot* in 1976, produced by Brian Holland, marked a move towards the burgeoning disco market, which was confirmed on two further albums that year, Walker's first as a solo artist. In 1979, he was one of several Motown artists to move to Whitfield Records. Finding his career deadlocked, Walker returned to Motown in 1983, issuing *Blow The House Down*, an exercise in reclaiming lost ground. The novelty single 'Sex Pot' rekindled memories of his classic hits, though

Walker's greatest commercial success in the 80s came when he guested with Foreigner on their hit single 'Urgent'.

Albums: *Shotgun* (1965), *Soul Session* (1966), *Road Runner* (1966), *Live!* (1967), *Home Cookin'* (1969), *What Does It Take To Win Your Love?* (1969), *Live* (1970), *A Gasssss* (1970), *Rainbow Funk* (1971), *Moody Jr.* (1971), *Peace And Understanding Is Hard To Find* (1973), *Hot Shot* (1976), *Sax Appeal* (1976), *Whopper Bopper Show Stopper* (1976), *...Smooth* (1978), *Back Street Boogie* (1979), *Blow The House Down* (1983). Compilations: *Greatest Hits* (1969), *Anthology* (1981), *Junior Walker's Greatest Hits* (1982), *19 Greatest Hits* (1987, CD only).

Walker Brothers

Walker Brothers

Hailing from America but transposed to England in the mid-60s, this hit trio comprised Scott Walker (b. Noel Scott Engel, 9 January 1944, Hamilton, Ohio; USA), John Walker (b. John Maus, 12 November 1943, New York; USA) and Gary Walker (b. Gary Leeds, 3 September 1944, Glendale, California; USA). Leeds, an ex-member of the Standells, had discovered former Routers' bassist Engel appearing with Maus in an ensemble called the Dalton Brothers. In 1964, the trio changed their name to the Walker Brothers and following a false start at home decided to relocate to the UK. After arriving in February 1965, they fell into the hands of manager Maurice King and were soon signed to Philips Records. Their debut 'Pretty Girls Everywhere', featured Maus as lead vocalist, but it was the Engel-voiced follow-up 'Love Her' which cracked the UK Top 20 in May 1965. By this time, Scott was the chosen 'a-side' main vocalist, with Maus providing the strong high harmony. The group neatly slotted into the gap left by Phil Spector's proteges the Righteous Brothers, who had topped the charts earlier in the year but failed to sustain their impact in the UK. As well as emulating their rivals' vocal power, the Walkers boasted film star looks and swiftly emerged as pin-up idols with a huge teenage following. On album, the trio played a contrasting selection of ballads, soul standards and occasional upbeat pop, but for the singles they specialized in high melodrama, brilliantly augmented by the string arrangements of Johnny Franz, with accompaniment directed by either Ivor Raymonde or Reg Guest.

The lachrymose Burt Bacharach/Hal David ballad 'Make It Easy On Yourself' (originally a US hit for Jerry Butler) gave them a UK chart number 1, while the similarly-paced 'My Ship Is Coming In' reached the Top 3. Their neurotic romanticism reached its apogee on the Bob Crewe/Bob Gaudio composition, 'The Sun Ain't Gonna Shine Anymore', in which Scott's deep baritone was wonderfully balanced by John's Four Seasons-styled soaring harmony. The song topped the UK listings for a month and gave them their second and last US Top 20 hit. Thereafter, there was immense friction in the Walkers' camp and their second EP *Solo Scott, Solo John* (1967) neatly summarized their future intentions.

Although they continued to chart in the UK between 1965-67, the quality of their material was generally less impressive. Pete Autell's '(Baby) You Don't Have To Tell Me' seemed a weak follow-up to their grandiose number 1 and commenced their gradual commercial decline. Another Bacharach/David composition 'Another Tear Falls' fared little better at number 12, while the film theme, 'Deadlier Than The Male' could only scrape the Top 30. The much-covered Bert Berns' composition 'Stay With Me Baby' retained the melodrama, but there was no emphatic comeback and in early 1967 the group elected to split-up. The emotional impact of the break-up on their loyal fan base should have pushed their farewell single, 'Walking In The Rain', to the upper echelons of the chart but as the **New Musical Express'** reviewer Derek Johnson sadly noted: 'Walkers Last Not So Great'.

As soloists, the Walkers suffered mixed fortunes, but it was still a surprise when the trio reunited in 1975. Their comeback album, *No Regrets*, consisted largely of extraneous material, but the classy Tom Rush title track returned the group to the Top 10 for the first time since 'The Sun Ain't Gonna Shine Anymore', released nearly a decade before. A follow-up album, *Lines*, was similar in style to its predecessor, but for their swansong, the self-penned *Nite Flights*, the trio produced a brave, experimental work, with oblique, foreboding lyrics and unusual arrangements. The album was a commercial failure, but by the time the initial sales figures had been computated, Scott, John and Gary had returned to their individual ventures and concomitant obscurity.

Albums: *Take It Easy With The Walker Brothers* (1965), *Portrait* (1966), *Images* (1967), *No Regrets* (1975), *Lines* (1977), *Nite Flights* (1978), *The Walker Brothers In Japan* (1987, rec. 1968). Compilations: *After The Lights Go Out - The Best Of 1965-1967* (1990), *No Regrets - The Best Of The Walker Brothers* (1991).

Warm Sounds

Warm Sounds

In 1965, Denver Gerrard (b. 1945, Johannesburg, South Africa) and Barry (Young) Husband (formerly of Tuesday's Children) were two young UK-based songwriters in search of a hit. After traipsing around London's Tin Pan Alley they decided to pool their resources and briefly switch to recording their own work. Producer Mike Hurst recognized their potential and in 1967 they signed to the highly fashionable Deram Records label under the name Warm Sounds. They enjoyed a small hit that year with the harmonious 'Birds And Bees', but subsequent releases such as 'Nite Is A-Comin'' and 'Sticks And Stones' (the latter on Andrew Loog Oldham's label, Immediate) sold poorly. The team soon split and Gerrard went on to record a commercially unsucessful album, *Sinister Morning*.

Warwick, Dionne

b. Marie Dionne Warrick, 12 December 1940, East Orange, New Jersey, USA. One of soul music's truly sophisticated voices, Dionne first sang in Newark's New Hope Baptist Church choir. She played piano with the Drinkard Singers, a gospel group her mother managed, and studied at Connecticut's Hart School of Music. During the same period, Warwick also formed the Gospelaires with her sister, Dee Dee and aunt Cissy Houston. Increasingly employed as backing singers, the trio's voices appeared on records by the Drifters and Garnet Mimms. Through such work Dionne came into contact with songwriters Burt Bacharach and Hal David. Her first solo single, on the Scepter label, 'Don't Make Me Over' (1963), was a fragile slice of 'uptown R&B' and set the tone for such classic collaborations as 'Anyone Who Had A Heart' and 'Walk On By'. Bacharach's sculpted, almost grandiose compositions were the perfect setting for Warwick's light yet perfect phrasing, delicate almost to the point of vulnerability. 'You'll Never Get To Heaven (If You Break My Heart)', 'Reach Out For Me' (both 1964) and 'Are You There (With Another Girl)' (1966) epitomized the style. Although many of her singles charted, few were Top 10 hits, and the soulful edge, prevalent for the first two years, was gradually worn away. As her songwriters moved ever closer to the mainstream, so Dionne too embraced a safer, albeit classier, approach with such successes as the uplifting 'I Say A Little Prayer' (1967) and 'Do You Know The Way To San Jose?' (1968).

In 1971 Warwick abandoned both her label and mentors for Warners Brothers, but despite several promising releases, the relationship floundered. Around this time she also temporally added an extra 'e' to the end of her name, on the advice given to her by an astrologer. Her biggest hit came with the (Detroit) Spinners on the Thom Bell-produced 'Then Came You' (1974). Warwick moved to Arista Records in 1979 where work with Barry Manilow rekindled her commercial standing. *Heartbreaker*, her collaboration with the Bee Gees, resulted in several hit singles while a pairing with Luther Vandross on 'How Many Times Can We Say Goodbye?' was also a success. 'That's What Friends Are For' pitted Dionne with Elton John, Gladys Knight and Stevie Wonder, and became a number 1 in both the US R&B and pop charts. Duets with Jeffrey Osborne, Kashif and Howard Hewitt, of Shalamar, maintained this newly-rediscovered profile in the 80s.

Albums: *Presenting Dionne Warwick* (1963), *Anyone Who Had A Heart* (1964), *Make Way For Dionne Warwick* (1964), *The Sensitive Sound Of Dionne Warwick* (1965), *Here I Am* (1966), *Dionne Warwick In Paris* (1966), *Here Where There Is Love* (1967), *Dionne Warwick Onstage And In The Movies* (1967), *The Windows Of The World* (1968), *Dionne In The Valley Of The Dolls* (1968), *Magic Of Believing* (1968), *Promises Promises* (1968), *Soulful* (1969), *Dionne Warwick's Greatest Motion Picture Hits* (1969), *I'll Never Fall In Love Again* (1970), *Very Dionne* (1970), *The Love Machine* (1971), *The Dionne Warwick Story - Live* (1971), *From Within* (1972), *Dionne* (1972), *Just Being Myself* (1973), *Then Came You* (1975), *Track Of The Cat* (1975), with Isaac Hayes *A Man And A Woman* (1977), *Only Love Can Break A Heart* (1977), *Love At First Sight* (1979), *Dionne* (1979), *No Night So Long* (1980), *Hot! Live And Otherwise* (1981), *Friends In Love* (1982), *Heartbreaker* (1982), *How Many Times Can We Say Goodbye* (1983), *So Amazing* (1983), *Friends* (1985), *Finder Of Lost Loves* (1985), *Without Your Love* (1985), *Rendezvous For Two* (1988), *Dionne Warwick Sings Cole Porter* (1989). Compilations: *Dionne Warwick's Golden Hits, Part 1* (1967), *Dionne Warwick's Golden Hits, Part 2* (1969), *From Within* (1972), *The Best Of Dionne Warwick* (1983), *The Original Soul Of Dionne Warwick* (1987), *The Love Songs* (1989).

Webb, Jim

b. 15 August 1946, Elk City, Oklahoma, USA. A music major at California's San Bernadino Valley College, Webb abandoned his studies in 1966 for a career in songwriting. His work impressed singer Johnny Rivers, who paired the composer with proteges Fifth Dimenson. Their partnership flourished with 'Up, Up And Away', a breezy recording indebted to west coast harmony groups and uptown soul, which sold over one million copies and was later adopted by the TWA corporation for a series of commercials. Links with the group were maintained on an attendant album, *Magic Garden*, while another Webb original, the reflective 'By The Time I Get To Phoenix', provided Glen Campbell with a Grammy as the Best Vocal Performance of 1967. The following year Richard Harris scored a major international smash with 'MacArthur Park', a melodramatic epic marked by lyrical extravagance and a sumptuous melody. Webb also composed material for Harris's albums *A Tramp Shining* and *The Yard Went On Forever*, but was reportedly dismayed when his own solo debut, *Jimmy Webb Sings Jimmy Webb* was issued, as it featured unfinished recordings. Further success for Campbell with 'Wichita Lineman' (1968) and 'Galveston' (1969) demonstrated Webb's songwriting ability at its zenith. These moving stories in song expressed Webb's immense feeling for a traditional, rural America and are rightly regarded as standards. Webb also composed the film scores for *Tell Them Willie Boy Is Here* (1969), but grew impatient with a public perception of him as merely a songwriter.

A 1970 tour revealed his inexperience as a performer, although *Words And Music* showed the episode had engendered a tighter, rock-based style. Webb continued to write and produce for other acts, notably Cher and the Supremes, but was curiously unable to attain the same success with his own

recordings. *Land's End*, *El Mirage* and *Angel Heart* were all released to critical acclaim, but when sales again proved negligible, their creator sought solace in other musical avenues. The relative failure of *El Mirage* was particularly disappointing as it featured some of Webb's best work, including 'The Highwayman' and was produced, conducted and arranged by George Martin. Webb continued to score film soundtracks for *Voices* and *Hanoi Hilton* and by the end of the 80s was completing work on two musicals, *The Children's Crusade* and *Dandelion Wine*. His main supporter and arguably his best interpreter during the 80s was Art Garfunkel. Webb contributed heavily to Garfunkel's albums, but although of excellent quality, they were largely ignored. He undertook several live shows in 1988 - the first in over a decade - but it is as a gifted composer, rather than performer, that Webb is better known.
Albums: *Jimmy Webb Sings Jimmy Webb* (1968), *Words And Music* (1970), *And So On* (1971), *Letters* (1972), *Land's End* (1974), *El Mirage* (1977), *Voices* (1979, film soundtrack), *Angel Heart* (1982), *Hanoi Hilton* (1987, film soundtrack).

Wells, Mary

b. 13 May 1943, Detroit, Michigan, USA. At the age of 17, Mary Wells composed 'Bye Bye Baby', a song which she offered to R&B star Jackie Wilson. His producer, Berry Gordy, was sufficiently impressed to offer her a contract with the newly-formed Motown label, and Wells's rendition of her song became one of the company's first Top 50 hits in 1960. Gordy entrusted her career to Smokey Robinson, who masterminded all her subsequent Motown releases. Smokey composed a remarkable series of clever, witty soul songs, full of puns and unexpected twists, and set to irresistible melody lines. Wells responded with the fluency of the natural vocalist and the results were Motown's most mature and adventurous records of the early 60s. 'The One Who Really Loves You' set the pattern as a Top 10 hit in 1962, while 'You Beat Me To The Punch' and 'Two Lovers' matched that success and offered two of Robinson's more subtle lyrics. 'What's Easy For Two Is So Hard For One' was Wells' answer to the predominant New York girl-group sound, and another Top 30 hit in 1963. The pinnacle of the Robinson/Wells partnership, though, was 'My Guy', a US number 1 and UK Top 5 contender in 1964. Sophisticated and assured, it introduced the Motown sound to a worldwide audience, and marked Wells out as America's most promising soul vocalist. At the same time, Berry Gordy encouraged her to record an album of duets with Motown's top male star, Marvin Gaye, from which 'Once Upon A Time' was pulled as another major hit single. Just as Mary's career reached its peak, she chose to leave Motown, tempted by an offer from 20th Century Fox which included the promise of film work. Without the guidance of Smokey Robinson, she was unable to capture her hit form, and she left the label the following year. In 1966, she married Cecil Womack of the Valentinos, and moved to Atco Records, where she scored a minor hit with 'Dear Lover'. That marked the end of her chart career: subsequent sessions for a variety of US labels proved less than successful, and after a long period without a contract she was reduced to re-recording her Motown hits for Allegiance in the early 80s. Despite being diagnosed as having throat cancer she continued touring during the late 80s. Wells signed to Ian Levine's Motor City label in 1987 and released *Keeping My Mind On Love* in 1990.
Albums: *Bye Bye Baby, I Don't Want To Take A Chance* (1961), *The One Who Really Loves You* (1962), *Two Lovers And Other Great Hits* (1963), *Recorded Live On Stage* (1963), with Marvin Gaye *Together* (1964), *Mary Wells Sings My Guy* (1964), *Mary Wells* (1965), *Mary Wells Sings Love Songs To The Beatles* (1965), *The Two Sides Of Mary Wells* (1966), *Ooh!* (1966), *Servin' Up Some Soul* (1968), *In And Out Of Love* (1981), *Keeping My Mind On Love* (1990). Compilations: *Greatest Hits* (1964), *The Old, New And Best Of Mary Wells* (1984).

West, Dodie

Her investors visualized this singer as the UK's own Mary Wells. Many who saw her on the supporting programme on round-Britain package tours in the mid-60s agreed - but not sufficiently to guarantee her lasting success. Her lone hit occurred in January 1966 after Decca Records hedged its bets by issuing the Zombies and West's simultaneous covers of Little Anthony And The Imperials' 'Goin' Out Of My Head'. Peaking at number 39, Dodie's eclipsed both the original version (at least, in the UK) and the Zombies' cover. Her only other flash of glory was in July 1967 when she was selected by NEMS Enterprises to represent England in the Eurovision Song Contest held in Knokke-le-Zoute, Belgium.
Album: *Walk Through This World* (1976).

West, Keith

b. Keith Hopkins, 6 December 1943, Dagenham, Essex, England. Lead vocalist with the In Crowd and Tomorrow, West embarked on a concurrent solo career while still a member of the latter group. His debut single, 'Excerpt From A Teenage Opera (Grocer Jack)', was a UK Top 10 hit in 1967, but when 'Sam', another song from the same project, failed to emulate its predecessor, West withdrew from further involvement. Tomorrow broke up in 1968 and West temporarily abandoned performing when his third release, 'On A Saturday', failed to chart. He resumed recording in 1973 with two low-key singles, before founding Moonrider with ex-Animals' guitarist John Weider.

Weston, Kim

b. Agatha Natalie Weston, 20 December 1939, Detroit, Michigan, USA. Kim Weston received her musical education with the Wright Specials gospel group, an influence that survived throughout her subsequent career. Torn between pursuing music or acting, she was persuaded to join the Motown label in the early 60s by Johnny Thornton, the cousin of two of the label's top producers, Eddie and Brian Holland. After a minor hit with 'Love Me All The Way' in 1963, Weston joined Marvin Gaye's soul revue, forming a partnership that was captured on record in 1964 and again in 1967. In between, Weston was produced by Holland/Dozier/Holland on a series of classic dance records which highlighted her versatile, gospel-tinged vocals. 'Take Me In Your Arms' was a substantial soul hit in 1965, followed the next year by the equally fluent 'Helpless'. In 1967, she and Gaye recorded 'It Takes Two', one of the finest of Motown's love duets. That same year, Weston married Motown producer Mickey Stevenson, who encouraged her to join him in a new venture at MGM Records. The move proved a commercial disappointment, and later releases on People and Pride failed to restore Weston to the charts. In the 70s, she devoted much time to community projects and art groups, besides finding time to record an album of jazz standards with the Hastings Street Jazz Experience. More recently, she was one of several Motown artists to re-record her hits on Ian Levine's Nightmare label. In 1987 she became the first ex-Motown artist to work with producer Ian Levine, who proceeded to sign virtually every Motown act during the next three years. Weston teamed up with Marvin Gaye's brother Frankie for a remake of 'It Takes Two' in 1989. She has so far released two new albums which mix new material with fresh versions of 60s Motown hits.
Albums: with Marvin Gaye *Take Two* (1966), *For The First Time* (1967), *This Is America* (1968), *Kim Kim Kim* (1970), *Investigate* (1990), *Talking Loud* (1992).

Whitcomb, Ian

b. 1941, Surrey, England. This former Dorset public schoolboy enjoyed fleeting success in North America when the continent's fascination with UK pop peaked in 1964. While a student, at Dublin's Trinity College in Eire, he fronted Bluesville who recorded 'Soho', a harmonica-led instrumental. During a summer holiday in the states, he secured the US release of 'Soho' through Zoom, a Capitol Records subsidiary. To the rest of Bluesville's consternation, only Whitcomb's name was printed on the record label. His follow-up - an arrangement of the skiffle standard, 'This Sporting Life' - slipped briefly into the Hot 100. During a session for the next a-side, the intended 'No Tears For Johnny', a Hal Shaper protest song, was rejected in favour of an off-the-cuff blues shuffle topped by Whitcomb's stammering falsetto. Titled 'You Turn Me On', it missed at home but, thanks to saturation publicity, reached the US Top 10. As the failure of a fourth single, 'N-N-Nervous', indicated, he went off the boil abruptly despite an intense coast-to-coast touring schedule supporting Jan And Dean, Sam The Sham and the Righteous Brothers. A 1966 fad for olde-tyme whimsy prompted a camp revival of the ragtime novelty, 'Where Did Robinson Crusoe Go With Friday On Saturday Night?'. By the early 70s, he was a radio presenter in Los Angeles, California, USA but he became better known for his witty chronicling of pop history - which included hefty segments of his own saga.
Albums: *You Turn Me On* (1965), *Under The Ragtime Moon* (1972), *You Turn Me On* (1973), *Hip Hooray For Neville Chamberlain* (1974), *Red Hot Blue Heaven* (1977), *Boogie Woogie Jungle Snake* (1983), *Rag Odyssey* (1984), *Oceans Of Love* (1987), *Steppin' Out* (1987), *Pianomelt* (1987), *On The Streets Of Dreams* (1987), *Don't Say Goodbye* (1988), *At The Ragtime Ball* (1988), *Treasures Of Tin Pan Alley* (1988), *Happy Days Are Here Again* (1989).
Further reading: *After The Ball*, Ian Whitcomb, London, 1972. *Whole Lotta Shakin'*, Ian Whitcomb, London, 1982.

Who

Who

Formed in Shepherd's Bush London in 1964, the Who evolved out of local youth club band the Detours. Pete Townshend (b. 19 May 1945, Chiswick, London, England; guitar/vocals), Roger Daltrey (b. 1 March 1944, Hammersmith, London, England; vocals) and John Entwistle (b. 9 October 1946, Chiswick, London, England; bass) founded this attraction, and having jettisoned Colin Dawson (vocals) and Doug Sanden (drums), recruited Keith

Moon (b. 23 August 1947, Wembley, London, England, d. 23 August 1978) as a replacement for the latter in a unit now bearing their more dynamic appellation. The restructured quartet was adopted by manager/publicist Peter Meadon, who changed the group's name to the High Numbers, dressed them in stylish clothes and determinedly courted a mod audience. Their sole single, 'I'm The Face', proclaimed this allegiance although Meadon shamelessly purloined its melody from Slim Harpo's 'Got Love If You Want It'. Two budding film directors, Kit Lambert and Chris Stamp, then assumed management responsibilities and having reverted to their Who sobriquet, the group assiduously began courting controversial publicity.

Townshend's guitar pyrotechnics were especially noteworthy; the instrument was used as an object of rage as he smashed it against floors and amplifiers in simulation of painter Gustav Metzke's auto-destructive art, although the origins of the act derived from when Townshend accidentally broke the neck of his guitar in a low-ceilinged club to the perverse delight of the crowd. Their in-person violence matched an anti-social attitude and despite a highly successful residency at the famed Marquee club, the Who were shunned by major labels. They eventually secured a deal through Shel Talmy, an independent producer who placed the group with American Decca. Their recordings were then sub-contracted through UK subsidiary, Brunswick, a perilous arrangement bearing later repercussions. 'I Can't Explain', released in January 1965, rose to the UK Top 10 on the strength of appearances on television's *Ready Steady Go* and *Top Of The Pops*, the latter transpiring when another act dropped out. Written by Townshend - already the group's established composer - but modelled on the Kinks, the song's formal nature surprised those expecting a more explosive performance. Such hopes were answered by the innovative 'Anyway, Anyhow, Anywhere' and 'My Generation', the latter of which encapsulated the frustrations of an amphetamine-charged adolescent, both in its stuttered intonation and smash-and-grab instrumental section. This pivotal release - one of the benchmarks of British 60s pop - served as the title track to the Who's debut album, the release of which was delayed to accommodate new Townshend originals at the expense of now *passé* cover versions. 'The Kids Are Alright' and 'Out In The Street' articulated a sense of cultural affinity and if the songwriter's attachment to the mod phenomenon was undoubtedly expedient, the cult held a lasting fascination for him.

However, despite artistic and commercial success, the Who wished to sever their punitive contract with Talmy. When he refused to renegotiate their terms of contract, the group simply refused to honour it,

completing a fourth single, 'Substitute', for a new label and production company. The ensuing wrangle was settled out of court, but although the unit achieved their freedom, Talmy retained royalty rights on all recordings made until the end of the decade. The Who continued to enjoy chart success, adeptly switching subject matter from a parochial clique to eccentric characterizations involving transvestism ('I'm A Boy') and masturbation ('Pictures Of Lily'). Townshend's decidedly English perceptions initially precluded a sustained international success. *A Quick One* and *The Who Sell Out*, the latter of which was, in part, programmed as a homage to pirate radio, thus proved more acceptable to the UK audience. The Who's popularity in the USA flourished only in the wake of their appearance at the 1967 Monterey Pop Festival.

They returned to the UK Top 10 in the winter of 1967 with the powerful 'I Can See For Miles'. Despite their strength as singles artists, however, the group failed to achieve a number 1 hit on either side of the Atlantic. The group embraced the album market fully with *Tommy*, an extravagant rock opera which became a staple part of their increasingly in-demand live appearances. The set spawned a major hit in 'Pinball Wizard' but, more crucially, established the group as a serious act courting critical respectability. *Tommy* was later the subject of a film, directed by the suitably eccentric Ken Russell, as well as an orchestrated interpretation, recorded under the aegis of impresario Lou Reizner. This over-exposure undermined the power of the original, and fixed a musical albatross around its creator's neck. The propulsive *Live At Leeds* was a sturdy concert souvenir (regarded by many as one the best live albums ever recorded), while Townshend created his next project, *Lighthouse*, but this ambitious work was later aborted, with several of its songs incorporated into *Who's Next*. Here the Who asserted a position as one of rock's leading attractions and the set which, in 'Baba O'Reilly' and 'Won't Get Fooled Again', contained two songs destined to form an integral part of the group's 70s' lexicon. The latter reached the UK Top 10 and was the prelude to a series of specifically created singles - 'Let's See Action' (1971), 'Join Together' (1972), 'Relay' (1973) - which marked time as Townshend completed work on *Quadrophenia*. This complex concept album was a homage to the mod sub-culture which provided the artist with his first inspiration. Although compared unfavourably with *Tommy*, the set's plot and musical content - while stylistically the antithesis of the group's early outburst - has shown a greater longevity and was the subject of a commercially successful film, featuring future stars Toyah and Sting. Commitments to solo careers undermined the parent unit's progress and *The Who By Numbers*, although a relevant study of the ageing rock star, was deemed low-key in comparison with earlier efforts. Another hiatus ensued, during which the ever self-critical Townshend reassessed his progress in the light of punk.

The quartet re-emerged with the confident *Who Are You*, but its release was sadly overshadowed when, on 23 August 1978, Keith Moon died following an overdose of medication taken to alleviate alcohol addiction. His madcap behaviour and idiosyncratic, exciting drumming had been an integral part of the Who fabric and rumours of a permanent split abounded. A retrospective film, *The Kids Are Alright*, enhanced a sense of finality, but the group resumed recording in 1979 having added former Small Faces/Faces drummer Kenney Jones to the line-up. However, any newfound optimism was undermined that year when 11 fans were killed prior to a concert in Cleveland, Ohio during a rush to secure prime vantage points, and neither *Face Dances*, nor *It's Hard*, recaptured previous artistic heights although the former contained the fiery 'You Better You Bet', which restored them to the UK Top 10. A farewell tour was undertaken in 1982-83 and although the group did reunite for an appearance at Live Aid, they remained estranged until the end of the decade. Townshend's reticence to tour - he now suffered from tinnitus - and his much-publicized period of heroin addiction, were major stumbling blocks, but in 1989 he agreed to undertake a series of US dates to celebrate the group's 25th anniversary (with Simon Phillips; drums). Townshend, Daltrey and Entwistle were augmented by a large ensemble of supporting musicians for a set indebted to nostalgia, which culminated in Hollywood with an all-star gala rendition of *Tommy*. As such, the tour confirmed the guitarist's fears - a request to include material from his concurrent solo album *The Iron Man* was vetoed. His desire to progress and challenge preconceptions has marked the very best of the Who's extensive and timeless catalogue.

Albums: *My Generation* (1965), *A Quick One* (1966), *The Who Sell Out* (1967), *Happy Jack* (USA 1967), *Magic Bus-The Who On Tour* (USA 1968), *Tommy* (1969), *Live At Leeds* (1970), *Who's Next* (1971), *Quadrophenia* (1973), *The Who By Numbers* (1975), *Who Are You* (1978), *The Kids Are Alright* (1979, film soundtrack), *Face Dances* (1981), *It's Hard* (1982), *Joined Together* (1990). Compilations: *Magic Bus* (1967), *Direct Hits* (1968), *Meaty Beefy Big And Bouncy* (1971), *Odds And Sods* (1974), *The Story Of The Who* (1976), *Hooligans* (1982), *Rarities Volume 1 (1966-1968)* (1983), *Rarities Volume 2 (1970-1973)* (1983), *Once Upon A Time* (1983), *The Singles* (1984), *Who's Last* (1984), *Who's Missing* (1985), *Two's Missing* (1987), *Who's Better Who's Best* (1988).
Further reading: *The Who*, Gary Herman. *Maximum*

R&B, Richard Barnes. *Before I Get Old*, Dave Marsh.

Williams, Danny

b. 7 January 1942, Port Elizabeth, South Africa. Williams started singing professionally at the age of 13 and was spotted by producer Norman Newell when touring England in *The Golden City Dixies* show in 1959. The ultra-smooth ballad singer, often called 'Britain's Johnny Mathis', joined HMV Records and released his first single 'Tall A Tree' in 1959. A regular on television pop show *Drumbeat*, he had a couple of small hits before his version of the much-recorded 'Moon River' shot to number 1 in 1961. Follow-ups 'Jeannie' (co-written by Russ Conway) and a cover of Andy Williams' 'Wonderful World Of The Young' also made the UK Top 10 in 1962. In 1964 'White On White', a UK flop, gave him a US Top 10 hit. For the next decade he worked the clubs, and recordings on Deram and Philips meant little. In 1977 he briefly returned to the Top 40 on Ensign with 'Dancing Easy', a re-work of a Martini television commercial. He later recorded without success on Piccadilly and EMI/Columbia and in 1991 joined Prestige Records.
Selected albums: *White On White* (1964), *I'm A Song - Sing Me* (1973), *Any Time, Any Place, Anywhere* (1977). Compilation: *Moon River And Other Great Songs* (1977).

Williams, Mason

b. 24 July 1936, Abilene, Texas, USA. This Oklahoma City University mathematics student was a self-taught guitarist who, after moonlighting in local venues, toured North America with the Wayfarers Trio before enlistment in the US Navy. On demobilization, he peddled topical tunes on the Los Angeles folk club circuit where he met the Limeliters' Glenn Yarbrough who introduced him to the Smothers Brothers. When this comedy duo began performing his compositions on their nationally-broadcast television series, other acts - among them the Kingston Trio and Petula Clark - began recording his material. His most lucrative song was the 1968 novelty UK number 1 'Cinderella Rockefella', (with Nancy Ames) for Esther And Abi Ofarim. That year, he scored a million-seller in his own right with the Grammy-winning 'Classical Gas', an orchestrated instrumental (from The Mason Williams Phonograph Record song cycle). A one-hit-wonder, he, nevertheless, protracted a prolific recording career into the 70s with accompaniment by such LA session colleagues as Hal Blaine, Ron Tutt, Milt Holland and Al Casey. He also achieved a qualified success as a poet, author, cabaret entertainer and concept artist with one of his exhibitions at Pasadena Arts Museum the subject of a feature in *Life* magazine. A reissue of 'Classical Gas' in 1978 met with further success.

Selected Albums: *Them Poems And Things* (1968), *The Mason Williams Phonograph Record* (1968), *The Mason Williams Ear Show* (1968), *Music By Mason Williams* (1969), *Hand Made* (1970), *Improved* (1971).

Williams, Maurice, And The Zodiacs

This R&B vocal group from Lancaster, South Carolina, USA, was led by Maurice Williams (lead/pianist/songwriter). The hit record 'Stay', which went to number 3 R&B and number 1 pop in 1960, immortalized the Zodiacs as a one-hit-wonder group. (In the UK 'Stay' went to number 14 in 1961.) Williams, however, had a long history before and after the hit, forming his first group, the Gladiolas, in 1955. Besides Williams (b. 26 April 1938, Lancaster, South Carolina, USA), the group consisted of Earl Gainey (tenor), William Massey (tenor/baritone), Willie Jones (baritone), and Norman Wade (bass). Their one hit for the Nashville-based Excello label was 'Little Darlin'', which went to number 11 R&B and number 41 pop in 1957. The record was covered with greater success by the Canadian group, the Diamonds. In 1960 Williams formed the Zodiacs, consisting of Wiley Bennett (tenor), Henry Gaston (tenor), Charles Thomas (baritone), Albert Hill (double bass), and Little Willie Morrow (drums). After the unforgettable 'Stay' the group honoured themselves with many outstanding sides, most notably 'I Remember' (number 86 pop in 1961), 'Come Along' (number 83 pop in 1961), and 'May I' (1966), but nothing close to a hit resulted. The latter song was remade in 1969 by Bill Deal And The Rhondels as a Top 40 national hit with it. The most frequently remade Williams' song was 'Stay', which the Hollies in the UK (1963), the Four Seasons (1964), and Jackson Browne (1978) all placed on the charts. Its timeless lyric of teenage lust and angst has been passed through the decades; 'Well your mama don't mind, well your papa don't mind', leading to the punch line; 'Oh won't you stay, just a little bit longer'. During the 70s and 80s Williams sustained a career with a new group of Zodiacs playing their classic catalogueto the Beach Music club circuit in the Carolinas.
Albums: *Stay* (1961), *At The Beach* (early 60s), *Maurice Williams And The Zodiacs* (1988). Compilations: *Best Of Maurice Williams & the Zodiacs* (1989), *Little Darlin'* (1991), *Best Of Maurice Williams & The Zodiacs* (1991).

Wilson, Jackie

b. 9 June 1934, Detroit, Michigan, USA, d. 21 January 1984, New Jersey, USA. When parental pressure thwarted his boxing ambitions, Wilson took to singing in small, local clubs. He sang with the Thrillers (a predecessor group to the Royals) and recorded some solo tracks for Dizzy Gillespie's Dee Gee label as Sonny Wilson, before replacing Clyde McPhatter in Billy Ward And The Dominoes. Jackie joined this notable group in 1953, but embarked on a solo career four years later with Brunswick Records. His first single for that label, was the exuberant 'Reet Petite', a comparative failure in the USA where it crept to a lowly pop position and missed the R&B lists altogether. In the UK, however, it soared to number 6 thereby establishing Wilson in the minds of the British pop purchasing audience. 'Reet Petite' had been written by Berry Gordy and Tyran Carlo (Roquel 'Billy' Davis), who went on to compose several of Wilson's subsequent releases which included the hits 'Lonely Teardrops' (1958), 'That's Why (I Love You So)' (1959) and 'I'll Be Satisfied' (1959).

In 1960, Jackie enjoyed two R&B number 1 hits with 'Doggin' Around' and 'A Woman, A Lover, A Friend'. His musical direction then grew increasingly erratic, veering from mainstream to pseudo-opera. There were still obvious highlights such as 'Baby Workout' (1963), 'Squeeze Her Please Her' (1964), 'No Pity (In The Naked City)' (1965), but all too often his wonderfully fluid voice was wasted on cursory, quickly-dated material. The artist's live appearances, however, remained both exciting and dramatic, capable of inspiring the ecstasy his sometimes facile recordings belied. Wilson's career was rejuvenated in 1966. Abandoning his New York recording base, he moved to Chicago where he worked with producer Carl Davis. Here, at last, was a more consistent empathy and 'Whispers (Gettin' Louder)' (1966), '(Your Love Keeps Lifting Me) Higher And Higher' (1967) and the sublime 'I Get The Sweetest Feeling' (1968), stand amongst his finest recordings. It was not to last. 'This Love Is Real (I Can Feel Those Vibrations)' (1970) proved to be Wilson's last Top 10 R&B entry, by which time his work was influenced by trends rather than setting them. In September 1975, while touring with the Dick Clark revue, Wilson suffered a near fatal heart attack onstage at New Jersey's Latin Casino. He struck his head on falling and the resulting brain damage left him comatose. He remained hospitalized until his death on 21 January 1984.

Wilson's career remains a puzzle; he never did join Berry Gordy's Motown empire, despite their early collaboration and friendship. Instead the singer's legacy was flawed; dazzling in places, disappointing in others. Immortalized in the Van Morrison song, 'Jackie Wilson Said', which was also a UK Top 5 hit for Dexy's Midnight Runners in 1982, his name has remained in the public's eye. Fate left its final twist for in 1987, when an imaginative video (which some claimed belittled the singer's memory) using plasticine animation, propelled 'Reet Petite' to number 1 in the UK charts.
Albums: *He's So Fine* (1958), *Lonely Teardrops* (1959),

Doggin' Around (1959), *So Much* (1960), *Night* (1960), *Jackie Wilson Sings The Blues* (1960), *A Woman A Lover A Friend* (1961), *Try A Little Tenderness* (1961), *You Ain't Heard Nothing Yet* (1961), *By Special Request* (1961), *Body And Soul* (1962), *Jackie Wilson At The Copa* (1962), *Jackie Wilson Sings The World's Greatest Melodies* (1962), *Baby Workout* (1963), *Merry Christmas* (1963), with Linda Hopkins *Shake A Hand* (1963), *Somethin' Else* (1964), *Soul Time* (1965), *Spotlight On Jackie Wilson* (1965), *Soul Galore* (1966), *Whispers* (1967), *Higher And Higher* (1967), with Count Basie *Manufacturers Of Soul* (1968), with Basie *Too Much* (1968), *I Get The Sweetest Feeling* (1968), *Do Your Thing* (1970), *This Love Is Real* (1970), *You Got Me Walking* (1971), *Beautiful Day* (1973), *Nowstalgia* (1974), *Nobody But You* (1976). Compilations: *My Golden Favourites* (1960), *My Golden Favourites - Volume 2* (1964), *Jackie Wilson's Greatest Hits* (1969), *It's All Part Of Love* (1969), *Classic Jackie Wilson* (1984), *Reet Petite* (1985), *The Soul Years* (1985), *The Soul Years Volume 2* (1986), *Higher And Higher* (1986), *The Very Best Of Jackie Wilson* (1987).

Wonder, Stevie

b. Steveland Judkins, 13 May 1950, Saginaw, Michigan, USA. Born Judkins, Stevie now prefers to be known as Steveland Morris after his mother's married name. Placed in an incubator immediately after his birth, baby Steveland was given too much oxygen, causing him to suffer permanent blindness. Despite this handicap, Wonder began to learn the piano at the age of seven, and had also mastered drums and harmonica by the age of nine. After his family moved to Detroit in 1954, Steveland joined a church choir, the gospel influence on his music balanced by the R&B of Ray Charles and Sam Cooke being played on his transistor radio. In 1961, he was discovered by Ronnie White of the Miracles, who arranged an audition at Motown Records. Berry Gordy immediately signed Steveland to the label, renaming him Little Stevie Wonder (the 'Little' was dropped in 1964). Wonder was placed in the care of writer/producer Clarence Paul, who supervized his early recordings. These accentuated his prodigal talents as a multi-instrumentalist, but did not represent a clear musical direction. In 1963, however, the release of the ebullient live recording 'Fingertips (Part 2)' established his commercial success, and Motown quickly marketed him on a series of albums as 'the 12-year-old genius' in an attempt to link him with the popularity of 'the genius', Ray Charles. Attempts to repeat the success of 'Fingertips' proved abortive, and Stevie's career was placed on hold during 1964 while his voice was breaking. He re-emerged in 1965 with a sound that was much closer to the Motown mainstream, scoring a worldwide hit with the dance-orientated 'Uptight (Everything's Alright)', which he co-wrote with Henry Cosby and Sylvia Moy. This began a run of US Top 40 hits which continued unbroken (apart from seasonal Christmas releases) for over six years.

From 1965-70, Stevie Wonder was marketed like the other major Motown stars, recording material that was chosen for him by the label's executives, and issuing albums that mixed conventional soul compositions with pop standards. His strong humanitarian principles were allowed expression on his version of Bob Dylan's 'Blowin' In The Wind' and Ron Miller's 'A Place In The Sun' in 1966. He co-wrote almost all of his singles from 1967 onwards, and also began to collaborate on releases by other Motown artists, most notably co-writing Smokey Robinson And The Miracles' hit 'The Tears Of A Clown', and writing and producing the (Detroit) Spinners' 'It's A Shame'.

His contract with Motown expired in 1971; rather than re-signing immediately, as the label expected, Wonder financed the recording of two albums of his own material, playing almost all the instruments himself, and experimenting for the first time with more ambitious musical forms. He pioneered the use of the synthesizer in black music, and also widened his lyrical concerns to take in racial problems and spiritual questions. Wonder then used these recordings as a lever to persuade Motown to offer a more open contract, which gave him total artistic control over his music, plus the opportunity to hold the rights to the music publishing in his own company, Black Bull Music. He celebrated the signing of the deal with the release of the solo recordings, *Where I'm Coming From* and *Music Of My Mind*, which despite lukewarm critical reaction quickly established him at the forefront of black music.

Talking Book in 1972 combined the artistic advances of recent albums with major commercial success, producing glorious hit singles with the poly-rhythmic funk of 'Superstition' and the crafted ballad, 'You Are The Sunshine Of My Life'. Wonder married fellow Motown artist Syreeta on 14 September 1970; he premiered many of his new production techniques on *Syreeta* (1972) and *Stevie Wonder Presents Syreeta* (1974), for which he also wrote most of the material. *Innervisions* (1973) consolidated his growth and success with *Talking Book*, bringing further hit singles with the socially aware 'Living For The City' and 'Higher Ground'. Later that year, Wonder was seriously injured in a car accident; his subsequent work was tinged with the awareness of mortality, fired by his spiritual beliefs. The release of *Fulfillingness' First Finale* in 1974 epitomized this more austere approach. The double album *Songs In The Key Of Life* (1976) was widely greeted as his most ambitious and satisfying work to date. It showed a mastery and variety of musical forms and instruments, offering a joyous tribute to Duke Ellington on 'Sir Duke', and heralding a pantheon of major black figures on 'Black Man'. This confirmed Wonder's status as one of the most admired musicians and songwriters in contemporary music.

Surprisingly after this mammoth success, no new recordings surfaced for over three years, as Wonder concentrated on perfecting the soundtrack music to the documentary film, *The Secret Life Of Plants*. This primarily instrumental double album was greeted with disappointing reviews and sales. Wonder quickly delivered the highly successful *Hotter Than July* in 1980, which included a tribute song for the late Dr. Martin Luther King, 'Happy Birthday', and a notable essay in reggae form on 'Masterblaster (Jamming)'.

The failure of his film project brought an air of caution into Wonder's work, and delays and postponements were now a consistent factor in his recording process. After compiling the retrospective double album *Stevie Wonder's Original Musiquarium I* in 1982, which included four new recordings alongside the cream of his post-1971 work, Wonder scheduled an album titled *People Move Human Play* in 1983. This never appeared; instead, he composed the soundtrack music for the film *The Woman In Red*, which included his biggest-selling single to date, the sentimental ballad 'I Just Called To Say I Loved You'.

The album which he had been working on since 1980 eventually appeared in 1985 as *In Square Circle*. Like his next project, *Characters* in 1987, it heralded a return to the accessible, melodic music of the previous decade. The unadventurous nature of both projects, and the heavy expectations engendered by the delay in their release, and led to a disappointing reception from critics and public alike.

Wonder's status as an elder statesman of black music, and a champion of black rights, was boosted by his campaign in the early 80s to have the birthday of Dr. Martin Luther King celebrated as a national holiday in the USA. This request was granted by President Reagan, and the first Martin Luther King Day was celebrated on 15 January 1986 with a concert at which Wonder topped the bill. Besides his own recordings, Wonder has been generous in offering his services as a writer, producer, singer or musician to other performers. His most public collaborations included work with Paul McCartney, which produced a cloying but enormous hit, 'Ebony And Ivory', Gary Byrd, Michael Jackson, and Eurythmics, and on the benefit records by USA For Africa and Dionne Warwick & Friends.

Albums: *Tribute To Uncle Ray* (1963), *The Jazz Soul Of Little Stevie* (1963), *The 12-Year-Old Genius Live* (1963), *With A Song In My Heart* (1963), *Stevie At The Beach* (1964), *Uptight (Everything's Alright)* (1966),

Down To Earth (1966), *I Was Made To Love Her* (1967), *Someday At Christmas* (1967), *For Once In My Life* (1968), *My Cherie Amour* (1969), *Stevie Wonder Live* (1970), *Stevie Wonder Live At The Talk Of The Town* (1970), *Signed, Sealed And Delivered* (1970), *Where I'm Coming From* (1971), *Music Of My Mind* (1972), *Talking Book* (1972), *Innervisions* (1973), *Fulfillingness' First Finale* (1974), *Songs In The Key Of Life* (1976), *Stevie Wonder's Journey Through The Secret Life Of Plants* (1979), *Hotter Than July* (1980), *The Woman In Red* (1984, film soundtrack), *In Square Circle* (1985), *Characters* (1987). Compilations: *Greatest Hits* (1968), *Greatest Hits, Volume Two* (1971), *Anthology* aka *Looking Back* (1977, recordings from 1962-71), *Stevie Wonder's Original Musiquarium I* (1982, recordings from 1972-82).

Wonder Who

At the 1966 apogee of their chart career, Nick Massi was replaced by Joe Long in the Four Seasons. Included in the new line-up's year of hits was a curious joke adaptation of Bob Dylan's 'Don't Think Twice It's All Right' under the *nom de turntable*, Wonder Who. The song itself mattered less than lead vocalist Frankie Valli's 'baby' falsetto - supposedly his impersonation of jazz singer Rose Murphy. Although it reached the US Top 5, the group did intend to seriously pursue this vocational tangent beyond a couple more singles, having made the point to their record company that the number *per se* was commercial enough without buyers knowing it was by the Four Seasons.

Wood, Brenton

b. Alfred Jesse Smith, 26 July 1941, Shreveport, Louisiana, USA. Smith was a veteran of several vocal groups, including the Dootones, the Quotations and Little Freddie And The Rockets, before assuming the name Brenton Wood in deference to his home district in Los Angeles. As a solo act he enjoyed fame with 'The Oogum Boogum Song' (1967), a nonsense novelty record. The follow-up, 'Gimme Little Sign' (although not a novelty), was in a similar style, but its more lasting appeal was confirmed when the single reached the UK and US Top 10. Further releases, 'Baby You Got It' (1967) and 'Some Got It, Some Don't' (1968), diluted the pattern and were less successful. Wood later recorded a duet with Shirley Goodman, before making a belated return to the US R&B chart in 1977 with 'Come Softly To Me'.

Albums: *The Oogum Boogum Man* (1967), *Baby You Got It* (1967).

Woodstock Festival

The original Woodstock Art and Music Fair was forcibly moved from its planned location after protest from local townsfolk of Wallkill, New York State,

USA. Their opposition to 'long-haired weirdos' was indigenous to 1969. The new location was 40 miles away at a 600-acre dairy farm in Bethel owned by Max Yasgur. If the Monterey Pop Festival in 1967 was the birth of the new music revolution, Woodstock was its coming of age.

A steady trail of spectators arrived up to a week before the event, to make sure they had a reasonable chance to catch a glimpse of at least one of the dozens of stars scheduled to appear. The line-up was intimidating in its scale: the Who, Jimi Hendrix, Crosby, Stills, Nash And Young, John Sebastian, Jefferson Airplane, Grateful Dead, Santana, Joe Cocker, Sly And The Family Stone, Country Joe And The Fish, Ten Years After, the Band, Johnny Winter, Blood Sweat And Tears, the Paul Butterfield Blues Band, Sha Na Na, Janis Joplin, Ravi Shankar, the Keef Hartley Band, the Incredible String Band, Canned Heat, Melanie, Sweetwater, Tim Hardin, Joan Baez, Arlo Guthrie, Richie Havens and Creedence Clearwater Revival. Estimates vary but it was generally felt that no less than 300,000 spectators were present at any one time, sharing 600 portable lavatories and inadequate water facilities. Nobody was prepared for the wave of bodies that formed, choking the highways from all directions. The world press which had previously scorned the popular hippie movement and the power of their musical message, were at last speaking favourably, as one. It was possible for vast amounts of youngsters to congregate for a musical celebration, without violence and regimented supervision. Joni Mitchell (who was not present) was one of the artists who eulogized the event in her song 'Woodstock': 'I'm going down to Yasgur's Farm, I'm gonna join in a rock 'n' roll band, I'm gonna camp out on the land and set my soul free'.

The subsequent film and live albums have ensured Woodstock's immortality, and though there are some critics of the 'love generation' few can deny that Woodstock was a milestone in musical history. It is no exaggeration to claim that the festival totally changed the world's attitude towards popular music.
Albums: *Woodstock* (1969), *Woodstock II* (1970).
Further reading: *Woodstock: The Oral History*, Joel Makower.

Wynter, Mark

b. Terence Lewis, 29 January 1943, Woking, Surrey, England. Wynter was one of several UK heart-throbs in the early 60s who took their lightweight cue from the USA. Once the extrovert champion of many a school sports day, he was serving in a general store by day and singing with the Hank Fryer Band in Peckham Co-op Hall, London in the evening when his well-scrubbed, good looks betrayed star potential to Ray Mackender, a Lloyds underwriter who

dabbled in pop management. As 'Mark Wynter', the boy was readied for his new career with vocal exercises, tips on stage demeanour from a RADA coach and advice about a middle-of-the-road repertoire from Lionel Bart. After exploratory intermission spots in metropolitan palais, he was signed to Decca Records who he rewarded with UK hit parade entries until 1964 - beginning with 'Image Of A Girl' (1960) at number 11. At the height of his fame two years later, he breached the Top 10 with covers of Jimmy Clanton's 'Venus In Blue Jeans' and Steve Lawrence's 'Go Away Little Girl' before subsequent singles hovered - as they had previously - mostly between 20 and 40. He resorted to a-side revivals of such 50s chestnuts as 'It's Almost Tomorrow' and 'Only You' but, with the levelling blow of the beat boom, he continued to perform in venues where current chart standing had no meaning.

Yardbirds

Yardbirds

This pivotal UK R&B group was formed in London in 1963 when Keith Relf (b. 22 March 1944, Richmond, Surrey, England, d. 14 May 1976; vocals/harmonica) and Paul Samwell-Smith (b. 8 May 1943; bass), both members of semi-acoustic act the Metropolis Blues Quartet, joined forces with Chris Dreja (b. 11 November 1944, Surbiton, Surrey, England; rhythm guitar), Tony 'Top' Topham (guitar) and Jim McCarty (b. 25 July 1944, Liverpool, England; drums). Within months Topham had opted to continue academic studies and was replaced by Eric Clapton (b. Eric Clapp, 30 March 1945, Ripley,

Surrey, England). The reconstituted line-up forged a style based on classic Chicago R&B and quickly amassed a following in the nascent blues circuit. They succeeded the Rolling Stones as the resident band at Richmond's popular Crawdaddy club, whose owner, Giorgio Gomelsky, then assumed the role of group manager. Two enthusiastic, if low-key singles, 'I Wish You Would' and 'Good Morning Little Schoolgirl', attracted critical interest, but the quintet's fortunes flourished with the release of *Five Live Yardbirds*. Recorded during their tenure at the Marquee club, the set captured an in-person excitement and was marked by an exceptional rendition of Howlin' Wolf's 'Smokestack Lightning'. Clapton emerged as the unit's focal point, but a desire for musical purity led to his departure in 1965 in the wake of a magnificent third single, 'For Your Love'. Penned by Graham Gouldman, the song's commerciality proved unacceptable to the guitarist despite its innovative sound. Clapton later resurfaced in John Mayall's Bluebreakers. Jeff Beck (b. 24 June 1944, Surrey, England), formerly of the Tridents, joined the Yardbirds as the single rose to number 1 in the UK's *New Musical Express* chart. Gouldman provided further hits in 'Heartful Of Soul' and 'Evil Hearted You', the latter of which was a double-sided chart entry with the group-penned 'Still I'm Sad'. Based on a Gregorian chant, the song indicated a desire for experimentation prevailing in the rage-rock 'Shapes Of Things', the chaotic 'Over Under Sideways Down' and the excellent *Yardbirds*. By this point Simon Napier-Bell had assumed management duties, while disaffection with touring, and the unit's sometimes irreverent attitude, led to the departure of Samwell-Smith in June 1966. Respected session guitarist Jimmy Page (b. 9 January 1944, London, England) was brought into a line-up which, with Dreja switching to bass, now adopted a potentially devastating twin-lead guitar format. The experimental 'Happenings Ten Years Time Ago' confirmed such hopes, but within six months Beck had departed during a gruelling USA tour.

The Yardbirds remained a quartet but, despite a growing reputation on the American 'underground' circuit, their appeal as a pop attraction waned. Despite late-period collaborations with the commercially-minded Mickie Most, singles, including 'Little Games' (1967) and 'Goodnight Sweet Josephine' (1968), failed to chart. The disappointing *Little Games* was denied a UK release but found success in the USA. They followed with two bizarre minor successes in America; 'Ha Ha Said The Clown' and Harry Nilsson's 'Ten Little Indians'. When Relf and McCarty announced a desire to pursue a folk-based direction, the group folded in June 1968. Page subsequently founded Led Zeppelin, Dreja became a highly successful photographer while the remaining duo forged a new career, firstly as Together, then Renaissance. Nonetheless, the legacy of the Yardbirds has refused to die, particularly in the wake of the fame enjoyed by its former guitarists. Relf was fatally electrocuted in 1976, but the following decade McCarty and Dreja joined Samwell-Smith - now a respected record producer - in Box Of Frogs. When this short-lived attraction folded, the former colleagues reverted to their corresponding careers, with McCarty remaining active in music as a member of the British Invasion All-Stars. The allure of his first group still flourishes and they remain acclaimed as early practitioners of technical effects and psychedelic styles. The 'blueswailing' Yardbirds have maintained enormous credibility as true pioneers of British R&B, classic experimental pop and early exponents of heavy rock.

Albums: *Five Live Yardbirds* (1964), *For Your Love* (1965), *Having A Rave Up With The Yardbirds* (1966), *Yardbirds* aka *Roger The Engineer* (1966), *Little Games* (1968). Compilations: *The Yardbirds With Sonny Boy Williamson* (1966), *Greatest Hits* (1967), *Remember The Yardbirds* (1971), *Live Yardbirds* (1971), *Yardbirds Featuring Eric Clapton* (1977), *Yardbirds Featuring Jeff Beck* (1977), *Shapes Of Things (Collection 1964-1966)* (1978), *The First Recordings* (1982), *Shapes Of Things* (Boxed Set - 1984), *The Studio Sessions* (1989), *Yardbirds....On Air* (1991).

Further reading: *Yardbirds*, John Platt, Chris Dreja and Jim McCarty.

Young, Neil

b. 12 November 1945, Toronto, Canada. Having moved to Winnepeg as a child, Young began his enigmatic career as a member of several high-school bands, including the Jades and Classics. He later joined the Squires, whose indebtedness to British act the Shadows was captured on the Young-penned 'Aurora'/'The Sultan'. In 1965 the artist embarked on a folk-based direction with appearances in Toronto's bohemian Yorkville enclave. A demonstration tape from this era contains early versions of 'Sugar Mountain', a paean to lost childhood later placed on 10 different single releases, and 'Don't Pity Me', revived a decade later as 'Don't Cry No Tears'. Young then joined the Mynah Birds, a pop-soul attraction which also featured Rick James, but this act folded prematurely upon the latter's arrest for draft evasion. Group bassist Bruce Palmer accompanied Neil on a subsequent move to California where they teamed with Stephen Stills and Richie Furay to form the Buffalo Springfield. Young's tenure in this seminal 'west coast' act was tempered by several sabbaticals, but two luxurious, atmospheric compositions, 'Broken Arrow' and 'Expecting To Fly', established the highly-sculptured orchestral-tinged sound prevalent on *Neil Young*.

Although blighted by a selfless mix which buried the artist's vocals, the album contained several excellent compositions, notably 'The Loner', 'The Old Laughing Lady', 'I've Been Waiting For You' and 'Here We Are In The Years'. The set also featured two highly effective instrumentals, Young's evocative 'Emperor Of Wyoming' and 'String Quartet From Whiskey Boot Hill', a sublime arrangement and composition by Jack Nitzsche. The closing track, 'The Last Trip To Tulsa', was unique in Young's canon, a surreal narrative whose performance betrayed the strong influence of Bob Dylan. Following his first album, Young was joined by Danny Whitten (guitar), Billy Talbot (bass) and Ralph Molina (drums) - three former members of the Rockets - in a new backing group dubbed Crazy Horse.

Everybody Knows This Is Nowhere captured a performer liberated from a previous self-consciousness with the extended 'Down By The River' and 'Cowgirl In The Sand' allowing space for his stuttering, yet enthralling, guitar style. While the epical guitar pieces dominated the set, there were other highlights including the zestful 'Cinnamon Girl' and the haunting 'Running Dry', a mournful requiem featuring Bobby Notkoff on violin. The album underlined the intense relationship between Young and Crazy Horse. An attendant tour confirmed the strength of this newfound partnership, while Young also secured acclaim as a member of Crosby, Stills, Nash And Young. His relationship with Crazy Horse soured as Whitten grew increasingly dependent on heroin and the group was dropped following the recording of *After The Goldrush*. The set provided a commercial breakthough and included several of Young's best-known compositions, including the haunting title track, 'Only Love Can Break Your Heart', a US Top 40 hit and the fiery 'Southern Man'. The highly commercial *Harvest* confirmed this newfound ascendancy and spawned a US chart-topper in 'Heart Of Gold' and remains one of the artist's best-selling albums. This commercial peak ended abruptly with *Journey Through The Past*, a highly-indulgent soundtrack to a rarely-screened autobiographical film. A disastrous tour with new backing group the Stray Gators exacerbated the gap between the artist and his potential audience, although *Time Fades Away*, a collection of new songs culled from the concerts, reclaimed the ragged feistiness of the Crazy Horse era. The set included the passionate 'Last Dance' and the superb 'Don't Be Denied', an unflinching autobiographical account of Young's early life.

The deaths of Whitten and road crew member Bruce Berry inspired the harrowing *Tonight's The Night*, on which Young's bare-nerved emotions were expounded over his bleakest songs to date. 'I'm singing this borrowed tune, I took from the Rolling Stones, alone in this empty room, too wasted to write my own', he intoned in world-weary fashion on 'Borrowed Tune', while in-concert Young would offer multiple versions of the grief-stricken title song. However the final set was shelved in favour of *On The Beach*, released to coincide with a Crosby, Stills, Nash And Young reunion tour. The work was initially greeted coolly and *Rolling Stone* described it as one of the 'most despairing albums of the decade'. This was a severe misinterpretation since *On The Beach* was actually a therapeutic work, enacting Young's shift to a more positive state of mind. In common with John Lennon's Plastic Ono Band, *On The Beach* saw Young stripping away his personality in a series of intense songs. The undoubted highlight of the set was the closing 'Ambulance Blues', arguably the most accomplished work of Young's career. In analysing his place in the rock music world, Young offered a sardonic riposte to his detractors: 'So all you critics sit alone/You're no better than me for what you've shown/With your stomach pump and your hook and ladder dreams/We could get together for some scenes'. On The Beach was a consummate album and a crucial turning point in Young's career. The belatedly issued *Tonight's The Night* was no longer a shock, but testified to Young's absolute conviction. The album sold poorly but was retrospectively acclaimed as one of the bravest and most moving albums of the decade.

Young next chose to team up Crazy Horse - Talbot, Molina and new guitarist Frank Stampedro - for *Zuma*. The set's highlight was provided by a guitar strewn 'Cortez The Killer' but, despite often ecstatic reviews, the overall performance was generally stronger than the material it supported. Another gripping recording, 'Like A Hurricane', was the pivotal feature of *American Stars 'N' Bars*, an otherwise piecemeal collection drawn from extant masters and newer, country-oriented recordings. The latter direction was maintained on *Comes A Time*, Young's most accessible set since *Harvest*, on which female vocalist Nicolette Larson acted as foil. The album's use of acoustic settings enhanced Young's pastoral intentions and the singer was moved to include a rare cover version; Ian Tyson's folk standard 'Four Strong Winds'. Characteristically, Young chose to follow this up by rejoining Crazy Horse for *Rust Never Sleeps*. The album rightly stands as one of Young's greatest and most consistent works. The acoustic 'My My, Hey Hey (Out Of The Blue)' and its electric counterpart 'Hey Hey, My My (Into The Black)' explained the central theme of the work - the transience of rock stardom. 'The Thrasher', one of Young's most complex and rewarding songs, reiterated the motif. 'Ride My Llama', 'Pocahontas' and 'Powderfinger' were all worthy additions to Young's classic canon. The album was preceded by a

Young film of the same name and followed by a double live album.

During the 80s the artist became increasingly unpredictable as each new release denied the musical directions offered by its predecessor. The understated and underrated *Hawks And Doves* was followed by excursions through electric R&B (*Re-Ac-Tor*), techno-pop (*Trans*) and rockabilly (*Everybody's Rockin'*), before embracing country (*Old Ways*), hard rock (*Landing On Water*) and blues (*This Note's For You*). The last-named achieved notoriety when a video for the title song, which attacked the intertwining of rock with corporate sponsorship, was banned by MTV. The blues experiment also saw Young regain some critical acclaim. Young's next project was culled from an aborted release, tentatively entitled *Times Square*. *Eldorado* invoked the raw abandonment of *Tonight's The Night*, but the 5-song set was only issued in Japan and Australia. Three of its songs were latterly placed on *Freedom*, an artistic and commercial triumph which garnered positive reviews and assuaged those viewing its creator as merely eccentric. The set was generally acclaimed as Young's finest work in a decade and included some of his most intriguing lyrics, most notably the lengthy 'Crime In The City', itself an extract from an even longer piece, 'Sixty To Zero'. Young affirmed this regeneration with *Ragged Glory*, a collaboration with Crazy Horse marked by blistering guitar lines, snarled lyrics and a sense of urgency and excitement few from Neil's generation could hope to muster. Contemporary new wave band Sonic Youth supported the revitalized partnership on the US *Spook The Horse* tour, cementing Young's affection for pioneers.

An ensuing in-concert set, *Weld* (accompanied by an album of feedback experimentation, *Arc*), was rightly applauded as another milestone in Young's often contrary oeuvre, and as the dawn of the 90s his artistic standing remains at all-time high. However, he retains the right to surprise, and even baffle, while a reluctance to court easy popularity must be applauded. More than any other artist working in the rock field, Young is the greatest chameleon. His many admirers never know what to expect, but the reaction whenever it arrives is almost universally favourable.

Albums: *Neil Young* (1969), *Everybody Knows This Is Nowhere* (1969), *After The Goldrush* (1970), *Harvest* (1972), *Journey Through The Past* (1972), *Time Fades Away* (1973), *On The Beach* (1974), *Tonight's The Night* (1975), *Zuma* (1975), *American Stars 'N' Bars* (1977), *Comes A Time* (1978), *Rust Never Sleeps* (1979), *Live Rust* (1979), *Hawks And Doves* (1980), *Re-Ac-Tor* (1981), *Trans* (1983), *Everybody's Rockin'* (1983), *Old Ways* (1985), *Landing On Water* (1986), *Life* (1987), *This Note's For You* (1986), *Eldorado*

(1989), *Freedom* (1989), *Ragged Glory* (1990), *Weld* (1991), *Arc/Weld* (1991). Compilations/archive sets: *Decade* (1977), *Greatest Hits* (1985).
Further reading: *Neil Young: Here We Are In The Years*, Johnny Rogan. *Neil And Me*, Scott Young.

Youngbloods

Formed in 1965 in Boston, Massachusetts, the Youngbloods evolved from the city's thriving traditional music circuit. The group was formed by folk-singers Jesse Colin Young (b. Perry Miller, 11 November 1944, New York City, New York, USA) and Jerry Corbitt (b. Tifton, Georgia, USA) who together completed a single, 'My Babe', prior to the arrival of aspiring jazz drummer Joe Bauer (b. 26 September 1941, Memphis, Tennessee, USA) and guitarist/pianist Lowell Levinger III, better-known simply as Banana (b. 1946, Cambridge, Massachusetts, USA). Jesse began playing bass when several candidates, including Felix Pappalardi and Harvey Brooks, proved incompatible, and the quartet took the name 'Youngbloods' from the singer's second solo album. Having secured a residency at New York's famed Cafe Au Go Go, the group established itself as a leading folk-rock cum good-time attraction. Their debut *The Youngbloods*, captures this formative era and mixes excellent original songs, including the ebullient 'Grizzly Bear', with several choice cover versions. The group's reading of Dino Valenti's 'Get Together' subsequently became a hit in California where it was adopted as a counter-culture anthem. The lyric 'Come on now people, smile on your brother, everybody get together, try and love one another right now', perfectly captured the mood of late-60s Californian rock music.

The Youngbloods then settled on the west coast. *Elephant Mountain*, their most popular album, reflected a new-found peace of mind and included several of the group's best-known songs, including 'Darkness Darkness' and 'Sunlight'. Jerry Corbitt had left the line-up during the early stages of recording allowing Bauer and Banana space to indulge in improvisational interludes. The Youngbloods gained complete artistic freedom with their own label, Racoon. However releases by Bauer, Banana and Young dissipated the strengths of the parent unit whose final releases were marred by inconsistency. A friend from the Boston days, Michael Kane, joined the band in the spring of 1971, but they split the following year when Jesse resumed his solo career. Banana, Bauer and Kane continued as Banana And The Bunch, but this occasional venture subsequently folded. In 1984 Levinger reappeared in the Bandits, before retiring from music to run a hang-gliding shop.
Albums: *The Youngbloods* (1967), *Earth Music* (1967), *Elephant Mountain* (1969), *Rock Festival* (1970), *Ride*

The Wind (1971), Good 'N' Dusty (1971), High On A Ridgetop (1972). Compilations: Two Trips (1970 - one side only), The Best Of The Youngbloods (1970), Sunlight (1971), Get Together (1971), This Is The Youngbloods (1972), Point Reyes Station (1987), From The Gaslight To The Avalon (1988).

Young Rascals (see Rascals)

Young Tradition

One of the leading practitioners of the English folk revival, the Young Tradition was formed in 1964 by Heather Wood (b. 1945; vocals), Royston Wood (b. 1935, d. 8 April 1990; vocals/tambourine) and Peter Bellamy (b. 8 September 1944, Bournemouth, Dorset, England, d. September 1991; guitar/concertina/vocals). The trio continued the oral harmony tradition of the influential Copper Family, while simultaneously enjoying the patronage of the Soho circuit and the emergent 'underground' audience. Their choice of material and powerful harmonies captured what was regarded as the essence of rural folk music. The group completed three albums during their brief sojourn. Their debut included guest performances from Dave Swarbrick and Dolly Collins and their much heralded Galleries, highlighted the divergent interests which eventually pulled them apart. Several selections featured support from David Munrow's Early Music Ensemble, a trend towards medieval perspectives which Bellamy felt unwelcome. Unable to make a commercial breakthrough, the Young Tradition split up in 1969, although Heather and Royston Wood remained together to record No Relation. The latter musician enjoyed a brief association with the Albion Country Band, before forming Swan Arcade. He died in April 1990, following a three-week coma after being run over by a car in the USA. Heather Wood teamed up with Andy Wallace to form the duo, Crossover. Pete Bellamy, meanwhile, enjoyed a successful solo career. This was abruptly cut short in 1991 when Bellamy committed suicide.
Albums: The Young Tradition (1966), So Cheerfully Round (1967), Galleries (1968). Compilations: The Young Tradition Sampler (1969), The Young Tradition (1989).

Zager And Evans

One of the biggest-selling hits of 1969 was the pessimistic look into the future, 'In The Year 2525 (Exordium & Terminus)' by Zager and Evans. The duo was Denny Zager (b. 1944, Wymore, Nebraska, USA) and Rick Evans (b. 1943, Lincoln, Nebraska, USA), who had met in 1962 and joined a band called the Eccentrics. Evans left that band in 1965 but the pair teamed up again at the end of the decade. Zager had written 'In The Year 2525' five years earlier, and

they recorded it in Texas in 1968. It was released on the local Truth label and picked up the following year by RCA Records, climbing to number 1, where it remained for six weeks in the US charts and three weeks in the UK, ultimately selling a reported five million copies. Unable to follow this success, Zager quit in 1970; neither he nor Evans were heard from again, although RCA continued to release their recordings for some time in attempts to make lightning strike twice.
Albums: 2525 (Exordium & Terminus) (1969), Zager And Evans (1970), Food For The Mind (1971).
991) 'Tis The Season To Be Jelly (1967), The Ark (1968), Freaks And Motherfuckers (1970), Piquantique (1973), Unmitigated Audacity (1974), Saarbrucken 1978 (1978), Any Way The Wind Blows (1979), As An Am Zappa (1981). Compilations: Rare Meat (1962-63), You Can't Do That On Stage Any More Vol 1 (1969-88), You Can't Do That On Stage Any More Vol 2 (1974), You Can't Do That On Stage Any More Vol 3 (1971-88), You Can't Do That On Stage Any More Vol 4 (1969-88).

Zombies

Rod Argent (b. 14 June 1945, St. Albans, Hertfordshire, England; piano), Colin Blunstone (b. 24 June 1945, St. Albans, Hertfordshire, England; vocals), Paul Atkinson (b. 19 March 1946, Cuffley, Hertfordshire, England; guitar), Paul Arnold (bass) and Hugh Grundy (b. 6 March 1945, Winchester, Hampshire, England; drums) formed the Zombies in 1963, although Chris White (b. 7 March 1943, Barnet, Hertfordshire) replaced Arnold within weeks of their inception. This St. Albans-based quintet won the local Herts Beat competition, the prize for which was a recording deal with Decca Records. The Zombies' debut single, 'She's Not There', rose to number 12 in the UK, but proved more popular still in America, where it reached number 2. Blunstone's breathy voice and Argent's imaginative keyboard arrangement provided the song's distinctive features and the group's crafted, adventurous style was then maintained over a series of excellent singles. Sadly, this diligence was not reflected in success, and although 'Tell Her No' was another US Top 10 entrant, it fared much less well at home while later releases, including 'Whenever You're Ready' and 'Is This The Dream' unaccountably missed out altogether.
The group, not unnaturally, grew frustrated and split up in 1967 on completion of Odyssey And Oracle. The promise of those previous releases culminated in this magnificent collection which adroitly combined innovation, melody and crafted harmonies. Its closing track, 'Time Of The Season', became a massive US hit, but despite several overtures, the original line-up steadfastly refused to reunite. Argent and Grundy

were subsequently joined by Jim Rodford (bass - ex Mike Cotton) and Rick Birkett (guitar) and this reshaped ensemble was responsible for the Zombies' final single, 'Imagine The Swan'. Despite the label credit, this release was ostensibly the first recording by the keyboard player's new venture, Argent. Colin Blunstone, meanwhile embarked on a solo career.

Albums: *Begin Here* (1965), *Odyssey And Oracle* (1968), *The Zombies Live On The BBC 1965-1967* (1985). Selected compilations: *The World Of The Zombies* (1970), *Time Of The Zombies* (1973), *The Zombies* (1984), *Meet The Zombies* (1988).

The Guinness Encyclopedia of Popular Music

Compiled by Colin Larkin

The most comprehensive and authoritative guide to popular music that has ever been published, *The Guinness Encyclopedia of Popular Music* covers every important artist, band, genre, group, event, instrument, publisher, promoter, record company and musical style from the world of popular music in four 832-page volumes.

The product of over four years of intensive labour by an international group of more than 100 skilled writers, musicologists and advisors, its scope is truly global. Compiled in an A-Z format, it covers all forms of popular music from 1990 to 1992 and contains over 9,000 entries varying in length from 100 to 5,000 words.

A bibliography of over 5,000 entries is included along with a full index of artists' names.

For further details of this essential reference work, please write to:
Section A,
The Marketing Department,
Guinness Publishing,
33 London Road,
Enfield,
Middlesex EN2 6DJ,
England.

Proposed Titles for Inclusion in the

'Guinness Who's Who of Popular Music Series'

The Guinness Who's Who of 50s Music
The Guinness Who's Who of 60s Music★
The Guinness Who's Who of 70s Music
The Guinness Who's Who of 80s Music
The Guinness Who's Who of Indie and New Wave Music★
The Guinness Who's Who of Blues Music
The Guinness Who's Who of Folk Music
The Guinness Who's Who of R&B Music
The Guinness Who's Who of Soul Music
The Guinness Who's Who of Country Music
The Guinness Who's Who of Jazz★
The Guinness Who's Who of Heavy Metal★
The Guinness Who's Who of Gospel Music
The Guinness Who's Who of UK Rock and Pop
The Guinness Who's Who of USA Rock and Pop
The Guinness Who's Who of Danceband Pop
The Guinness Who's Who of World Music
The Guinness Who's Who of Stage Musicals

★ Already published

For further information on any of these titles please write to:
Section A,
The Marketing Department,
Guinness Publishing,
33 London Road,
Enfield,
Middlesex EN2 6DJ,
England